International Federation of Library Associations and Institutions
Fédération Internationale des Associations de Bibliothécaires et des Bibliothèques
Internationaler Verband der bibliothekarischen Vereine und Institutionen
Международная Федерация Библиотечных Ассоциаций и Учреждений

IFLA Publications 52/53

World Guide to Library, Archive, and Information Science Associations

Josephine Riss Fang and Alice H. Songe
with the assistance of
Anna J. Fang and Alexandra Herz

K·G·Saur
München · London · New York · Paris 1990

IFLA Publications
edited by Carol Henry

Recommended catalog entry:
World guide to library, archive, and information
science associations / Josephine Riss Fang and Alice H. Songe.
With the assistance of Anna J. Fang and Alexandra Herz.
Intern. Fed. of Library Assoc. and Inst. – München; London;
New York; Paris: Saur, 1990.
XXVII, 517 p., 21 cm. –
(IFLA Publications; 52/53)
ISBN 3-598-10814-1

CIP-Titelaufnahme der Deutschen Bibliothek

Fang, Josephine Riss:
World guide to library, archive, and information science
associations / Josephine Riss Fang and Alice H. Songe. With
the assistance of Anna J. Fang and Alexandra Herz. [Internat.
Fed. of Library Assoc. and Inst.]. – München ; London ; New
York ; Paris : Saur, 1990
    (IFLA publications ; 52/53)
    ISBN 3-598-10814-1
NE: Songe, Alice H.:; HST; International Federation of Library
    Associations and Institutions: IFLA publications

Printed on acid-free paper / Gedruckt auf säurefreiem Papier

Druck/Printed by Strauss Offsetdruck GmbH, Hirschberg
Binden/Bound by Buchbinderei Schaumann, Darmstadt

ISBN 3-598-10814-1
ISSN 0344-6891 (IFLA Publications)

Contents

Preface

We are pleased to join the distinguished list of reference publications of K.G. Saur Publishers with this contribution to the field. Librarians, archivists, information scientists and documentalists find an increasing need and pressure to communicate, exchange information, and cooperate at national and international levels. Knowledge and information, contained both in the records of the past and in the technology of the present and future, are regarded vital to the welfare of nations and of the world community. Professionals from all countries are striving to cope with the volume of created information and the increasing demands by users for specialized and sophisticated services, while still supplying basic information needs in developing areas of the world.

With this reference tool we hope to provide information professionals in all countries with a means for professional communication of global dimensions.

Several significant trends in the organization of the information professions can be identified:

1.   An increase in the number of international associations (from 33 in 1973, 41 in 1976, 58 in 1980, to 76 in 1990).

2.   An increase in the number of national associations (from 285 in 1973, 317 in 1976, 450 in 1980, to 511 in 1990). In emerging nations new associations were formed as soon as a body of professionals existed. In highly industrialized countries there are also a number of new associations. They may be concerned with serving special interest groups, such as the handicapped, ethnic groups, etc., through an intensified awareness by our service-oriented profession, or they are the result of rapid developments in high technology and the need for sophisticated information management and cooperation among professionals.

3.   An increase in the number of official journals and newsletters published by the associations as part of their service to members (from 256 in 1976, 301 in 1980, to 406 in 1990).

4.   The growth and diversification of activities of the associations, especially in working for legislative support, and the use of high technology in managing the association. There is an increasing awareness of members' needs for professional information exchange, professional development (e.g., continuing education), and public recognition of the profession within the framework of the culture and civilization of a nation as well as of the world community.

When preparing a reference work of this kind, we have to accept the fact that there is continuing change taking place within each association, not only in the names and terms of officers, membership, assembly, but also in an association's activities, publications, goals, and ever-present striving for improvement. Nevertheless, it is important and useful to establish a record at a given point in time. This reference source shows an association's growth and its attempts to adapt to the changing needs of users and society, it helps gaining a historic perspective, and provides a means for obtaining further information directly from the associations as well as through the researched bibliographies.

This book shows an impressive record of the information professions. Much has still to be done to bridge the great chasm between the young and struggling associations of emerging and economically deprived countries and the well-established and strong associations in other parts of the world. Here international associations such as the International Federation of Library Associations and Institutions (IFLA) can play an important role in aiding the development of professional organizations with the help of the expertise of their members and the establishment of the IFLA Clearing House on Associations in the Information Fields at the Graduate School of Library and Information Science at Simmons College in Boston, Massachusetts.

Each association was contacted for providing up-to-date information, which was supplemented by research of the literature. All pertinent information obtained for each association has been included.

We are greatly indebted to the many people who assisted us, foremost the officers of the associations who took the time and effort to fill out questionnaires and provide us with information. We are very grateful for the many responses from our colleagues all over the world. The comments and advice from this international community were essential and important in making this book a useful information source and an aid in making professional contacts throughout the world.

We wish to thank particularly the IFLA Secretary General Paul Nauta and his associates, Deputy Secretary General Guust van Wesemael, Executive Officer Carol Henry, Hilda Urai and all the IFLA Headquarters Staff for generous and invaluable assistance, and for the support of the IFLA Clearing House on Associations in the Information Fields at Simmons College. Among the many colleagues from all over the world who kindly assisted, we like to acknowledge Ben G. Goedegebuure, Executive Director, FID, Dr. Magda Strebl and Dr. Laurenz Strebl for valuable help with Austria, Kyoko Toyoda for help with Japan, and Daniel Ortíz for help with entries in Spanish and Portuguese. In the early stages Donna Gagnon and Paula Gahagan were dedicated and highly competent assistants.

Our special thanks go to the Simmons College community for encouragement in our international activities and support from the Emily Hollowell Research Fund. We are grateful for President William J. Holmes' continuous interest, and the many helpful discussions with Dean Robert D. Stueart and our colleagues. Our own activities in professional associations at the national and international levels have given us opportunities to communicate and consult with our colleagues worldwide.

We are most grateful for indispensable assistance in research from Linda Watkins and Charlotte Hegyi at Simmons College, as well as Linda Willey for generous help throughout this project.

The statistical data were prepared by Joseph H. Fang. Our special gratitude and appreciation to Dr. Alexandra Herz for exacting scholarship in editing and meticulous proofreading.

Anna Fang devoted a great amount of time and effort to this project and guided it expertly from the beginning to the end. She is responsible for all the technical aspects of this publication, for design, formatting and planning of text and indexes, using Interleaf Technical Publishing Software, and preparing the printout for the camera-ready copy.

Last not least, our sincere thanks to our publisher, Dr. Klaus G. Saur, for his unfailing support and encouragement, and our editor, Manfred Link, for his patience and counsel.

Josephine Riss Fang
Alice H. Songe

April 1990
Graduate School of Library and Information Science
Simmons College
Boston, Massachusetts 02115
U.S.A.
Telephone: 1 (617) 738-2223
Fax: 1 (617) 738-2099

Introduction

The associations included in this reference work are nonprofit associations in the fields of librarianship, documentation, information science, and archives, including associations formed by institutions, staff (both professional and nonprofessional), and associations for professional education. Associations depending on commercial support are omitted. The term "library association" is used throughout the book for the sake of simplification and also because it seems to be accepted in many countries. However, the meaning should be understood in the broadest context of including all types of associations in the information fields.

The associations selected belong to two categories:
1. International Associations: Those organizations whose membership includes two or more countries (e.g., Scandinavia, Africa, Europe, Southeast Asia). They may be general in nature (e.g., the International Federation of Library Associations and Institutions), or specialized (e.g., the International Association of Law Libraries).
2. National Associations: Those organizations operating on a national level, either general in nature or specialized by subject, type of library, staff, etc., but open to all qualified members of a country. Associations covering only certain districts, provinces, or regions within a country are generally not within the scope of this *World Guide*.

The format of the book is designed to facilitate use and allow for easy identification and comparison of different aspects concerning the associations. Thus, the outline for each association follows the same pattern under established uniform headings. Whatever pertinent information could be obtained is listed, and if a negative answer was ascertained, it is so stated (e.g., *Staff*: None). When no definite information was available, or could be verified, headings are usually omitted.

The associations are grouped according to the two above-mentioned categories: First, the international associations in alphabetical order (totaling 76 active associations); second, the national associations listed by countries of the world (511 associations). The countries are in alphabetical order, and the associations are listed alphabetically under each country. Countries without evidence of existing associations are not listed. All efforts were made to be as inclusive as possible of newly established independent nations. A bibliography of *Selected Information Sources on Librarianship in the Third World* provides further information on these areas.

Guide to Use

The information for each association is given as follows:

Name. Each association is entered under its official name as listed by the association, followed by the acronym, if one is used, and in parenthesis the English translation of the official name. In the case of languages using a non-Roman alphabet, some associations may list the English version first. In the case of associations using more than one official language for their name, the first title is in the language officially used by the association itself, separated by a slash from the titles in other languages (e.g., the International Council on Archives is listed under the French name, Conseil International des Archives; FID under Fédération Internationale d'Information et de Documentation; IFLA under International Federation of Library Associations and Institutions). Each association is assigned an Arabic number for identification purposes. This number is referred to in the various indexes.

Address. The current mailing address is given and, whenever possible, whether or not the address is permanent. If the address of the headquarters differs from the mailing address, it is also provided. Telephone, telex, and fax numbers are given whenever available.

Officers. The main executive officers, whether they are elected or appointed, and their term of office are listed. The total number of members on the Executive Board/Committee is given.

Staff. Whether there is any staff at Headquarters, and if so, number of staff and whether paid or voluntary.

Languages. The official language(s) used by the association in its publications and activities.

Established. Date, place, and occasion of founding. A brief summary of any changes in the name of the association, the constitution or bylaws, with corresponding dates.

Major Fields of Interest. The broad areas of concern of the association.

Major Goals and Objectives. The mission statement and objectives of the association as specified in the statutes.

Structure. How the association is governed and name of the governing body. Affiliations with other organizations, e.g., IFLA, FID, and whether the association is part of a parent organization.

Sources of Support. How the association is financed, whether through membership dues, sale of publications, and any other means, especially, whether any forms of government subsidies are received. Amount of Budget in latest available figures.

Membership. Total number of members, both individual and institutional members. Number of chapters, divisions, sections, or any other subgroups (with brief listings). Types of membership available. Requirements for joining the association for each type of membership. Amount of dues for each category of membership, usually in the currency of the country.

General Assembly. How often the general membership meets; date and place of recent and future meetings whenever available.

Publications. Official journal and any newsletters of the association with all available bibliographical information: Title (also in English translation, if needed), date of founding, frequency, price, name of editor, address (if different from that of the association), telephone number, language(s), circulation, and where indexed and/or abstracted. Other major publication programs. Types of material published (including annual reports, proceedings of conferences, bibliographies). Some recent publications representative of the association's publishing activities. Whether publications are for sale, whether price lists are available, whether publications are listed in the journal. Any publications exchange programs in existence.

Activities. Major accomplishments in recent years. Current major activities and projected activities in the immediate future. Library legislation with which the association has been involved. Specific information on any continuing education programs, and sponsorship of Book Week, Exhibits, and other activities.

Use of High Technology. Whether the association uses computers (specifying types), databases, and other types of automation for its management and other activities.

Bibliography. Useful references resulting from an extensive literature search from the years 1981 to 1990, with emphasis on the most recent years, or highlights of the association's past, are appended whenever possible, providing additional information on policies, activities, and the history of the organization. Works in the English language are given preference, and for reasons of space the listings are selective. It is assumed that the reader will consult the official journal of an association for direct information on activities, and therefore listings from official journals are restricted. Bibliographies vary in length, revealing areas where further research and publications are needed. The entries in the Bibliography are chronologically arranged, with the most recent publications last.

Special Features

List of Acronyms. An alphabetical index of acronyms used by the associations, with the full name and entry number of the association, followed by the page number in bold-face, to facilitate quick identification and reference. This feature is useful due to the extensive use of acronyms in current publications.

General Bibliography: 1981-1990. A worldwide listing of reference sources on professional associations in the information fields, including monographs, series, articles, journals and general reference works of importance. This bibliography supplements the bibliographies of earlier editions, which should be consulted for retrospective sources.

Selected Information Sources on Librarianship in the Third World. Some selected references are provided on developing countries that have not yet been able to form a professional organization.

Official Journals. The official journals and selected newsletters published by the associations are grouped together in one alphabetical listing. Each entry is followed by the name and identification number of the association in parenthesis, and the page number for easy reference.

Official Names of Associations. An alphabetical listing of all associations, both international and national, usually by the official name, but occasionally by the English version, if the official name was not available. This index is useful for locating an association known only by name and not by country of origin. The country of origin (or "International"), and the entry number of the association are listed in parenthesis, followed by the page number.

Chief Officers of the Associations. An alphabetical index of the presidents or chairpersons of the associations, with the country (or "International") and entry number of the corresponding association in parenthesis, followed by the page number. This is a worldwide guide to prominent professionals active in associations in the information fields.

Subject Index. This index of broad areas of concern to associations in the information fields gives an indication of the extent of specialization and identifies current issues. Subject entries are followed by the total number of associations cited under this topic (in parenthesis), followed by the entry number for each association. This index is useful for identifying similar interest groups in other parts of the world. The total number of associations listed for each subject reveals interesting trends in professional cooperation.

Countries with International Associations. This alphabetical list identifies 40 countries in which international associations in the information fields are currently located. The entry number for each association, as well as the page number are provided. This index is useful for identifying countries that are internationally active.

Countries with National Associations. An alphabetical index by the English names of the 127 countries with national associations, for which information has been given in the book. For each country the page numbers are provided.

Statistical Data. The following comparative statistics (number and percentage) are given for the years 1976, 1980, and 1989/90.
1. Total number of associations listed (international and national)
2. Associations with full- or part-time paid staff
3. Associations affiliated with IFLA
4. Associations affiliated with other organizations
5. Associations receiving government aid
6. Associations having a publications exchange program
7. Associations having continuing education programs

8. Associations involved in library legislation
9. Associations using high technology in management
10. Total membership in associations
    a. Individual membership
    b. Institutional membership
    c. Not established (assumed majority individual)
    d. Membership in international associations
    e. Membership in national associations
11. Total number of official journals published
    a. International associations
    b. National associations
12. Number of journals indexed and/or abstracted
    a. Indexed in *Library and Information Science Abstracts (LISA)*
    b. Indexed in *Library Literature*
    c. Indexed in *Information Science Abstracts (ISA)*
    d. Indexed in other sources

List of Acronyms

Acronyms used by the associations, with the full name and entry number of the association, followed by the page number in bold face, to facilitate quick identification and reference.

AABDFC, Association des Archivistes, Bibliothécaires, et Documentalistes Francophone de la Caraïbe 013, **9**

AABevK, Arbeitsgemeinschaft der Archive und Bibliotheken in der Evangelischen Kirche 233, **172**

AACOBS, Australian Advisory Council on Bibliographical Services 089, **69**

AAE, Associazione Archivistica Ecclesiastica 297, **219**

AAHLIS, Australian Association for Health Literature and Information Services, Incorporated 090, **69**

AAHSLD, Association of Academic Health Sciences Library Directors 507, **391**

AAL
   Association of Architectural Librarians 508, **392**
   Association of Assistant Librarians 465, **351**

AALL, American Association of Law Libraries 487, **369**

AAS
   Association des Archivistes Suisses 447, **333**
   Associazione degli Archivisti Svizzeri 447, **333**

AASL, American Association of School Librarians 488, **370**

AATLH, Australian Association of Toy Libraries for the Handicapped 091, **70**

ABADCAM, Association des Bibliothécaires, Archivistes, Documentalistes et Muséographes du Cameroun 140, **107**

ABAH, Asociación de Bibliotecarios y Archiveros de Honduras 267, **196**

ABB, Asociación Boliviana de Bibliotecarios 121, **95**

ABD, Association Belge de Documentation 111, **87**

ABDOSD, Arbeitsgemeinschaft der Bibliotheken und Dokumentationsstellen der Osteuropa-, Südosteuropa- und DDR-Forschung 234, **173**

ABEA, Asociación Bibliotecarios Económicos y Administrativos 083, **67**

ABEBD, Associaçao Brasileira de Escolas de Biblioteconomía e Documentaçao 123, **97**

ABEF, Association des Bibliothèques Ecclésiastiques de France 223, **163**

ABES, Asociación de Bibliotecarios de El Salvador 206, **151**

ABF, Association des Bibliothécaires Français 222, **162**

ABGRA, Asociación de Bibliotecarios Graduados de la República Argentina 084, **67**

ABI, Association des Bibliothèques Internationales 022, **15**

ABIESI, Asociación de Bibliotecarios en Institucións de Enseñanza Superior e Investigación 351, **261**

ABIISE, Agrupación de Bibliotecas para la Integración de la Información Socio–Económica 396, **294**

ABIPALC, Asociación de Bibliotecas Públicas de América Latina y el Caribe 009, **7**

ABIPAR, Asociación de Bibliotecarios del Paraguay 394, **292**

ABL, Association des Bibliothèques Libanaises 339, **248**

ABLISS, Association of British Library and Information Studies Schools 466, **353**

ABPAC, l'Association des Bibliothécaires Parlementaires au Canada 143, **109**

ABRC, Association des Bibliothèques de Recherche du Canada 153, **117**

ABS
  Association des Bibliothécaires Suisses 448, **334**
  Associazione dei Bibliotecari Svizzeri 448, **334**

ABSC, Association des Bibliothèques de la Santé du Canada 157, **120**

ABTAPL, Association of British Theological and Philosophical Libraries 467, **353**

ABU
  Agrupación Bibliotecológica del Uruguay 561, **442**
  Asociación de Bibliotecarios del Uruguay 562, **442**

ABUEN, Asociación de Bibliotecas Universitarias y Especializadas de Nicaragua 373, **278**

ABUP, Asociación de Bibliotecarios Universitarios del Paraguay 395, **292**

ABYDAP, Asociación de Bibliotecarios y Documentalistas Agrícolas del Perú 397, **294**

ACA, Association of Canadian Archivists 141, **108**

ACAR, Asociación Colombiana de Archivistas 176, **132**

ACB, Asociación Costarricense de Bibliotecarios 182, **135**

ACBCU, Association Canadienne des Bibliothèques de Collège et d'Université 149, **114**

ACBD, Association Canadienne des Bibliothèques de Droit 150, **115**

ACBM, Association Canadienne des Bibliothèques Musicales 151, **115**

ACDBA, Association Congolaise pour le Développement de la Documentation, des Bibliothèques et des Archives 181, **134**

ACESBASI, Association Canadienne des Études Supérieures en Bibliothéconomie, Archivistique, et Sciences de l'Information 146, **111**

ACL, Association of Christian Librarians 509, **393**

ACLIS, Australian Council of Libraries and Information Services 092, **70**

ACML, Association of Canadian Map Libraries and Archives 142, **108**

ACRL, Association of College and Research Libraries 510, **394**

ACSI, Association Canadienne des Sciences de l'Information 147, **112**

ACURIL, Association of Caribbean University, Research and Institutional Libraries 021, **13**

ADBACI, Association pour le Développement de la Documentation, des Bibliothèques et Archives de la Côte d'Ivoire 305, **223**

ADBS, Association Française des Documentalistes et des Bibliothécaires Spécialisés 225, **165**

ADBU, Amicale des Directeurs de Bibliothèques Universitaires 218, **160**

ADEBD, Association des Diplômés de l'École de Bibliothécaires–Documentalistes 224, **164**

AEB, Asociación Ecuatoriana de Bibliotecarios 202, **148**

AENSB, Association de l'École Nationale Supérieure des Bibliothécaires 219, **160**

AFFIRM, Association for Federal Information Resources Management 501, **385**

AFIPS, American Federation of Information Processing Societies 489, **372**

AFLI, Arab Federation for Libraries and Information 003, **4**

AFVA, American Film and Video Association 490, **372**

AFVL, American Friends of the Vatican Library 491, **373**

CHLA, Canadian Health Libraries Association 157, **120**

CIA, Conseil International des Archives 033, **22**

CLA
Canadian Library Association 159, **121**
Catholic Library Association 521, **405**
Cyprus Library Association 186, **137**

CLEA, Canadian Library Exhibitors Association 160, **123**

CLENERT, Continuing Library Education Network and Exchange Round Table of the American Library Association 528, **410**

CLOSH, Canadian Libraries in Occupational Safety & Health 158, **121**

CLR, Council on Library Resources, Inc. 532, **414**

CLS, Cumann Leabharlannaithe Scoile 290, **214**

CLTA, Canadian Library Trustees Association 161, **123**

CNLIA, Council of National Library and Information Associations, Inc. 529, **411**

COLBAV, Colegio de Bibliotecólogos y Archivólogos de Venezuela 566, **444**

COLT, Council on Library/Media Technicians 533, **414**

COMLA, Commonwealth Library Association 030, **19**

COMLIS, (Congress of Muslim Librarians and Information Scientists) 028, **18**

CONSAL, (Congress of South–East Asian Libraries) 032, **21**

CONSALD, Committee on South Asian Libraries and Documentation of the Association for Asian Studies, Inc. 527, **410**

COSLA, Chief Officers of State Library Agencies 523, **406**

CPL, Council of Planning Librarians 530, **412**

CRL, Center for Research Libraries 522, **406**

CSL, Circle of State Librarians 472, **356**

CSLA
Canadian School Library Association 162, **123**
Church and Synagogue Library Association 525, **408**

CSLS, China Society of Library Science 172, **129**

CSSTI, Chinese Society of Scientific and Technical Information 173, **130**

CUTA, Chama Cha Ukutubi, Tanzania 450, **337**

D

DAR BiH, Drustvo Arhivskih Radnika Bosne i Hercegovine 573, **449**

DB, Danmarks Biblioteksforening 191, **142**

DB BiH, Drustvo Bibliotekara Bosne i Hercegovine 575, **450**

DBK, Deutsche Bibliothekskonferenz 248, **180**

DBV, Deutscher Bibliotheksverband e.V. 250, **182**

DF, Danmarks Forskningsbiblioteksforening 192, **143**

DGD, Deutsche Gesellschaft für Dokumentation e.V. 249, **181**

DVEB, Deutscher Verband Evangelischer Büchereien e.V. 251, **183**

E

EAHIL, European Association for Health Information and Libraries 037, **25**

K

KBF, Kommunale Bibliotekarbeideres Forening 381, **283**
KKL, Kirjastonhoitajien Keskusliitto – Bibliotekariernas Centralföbund 213, **155**
KLA, Korean Library Association 335, **245**
KLSS, Korean Library Science Society 334, **244**
KODAIKYO, Kouritsu Daigaku Kyokai Toshokan Kyogikai 314, **229**
KORDELA, Korean Research and Development Library Association 337, **246**
KOTANTOKYO, Kouritsu Tanki Daigaku Toshokan Kyogikai 315, **230**
KÜT–DER, Universite Kütüphanecilik Bölümü Mezunlari Dernei 457, **343**

L

LA
  Library Association 348, **257**
  The Library Association 476, **359**
LA (NI), The Library Association, Northern Ireland Branch 378, **281**
LAB
  Library Association of Bangladesh 108, **84**
  Library Association of Barbados 109, **85**
LAC, Library Association of China 174, **131**
LAI, The Library Association of Ireland 289, **213**
LAMA, Library Administration and Management Association 541, **420**
LAS, Library Association of Singapore 421, **313**
LATRA, Library Association of Transkei 424, **316**
LATT, Library Association of Trinidad and Tobago 454, **341**
LCF, Librarians' Christian Fellowship 475, **359**
LCLA, Lutheran Church Library Association 544, **423**
LIBER, Ligue des Bibliothèques Européennes de Recherche 059, **48**
LITA, Library and Information Technology Association 542, **421**
LLA
  Liberian Library Association 341, **250**
  The Lebanese Library Association 339, **248**
LNAC, Librarians for Nuclear Arms Control 540, **420**
LPB, Library Promotion Bureau 386, **286**
LPRC, Library Public Relations Council 543, **423**

M

MALA, Malawi Library Association 344, **253**
MELA, Middle East Librarians Association 060, **49**
MKE, Magyar Könyvtárosok Egyesülete 270, **199**
MLA
  Marine Librarians' Association 478, **361**
  Medical Library Association 546, **425**
  Music Library Association, Inc. 547, **426**
MLAJ, Music Library Association of Japan 323, **236**
MTESZ – TTT, MTESZ Tájékoztatási Tudományos Tanács 271, **200**

N

NAALD, Nigerian Association of Agricultural Librarians and Documentalists 376, **280**

NAFIPS, North American Fuzzy Information Processing Society 062, **50**

NAGARA, National Association of Government Archives and Records Administrators 548, **427**

NAL, Nippon Association for Librarianship 320, **233**

NBF, Norsk Bibliotekforening 382, **283**

NBLC, Nederlands Bibliotheek en Lektuur Centrum 357, **265**

NCS, Nederlandse Stichting voor Classificatie en Andere Ontsluitingsmethoden 358, **267**

NFAIS, National Federation of Abstracting and Information Services 549, **428**

NFF, Norsk Fagbibliotekforening 384, **284**

NITOKYO, Nihon Toshokan Kyokai 321, **234**

NITTOKEN, Nihon Toshokan Kenkyukai 320, **233**

NLA
  National Librarians Association 550, **430**
  Nigerian Library Association 377, **280**

NOTOKYO, Nihon Nougaku Toshokan Kyogikai 318, **232**

NTLA, Play Matters / The National Toy Libraries Association / ACTIVE 479, **362**

NVB, Nederlandse Vereniging van Bibliothecarissen, Documentalisten en Literatuuron-derzoekers 360, **268**

NVBA, Nederlandse Vereniging van Bedrijfsarchivarissen 359, **267**

NVBF, Nordisk Videnskabeligt Bibliotekarforbund 061, **50**

NZLA, New Zealand Library Association 372, **277**

O

OEGI, Österreichische Gesellschaft für Öffentlichkeitsarbeit des Informationswesens 105, **81**

OGDI, Österreichische Gesellschaft für Dokumentation und Information 104, **80**

OLM, Office du Livre Malagasy 342, **251**

ONTOKYO, Ongaku Toshokan Kyogikai 323, **236**

P

PAARL, Philippine Association of Academic and Research Libraries 403, **298**

PARBICA, Pacific Regional Branch of the International Council on Archives 063, **51**

PASL, Philippine Association of School Librarians 404, **299**

PATLS, Philippine Association of Teachers of Library Science 405, **300**

PBWG, Pakistan Bibliographical Working Group 388, **287**

PLA
  Pakistan Library Association 389, **287**
  Private Libraries Association 480, **363**
  Public Library Association 551, **430**

PLAI, Philippine Library Association, Inc. 406, **301**

PLAP, Public Libraries Association of the Philippines 407, **302**

PNGLA, Papua New Guinea Library Association 393, **291**

PPM, Persatuan Perpustakaan Malaysia 345, **254**

R

REFORMA, REFORMA (National Association to Promote Library Services to the Spanish Speaking) 552, **432**

S

SAA, Society of American Archivists 553, **433**

SAB, Sveriges Allmänna Biblioteksförening 439, **329**

SACAS, Standing Conference of National and University Libraries. SCONUL Advisory Committee on American Studies 486, **367**

SAIBI, Suid–Afrikaanse Instituut vir Bibliotek en Inligtingwese 425, **316**

SAILIS, South African Institute of Librarianship and Information Science 4255, **316**

SAILIS–SWA/Namibia Branch, South African Institute of Librarianship and Information Science. South West Africa/Namibia Branch 355, **264**

SALALM, Seminar on the Acquisition of Latin American Library Materials 064, **52**

SALIS, Sudan Association for Library and Information Science 432, **323**

SAP, Stowarzyszenie Archivistów Polskich 408, **303**

SARBICA, Southeast Asian Regional Branch of the International Council on Archives 067, **54**

SARJ, Savez Arhivskih Radnika Jugoslavije 580, **453**

SBC, La Société Bibliographique du Canada 145, **111**

SBP, Stowarzyszenie Bibliotekarzy Polskich 409, **303**

SBPR, Sociedad de Bibliotecarios de Puerto Rico 411, **306**

SBS, Svenska Bibliotekariesamfundet 436, **327**

SCAD, Société Canadienne pour l'Analyse de Documents 167, **127**

SCALS, Standing Conference of African Library Schools 068, **55**

SCAUL, Standing Conference of African University Libraries 069, **56**

SCAULEA, Standing Conference of African University Libraries, Eastern Area 070, **56**

SCAULWA, Standing Conference of African University Libraries, Western Area 071, **57**

SCECSAL, Standing Conference of Eastern, Central and Southern African Librarians 072, **58**

SCL, Society of County Librarians 483, **365**

SCOCLIS, Standing Conference of Co–operative Library and Information Services 484, **366**

SCOLMA, Standing Conference on Library Materials on Africa 074, **58**

SCONUL, Standing Conference of National and University Libraries 485, **366**

SCOPAL, Standing Conference of Pacific Librarians 073, **58**

SDARM, Sojuz na Drustvata na Arhivskite Rabotnici na Makedonija 581, **454**

SDF, Sammenslutningen af Danmarks Forskningsbiblioteker 198, **146**

SEDIC, Sociedad Española de Documentación e Información Científica 429, **320**

SENTOKYO, Senmon Toshokan Kyogikai 324, **236**

SFF, Svenska Folkbibliotekarieförbundet 437, **328**

SHITANTOKYO, Shiritsu Tanki Daigaku Toshokan Kyogikai 326, **238**

SIBMAS, Société Internationale des Bibliothèques et des Musées des Arts du Spectacle 065, **53**

SLA
School Library Association 481, **364**
Scottish Library Association 415, **308**
Special Libraries Association 555, **435**
Sudan Library Association 431, **323**

SLAALIS, Sierra Leone Association of Archivists, Librarians and Information Scientists 419, **312**

SLLA, Sri Lanka Library Association 430, **322**

SPIL, Society for the Promotion and Improvement of Libraries 390, **288**

SVD, Schweizerische Vereinigung für Dokumentation 446, **333**

SVSF, Sveriges Vetenskapliga Specialbiblioteks Förening 440, **329**

SWALA, Swaziland Library Association 433, **325**

SWARBICA, South and West Asian Regional Branch of the International Council on Archives 066, **54**

T

TEBA, Tutmonda Esperantista Biblioteka Asocio 075, **59**

TKD, Türk Kütüphaneciler Dernegi 456, **343**

TLA
Tanzania Library Association 450, **337**
Thai Library Association 451, **338**
Theatre Library Association 556, **437**
Tonga Library Association 453, **340**

TLS, Tekniska Litteratursällskapet 442, **330**

TOHYOP, Hanguk Tosogwan Hyophoe 335, **245**

TOMONKEN, Toshokan Mondai Kenkyukai 327, **238**

TSMA, Transvaal School Media Association 426, **317**

TSMV, Transvaalse Skoolmediavereniging 426, **317**

U

UBTA, Ukrains'ke Bibliotechne Tovarystvo Ameryky 557, **437**

UKB, UKB (Samenwerkingsverband van de Universiteitsbibliotheken, de Koninklijke Bibliotheek en de Bibliotheek van de Koninklijke Nederlandse Akademie van Wetenschappen) 362, **270**

UKR CSR, Ustřední Knihovnická Rada CSR 187, **139**

ULAA, Ukrainian Library Association of America, Inc. 557, **437**

ULC, Urban Libraries Council 558, **438**

USLA, Uganda School Library Association 459, **345**

V

VAN, Vereniging van Archivarissen in Nederland 363, **270**

VBB, Verein der Bibliothekare an Öffentlichen Bibliotheken e.V. 256, **186**

VBT, Vetenskapliga Bibliotekens Tjänstemannaförening 443, **331**

VdA, Verein Deutscher Archivare 258, **188**

VDB, Verein Deutscher Bibliothekare e.V. 259, **188**

VDD, Verein Deutscher Dokumentare e.V. 260, **189**

Part I
International Associations

001   African Standing Conference on Bibliographic Control/Conférence Africaine Permanente sur la Contrôle Bibliographique (ASCOBIC)

Address   c/o M. Saliou Mbaye, Executive Secretary, Archives du Sénégal, Immeuble Administratif, Avenue Roume, Dakar, SENEGAL (permanent).   Tel: (221) 215072
Officers   Exec.Sec: Saliou Mbaye
Languages   English, French
Established   1979
Major Fields of Interest   Bibliographic control in Sub-Saharan Africa
Major Goals and Objectives   Exchange documents of information concerning bibliographies between the member countries.
Sources of Support   Unesco
Membership   20 members, all institutional, 20 countries represented. Requirements: Must be a national bibliographic agency.
General Assembly   Meets every 18 months. 1986: Nairobi, Kenya; 1988: Antananarivo, Madagascar.
Publications   *Official journal:* Afribiblios. 1975-. 2/yr. Editor: Olu Olafioye. Address: National Library of Nigeria, Lagos, Nigeria. English,French. Publishes proceedings of meetings, reports on seminars and workshops. Has publications exchange program.
Activities   To extend the control of bibliography in Africa; to adopt laws to provide for the legal deposit of documents pertaining to bibliography in the ISDS Centres of member countries. Future: To keep in touch with the countries south of the Sahara concerning bibliographic activities. Active in promoting legislation pertaining to the legal deposit of documents. Sponsors continuing education lectures, seminars and workshops.
Use of High Technology   No computers yet, but Exec. Sec. attended seminars dealing with computerization of library activities.
Bibliography   Manual ASCOBIC sur la contrôle bibliographique en Afrique préparé par Saliou Mbaye. Programme Général d'information et UNISIST (et pour la) conférence africaine permanente sur la contrôle bibliographique. Paris, Unesco, 1981. iii, 61 p. (PGI-81/WS/29); Armstrong, J.C., "Sixth ASCOBIC Conference is Held in Nairobi, Kenya," Library of Congress Information Bulletin 46 (Jan. 19, 1987):35.

002   Agricultural Information Bank for Asia (AIBA)

Address   c/o Josephine C. Sison, Project Officer, SEAMEO Regional Center for Graduate Study and Research in Agriculture (SEARCA) College, Laguna 3720, PHILIPPINES (permanent).   Tel: 2477, 2290, or 2317; Telex: (ITT) 40904 SEARCA PM
Officers   Josephine C. Sison, Project Officer. Board of Directors: 5
Staff   9 (paid)
Languages   English
Established   1974
Major Fields of Interest   Information services in agriculture and related fields.
Major Goals and Objectives   To promote new and improved techniques for handling and disseminating information in the field of agriculture and related disciplines; to serve as a coordinating center in Southeast Asia for the FAO's international agricultural systems such as AGRIS and CARIS.
Structure   Governed by SEAMEO Regional Center for Graduate Study and Research in Agriculture (SEARCA). Affiliations: ALAP (Agricultural Libraries Association of the Philippines).
Sources of Support   SEAMEO (Southeast Asian Ministers of Education Organization). Budget: Confidential.

General Assembly   General membership meets once a year.
Publications   *Official journals:* AGRIASIA. 1977-. 4/yr. Editor: Sergia C. Baldos. Address: AIBA/SEARCA, College, Laguna 3720. Circ: Membership. English; CARIS-SEA. 1984-. 1/yr. Editor: Alicia H. Rillo. Address same as above. English. Indexed in AIBA using AGRIS/CARIS systems. Other official publications: Special bibliographies. No publications exchange program.
Activities   Creation of database in agriculture and all related fields, providing online bibliographic literature searching services and training in relation to information work. Future activities will concentrate on providing training in relation to information work. Sponsors continuing education lectures, seminars, and training workshops.
Use of High Technology   Computers (mini- and micro-computers), databases for management.

003   Arab Federation for Libraries and Information (AFLI)

Address   BP 1603, Tunis 1055, TUNISIA
Officers   Pres: Wahid Gdoura (Tunisia); VP: Yessef Qandel (Jordan); Treas: Rachid Abdulhak (Tunisia); Gen-Sec: Jassim Muhammed Jirjees (Iraq). Exec.Board: 7, elected.
Established   Dec. 1986, during Fourth Arab Conference organized by the Institut Supérieur de Documentation in Hammamet, Tunisia.
Major Fields of Interest   Cooperation between library associations and institutions in the Arab world.
Major Goals and Objectives   To re-enforce cooperation between library associations and institutions in the Arab world; to conserve the Arab heritage everywhere in its written or audiovisual form and to make it known; to promote the profession; to prepare and encourage scientific research and studies in the field of librarianship and to organize special conferences and seminars; and to try to improve the quality of curricula dispersed in schools and institutes which educate and train librarians and information specialists.
Activities   Establish mutual help relationships with national, Arab, and international organizations and institutions which share the same concerns; publish a magazine and yearbook on libraries and information in the Arab world; hold conferences on the Arab level which deal with technical subjects in the field of information; form working commissions such as: Intellectual production, Bibliographical, Education and training, and standards and professional lexicon.

004   Arab Regional Branch of the International Council on Archives (ARBICA)

Address   Ezz Eldin Ismail, President, c/o The National Library & The General Egyptian Book Organization, Corniche El-Nil, Ramlat Boulaq, Cairo, EGYPT (not permanent). Tel: 20 (2) 762971/765436. Telex: 93932.
Officers   Pres: Ezz Eldin Ismail (Egypt); Sec.Gen: M.J. Abdusalim (Sudan).
Languages   Arabic, English
Established   1972, Rome, by leading archivists from 9 Arab countries: M. Touili (Algeria), E.M. ElSheneti (Egypt), M. Abdulhamid (Iraq), S. Mousa (Jordan), C. Muemne (Lebanon), W. Wakili (Morocco), M. J. Abdusalim (Sudan), A. Rifai (Syria), and O. Salah Ahmed (People's Republic of Yemen).
Major Fields of Interest   Regional cooperation among national archival institutions of Arab States.
Major Goals and Objectives   To establish, maintain, and strengthen relations between archivists of all countries in the region and between all institutions, professional bodies, and organizations that are concerned with the custody, organization, or administration of

archives; to promote preservation and conservation of archives; to facilitate use of archives through publicity and greater ease of access; to promote, organize, and coordinate activities in the field of archives in the region; to sponsor professional training of archivists; to cooperate with other organizations or institutions concerned with the documentation of human experience and the use of that documentation for the benefit of mankind.
Structure   Governed by Executive Board. Affiliation: ICA
Membership   Total members: 29. Type of membership: National archival institutions of Arab States, and other institutions and organizations of the region concerned with archives. 3 committees (archival development and training; financial and legal affairs; technical matters, such as buildings, reprography, restoration).
Publications   *Official journal:* The Arab Archives (al-Watha'ig al Arabiyah). 1975-. 1/yr. Address: Ezz Eldin Ismail, Pres., The National Library & The General Egyptian Book Organization, Corniche El-Nil, Ramlat Boulaq, Cairo, Egypt. English, Arabic. Issues occasional publications.
Activities   To establish regional cooperation among national archival institutions of Arab States; to create a regional training center for archivists; to promote the creation of national archives services in Arab countries.

005   Arab University Library Association (AULA)

Address   c/o Chief Librarian, Kuwait University, Kuwait, KUWAIT. Further information may be obtained from Arab League Educational, Cultural & Scientific Organization (ALECSO), c/o M.T. Khafagi, Director, Information, Documentation Department, B.P. 1120, Tunis, TUNISIA. Tel: 216 (1) 781519. Telex 13825. Fax: 216-1784965.

006   ARLIS NORDEN

Address   c/o Uppsala University Library, Box 510, S-75120 Uppsala, SWEDEN (not permanent). Tel: 46 (18) 183900. Telex 76076
Officers   Pres: Ms. A. L. Thygesen
Established   1986
Major Fields of Interest   Art librarianship
Major Goals and Objectives   To promote art librarianship in the Scandinavian countries.
Structure   Affiliations: IFLA.

007   ARMA International: Association of Records Managers and Administrators, Inc. (ARMA)

Address   c/o James P. Souders, Executive Director, 4200 Somerset Drive, Suite 215, Prairie Village, Kansas 66208, USA (permanent). Tel: (913) 341-3808; Fax: 913-341-3742
Officers   (elected for 1-yr. term) Pres. and CEO: Martin Richelsoph, CRM; Exec. VP: David O. Stephens, CRM; Sec/Treas. (2-yr.-term): Manker R. Harris, CRM; Chairman of the Board (Immed. Past Pres.): John Moss Smith, COAP; Regional VPs for 11 regions; Exec.Dir. (appointed): James P. Souders.
Staff   10 (paid)
Languages   English
Established   1955
Major Fields of Interest   Information retrieval, files and forms management, historical documentation, micrographics, retention schedules, vital records protection, computer-assisted information management programs, correspondence and reports management.

Major Goals and Objectives　To promote a scientific interest in records and information management; to provide a forum for research and the exchange of ideas and knowledge; to foster professionalism; to develop and promulgate workable standards and practices; and to furnish a source of records and information management guidance through education and publication.

Sources of Support　Membership dues, sale of publications, annual conference. Budget (US Dollar): 1987/88: 1.3 million.

Membership　Total members: 9,000 (all individual). Sections: 32. Chapters: 130. 20 countries represented. Requirements: Interest in profession of records and information management. Dues (US Dollar): $65, international, plus chapter dues of $10-30.

General Assembly　General membership meets once a year. 1988: Baltimore, Maryland, Oct. 3-6; 1989: New Orleans, Louisiana, Oct. 2-5; 1990: San Francisco, California, Nov. 5-8.

Publications　*Official journal:* Records Management Quarterly. 1967-. 4/yr. $45, $38 (libraries). Free to members. Editor: Ira A. Penn, CRM. Address: PO Box 4580, Silver Spring, MD 20904, USA. Circ: 10,500. English. Publications available for sale: Quarterly newsletter; Handbook for the Recovery of Water Damaged Business Records; Alphabetic Filing Rules; many others. Price lists available twice a year.

Activities　Past achievements: Worked on ELF (Eliminate Legal-size Filing) legislation passed by U.S. federal and several state governments; growth of Canadian membership (to 15% of total); growth in Industry Action Committee program; growth in Annual Conference program and exhibits. Currently working for default 3-year retention period in all statutes and regulations not specifying a longer period, and seeking additional international growth.

Use of High Technology　Computers (Alpha Micro) for management. Journal and other materials available on microfiche.

Bibliography　"ARMA International," in The Bowker Annual: Library and Book Trade Almanac, 34th Edition 1989-90, pp. 665-666. New York: R.R. Bowker, 1989.

008　Art Libraries Society of Australia and New Zealand (ARLIS-ANZ)

Address　c/o 6 Hardy Terrace, East Ivanhoe, Victoria 3079, AUSTRALIA. Tel: (61) 6699846. Telex: 38104. Fax: 61-6631480.

Languages　English

Established　1975, Melbourne. Founders: Joyce McGrath, Sue Boaden, Patricia Foster, Bronwen Merrett.

Major Fields of Interest　Art librarianship

Major Goals and Objectives　To promote the development of art librarianship and art library resources, particularly by creating a forum for the exchange of ideas.

Structure　Governed by Executive Committee, meeting monthly. Affiliation: IFLA.

Sources of Support　Membership dues, grants from the Australia Council

Membership　Total members: 75 (50 individual, 25 institutional). 3 countries represented. Types of membership: Individual, institutional. Requirements: Interest in the aims of the Association. Dues (Australian Dollar): 5, individual; 10, institutional.

General Assembly　Entire membership meets annually in seminars with overseas guest speakers.

Publications　*Official journal:* ARLIS-ANZ News. 1975-. 4/yr (approx.). (Australian Dollar) 5, individuals; 10, institutions. Not free to members. Address same as Association. English. Publications exchanged with other associations, libraries, nonlibrary institutions and organizations.

Activities   Exchanging information at conferences and seminars, organizing special studies seminars during LAA Conferences. Association has provided a support system for art librarians from wide-spread areas, encouraged the establishment of local interest groups, and furthered cooperation beetween art libraries in art galleries and museums, universities, schools of art and national resource libraries. Sponsors lectures open to the public, seminars, workshops, and other continuing education activities.
Bibliography   Richards, V., "ARLIS/ANZ and Art Libraries in the Antipodes," Art Libraries Journal 11 (1986):12-16.

009   Asociación de Bibliotecas Públicas de América Latina y el Caribe (ABIPALC) (Association of Public Libraries of Latin America and the Caribbean)

Address   c/o Biblioteca Nacional, Las Mercedes, Calle Paris cruce con Caroni, Edificio Macanao, Piso 2. Apartado postal 6525, Caracas, VENEZUELA (permanent). Tel: 58 (2) 913408. Fax: 58-2-919545
Officers   (elected) Pres: Graciela Lovera de Mantellini (Venezuela); VP: Miriam Mejía (Colombia); Sec: María Elena Zapata (Venezuela); Treas: Marta Terry (Cuba); Other officers: Eduardo Puente (Ecuador); Teresa Naveillan (Chile); Fidel Coloma (Nicaragua). Exec.Board: 7.
Staff   None
Languages   Spanish
Established   Nov.13-17, 1989, Caracas, Venezuela, at the Seminario Regional sobre Sistemas de Bibliotecas Públicas de América Latina y el Caribe (Regional Seminar on Public Library Systems of Latin America and the Caribbean), as a result of recommendations made at the First Regional Seminar in Caracas in 1982. Constitution signed by representatives of Brazil, Colombia, Cuba, Chile, Ecuador, Nicaragua and Venezuela.
Major Fields of Interest   Public libraries
Major Goals and Objectives   To contribute to the development, cooperation and promotion of public libraries in the region. (Association is in the process of formulating goals and objectives)
Structure   Governed by executive officers. Affiliations: IFLA
Sources of Support   Membership dues.
Membership   Association is in the process of asking governmental bodies in charge of the development of public libraries to join, as well as institutions and individuals that might be interested.
General Assembly   Not yet determined
Publications   Not yet determined
Activities   As a new Association, a plan of action is being developed.

010   Asociación Interamericana de Bibliotecarios y Documentalistas Agrícolas (AIBDA) (Inter-American Association of Agricultural Librarians and Documentalists)

Address   Secretaría Técnica Ejecutiva, c/o IICA-CIDIA, Apartado 55, 2200 Coronado, San José, COSTA RICA (permanent). Tel: (506) 290222. Fax: 506-294721.
Officers   (elected for 3-yr.term) Pres: Lupita Rodríguez de M.; Past Pres: Nitzia Barrantes (Panama); VP: Guadalupe Bustamente (Colombia); Sec: Ms. I. Cortés P.; Treas: Lupita Rodríguez (Costa Rica); Members: Celia Fernández (Argentina); Exec. Dir: Ana María Paz de Erickson (appointed); Fiscal: Ligia López (Costa Rica, elected). Board of Directors: 6, plus 2 substitute members.
Languages   Spanish, Portuguese or English for articles in the AIBDA Journal.

Staff   2 (paid)

Established   1953, at the First Inter-American Meeting of Agricultural Librarians and Documentalists. Reactivated 1965 at the Third World Congress of the International Association of Agricultural Librarians and Documentalists (IAALD), in Washington, DC.

Major Fields of Interest   Agricultural librarianship and information; training of agricultural librarians; continuing education.

Major Goals and Objectives   To promote librarianship and documentation in the field of agriculture in Latin America and the Caribbean; to establish cooperation among librarians and information science specialists; to promote professional education.

Structure   Governed by executive officers and council meeting annually. Affiliations: IFLA, IAALD.

Sources of Support   Membership dues, sale of publications, annual economic support of the Inter-American Institute of Cooperation for Agriculture. Donations for special projects from other donor organizations. Budget (US Dollar): Approx.18,000.

Membership   Total members: 479 (392 individual, 87 institutional). Chapters: 6. 31 countries represented. Requirements: Individuals working in agricultural library or documentation centers, librarians working in other fields, library school professors, individuals in other fields interested in the aims of the Association. Institutions with an agricultural interest. Dues (US Dollar): 20, individual; 50, institution, 100, contributor.

General Assembly   General membership meets every 3 years. 1987: Guatemala City, July 13-17.

Publications   *Official journal:* Revista AIBDA. 1980-. 2/yr. (US Dollar) 25. Free to members. Editor: Ana María Paz de Erickson. Address: AIBDA, c/o CATIE 7170, Turrialba, Costa Rica. Circ: 800. Spanish, English, Portuguese. Indexed in LISA, IREBI, Páginas de Contenido: Ciencias de la Información, INSPEC, PASCAL THEMA T 205. Other publications: Annual report, reports of seminars, workshops; Boletín Informativo. 1966-. 4/yr. Free to members. Editor: Ana María Paz de Erickson; Páginas de Contenido: Ciencias de la Información. 1979-. 4/yr. Editor: Lupita Rodriguez Mendex; AIBDA Actualidades. 1981-. irreg.; Boletín Especial. 1966-. irreg.; Diccionario Historico del Libro y de la Biblioteca; Guía para Bibliotecas Agrícolas. Publications listed in Journal, available for sale. Publications exchange program in effect.

Activities   Past achievements: Inter-American meetings (Dominican Republic, 1981; Brasilia, Brazil, 1984); training courses in preparation for library projects and on information for librarians; participation in a World Congress (Ottawa, Canada, 1985); promotion of professional education for librarians; preparation of a major project for establishing a clearing house and training facilities. Current: Continue past activities, improve publications program. Future: Establish a clearinghouse on training facilities, offer short courses, prepare textbooks and other teaching materials. Association sponsors exhibits, continuing education, short courses. Members participate in congresses, seminars and meetings.

Bibliography   Moretti, D.M.B., "A evoluçao de AIBDA," Revista AIBDA 4 (1983):53-54 (in Spanish); Chavez, M., "Las Filiales de AIBDA," Revista AIBDA 4 (1983):55-58 (in Spanish); "AIBDA ha cumplido viente años," Boletín de Informativa de AIBDA 21 (1986):1-2 (in Spanish); Paz de Erickson, A.M., "Recursos humanos: un recurso renovable?" (Human Resources: A Renewable Resource? Revista AIBDA 7 (1986):85-94 (AIBDA's program for continuing education); Márquez, O., "La Asociación Interamericana de bibliotecarios y Documentalistas Agrícolas (AIBDA) y sus organismos componentes - Cronología y análisis de actividades," (The Interamerican Association of Agricultural Librarians and Documentalists (AIBDA) and its consistituent bodies - chronology and analysis of activities) Revista AIBDA 7 (1986):63-83 (survey and evaluation of activities 1966-83); "AIBDA in Guatemala: Looking to the Future," (80th Conference, 1987); Quarterly Bulletin of IAALD 32 (1987):229-230; "Inter-American Association of Agricultural Librarians and Documentalists," in The Bowker Annual: Library and Book Trade Almanac, 34th Edition 1989-90, p. 728. New York: R.R. Bowker, 1989.

011   Asociación Latinoamericana de Archivos (ALA)
(Latin American Association of Archives)

Address   c/o Guillermo Durand Florez, President, Director del Archivo General de la Nacion, Palacio de Justicia, Jiron Manuel Cuadros s/n Apartado 3124, Lima, PERU
Officers   Pres: Guillermo Durand Florez (Peru); VPs: Raul do Rego Lima (Brazil) and Vicente de la O Gutierrez (Cuba); Sec.Gen: Alberto Lee Lopez (Director del Archivo Nacional, Calle 24 no.5-60, 4 piso, Bogota, DE, Colombia).
Structure   A regional branch of ICA
Membership   Members from 18 Latin American countries. Dues: According to 5 classes ranging from 15 to 100 US Dollars.
Publications   *Official journal:* Boletín Interamericano de Archivos. 1/yr. Address: Centro Interamericano de Formación de Archiveros, Cordoba, Argentina.
Activities   Sponsors regional and international seminars and meetings

012   Asociación Latinoamericana de Escuelas de Bibliotecología y Ciencias de la Información (ALEBCI)
(Latin American Association of Schools of Library and Information Science)

Address   c/o Octavio Castillo Sánchez, Executive Secretary, ALEBCI, Escuela de Bibliotecología, Centro Regional Universitario de Veraguas, Santiago de Veraguas, PANAMA (not permanent). Tel: (507) 984587/984703.
Officers   Exec.Sec: Octavio Castillo Sánchez. Board of Directors: 6
Staff   None.
Languages   Spanish
Established   Sept. 1970, Buenos Aires, Argentina, during the International Congress of Documentation.
Major Fields of Interest   Library education in Latin America and the Caribbean
Major Goals and Objectives   To further library education through cooperation among library schools and library school teachers.
Structure   Governed by executive officers and library school members. Affiliations: FID, IFLA.
Sources of Support   Membership dues.
Membership   Total members: 40 (35 individual, 5 institutional)
General Assembly   General membership meets every 2 years.
Publications   *Official journal:* ALEBCI Informa (until 1987, ALEBCI: Boletín Informativo). 1972-. 3/yr. Free to members. Editor: Judith Licea de Arenas. Address: Colegio de Bibliotecología, Universidad Nacional Autonoma de Mexico, Mexico 20, DF, MEXICO. Circ: Membership. Spanish. Publications exchanged with libraries and other library associations.
Activities   Promotion of membership. Regional reunions of library school educators.

013   Association des Archivistes, Bibliothécaires, et Documentalistes Francophone de la Caraïbe (AABDFC)
(Caribbean Association of French-Speaking Archivists, Librarians and Information Scientists)

Address   BP 751, Fort de France 97201, MARTINIQUE (not permanent)

Languages French
Established 1979
Major Fields of Interest Archives, libraries and information centers
Major Goals and Objectives To promote the development of archives, libraries and information centers in the French-speaking Caribbean.
Membership Total members: 106 (individual, institutional). Sections: 4 (Guadeloupe, Guyana, Haiti, Martinique).
Publications *Official journal:* Notes Bibliographiques Caraïbes. 3/yr. Free to members. French; Bulletin de Liaison. 2/yr. Membership only. Other publications: Guide des sources disponibles sur la Révolution de Saint-Domingue, en Guadeloupe, Guyane, Haïti et Martinique, etc.

**014 Association des Bibliothèques de l'Enseignement Supérieur de l'Afrique de l'Ouest
(Association of Libraries of Higher Education in West Africa)**

Address BP 1093, Yamoussoukro, IVORY COAST (permanent). Tel: (225) 640541/640353/640698
Officers Pres: Koffi Koffi; Sec: Ama Ekue
Languages French
Major Fields of Interest Higher Education
Major Goals and Objectives To promote the development of libraries in higher education in West Africa.
Structure Governed by executive officers. Affiliations: IFLA member since 1987.
Sources of Support Membership dues. No further information on Association available.

015 Association for Health Information and Libraries in Africa (AHILA) (formerly Africal Medical Library Association / AMLA)

Address c/o World Health Organization AFRO, Regional Office Library, POB 6, Brazzaville, CONGO (permanent). Tel: (242) 833860/65. Telex: 5217. Fax: 242-831879.
Officers Pres: Alphonse Ikama-Obambi; Sec: C.J.J. Chisanga.
Languages English
Established 1984, as African Medical Library Association (AMLA); new name adopted 1988.
Major Fields of Interest Medical librarianship and health information services
Major Goals and Objectives To promote medical libraries and health sciences information in Africa.
Structure Affiliations: IFLA
Sources of Support Membership dues. No further information on Association available.

016 Association for Population/Family Planning Libraries and Information Centers - International (APLIC - International)

Address c/o S. Pasquariella, President, Population Council Library, 1 Dag Hammerskjold Plaza, New York, New York 10017, USA. Tel: 1 (212) 6441620. Telex: 234722.
Officers (elected for 1-yr.term). Pres: S. Pasquariella; Sec: J. Heide.
Staff None
Languages English

Established 1968, at the Carolina Population Center, Chapel Hill, North Carolina.
Major Fields of Interest Population and family planning information centers.
Major Goals and Objectives (1) The professional development of effective documentation and information systems and services in the field of population and family planning; (2) professional contact among population documentalists, librarians, and information and communication specialists; (3) the worldwide exchange of population information through international programs and activities; (4) an international cooperative network of population information centers for the exchange, dissemination, and communication of population information; (5) continuing education to encourage professional development among population documentalists, librarians, and information specialists.
Structure Governed by executive officers. Affiliations: AICIP, ASIS, MLA, IFLA.
Sources of Support Membership dues, private gifts.
Membership Total members: 130. Type of membership: Individual, institutional. Requirements: Payment of fee for both categories. Dues (US Dollar): 15, individual; 75, institutional.
General Assembly Entire membership meets annually in April.
Publications *Official journal:* AppliCommunicator. irreg. Free to members. Editor varies. Address same as Association. Circ: 200. English. Issues proceedings of annual meetings, proceedings of seminars, workshops, conferences sponsored by the Association. Other publications: Union List of Population/Family Planning Periodicals: A Serials Holding List of 36 North American APLIC Member Libraries; Guide to Population/Family Planning Information Sources; Some Holding Library Tools for Population Information: Indexing and Abstracting Services; etc. Publications issued for sale.
Activities International technical assistance in development of population/family planning librarianship. Training seminars for Africa and Latin America. Special publications, international family planning population networking. Active in promoting library-related legislation in the field of training seminars and development of teaching materials. Sponsors exhibits, seminars, workshops, continuing education.

017 Association Internationale de Bibliophilie (AIB) (International Association of Bibliophiles)

Address c/o Bibliothèque Nationale, 58 Rue de Richelieu, F-75084 Paris, Cedex 02, FRANCE (permanent). Tel: 33 (42) 723314
Officers (elected for 4-yr.term) Pres: Anthony R.A. Hobson; Treas: Bernard Skalli; Gen. Sec: Antoine Coron. Board of Directors: 16.
Staff 1 (paid)
Languages French, English
Established 1963
Major Fields of Interest Books, collections of precious books, bibliophily, bindings, typography, illuminations.
Major Goals and Objectives To establish a link between bibliophiles of various countries, to encourage all actions in relation with bibliophily.
Sources of Support Membership dues. Budget (French Franc): Approx.200,000.
Membership Total members: 500 (430 individual, 70 institutional). 32 countries represented. Requirements: To be presented by 2 members of the Association. Dues (US Dollar): 77, individual; 245, institutional.
General Assembly General membership meets once a year. 1988: Manchester, UK; 1989: Hungary.
Publications *Official journal:* Bulletin du Bibliophile (until 1920, Librairie Ancienne et Moderne. Bulletin). 1834-. 4/yr. (French Franc) 368. Free to members. Address: Promo-

dis (Syndicat National de la Librairie Ancienne et Moderne), 18 rue Dauphine, 75006 Paris, France. Circ: 500. French (English, German). Other publications: Proceedings of meetings. Publications for members only.

018 Association Internationale des Documentalistes et Techniciens de l'Information (AID)
(International Association of Documentalists and Information Officers) (IAD)
Address 74 Rue des Saints Pères, F-75007 Paris, FRANCE
Officers (elected for 4-yr.term) Pres: G. Picard; Exec.Sec: Jacques Samain
Staff None
Languages French, English
Established 1962, Paris
Major Fields of Interest Information and documentation
Major Goals and Objectives Promotion of information and documentation
Sources of Support Membership dues
Membership Total members: 300 (individual). Types of membership: Individual only. Requirements: Acceptance by the Direction Council. Dues (French Franc): 50
General Assembly Entire membership meets annually in October, in Paris at Association headquarters

019 Association Internationale des Écoles des Sciences de l'Information (AIESI)
(International Association of Schools of Information Science)
Address c/o Secretariat: AUPELF, BP 6128, Succ. A, Montreal, Quebec H3C 3J7, CANADA (permanent). Tel: 1 (514) 3436630. Telex: 05560955
Officers (elected for 2-yr.term) Pres: Catherine Lermyte (Institut National des Techniques de la Documentation, 202 rue St- Martin, 75141 Paris Cedex 03, France. Tel: 33 (1) 42712414 P 517; telex: 240247); VP: Gilles Deschatelets (Canada); Treas: Yolande Estermann (Switzerland); Secs: Roland Ducasse (France) and Bechir El Fani (Tunisia). Board of Directors: 5
Staff None
Languages French
Established 1977, Geneva, Switzerland. Founders: Georges Cartier, Jean Meriat, Gerard Hertzaff, Michel Merland.
Major Fields of Interest All fields related to the training of specialists in information science.
Major Goals and Objectives To encourage the development of the education of librarians, information scientists and other information professionals and to encourage a higher quality of such personnel; to stimulate original French-language research in this area; to establish and maintain a liaison between French-language schools, and promote instructional material in the French language.
Structure Governed by an Executive Board and a Secretariat meeting twice yearly. Affiliations: IFLA, AUPELF (Association des Universités Partiellement ou Entièrement de Langue Française).
Sources of Support Membership dues. Receives financial aid from FICU (Fonds International de Coopération Interuniversitaire). Budget (Canadian Dollar): Approx.$18,000.
Membership Total members: 45 (15 individual, 30 institutional). 8 countries represented. Requirements: Affiliation with school of information science or educational program of university level of an organization that uses French. Dues (Swiss Francs): 20, individual; 200, institutional; 150, associate member.

General Assembly   General membership meets every 2 years. 1988: Montreal, May 12-21.
Publications   No official journal.   Other publications: <u>Répertoire des Écoles franco-phones en sciences de l'Information</u> (Directory of French-language Schools of Information Science)
Activities   Major accomplishments in the last 5 years: sponsored workshops on "Teaching Methods and the Information Sciences" (Rabat, Morocco, 1984); "Continuing Education and Information Science" (University of Bordeaux, France, 1986). Current: Cooperation between schools of information sciences. Future: Further cooperation between schools, publication of teaching materials in French.
Bibliography   Lajeunesse, M., "Les relations internationales à l'École de Bibliothéconomie et des Sciences de l'Information," (The International Relations of the School of Library and Information Science [University of Montreal], <u>Argus</u> 16 (1987):31-33.

020   Association Internationale pour le Développement de la Documentation, des Bibliothèques et des Archives en Afrique / International Association for the Development of Documentation, Libraries and Archives in Africa (AIDBA/IADLA)

Address   Commission de Bibliothèques, BP 375, Dakar, SENEGAL (permanent). Tel: (221) 210954.
Officers   Pres: B. Dadie; Sec.Gen: Zacheus Sunday Ali
Languages   French, English
Established   1957, as Association pour le Développement des Bibliothèques Publiques en Afrique. Present name assumed 1968.
Structure   Affiliations: IFLA
Activities   Works for the development of national information policies in cooperation with Unesco.
Bibliography   "National Information Policies in West African Countries," <u>Herald of Library Science</u> 28 (1989):294.

021   Association of Caribbean University, Research and Institutional Libraries (ACURIL)
(formerly Association of Caribbean University and Research Libraries)

Address   c/o Oneida R. Ortiz, Executive Secretary, PO Box S, University of P.R. Station, San Juan 00931, PUERTO RICO (permanent). Headquarters: José M. Lázaro Library, University of Puerto Rico, San Juan, Puerto Rico. Tel: 1 (809) 7908054
Officers   (elected for 1-yr.term) Pres (1989-90): Jean-Wilfrid Bertrand (Bibliothèque nationale d'Haïti, 193, rue du Centre, Port-au-Prince, Haiti); VP/Pres-Elect: Blanca Hodge; Past Presidents: Alma Jordan (University Librarian, University of the West Indies, St. Augustine, Trinidad and Tobago), Albertina Jefferson; Exec.Sec.(perm.): Oneida R. Ortiz; Treas. (perm.): Joan Hayes. Board of Directors: 15.
Staff   2 (volunteer, partial pay)
Languages   Spanish, French, Dutch, English
Established   June, 1969 in San Juan during the East Caribbean Conference. Originally founded as the Association of Caribbean University and Research Institute Libraries (hence the acronym ACURIL), but changed to present name in order to broaden the membership to include public libraries, which in many areas serve as research sources.
Major Fields of Interest   Libraries, archives, information services and library associations and workers in these areas in the Caribbean.
Major Goals and Objectives   To facilitate the development and use of libraries, archives, and information services, and the identification, collection and preservation of in-

formation resources in support of the whole range of intellectual and educational endeavors throughout the Caribbean area; to strengthen the archival, library and information professions in the region; to unite workers in them; and to promote cooperative activities in pursuit of these objectives.

Structure   Governed by Executive Council. Affiliations: IFLA, UNICA (Association of Caribbean Universities and Research Institutions)

Sources of Support   Membership dues.

Membership   Total members: 200 (50 individual, 150 institutional). 26 countries represented. Standing Committees: 16 (Acquisitions, Bibliography, Microfilming, Indexing and Personnel, Library Education, Planning and Research, etc.). Requirements: Institutional: Libraries, archives and schools conducting programs of library or archival education; Organizational (since 1986): National, regional library associations, special associations; Individual: Librarians, archivists, students, retired librarians. Associate membership in each category available to members outside the Caribbean region. Dues: Regular and associate institutional members pay .0005 of budget with maximum of (US Dollar) 150 and minimum of 25; organizations, 20 per member; individual, 25 (associate 20); student, 10 (associate 7); retired, 10 (associate 7); honorary member free.

General Assembly   General membership meets annually in May. 1988: Martinique; 1989: Jamaica; 1990: Port-au-Prince, Haiti, April 22-27. The Executive Council usually meets in November and during the annual meetings.

Publications   *Official journal:* ACURIL Newsletter/Carta Informativa. 1972-. 4/yr. (US Dollar) 8. Free to members. Address same as Association. Editors: Oneida Ortiz, Neida Pagaú, Almaluces Figuera. Circ: 200+. Spanish, English. Other publications: Proceedings of meetings; reports of seminars, workshops; CARINDEX: Social Sciences and Humanities. 1977-; bibliography. Publications available for sale. No publications exchange program.

Activities   Past accomplishments: Restructuring of the Association to widen its scope; the SALALM-ACURIL Conference in 1987; publication of proceedings. Current: Annual meetings, committees' activities, publications. Cooperative activities, such as acquisitions, bibliography, microfilming and indexing. Future: Membership drive; strengthening of Association through use of new technologies; promoting role of information for national development; enhancing professional education; strengthening cooperation with similar associations, e.g. SALALM, etc. Sponsors continuing education lectures, seminars, workshops.

Bibliography   Jordan, A., "ACURIL - Treasure of My Dreams," COMLA Newsletter 35 (Mar. 1982):3-4; de la Garza, P.J., "Report on the 16th Annual Meeting of ACURIL," Library of Congress Information Bulletin 44 (Aug. 12, 1985):225-228; "ACURIL XVII Stresses Continuing Education," Quarterly Bulletin of IAALD 31 (1986):175; Douglas, D., "Association of Caribbean University, Research and Institutional Libraries," in ALA World Encyclopedia of Library and Information Services, 2nd ed., pp. 81-82. Chicago: American Library Association, 1986; de la Garza, P.J., "Report on the 17th Annual Meeting of the Association of Caribbean University, Research and Institutional Libraries," Library of Congress Informaton Bulletin 45 (Sept. 8, 1986):312-315; "SALALM and ACURIL Consider Strategies for Coping with Shrinking Budgets," Library of Congress Information Bulletin 46 (Nov.16, 1987):483-491; Jordan, A., "The Association of Caribbean University, Research and Institutional Libraries (ACURIL)," IFLA Journal 15 (1989):233-236.

022   Association of International Libraries/ Association des Bibliothèques Internationales (AIL/ABI)

Address   PO Box 117, CH-1211 Geneva 19, SWITZERLAND. Tel: 41 (22) 998667
Officers   (elected for 3-yr.term). Pres: Laura Alpern; Sec: Catherine Theissens; Treas: Edgar John. Exec. Comm: 5
Staff   None
Languages   English, French
Established   1963, Sofia, Bulgaria, at the 29th session of the IFLA Council.
Major Fields of Interest   International documentation
Major Goals and Objectives   To promote cooperation among international libraries.
Structure   Governed by Executive Committee. Affiliation: IFLA.
Sources of Support   Membership dues.
Membership   Total members: 80. 10 countries represented. Requirements: International libraries, individuals working in international libraries or interested in the goals of the association.
General Assembly   Entire membership meets every 2 years.
Publications   No official journal.
Activities   The Association was revived in 1987 after some years of inactivity. As a first step, the Geneva chapter has been reactivated and an acting Executive Board constituted. Current: Visits to international libraries in the Geneva area; meetings and discussions of problems common to librarians in international (or internationally-oriented) organizations. Future: Organization of a European Seminar in 1990; re-establishment of chapters in other international centers (New York, Paris). Sponsors continuing education offerings and visits to international libraries.

023   Association of Libraries of Judaica and Hebraica in Europe / Association des Bibliothèques de Judaica et Hebraica en Europe

Address   c/o Bibliothèque de l'Alliance Israélite Universelle, 45 Rue la Bruyère, F-75425 Paris Cedex 09, FRANCE (not permanent). Tel: 33 (1) 2803500
Officers   Pres: Georges Weill
Staff   Volunteers
Languages   English, French
Established   1955, Paris
Major Fields of Interest   Libraries of Judaica and Hebrew studies
Major Goals and Objectives   To encourage and facilitate the use of the Judaica and Hebraica held in European libraries.
Structure   Governed by executive officers who meet annually. Affiliations: IFLA.
Sources of Support   Membership dues and partly by subsidies.
Membership   Total members: 19 in 11 European countries. Types of membership: Institutional only. Requirements: Open to member libraries prepared to grant research facilities. Dues (Pound Sterling): 5.
General Assembly   Entire membership meets occasionally. No special time set.
Publications   Publications for internal use only; chairman issues an occasional newsletter. Annual reports published in IFLA Annual.
Activities   Members are encouraged to make interlibrary loans, assist in the establishment and maintenance of central information service, compile catalogs of their existing stock, exchange duplicates, arrange exhibits to arouse interest in Jewish writings. Association sponsors conferences. A union catalog is being created at the Copenhagen Royal Library.

024   Beta Phi Mu (International Library Science Honor Society) (BPM)

Address   c/o Blanche Woolls, Executive Secretary, School of Library and Information Science, University of Pittsburgh, Pittsburgh, Pennsylvania 15260, USA (permanent). Tel: 1 (412) 6249435. Fax: 1-602-6213279.
Officers   (elected for 1-yr.term) Pres: Joseph J. Mika; VP/Pres-Elect: Norman Horrocks; Past Pres: Elaine F. Sloan; Treas: Dennis K. Lambert; Exec.Sec: Blanche Woolls (appointed); Admin. Sec: Mary Y. Tomaino. Board of Directors: 14; elected.
Staff   1 (paid)
Languages   English
Established   Aug. 1948, at the University of Illinois.
Major Fields of Interest   Librarianship
Major Goals and Objectives   The society was proposed by a group of leading librarians and library educators who were aware of the notable achievements of honorary societies in other professions and who believed that such a society might have much to offer in the service of librarianship and library education. Its objectives are to recognize high scholarship in the study of librarianship and to sponsor appropriate professional and scholarly projects.
Structure   Governed by Executive Council.
Sources of Support   Membership dues, sale of publications. Budget (US Dollar): Approx.35,000.
Membership   Total members: 22,000. Chapters: 44. 15 countries represented. Requirements: Graduates of ALA-accredited schools who complete course requirements leading to a fifth year or other advanced degree in librarianship with a scholastic average of 3.75 on a 4.0 scale and recommended by the dean of their school. Dues (US Dollar): 50 for lifetime membership.
General Assembly   General membership meets yearly during ALA annual conference. 1988: New Orleans, LA, July; 1989: Dallas, TX, June; 1990: Chicago, July.
Publications   *Official journal:* Beta Phi Mu Newsletter. 1954-. 2/yr. Free to members. Address same as Association. Editor: Charles A. Seavey. Address: Graduate Library School, University of Arizona, 1515 East First Street, Tucson, AZ 85719. English. Circ: Membership. Publishes a numbered BPM Monograph Series (replacing the former Chapbook Series); Editor: Wayne A. Wiegand. vol.1: Wiegand, W., "An Active Instrument for Propaganda," The American Public Library during World War I (1989). Publications available for sale. The publication of a scholarly official journal is under consideration.
Activities   Scholarship program. Association offers annually the Distinguished Service Award to an individual, and funds an annual Distinguished Lecturer Series.
Bibliography   Holley, E. G., "Beta Phi Mu," in ALA Yearbook 1989, pp. 62-63. Chicago: American Library Association, 1989; "Beta Phi Mu," in The Bowker Annual: Library and Book Trade Almanac, 34th Edition 1989-90, pp. 677-679. New York: R.R. Bowker, 1989.

025   Bibliographical Society of Australia and New Zealand (BSANZ)

Address   c/o Rose T. Smith, Secretary, 76 Warners Aveenue, Bondi Beach, NSW 2026, AUSTRALIA (not permanent). Tel: 61 (2) 301014
Officers   (elected for 1-yr.term) Pres: Trevor Mills; Treas: Jennifer Alison; Sec: Rose T. Smith. Board of Directors: 5.
Staff   6 (volunteers)
Languages   English
Established   1969

Major Fields of Interest   Bibliography of all types.
Major Goals and Objectives   To encourage and promote research in all aspects of physical bibliography in Australia and New Zealand.
Structure   Governed by Council.
Sources of Support   Membership dues, sale of publications.
Membership   Total members: 340 (individual and institutional). 10 countries represented. Requirements: None. Dues (Australian Dollar): 24, individual; 30, institutional.
General Assembly   General membership meets once a year. 1987: Canberra, May 15-16; 1988: Sydney, Australia, Sept.
Publications   *Official journal:* The Bibliographical Society of Australia and New Zealand Bulletin. 1969-. 4/yr. Free to members. Editor: Trevor Mills. Address: Fisher Library, University of Sydney, NSW 2006, Australia. Circ: 350. English. Other publications: Broadsheet (newsletter), 3/yr.; occasional publications. Publications available for sale, address inquiries to editor. No publications exchange program.
Activities   Past achievements: Good standard of publications; recording material for Australian and New Zealand Early Imprints Project (EIP) under the aegis of the Society. Current: Annual conference, local meetings, participation in planning of EIP. Future: Continue with EIP project; improve communications.

026   Caribbean Archives Association - Regional Branch of the International Council on Archives (CARBICA)

Address   c/o Secretary, BP 74, Department of Archives, Basse-Terre, GUADELOUPE (not permanent); or c/o President.
Officers   (elected for 4-yr.term) Pres: Christine Matthews (Chief Archivist, Department of Archives, Black Rock, St. Michael, Barbados, West Indies. Tel: 4251380/1). Exec.Comm: 8; elected.
Staff   None
Languages   English, French
Established   1965, Mona Kingston, Jamaica.
Major Fields of Interest   Archival science
Major Goals and Objectives   To establish, maintain and strengthen relations between archivists of the Caribbean; to study problems concerned with the conservation of archives in tropical countries; to contribute to a better mutual understanding among peoples of the Caribbean.
Structure   Governed by an Executive Committee, meeting once or twice a year. Affiliations: ICA, OAS (Organization of American States), Unesco.
Sources of Support   Membership dues, sale of publications.
Membership   Total members: 40. Types of membership: Individual, institutional, honorary. Requirements: Individual: Archivists, historians, librarians, or persons approved by the Association for membership. Institutional: National or other institutions concerned with the custody and preservation of archives.
Publications   *Official journal:* Caribbean Archives. 1975-. 2/yr. (US Dollar) 3. Free to members. Address same as Association. English and French. Circ: 40. Issues proceedings of meetings. Publications issued for sale, price lists available. Publications exchanged with other associations.
Activities   Holding Caribbean Archives Conferences; publication of journal. Establishing a training program for Caribbean archivists. The Association has succeeded in bringing together archivists of the English- and French-speaking Caribbean. The Spanish-speaking archivists have their own association (Asociación Latinoamericana de Archivos/Latin American Association of Archives).

027   Central Africa Regional Branch of the International Council on Archives (CENARBICA)

Address   c/o Kiobe Lumenga-Neso, President, Director, Archives Nationales, Avenue de la Justice, 42, BP 3428, Kinshasa, ZAIRE (not permanent). Tel: 31083. Correspondence can also be directed to the Headquarters of the Conseil International des Archives/ International Council on Archives in Paris.

028   COMLIS (Congress of Muslim Librarians and Information Scientists)

Address   c/o Milli kütüphane (National Library), 06490 Bahcelievier, Ankara, TURKEY (not permanent). Tel: 90 (4) 2223812 / 2224158 / 2224768.
Officers   Pres: Dr. Oli Mohamed (c/o COMLIS Secretariat, Library, University Utara Malaysia, Bandar Darulaman, 06000 Jitra, Kedah, MALAYSIA); Chairman, COMLIS III Organising Committee: Hasan Duman, c/o Ministry of Culture and Tourism, Ankara, Turkey. Tel: 90 (4) 1312610. Fax: 90-4-1337140.
Staff   None
Languages   English and other languages
Established   1985
Major Fields of Interest   Muslim libraries and Islamic studies
Major Goals and Objectives   To promote cooperation and communication among libraries with Islamic collections; to promote Islamic studies; to establish an international information network on Islamic studies; to further the development of libraries in the Muslim world; to promote the standardization of certain basic practices such as, classification schedules, cataloging of Muslim names, and Islamic subject headings.
Structure   Governed by Executive Board.
Sources of Support   Host country takes care of expenses for the Congress.
Membership   Muslim and non-Muslim countries, such as Malaysia, Pakistan, Iran, Egypt, Bangladesh, Singapore, Turkey, China, Philippines, UK, USA, etc.
General Assembly   COMLIS III met at the Ataturk Cultural Centre, Istanbul, Turkey, May 24-26, 1989.
Publications   A quarterly journal is being planned on issues and ideas on library and information services in Muslim nations. It should serve as a scholarly instrument to promote the cause of COMLIS. Publishes proceedings of conferences.
Activities   Each Congress has a theme and ends with resolutions for acceptance by members. "Planning an Information Strategy for the Muslim World" was the theme for COMLIS III. Among the 13 resolutions, the following activities were planned: To prepare a proposal to the Organisation of Islamic Conference (OIC) for further support; to prepare a comprehensive Information Programme for the Muslim World, an International Muslim Information Network (IMIN); to promote compatibility and standardization in subject access, in networking query language, standards, Arabization of automated systems, and dissemination of research and development results among COMLIS members; to establish standards for bibliographic tools to meet the specific needs of the Muslim world and Islamic studies, such as, classification schedules, cataloging of Muslim names, and Islamic subject headings.
Use of High Technology   Depending on facilities of host country.
Bibliography   Anees, Munawar Ahmad, "Planning an Information Strategy for the Muslim World," Pakistan Library Bulletin 19 (1988):6; Rosdi, S., "Congress of Muslim Librarians III (COMLIS III) 24 - 26 May 1989, Istanbul," COMLA Newsletter 65 (1989):12; The Third Congress of Muslim Librarians and Information Scientists. Ankara: General Directorate of Libraries and Publications, Ministry of Culture, Turkey, 1989.

029 Commonwealth Archivists Association (CAA)

Address   c/o Anthony J. Farrington, Secretary, Public Record Office, Chancery Lane, London WC2A 1LR, UNITED KINGDOM (not permanent). Tel: 44 (1) 4050741 x223
Officers   (elected for 4-yr.term) Chair: G.H. Martin CBE; Sec: A.J. Farrington; Treas: A. Burnett. Exec.Comm: 7, plus officers.
Staff   Volunteers (officers)
Languages   English
Established   Sept., 1984, at 10th International Congress on Archives.
Major Fields of Interest   Archives and records management.
Major Goals and Objectives   Promote the development of professional archival standards in the Commonwealth; reaffirm the importance of archives in national heritage and development; exchange experiences and disseminate information.
Structure   Governed by officers and Executive Committee. Affiliations: ICA
Sources of Support   Membership dues, quasi-government subsidies from the Commonwealth Foundation. Budget (Pound Sterling): 1987/88: 7,000.
Membership   Total members: 86 (23 individual, 63 institutional). 33 countries represented. Requirements: Archival institution, practicing archivist, or general interest in objectives. Dues (Pound Sterling): 5, individual; 25, institutional.
General Assembly   General membership meets every 4 years. 1988: Paris, France, Sept. (during 11th International Congress on Archives).
Publications   *Official journal:* Commonwealth Archivists Association Newsletter. 1985-. 2/yr. Free to members. Editor: G. Bolotenko. Address: Public Archives of Canada, 395 Wellington St., Ottawa, Ontario, Canada K1A ON3. Circ: 100+. English. Other publications: Surveys of archival sources. Publications available for sale, listed in Journal. No publications exchange program.
Activities   Past accomplishments: Audio-visual training seminar, Malaysia/Singapore, 1985; Conservation training workshop, Barbados, 1986. Current: Conservation training workshop, Zimbabwe, 1987/88. Future: Involvement in records management programs for Commonwealth governments. Association sponsors continuing education lectures, seminars, and workshops.

030 Commonwealth Library Association (COMLA)

Address   c/o Joan E. Swaby, Executive Secretary, PO Box 40, Mandeville, JAMAICA, WEST INDIES. Headquarters: PO Box 534, Kingston 10, Jamaica (permanent). Tel: 1 (809) 9620703. Fax: 1-809-9622770.
Officers   (elected for 3-yr.term) Pres: Stephney Ferguson (1986-, c/o National Library of Jamaica, 12 East Street, PO Box 823, Kingston, Jamaica, WI); VP: Judith Baskin (Australia); Ex.Sec: Joan E. Swaby (appointed); Treas: Maurice Lundu (Zambia). Chief Exec.Comm: 8.
Staff   2 (paid)
Languages   English
Established   1972, Lagos, Nigeria, at an inaugural conference. Sponsored by the Commonwealth Foundation, Mr. John Chadwick, Director. Constitution amended 1979 to restructure on a regional basis.
Major Fields of Interest   Development of all types of libraries and library services in the Commonwealth.
Major Goals and Objectives   (1) To improve libraries in the Commonwealth; (2) to forge, maintain and strengthen professional links between librarians; (3) to support and encourage library associations; (4) to promote the status and education of librarians and the reciprocal recognition of qualifications; (5) to initiate research projects.

Structure   Governed by 6 Regional Councils, which send delegates to General Council meetings every 3 to 4 years. Regional Vice Presidents sit on the Chief Executive Committee, which meets every 12 to 18 months. Affiliations: ACURIL, FID, IFLA

Sources of Support   Membership dues, grants from the Commonwealth Foundation.

Membership   Total members: 230 (50 regular, 180 affiliates). 50 countries represented. Types of membership: Full: National associations; affiliates: Libraries, documentation centers, etc. Requirements: Open to all associations, libraries, information centers, etc. in and out of the Commonwealth. Dues (Pound Sterling): 20-350, full members; 20, affiliates.

General Assembly   General membership, Executive Committee, and COMLA Council meet every 3-4 years. 1983: COMLA Council IV, Nairobi, Kenya; 1986: Council V, Ottawa, Canada; 1990: Council VI, Malta, April 2-7.

Publications   *Official journal:* COMLA Newsletter. 1973-. 4/yr. (US Dollar) 35. Free to members. Hon.Editor: Paul Xuereb. Address: c/o University of Malta Library, Msida, MALTA. Circ: 600. English. Issues proceedings of seminars, workshops sponsored by the Organization. Has other occasional publications: Mungo, K.M. and Robertson, A., comps., Policy Guidelines for School Library Development (1987); Xuereb, P., ed., The Impact of Automation on the Functions, Administration and Staffing of Libraries: A COMLA Seminar, Singapore, Nov.1-2, 1985 (Malta, 1988); etc. Publications issued for sale, price lists available, listed in official Journal, exchanged with other international associations and Commonwealth professional associations. Some publications sent free on request.

Activities   Past accomplishments: Greater emphasis on development of COMLA member organizations within their own regions through the activities of the Regional Councils (Europe, West Africa, Asia, East, Central and Southern Africa, Americas and Caribbean). COMLA seminar on library services in rural areas, Sydney, Australia, Aug. 1988. Current and future: Promotion of rural libraries and resource centers; furthering of library and information work in developing countries; promotion of library skills amongst young readers. Proposed amendments to the Constitution to clarify certain articles. Active in promoting library-related legislation by providing background information and promotional activities. Sponsors conferences, seminars, workshops, and other continuing education programs. Since its founding in 1972, the COMLA Secretariat was located at the Jamaica Library Association and subsidized by the Government of Jamaica. In 1989, COMLA requested other member associations to host the COMLA Secretariat and the expenses of the Executive Secretary, so that the Secretariat could be moved after the General Council meeting in April 1990.

Bibliography   "COMLA: A Decade of Growth," COMLA Newsletter 37 (Sept. 1982):1-5, 12-13; Swaby, J.E., "Commonwealth Library Association," in ALA World Encyclopedia of Library and Information Services, 2nd ed., pp. 215-216. Chicago: American Library Association, 1986; "COMLA and the Library Profession," COMLA Newsletter 53 (Sept.1986):1; Ferguson, S., "Organising Library Associations in Small Countries," COMLA Newsletter 54 (Dec. 1986):8-9; "The Sydney Workshop on Rural Libraries," COMLA Newsletter 63 (Mar. 1989):1-4 (COMLA organized a Workshop on Rural Libraries and Community Resource Centres in Sydney, Australia, 5-7 Sept.1988); "Location of COMLA Secretariat," COMLA Newsletter 63 (Mar. 1989):6; "The COMLA Connection: An Interview between Michael Wooliscroft (Regional Councillor, COMLA South Pacific Region) and John Stringleman (former COMLA President)," New Zealand Libraries 46 (Mar. 1989):12-16; Swaby, J.E., "COMLINKS: News and Views from the COMLA Secretariat," COMLA Newsletter 64 (June 1989):1-2, 12; Benoit, M., "COMLA Workshop, Malta, 2-5 April 1990," COMLA Newsletter 65 (Sept. 1989):1,2; Swaby,

J., "Regional Cooperation: The Role of COMLA in International Librarianship," IFLA Journal 15 (1989):243-245.

031   Conference of Directors of National Libraries (CDNL)

Address   c/o Marianne Scott, Chair, National Library of Canada, 395 Wellington Street, Ottawa, Ontario K14 0N4, CANADA (not permanent). Tel: 1 (613) 9961623. Fax: 1-613-9964424.
Officers   Chair: Marianne Scott (Canada); Past Chair: Magda Strebl (Austria)
Staff   None
Languages   English
Established   1974
Major Fields of Interest   Those aspects of librarianship that are pertinent among directors of national libraries.
Major Goals and Objectives   To provide a forum for communication among directors of national libraries.
Structure   Affiliations: IFLA
Sources of Support   Not applicable.
Membership   Total members: 112, representing 112 countries.   Requirements: Open to directors of national libraries.
General Assembly   Entire membership meets once a year. 1987: British Library, London; 1988: National Library of Australia, Canberra.
Publications   No official journal.
Activities   Past achievements: Sponsored the Conference on Preservation of Library Materials (Vienna, 1986); provided guidance and support to international MARC activities and developments.   Current: Support of IFLA Core Programmes; annual meetings which facilitate communication and dialogue among national libraries.   Future: Continue supporting IFLA Core Programmes.
Use of High Technology   Computers (IBM PC) for management.
Bibliography   Strebl, M., "La préservation des resources documentaires dans les bibliothèques. Rapport de la conférence internationale de Vienne, 7-10 avril 1986," (The Preservation of Documentation Resources in Libraries. Report of the Vienna International Conference, 7-10 April 1986) Bulletin d'Information de l'Association des Bibliothécaires Français 137 (1987):19-22;   Carroll, F.L., and Schwartz, P.J., Biographical Directory of National Librarians (London: Mansell, 1989).

032   CONSAL (Congress of South-East Asian Libraries)

Address   c/o Mastini Hardjo Prakaso, Chairperson, National Library of Indonesia, Jalan Salemba Raya 28, PO Box 6324, Jakarta 10002, INDONESIA (not permanent). Tel: 62 (21) 3101411 or 3103553. Fax: 62-21-3103554.
Officers   CONSAL Committee of host country: Chair of Exec.Board, 8th CONSAL: M. Hardjo Prakaso; Vice-Chairman; Hon.Sec.; Hon.Treas). Exec.Board: Includes 3 members from each participating country
Staff   None
Established   1970, Singapore, as First Conference of Southeast Asian Librarians by the Library Associations of Malaya and Singapore.   Current name assumed and constitution revised in 1975
Major Fields of Interest   Libraries and librarianship in the Southeast Asian region
Major Goals and Objectives   (1) To establish, maintain and strengthen relations among librarians, library schools, library associations and related organizations in the re-

gion; (2) to promote cooperation in the fields of librarianship, bibliography, documentation and related activities in the region; (3) to cooperate with other regional or international organizations and institutions in the fields of librarianship, bibliography,
documentation and related activities
Structure   Governed by the CONSAL Committee, which includes the Executive Board
and 3 delegates from each participating country.
Sources of Support   Library association of host country; membership dues; subventions from various foundations and other private sources; sale of publications
Membership   Open to all national library associations of the Southeast Asian region
(Brunei, Burma, Cambodia, Indonesia, Laos, Malaysia, the Philippines, Singapore, Thailand and Vietnam). National membership: National library associations; the national library and all libraries and related organizations within the member countries. Associate
membership: Libraries and related organizations of non-member countries; and individuals interested in the objectives of CONSAL
General Assembly   CONSAL members meet at least once every 3 years with one
member country acting as host for the conference.   CONSAL VI: Singapore, 1983, May;
CONSAL VII: Manila, 1987, Feb. 15-21; CONSAL VIII: Jakarta, Indonesia, 1990, June
11-14.
Publications   No official journal. Publishes newsletter, proceedings, and other publications. Southeast Asian Microfilms Newsletter. 1972-; Masterlist of Southeast Asian Micro-
forms (1978) and Supplements
Activities   Provides opportunities for Southeast Asian librarians to come together to discuss matters of common professional interest.   The CONSAL Committee is charged with
carrying out the resolutions of the conference. CONSAL has held 7 conferences to date.
CONSAL VII (Manila, 1987; Chairman: Serafin D. Quiason) had 633 participants from
the 5 ASEAN (Association of Southeast Asian Nations) countries (Indonesia, Malaysia,
the Philippines, Singapore and Thailand).   The theme for CONSAL VIII is "New Challenges in Library Services in the Developing World."   Works with the Association of
Southeast Asian Nations (ASEAN) for the establishment of a Southeast Asian University
Network (SAULNET).
Bibliography   Soosai, J.S., "Fifth Congress of the South-East Asian Librarians (CON-
SAL V)," IFLA Journal 7 (1981):416-418; Horton, A.R., "CONSAL VI," Australian Academic and Research Libraries 14 (1983):249-251; Mansor, N., "CONSAL VI: A Report
and Personal Impressions," Singapore Libraries 13 (1983):28-30; Lim Pui Huen, P.,
"Congress of Southeast Asian Librarians (CONSAL)," in ALA World Encyclopedia of
Library and Information Services, 2nd ed., pp. 218-219. Chicago: American Library Association, 1986; Khurshid, A., "Library Associations in Asia," Herald of Library Science 28
(1989):3-10; Anuar, H., "The Why and How of CONSAL as a Regional Library Association," IFLA Journal 15 (1989):237-242.

**033   Conseil International des Archives/International Council on Archives
(CIA/ICA)**

Address   Charles Kecskeméti, Executive Director, 60 Rue des Francs-Bourgeois,
F-75003 Paris, FRANCE (permanent).   Tel: 33 (1) 42771130/40276000 x 6349. Fax:
33-1-48870608.
Officers   (elected for 4-yr.term) Pres: Jean Favier (France); Past Pres: Hans Booms
(FRG); VPs: Angeline S. Kamba (Zimbabwe) and Jean P. Valeaux (Canada); Ex.Sec (ap-
pointed): Charles Kecskeméti (Paris).   Exec.Comm: 30
Staff   4 (paid)

Languages   Documents: English, French; Congresses: English, French, German, Spanish and Russian
Established   1948, as provisional ICA; first congress held in 1950.
Major Fields of Interest   Archives, including records management.
Major Goals and Objectives   To promote international archival cooperation, preservation of the archival heritage, archival development, professional training, facilitating access to archives.
Structure   Governed by Executive Committee. Affiliations: National administrations members have a consultative status with Unesco.
Sources of Support   Membership dues, sale of publications, government subsidies (support of projects from various governments), subventions and contracts from Unesco.
Membership   Total number: 860 (150 individual, 550 institutional, 160 national administrations and associations). Regional Branches: 9 (Asociación Latinoamericana de Archivos (ALA), Arab Regional Branch (ARBICA), Caribbean Regional Branch (CARBICA), Central Africa Regional Branch (CENARBICA), Eastern and Southern Africa Regional Branch (ESARBICA), Pacific Regional Branch (PARBICA), Southeast Asian Regional Branch (SARBICA), South and West Asian Regional Branch (SWARBICA), West African Regional Branch (WARBICA). Sections: 3. Committees: 10. 127 countries represented. Requirements: Archival administrations, institutions, services, training centers, professional associations, professional archivists. Dues (US Dollar): Cat.A (national administrations), 115 - 230; Cat.B (associations), 50-100; Cat.C (institutions), 50; Cat.D (individuals), 30
General Assembly   Entire membership meets every 4 years. 1988: Paris, France; 1992: Montreal, Canada. International Round Table Conferences on Archives, of leaders in the profession, dealing with major issues and problems, are held annually except in years when congress convenes.
Publications   *Official journal:* Archivum. 1950-. 1/yr. Free to members. Address same as Association. Editor: M. André Vanrie. Address: Archives Générales du Royaume, 2-6 rue de Ruysbroeck, 1000 Brussels, Belgium. English, French, German, Spanish, Russian, Italian. Other publications: ICA Bulletin. 2/yr.; ICA Directory; C. Crespo Nogueira, ed., Glossary of Basic Archival and Library Conservation Terms (1988; ICA Handbook Series 4); Duchein, M., Archive Buildings and Equipment (2nd rev. ed., ed. P. Walne, 1988; ICA Handbook Series 6); Bulletin of the Business Archives Committee; Bulletin of the Commission for Archival Development; and many others. Guide to the Sources for the History of Nations, a monumental series of archival guides, is being published jointly with Unesco. Lists of publications for sale available. Publications listed in Directory. No publications exchange program.
Activities   Past achievements: Production of 43 RAMP (Records and Archives Management Programme) studies for Unesco, published between 1981 and 1986; production of various guides; strengthening of the regional structures; organization of new sections, such as of municipal archives; of business and trade union archives, and professional education and training; conducting survey on the preservation of the world's archival and library heritage; adopting 3d Medium Term Plan 1988-1992. Current priority areas: Professional training, conservation, automation, microfilming for developing countries, archival development and research in archives, administration (including records management). XIth International Congress on Archives, Paris, 1988. Sponsored Second European Conference on Archives, University of Michigan, 1989, May. Future: XIIth International Congress on Archives, Montreal, 1992; reconstitution of archival heritages through microfilming. Association has devoted 3 volumes of Archivum to archival legislation and

conducted 3 RAMP studies on legal matters. Association sponsors continuing education lectures, seminars, workshops.
Use of High Technology   Computers (microcomputer HERMES 100 - IBM-compatible) for management. Automation underway.
Bibliography   Franz, E.G., "Le Conseil International des Archives, ses Realisations et son Avenir," Archives et Bibliothèques de Belgique 55 (1984):3-27 (in French); Kecskeméti, C., "Rapport Général du Secrétaire Exécutif du CIA à l'Assemblée Générale, Bonn 17-21 Septembre 1984," Rassegna degli Archivi de Stato 45 (1985):547-575; Rhoads, J.B. and Kecskeméti, C., "International Council on Archives," in ALA World Encyclopedia of Library and Information Services, 2nd ed., pp. 373-374. Chicago: American Library Association, 1986; Rhoads, J.B., "North American Contributions to International Archival Endeavours," in Miscellanea Carlos Wyffels, pp. 309-322. Brussels, 1987; Kecskeméti, C., "International Council on Archives," in The Bowker Annual of Library and Book Trade Information, 1986, 31st ed., pp. 50-60. New York: R.R. Bowker, 1986; Broom, A., "The ICA Committee on Conservation and Restoration," IFLA Journal 12 (1986):314-316; Daniels, M.F., "The Genesis and Structure of the International Council on Archives: An American View," American Archivist 50 (1987):414-419; Blouin, F.X., "International Council on Archives, Committee on Professional Education and Training Meeting, April 1987, Grenada, Spain," ibid.:598+; Warner, R.M., "International Council on Archives, Executive Committee Annual Meeting and the International Round Table Conference on Archives, Sept. 1987," American Archivist 51 (1988):139-141; Crush, P., "Report on the President's Attendance at the XIth ICA Congress, Paris 1988," Archives and Manuscripts 17 (1989):9-24; Pizer, I., "Second European Conference on Archives," IFLA Journal 15 (1989):261-263; "International Council on Archives," in The Bowker Annual: Library and Book Trade Almanac, 34th Edition 1989-90, p. 734. New York: R.R. Bowker, 1989.

034   Conseil International des Associations de Bibliothèques de Théologie (International Council of Theological Library Associations)

Address   c/o Juan Antonio Cervelló-Margalef, General Secretary, Postfach 100690, Kardinal-Frings-Strasse, D-5000 Cologne 1, FEDERAL REPUBLIC OF GERMANY (permanent). Tel: 49 (221) 133587
Officers   (elected for 5-yr.term) Pres: Herman Morlion (Heverlee-Leuven, Belgium); VP: Andreas Geuns (Tilburg, Netherlands); Gen.-Sec: Juan Antonio Cervelló-Margalef (Cologne, FRG). Exec.Comm: 3.
Established   Oct. 18, 1961 under the name "Comité International de Coordination des Associations de Bibliothèques de Théologie Catholique (CIC);" adopted present name under statutes, 1972, as registered association with seat in Nijmegen
Major Fields of Interest   Theological library associations.
Major Goals and Objectives   To promote national and international cooperation among members and contribute to the general improvement of theological libraries.
Structure   Governed by executive officers meeting several times a year. Affiliations: IFLA
Sources of Support   Membership dues.
Membership   Total members: 11 (9 regular, 2 extraordinary). Requirements: None, but membership comprises mainly theological associations.
General Assembly   1987: Maredsous, Sept.1-3.
Publications   No official journal, but maintains an extensive publications program.
Activities   Furthering the aims of the association and carrying out an extensive publications program.

Bibliography   Cervelló-Margalef, J.A., ed., <u>Le Conseil International des Associations de Bibliothèques de Théologie, 1961-1981</u>. Cologne: Secrétariat du Conseil, 1982; Cervelló-Margalef, J.A., "Der Internationale Rat der Vereinigung Theologischer Bibliotheken," <u>Zeitschrift für Bibliothekswesen und Bibliographie</u> 30 (1983):257-262.

035   Consejo Interamericano de Archivos (Inter-American Council of Archives)

Address   c/o Professor J. Ignacio Rubio Mane, Director, Archivo General de la Nación, Palacio Nacional, Mexico DF, MEXICO

036   Eastern and Southern Africa Regional Branch of the International Council on Archives (ESARBICA)

Address   c/o Musila Musembi, Secretary-Geneneral, PO Box 49210, Nairobi, KENYA (not permanent). Tel: 28959; Telex: archives nairobi
Officers   (elected for 2-yr.term) Chair: J.S. Dlamiwi (Swaziland); Vice-Chair: P. Mukula (Zambia); Sec.-Gen: M. Musembi (Kenya); Treas: T.M. Lekaukau (Botswana); Ed: P. Mazikama. Board of Directors: 10.
Staff   Volunteers (officers)
Languages   English
Established   1969
Major Fields of Interest   Records and archives management.
Major Goals and Objectives   To facilitate faster development in records and archives management in the entire region.
Structure   Governed by Executive Board. Affiliations: A regional branch of ICA; IFLA
Sources of Support   Membership dues, sale of publication, government subsidies.
Membership   Total members: 20 (5 individual, 15 regular). 10 countries represented. Requirements: Open to national archives in Eastern and Southern Africa; other interested institutions and persons working in these institutions.
General Assembly   General membership meets every 2 years. 1988: Lusaka, Zambia.
Publications   *Official journal:* ESARBICA Journal, 1969-. 1/yr. Address same as Association. Editor: Peter Mazikama. Address: National Archives of Zimbabwe, Private Bag 779, Causeway, Harare, Zimbabwe. English. Other publications: Proceedings of meetings; reports of seminars, workshops. Publications available for sale. No publications exchange program.
Activities   Past achievements: Improvement of records and archives management in the entire region through discussions and guidance among members. Current and future: Publication of journal and 1986 conference proceedings; conservation programs, guiding projects. Actively promoted legislation related to libraries and information services in countries which did not have any legislation, e.g. Zanzibar. At times, Association sponsors attendance at conferences.
Use of High Technology   Electronic publishing for management
Bibliography   More detailed information can be obtained from the 1986 proceedings of the ESARBICA conference.

037   European Association for Health Information and Libraries (EAHIL)

Address   Rue de la Concorde 60, B-1050 Brussels, BELGIUM. Tel: 32 (2) 5118063. Fax: 32-2-5123265.
Officers   Acting Pres: Ms. U. Hausen; Exec.Sec: Ms. B. Blum; Past Pres: Marc Walckiers (Director, Medical Library, University of Louvain, Ave. Hippocrate 50, B-1200 Brussels, Belgium).

Established 1987
Major Fields of Interest Health sciences and medical librarianship
Major Goals and Objectives To promote information and libraries in the health
sciences in Europe
Structure Affiliations: IFLA
Activities Sponsors workshops on topics of current interest, e.g., a Workshop on Human Issues in Library Automation, on CD-ROM training and implementation, in Brussels, May 7-8, 1990.

038 European Association of Information Services (EUSIDIC)

Address c/o Barbara Sarjeant, Administrative Secretary, EUSIDIC, 9A High Street, 1st Floor, Calne, Wiltshire SN11 0BS, UNITED KINGDOM (permanent headquarters). Tel: 44 (249) 814584. Fax: 44-249-813656.
Officers Adm.Sec. (appointed): Barbara Sarjeant.
Staff 1 (paid)
Languages English
Established 1970
Major Fields of Interest Electronic transfer of information
Major Goals and Objectives To promote the unimpeded and efficient flow of information in machine-readable form both within Europe and between Europe and the rest of the world.
Structure Governed by Executive Board and Council, elected annually from full membership. Affiliations: INTUG (International Telecommunications User Group).
Sources of Support Membership dues, subsidies.
Membership Total members: 200+ (institutional). Committees: 2 (Barriers to Information Flow, European Online User Group). 27 countries represented. Requirements: Any organization involved in the electronic transfer of information. European members: Full membership with voting rights; outside Europe: Associate membership.
General Assembly Entire membership meets annually. 1989: Abano Terme, Italy, Oct. 16-19; 1990: Helsinki, Finland, 3rd week of Oct.
Publications *Official journal:* Newsidic (newsletter). 6/yr., circulated to members only. Other publications: EUSIDIC Members Directory (1/yr.); EUSIDIC Database Guide; various reports, Guidelines, and Codes of Practice, etc. on topics of interest to members.
Activities Association has become an international forum for information producers, hosts, users, and all groups interested in the handling, production, and dissemination of information in electronic form. Activities cover online services (both bibliographic and nonbibliographic), telecommunications, economics of information processing, microcomputing, office systems, transborder data flow, etc. Organizes yearly monitoring week of public data networks (PDNs) in Europe to determine the failure rate via the public data networks of members. Sponsors workshops, usually at end of annual conference. Maintains close contacts with relevant organizations.
Use of High Technology Computers for management
Bibliography Henderson, H., "European Association of Information Services (EUSIDIC)," in ALA World Encyclopedia of Library and Information Services, 2nd ed., p. 272. Chicago: American Library Association, 1986; "EUSIDIC Survey of Public Data Network," Herald of Library Science 28 (1989):289; "EUSIDIC 1989 Monitoring Week: The Results," Program: Automated Library and Information Systems 24 (1990):94.

039   Federación Internacional de Información e Documentación. Comisión Latino-americana (FID/CLA) (FID Commission for Latin America)

Address   c/o Ricardo A. Gietz, FID/CLA President, Director, Centro Argentino de Información Científica y Tecnológica (CAICYT), Moreno 433, Buenos Aires 1091, ARGENTINA
Officers   (elected for 4-yr.term). Pres: Ricardo A. Gietz (Argentina); Sec: María de las Mercedes Patalano (Argentina). Exec.Comm: 3.
Staff   Volunteer librarians
Languages   Spanish, Portuguese
Established   1960, at the 26th General Conference of FID, Rio de Janeiro, Brazil
Major Fields of Interest   Documentation in Latin American countries
Major Goals and Objectives   To promote the FID program and activities in the region; to initiate, promote and support the development of national documentation and information services in the region; to encourage and facilitate cooperation in the documentation and information fields among the countries of the region and with other countries, especially with ones that, owing to linguistic and cultural factors, are most closely related, that is to say, Spain and Portugal
Structure   Governed by Executive Committee meeting annually. Affiliations: FID
Sources of Support   Membership dues
Membership   National members: Argentina, Bolivia, Brazil, Chile, Colombia, Costa Rica, Cuba, Ecuador, Mexico, Nicaragua, Uruguay and Venezuela. Types of membership: Representatives of national members; associate members.
General Assembly   Entire membership meets every two years
Publications   *Official journal:* Informaciónes FID/CLA. 1964-. 4/yr. Free to members. Address same as Association. Portuguese and Spanish. Circ: 400. Other publications: Folletos de Difusion (series); Guía de servicos de reprografía de America Latina, etc. Publications deal with scientific and technical progress in Latin America, exchange of technical information, training of personnel. Issues the papers given at the regional congresses. Publications available for sale.
Bibliography   Miranda, A., "Objectives and Achievements of the FID Latin American Commission," Revista Latinoamericana de Documentación 2 (1982):2-3 (in Spanish); Gietz, R.A., "FID Latin American Commission and Its Activities," International Forum on Information and Documentation 8 (1983):32-34; Gietz, Ricardo A., "FID Commission for Latin America (FID/CLA)," International Forum on Information and Documentation 11 (1986):26-28.

040   Fédération Internationale d'Information et de Documentation / International Federation for Information and Documentation (FID)

Address   Prins Willem-Alexanderhof 5, 2595 BE The Hague. Postal address: PO Box 90402, 2509 LK The Hague 2509, NETHERLANDS (permanent). Tel: 31 (70) 140671; Telex: 34402 KB GVNL Atttn:FID; Fax: 31-70-3834827
Officers   (elected for 4-yr.term) Pres: Michael W. Hill; VPs: Ritva T. Launo, P.V. Nesterov, M. H. Wali; Treas: Peter P. Canisius; Exec.Dir: Ben G. Goedegebuure (appointed). Exec.Board: 5 members (elected). Council: 21 members (elected).
Staff   6 (paid)
Languages   English, French
Established   1895, Brussels, by Paul Otlet and Henri La Fontaine as the Institut Internationale de Bibliographie (IIB). Later became the Fédération Internationale de Docu-

mentation / International Federation for Documentation (FID). In 1986 the General Assembly voted to adopt the present name to reflect FID's increasing concern with modern information developments.

Major Fields of Interest   Information management; information science (theory and practice; classification, etc.); documentation; Universal Decimal Classification (UDC); information policy

Major Goals and Objectives   To promote, through international cooperation, research in and development of information science in all fields, including science, technology, the social sciences and the humanities; to promote the use of information and documentation; to develop access to information; to develop tools for information work; to contribute to the creation of an international network of information systems..

Structure   Governed by General Assembly meeting every two years. Affiliated with ICSU (International Council of Scientific Unions); member of ICSSD (International Committee for Social Sciences Information and Documentation), ICOM (International Council of Museums), and UIA (Union of International Associations). Consultative relations with 12 international organizations, e.g. IFLA, ICA, ECOSOC (Economic and Social Council of the UN), FAO (Food and Agriculture Organization of the UN), IAEA (International Atomic Energy Agency), CIB (International Council for Building Research, Studies and Documentation), ISO (International Organization for Standardization), ITU (International Telecommunication Union), Unesco, UNIDO (United Nations Industrial Development Organization), WIPO (World Intellectual Property Organization), etc.

Sources of Support   Membership dues, sale of publications, Unesco subvention, international contract work.

Membership   Total members: 371 (66 national, 5 international, 300 affiliated members in the following categories: Educational, governmental, industrial, international, and personal). 2 Regional Commissions: FID/CAO - Commission for Asia and Oceania; FID/CLA - Commission for Latin America. 2 Regional Commissions in preparation: FID/NANE - Commission for North Africa and the Near East; FID/CAF - Commission for Western, Eastern and Southern Africa. 82 countries represented. Committees: 9 (Research on Theory of Information, Linguistics in Documentation, Information for Industry, Education and Training, Classification Research, Terminology of Information and Documentation, Patent Information and Documentation, Social Sciences Documentation, and Informatetrics). Requirements: Only 1 organization in a country can take national membership in FID. This organization should be directly or indirectly involved in the information chain or be responsible for part of the provision of information in its country. National members and international members have voting power within the General Assembly. National members take on the role of National Focal Point for FID in their country. Affiliate members (individuals and institutions) can come from all categories of information organizations mentioned above. Dues (Dutch Guilder): National members dues based on United Nations scales of assessment; affiliated members dues: 235, educational organizations; 425, governmental and industrial organizations; 325, international nongovernmental organizations; 1,500, international governmental organizations; 110, personal affiliates

General Assembly   Entire membership meets every 2 years. 1988: Ljubljana, Yugoslavia; 1990: Havana, Cuba, Sept. 19-22; 1992: Madrid, Spain, Sept.

Publications   *Official journals:* (1) International Forum on Information and Documentation (IFID). 1975-. 4/yr. (US Dollar) 78 (41 Pound Sterling for EEC countries). Address same as Association. Editor-in-Chief: P.V. Nesterov. Address: Director, VINITI, Ul. Usievicha 20a, Moscow 125219, USSR. Circ: 500. English, Russian, and Spanish language editions. Indexed in ERIC, Pascal 205, LISA, Informatika, ISA; (2) FID News Bulletin.

12/yr. (US Dollar) 67 (35 Pound Sterling for EEC countries). Address same as Association. Editor: Ben G. Goedegebuure, Exec. Director, FID. Circ: 1500. English (occasionally French). Issues proceedings of meetings, reports of seminars, workshops. Other publications include Research Review in Information and Documentation. 1989-. 4/yr. (replaces R & D Projects in Documentation and Librarianship, 6/yr.). Editor: Stella Keenan. Address: Rooftops, 27 Hill Place, Oxenholme, Kendal, Cumbria LA9 7HB, United Kingdom; directories, studies, FID Occasional Paper Series, e.g., Dosa, M., Farid, M. and Vasarhelyi, P., From Informal Gatekeeper to Information Counselor: Emergence of a New Professional Role (1989, FID 677); Hill, M.W., National Information Policies: A Review of the Situation in 17 Industrialised Countries, with Particular Reference to Scientific and Technical Information (1989; FID 678), etc. Publications available for sale: Monographs from FID General Secretariat, serials from FID Distribution Centre, Letchworth, Leics., United Kingdom). Price lists issued for monographs and serials. Publications listed in FID News Bulletin

Activities The FID Professional Programme is organized in the following Major Programme Areas (according to the new Strategic Plan, endorsed by the General Assembly in 1986): (1) Improvements in the availability and applicability of information resources; (2) developing the information marketplace; (3) development of tools for information work; (4) increasing basic understanding of the properties of information; (5) professional development, especially education and training of documentalists and information specialists. Industrial information (to include all above areas). A panel oversees the Broad System of Ordering (BS0), and a management board is in charge of the Universal Decimal Classification (UDC). Activities take place through workshops, seminars, publications, directories. Active in promoting legislation related to information services. Sponsors exhibits, continuing education offerings

Use of High Technology Computers (PCs) for management

Bibliography "85 Years of FID," International Forum on Information and Documentation 6 (1981), entire issue; Hill, M., "The International Federation for Documentation and Aslib," Aslib Information 10 (1982):301-304; FID Statutes, Rules of Procedure, Terms of Reference. The Hague: FID, 1983 (FID Publication 621); Vig, M.L., "FID and UDC: General Background and New Developments," Inspel 17 (1983):251-258; Keenan, S., "International Federation for Documentation (FID)," in ALA World Encyclopedia of Library and Information Services, 2nd ed., pp. 374-376. Chicago: American Library Association, 1986; "FID/ICA/IFLA Experts Meeting, Veldhoven, The Netherlands (1985)," IFLA Journal 12 (1986):46-49; Gietz, R.A., "La historia de la FID," (The History of FID) Revista Española de Documentación Científica 9 (1986):237-247 (in Spanish, includes summary of Spanish involvement in FID); Rajagopalan, T.S. and Rajan, T.N., "India and the International Federation for Documentation," International Forum on Information and Documentation 11 (1986):35-37; "FID 90th Anniversary," International Forum on Information and Documentation 11 (July 1986):1-68 (special issue); some of the articles appeared in Spanish translation in Revista Española de Documentación Científica 9 (1986), issue 3; Dosa, M., "FID: Information for Development," Library Times International 3 (1986):20 (guest editorial); Goedegebuure, B.G. and Keenan, S., "Unesco at Forty: FID Reflections," International Forum on Information and Documentation 12 (1987):8-12; Farkas-Conn, I., "FID Report," Bulletin of the American Society for Information Science 13 (1987):36; "International Federation for Information and Documentation (FID)," in The Bowker Annual: Library and Book Trade Almanac, 34th Edition 1989-90, pp. 734-735. New York: R.R. Bowker, 1989; Seiful-Mulyukov, R.B., "The 44th Conference and Congress of FID (Helsinki, Finland, Aug. 28-Sept.1, 1988)," International Forum on Information and Documentation 14 (1989):28-35; Satija, M.P.,

"44th FID Conference and Congress," Herald of Library Science 28 (1989):230-231; Hill, M.W., "Co-operation between FID and Other Organizations Involved in the Library and Information Fields," IATUL Quarterly 3 (1989):158-161.

041   Fédération Internationale des Archives du Film (FIAF)
(International Federation of Film Archives)

Address   c/o Brigitte van der Elst, Executive Secretary, Coudenberg 70, B-1000 Brussels, BELGIUM (permanent). Tel: 32 (2) 5111390
Officers   (elected for 2-yr.term) Pres: Anna-Lena Wibom (Sweden); VPs: Hector Garcia Mesa (Cuba), Wolfgang Klaue (GDR); Sec.-Gen: Guido Cincotti (Italy); Treas: Raymond Borde (France); Exec.Sec: Brigitte Van der Elst (Belgium). Exec.Comm: 13
Staff   2 (paid)
Languages   English, French; Spanish also used as a working language.
Established   1938, Paris
Major Fields of Interest   The preservation of film as art and historical document, including all forms of the moving image
Major Goals and Objectives   To promote the preservation of films; encourage the formation and development of film archives in all countries; facilitate the collection and the international exchange of films and documents relating to the cinema; develop cooperation among its members.
Structure   Governed by general assembly and executive committee. Affiliations: Unesco
Sources of Support   Membership dues. Budget (US Dollar): Approx.125,000.
Membership   Total members: 78 (institutional). Divisions: 2. 56 countries represented. Types of membership: Institutional. Requirements: Autonomous, non-profit film archives, working on a national level, accessible to the public, devoted to the history and aesthetics of the cinema. Dues (Swiss Franc): 2,850, regular; 400, observer.
General Assembly   General membership meets once a year in different countries. 1988: Paris, France; 1989: Lisbon, Portugal; 1990: Havana, Cuba.
Publications   No official journal. Publications available for sale: Handbook for Film Archives (1980; also in French version); Preservation and Restoration of Moving Images and Sound (1986); Bibliography of National Filmographies; Annual Bibliography of FIAF Members' Publications; International Index to Film and TV Periodicals (1/yr.); Glossary of Filmographic Terms (in 5 languages); Smither, R. Evaluating Computer Cataloguing Systems: A Guide for Film Archivists (1988); Opela, V. Problems of Fungus in Film and TV Archives (in preparation), etc. Price list available.
Activities   Publication of several manuals on film preservation, film cataloging, and bibliographical tools. The Association's practical work is also carried out by individual archives and by commissions of experts drawn from its members to investigate areas such as preservation, documentation, cataloging, etc.
Use of High Technology   Computers (IBM PC AT) for management.
Bibliography   King, B.E., "International Federation of Film Archives," Archives and Manuscripts 9 (1981):87-91; "Fourth Round Table Meeting on Audiovisual Archives," IFLA Journal 10 (1984):421-422 (repr. from Unisist Newsletter); "International Federation of Film Archives," in The Bowker Annual: Library and Book Trade Almanac, 34th Edition 1989-90, pp. 735-736. New York: R.R. Bowker, 1989; Smither, R.B.N., "Formats and Standards: A Film Archive Perspective on Exchanging Computerized Data (paper given at 42nd Annual Congress of FIAF)," American Archivist 50 (1987): 324-339; "News in the Field of Audio-visual Archives," Unisist Newsletter 17 (1989):66-67.

042   International Association for Social Sciences Information Services and Technology (IASSIST)

Address   c/o Judith S. Rowe, US Secretariat-IASSIST, Princeton University Computer Center, 87 Prospect Avenue, Princeton, New Jersey 08540, USA (not permanent). Tel: 1 (609) 2586052
Staff   None
Languages   English, some French
Major Fields of Interest   Social Sciences information services
Membership   Over 40 countries represented
General Assembly   Entire membership meets annually in May. 1987: Vancouver, B.C., May 18-22; 1988: Washington, DC; 1989: Europe; 1990: California.
Use of High Technology   Computers, databases, electronic publishing, and electronic mail for management.
Bibliography   Geraci, D., "The International Association for Social Science Information Services and Technology (IASSIST) [1988 Annual Meeting]," College & Research Libraries News 8 (1988):530-532.

043   International Association of Agricultural Librarians and Documentalists (IAALD)

Address   c/o Jan van der Burg, Secretary/Treasurer, c/o Pudoc, PO Box 4, 6700 AA Wageningen, NETHERLANDS (not permanent). Tel: 31 (8370) 84440/84540. Telex: 45015 blhwg nl
Officers   (elected for 5-yr.term) Pres: E.J. Mann (UK); Sr.VP: P.J. Wortley (UK); Jr.VP: H. Haendler (FRG); Sec.-Treas: Jan van der Burg (Netherlands). Board of Directors: 19
Staff   1 (volunteer)
Languages   English
Established   1955, Ghent, Belgium
Major Fields of Interest   Agricultural librarianship and documentation on an international scale
Major Goals and Objectives   To promote internationally and nationally agricultural library science and documentation/information as well as the professional interests of agricultural information professionals.
Structure   Governed by executive officers meeting annually. Affiliations: FID, IFLA.
Sources of Support   Membership dues. Budget (Pound Sterling): Approx.12,000.
Membership   Total members: 650. 20 countries represented. No membership requirements. Dues (US Dollar): 20, individual; 40, institutional.
General Assembly   General membership meets every five years in a World Congress. Regional conferences held in between. 1985: 7th World Congress, Ottawa, Canada; 1988: Regional conference, Kuala Lumpur, Malaysia; 1990: 8th World Congress, Budapest, Hungary.
Publications   *Official journal:* Quarterly Bulletin of IAALD. 1956-. 4/yr. (US Dollar) 60. Free to members. Editor: Sue Harris. Address: 1275 4th St., Suite 380, Santa Rosa, CA 95404, USA. English, Spanish, French, German. Other publications: IAALD News. 1980-, an occasional newsletter from the President, conference proceedings, bibliographies, monographs, etc.
Activities   Current: Holding regional and worldwide meetings for members under special themes, such as "Agricultural Information to Hasten Development" (1980), "Information for Food" (1985). Future: Publish an updated version of the World Directory of Agricultural Libraries and Documentation/Information Centres.

Use of High Technology   Computers (IBM PC) for communications.
Bibliography   Butler, R.W., "International Association of Agricultural Librarians and Documentalists," in ALA World Encyclopedia of Library and Information Services, 2nd ed., p. 367. Chicago: American Library Association, 1986; Paz de Erickson, A.M., "Recursos humanos: un recurso renovable?" (Human Resources: A Renewable Resource?) Revista AIBDA 7 (1986):85-94 (reviews role of AIBDA in continuing education); "IAALD Members," Quarterly Bulletin of IAALD 33 (1988):13-45; "International Association of Agricultural Librarians and Documentalists," in The Bowker Annual: Library and Book Trade Almanac, 34th Edition 1989-90, pp. 728-729. New York: R.R. Bowker, 1989.

044   International Association of Law Libraries (IALL)

Address   c/o A. Sprudzs, President, The University of Chicago Law School Library, 1121 E 60th Street, Chicago, Illinois 60637, USA (not permanent). Tel: 1 (312) 7029599/9629599. Telex: 28213. Fax: 1-312-7020730. (Headquarters change with President)
Officers   (elected for 3-yr.term, 1989-92) Pres: Adolf Sprudzs (USA); 1st VP: John Lawrence Rodwell (Australia); 2nd VP: Yoshiro Tsuno (Japan); Sec: Timothy G. Kearley (USA); Treas: Ivan Sipkov (USA). Exec.Board: 8 members; 4 elected; 4 appointed
Staff   None
Languages   English, French, German, Spanish
Established   1959, New York, by European and American law librarians
Major Fields of Interest   Law libraries, international cooperation among legal resource libraries, acquisition and research of multinational legal material
Major Goals and Objectives   To promote the work of individuals, libraries, and other institutions and agencies concerned with the acquisition and bibliographic processing of legal materials collected on a multinational basis, and to facilitate the research and use of such materials on a worldwide basis
Structure   Governed by executive officers and Board of Directors meeting annually. Affiliations: FID, IFLA
Sources of Support   Membership dues, private gifts
Membership   Total members: 600 (420 individual, 180 institutional). 60 countries represented. Types of membership: Individual, institutional, life. Requirements: Any person or institution interested in the aims of the Association. Dues (Swiss Franc): 30, individual; 60, institutional; 120, sustaining
General Assembly   Entire membership meets annually
Publications   *Official journal:* International Journal of Legal Information (formerly International Journal of Law Libraries, 1973-82, and IALL Bulletin, 1960-72). 1982-. 3/yr. (US Dollar) 55, individual; 80, institutional. Free to members. Address: PO Box 5709, Washington, DC 20016-1309 USA. Editor: Ivan Sipkov. Address: 4917 Butterworth Place NW, Washington, DC 20016, USA. English, French. Circ: 1,200. Indexed in ISA, Index to Foreign Legal Periodicals, Lib.Lit., etc. Other publications: The IALL Messenger (newsletter, irreg.), Membership Directory.
Activities   Establishment of regular channels of communication among law librarians in 60 countries; dissemination of information through the official journal; establishment of the IALL Courses in Law Librarianship. Sponsors seminars, sessions within the IFLA General Council meetings
Use of High Technology   Computers (PCs) for management
Bibliography   Kavass, I. and Vlasman, G.W., "The International Association of Law Libraries," Juridische Bibliothecaris 3 (1982):12-14 (in Dutch); Sipkov, I., "International

Association of Law Libraries," in <u>ALA World Encyclopedia of Library and Information Services</u>, 2nd ed., pp. 367-368. Chicago: American Library Association, 1986; Sipkov, I., "International Association of Law Libraries," <u>Library of Congress Information Bulletin</u> 46 (May 11, 1987):198-199 (review of 1986 meeting, Tokyo, during IFLA conference); "International Association of Law Libraries," in <u>The Bowker Annual: Library and Book Trade Almanac, 34th Edition 1989-90</u>, p. 729. New York: R.R. Bowker, 1989.

045   International Association of Marine Science Libraries and Information Centers (IAMSLIC)

Address   c/o Kristen L. Metzger, Newsletter Editor, Harbor Branch Oceanographic Institution, 5600 Old Dixie Highway, Ft. Pierce, Florida 34946, USA (not permanent). Tel: 1 (407) 4652400
Officers   (elected for 1-yr term, Oct.1989-Oct.1990) Pres: Sharon Thomson (Canada); Pres-Elect: Kay Hale (USA); Sec: Eleanor Uhlinger (USA); Treas: Sheila Baldridge (USA); Past Pres: Cecile Thiery (USA). Exec.Board: 4, plus past presidents
Staff   None
Languages   English
Established   1975, Woods Hole, Massachusetts, USA
Major Fields of Interest   Libraries and information centers in marine science
Major Goals and Objectives   To promote the cooperation and sharing of resources among libraries and information centers which specialize in any aspect of marine science
Structure   Governed by Executive Board
Sources of Support   Membership dues, sale of publications
Membership   Total members: 206. Types of membership: Individual, institutional. Requirements: Interest in marine science librarianship/information/documentation. Members include all types and sizes of libraries and information centers, including marine research and policy institutions, government agencies, colleges, universities, non-profit and profit-making institutions. Dues (US Dollar): 25
General Assembly   Entire membership meets annually. 1989: Bermuda; 1990: Seattle, WA, Oct.1-5
Publications   No official journal. <u>IAMSLIC Newsletter</u>. 1977-. 4/yr. Editor: Kristen L. Metzger. Address same as Association. Circ: Membership only. English. Publishes proceedings of meetings.
Activities   Provides continuing education workshops for members. Promotes opportunities for members to exchange ideas and explore issues of mutual concern.
Use of High Technology   Computers (PC) for publication of newsletter. Most members have access to electronic mail.

046   International Association of Metropolitan City Libraries (INTAMEL)

Address   c/o W. N. Renes, Secretary/Treasurer, City Librarian, Dienst Openbare Bibliotheek, Bilderdijkstraat 1-3, 2513 CM The Hague, NETHERLANDS (not permanent) Tel: 31 (70) 469235
Officers   (elected for 3-yr.term) Chair: Constance B. Cooke (Queensborough Public Library, 89-11 Merrick Boulevard, Jamaica, NY 11432, USA; Tel: 1-718-9900794; Fax: 1-718-2918936); Sec/Treas: W. N. Renes (Netherlands); Past Pres: Sten Cedergren (Sweden). Exec.Comm: 8; elected
Staff   None
Languages   English
Established   1968, Liverpool, England; 1976, became a Round Table of IFLA.

Major Fields of Interest Metropolitan city libraries all over the world
Major Goals and Objectives To serve as a platform for professional communication and information for public libraries of cities with 400,000 or more inhabitants; to assist the worldwide flow of information and knowledge by promoting practical collaboration in the exchange of books, exhibitions, staff, and information in all phases of metropolitan city public library service; to organize conferences where the exchange of experience and ideas takes place on library systems, library buildings, and library activities.
Structure Governed by executive officers, meeting twice a year. Affiliation: IFLA (a Round Table of Division III, Libraries Serving the General Public)
Sources of Support Membership dues
Membership Total members: Approx. 100. 40 countries represented. Types of membership: Institutional only. Requirements: Open to metropolitan city libraries all over the world, serving populations of 400,000 people or more, and national libraries, when appropriate.
General Assembly Entire membership meets once a year during IFLA conferences (see IFLA entry for location and date of meetings)
Publications No official journal. INTAMEL Newsletter. 1970-. irregular. Free to members. English. Address same as Association. Annual reports appear in IFLA Annual. Papers of working party meetings appear in International Library Review. Issues Annual International Statistics of City Libraries (INTAMEL) and occasional monographs.
Activities Initiating studies to investigate problems and solutions of metropolitan city library service in developing countries. Promoting public library progress in metropolitan areas throughout the world. In accordance with the Medium-Term Programme, current activities focus on library networks in larger cities, library buildings, formation of special subject departments within city libraries, organization and use of catalogs, automation of circulation and catalogs, problems of library services to ethnic and linguistic minorities in large cities, research library work, and online information services.
Bibliography Alison, W.A.G., "INTAMEL Meets in Hungary: Big City Concerns," Library Association Record 83 (1981):575; Harrison, K.C., "Origin, Development and Tasks of INTAMEL," in Metropolitan Libraries on Their Way into the Eighties, ed. M. Beaujean, pp. 101-108. Munich: K.G. Saur, 1982; Eyssen, J., "To Meet Again after 15 Years: INTAMEL in Gothenburg," Buch und Bibliothek 36 (1984):692-694 (in German); Cedergren, S., "International Association of Metropolitan City Libraries (INTAMEL)," in ALA World Encyclopedia of Library and Information Services, 2nd ed., pp. 368-369. Chicago: American Library Association, 1986; Cooke, C.B., "The Work of INTAMEL," IFLA Journal 14 (1988):252-254; "International Association of Metropolitan City Libraries," The Bowker Annual: Library and Book Trade Almanac, 34th Edition 1989-90, p. 730. New York: R.R. Bowker, 1989.

047 International Association of Music Libraries, Archives and Documentation Centres/Association Internationale des Bibliothèques, Archives et Centres de Documentation Musicaux/Internationale Vereinigung der Musikbibliotheken, Musikarchive und Musikdokumentationszentren (IAML/AIBM/IVMB)

Address c/o Veslemöy Heintz, Secretary Gen7neral, Svenskt Musikhistoriskt Arkiv, Box 16326, S-10326 Stockholm, SWEDEN (not permanent). Tel: (46) 8119192
Officers (elected for 3-yr.term; Treas. and Sec.Gen. elected for 4-yr.term) Pres: Maria Calderisi Bryce (Music Division, National Library of Canada, 395 Wellington Street, Ottawa, Ont. K1A ON4, Canada. Tel: 1 (613) 9967514. Telex: 534311); Past Pres: Anders Lönn (Sweden); VPs: Barnard Huys (Belgium), Catherine Massip (France), Svetlana Sigi-

da (USSR), Malcolm Turner (UK); Treas: Don L. Roberts (USA); Sec. Gen: Veslemöy Heintz (Sweden). Board of Directors: 8
Staff   None
Languages   English, French, German
Established   1951, Paris
Major Fields of Interest   Source inventories in the field of music, music librarianship including cataloging.
Major Goals and Objectives   To encourage and promote the activities of music libraries, archives and documentation centers and to strengthen the cooperation among institutions and individuals in these fields of interest.
Structure   Governed by a Council, made up of national branch and professional branch representatives, a Board, made up of elected and appointed officers, and the General Assembly. Affiliations: IFLA, International Music Council, International Musicological Society (IMS).
Sources of Support   Membership dues. Budget (Deutsche Mark): 1987: 135,590; 1988: 128,041.
Membership   Total members: 1,934 (817 individual, 1,117 institutional). National Branches: 20. Professional Branches: 5 (Broadcasting and Orchestra Libraries, Music Teaching Institutions, Music Information Centers, Public Libraries, Research Libraries). Commissions/Committees: 5 (Bibliography, Cataloguing, Constitution, Publications, Service and Training). Requirements: Any person or institution wishing to further the goals of the Association. Dues (Deutsche Mark): 45, individual; 70, institutional
General Assembly   General membership meets once a year. 1988: Tokyo, Japan; 1989: Great Britain; 1990: Boulogne, France. General Assembly holds a Congress every 3 years.
Publications   *Official journal:* Fontes artis musicae. 1954-. 4/yr. Free to members. Editor: Brian Redfern. Address: 27 Plantation Road, Leighton Buzzard, Bedfordshire, LU7 7HJ, United Kingdom. English, French, German. Circ: Membership. Indexed in RILM abstracts (Dialog). Other publications: Notes. 4/yr. Editor: Michael Ochs (Eda Kuhn Loeb Music Library, Harvard University, Cambridge, MA 02138, USA), published by US Branch; BRIO. 2/yr. Editor: Ian Ledsham (Barber Institute of Fine Arts, Music Library, University of Birmingham, Box 363, Birmingham B15 2TS, United Kingdom), published by UK Branch. Extensive publication projects are the major activities of the Association. Publications for sale.
Activities   Through a series of joint Committees with other international organizations, IAML sponsors the preparation and publication of significant works in music and bibliographic scholarship: (1) Répertoire International des Sources Musicales (RISM)/International Inventory of Music Sources (RISM), 1952-, concerned with bibliographies of all sources in music until 1800; The Directory of Music Research Libraries (RISM Series C); (2) Répertoire International de Littérature Musicale (RILM)/International Inventory of Music Literature, 1966-, deals with current literature; sponsors RILM Abstracts, 1967-, also available online through Dialog database; (3) Répertoire International d'Iconographie Musicale (RIdIM)/The International Repertory of Musical Iconography, 1971-, concerned with visual materials relating to music; the Research Center for Musical Iconography at the City University of New York (founded 1972) serves as the international RIdIM center; (4) The International Repertory of the Musical Press (RIPIM). Other IAML-assisted publications include Documenta Musicologica, Catalogus Musicus, Terminorum Musicae Index Septum Linguis Redactus, The Guide for Dating Early Published Music. The Association has been involved in a Unesco-sponsored plan to assist Third World countries in developing music libraries and documentation centers.

Use of High Technology   Computers (PC) for management
Bibliography   "IAML Annual Conference, 1984 in Como, Italy," Fontis Artis Musicae
32 (Jan. 1985):1-86 (special issue); "1985 IAML/IASA Conference, Berlin, GDR, 7-14
September," Fontis Artis Musicae 33 (1986):1-91, 246-247; Brook, B.S. and Ratliff, N.,
"International Association of Music Libraries, Archives and Documentation Centres
(IAML)," in ALA World Encyclopedia of Library and Information Services, 2nd ed., pp.
369-370. Chicago: American Library Association, 1986; Crudge, R., "The Constitution of
IAML: A United Kingdom View," Brio 23 (1986):8-11; Lönn, A., "The IAML Constitu-
tion Revisited - A Progress Report," Fontes Artis Musicae 35 (1988):3-6; "International
Association of Music Libraries, Archives and Documentation Centres (IAML)," in The
Bowker Annual: Library and Book Trade Almanac, 34th Edition 1989-90, pp. 730-731.
New York: R.R. Bowker, 1989.

048   International Association of Orientalist Librarians (IAOL)

Address   c/o William S. Wong, Secretary/Treasurer, Asian Library, University of Illinois
Library, 1408 West Gregory Drive, Urbana, Ilinois 61801, USA (not permanent). Tel: 1
(217) 3331501
Officers   Pres: Warren Tsuneishi; Sec/Treas: William S. Wong; Ed: Om P. Sharma.
Board of Directors: 3
Staff   None
Languages   English
Established   August, 1967, at the 27th International Congress of Orientalists (now In-
ternational Congress for Asian and North African Studies) in Ann Arbor, Michigan, USA.
Major Fields of Interest   Oriental studies, librarianship
Major Goals and Objectives   To promote better communication between Orientalist
librarians and libraries and others in related fields throughout the world; to provide a fo-
rum for the discussion of problems of common interest; to improve international cooper-
ation among institutions holding research resources for Oriental studies.
Structure   Governed by the 3 elected officers. Affiliations: IFLA, International Con-
gress for Asian and North African Studies
Sources of Support   Membership dues
Membership   Total members: 250 (150 individual, 100 institutional). Dues (US Dollar):
10, individual; 12, institutional.
General Assembly   General membership meets every 3 years. 1989: Toronto, Canada.
Publications   *Official journal:*   IAOL Bulletin. 1967-. 2/yr. Free to members. Editor:
Om P. Sharma. Address: South Asia Division, University of Michigan Library, Ann Arbor,
MI 48109, USA. Circ: 250. English.
Activities   Centered in establishing better communication among librarians in Oriental
collections throughout the world
Bibliography   Tsuneishi, L., "International Association of Orientalist Librarians," Li-
brary of Congress Information Bulletin 45 (Dec. 8, 1986):400; "International Association
of Orientalist Librarians (IAOL)," in The Bowker Annual: Library and Book Trade Almanac, 34th Edition 1989-90, pp.731-732. New York: R.R. Bowker, 1989.

049   International Association of School Librarianship (IASL)

Address   c/o Jean E. Lowrie, Executive Secretary, PO Box 1486, Kalamazoo, Michigan
49005, USA (permanent). Tel: 1 (616) 3435728/3271390.
Officers   (elected for 3-yr.term, 1989-92) Pres: Lucille C. Thomas (USA); Past Pres: Michael J. Cooke (UK); VP: Sigrunklara Hannisdöttir (Iceland); Treas: Donald Adcock

(USA); Dir. of N.America: Gerald Brown (Canada); Dir. of Caribbean Region: Beatrice
Anderson (Jamaica); Dir. for Africa: Felix Tawete (Swaziland); Ex.Sec (perm.): Jean E.
Lowrie (USA). Board of Directors: 11
Staff 1 (paid), 1 (volunteer)
Languages English
Established July, 1970, in Jamaica, at conference of the World Confederation of Orga-
nizations of the Teaching Profession (WCOTP)
Major Fields of Interest Development of school library services throughout the world.
Major Goals and Objectives To encourage the development of school libraries and
library programs in all countries; promote professional and continuing education of
school librarians, teacher librarians, and media specialists; foster communication and research; promote publication and dissemination of information about school librarianship;
coordinate activities and initiate conferences.
Structure Governed by Board of Directors elected from 6 major geographic regions
and officers. Affiliations: IFLA, WCOTP
Sources of Support Membership dues, sale of publications. Budget (US Dollar): Ap-
prox.10,700.
Membership Total members: 725 (700 individual and institutional, 25 associations).
Sections: 1. 44 countries represented. Requirements: Interest in the development of
school library services. Dues (US Dollar): 15, individual and institutional; 20+ (gra-
duated scale), association.
General Assembly General membership meets yearly. 1988: Kalamazoo, MI; 1989:
Kuala Lumpur, Malaysia, July 22-26; 1990: Umea, Sweden, July 8-12 (Gunilla Janlert,
Chairperson, 19th IASL Conference, Skolbibliotekscentralen, PO Box 1007, S-90120
Umea, Sweden).
Publications *Official journal:* IASL Newsletter. 1971-. 4/yr. (US Dollar) 15. Free to
members. Address same as Association. Editor: Judith Higgins. Address: 3 Greenridge
Ave., White Plains, NY, USA. Circ: 950. English. Other publications: Proceedings of
conferences, monograph series, etc.. Publications for sale, price lists available.
Activities Past achievements: Expanded publications program; increased interest in conferences, i.e., wider international participation; made joint statement on role of school
library with World Confederation of Organizations of the Teaching Profession. Current:
Implement stronger research program; develop program for school library leaders in developing countries with emphasis on continuing education and conference seminars; carry
out IASL/Unesco co-action book program to raise money for books for school libraries
in developing countries. Future: Increase national representation; emphasis on younger
members.
Use of High Technology Computers (Apple IIe) for management.
Bibliography Cooke, M.J., "International Developments in School Librarianship: The
Work of the IASL," Education Library Bulletin 24 (1981):44-47; Wright, S., "International Association of School Librarianship Hawaian Conference 1984; an Eyewitness Report," School Libraries in Canada 4 (1984):23+; Lowrie, J.E., "International Association
of School Librarianship," in ALA World Encyclopedia of Library and Information Services, 2nd ed., pp. 370-371. Chicago: American Library Association, 1986; Wilslow, M.,
"IASL Jamaica Conference, 1985," IFLA Journal (1986):57-59; "IASL Meets in Halifax:
150 Delegates Attend," School Library Journal 33 (1986):80+; Suchy, K., "Report on
the 15th Annual Conference of IASL," Catholic Library World 58 (1986):109-110; Lowrie, J.E., "The International Association of School Librarianship," Ohio Media Spectrum
39 (1987):5-7; Malhan, I.V., "18th Annual IASL Conference Report," Library Times International 6 (1989):44; "Report on 18th Annual Conference IASL, Kuala Lumpur July

22-26, 1989," International Leads 3 (Winter 1989):2-3; "International Association of School Librarianship," in The Bowker Annual: Library and Book Trade Almanac, 34th Edition 1989-90, p. 732. New York: R.R. Bowker, 1989.

050   International Association of Sound Archives (IASA)

Address   c/o Helen P. Harrison, President, Open University, Media Library, Walton Hall, Milton Keynes MK7 6AA, UNITED KINGDOM (not permanent). Tel: 44 (908) 653530. Telex: 826739. Fax: 44-908653744.
Officers   (elected for 3-yr.term, 1987-90) Pres: Helen P. Harrison (UK); VPs: Hans Bosma (Netherlands), Magdalena Cseve (Hungary), Ulf Scharlau (FRG); Ed: Grace Koch (Australia); Treas: Anna Maria Foyer (Sweden); Sec.Gen: Jean-Claude Hayoz (Radio DRS, Studio Bern, Phonothek, Schwartorstrasse 21, CH-3000 Bern 14, Switzerland). Board of Directors: 7
Staff   None
Languages   English, German, French
Established   1969, Amsterdam, during IAML Conference
Major Fields of Interest   Preservation, organization and use of sound recordings, techniques of recording, restoration and methods of reproducing sound. Archives of music, history, literature, drama, folklife, ethnomusicology, bio-acoustic and musical sounds, linguistics, dialect, radio and television archives.
Major Goals and Objectives   To promote the archival preservation and use of recorded sound; to promote international cooperation among archives which preserve recorded sound documents; to provide and promote the use of archival principles in sound archives and collections.
Structure   Governed by Executive Board and General Assembly of members. Affiliations: IFLA, ARSC (Association for Recorded Sound Collections), IAML, FIAT (International Federation of Television Archives), FIAF (International Federation of Film Archives), ICA, Unesco.
Sources of Support   Membership dues, publication sales. Budget (Swedish Krona): Approx.96,000.
Membership   Total members: 440 (253 individual, 187 institutional). Committees: 7 (Cataloguing, Copyright, Discography, History of IASA, National Archives, Radio Sound Archives, Technical and Training). 41 countries represented. Types of membership: Individual, institutional, sustaining. Requirements: Open to individuals and institutions actively engaged in or having a serious interest in sound archive work and the goals of the Association. Dues (Swedish Krona): 100, individual; 230, institutional
General Assembly   General membership meets yearly. 1988: Tokyo, Japan, Sept. 11; 1989: Vienna, Austria, Sept.; 1990: Canberra, Australia, Aug.
Publications   *Official journal:* Phonographic Bulletin. 1969-. 3/yr. 230 Swedish Krona. Editor: Dietrich Schueller. Address: Phonogrammarchiv der Österreichischen Akademie der Wissenschaften, Liebiggasse 5, Vienna 1, Austria. Circ: 450. English, German, French. Indexed in LISA, RILM, etc. Other publications: Directory of Members; Harrison, H., ed., Selection in Sound Archives (1984); Lance, D., ed., Sound Archives: A Guide to Their Establishment and Development (1983). Publications available for sale (listed in Journal). Price lists issued. No publications exchange program.
Activities   Past achievements: Increased membership (almost doubled); instituted publications program; increased cooperation with other audiovisual archives associations, especially in Unesco Round Table. Current: Reorganization of main Executive Board; widening of interests of audiovisual archives; organized international technical symposium for 1987 with FIAF and FIAT. Future: Further cooperative ventures in training courses and a

training symposium; increase convergence with other audiovisual archive associations. Association has been active in promoting relevant legislation, e.g., archives, copyright, legal deposit, access, cataloging rules, preservation guidelines. Sponsors continuing education lectures, seminars, workshops.

Use of High Technology   Computers and electronic publishing for management.

Bibliography   "International Association of Sound Archives," IFLA Journal 9 (1983):370; "Report on the IAML/IASA Meeting," ibid.:371-372; Harrison, H.P., "International Association of Sound Archives (IASA)," in ALA World Encyclopedia of Library and Information Services, 2nd ed., p. 371. Chicago: American Library Association, 1986; Harrison, H.P., "Annual Conference of the International Association of Sound Archives (Berlin, 1985)," Fontes Artis Musicae 33 (1986):94-99; "News in the Field of Audio-visual Archives," Unisist Newsletter 17 (1989):66-67; "International Association of Sound Archives," in The Bowker Annual: Library and Book Trade Almanac, 34th Edition 1989-90, pp. 732-733. New York: R.R. Bowker, 1989.

051   International Association of Technological University Libraries (IATUL) / Association Internationale des Bibliothèques d'Universités Polytechniques / Internationale Vereinigung der Bibliotheken Technischer Universitäten / Asociación Internacional de Bibliotecas de las Universidades Tecnológicas

Address   c/o Nancy Fjällbrant, Secretary, The Library of Chalmers University of Technology, S-41296 Gothenburg, SWEDEN (not permanent). Tel: 46(31)810100 ext.1229; Telex: 2369

Officers   (elected for 3-yr.term, 1989-91) Pres: Dennis F. Shaw (Radcliffe Science Library, Oxford University, Parks Rd., Oxford OX1 3QP, UK); 1st VP: Dieter Schmidmaier (GDR); 2nd VP: Elin Törnudd (Finland); Sec: Nancy Fjällbrant (Sweden); Treas: Gerard A.J.S. van Marle (Netherlands). Board of Directors: 10

Staff   2 (part-time volunteers)

Languages   English

Established   1955, Düsseldorf, Federal Republic of Germany

Major Fields of Interest   Librarianship, information science, information technology.

Major Goals and Objectives   To provide a forum for library directors to meet for an exchange of views on matters of current significance in the libraries of Universities of Science and Technology, and to provide an opportunity for them to develop a collaborative approach to problems.

Structure   Governed by Board of Directors and General Assembly of ordinary members. Affiliations: IFLA, FID, Scientific Associate of ICSU

Sources of Support   Membership dues, sale of publications. Budget (US Dollar): 1986/87: $5,500; 1987/88: $6,000

Membership   Total members: 175 (25 individual, 150 institutional). 39 countries represented. Requirements: Open "normally to libraries of academic institutions which offer courses in engineering or technology to the doctoral level;" institutional membership. Other types of membership available: Official observer, sustaining, nonvoting associate. Dues (US Dollar): $40, institutional

General Assembly   General membership meets regionally once a year, and internationally every 2 years. 1987: Helsinki, Finland; Chicago, IL, regional; 1988: Australia and Hungary, regional; 1989: Ljubljana, Yugoslavia, May 22-26; 1991: Cambridge, MA, USA.

Publications   *Official journal:* IATUL Quarterly: A Journal of Library Management and Technology. 1987-. 4/yr. £30 Pound Sterling (UK), 70 US Dollar (North America); £35 Pound Sterling elsewhere. Address: Oxford Journals, Oxford University Press, Wal-

ton St., Oxford, OX2 6DP, UK. Editor: Joan Hardy. Address: Central Libraries, Imperial College of Science, Technology & Medicine, London SW7 2AZ, UK. Circ: 700. English. Indexed in LISA, ASLIB and INSPEC, etc. Journal is successor to IATUL Proceedings and IATUL Conference Proceedings (until 1986). Other publications: Annual reports, proceedings of meetings, reports of seminars, workshops. Publications available for sale. Price lists issued, publications listed in journal. No publications exchange program.
Activities   Past achievements: Establishment of international exchange of information on library management and information technology for university libraries of technology. Studies leading to a specification of function. Current: Biennial international meetings; cooperation with IFLA Section of Science and Technology Libraries; seminars on library user education; research programs on scientific serials, electronic data transfer. Future: Assistance to universities of technology libraries in developing countries. Collaborated in promoting legislation (UNISIST). Sponsors continuing education seminars and exchange visits.
Use of High Technology   Computers (ITL 8046 and IBM) for management. Telefacsimile and electronic mail services.
Bibliography   Schmidmaier, D., "30th Anniversary of IATUL and Its 11th Conference," Zentralblatt für Bibliothekswesen 99 (1985):554-555 (in German); Shaw, D.F., "International Association of Technological University Libraries," in ALA World Encyclopedia of Library and Information Services, 2nd ed., p. 372. Chicago: American Library Association, 1986; Schmidmaier, D., "Tendenzen in der Arbeit der International Association of Technological University Libraries," (Trends in the Work of IATUL) Zentralblatt für Bibliothekswesen 101 (1987):170-173 (in German); Lucker, J.K., et al., "Report on the 1987 Meeting of the North American Regional Group of IATUL," IATUL Quarterly 2 (1988):72-77; Schmidmaier, D., "International Association of Technological University Libraries (IATUL) 1955-1988," LIBER News Sheet 24 (1988):30-34; "International Association of Technological University Libraries (IATUL)," in The Bowker Annual: Library and Book Trade Almanac, 34th Edition 1989-90, pp. 733-734. New York: R.R. Bowker, 1989.

052   International Council of Library Association Executives

Address   c/o Margaret Bauer, President, c/o Pennsylvania Library Association, 3107 North Front Street, Harrisburg, Pennsylvania 17110 USA (not permanent). Tel: 1 (800) 6223308
Officers   (elected for 1-yr.term, July-June) Pres: Margaret Bauer; Past Pres: Sharilynn Aucoin (Louisiana Library Association, Box 3058, Baton Rouge, LA 70821. Tel: 1-504-3424928); Sec: Robert Greenfield (Maryland Library Association, 115 W. Franklin Street, Baltimore, MD 21201. Tel: 1-301-6855760); Treas: Raymond Means. Exec.Board: 6
Staff   None
Languages   English
Established   1975
Major Fields of Interest   Management of library associations
Major Goals and Objectives   To provide an opportunity for the exchange of information, experience, and opinion on a continuing basis through discussion, study and publication; to promote the arts and sciences of education association management; and to develop and encourage high standards of professional conduct.
Structure   Governed by Executive Officers
Sources of Support   Membership dues, workshop fees.
Membership   Requirements: Open to chief paid executives engaged in the management of library associations. Dues (US Dollar): $25.

General Assembly   Entire membership meets once a year at the annual conference of the American Library Association in June or July (see ALA entry for date and location of meetings).
Publications   No official journal.
Activities   Sponsors workshops, seminars and other continuing education offerings.

053   International Federation for Information and Documentation. Commission for Asia and Oceania (FID/CAO)

Address   c/o Lawrence W.H. Tam, Secretary General, Hong Kong Polytechnic Library, Kowloon, HONG KONG (permanent). Tel: 852 (3) 638344
Officers   Pres: B.L. Burton; Sec/Gen: Lawrence W.H. Tam. Board of Directors: 2
Staff   2 (volunteers)
Languages   English
Established   1968, at FID 34th General Assembly in The Hague, Netherlands.
Major Fields of Interest   Information and documentation.
Major Goals and Objectives   To promote the program of the FID in the region; to initiate, promote and support the development of national documentation and information services in the region; to encourage and facilitate cooperation in the documentation and information field among countries of the region and with other countries.
Structure   Governed by FID/CAO general assembly. Affiliations: FID
Sources of Support   FID Headquarters and Unesco. Budget (Hong Kong Dollar): Approx.7,000.
Membership   Requirements: Membership countries of FID; 23 member countries (representing over 60% of the world population). No dues.
General Assembly   General membership meets every 2 years. 1988: Beijing, May
Publications   *Official journal:* FID/CAO Newsletter. 1968-. 2/yr. Free to members. Editors: B.L. Burton and Lawrence W.H. Tam. Address same as Association. Circ: 500. English. Other publications: Proceedings of meetings; Guide to Agricultural Information Sources in Asia and Oceania (FID 592; available from FID Headquarters). Has publications exchange program.
Activities   Past achievements: Successfully carried out 2 conferences with themes of promoting information activities; organized workshop. FID/CAO covers an enormous area with vast distances and many spoken languages, presenting a challenge to communication and coordination efforts. Current: Compilation of a Directory/Index for Secondary Sources of Scientific and Technical Information of the national members. Association passed a resolution to urge national members to convince their governments to promote information legislation.
Use of High Technology   Computers (IBM PC) for management.
Bibliography   Burton, B.L. and Tam, L.W.H., "FID Commission for Asia and Oceania (FID/CAO)," International Forum for Information and Documentation 11 (1986):29-33.

054   International Federation for Information Processing (IFIP)

Address   c/o A.A. Verrijn Stuart, PO Box 9512, 2300 RA Leiden, NETHERLANDS. Tel: 31 (71) 277067. Telex: 39058. Fax: 31-71-275819
Established   Jan. 1, 1960, at first International Conference on Information Processing, sponsored by Unesco
Major Fields of Interest   All aspects of information processing
Major Goals and Objectives   To promote all aspects of information science and technology by fostering international cooperation in the field of information processing; stim-

ulating research, development, and the application of information processing in science and human activity; furthering the dissemination and exchange of information about the subject; encouraging education in information processing
Structure   Governed by the General Assembly and executive officers. Affiliations: IFLA, Unesco (Class B status), WHO (World Health Organization), ICSU (International Council of Scientific Unions), FIACC (Five International Associations Coordinating Committee)
Sources of Support   Membership dues, sale of publications, Unesco
Membership   Total members: 45 (organizations). 57 countries represented. Over 500,000 computer professionals represented worldwide. Requirements: Professional and technical organizations representing all branches of information processing.
General Assembly   Entire membership meets every 3 years at IFIP Congress. 1986: Dublin; 1989: San Francisco
Publications   *Official journal:* Information Bulletin. 1/yr.; Computers in Industry. 4/yr.; Computers and Society. 4/yr.; IFIP Newsletter. 4/yr. Extensive publication program. Publishes conference proceedings, etc.
Activities   Major activities: Sponsoring of international conferences and extensive publication program. Technical work is carried out in 9 program areas under Technical Committees: Programming, Education, Computer Applications in Technology, Data Communication, System Modeling and Optimization, Information Systems, Relationship between Computers and Society, Digital Systems Design, and Security and Protection in Information Processing Systems. Organizes triennial series on medical informatics (MEDINFO). Technical Committees sponsor international conferences on specialized topics
Bibliography   Glaser, G., "International Federation for Information Processing," in ALA World Encyclopedia of Library and Information Services, 2nd ed., pp. 376-377. Chicago: American Library Association, 1986.

055   International Federation of Library Associations and Institutions/Fédération Internationale des Associations de Bibliothécaires et des Bibliothèques (IFLA)

Address   c/o Paul Nauta, Secretary General, PO Box 95312, 2509 CH The Hague, NETHERLANDS (permanent). Tel: 31 (70) 3140884; Telex: 34402 kbnl. Fax: 31-70-3834827. Headquarters: Prinz Willem Alexanderhof 5, 2595 BE The Hague, Netherlands.
Officers   (elected for 4-yr.term) Pres (1989-91): Hans-Peter Geh (FRG); 1st VP: Robert Wedgeworth (USA); 2nd VP: P.B. Mangla (India); Treas: Marcelle Beaudiquez (France); Sec.Gen: Paul Nauta (appointed, 1987-). Exec.Board: 9 members; elected.
Staff   7 (paid)
Languages   English, French, German, Russian, Spanish
Established   1927, Edinburgh, Scotland, at the 50th Anniversary Conference of the British Library Association. Representatives of 15 countries signed resolution.
Major Fields of Interest   International cooperation in all areas of librarianship and information services.
Major Goals and Objectives   The Federation shall be an independent international nongovernmental association, without profit motive, whose purposes shall be to promote international understanding, cooperation, discussion, research and development in all fields of library activity, including bibliography, information services and the education of personnel; and to provide a body through which librarianship can be represented in matters of international interest.
Structure   Governed by Council, composed of the representatives nominated by members, and meeting biennially (odd years). The main IFLA steering bodies are the Execu-

tive Board, Professional Board, and the Programme Management Committee. Affiliations: Unesco (consultative status), WIPO, ISO (International Organization for Standardization; observer status), ICSU (associate status), FID, ICA, IBBY (International Board on Books for Young People), IAALD, ALECSO (Arab League Educational, Cultural & Scientific Organization), etc.

Sources of Support Membership dues, sale of publications, government subsidies, foundation grants, Unesco.

Membership Total members: 1,224. 2 categories: Members of national associations/institutions; and institutional and personal (nonvoting) affiliates. Divisions: 8 (General Research Libraries, Special Libraries, Libraries Serving the General Public, Bibliographic Control, Collections and Services, Management and Technology, Education and Research, Regional Activities). Sections: 32 (15 sections by type of library, e.g. National, University, Parliamentary, Administrative, Social Science, Geography and Map, Science and Technology, Public, Serving Disadvantaged Persons, Children's, School, Biological and Medical, Art, Serving the Blind, Serving Multicultural Populations; 7 sections by type of activity and material, e.g. Bibliography, Cataloguing, Acquisition & Exchange, Interlending & Document Delivery, Serials, Government Publications, Rare & Precious Books & Documents, Classification & Indexing; 10 sections on other aspects, e.g. Conservation, Library Buildings & Equipment, Statistics, Education & Training, Library Theory & Research, Regional Activities: Africa, Asia & Oceania, Latin America & Caribbean). Roundtables: 11 (Continuing Education, Audiovisual Media, Research in Reading, etc.). Requirements: Library associations, or national and international associations, or organizations with similar interests are admitted by the Exec. Board. Libraries and similar institutions and individuals are admitted by the Secretariat. Dues (Dutch Guilder): Full membership: 0.1 percent of assessment of country for Unesco (Dfl 600 min.); institutional membership: Dfl 600. Dues structure was revised at IFLA Council in Paris, 1989.

General Assembly General conferences held annually (without general business meetings); IFLA Council meets in odd years. 1988: Sydney, Aug.30-Sept.3; 1989: Paris, Aug.20-25; 1990: Stockholm, Aug.18-24; 1991: Moscow, USSR, Aug.18-24; 1992: New Delhi, India, Aug.18-24; 1993: Barcelona, Spain; 1994: Havana, Cuba.

Publications *Official journal:* IFLA Journal. 1975-. 4/yr. DM 120. Free to members. Editor: IFLA Hdq. Circ: 4,000. English, French, Spanish, German. Indexed in Lib. Lit., LISA. Issues IFLA Annual, IFLA Directory, IFLA Trends (biennial report), IFLA Medium Term Programme 1986-1991 (2nd ed. ed. Irwin H. Pizer), IFLA Statutes and Rules of Procedure. IFLA has an extensive publications program. Publications may be ordered from K.G. Saur, POB 711009, D-8000 Munich 71, FRG. Price lists available, publications listed in journal. No publications exchange program. Other publications include International Cataloguing and Bibliographic Control. 1972-. 4/yr. (Pound Sterling) 23 or (US Dollar) 44. (IFLA International Program for UBCIM). Address: Library Association Publishing Ltd., 7 Ridgmount St., London WC1E 7AE, UK. Some recent publications: Ray, C., ed., Library Service to Children (new ed.,1983); Genzel, P., ed., Studies in the International Exchange of Publications (1981); Bowden, R. Library Education Programmes in Developing Countries with Special Reference to Asia (1982); Hannesdóttir, S.K., ed., Education of School Librarians for Central America and Panama (1982); Massis, B.E., ed., Library Service for the Blind and Physically Handicapped (1982); Line, M.B. and Vickers, S. Universal Availability of Publications (1983); Overton, D. Planning the Administrative Library (1983); Patte, G. and Hannesdóttir, S.K., eds., Library Work for Children and Young Adults in the Developing Countries (1984); Clark, L.L. A Guide to Developing Braille and Talking Book Services (1984); Wolter, J.A., Grimm, R.E. and Carrington, D. World Directory of Map Collections (2nd ed., 1985); Fang, J.R. and Nauta, P. International Guide to Library and Information Science Education (1985); Loveday, A.J. and Gattermann, G. University Libraries in Developing Countries (1985); Pacey, P. A Reader in Art Librarianship (1985); Beaudiquez, M., comp., General Directory of Retrospective National Bibliographies (1986); Jones, A., comp., Guidelines for Public Libraries (3rd ed., 1986); Baxter, P.A., comp., International Bibliography of Art Librarianship (1987); Bossemeyer, C. and Massil, S.W., eds., Automated Systems for Access to Multilingual and Multiscript Library Materials (1987); Dewe, M., ed., Adaptation of Buildings to Library Use (1987); Smith, M.A., ed., Preservation of Library Materials (1987); Poland, U., ed., World Directory of Biological and Medical Sciences Libraries (1988); Tees, M., ed., Education and Research in Library and Information Science in the Information Age (1988); Smith, C.H., ed., Open Systems Interconnection: The Communications Technology of the 1990s (1988); Gibb, I., ed., Newspaper Preservation and Access (2 v.,1988); Rouit, H. and Dubouloz, J.-P., eds., A l'écoute de l'oeil. Les collections iconographiques et les bibliothèques (1989); Dewe, M., ed., Library Building: Preparations for Planning (1989); Johnson, I.M. and others, eds., Harmonisation of Education and Training Programmes for Library, Information and Archival Personnel (2 v.,1989). A series of IFLA Professional Reports are published by IFLA Headquarters, including IFLA Communications 1986: A Bibliography of IFLA Conference Papers (1988).

Activities   The activities of IFLA are carried out through the core programs (Programme Management Committee: Chair: A. Wysocki, Poland) and by the divisions, sections and round tables. Past achievements: Development of core programs and their focal points: Universal Bibliographic Control International MARC (UBCIM) (c/o Deutsche Bibliothek, Zeppelinallee 4-8, Frankfurt/Main 1, FRG); Universal Availability of Publications (UAP) (c/o The British Library Document Supply Centre, Boston Spa, Wetherby, West Yorkshire LS23 7BQ, UK); Preservation and Conservation (PAC) (c/o Library of Congress, Preservation Office, Washington, DC 20540, USA); Universal Dataflow and Telecommunications (UDT) (c/o National Library of Canada, 395 Wellington Street, Ottawa, Ontario K1A ON4, Canada); and Advancement of Librarianship in the Third World (ALP) (c/o IFLA Headquarters, provisionally). Current priorities: Intensification of program for Third World development; education and training; preservation and conservation; bibliographic control. Association sponsors continuing education seminars, and holds workshops and seminars at annual conference.

Use of High Technology   Computers (IBM XT, IBM AT, IBM PS/2), databases for management.

Bibliography   "IFLA in 1982: Highlights," IFLA Journal 9 (1983):133-140; "IFLA 1983," VSB/SVD Nachrichten 59 (1983):367-381 (in French); "IFLA, What It Should Mean to U.S. Librarians," ed. R. Dougherty, Journal of Academic Librarianship 9 (1983):68-74; "IFLA in 1983: Highlights," IFLA Journal 10 (1984):189-198; Fang, J.R., "First IFLA in Africa Inspires Delegates," American Libraries 15 (1984):689-690; Vosper, R., "IFLA and the Recent Growth of Organized International Librarianship," in Advances in Librarianship, vol. 13, pp. 129-134. Orlando, FL: Academic Press, 1984; "IFLA in 1984: Highlights," IFLA Journal 11 (1985):147-156; IFLA and the Library World: A Review of the Work of IFLA, 1981-1985, comp. P.J. Swigchem. The Hague: IFLA, 1985; DeLoach, M.L., "An African Odyssey: A Report on the First African and African-American IFLA Pre-Conference Seminar in Nairobi, Kenya," Library Journal 110 (Mar. 1, 1985):57-62; Kaegbein, P., "IFLA's Medium-Term Programme 1986-1991," Library Times International 1 (1985):75; Sylvestre, J.J.G., "Canadians, Unesco and IFLA," Canadian Library Journal 42 (1985):219-220; Wijnstroom, M., "IFLA in the Eighties," Library Times International 2 (1985):1, 17; Avram, H.D., "The Importance of IFLA," ibid.:26, 40 (guest editorial); Wijnstroom, M., "International Federation of Libary Associations and

Institutions," in <u>ALA World Encyclopedia of Library and Information Services</u>, 2nd ed., pp. 377-381. Chicago: American Library Association, 1986; Fang, J.R., "IFLA Moves Towards the 21st Century: Chicago 1985 to Tokyo 1986," in <u>The Bowker Annual of Library & Book Trade Information 1986</u>, 31st ed., pp.149-156. New York: R.R. Bowker, 1986; Lauster, A., "IFLA und Schulbibliotheken," (IFLA and School Libraries), <u>Schulbibliothek Aktuell</u> 1 (1986):56-61 (in German); Carroll, F.L., "Some Impressions of Former Presidents of IFLA 1963-79: Francis, Liebaers and Kirkegaard," <u>International Library Review</u> 18 (1986):147-152; Bourne, R., "The IFLA International Programme for Universal Bibliographic Control (UBC)," <u>IFLA Journal</u> 12 (1986):341-343; Hanitzsch, P., "Von Kopenhagen bis Chicago. Ein Rückblick auf die jüngste IFLA-Geschichte," (From Copenhagen to Chicago: Recent History of IFLA in Retrospect), <u>Zentralblatt für Bibliothekswesen</u> 100 (1986):482-488 (in German); Smith, M.A., "The IFLA Core Programme on Preservation and Conservation (PAC)," <u>IFLA Journal</u> 12 (1986):305-306; "Reports on the 51st Council and General Conference of IFLA, Chicago, Ill., Aug. 1985," <u>Library of Congress Information Bulletin</u> 45 (May 5, 1986):131-146, (May 12, 1986):151-169; Erratum (May 26, 1986):191; Negishi, M., "IFLA Tokyo Conference Report: A Japanese View," <u>Library Times International</u> 3 (Nov. 1986):35; Casey, D.W., "New Horizons of Librarianship Discussed at IFLA Conference," <u>ibid.</u>:33; "Africa at IFLA," <u>African Research & Documentation</u> 43 (1987):27-29; Matsumoto, S., "Post-Tokyo Conference of IFLA and Unesco's Expectation on Japan," <u>Toshokan Zasshi</u> 81 (1987):13-15 (in Japanese); Anuar, H., "The Library and Information Dimensions of the North-South Dialogue: Some Thoughts on the Threshold of the 21st Century," <u>IFLA Journal</u> 13 (1987):327-333; Molholt, P.A., "IFLA 1986: The New Horizons of Librarianship toward the 21st Century," <u>Special Libraries</u> 78 (1987):60-61; "IFLA Appoints Paul Nauta as New Secretary General," <u>Library of Congress Information Bulletin</u> 46 (Mar. 30, 1987):123; "Report on the 52nd General Conference of the IFLA, Tokyo, Japan," <u>Library of Congress Information Bulletin</u> 46 (Apr. 27, 1987):167-175; Kon, M., "Division of Regional Activities: Regional Section for Asia and Oceania," <u>Toshokan-Kai</u> 38 (1987):330-338 (in Japanese); Palmer, R., "Anatomy of an International Association Conference," (53rd, 1987, Brighton) <u>Library Association Record</u> 89 (1987):41-42; Spaulding, F.H., "IFLA 1987: Library and Information Services in a Changing World," <u>Special Libraries</u> 79 (1988):72-74; "IFLA 1987," <u>Library Association Record</u> 89 (1987):485-486, 513-522; Darrobers, M., "Les mystères de l'IFLA," (The Mysteries of IFLA), <u>Bulletin des Bibliothèques de France</u> 32 (1987):374-380; 448-455; Bowden, R., "Key Role for Britons in IFLA's Growth," <u>Library Association Record</u> 89 (1987):362; "Multiculturalism and Libraries: Issues and Trends," (Pre-Conference Seminar held 13-15 Aug. 1987), <u>IFLA Journal</u> 13 (1987):404-405; Meyriat, J., "53e Conférence Générale de l'IFLA: Library and Information Services in a Changing World (Brighton, 16-21 Août 1987)," <u>Documentaliste</u> 25 (1988):41-42 (in French); Thi, K.W., "Four Decades of International Library Statistics," <u>IFLA Journal</u> 14 (1988):149-154; Cylke, F.K., "Report on the 53rd Council and General Conference of IFLA, Held in Brighton, UK," <u>Library of Congress Information Bulletin</u> 47 (Apr.11, 1988):135-159; Doyle, R.P., "International Federation of Library Associations and Institutions Conference, 1987," in <u>Bowker Annual of Library and Book Trade Information, 1988</u>, 33rd ed. New York: R.R. Bowker, 1988. pp. 143-146; Tees, M.H., "Harmonization of Education and Training Programmes for Library, Information and Archival Personnel: A Report of the Colloquium Held in London, 9-15 Aug.1987," <u>IFLA Journal</u> 14 (1988):234-236; Wijasuriya, D.E.K., "IFLA's Core Programme on the Advancement of Librarianship in the Third World: Orientation, Mechanisms and Priorities," <u>IFLA Journal</u> 14 (1988):324-333; Rayward, W.B., "Robert Wedgeworth: IFLA's Reach Exceeds Its Grasp: An Interview," <u>American Libraries</u> 19 (1988):854; Spaulding, F.H., "IFLA 1988: Living Together: People, Libraries, Information," Special Libraries (1988):66-6; Dyer, E.R., "IFLA Meets Down Under," Wilson Library Bulletin 53 (1988):69-70; "Reports from the 54th General Conference of The International Federation of Library Associations and Institutions, Sydney, Australia," Library of Congress Information Bulletin 48 (Jan. 30, 1989):39-52; Geh, H.-P., "IFLA," in ALA Yearbook 1989, pp. 129-130. Chicago: American Library Association, 1989; Bloss, M.E., "International Federation of Library Associations and Institutions," in The Bowker Annual: Library and Book Trade Almanac, 34th Edition 1989-90, pp. 188-192. New York: R.R. Bowker, 1989; Razumovsky, M., "Eindrücke von der 55. IFLA-Konferenz in Paris," (Impressions of the 55th IFLA Conference in Paris), Mitteilungen der Vereinigung Österreichischer Bibliothekare 42 (1989):26-29; "Das Gespräch: IFLA Präsident Dr. Hans-Peter Geh sprach mit Marianne Jobst-Rieder" (Discussion between IFLA President H.-P. Geh and M. Jobst-Rieder), ibid.:35-41; "International Federation of Library Associations and Institutions (IFLA)," in The Bowker Annual: Library and Book Trade Almanac, 34th Edition 1989-90, pp. 736-737. New York: R.R. Bowker, 1989; "Report of the 55th Council and General Conference of The International Federation of Library Associations and Institutions, Paris, France, August 1989," Library of Congress Information Bulletin 49 (Jan. 15, 1990):19-45.

056   International Group of Publishing Libraries (IGPL)

Address   c/o David Way, Secretary, Marketing and Publishing Office, The British Library, Great Russell Street, London WL1B 3DG, UNITED KINGDOM (not permanent). Tel: 44 (1) 3237704. Telex: 21462
Officers   Chair: Co-opted for each conference, Sec: David Way
Staff   None
Languages   English
Established   April, 1983, after inaugural meeting at the British Library
Major Fields of Interest   Library publishing
Major Goals and Objectives   To share experience and explore the possibilities of active collaboration between research libraries which operate publishing programs.
Sources of Support   Conference fees.
Membership   Total members: 40 (30 individual, 10 institutional). 8 countries represented. Requirements: Members must belong to research and/or national libraries which are either active in publishing or are considering initiating publishing programs. No dues.
General Assembly   General membership meets every 2 years. 1987: Washington, D.C., May 20-22; 1989: Edinburgh, Scotland, May.
Publications   *Official journal:* IGPL Newsletter. 1986-. 1/yr. Free to members. Editor: David Way. Address same as Association. Circ: 150. English. Other publications: Reports of seminars and workshops. Publications available for sale.
Activities   Past achievements: Acted as a focus for international collaboration between national and research libraries for publishing, collaborated on mailings and joint publishing projects.
Use of High Technology   Computers (SIRIUS) for management.
Bibliography   "Library Publishing." British Library Occasional Paper 2, 1985; "Meeting of International Group of Publishing Libraries," Library of Congress Information Bulletin 46 (June 29, 1987):294.

057   International Society for Knowledge Organization (ISKO)

Address   c/o ISKO General Secretariat, Woogstrasse 36a, D-6000 Frankfurt am Main 50, FEDERAL REPUBLIC OF GERMANY (permanent). Tel: 49 (69) 523680.

Officers (elected) Pres: I. Dahlberg; VPs: R. Fugmann, N. Meder; Treas: I. Stoltzenburg; other officers: B. Kelm, E. Svenonius, R. Ungvary. Scientific Council: 21.
Staff None
Languages English
Established July 22, 1989, Frankfurt, at the central railway station, by a group of interested specialists.
Major Fields of Interest Conceptual organization of knowledge by classification, indexing, systematic terminology, concept analysis, etc.
Major Goals and Objectives "To promote research, development and application of all methods for the organization of knowledge in general or of particular fields by integrating especially the conceptual approaches of classification research and artificial intelligence. The Society emphasizes philosophico-logical, psychological and semantic approachers of conceptual order." (Charter, Art. 4.1).
Structure Governed by Executive Board and the consulting Scientific Council.
Sources of Support Membership dues.
Membership Types of membership: Individual, institutional. Requirements: Interest in goals and objectives of Society. Dues (US Dollar): 25, individual; 50, institutional.
General Assembly Entire membership meets annually. First international conference planned for Aug. 14-17, 1990 at the Technical University of Darmstadt.
Publications The existing journal International Classification will serve as communication tool.
Activities Society unites experts from all over the world in this field. One concern is to underline the human element in scientific work, thus the theme of the first conference: "Knowledge Organization and the Human Interface."
Use of High Technology Computers for management.
Bibliography "International Society for Knowledge Organization (ISKO) Founded," Library Times International 6 (1989):47; "International Associations and Groups," Focus on International and Comparative Librarianship 20 (1989):57-59.

058 Internationale Arbeitsgemeinschaft der Archiv-, Bibliotheks-, und Graphikrestauratoren (IADA)
(International Working Group of Archival, Library and Graphic Restorers)

Address c/o Ludwig Ritterpusch, Secretary, Friedrichsplatz 15, Postfach 540, D-3550 Marburg, FEDERAL REPUBLIC OF GERMANY (permanent). Tel: 06421/25078
Officers Gen.Sec: Ludwig Ritterpusch
Languages German (80%), English (20%)
Established 1957, Marburg
Major Fields of Interest Restoration and conservation of paper
Sources of Support Membership dues, sale of publications.
Membership Total members: 650. Requirements: Interest in the aims of the Association. Dues (Deutsche Mark): 60.
General Assembly General membership meets every 4 years. 1987: Berlin, Oct.
Publications Official journal: Maltechnik-Restauro: Mitteilungen der IADA. 1976-. 4/yr. Free to members. Address: c/o Verlag Georg D.W. Callwey KG, Streitfeldstr. 35, D-8000 Munich 80, FRG.
Activities Seminars and other types of continuing education programs.

059   Ligue des Bibliothèques Européennes de Recherche (LIBER)
(League of European Research Libraries)

Address   c/o Hans-Albrecht Koch, Secretary, Staats- und Universitätsbibliothek Bremen, Postfach 330160, D-2800 Bremen 33, FEDERAL REPUBLIC OF GERMANY (not permanent). Tel: 49 (421) 2182601. Telex: 245811.
Officers   (elected for 3-yr.term) Pres: J.M. Smethurst; Past Pres: Franz Kroller (Austria); VP: Thomas Tottie (Sweden); Sec: Hans-Albrecht Koch (FRG); Treas: Jakob van Heijst (Netherlands). Board of Directors: 7
Staff   None
Languages   English, French, German
Established   1971 in Strasbourg at Council of Europe
Major Fields of Interest   Cooperation between European research libraries.
Major Goals and Objectives   "The aim of LIBER is to establish close collaboration between the general research libraries of Europe, and national and university libraries in particular. Its intention is to help in finding practical ways of improving the quality of the services these libraries provide." (Statutes, Art. 2)
Structure   Governed by Executive Committee. Affiliation: IFLA
Sources of Support   Membership dues, sale of publications, subsidies, gifts and bequests, ad hoc grants.
Membership   Total members: 180. Working groups: 7. 18 countries represented. Requirements: "Membership shall be granted by the decision of the Executive Board to European research libraries within the meaning of Article 2 which undertake to abide by this constitution and hence to take out annual subscriptions to LIBER publications. Appeals may be made to the General Assembly against any decision by the Executive Board concerning granting of membership." (Statutes, Art. 4). For the time being, libraries in the following countries may become members: Austria, Belgium, Cyprus, Denmark, Finland, France, FRG, Greece, The Holy See, Iceland, Ireland, Italy, Luxembourg, Malta, Netherlands, Norway, Portugal, Spain, Sweden, Switzerland, Turkey, and the UK. Dues (Deutsche Mark): 120.
General Assembly   General membership meets once a year. 1988: Copenhagen, Denmark; 1989: Madrid, Spain.
Publications   *Official journals:* LIBER Bulletin and LIBER News Sheet. 1972-. irreg. (Deutsche Mark) 165 (both); DM 120 Bull. only; DM 45 News Sheet only. Both free to members. Bulletin Editor: Dr. Roland Matys, Zentralbibliothek, Zähringerplatz 6, Postfach, CH-8025, Zurich, Switzerland. News Sheet Editor: Heiner Schnelling, Bibliothek der Universität Konstanz, Postfach 5560, D-7750 Constance, FRG. Circ: 340. English, French, German. Other publications: Annual reports, proceedings of meetings, reports of seminars and workshops. Festgabe für Franz Kroller zum 65. Geburtstag. Die Universitätsbibliothek Graz: Eine Bibliothek im Wandel. Bibliothekskooperation: Möglichkeiten u. Grenzen (Festschrift for Franz Kroller's 65th Birthday. The University Library Graz: A Library undergoing Changes. Library Cooperation: Chances and Limitations), ed. by S. Reinitzer and H.-A. Koch (LIBER Bulletin 32/33, 1989). Publications available for sale: LIBER Bulletin, LIBER News Sheet.
Activities   Current: Involved in European Register of Microform Masters (sponsored by the Council of Europe); Retrospective Cataloguing (sponsored by the Council of Europe); Optical Disks (under the auspices of the Council of Europe); promotion of the Conspectus Method (in cooperation with the British Library). Future: Setting up a working party on retrospective cataloging which will consist of 10-12 experts from member states of the European Community and other European countries; preparing a European Register of Microform Masters as a computerized database.

Bibliography Clavel, J.-P., "LIBER - a Brief Account of Its Origins," LIBER Bulletin 1 (1972):3-5; Kroller, F., "Harmonisierung der Konzeption und Realisierung der europäischen Bibliothek aus bibliothekarischer Sicht," (Harmonization and Realization of the Concept of the European Library from a Library Perspective) in Zur Internationalität wissenschaftlicher Bibliotheken. 76. Bibliothekartag in Oldenburg, 1986. (Zeitschrift für Bibliothekswesen und Bibliographie. Sonderheft 44) pp. 40-47 (in German); Schnelling, H., "New European Perspectives for LIBER," LIBER Bulletin 27 (1985):60-64; Munthe, G., "LIBER," in ALA World Encyclopedia of Library and Information Services, 2nd ed., p. 452. Chicago: American Library Association, 1986; Munthe, G., "LIBER - A Library Organization, Its Origin, Its Objectives and Its Achievements," Libri 38 (1988):45-50; Koch, H.-A., "The Ligue des bibliothèques européennes de recherche (LIBER) and International Library Co-operation," IATUL Quarterly 3 (1989):173-79.

060 Middle East Librarians Association (MELA)

Address c/o James Weinberger, Secretary/Treasurer, Princeton University Library, Box 190, Princeton, New Jersey 08540, USA (not permanent). Tel: 1 (609) 4523248/3279.
Officers (elected for 1-3-yr.term) Pres: Janet Heineck; VP and Pres.-Elect: Edward Jajko; Sec/Treas: James Weinberger; Ed: Brenda E. Bickett. Exec.Board: 5
Staff None
Languages English
Established 1972, Binghamton, New York, during annual meeting of the Middle East Studies Association of North America (MESA).
Major Fields of Interest Middle East and North African studies, including the Arab world, Turkey, Israel, Iran; library collections all over the world concerned with this area.
Major Goals and Objectives To facilitate communication among members through meetings and publications; to improve the quality of area librarianship through the development of standards for the profession and education of Middle East library specialists; to compile and disseminate information concerning Middle East libraries and collections and represent the judgment of the members in matters affecting them; to encourage cooperation among members and Middle East libraries, especially in the acquisition of materials and the development of bibliographic controls; to cooperate with other library and area organizations in projects of mutual concern and benefit; to promote research in and development of indexing and automated techniques as applied to Middle East materials.
Structure Governed by executive officers meeting at least once a year.
Sources of Support Membership dues, sale of publications.
Membership Total members: 173 (123 individual, 50 institutional). 17 countries represented. Types of membership: Full, associate. Dues (US Dollar): $15, individual and institutional.
General Assembly Entire membership meets once a year. 1988: Los Angeles, CA; 1989: Toronto, Canada.
Publications *Official journal:* MELA Notes. 1973-. 3/yr. 10 (US Dollar). Free to members. Editor: Brenda E. Bickett. Address: Cataloging Department, Georgetown University Library, PO Box 37445, Washington DC 20013 USA. Circ: 173 (membership). English. Indexed in Quarterly Index Islamicus. Other publications: Occasional Papers in Middle Eastern Librarianship (No. 1, 1981-). Price lists available. Publications exchanged with editors of other library journals.
Activities Past achievements: Sponsored coordinating effort to start up Middle East Microform Project; Middle East materials held at Center for Research Libraries (CRL).

Current: Interested in computerized representation of Arabic script. Future: Directory of Middle East Collections in North America.
Use of High Technology   Computers (IBM-PC) for management.
Bibliography   Albin, M.W., "Report from Meetings of Middle East Specialists in New Orleans," Library of Congress Information Bulletin 45 (Mar. 3, 1986):75; Filstrup, E.C., "Report from Meetings of Middle East Specialists," Library of Congress Information Bulletin 46 (Apr. 13, 1987):151-152; Albin, M.W. and Filstrup, C., "Report from the Middle East Librarians' Association [annual meeting]," Library of Congress Information Bulletin 47 (Feb. 29, 1988):86-88.

061   Nordisk Videnskabeligt Bibliotekarforbund (NVBF)
(Scandinavian Federation of Research Librarians/Nordic Union of Research Librarians)

Address   c/o Forstebibliotekar Ulla Hojsgaard, President, IDE Danish Institute of International Exchange, Amaliegade 38, DK-1256 Copenhagen K, DENMARK (not permanent). Tel: 45 (1) 156521.
Officers   Pres: Ulla Hojsgaard. Exec.Comm: 9
Staff   None
Languages   Danish, Swedish, Norwegian
Established   1947, Copenhagen
Major Fields of Interest   Cooperation of Nordic research libraries and librarians
Major Goals and Objectives   To develop contacts between Scandinavian and Icelandic research librarians; to develop the cooperation and coordination of the libraries; and to encourage joint Scandinavian education of librarians.
Structure   Governed by officers and Executive Council meeting twice a year. Affiliations: Coordinating organization for five research libraries organizations in Denmark, Finland, Norway, Sweden, and Iceland. Member associations nominate 2 representatives each to the NVBF Board; chair rotates among countries every 2 years.
Sources of Support   Membership dues, sale of publications, government subsidies.
Membership   Total members: Five associations. 5 countries represented. Types of membership: Institutional. Requirements: Status of research library.
General Assembly   Entire membership meets very two years.
Publications   No official journal. Issues annual reports, proceedings of annual meetings, workshops, seminars, etc. Published several editions of a general handbook on librarianship. Publications available from Bibliotekcentralen, Tempovej 5-7, DK-2750 Ballerup, Denmark.
Activities   Initiated and sponsored regular annual Round Table Conferences on topics of current interest; initiated two major projects, the "Scandia Plan," coordinating acquisitions among Scandinavian libraries, and the Nordic Union Catalogue for Periodicals (NOSP). The Nordic Countil for Scientific and Technical Information (NORDINFO) was put in charge of these two projects and continues to support projects of NVBF.
Bibliography   Sanner, L.-E., "Scandinavian Federation of Research Libraries," in ALA World Encyclopedia of Library and Information Science, 2nd ed., pp. 728-729. Chicago: American Library Association, 1986.

062   North American Fuzzy Information Processing Society (NAFIPS)

Address   c/o E.H. Ruspini, 3720 Carlson Circle, Palo Alto, California 94306, USA (not permanent). Tel: 1 (415) 8562837
Officers   (elected for 3-yr.term) Pres: James T.P. Yao (Tel: (317) 4942238); Lifetime Chair, Board of Directors: Lotfi A. Zadeh; Sec-Treas: B. Buckles; Registered Agent in

CA: E.H. Ruspini; Past Pres. and Ed: J.C. Bezdek. Further contact: Felix S. Wong, Weidlinger Associates, 620 Hansen Way, Suite 100, Palo Alto, CA 94304. Board of Directors: 10
Staff   20 (volunteers)
Languages   English
Established   1981
Major Fields of Interest   Theory of fuzzy sets
Major Goals and Objectives   To promote the scientific study of, to develop an educational institution for the instruction in, and to disseminate educational materials in the public interest including, but not limited to, theories of fuzzy sets.
Structure   Governed by the Board of Directors (elected 3 members per year for 3-yr. terms).
Sources of Support   Membership dues. Budget (US Dollar): 1986/87: $3,000; 1987/88: $11,000.
Membership   Total members: 150 (individual). Divisions: 6. 10 countries represented. Requirements: Interest in promoting the purpose of the Society. Dues (US Dollar): $55, individual; $36, student; $5, student (without journal)
General Assembly   Entire membership meets once a year. 1988: San Francisco Bay Area, CA; 1989: Joint meeting with International Fuzzy Systems Association, USA; 1990: Toronto, Ont., Canada; 1991: Dallas-Ft. Worth, TX, USA.
Publications   *Official journal:* (IJAR) International Journal of Approximate Reasoning. 1986-. 6/yr. (US Dollar) 128. Free to members. Editor: James C. Bezdek. Address: Computer Science Department, University of South Carolina, Columbus, SC 29208, USA. English. Other publications: Annual reports, proceedings of meetings. Publications available for sale: Contact J.C. Bezdek, Chairman, Publications Committee (address above).
Activities   Past achievements: Annual meetings since 1982, and publication of conference and workshop proceedings. Current: Planning future meetings, and publication of the International Journal of Approximate Reasoning. Sponsors continuing education workshops, lectures, seminars.
Use of High Technology   Computers (VAX, IBM PC, Apple), databases for management. Newsletter disseminated through automated means.

063   Pacific Regional Branch of the International Council on Archives (PARBICA)

Address   c/o Setareki Tuinaceva, President, Chief Archivist, National Archives of Fiji, Suva, FIJI (not permanent)
Officers   Pres: Setareki Tuinaceva; VP: George Paniani; Sec.Gen: Lindsay Cleland; Dep.Sec.Gen: Richard Overy; Treas: Bruce Burne. Exec.Board: Siavata Gale, Judith Hornabrook, Edward Iamae, Tina Rehuher, Magdalena Taitano, Willie Toa
Staff   None
Languages   English
Established   1980, London. Inaugural Conference, Suva, Fiji, Oct.25-27, 1981.
Major Fields of Interest   Archives and records management
Major Goals and Objectives   Promote the establishment and development of archives in the Pacific region
Structure   Governed by Executive Board. Affiliations: ICA, Commonwealth Archivists Association
Sources of Support   Membership dues and other subsidies
Membership   14 countries of the Pacific region represented. Requirements: Archival institution, practicing archivist, or interest in aims of the Association.

General Assembly General membership meets every 4 years.
Publications Newsletter and other publications: Hornabrook, Judith, <u>Manual for Pacific Archivists</u>.
Activities Engaged in Fact Finding Advisory Mission, South Pacific, under Bruce Burne, to assess the situation in various member countries; holding archives and records management training seminars in the region. Members participate in activities of the Commonwealth Archivists Association and International Council on Archives.
Bibliography Cleland, L., "PARBICA 1984-1985," <u>Archives and Manuscripts</u> 13 (1985):189-195.

064 Seminar on the Acquisition of Latin American Library Materials (SALALM)

Address c/o Suzanne Hodgman, Executive Secretary, SALALM Secretariat, 728 State Street, Madison, Wisconsin 53706, USA (not permanent). Tel: (608) 2623240. Headquarters: SALALM Secretariat, Memorial Library, University of Wisconsin-Madison, Madison, WI 53706, USA.
Officers (elected for 1-yr.term) Pres: Ann Harness (University of Texas at Austin); VP/Pres-Elect: Deborah Jakubs (Duke University); Past Pres: Barbara Robinson; Treas: Jane Garner (appointed for indefinite period); Exec. Sec: Suzanne Hodgman (appointed for 5-yr. term); also 6 members at large (elected for 3-yr.term). Executive Board: 12.
Staff 1 (paid)
Languages English, Spanish
Established 1956 at Chinsegut Hill, Florida, under the auspices of the Columbus Memorial Library of the Pan American Union and the University of Florida Libraries, by Stanley, L. West and Marietta Daniels Shepard, who served as Permanent Secretary, 1956-68, and Executive Secretary, 1968-73. In 1968, Association was incorporated, and present constitution and bylaws adopted. Since 1973, the Secretariat has moved to designated academic member libraries with strong Latin American programs, every 3 to 5 years.
Major Fields of Interest Latin American bibliography, acquisitions, networking, collection development, library operations and services in Latin America.
Major Goals and Objectives Control and dissemination of bibliographic information about all types of Latin American publications; development of library collections of Latin Americana; promotion of cooperative efforts to improve library service for individuals and institutions; improving library service to the Spanish- and Portuguese-speaking population of the United States.
Structure Governed by Executive Board and constitution.
Sources of Support Membership dues, sale of publications, return on investments, support by host institution. Budget (US Dollar): 1986/87: $16,900; 1987/88: $22,380
Membership Total members: 475 (350 individual, 125 institutional). Committees and Subcommittees: 28. 35 countries represented. Types of membership: Individual, student, emeritus, institutional. Requirements: Any person, institution, or other organization interested in the aims of SALALM. Dues (US Dollar): $35, individual; $80, institutional; $17.50, student and emeritus. Dues for members from Latin America, Puerto Rico, Caribbean: $25, individual; $80, institutional; $12.50, student and emeritus.
General Assembly Entire membership meets once a year; sometimes also mid-winter meetings. 1988: University of California, Berkeley; 1989: University of Virginia
Publications *Official journal:* <u>SALALM Newsletter</u>. 1964-. 4/yr. $10. Free to members. Editor: Laurence Hallewell. Address: 5 Wilson Library, University of Minnesota Libraries, 309 Nineteenth Avenue South, Minneapolis, MN 55455-0414, USA. Tel:1 (612) 6245860. Fax: 1-612-6267385. Circ: 525. English, Spanish, Portuguese, French. Other

publications: Proceedings of meetings, and Bibliography and Reference Series, e.g., Il-gen, W. and Jakubs, D., An Acquisitions Manual/Manual de Adquisiçóes (1988, Bibl. & Ref. Series, 21); Karno, H. and Block, D., Directory of Vendors of Latin American Library Materials (3rd ed., 1988, Series, 22); Loroña, L., ed., A Bibliography of Latin American and Caribbean Bibliographies, 1987-1988 (1988, Series, 23), etc. Issues annual Microfilming Projects Newsletter. Publications available for sale. Price lists issued. No publications exchange program.

Activities   "Members include libraries, librarians, book dealers, and scholars interested in the control and dissemination of bibliographical information about all types of Latin American publications and also in the development of library collections in support of Latin American studies." (S. Hodgman, p. 224, below). Past achievements: Establishment of Marietta Daniels Shepard Scholarship at University of Texas; publications. Current: Preparation for the annual conference, publications, committee projects, scholarship program.

Use of High Technology   Computers (IBM) for management.

Bibliography   "SALALM at Chapel Hill: A Time for Understanding Latin America," Library Journal 109 (1984):1274; Kahler, M.E., "Report on the Seminar on the Acquisition of Latin American Library Materials, SALALM XXX," Library of Congress Information Bulletin 44 (Sept. 2, 1985); Hazen, D. H., "Seminar on the Acquisition of Latin American Material," in ALA World Encyclopedia of Library and Information Services, 2nd ed., pp. 753-755. Chicago: American Library Association, 1986; "Report from the 23rd Seminar on the Acquisition of Latin American Library Materials," Library of Congress Information Bulletin 45 (Aug. 11, 1986):284-288; "SALALM and ACURIL Consider Strategies for Coping with Shrinking Budgets," Library of Congress Information Bulletin 46 (Nov. 16, 1987):483-491; Hodgman, S., "Seminar on the Acquisition of Latin American Library Materials," in ALA Yearbook 1989, pp. 223-224. Chicago: American Library Association, 1989.

065   Société Internationale des Bibliothèques et des Musées des Arts du Spectacle (SIBMAS)
(International Society of Libraries and Museums of the Performing Arts)

Address   c/o Alexander Schouvaloff, Secretary General, c/o Theatre Museum, Victoria and Albert Museum, London SW7 2RL, UNITED KINGDOM (not permanent). Tel: 44-1-5895371. Postal address: 59 Lyndhurst Grove, London SE15, United Kingdom. Tel: 44-1-8367891.

Officers   (elected for 2-yr.term) Pres: Oskar Pausch; Sec: Alexander Schouvaloff; Treas: Martin Dreier. Exec. Board: 17

Staff   None

Languages   English, French

Established   1954, Zagreb, Yugoslavia. Originally founded as section of IFLA under name Section Internationale des Bibliothèques-Musées des Arts du Spectacle. Became autnomous association under present name in 1972.

Major Fields of Interest   Theater libraries, theater documentation centers, theater museums, and dance

Major Goals and Objectives   To promote research, practical and theoretical, in the documentation of the performing arts; establish international contacts between theater libraries and documentation centers, and coordinate the work of members

Structure   Governed by a Council. Affiliations: IFLA, ICOM

Sources of Support   Membership dues

Membership   Total members: 30 (institutional)

General Assembly   Entire membership meets every 2 years. 1988: Mannheim, FRG, Sept. 4-9
Publications   *Official journal:* SIBMAS Bulletin. 1876-, 2/yr. Free to members. Editor: Liliana Alexandrescu. Address: Waalstreet 3 III, 1078 BN Amsterdam, Netherlands. Circ: 400. English, French. Issues proceedings of meetings.
Activities   Cooperative project of international theater bibliography. Holding congresses.

066   South and West Asian Regional Branch of the International Council on Archives (SWARBICA)

Address   c/o R. K. Perti, President, Director, National Archives of India, Janpath, 110001 New Delhi, INDIA (not permanent). Tel: 91 (11) 383436.
Officers   Pres: R. K. Perti
Staff   None
Languages   English
Established   1976, New Delhi
Major Fields of Interest   Archives
Major Goals and Objectives   To promote conservation, administration, and utilization of archive material in the region; establish, maintain, and strengthen relations among all having such materials in their custody
Structure   Governed by executive officers and committee, meeting annually. Affiliations: A Regional Branch of the International Council on Archives.
Sources of Support   Membership dues, sale of publications, private gifts, government grants, subsidies from ICA.
Membership   Total members: 50 (22 individual, 21 institutional; 7 national). 7 countries represented. Types of membership: Individual, institutional, honorary, national. Requirements: Individual: Interest in archives; institutional: Custody of archival materials, interest in archives by association. Dues (Indian Rupee): 100, individual; 500 institutional.
General Assembly   Entire membership meets every 2 years.
Publications   *Official journal:* SWARBICA Journal, 1977-. 1/yr. (Indian Rupee) 25. Free to members. Editor: Dr. N.H. Kulkarnee. Address same as Association. English. Circ: Membership. All transactions of the Association appear in the official journal. Newsletter published occasionally.
Activities   Sponsors seminars, workshops and other continuing education programs, e.g., on archival training requirements of the region and on records management. Participates in programs and meetings of ICA.

067   Southeast Asian Regional Branch of the International Council on Archives (SARBICA)

Address   Ms. Azizah bt. Kasah, Secretary General, SARBICA Secretariat, c/o National Archives of Malaysia, Jalan Duta, Kuala Lumpur 50568, MALAYSIA (permanent). Tel: 60 (3) 2543244.
Officers   (elected for 2-yr.term) Chair: Dra Soemartini (Indonesia); Vice Chair: Ms. Zakiah Hanum Nor (Malaysia); Sec.Gen: Ms. Azizah bt. Kasah (Malaysia); Treas: Hassan Mohd (Malaysia). Exec.Board: 8
Staff   Staff of the National Archives of Malaysia
Languages   English
Established   July 9, 1968, at the Inaugural Conference of SARBICA held in Kuala Lumpur, Malaysia. First regional branch of ICA.

Major Fields of Interest   Administration of archives
Major Goals and Objectives   (1) To establish, maintain and strengthen relations between archivists of all countries in the region and between all institutions, professional bodies and organizations which are concerned with the custody, organization or administration of archives; (2) to promote all measures for the preservation, protection and defense against all manner of hazards to the archival heritage of the region, and to further the progress of all aspects of the administration and preservation of these archives; (3) to facilitate the use of archives of the region by making them more widely known and by encouraging greater ease of access; (4) to promote, organize and coordinate activities in the field of archives in the region; (5) to sponsor professional training of archivists in the region; (6) to cooperate with other organizations or institutions concerned with the documentation of human experience and the use of that documentation for the benefit of mankind; (7) to generally carry out the aims and objectives of the International Council on Archives.
Structure   Governed by constitution. Affiliations: Regional Branch of ICA.
Sources of Support   Membership dues, sale of publications, government subsidies, international organizations (including ICA). Budget (Malaysian Ringgit): 1986/87: 10,000; 1987/88: 18,000.
Membership   Total members: 6 (institutional). 6 countries represented. Requirements: Open to archival institutions in countries of Southeast Asia only. Dues (Malaysian Ringgit): 700
General Assembly   Executive Board meets once a year. General conference every 2 years. 1988: Bangkok/Brunei, 2nd Meeting of the 8th SARBICA Executive Board; 1989: 8th SARBICA General Conference, Malaysia.
Publications   *Official journal:* SARBICA Journal. 1968-. 1/yr. (Malaysian Ringgit) 15. Editor: Zawawi Abdullah. Address same as the Association. Circ: 500. English. Other publications: Southeast Asian Microfilms Newsletter (SARBICA/CONSAL publication). Publications available for sale. Price list issued.
Activities   Past achievements: (1) Projects completed under contract with the Regional Office of Unesco for Asia and Pacific: Inventory of cartographic records in the Arsip Nasional, 1612-1816 (Indonesia); Guide to the Royal Archives of Perak (1945-69), Johore (1874-1984) and Perlis (1984-1985) (Malaysia); Purchase of aerial photographs of Thailand preserved in the Williams Hunt Collection, United Kingdom (Thailand); (2) Testing of Records and Archives Management Programme (RAMP) Guidelines Projects: Appraisal of moving images (Indonesia); Sampling techniques; legislation and regulations; and preservation and restoration of paper records (Malaysia); Surveying archival records management systems; and preservation and restoration of photographic materials (Thailand); (3) Training courses in archival handling of audiovisual materials in Malaysia and Singapore; (4) Colloquium on Access and Use of Archives in Jakarta, in conjunction with the 7th General Conference of SARBICA, 1987. Current: Project on Guide to the Sources of Asian History; publications. Future: (1) Preparation of a model kit for the training of users of archives; (2) guidelines for simplified access procedures. Association sponsors exhibits and continuing education lectures, seminars, workshops.
Bibliography   Tan, L., "SARBICA," Singapore Libraries 12 (1982):21-23.

068   Standing Conference of African Library Schools (SCALS)

Address   c/o École des Bibliothécaires, Archivistes et Documentalistes de l'Université Ceikh Anta Diop de Dakar (School of Librarians, Archivists, and Documentalists, University of Dakar), BP 3252, Dakar, SENEGAL. Tel. (221) 227660/230542
Languages   English, French

Established   1973, Dakar, at meeting of heads of African library schools, organized by the School of Librarians, Archivists, and Documentalists, University of Dakar. 20 participants from Ethiopia, Ghana, Nigeria, Senegal, and Uganda attended.
Major Fields of Interest   Education of librarians, archivists and information professionals in Africa
Major Goals and Objectives   To further undergraduate and graduate professional education of information professionals in Africa. To promote cooperation among schools through exchange of teachers and information
Publications   Official journal: SCALS Newsletter. irreg.

069   Standing Conference of African University Libraries (SCAUL)

Address   c/o PO Box 46, University of Lagos Post Office, Akoka, Yaba, Lagos, NIGERIA
Officers   (elected for 2-yr. term) Chair: J.K.T. Kafe; Treas: S.A. Orimoloye; Ed: E.B. Bankole
Staff   None
Languages   English, French
Established   August, 1969, at the Conference of Librarians from Commonwealth Universities in Africa, as a result of resolutions of earlier conference of university librarians in 1964
Major Fields of Interest   Academic library development
Major Goals and Objectives   (1) To keep members informed of each other's activities and, whenever possible, to correlate such activities in the common interest; (2) to support and develop university library services in Africa.
Structure   Governed by 2 area organizations: SCAULEA (SCAUL Eastern Area) and SCAULWA (SCAUL Western Area) coordinated by a Central Committee. Affiliations: Association of African Universities
Sources of Support   Membership dues, sale of publications.
Membership   Total members: 52 (institutional). Divisions: 2. Requirements: Libraries of institutions in countries eligible for membership in the Association of African Universities. Dues (US Dollar): 250, institution; associate institution (by selection) free.
General Assembly   General membership meets every 2 years. 1988: Freetown, Sierra Leone; 1989: East Africa; 1990: East Africa.
Publications   *Official journal:* African Journal of Academic Librarianship (supersedes SCAUL Newsletter. 1965-82). 1983-. 2/yr. (US Dollar) 50. Editor: E. Bejide Bankole. Address same as the Association. English, French. Indexed in LISA. Other publications: Proceedings of meetings. Publications available for sale; listed in Journal. No publications exchange program.
Activities   Past achievements: Established medium for exchange of ideas, sharing professional views and seeking solutions; established professional journal. Current: Journal publication; cooperative acquisition of African publications; organizing conferences and meetings. Future: Publication of books and reports; staff training and exchanges. Association sponsors continuing education seminars, lectures, and workshops.
Bibliography   Bankole, E. B., "Standing Conference of African University Libraries (SCAUL)," in ALA World Encyclopedia of Library and Information Services, 2nd ed., p. 785. Chicago: American Library Association, 1986.

070   Standing Conference of African University Libraries, Eastern Area (SCAULEA)

Address   c/o University Library, University of Nairobi, Nairobi, KENYA

Languages English, French
Established 1971, Addis Ababa, Ethiopia, as an area organization of SCAUL.
Major Fields of Interest Academic library development
Major Goals and Objectives To support and promote the aims of SCAUL in the region and to specifically further and coordinate development of university libraries in Eastern Africa; to develop and coordinate such matters as regional acquisition, cataloging, bibliographic programs, and library education; to organize and encourage the exchange of information and the holding of conferences and seminars concerning university libraries.
Structure Governed by conference membership meeting every 2 years. Together with SCAULWA forms Central Committee which coordinates activities of SCAUL.
Sources of Support Membership dues.
General Assembly Entire membership meets every 2 years
Publications See SCAUL for official journal
Activities Holding conferences and other activities to carry out the goals of the Association.
Bibliography Bankole, E. B., "Standing Conference of African University Libraries (SCAUL)," in ALA World Encyclopedia of Library and Information Services, 2nd ed., p. 785. Chicago: American Library Association, 1986.

071   Standing Conference of African University Libraries, Western Area (SCAULWA)

Address c/o M. Jean Aboghe-Obyan, Bibliothèque Universitaire, Université Omar Bongo, Libreville, GABON
Officers (elected for 2-yr. term) Pres. and Exec.Sec: M. Jean Aboghe-Obyan
Languages English, French
Established 1972, Lagos, at Conference of University Librarians, as an area organization of SCAUL
Major Fields of Interest University libraries
Major Goals and Objectives To support and further the aims of SCAUL in the area and to specifically further and coordinate development of university libraries in Western Africa; to develop and coordinate such matters as regional acquisition, cataloging, bibliographic programs, and library education; to organize and encourage the exchange of information and the conduct of conferences and seminars concerning university libraries
Structure Governed by conference membership meeting every 2 years. Together with SCAULEA forms Central Committee which coordinates activities of SCAUL.
Sources of Support Membership dues, sale of publications
Membership Total members: 33 (institutional). 12 countries represented. Requirements: Membership in the West African Conference of the Association of African Universities. Dues (US Dollar): 300 (institutional)
General Assembly Entire membership meets every 2 years
Publications *Official journal:* African Journal of Academic Librarianship, 1983-. 2/yr. Same journal as SCAUL. Publishes conference proceedings.
Activities Holding conferences and other activities to carry out the goals of the Association
Bibliography "Sixth Standing Conference of African University Libraries, Western Area," Unesco Journal of Information Science, Librarianship and Archives Administration 4 (1982):218; Bankole, E. B., "Standing Conference of African University Libraries (SCAUL)," in ALA World Encyclopedia of Library and Information Services, 2nd ed., p. 785. Chicago: American Library Association, 1986.

072   Standing Conference of Eastern, Central and Southern African Librarians (SCECSAL)

Address   c/o The Secretary, SCECSAL IX, Makerere University Library, PO Box 7062, Kampala, UGANDA (not permanent)
Officers   Chair: I.M.N. Kigongo-Bukenya
Staff   Provided by host country of Conference
Languages   English
Established   1974, Dar es Salaam, Tanzania, first conference, SCECSAL I, hosted by Tanzania Library Association
Major Fields of Interest   Libraries and librarianship in region
Major Goals and Objectives   (1) To promote and support the development of libraries in member countries; (2) to forge, maintain and strengthen professional links between librarians in member countries; (3) to discuss matters of mutual benefit and interest
Structure   Governed by decision of the general meeting during the Conference. Management of business of Standing Conference rests with Library Association of host country, which provides an acting Executive Committee that adheres to the policy guidelines of SCECSAL
Sources of Support   Membership dues, conference fees, support by host country of conference; government and private subsidies
Membership   Requirements: Open to all independent countries in Eastern, Central and Southern Africa (Angola, Botswana, Burundi, Ethiopia, Kenya, Lesotho, Madagascar, Malawi, Mauritius, Mozambique, Namibia, Rwanda, Seychelles, Somalia, Swaziland, Tanzania, Uganda, Zambia, and Zimbabwe)
General Assembly   Conference takes place every 2 years. 1986 (SCECSAL VII): Botswana; 1988 (SCECSAL VIII): University of Swaziland, Manzini, Swaziland, July 26; 1990 (SCECSAL IX): Kampala, Uganda, July/Aug.
Publications   No official journal. Library association or national library of host country is responsible for publication of proceedings
Activities   Center around the goals of the Association.
Bibliography   "Regional Council Meeting for East, Central and Southern Africa," COMLA Newsletter 62 (Dec. 1988):3

073   Standing Conference of Pacific Librarians (SCOPAL)

Address   c/o Leigh Baker, Chairperson, Lae, PAPUA NEW GUINEA
Languages   English
Established   Oct. 1979, Suva, Fiji, at headquarters of SPEC (South Pacific Bureau of Economic Co-operation)
Major Fields of Interest   Librarianship in Pacific region
Major Goals and Objectives   To further the development of library services and librarianship in Pacific region
Activities   Development of school libraries (with Unesco's assistance); education of teacher-librarians; production of regional bibliography (with Unesco's assistance); utilization of the register of research projects established by the South Pacific Commission and the University of the South Pacific in Suva.
Bibliography   Flores, B., "SCOPAL," COMLA Newsletter 33 (Sept. 1981):5-6, 13.

074   Standing Conference on Library Materials on Africa (SCOLMA)

Address   c/o P.M. Larby, Secretary, The Institute of Commonwealth Studies, University of London, 27-28 Russell Square, London WC1B 5DS, UNITED KINGDOM (not permanent). Tel: 44 (1) 5805876

Officers   (elected for 1-yr.term) Chair: P.B. Freshwater; Sec: P.M. Larby; Treas: B. Burton. Exec.Comm: 12
Staff   1 (volunteer)
Languages   English
Established   1962
Major Fields of Interest   Library materials on Africa
Major Goals and Objectives   To improve the acquisition of materials on Africa; to
sponsor and publish bibliographical projects and works; to organize conferences and
seminars on African bibliographical topics.
Structure   Governed by Executive Committee.
Sources of Support   Membership dues, sale of publications. Budget (Pound Sterling):
1986/87: 900; 1987/88: 1,000
Membership   Total members: 100 (institutional). 20 countries represented. Requirements: Libraries interested in African studies. Dues (Pound Sterling): 9, institutional.
General Assembly   General membership meets once a year, usually in London.
Publications   *Official journal:* African Research & Documentation. 1973-. 3/yr. (Pound
Sterling) 7.5. Free to members. Address: University of Birmingham, PO Box 363, Birmingham B15 2TT, United Kingdom. Editor: J.H. St. J. McIlwaine. Address: School of
Library, Archive and Information Studies, University College, London WCIE 6BT,
United Kingdom. Circ: 500. English. Publications available for sale: UK Publications
and Theses on Africa; Periodicals from Africa: A Bibliography and Union List; census
reports, directories, and others. Price lists issued.
Activities   Conferences and publications.

**075   Tutmonda Esperantista Biblioteka Asocio/World Association of Esperantist
Librarians (TEBA)**

Address   c/o Geoffrey King, Secretary, 228 Capworth Street, London E10 7HL,
UNITED KINGDOM (permanent). Tel: 44 (1) 5560894
Officers   (elected for 1-yr.term) Sec: Geoffrey King; Ed: Douglas Postmann.
Exec.Comm: 2
Staff   2 (volunteers)
Languages   Esperanto
Established   1984
Major Fields of Interest   Application of Esperanto to librarianship and comparative
librarianship.
Major Goals and Objectives   Furthering the use of Esperanto in librarianship; contact
between Esperanto-speaking librarians; services to members.
Structure   Governed by members. Affiliations: Monda Federacio de Kulturaj Asocioj
(Metz, France)
Sources of Support   Membership dues, sale of publications.
Membership   Dues (US Dollar): $8, regular.
General Assembly   Entire membership meets once a year.
Publications   *Official journal:* Biblioteka Bulteno. 1986-. (US Dollar) 8. Free to members. Editor: Douglas Postmann. Address same as Association. Circ: 100. Esperanto.
Activities   Publication of magazine; Conferences. Future: Publication of specialist
works.
Bibliography   "Worldwide Esperanto Library Association," Herald of Library Science
25 (1986):134.

076   West African Regional Branch of the International Council on Archives (WARBICA)

Address   c/o Akintunde Akinfemiwa, Chair, WARBICA, Director, National Archives of Nigeria, PMB 4 UI, PO Ibadan, NIGERIA (not permanent).
Officers   (elected for 3-yr.term) Chair: A. Akinfemiwa, Director of National Archives of Nigeria; Vice Chair: D. Tchriffo, Director of National Archives, Ivory Coast; Sec.Gen: M. Senghor, Chief of National Archives, Togo; Ed: S. Mbaye, Director of Archives of Senegal. Board of Directors: 6
Staff   None
Languages   French, English
Established   Dec. 1977
Major Fields of Interest   Archives
Major Goals and Objectives   To preserve the regional archives, promote the regional archives and cooperation among them.
Structure   Affiliations: Regional Branch of ICA
Sources of Support   Membership dues, government subsidies
Membership   Total members: 15 (institutional). 15 countries represented. Requirements: National archival institutions in West Africa. Dues (US Dollar): 150.
General Assembly   Entire membership meets once a year. 1987: Yamoussoukro, Ivory Coast; 1988: Paris, France during the XIth Congress on Archives.
Publications   *Official journal:* African Archivist: Journal of WARBICA. 1977-. 2/yr. Free to members. Editor: Saliou Mbaye. Address: Directeur des Archives du Sénégal, Immeuble Administraif, Avenue Roume, Dakar, Senegal. Tel: (221) 215072. French, English. Other publications: Proceedings of meetings, reports of seminars, workshops. Publications available for sale.
Activities   Past achievements: 2 seminars in management of archives and conservation for technicians. Future: Use of computers in archival work. Association is promoting library-related legislation as one of the topics of its Medium Term Plan. Sponsors continuing education seminars, workshops, lectures.

Part II
National
Associations

Afghanistan

077   Anjuman Ketab-khana-e-Afghanistan (Afghanistan Library Association / ALA)

Address   PO Box 3142, Kabul (permanent).
Officers   No information available
Languages   Dari, Pushtu, English
Established   June 13, 1971, Kabul, by Kabul University Librarian Abdul Rasoul Fahim, to commemorate International Book Year, 1972.
Major Fields of Interest   Promotion and development of national library system
Major Goals and Objectives   To promote library movement, library education, and bibliographic works; to improve the status and condition of librarians; to work toward training in-service librarians; to nationalize the library system of Afghanistan.
Structure   Governed by executive officers. Affiliations: None.
Sources of Support   Membership dues, subsidies, grants.
Membership   Total members: 200+. Types of membership: Individual, honorary, student, life, emeritus. Requirements: Interest in aims of Association. Dues: No information available.
General Assembly   Entire membership meets annually in Kabul.
Publications   *Official journal:* Afghan Library Association Bulletin. 1972-. irreg. Other publications: Annual reports, proceedings of conferences, seminars, and, irregularly, the Afghan National Bibliography.
Activities   Works to raise the literacy level in Afghanistan, and to establish a library school at Kabul University. Sponsors conferences, seminars, workshops, and other continuing education programs.
Bibliography   Urquidi, J. de Belfort,"Afghanistan," in ALA World Encyclopedia of Library and Information Services, 2nd ed., pp. 34-35. Chicago: American Library Association, 1986; Khurshid, Anis, "Library Associations in Asia," Herald of Library Science 28 (1989):3-10.

Albania

078   Council of Libraries

Address   Rruga "Abdi Toptani," no.3, Tirana. Tel: 7984 or 7823.
Officers   Pres: M. Domi
Languages   Albanian
Structure   Affiliations: IFLA since 1977.
Activities   No further information available. See Bibliography for general information on librarianship in Albania.
Bibliography   Domi, Mahir, "Albania," in <u>ALA World Encyclopedia of Library and Information Services</u>, 2nd ed., pp. 38-39. Chicago: American Library Association, 1986

Antigua and Barbuda

079   Library Association of Antigua and Barbuda

Address   c/o Documentation Centre, OECS Economic Affairs Secretariat, PO Box 822, St. John's, ANTIGUA, WEST INDIES (permanent). Tel: 1 (809) 4623500. Fax: 1-809-4621537.
Officers   Pres: Ms. S. Evan-Wong; Sec: Ms. J. Josiah.
Languages   English
Established   1983
Major Fields of Interest   Library services in Antigua and Barbuda
Major Goals and Objectives   To promote the development of library services in Antigua and Barbuda
Structure   Affiliation: IFLA since 1984

Argentina

080 Asociación Archivistica Argentina
(Association of Argentine Archivists)

Address Avenida Córdoba 1556, Buenos Aires
Officers Pres: Luis F. Piazzoli
Languages Spanish
Major Fields of Interest Archives
Major Goals and Objectives To promote the development of archives in Argentina
Structure Governed by executive officers.
Sources of Support Membership dues.
General Assembly Entire membership meets annually.
Activities Sponsors conferences, seminars.

081 Asociación Argentina de Bibliotecas Biomédicas
(Association of Argentine Biomedical Libraries)

Address Cangallo 2683, Buenos Aires.
Languages Spanish
Major Fields of Interest Biomedical librarianship
Major Goals and Objectives To promote the development of biomedical libraries in Argentina
Sources of Support Membership dues
General Assembly Entire membership meets annually
Activities Sponsors conferences, seminars, workshops.

082 Asociación Argentina de Bibliotecas y Centros de Información Científicos y Técnicos
(Argentine Association of Scientific and Technical Libraries and Information Centers)

Address Santa Fé 1145, Buenos Aires (permanent). Tel: 54 (1) 411405
Officers (elected for indefinite term) Pres: Abilio Bassets; VP and Tec.Dir: Ernesto G. Gietz; Exec.Sec: Olga E. Veronelli; Treas: José A. Villegas.
Staff None
Languages Spanish
Established 1937, Buenos Aires, as Permanent Committee of Librarians (Comité Permanente de Bibliotecarios) at meeting of Scientific Society of Argentina (Sociedad Científicos Argentina).
Major Fields of Interest Library services in science and technology
Major Goals and Objectives To establish communication between technical and scientific libraries, foreign libraries; to assist professionals and scientists in their research.
Structure Governed by executive officers
Sources of Support Membership dues, sale of publications
Membership Total members: 84 (institutional). Types of membership: Institutional only. Requirements: Scientific and technical libraries.
General Assembly Entire membership meets regularly.
Publications No official journal. Issues reports on meetings.
Activities Publication and updating of <u>Collective Catalogue of Scientific and Technical Publications</u>

083   Asociación Bibliotecarios Económicos y Administrativos (ABEA) (Association of Economics and Administration Librarians)

Address   c/o Universidad Nacional de Córdoba, Facultad de Ciencias Económicas, Biblioteca, Ciudad Universitaria, Estafeta 32, Ciudad de Córdoba
Languages   Spanish
Major Fields of Interest   Economics and Administration
Major Goals and Objectives   To promote libraries in the fields of economics and administration in Argentina
Sources of Support   Membership dues

084   Asociación de Bibliotecarios Graduados de la República Argentina (ABGRA) (Association of Graduate Librarians of the Argentine Republic)

Address   Montevideo 581 5 "F," 1019 Buenos Aires (not permanent). Tel: 54 (1) 409728. Telex: 18201.
Officers   Pres: Ms. S. Maris Fernández; Sec: E. del Cano. Exec.Comm: 12
Staff   None
Languages   Spanish
Established   Nov. 5, 1953, Buenos Aires, as Asociación de Bibliotecarios Graduados de la Capital Federal (Association of Graduate Librarians of the Federal Capital), succeeding the Centro de Estudios Bibliotecologicos del Museo Social Argentino, founded in 1943.
Major Fields of Interest   All areas of library science, documentation, and information; library education, particularly postgraduate level.
Major Goals and Objectives   To develop and maintain the librarian's profession by working for the professional status of librarians, defending their interests, and working toward solutions of problems encountered in the exercise of librarianship; to cooperate with the State in matters pertaining to libraries and librarians and maintain relations with other organizations with similar interests; to promote the annual conferences and to publish materials related to the activities of the library profession.
Structure   Governed by Executive Council in cooperation with other groups of the Association. Affiliations: Comisión Nacional Argentina para la Unesco, IFLA.
Sources of Support   Membership dues, private donations, government subsidies.
Membership   Total members: 800+ (individual). Subcommissions: 9. Types of membership: Individual, honorary. Requirements: Open to officially recognized professional librarians.
General Assembly   Entire membership meets annually.
Publications   *Official journal:* Boletín Informativo ABGRA. First series, 1968-75; second series, 1984-. 4/yr. Free to members. Editor: Juan Miguel Roig. Address same as Association. Circ: 900. Spanish. Indexed in IREBI (Madrid). Other publications: Bibliotecología y documentacíon (2/yr.); conference proceedings, annual reports, and others. Exchange of publications with other library associations and libraries in effect.
Activities   Past achievements: The national reunion of librarians (Las Reuniones Nacionales de Bibliotecarios) held every year since 1962. Current: Sponsors continuing education programs, workshops, seminars, etc. Future: Automation of libraries, greater coordination and cooperation in information processing. Association has been active in promoting federal library legislation, such as, for library education, the status of librarians, and the establishment of Librarians' Day (Día del Bibliotecario).
Bibliography   Gravenhorst, H. and Suarez, R.J. (tr. by E.S. Gleaves), "Argentina," in ALA World Encyclopedia of Library and Information Services, 2nd ed., pp.76-78. Chicago: American Library Association. 1986.

085   Asociación de Bibliotecarios Profesionales
(Association of Professional Librarians)

Address   Mitre 1434, 2000 Rosario. Tel: 216544.
Languages   Spanish
Established   1952
Major Fields of Interest   Professional education and professional development of librarians
Major Goals and Objectives   To promote professional status and further professional development of librarians
Sources of Support   Membership dues
Membership   Total members: Approx.200 librarians with diploma
Publications   *Official journal:* Boletín: Asociación de Bibliotecarios Profesionales. Other publications: Manuals, guides, and others.
Activities   Offering seminars, workshops, and other continuing education programs; professional evaluations at requesting institutions. Association sponsors cultural and professional activities for members.

086   Junta de Bibliotecas Juridicas
(Council of Law Libraries)

Address   c/o Universidad Nacional de la Plata, Biblioteca de la Facultad de Ciencias Juridicas y Sociales "Joaquin V. Gonzalez." Calle 7, no. 776, La Plata, Buenos Aires. No further information available

087   Junta de Bibliotecas Universitarias Nacionales Argentinas (JUBUNA)
(Council of National University Libraries of Argentina)

Address   Casilla de Correo 167, San Miguel de Tucuman
No further information available.

088   Reuniónes de Bibliotecas Teológicas
(Union of Theological Libraries)

Address   c/o Facultad de Teologia, José Cubas 3543, Buenos Aires 19. No further information available.

Australia

089 Australian Advisory Council on Bibliographical Services (AACOBS)

Address   c/o AACOBS Secretariat, National Library of Australia, Canberra, Australian Capital Territory 2600 (permanent)
Officers   Chair: F.D.O. Fielding
Staff   Provided by National Library
Languages   English
Major Fields of Interest   Bibliographical services; information resources; user needs; research and development; systems and communications.
Major Goals and Objectives   To improve library and information services in Australia through establishing national policies and guidelines for national planning.
Structure   The association functions through five working parties: bibliography, information resources, user needs, research and development, systems and communications.
Sources of Support   The National Library supports the Secretariat and the activities of the five working groups.
Membership   AACOBS is a voluntary association of major library, archive, and information services in Australia. Committees: State and regional.
Publications   No official journal. Other publications: Library Services for Australia: The Work of AACOBS; Current Australian Reference Books: A List for Medium and Small Libraries; DIALS: Developments in Australian Library Science (annual); 'Pinpointer' Popular Periodicals on Microfiche (annual), and others.
Activities   Carried out through the five working groups. The Association provides a forum for information exchange and cooperation for its members with the set goals in mind. Acts in advisory capacity to government and the National Library.
Bibliography   Bryan, H., "Australia," in ALA World Encyclopedia of Library and Information Services, 2nd ed., pp.88-91, Chicago: American Library Association, 1986.
Additional Information   The work of AACOBS was continued by ACLIS, the Australian Council of Library and Information Services, established in 1988. See: Averill M.B. Edwards, "Frontline (Editorial)," InCite 10 (Apr.1989):2.

090 Australian Association for Health Literature and Information Services, Incorporated (AAHLIS)

Address   PO Box 760, Woden, Australian Capital Territory 2606 (permanent)
Officers   (elected for 1-yr.term) Convenor: Ms. P. Woolcock; Minute Sec: Jane McGlew. Exec.Comm: 7
Staff   None
Languages   English
Established   May 1987; formerly Australian Medical Librarians Group (A.C.T. Branch)
Major Fields of Interest   Medical librarianship and literature
Major Goals and Objectives   To promote the efficient organization and dissemination of health and medical literature; to promote library and information services and research in this field; to provide a common forum for discussion and cooperation between librarians and others in this field; to provide for continuing education of its members.
Structure   Governed by Executive Committee
Sources of Support   Sale of publications
Membership   Total numbers: No information available. Requirements: Open to individuals and institutions interested in health literature and library services.

General Assembly   Meetings every 2 months
Publications   No official journal.   Published <u>Directory of Life Science Libraries in Australia and New Zealand</u> (2nd ed.)
Activities   Publication of <u>Directory</u>.   Sponsors seminars and meetings with guest speakers

091   Australian Association of Toy Libraries for the Handicapped (AATLH)

Address   c/o Narrabeen Community Learning Centre, Pittwater Road, Narrabeen, New South Wales 2101 (not permanent).   Tel: 9131474
Officers   (elected for 2-yr.term) Pres: Nan Bosler; Sec: Helen Stark; Treas: Neal Palmer. Exec.Comm: 11
Staff   3 (volunteers)
Languages   English
Established   1976, Canberra
Major Fields of Interest   Toy libraries for the handicapped
Major Goals and Objectives   To establish an effective communication network between toy libraries for the handicapped throughout Australia.
Structure   Governed by executive officers
Sources of Support   Membership dues, sale of publications, government subsidies, private donations
Membership   Total members: 98 (26 individual, 72 institutional).   4 countries represented in membership.   Requirements: Available to organizations and individuals seeking liaison with the Association.   Each member library can represent from 50 to 3000 members.   Dues (Australian Dollar): 30, full member; 20, associate; 12, individual.
General Assembly   Entire membership meets once a year.
Publications   *Official journal:* <u>Australian Journal of Toy Libraries for the Handicapped</u>. 1980-. 3/yr. (Australian Dollar) 12. Free to members. Editor: Melva White. Address: Torrens Toy Library, Sturt Rd., Bedford Park, S.A. 5042. Circ: 120. English. Other publications: Annual report, proceedings of meetings. Publications exchange program in effect.
Activities   Past achievements: Promotion of the value of play therapy through toys. Current: Annual conference. Future: To establish an effective communication network between toy libraries for the handicapped throughout Australia and to assist with the development from the earliest stage of all handicapped people, in areas covered by toy libraries.
Bibliography   <u>Toys in Australia</u>, June 1987; <u>Reader's Digest</u>, January 1985; <u>Family Circle</u>, April 1986.

092   Australian Council of Libraries and Information Services (ACLIS)

Address   c/o National Library of Australia, Canberra, Australian Capital Territory 2600. Tel: 61 (62) 621111. Telex: 62100.
Officers   Pres: Earle Gow; Exec.Dir: Gordon Bower
Languages   English
Established   Oct, 1988, based on the former AACOBS (Australian Advisory Council on Bibliographic Services)
Major Fields of Interest   Library and information services
Major Goals and Objectives   To coordinate library and information services; to promote a national information policy.
Structure   Governed by executive officers. Affiliations: ALIA

Sources of Support   Membership dues, government subsidies.
Membership   Total members: State and Territory Committees.
General Assembly   Entire membership meets annually.
Activities   Close cooperation with ALIA, and exploration of possible merger in the future. Sponsors conferences, seminars, workshops, and other continuing education programs.
Bibliography   Edwards, Averill M.B., "Frontline (Editorial)," InCite 10 (Apr.1989):2.

093   Australian Law Librarians' Group (ALLG)

Address   PO Box 78, St. Pauls, New South Wales 2031 (permanent). Tel: 61 (2) 6972656
Officers   Convenor: John Rodwell. Exec. Comm: 12
Staff   2 (volunteers)
Languages   English
Established   1969, Sydney
Major Fields of Interest   Law libraries; law librarianship; legal information.
Major Goals and Objectives   Promote and exchange information and ideas on all aspects of law libraries and law librarianship; dissemination of legal information generally; cooperation and joint projects among members; opportunities for continuing education for law librarians.
Structure   Governed by National Board
Sources of Support   Membership dues, sale of publications. Budget (Australian Dollar): Approx.4,500.
Membership   Total members: 240 (230 individual, 10 institutional). Divisions: 6. 6 countries represented in membership. Requirements: Interest in objectives of Association. Dues (Australian Dollar): 16, for all membership categories.
General Assembly   Entire membership meets every two years. 1988: Sydney, August.
Publications   *Official journal:* Australian Law Librarians' Group Newsletter. 1973-. 6/yr. (Australian Dollar) 16. Free to members. Editor: Colin Fong. Address: Allen Allen & Hemsley, Mill Centre, 19-29 Martin Place, Sydney (Postal: Box 50, GPO Sydney N.S.W. 2001). Circ: 250. English. Indexed in Legal Information Management Index, ALISA. Full text on CLIRS (Computerised Legal Information Retrieval System). Other official publications: Reports of seminars, workshops; National Survey of Law Libraries in Australia (1984); Australian Legal Periodicals and Loose-leaf Services Abbreviations (1986); Executive Responsibility for the Administration of Commonwealth Statutes (1984), and others. Publications available for sale.
Activities   Past achievements: Completion of national survey of law libraries; publications; workshops and conferences. Current: Implementation of recommendations of national survey. Sponsors seminars, workshops.
Use of High Technology   Computers used for mailing list. Newsletter available online on CLIRS

094   Australian Library and Information Association (ALIA)
(formerly Library Association of Australia (LAA))

Address   Postal address: PO Box E441, Queen Victoria Terrace, Astralian Capital Territory 2600. Tel: 61 (62) 851877. Fax: 61-62-822249. Headquarters: 40 Brisbane Avenue, Barton (not permanent). Tel: 61 (2) 6929233. (A national headquarters building is being constructed in Canberra, to be completed by mid-1990)

Officers (elected for 1-yr.term) Pres: Averill M.B. Edwards (PO Box 3381, Manuka, ACT 2603); VP/Pres.-Elect: Lynn Allen (State Librarian, State Library Service of WA, Alexander Library Building, James Street, Perth, WA 6000); Past Pres: Alan Bundy; Exec.Dir.(appointed): Sue Kosse. Exec. Board: 6

Staff 11 (paid); 300 (volunteers, throughout Australia)

Languages English

Established 1937, as Australian Institute of Librarians. 1949 name changed to Library Association of Australia (LAA). Incorporated by Royal Charter, 1963. Present name adopted 1988.

Major Fields of Interest Librarianship; library education; library management; library and information studies; related information technology.

Major Goals and Objectives (1) To promote, establish and improve libraries and library services; (2) to improve the standard of librarianship and the status of the library profession; (3) to promote the association for the foregoing objectives of persons engaged in or interested in libraries or library services.

Structure Governed by General Council meeting 3 times a year. Affiliation: IFLA, ASLA.

Sources of Support Membership dues, sale of publications, continuing education conferences. Budget (Australian Dollar): 1986/87: 1,137.000; 1987/88: 1,280,000.

Membership Total members: 7,676 (6,330 individual, 1,346 institutional). Divisions: 9. Sections: 13. Branches: 8. Requirements: Open to all librarians and others interested in the goals of the Association. Professional membership for recognized librarians. Dues (Australian Dollar): 120, individual (professional); 90, individual (other); 30-550, institutional, according to budget.

General Assembly Entire membership meets every year. 1989: Adelaide, July 20; 1990: Perth, Sept.30-Oct.5

Publications *Official journal:* Australian Library Journal. 1951-. 4/yr. (Australian Dollar) 27. Free to members. Address same as the Association. Editor: John Levett. Address: 'Hill Farm,' PO Box 12, Middleton, Tasmania 7163. Circ: 9,000+. English. Indexed in Lib.Lit., Australian Public Affairs Information Service, LISA, and others. Other journals: InCite (Newsletter of ALIA). Managing Editor: Tanya Vojsk. Address: PO Box E441, Queen Victoria Terrace, ACT 2600; Australian Academic & Research Libraries. 4/yr; Australian Special Libraries News. 4/yr; Cataloguing Australia; Orana (Children and school libraries newsletter). 4/yr.; Education for Librarianship. 4/yr; Teacher-Librarian. 4/yr. Other publications: Annual reports, proceedings of meetings, monographs, manuals, e.g. Australian Librarian's Manual; Directory of Special Libraries; Library Services in Distance Education; Bryan, H., ed., ALIAS - Australia's Library, Information and Archives Services: An Encyclopedia of Practice and Practitioners (3 vol., 1989); and many more. A newsletter, ALIA Alert, was initiated in 1989 to reflect the increasing lobbying efforts of the Association and to inform all members of activities of the Federal Parliament concerning libraries and information services. Editor: Michael Evans, ANU, Canberra. Issues annual price lists. Publications listed in journal. Publications exchange program in effect. The General Council resolved in March 1989 to establish ALIA Press to publish Association monograph titles on a commercial basis, with reduced rates for members.

Activities Past achievements: A total review of the Association has been carried out during 1984-86, which led to a change of name and objectives and a broader membership base; the downturn in membership was halted (in 1975 there were 8,878 members) and membership has been increasing; Australian Libraries Summit in Canberra, October 1988; success in influencing related legislation. Current: Campaign for federal funding

for public libraries; national information policy; library standards; promotion of the profession. 50th anniversary of the Association in 1987; IFLA Conference in Sydney, 1988; encouraging the development of regional groups that have strong contacts with their State branch (there are 15 regional groups widely distributed geographically). Future: Continued pressure on the Government in areas relating to libraries; increase in Association membership; publication of national public library standards; resolving issues concerning user charges for certain library services in public libraries. A number of joint projects with ASLA (Australian School Library Association) as outcome of the Australian Libraries Summit. Active in promoting library-related legislation regarding copyright, freedom of information, taxation on books, etc. These and other issues, such as telecommunication, education, information industry policy, science and technology policy, are reported in the newsletter ALIA Alert, which aims to strengthen the involvement of the profession in any legislation in these areas. Sponsors exhibits and continuing education programs.
Use of High Technology   Computers (dataprint), databases, VIATEL Videotext System, Minerva Electronic mail used for management.
Bibliography   Tilley, C.M., "Australian Public Libraries, the Library Association of Australia and Literacy," International Library Review 16 (1984):143-156; Chou, M.P., "Seven Down Under: Synopsis of a Trip to New Zealand and Australia," (Joint LAA/NZLA Conference, Aug. 1984), Hawaii Library Association Journal 41 (1984):27-31; Bryan, H., "Australia," in ALA World Encyclopedia of Library and Information Services, 2nd ed., pp. 88-91. Chicago: American Library Association, 1986; Mackinnon, M., "Professionalism: The LAA Board of Education and the Decade Ahead," Australian Library Journal 34 (1987):5-13; Flowers, T., "To the Association's Credit," ibid.:226-228; Conochie, J., "AIL/LAA Major Achievements in the Area of Special Librarianship," ibid.:236-238; Bryan, H., "The Achievements of the LAA (and the AIL) over the First Fifty Years," ibid.:244-246; Horton, W., "Objectives for the Future," ibid.:261-263; Adams, J., "The Individual Member and the Future: The View from Head Office," ibid.:267-272; Judge, P., "The Professional Future," ibid.:272-278; Webb, M., "The Library Association of Australia's Library and Information Services for People with Disabilities," Link-up 50 (1988):24-25; "The Australian Libraries Summit: A Report by Warren Horton," InCite 9 (Nov. 1988):1,6-7; "ALIA's Royal Charter," InCite 10 (Feb. 1989):12-13.

095   Australian Library Promotion Council (ALPC)

Address   c/o Executive Director, 328 Swanston Street, Melbourne, Victoria 3000 (permanent). Tel: 61 (3) 6637194.
Officers   Pres: John Ward; Hon.Sec (appointed): Stewart Edwards
Staff   3 (paid)
Languages   English
Established   1967, Melbourne.
Major Fields of Interest   All types of libraries
Major Goals and Objectives   (1) To raise the level of public awareness of the value, role and importance of libraries in Australia; (2) to promote appreciation of library services in and for all aspects of society - education, culture and the arts, community affairs, government, the sciences, industry, commerce, agriculture, leisure; (3) to promote, and assist in the promotion of, the use of libraries of all types; (4) to promote the value of libraries in preserving and enhancing Australia's multicultural heritage in literature and other media; (5) to encourage appreciation of the value of reading, of books, and of personal libraries in the home; (6) to promote the role of libraries in the field of information service; (7) to assist in the establishment and development of libraries and library services and to promote the utilization of new techniques; (8) to assist in the development of the

professions and occupations concerned with providing library service; (9) to support efforts, direct and indirect, to gain financial and other support for the establishment and growth of libraries of all kinds; (10) to provide a forum of consultation among all groups and interests concerned with the aims of the Council; (11) to promote evaluation and assessment of the performance of libraries in relation to their stated objectives; (12) to promote the formulation and implementation of minimum standards for libraries of all types.

Structure   Governed by executive officers and subcommittees, meeting monthly. Affiliations: Australian Book Publishers Association, ALIA.

Sources of Support   Membership dues; sale of publications, government grants.

Membership   Total members: 35 (14 individual, 15 institutional, 6 chapters). Requirements: Individual, approval by Council; institutional, national organizations in the fields of library and information science, books, media retailing, government, profesional and commercial organizations.

General Assembly   Entire membership meets annually.

Publications   *Official journal:* <u>Australian Library News</u>. 1969-. 10/yr. Address same as Association. English. Circ: 2,700+. Other publications: Annual report, proceedings of meetings, etc.

Activities   Carried out in accordance with the goals and objectives. Active in promoting library-related legislation.

Additional Information   The Australian Library Promotion Council was dissolved in 1988/89, when the Australian Council of Library and Information Services (ACLIS) was established.

096   Australian Map Circle (AMC)
(formerly Australian Map Curators' Circle)

Address   PO Box E 133, Queen Victoria Terrace, Australian Capital Territory 2600 (permanent).

Officers   (elected for 1-yr.term) Pres: Dorothy F. Prescott; VP: Ms. J.M. Scurfield; Sec: R.H.L. Bartlett; Business Manager: J.D. Lines. Exec.Board: 4

Staff   4 (volunteers)

Languages   English

Established   1973, following a meeting for map keepers at the National Library, Canberra, April 1973. Original name was Australian Map Curators' Circle.

Major Fields of Interest   The making, use and care of cartographic materials within the entire information milieu

Major Goals and Objectives   To establish maps as an important source of information in their own right; to promote the use of map collections; to encourage training and education of personnel in the field of map librarianship.

Structure   Governed by membership and executive officers. Affiliation: IFLA

Sources of Support   Membership dues, sale of publications. Budget (Australian Dollar): Approx.5,500+.

Membership   Total members: 220 (115 individual, 105 institutional). Divisions: 2.   4 countries represented in membership. Requirements: Interest in maps. Dues (Australian Dollar): 18, individual; 25, institutional.

General Assembly   Entire membership meets once a year.

Publications   *Official journal:* <u>The Globe</u>. 1974-. 2/yr. Free to members. Editor: Ms. G. Faragher, 4 Grange Ave., Canterbury, Victoria 3126. Circ: 250. English. Indexed in <u>LISA</u>, <u>Lib.Lit.</u>, <u>Australian Public Affairs Information Service</u>. Other publications: Con-

Additional Information   ASLA is a federation of State associations, each with its own constitution, objectives, membership conditions, and fees. Each State association has its own name, and often own acronym. ASLA is a coordinating body for over 2,000 teacher-librarians in Australia.

098   Australian Society of Archivists (Inc.) (ASA)

Address   PO Box 83, O'Connor, Australian Capital Territory 2601 (permanent).
Officers   (elected for 2-yr.term, 1987-89) Pres: Peter Crush; Treas: Gunna Kinne; VP: Christopher Hurley; Ed: Averil Condren; Sec: Nancy U'Ren; Exec.Sec: Barbara Reed. Exec.Board: 5
Staff   7+ (volunteer)
Languages   English
Established   1975, Canberra
Major Fields of Interest   Archives; archival material
Major Goals and Objectives   A professional organization for archivists concerned with the care and preservation of archives, promotion of standards, archival training, publication of a journal, and promotion of a professional identity.
Structure   Governed by Council consisting of 10 professional members of the Society elected every 2 years and the immediate past president ex-officio. Affiliations: ICA, Australian Council of Archives.
Sources of Support   Membership dues, sale of publications.
Membership   Total members: 452 (361 individual, 91 institutional). Branches: 6. Requirements: No requirement for associate/institutional membership; professional membership: Graduate of university plus 2 years experience in recognized archival institution, or, graduate training in archives administration plus 1 year experience in recognized archival institution. Dues (Australian Dollar): 50-80, professional; 45, associate; 80, institution; 40, voluntary institution.
General Assembly   Entire membership meets every 2 years. 1987: Perth; 1989: Hobart, Tasmania, June.
Publications   *Official journal:* Archives and Manuscripts. 1955- .2/yr. (Australian Dollar) 25. Free to members. Address same as Association. Editor: Averil Condren. Address: The Editor, Australian Society of Archivists, c/o School of Librarianship, University of New South Wales, PO Box 1, Kensington 2033. Circ: 500+. English. Indexed in Australian Public Affairs Information Service, LISA, Historical Abstracts. Other publications: Bulletin. Editor: Ross Connell; Our Heritage: A Directory of Archives and Manuscript Repositories in Australia; conference proceedings, and others. Price lists available. Publications exchange program in effect.
Activities   Past achievements: Establishment of Australian Council of Archives; growing recognition of profession; high reputation of journal. Current: Formulation of Code of Ethics; publications; examination of issues surrounding extension/continuing education courses; high public profile during bicentennial year. Future: Cooperation with Pacific Region; international contacts. Association has been active in input into legislation at federal and state levels, and submission to state government on status of archival/records management services.
Use of High Technology   Computers (datebases) used for management.
Bibliography   Sallier, Michael, "Ten Years of the Australian Society of Archivists in Retrospect," Archives and Manuscripts 13 (1985):145-147; Berrins, Baiba, "Thoughts about the Next Decade," ibid.:147-150.

099   East Asian Librarians Association of Australia (EALGA)

Address   c/o Orientalia, National Library of Australia, Canberra, Australian Capital
Territory 2600 (permanent). Tel: 61 (62) 621286.
Officers   (elected for 2-yr.term) Chair: Y. S. Chan; Vice-Chair/Ed: S.W. Wang; Sec/
Treas: Andrew Gosling. Exec.Comm: 3
Staff   None
Languages   English
Established   1977, as East Asian Librarians Group of Australia (EALGA)
Major Fields of Interest   East Asian librarianship in Australia
Major Goals and Objectives   To promote standards of East Asian librarianship; to en-
courage exchange of information among members and similar organizations; to develop
an effective bibliographic control of East Asian collections in Australia.
Structure   Governed by members through executive officers. Affiliations: Asian Stu-
dies Association of Australia
Sources of Support   Membership dues
Membership   Total members: 91 (51 individual, 40 institutional). 12 countries repre-
sented in membership. Requirements: Any individual or institution interested in East
Asian library services. Dues (Australian Dollar): 5, for all members.
General Assembly   Entire membership meets every 2 years. 1988: Canberra, during
Asian Studies Association of Australia conference.
Publications   *Official journal:* EALGA Newsletter. 1978-. irregular. (Australian Dollar)
5. Free to members. Editor: S.W. Wang. Address same as Association. Circ: 100. English.
Activities   Past achievements: Production of a high quality newsletter communicating
developments in East Asian librarianship in Australia and overseas; Association has
brought together professional librarians in this specialized field formerly isolated in different parts of Australia. Current: Newsletter. Future: Seeking suitable automation for
East Asian language (Chinese, Japanese, Korean) collections in Australia.

**100   International Association of Music Libraries, Archives and Documentation
Centres, Australian Branch (IAML-Australian Branch)**

Address   c/o Laurel Garlick, Music Librarian, State Library of Queensland, William
Street, Brisbane, Queensland 4000 (not permanent).
Officers   Pres: Mary O'Mara; Sec: Laurel Garlick
Languages   English
Established   1970, IAML-Australia and New Zealand Branch formed in Australia;
1982, two separate Branches established, IAML-New Zealand Branch, and IAML-Austra-
lian Branch
Major Fields of Interest   Music bibliography; music librarianship
Major Goals and Objectives   To encourage and promote the development of music
libraries, archives and documentation centers in Australia; to strengthen the cooperation
among member institutions and individuals.
Structure   Governed by executive officers under the parent body. Affiliations: A branch
of IAML
Sources of Support   Membership dues, sale of publications.
General Assembly   Entire membership meets once a year.
Publications   *Official journal:* Continuo. 1982-. Other publications: Annual reports, proceedings of conferences, seminars, etc.
Activities   Sponsors conferences, seminars, workshops, and other continuing education
programs.

101   State Librarians' Council of Australia

Address   c/o D. W. Dunstan, Chair, State Librarian, State Library of Tasmania, 91 Murray Street, Hobart, Tasmania 7000 (not permanent)
Officers   (elected for 5-yr.term) Chair: D.W. Dunstan.   Exec.Comm: 6 (appointed)
Staff   None
Languages   English
Established   1973, Melbourne
Major Fields of Interest   Administration of Australian state libraries and public library systems
Major Goals and Objectives   To improve the efficiency of library services to the public in Australia by discussion and sharing of information
Structure   No formal governing body
Sources of Support   No financial support required
Membership   Total members: 6 (institutional). The Council consists of the six State Librarians of Australia.
General Assembly   Entire membership meets twice a year.
Activities   Past achievements: Advancing the special needs of State Library collections to have a voice on the Australian Government's Committee on Taxation Incentives for the Arts; bringing uniformity in the collection and recording of state and public library statistics. Current and future: Playing a part in the adoption by the Australian federal and state governments of a public information policy. Active in promoting library-related legislation. Involved in Australian government participation in bibliographical listing of state government publications.

Austria

102   Arbeitsgemeinschaft audiovisueller Archive Österreichs (AGAVA) (Working Group of Austrian Audiovisual Archives)

Address   c/o Programmarchiv der Österreichischen Akademie der Wissenschaften, Liebiggasse 5, A-1010 Vienna (permanent). Tel: 43 (1) 43002743
Officers   (elected for 3-yr. term) Chair: Gerhard Jagschitz; Vice-Chair: Armgard Schiffer; Sec.Gen: Dietrich Schüller; Ed: Rainer Hubert; Treas: Walter Schollum. Exec.Board: 5
Staff   2 (volunteer)
Languages   German
Established   1976, as Arbeitsgemeinschaft Österreichischer Schallarchive, restructured 1987 to AGAVA.
Major Fields of Interest   Audiovisual archives
Major Goals and Objectives   Co-ordination of audiovisual archives in Austria; improvement of cooperation, cataloging, acquisition and distribution, conservation and restoration; training of audiovisual archivists and librarians.
Structure   Governed by executive officers. Affiliations: IASA (International Association of Sound Archives)
Sources of Support   Membership dues, sale of publications, government subsidies, sponsorships.
Membership   Total members: 40 (19 individual, 21 institutional). Requirements: Institutional: Audiovisual archive or collection; individual: Audiovisual archivist.
General Assembly   Entire membership meets at least every 3 years. 1987: Vienna, October 2.
Publications   *Official journal:* Das audiovisuelle Archiv. 1988-. (formerly Das Schallarchiv. 1976-1987). 2/yr. Free to members. Address same as Association. Editor: Rainer Hubert. Address: c/o Österreichische Phonothek, Webgasse 2a, A-1060 Vienna. Circ: 150. German, with English abstracts. Other publications: Annual reports, proceedings of meetings, and a monograph series: Holzbauer, R., Jagschitz, G., and Malina, P. Handbuch Audiovisueller Medien in Österreich (Handbook of Audiovisual Media in Austria) (1989). Publications available for sale.
Activities   Past and current: Training courses for av-media archivists and librarians; widening of the scope of the former Arbeitsgemeinschaft Österreichischer Schallarchive to the entire field of audiovisual archive studies. Future: Improvement of funding for audiovisual archives by governmental authorities and private organizations; re-structuring of Austrian audiovisual archives. Association active in promoting related legislation, e.g., it took several initiatives to give audiovisual archives the same stature as libraries and museums. Sponsors continuing education programs.
Bibliography   Holzbaum, Jagschitz, Malina, Fachinformationsführer audiovisuelle Medien; "News in the Field of Audio-visual Archives," Unisist Newsletter 17 (1989):66-67.

103   Büchereiverband Österreichs (BVÖ) (Association of Austrian Public Libraries) (formerly Verband Österreichischer Volksbüchereien und Volksbibliothekare)

Address   Langegasse 37, A-1080 Vienna (permanent). Tel: 43 (1) 439722.
Officers   (elected for 2-yr. term) Chair: Franz Pascher; 2nd Chair: Magdalena Pisarik; 3rd Chair: Michael Neureiter; Sec: Heinz Buchmüller. Exec.Comm: 28

Staff   9 (paid)
Languages   German
Established   1948, Vienna, as Verband Österreichischer Volsbüchereien; name changed
to Verband Österreichischer Volksbüchereien und Volksbibliothekare.
Major Fields of Interest   Public libraries and librarianship
Major Goals and Objectives   To serve the needs of public libraries and the training of
librarians; to represent the interests of the public library community; to give guidelines
regarding furnishing and equipment; to provide bibliographical services.
Structure   Governed by Executive Committee: Affiliations: IFLA
Sources of Support   Membership dues, government subsidies. Budget (Austrian Schil-
ling): 1986/87: 3,900.000; 1987/88: 3,400.000.
Membership   Total members: 1,024. Divisions: 8. Types of membership: Individual,
institutional. Requirements: Open to Austrian public libraries and librarians.
General Assembly   Entire membership meets every 2 years. 1988: Graz; 1990: Vienna.
Publications   *Official journal:* Bücherei Perspektiven. 1984-. 4/yr. Address same as As-
sociation. Free to members. Editor: BVÖ. Circ: 1,400. German. Other publications:
Öffentliche Büchereien in Österreich, ed. J. Sonnleitner (1988).
Activities   Past and current: Development of public library plan to improve library education; publication of training material; promoting libraries; 1987 held first "Open-
Week" of public libraries. Future: To build a network of provincial libraries. Association
has been active in promoting legislation, such as the Library Act. Sponsors continuing
education seminars, workshops, and the Andersen Day.
Bibliography   Strassnig-Pachner, M.R., "Austria," in ALA World Encyclopedia of Library and Information Services, 2nd ed., pp.91-93. Chicago: American Library Association, 1986; Pascher, F., "Büchereien für morgen," (Public Libraries for Tomorrow) Er-
wachsenenbildung in Österreich 4 (1987):1-3.

**104   Österreichische Gesellschaft für Dokumentation und Information (ÖGDI)
(Austrian Society for Documentation and Information)**

Address   c/o Österreichisches Normungsinstitut, Heinestrasse 38, A-1021 Vienna (per-
manent). Tel: 43 (1) 267535. Telex: 115960 onorm a
Officers   (elected for 3-yr. term) Pres: H. Jobst; VPs: F.H. Lang, W. Koch; Sec: B. Ho-
fer; Treas: F. Wimmer. Exec.Comm: 14
Staff   None
Languages   German, (English)
Established   1951, as Österreichische Gesellschaft für Dokumentation und Bibliographie. Present name adopted 1971.
Major Fields of Interest   Information and documentation science; technology, economy, social sciences
Major Goals and Objectives   Promotion of cooperation between existing documentation units; education of documentation personnel; propagation of the application of documentation for decision-making.
Structure   Governed by executive officers. Affiliations: FID, Vereinigung Österreichischer Bibliothekare (VÖB), Österreichische Gesellschaft für Öffentlichkeitsarbeit des Informationswesens (OEGI).
Sources of Support   Membership dues, sale of publications, government subsidies,
dues from courses. Budget (Austrian Schilling): 1986/87: 170,000 (includes a special
meeting); 1987/88: 60,000

Membership   Total members: 152 (128 individual, 24 institutional).   Requirements: Interest in documentation and information.   Dues (Austrian Schilling): 150, individual; 800, institutional.

General Assembly   Entire membership meets once a year.   Special meetings take place irregularly.

Publications   *Official journal:* Fakten, Daten, Zitate. 4/yr.   Free to members.   Editor: Ms. B. Schmeikal.   Address: Sozialwissenschaftliche Dokumentation, Kammer für Arbeiter und Angestellte in Wien, Prinz Eugen-Strasse 20-22, A-1040 Vienna.   Circ: 1,100. German.   Other official publications: Proceedings of special meetings.   Publications exchange program in effect.

Activities   Past achievements: Establishment of a regular course for professional documentation and information personnel; establishment of an official "profile of the profession" for documentalists.   Current: Promoting the application of documentation and information in research, science, industrial projects, and especially in innovations benefitting the Austrian economy.   Future: Enhancing and establishing contacts with foreign and international bodies with similar objectives.   Association has been active in library-related legislation, such as intervening in regard to the Austrian law for personal data protection.   Sponsors continuing education programs and special meetings on current themes; provides forum for exchange of experiences among members.

Use of High Technology   Computers for management.

Bibliography   Strassnig-Bachner, M.R., "Austria," in ALA World Encyclopedia of Library and Information Services, 2nd ed., pp. 91-93. Chicago: American Library Association, 1986.

105   Österreichische Gesellschaft für Öffentlichkeitsarbeit des Informationswesens (OEGI)
(Austrian Society for Information Public Relations)

Address   Prinz Eugen-Strasse 20, A-1040 Vienna (permanent). Tel: 43 (1) 653765/393

Officers   (elected for 2-yr. terms) Pres: Maria Biebl; Exec.Sec: Bettina Schmeikal-Frey; Treas: Elisabeth Glantschnig. Exec.Comm: 12

Staff   None

Languages   German

Established   1977, Vienna

Major Fields of Interest   Public relations of libraries, documentation centers, archives

Major Goals and Objectives   To promote publicity for libraries, documentation centers, and archives.

Structure   Governed by Executive Committee meeting irregularly.   Affiliations: Österreichische Gesellschaft für Dokumentation und Information (ÖGDI), Büchereiverband Österreichs (BVÖ), Vereinigung Österreichischer Bibliothekare (VÖB).

Sources of Support   Membership dues, government subsidies.

Membership   Types of membership: Individual, institutional.

General Assembly   Entire membership meets every 2 years in December.

Publications   *Official journal:* Fakten, Daten, Zitate. 1981-. 4/yr. (Austrian Schilling) 200. Editor: Ms. B. Schmeikal.   Address: c/o Sozialwissenschaftliche Dokumentation, Kammer für Arbeiter und Angestellte in Wien, Prinz Eugen-Strasse 20-22, A-1040 Vienna. Circ: 1,100.   German.   Journal serves jointly ÖGDI and OEGI.   Other official publications: Conference proceedings.

Activities   Past achievements: Publicity reports on libraries, documentation centers, and archives in newspapers and on television; posters printed and distributed; forming an information file on libraries and documentation centers with videotext; organization of sym-

posiums; editing calendar with information on libraries, documentation centers, databases in Austria. Current: Publication of journal.
Bibliography   Strassnig-Bachner, M.R., "Austria," in ALA World Encyclopedia of Library and Information Services, 2nd ed., pp. 91-93. Chicago: American Library Association, 1986.

106   Verband Österreichischer Archivare (VÖA)
(Association of Austrian Archivists)

Address   Postfach 164, A-1014 Vienna (permanent). Tel: 43 (1) 53110/2042
Officers   (elected for 2-yr.term) Pres: Gerhard Pferschy; VPs: Friderike Zaisberger, Rainer Egger; Exec.Secs: Anton Eggendorfer, Michael Göbl; Treas: Annemarie Fenzl, Karl Rehberger. Exec.Comm: 20.
Staff   None
Languages   German
Established   1967, Linz
Major Fields of Interest   Archives; history
Major Goals and Objectives   As a professional association, to promote Austrian archives and the interests of its members nationally and internationally.
Structure   Governed by Executive Committee.
Sources of Support   Membership dues.
Membership   Total members: 333 (232 individual, 101 institutional). Types of membership: Individual, institutional. Requirements: Archivists and archives. Dues (Austrian Schilling): 150, individual; 300, institutional.
General Assembly   Entire membership meets once a year. 1987: Eisenstadt, Burgenland; 1988: Vienna; 1989: Radstadt, Salzburg; 1990: Linz, Oberösterreich.
Publications   *Official journal:* Scrinium: Zeitschrift des Verbandes Österreichischer Archivare. 1969-. 2/yr. Free to members. Address same as Association. Circ: Membership. German. Abstracted in Historical Abstracts.
Activities   Meetings, publication of journal.
Bibliography   Strassnig-Bachner, M.R., "Austria," in ALA World Encyclopedia of Library and Information Services, 2nd ed., pp. 91-93. Chicago: American Library Association, 1986.

107   Vereinigung Österreichischer Bibliothekare (VÖB)
(Association of Austrian Librarians)

Address   c/o Österreichische Nationalbibliothek, Josefsplatz 1, A-1015 Vienna (permanent). Tel: 43 (1) 53410/389. Telex: 112624.
Officers   (elected for 2-yr. term, 1988-90) Pres: Magda Strebl; Past Pres. & 1st VP: Ferdinand Baumgartner; 2nd VP: Eberhard Tiefenthaler; Sec: Marianne Jobst-Rieder. Exec.Board: 8
Staff   None
Languages   German
Established   1896, Vienna, as Österreichischer Verein für Bibliothekswesen, until 1919. Reorganized 1945 under present name.
Major Fields of Interest   National and international librarianship
Major Goals and Objectives   To promote librarianship in Austria; to represent the interests of Austrian librarians at home and abroad; to further advanced training of members.
Structure   Governed by Executive Board (Präsidium). Affiliations: IFLA

Sources of Support   Membership dues, sale of publications.
Membership   Total members: 902 (897 individual, 5 institutional). Divisions: 15. Requirements: Open to persons who work in libraries, in documentation or information. Dues (Austrian Schilling): 100 to 150, regular member; 300+, sustaining member.
General Assembly   Entire membership meets every 2 years: 1988: Linz, Sept. 5-9; 1990: Bregenz, Sept. 4-8.
Publications   *Official journals:* Mitteilungen der Vereinigung Österreichischer Bibliothekare. 1950-. 4/yr. (Austrian Schilling) 320, for foreign countries. Free to members. Editorial Board: Marianne Jobst-Rieder, Gabriele Mauthe, Helga Weinberger. Address same as Association. Circ: 1,000 (approx.). German; Biblos: Österreichische Zeitschrift für Buch- und Bibliothekswesen, Dokumentation, Bibliographie und Bibliophilie. 1952-. 4/yr. Editor: Walter G. Wieser. Address same as Association. Indexed in LISA (Dialog). Other official publications: Conference proceedings, reports of seminars, workshops, and the scholarly series Biblos Schriften, e.g., Hirschegger, M., Geschichte der Universitätsbibliothek Graz 1918-1945 [History of the University Library Graz 1918-1945] (vol. 148, 1989); Oberhauser, O., Die Universitätsbibliothek der Technischen Universität Wien aus der Sicht ihrer Benutzer [The Technical University Library Vienna from the Users' Point of View] (vol. 149, 1989). Publications available for sale; price lists issued. Publications exchanged through the Austrian National Library.
Activities   Past achievements: International interlibrary loan; directives for professional education and training of librarians, documentalists, and information personnel; directives for users; planning for automation. Current: Preservation and conservation of libraries and library material; automation of libraries. Future: Automation of libraries and a national network. Association was active in promoting library-related legislation, such as directives for professional status of librarians, documentalists, and information personnel. Sponsors continuing education programs.
Bibliography   Strassnig-Bachner, M.R., "Austria" in ALA World Encyclopedia of Library and Information Services, 2nd ed., pp. 91-93. Chicago: American Library Association, 1986.

Bangladesh

108   Bangladesh Granthagar Samiti / Library Association of Bangladesh (BGS/LAB)

Address   c/o Library, Bangladesh University of Engineering and Technology, Dacca 2.
Officers   (elected for 3-yr. term) Pres: Zaki Uddin Ahmed; Gen.Sec: Sultan Uddin Ahmad   (Library Training Institute, Bangladesh Central Public Library Building, Shahbagh, Dacca. Tel: 504269). Exec.Comm: 17
Staff   2 (paid), 5 (volunteer)
Languages   Bengali, English
Established   1956, Dacca; originally the East Pakistan Library Association (EPLA) before the establishment of Bangladesh in 1971.
Major Fields of Interest   Library and information science
Major Goals and Objectives   (1) Promotion of library service to the people of the country; (2) provision and promotion of facilities for training for librarianship and research in library science; (3) cooperation with libraries, library organizations, and with associations with similar aims and objectives in and outside the country, in furtherance of the cause of service to the people in the field of librarianship; (4) improvement of the status and service conditions of library personnel.
Structure   Governed by Executive Council. Affiliations: COMLA, IFLA.
Sources of Support   Membership dues, sale of publications, government subsidies, donations by national and international organizations and firms.
Membership   Total members: 710 (690 individual, 20 institutional). Types of membership: Individual, honorary, life, institutional, associate. Requirements: Professional library personnel and individuals interested in libraries and information services. Dues (Taka): 20 to 200.
General Assembly   Entire membership meets once a year.
Publications   *Official journal:* Eastern Librarian. 1966-. 2/yr. Free to members. Editor: Ahmad Hussain. Address: Library Training Institute, Bangladesh Central Public Library Building, Shahbagh, Dacca. Circ: 300. English, Bengali (Publication was temporarily suspended in 1978). Other publications: Annual reports, proceedings of meetings, reports of seminars, workshops.
Activities   Past achievements: National seminars; recommendations to the government for the development of libraries in Bangladesh. Current: Training Course for catalogers and library assistants. Future: Training course for technical services college librarians. Association has been active in promoting relevant legislation by presenting a proposal to the government for passing a bill for library legislation. Sponsors continuing education seminars, workshops.
Bibliography   Hossain, S., "Library Associations in Bangladesh," International Library Review 13 (1981):323-327; Foote, J.B., "Bangladesh," in ALA World Encyclopedia of Library and Information Services, 2nd ed., pp. 98-100. Chicago: American Library Association, 1986; Khurshid, A., "Library Associations in Asia," Herald of Library Science 28 (1989):3-10.
Additional Information   Other associations reported in Bangladesh are Granthagar Parishad (The Special Libraries Association of Bangladesh), Bangladesh Library Council (founded 1968), the Bangladesh Medical Library Association (founded 1975), the Association for Librarians and Information Scientists (founded 1976), and the Bangladesh Society for Indexers and Bibliographers (founded 1978).

Barbados

109   Library Association of Barbados (LAB)

Address   PO Box 827 E., Bridgetown (permanent).
Officers   (elected for 1-yr.term, 1989-90) Pres: Elizabeth Campbell; VP: Joan Brath-
waite; Sec: Angela Skeete (Tel: 809-4295716 / 809-4295724); Asst.Sec: Shirley Yearwood;
Treas: Cathy Carter; Hon.Ed: Hazelyn Devonish. Exec.Comm: 9
Staff   None
Languages   English
Established   1968, Bridgetown
Major Fields of Interest   Library and information science
Major Goals and Objectives   (1) To unite qualified librarians, archivists and information specialists, and all other persons engaged or interested in information management
and dissemination in Barbados, and to provide opportunities for their meeting together;
(2) to promote the active development and maintenance of libraries and related institutions throughout Barbados, and to initiate and foster cooperation between these institutions; (3) to promote high standards of education and training for staffs of information
services and to take such steps as are requisite to improve their status; (4) to consider any
matter affecting information units, and to assist in the promotion of activities which
would enhance their management, regulation and extension; (5) to promote a wide
knowledge of information work.
Structure   Governed by Executive Council. Affiliations: IFLA, ACURIL, COMLA
Sources of Support   Membership dues.
Membership   Total members: 69 (60 individual, 9 institutional). Types of membership:
Personal, associate, corresponding, institutional, honorary. Requirements: Individual:
Open to all persons qualified in library and information science and related disciplines,
and to other persons who by their services in the field of information management and
dissemination in Barbados, are considered eligible by the Exec.Comm.; Associate: All
other persons interested in the information profession; Corresponding: Persons living outside Barbados who otherwise meet the requirements for membership; Institutional: Libraries, other institutions or associations which may nominate a delegate as representative; Honorary: Persons who have rendered outstanding service to the information
profession and are recommended by the Exec.Comm. Dues (Barbados Dollar): 20, individual; 10, associate; 20, corresponding; 50, institutional.
General Assembly   Entire membership meets at least 3 times a year.
Publications   *Official journal:* Bulletin of the Library Association of Barbados.
1968-1985. Irreg. Free to members. Address same as Association. Circ: 100. English;
temporarily discontinued. Update: Occasional Newsletter of the Library Association of
Barbados. There are plans for an Occasional Papers series.
Activities   Past achievements: Has been actively involved in educational programs; sponsored seminars and workshops in areas of major interest to libraries: 1986, Introduction
to Library Automation; 1982, co-sponsored Seminar on Audio-visual Materials in Libraries; Association has also been involved in getting the Barbados Community College
to offer a course for library assistants (technical staff) and assist in its coordination; Association co-sponsored with the Organization of American States (OAS) and the Department of Library Studies a regional workshop on the computer program CDS-ISIS (mini-
micro version) developed by Unesco for information storage and retrieval; sponsored
Public Relations Seminar, and hosted a number of regional meetings. Current: Initiated
regional quiz conducted over the University of the West Indies Distance Teaching Experi-

ment (UWIDITE), a teleconferencing system linking Jamaica, Trinidad & Tobago, Barbados, Antigua, Dominica, Grenada and St. Lucia, which brings together young people of the Caribbean through the libraries; continuing fund raising efforts. Initiated relief efforts to donate children's books to Jamaican libraries devastated by Hurricane Gilbert in September 1988. Future: Improvement of professional image and status; provision of training opportunities at all levels; establishment of additional professional posts; realization and acceptance of the broadening role of the professional librarian. Sponsors Book Week and continuing education programs.

Bibliography   Blackman, J., "Barbados," in ALA World Encyclopedia of Library and Information Services, 2nd ed., pp. 100-101. Chicago: American Library Association, 1986; Campbell, E.F., "Library Association of Barbados - 20 Years On," COMLA Newsletter 64 (1989):9 (gives an excellent overview of the Association by the current President).

Belgium

110 Archives et Bibliothèques de Belgique / Archief- en Bibliotheekwezen in België (ASBL/VZW)
(Belgian Association of Archives and Libraries)

Address c/o Bibliothèque Royale Albert I, 4 Boulevard de l'Empereur, B-1000 Brussels. Tel: 32 (2) 5195351. Telex: 21157.
Officers Ex.Sec: Tony Verschaffel
Staff None
Languages French, Dutch
Established 1907, Brussels
Major Fields of Interest Libraries and archives
Major Goals and Objectives To promote study and research relating to archives, librarianship, and related disciplines, and to contribute publications in these areas.
Structure Governed by executive officers. Affiliations: IFLA, ICA.
Sources of Support Membership dues, government subsidies, donations.
Membership Total members: 500 (individual). Sections: 2 (librarians, archivists). Types of membership: Individual only. Requirements: Professional librarians and archivists. Dues (Belgian Franc): 300.
General Assembly Entire membership meets annually in Brussels
Publications *Official journal:* Archives et Bibliothèques de Belgique/Archief- en Bibliotheekwezen in België. 1923-. 2/yr. 450 (Belgian Franc). Address same as Association. Circ: 600. French, Dutch. Publishes various specialized publications.
Activities Sponsors meetings, continuing education programs.
Bibliography Vanderpijpen, W., "Belgium," in ALA World Encyclopedia of Library and Information Services, 2nd ed., pp. 103-105. Chicago: American Library Association, 1986.

111 Association Belge de Documentation / Belgische Vereniging voor Documentatie (ABD/BVD)
(Belgian Association for Documentation)

Address PO Box 110, B-1040 Brussels 26
Officers Pres: Paul Hubot; Past Pres: R.de Backer.
Staff None
Languages French, Dutch
Established 1947, Brussels
Major Fields of Interest Documentation
Major Goals and Objectives To promote documentation services in Belgium
Publications *Official journal:* Cahiers de la Documentation/Bladen voor de Documentatie. 1949-. 4/y. (Belgian Franc) 740. Editor: P. Hubot. Address same as Association. Circ: 360+. French, Dutch, English.
Bibliography Vanderpijpen, W., "Belgium," in ALA World Encyclopedia of Library and Information Services, 2nd ed., pp. 103-105. Chicago: American Library Association, 1986.

112 Association des Bibliothécaires Belges d'Expression Française (ASBL)
(Belgian Association of French-Speaking Librarians)

Address c/o Bibliothèque Principale de la Ville de Bruxelles, Rue des Riches Claires 24, B-1000 Brussels. Tel: 32 (2) 5129569/5124012.

Officers   (elected for 3-yr.term) Pres: L. Buxin; Exec.Sec: M. Dagneau. Exec.Comm: 19
Staff   4 (volunteer)
Languages   French
Established   1964, Namur. Earlier name: Association Nationale des Bibliothécaires d'Expression Française (ANBEF).
Major Fields of Interest   The status of librarians and public libraries
Major Goals and Objectives   To assist members in professional development and professional status
Structure   Governed by executive officers. Affiliations: IFLA
Sources of Support   Membership dues, sale of publications, government subsidies.
Membership   Total members: 1,900 (450 individual, 1,450 institutional). Requirements: Open to librarians, particularly those in public libraries. Dues (Belgian Franc): 75, individual; no dues, institutional.
General Assembly   Entire membership meets once a year.
Publications   *Official journal:* Le Bibliothécaire: Revue d'Information Culturelle et Bibliographique. 1950-. 12/yr. 300 (Belgian Franc). Editorial Board. Address same as Association. French. Circ: 2,200. Indexed in Library Literature, LISA, ISA. Issues annual reports, conference proceedings, and other publications.
Activities   Past achievements: Effective in obtaining higher salaries for librarians; involved in a new law concerning public reading. Sponsors continuing education programs, lectures, seminars, workshops, to improve library services.
Bibliography   Vanderpijpen, W., "Belgium," in ALA World Encyclopedia of Library and Information Services, 2nd ed., pp. 103-105. Chicago: American Library Association, 1986.

113   Association des Bibliothécaires-Documentalistes de l'Institut Supérieur d'Études Sociales de l'État
(Association of Librarian-Documentalists of the Higher State Institution for Social Studies)

Address   26 rue de l'Abbaye, B-1050 Brussels (permanent). Tel: 32 (2) 6493443.
Officers   (elected for 3-yr.term) Pres: A. Massaux; Exec.Sec: C. Gerard.
Staff   None
Languages   French
Established   1971
Major Fields of Interest   Libraries and documentation in the social sciences
Major Goals and Objectives   To promote and advance the status and professional development of members
Structure   Governed by Executive Council.
Sources of Support   Membership dues.
Membership   Total members: 200+ (individual). Divisions: 4 (public libraries, documentation services, education and training, official journal). Requirements: Student or graduate of the Institute. Dues (Belgian Franc): 300, individual; 150, student.
General Assembly   Entire membership meets annually at the Institute of Social Studies.
Publications   *Official journal:* Gazette B.D. 1972-. 12/yr. Free to members. Address same as Association.
Activities   Sponsors conferences, job placement office for librarians and documentalists. Planning coordination and possible merger with the other associations for French-speaking librarians and documentalists in Belgium.
Bibliography   Vanderpijpen, W., "Belgium," in ALA World Encyclopedia of Library and Information Services, 2nd ed., pp. 103-105. Chicago: American Library Association, 1986.

114   Association Professionnelle des Bibliothécaires et Documentalistes (APBD) (Professional Association of Librarians and Documentalists)

Address   BP 31, B-1070 Brussels (permanent)
Officers   (elected for 4-yr. term) Pres: J. Lheureux; Sec: G. Lecocq; Past Pres: Jean-François Gilmont (rue Louis Hymans 8, B-1060 Brussels; Tel: (02)3456829); Treas: Thierr J. De Bry; VP: Marie-Blanche Delattre. Exec.Board: 3
Staff   17 (paid)
Languages   French
Established   1975, Namur
Major Fields of Interest   All types of libraries
Major Goals and Objectives   To unite professional librarians and documentalists of public, scientific, special, and research libraries; to promote the work of documentalists and librarians; to encourage professional development; to participate in scientific research; to create a general policy of the book and documentation
Structure   Governed by the President and executive officers. Affiliations: IFLA
Sources of Support   Membership dues, sale of publications, government subsidies.
Membership   Total members: 350 (individual). Divisions: 2. Sections: 4. 5 countries represented. Requirements: Professional librarian/documentalist, or student. Dues (Belgian Franc): 400, individuals working fulltime; 200, individuals working halftime, students.
General Assembly   Entire membership meets once a year, in April.
Publications   *Official journal:* BLOC-Notes. 1978-. 10/yr. Membership only. Address: 35, rue Puits-en-Sock, B-4020 Liege. French.
Activities   Past achievements: Publication of works related to cataloging standards, author and title entries. Current and future: Continue publication of journal; organization of seminars; presenting the utility of the INTERMARC format. Association has been active in promoting library-related legislation. Sponsors continuing education programs.
Use of High Technology   Mini-computer for management.
Bibliography   Vanderpijpen, W., "Belgium," in ALA World Encyclopedia of Library and Information Services, 2nd ed., pp. 103-105. Chicago: American Library Association, 1986.

115   Nationaal Bibliotheekfonds / Office National des Bibliothèques et des Bibliothécaires Socialistes (National Office of Socialist Libraries and Librarians)

Address   13, Boulevard de l'Empereur, B-1000 Brussels.
Languages   Dutch
Major Fields of Interest   Flemish socialist libraries and librarians
Major Goals and Objectives   To serve Flemish socialist libraries and librarians
Publications   Lektuurgids
Bibliography   Vanderpijpen, W., "Belgium," in ALA World Encyclopedia of Library and Information Services, 2nd ed., pp. 103-105. Chicago: American Library Association, 1986.

116   Vereniging van Religieus-Wetenschappelijke Bibliothecarissen (VRB) (Association of Theological Librarians)

Address   Minderbroederstraat 5, B-3800 Sint-Truiden (permanent)
Officers   Pres: Herman Morlion; VP: Herwig Ooms; Exec.Sec: Kris Van De Casteele (Spoorweglaan 237, B-2610 Wilrijk)
Staff   6 (volunteer)

Languages   Dutch, French
Established   1965
Major Fields of Interest   Theological libraries and librarians
Major Goals and Objectives   Establishment, development and promotion of librarianship and documentation services in the field of scientific-religious knowledge; improvement of the status and working conditions of personnel; discussion of problems concerning theological libraries.
Structure   Governed by Executive Council. Affiliations: Conseil International des Associations de Bibliothèques de Théologie (International Council of Theological Library Associations)
Sources of Support   Membership dues
Membership   Total members: 65 (individual and institutional). Requirements: Theological libraries and individuals interested in the aims of the Association. Dues (Belgian Franc): 450.
General Assembly   Entire membership meets twice a year.
Publications   *Official journal:* V.R.B.-Medelingen. 1970-. 2/yr. (Belgian Franc) 200. Free to members. Address same as Association. Dutch. Other publications for sale: Ooms,H. and Braive,G., Gids voor de kerkelijke wetenschappelijke bibliotheken in België (Guide to Theological Libraries in Belgium); Gide voor theologische bibliotheken in Nederland en Vlaanderen (Guide to Theological Libraries in the Netherlands and Flemish Belgium), and others.
Activities   Publication of reference sources; sponsoring of meetings.
Bibliography   Vanderpijpen, W., "Belgium," in ALA World Encyclopedia of Library and Information Services, 2nd ed., pp. 103-105. Chicago: American Library Association, 1986.

117   Vlaamse Vereniging voor het Bibliotheek-, Archief- en Documentatiewezen (VVBAD)
(Flemish Association of Librarians, Archivists and Documentalists)

Address   Goudbloemstraat 10, B-2008 Antwerp (permanent). Tel: 32 (3) 2318349.
Officers   (elected for 4-yr.terms) Pres: Frans Heymans; Sec: L. van den Bosch; Treas: Lee Noels; Ed: Marianne Dossche. Exec.Board: 15
Staff   1 (paid)
Languages   Dutch (with English abstracts in publications)
Established   1921, Antwerp, as Vlaamse Vereniging van Bibliotheek- en Archiefpersoneel (VVBAP). 1974, new statutes, and name changed to Vlaamse Vereniging van Bibliotheek-, Archief- en Documentatiepersoneel (VVBADP).
Major Fields of Interest   Libraries, archives and information services
Major Goals and Objectives   To promote the status and professional education of librarians, archivists and documentalists; to advance library and information systems for socioeconomic development.
Structure   Governed by Board of Directors. Affiliations: IFLA.
Sources of Support   Membership dues, sale of publications. Budget (Belgian Franc): 1986/87: 2,195.000; 1987/88: 2,575,750.
Membership   Total members: 782 (740 individual, 42 institutional). Sections: 3. Chapters: 3. Requirements: Working, studying or looking for employment in library, archive or documentation/information center. Dues (Belgian Franc): 500-700, individual; 1,000, institutional (less than 30 hours/week open to public); 2,000 institutional (more than 30 hours/week open to public).
General Assembly   Entire membership meets once a year.

Publications   *Official journal:* Bibliotheek- en Archiefgids. 1983-. (formerly Biblio-theekgids, 1922-83). 3/yr. 1,250 Belgian Franc. Address same as Association. Circ: 1,200. Dutch, with English abstracts. Indexed in LISA, Lib.Lit., ISA, Bull.Signal., etc. Other publications: Annual reports, conference proceedings, 2 series (Library knowledge; archive knowledge), INFO. 12/yr. (formerly Bibinfo), a newsletter for members.

Activities   Past achievements: Organization of study-days in library management, library automation; organization of an annual Week of the Public Library; bringing together on an informal basis librarians, archivists and documentalists. Current: Continue the same work; promoting standards for professional education; development of cooperative activities among school libraries; promoting the idea of the public library. Association has been active in promoting library-related legislation: A working group is making proposals for a new law concerning archives; another working group evaluates the public library law of 1978.

Use of High Technology   Computers (Apple IIe + Ramworks 512k) used for management.

Bibliography   Vanderpijpen, W., "Belgium," in ALA World Encyclopedia of Library and Information Services, 2nd ed., pp. 103-105. Chicago: American Library Association, 1986.

Belize

118   Belize Library Association (BLA)

Address   c/o Bliss Institute, PO Box 287, Belize City (permanent). Tel: 7267.
Officers   (elected for 1-yr.term) Pres: Horace Young; VP: Corinth Lewis; Exec.Sec:
Robert T. Hulse; Treas: Marlene Alford. Exec.Comm: 7
Staff   None
Languages   English
Established   1976, at a special meeting in the Children's Library, called to discuss the
formation of a library association.
Major Fields of Interest   Public and school libraries; book dealers
Major Goals and Objectives   To foster and promote the development of libraries, the
book trade, and information science; the highest standards of learning, efficiency, integri-
ty, and courtesy in librarianship; to represent the profession in matters concerning librari-
anship.
Structure   Governed by Executive Committee. Affiliations: COMLA, IFLA
Sources of Support   Membership dues, private gifts
Membership   Total members: 50 (48 individual, 2 institutional). Types of membership:
Individual, institutional, emeritus, student. *Requirements:* Open to any individual who
wishes to join; institutional: Must be either a school or bookstore. Dues (Belize Dollar):
20, individual; 30, institutional; 10, emeritus and student.
General Assembly   Entire membership meets once a month.
Publications   *Official journal:* Belize Library Association Bulletin. 1976-. 3/yr. Free to
members. Editor: Robert T. Hulse. Address same as Association. Circ: Membership. English. Publications issued for sale.
Activities   Sponsors "Annual Summer Programme on Basic Library Science" since 1977
to meet needs for basic training of library workers from all types of libraries; sponsors
advanced course since 1989 with the help of the National Library Service and the Department of Library Studies in Jamaica; sponsors book fairs with books donated by publishers; continues weekly radio programs on books for the National Library.
Bibliography   Vernon, L.G., "Belize," in ALA World Encyclopedia for Library and Information Services, 2nd ed., p.106; Hulse, R., "Library Education in Belize," COMLA
Newsletter 62 (Dec.1988):4; Vernon, L., "Library Service in Belize," COMLA Newsletter
64 (June 1989):9, 11.

Benin

119   National Association of Archivists, Librarians, Documentalists, Booksellers, Museologists and Museographers of Benin

Address   Noel H. Amoussou, Director, Bibliothèque Nationale, BP 401, Porto-Novo (permanent)
Languages   French
Major Fields of Interest   Archives, libraries, documentation, booktrade, museums
Major Goals and Objectives   To promote the development of archives, libraries, information services, museums, and the booktrade in Benin
Structure   Affiliations: Association Internationale pour le Développement de la Documentation, des Bibliothèques et des Archives en Afrique (AIDBA)
Activities   No further information available. The Bibliothèque Universitaire Centrale (B.P. 526, Cotonou, Benin; Tel: 360074, 360105, 360122) is a member of IFLA.
Bibliography   McHugh, N., "Benin," in ALA World Encyclopedia of Library and Information Services, 2nd ed., pp. 107-108. Chicago: American Library Association, 1986.

Bermuda

120 Library Association of Bermuda

Address c/o Bermuda Library, Par-la-Ville, Hamilton HM11. Tel: (809) 2952905. Telex: 3775
Languages English
Established 1983
Major Fields of Interest Librarianship
Major Goals and Objectives To promote library development in Bermuda
Structure Affiliations: Commonwealth Library Association (COMLA), IFLA
Sources of Support Membership dues, subsidies
General Assembly Entire membership meets annually.
Bibliography Packwood, C.O., "Bermuda," in <u>ALA World Encyclopedia of Library and Information Services</u>, 2nd ed., pp. 108-110. Chicago: American Library Association, 1986.

Bolivia

121   Asociación Boliviana de Bibliotecarios (ABB)
(Bolivian Association of Librarians)

Address   c/o Efraín Virreira Sánchez, President, Casilla 992, Cochabamba (not permanent). Headquarters: La Paz.
Officers   Pres: Efraín Virreira Sánchez
Staff   None
Languages   Spanish
Established   1974, Portales, Cochabamba
Major Fields of Interest   General and special libraries; library technology
Major Goals and Objectives   (1) Professionalization of librarians in general; (2) technical organization of libraries; (3) creation of additional libraries.
Structure   Governed by Executive Council. Affiliations: FID.
Sources of Support   Membership dues, private donations
Membership   Total members: 400 (375 individual, 25 institutional). Divisions: 9. Types of membership: Individual, institutional, student, honorary. Requirements: Open to all librarians, students, and libraries.
General Assembly   Entire membership meets once a year.
Publications   No official journal. Issues proceedings of annual meetings.
Activities   Sponsors continuing education programs for librarians; involved in the establishment of the first library school at the Universidad Mayor de San Andrés.
Bibliography   Aguirre Quintero, J., "Bolivia," in ALA World Encyclopedia of Library and Information Services, 2nd ed., pp. 129-130. Chicago: American Library Association, 1986.

Botswana

122 Botswana Library Association (BLA)

Address PO Box 1310, Gaborone (permanent). Tel: (267) 351151 ext.2297. Telex: 2429
Officers (elected for 1-yr. term) Chair: B. Garebakwena; Vice-Chair: J.R. Neill; Sec: Ms. D.M. Mbaakanyi; Asst.Sec: T. Kwelagobe; Treas: J. Tsonope; Ed: J.O. Asamani; Asst.Ed: S. Monageng. Exec.Comm: 7
Staff None
Languages English
Established 1978
Major Fields of Interest Library and information science
Major Goals and Objectives To unite persons interested in libraries; to promote development of libraries; to promote bibliographic research, studies in librarianship by means of articles, news briefs and reports on all aspects of library and information sciences, with emphasis on Southern Africa.
Structure Governed by Executive Committee. Affiliations: COMLA, IFLA
Sources of Support Membership dues, sale of publications. Budget (Pula): 1986/87: 900; 1987/88: 1,000.
Membership Total members: 50 (40 individual, 10 institutional). Requirements: Interest in aims of Association. Dues (Pula): 10, individual; 20, institutional.
General Assembly Entire membership meets annually.
Publications *Official journal:* Botswana Library Association Journal. 1979-. 2/yr. 15 Pula. Free to members. Address same as Association. Editor: J.O. Asamani. Address: University of Botswana, Private Bag 0022, Gaborone. Circ: 200. English. Indexed in LISA. Other publications: Annual reports; reports of seminars, workshops.
Activities Past achievements: (1) Increase in membership from about 10 in 1978 to 50 in 1988; (2) regular publication of the BLA Journal; (3) Organizing SCECSAL VII (Standing Conference of Eastern, Central and Southern African Librarians) Conference in August, 1986 in Gaborone, attended by all library associations in the region. Current: Implementation of SCECSAL VII Conference resolutions, i.e. propagation with a view to the establishment of library and information centers in rural areas. Future: Organization of: (1) refresher courses and in-service training for library staff at various levels; (2) intensive courses for school teachers interested in becoming tutor-librarians. Association has been active in promoting library-related legislation, such as pursuing tightening up of legal deposit legislation. Sponsors Book Week, continuing education programs.
Bibliography African Book Publishing Record 10 (1984):31-32; Raseroka, K., "Botswana," in ALA World Encyclopedia of Library and Information Services, 2nd ed., pp. 132-133. Chicago: American Library Association, 1986.

Brazil

123   Associaçao Brasileira de Escolas de Biblioteconomía e Documentaçao (ABEBD)
(Brazilian Association of Schools of Library and Information Science)

Address   c/o Escola de Biblioteconomia e Communicaçao, Universidade Federal de Bahia, Campus Universitário do Caneta, Salvador, Bahia 40,000 (not permanent). Tel: (55) 2476755.
Officers   Pres: Maria Stela Santos Pita Leite
Languages   Portuguese
Established   1967, Belo Horizonte, at the 5th Brazilian Library and Documentation Congress, as Brazilian counterpart to ALISE (formerly AALS).
Major Fields of Interest   Education for library and information science
Major Goals and Objectives   "To provide an opportunity for the faculties of the Brazilian library science and documentation schools to meet for the discussion and resolution of common problems; to provide an opportunity for the development and improvement of education for librarianship in general through such measures and plans as may make possible the improvement of the faculties." (Chapter II, article 2 of Statutes)
Structure   Governed by Executive Board
Sources of Support   Membership dues, subsidies
Membership   Types and requirements: (1) Institutional: Library science and documentation schools represented by the head of each school and an elected delegate from each faculty; (2) individual: Faculty members of the Brazilian library science and documentation schools; (3) honorary: Individuals who have actively demonstrated their interest in the cause and development of librarianship; (4) cooperating: Individuals or organizations who demonstrate an interest in the training for and development of librarianship and make annual contributions to the Association.
General Assembly   Entire membership meets annually.
Activities   Sponsors conferences, seminars, and regional meetings of library educators; seeks to improve information service for library education and to promote attendance at library schools; aims at stronger cooperation at the international level.
Bibliography   Fonseca, Edson Nery da, "Brazil," in ALA World Encyclopedia of Library and Information Services, 2nd ed., pp. 137-139. Chicago: American Library Association, 1986.

124   Associaçao dos Arquivistas Brasileiros
(Association of Brazilian Archivists)

Address   Praia de Botafogo 186, Sala B-217, CEP 22253 Rio de Janeiro, RJ. Tel: 55 (21) 5510748.
Officers   Pres: Jaime Antunes da Silva; Sec: Rosely Cury Rondinelli.
Staff   None
Languages   Portuguese
Established   1971
Major Fields of Interest   Archives
Major Goals and Objectives   To promote the work of archives and the archival profession.
Structure   Governed by executive officers. Affiliations: ICA.
Sources of Support   Membership dues, sale of publications

Membership Total members: 1,500 (individual and institutional)
General Assembly Entire membership meets every two years.
Publications *Official journal:* Arquivo e administraçao. 2/yr. Free to members. Address same as Association. Portuguese. Other publications: Annual reports, proceedings of conferences. Publications available for sale.
Activities Sponsors continuing education lectures, seminars, workshops on current topics, such as new techniques in archival management; encourages cooperation between archivists and exchange of information.

125 Associaçio Paulista de Bibliotecários (APB)
(Sao Paulo Library Association)

Address Rua Maestro Cardim, 94, Caixa Postal 343, 01323 Sao Paulo SP (permanent). Tel: 55 (11) 2853831
Officers (elected for 3-yr.terms) Pres: Oswaldo Francisco de Almeida Junior; 1st Sec: Marta Ligia Pomim Valentim; VP: José Fernando Modesto da Silva; 2nd Sec: Elizabeth Reis Cavalheiro; 1st Treas: Berenice Neubhaher; 2nd Treas: Silvia de Almeida; Exec.Sec: Madalena Sofía Mitiko Wada. Exec.Comm: 6
Staff 3 (paid)
Languages Portuguese
Established 1938, Sao Paulo
Major Fields of Interest Library science, documentation, information science, archival studies
Major Goals and Objectives Promote the status and professional development of librarians in Sao Paulo; represent their interests in salary matters; improve their work and working conditions; generally represent the library profession in society and contribute to the cultural and technical improvement of librarians, libraries, documentation centers and archives.
Structure Governed by Executive Committee. Affiliations: FEBAB, IFLA
Sources of Support Membership dues, sale of publications, fees from courses and events
Membership Total members: 1,500 (individual). Types of membership: Individual. Requirements: Librarians and students of librarianship
General Assembly Entire membership meets every 2 years. 1988: Sao Paulo, Sept.
Publications *Official journal:* APB Boletim. 1984-. 6/yr. Address same as Association. Circ: 1,700. Portuguese. Other publications: Palavra Chave (Library Review). 12/yr.; etc.. Publications issued for sale
Activities Sponsors continuing education seminars, workshops, lectures, and library-related events; provides scholarships to students of librarianship; improving publication program. Association has been active in promoting library-related legislation: Worked for the passage of laws to improve condition of public libraries and to improve working conditions in existing libraries. As the oldest library association in Brazil, it has great impact in promoting the profession of librarianship, and is active on both the national and international level.
Bibliography Fonseca, Edson Nery da, "Brazil," in ALA World Encyclopedia of Library and Information Services, 2nd ed., pp. 137-139. Chicago: American Library Association, 1986.

126   Associaçao Profissional de Bibliotecários do Estado do Rio de Janeiro (APBERJ) (formerly Associaçao Brasileira de Bibliotecários) (Library Association of Rio de Janeiro, formerly Brazilian Library Association)

Address   Rua Martins Torres 99, Santa Rosa, Niterói, 24000 Rio de Janeiro RJ (not permanent).
Officers   Pres: Antonio Caetano Dias; Exec.Sec: Nolka N. Freitas. Exec.Comm: 5
Staff   None
Languages   Portuguese
Established   1949, as Associaçao Brasileira de Bibliotecários (Brazilian Library Association); new name adopted, 1976.
Major Fields of Interest   Libraries and information services, generally and in specific fields, such as, medicine, agriculture, technology, law, technical processes
Major Goals and Objectives   To further library development and represent the interests of librarians
Structure   Governed by Executive Council. Affiliations: FEBAB
Sources of Support   Membership dues, sale of publications, registration for specialized courses
Membership   Total members: 500+ (individual).
General Assembly   Entire membership meets twice a year.
Publications   *Official journal:* Noticias da ABB. 1954-. 2/yr. Membership. Address same as Association. Circ: 500+. Portuguese. Other publications: Guia de Bibliografia Especializada (Guide to Special Libraries), and other professional monographs. Publications available for sale.
Activities   Special Interest Groups, such as, medical, agricultural, technological, law, technical processes. Active in promoting library-related legislation, e.g., professional status for librarians. Sponsors seminars, conferences, workshops, and other continuing education programs. Celebrates Book Week. Works for greater professional consciousness in the Association concerning the importance of information retrieval for cultural, scientific, and technological development.

127   Conselho Federal de Biblioteconomia (CFB) (Federal Council of Librarianship)

Address   SCLRN 712-713 - bloco A - entr 31 sobreloja - sala 02, 70760 Brasilia DF (permanent). Tel: 55 (61) 231561.
Officers   (elected for 3-yr.term) Pres: María Lucia Almeida; Exec.Sec: Etelvina Lima. Exec.Comm: 14
Staff   6 (2 paid)
Languages   Portuguese
Established   1962, Sao Paulo, by Laura García Moreno Russo, first president.
Major Fields of Interest   Economic status of the library profession
Major Goals and Objectives   To promote the status of librarians and libraries in Brazil
Structure   Governed by Executive Council and officers. The Association comprises librarians from 10 different areas (estados).
Sources of Support   Membership dues, sale of publications.
Membership   Total members: 5,000+ (individual). Types of membership: Individual. Requirements: Open to all librarians.
General Assembly   Entire membership meets every two years.
Publications   No publications program
Activities   Sponsors seminars, conferences, celebration of Book Week.

128   Federaçao Brasileira de Associaçoes de Bibliotecários (FEBAB) (Brazilian Federation of Library Associations)

Address   Rua Avanhandava 40 - conj. 110, 01306 Sao Paulo SP (permanent). Tel: 55 (11) 2579979. Fax: 55-11-2830747.
Officers   (elected for 2-yr.term) Pres: Elizabet María Ramos de Carvalho; Sec.Gen: Mirian Salvadore Nascimento; Past Pres: Antonio Gabriel. Exec.Comm: 5
Staff   100 (paid)
Languages   Portuguese
Established   1959, during the Second Brazilian Congress of Librarianship and Documentation, by Laura García Moreno Russo and Rodolpho Rocha, Jr.
Major Fields of Interest   Librarianship and documentation
Major Goals and Objectives   To unite the library associations of the country; to promote the interests of professional librarians; to assist in the solution of problems in libraries and documentation centers; to assist the member associations in the Federation.
Structure   Governed by Executive Committee and representatives of 8 specialized committees. Affiliations: IFLA
Sources of Support   Membership dues, sale of publications, government and private subsidies.
Membership   Total members: 24 associations. Commissions: 8 (University Libraries, Public and School Libraries, Agricultural Documentation, Biomedical Documentation, Social Sciences and the Humanities, Legal Documentation, Technological Documentation, and Technical Processes; each with their own organizational structure)
General Assembly   Entire membership meets every two years.
Publications   *Official journal:* Revista Brasileira de Biblioteconomía e Documentaçao (Brazilian Review of Librarianship and Documentation). 1973-. 2/yr. (US Dollar) 30. Free to members. Editor: Francisco José de Castro Ferreira. Address same as Association. Circ: 1,000 +. Portuguese, with English abstracts. Indexed in LISA, ISA, Lib.Lit.. Other publications: Codigo de Catalogaçao Anglo-Americano (Anglo-American Cataloging Rules); proceedings of conferences, seminars, annual reports, etc. Publications available for sale.
Activities   Activities center on improving state library associations, observing Book Week, sponsoring exhibits, conferences, and other continuing education programs. Sponsors the national specialized meetings of the eight standing committees of the Federation. Active in promoting library-related legislation.
Bibliography   McCarthy, C.M., "Achievements and Objectives in Brazilian Librarianship," International Library Review 15 (1983):131-145; Fonseca, Edson Nery da, "Brazil," in ALA World Encyclopedia of Library and Information Services, 2nd ed., pp. 137-139. Chicago: American Library Association, 1986.

129   Federaçao Brasileira de Associaçoes de Bibliotecários - Comissao Brasileira de Bibliotecas Centrais Universitárias (FEBAB/CBBCU) (Brazilian Federation of Library Associations - Brazilian Commission of University Libraries)

Address   c/o Zita Prates de Oliveira, Librarian, Biblioteca Central, Universidade Federal do Rio Grande do Sul (UFRGS), CP 2303, 90001 Pôrto Alegre RS (not permanent). Tel: 55 (512) 242431. Telex: 0511055.
Languages   Portuguese
Major Fields of Interest   University libraries

Major Goals and Objectives   To promote the development of university libraries in Brazil
Structure   Governed by executive officers.   Affiliations: FEBAB

130   Federaçao Brasileira de Associaçoes de Bibliotecários - Comissao Brasileira de Bibliotecas Públicas e Escolares (FEBAB/CBBPE) (Brazilian Federation of Library Associations - Brazilian Commission of Public and School Libraries)

Address   c/o Biblioteca Pública de Minas Gerais, Praça de Liberdade 21, 30000 Belo Horizonte, Minas Gerais MG (not permanent).
Languages   Portuguese
Major Fields of Interest   Public libraries and school libraries
Major Goals and Objectives   To promote the development of public and school libraries in Brazil
Structure   Governed by executive officers.   Affiliations: FEBAB
Sources of Support   Membership dues, sale of publications.

131   Federaçao Brasileira de Associaçoes de Bibliotecários - Comissao Brasileira de Documentaçao Agrícola (FEBAB/CBDA) (Brazilian Federation of Library Associations - Brazilian Commission of Agricultural Documentation)

Address   c/o Janeti L. Bombini de Moura, President, Ave. Pádua Dias, 11, PO Box 09, 13.400 Piracicaba, SP (not permanent). Tel: 55 (194) 330011 ext.382. Telex: (019) 1141.
Officers   (elected for 3-yr.term) Pres: Janeti L. Bombini de Moura; VP: Ademir G. Pietrosanto; 1st Sec: Marilia Garcia Henyei; Treas: Adriana Bueno Moretti; 2nd Sec: Ana Maria Rabetti. Exec.Board: 5
Staff   100 (paid)
Languages   Portuguese
Established   1967, in Cruz das Almas, Bahia, by 20 documentalists and librarians.
Major Fields of Interest   Agricultural information and documentation; sources of information; automation in agricultural libraries; library marketing; library management; information systems for agriculture
Major Goals and Objectives   To promote cooperation among librarians at the national level; to establish and define all basic activities that relate to documentation and agricultural sciences; to promote continuing education; to promote socio-cooperative activities; to sponsor technical meetings.
Structure   Governed by executive officers.   Affiliations: FEBAB, AIBDA.
Sources of Support   Membership dues, sale of publications, private contributions, foundation subsidies.
Membership   Total members: 370 (individual).   Requirements: Working in agricultural institution.
General Assembly   Entire membership meets every 2 years.
Publications   *Official journal:* Agrícolas. 1969-. 2/yr. Free to members. Address same as Association. Circ: Membership only. Portuguese. Other publications: Directory of Members and Institutions, occasional monographs. Publications available for sale. Publications exchange program in effect.
Activities   Past achievements: Training and continuing education. Current: Publications and technical meetings. Future: Professional improvement of members and socio-cooperative activities. Sponsors seminars, workshops, and other continuing education programs.

132 Federaçao Brasileira de Associaçoes de Bibliotecários - Comissao Brasileira de Documentaçao Biomédica (FEBAB/CBDB)
(Brazilian Federation of Library Associations - Brazilian Commission of Biomedical Documentation)

Address 04040 Rua Loefgren, CP 7144, 2473 Sao Paulo, or c/o Sistema de Bibliotecas da Universidade de Sao Paulo (SIBI), CP 8191, 05508 Sao Paulo SP.
Languages Portuguese
Established 1971, in Belo Horizonte
Major Fields of Interest Biomedical librarianship and documentation.
Major Goals and Objectives To unite biomedical librarians in order to promote the development of documentation in the field of biomedical science
Structure Governed by executive officers. Affiliations: FEBAB
Sources of Support Membership dues.
Membership Open to Biomedical Working Groups of the Brazilian library associations of the various states.
General Assembly Entire membership meets during FEBAB congress.

133 Federaçao Brasileira de Associaçoes de Bibliotecários - Comissao Brasileira de Documentaçao em Ciências Sociais e Humanidades (FEBAB/CBDCSH)
(Brazilian Federation of Library Associations - Brazilian Commission for Documentation in the Social Sciences and Humanities)

Address c/o Rua Avanhandava 40 - conj. 110, 01306 Sao Paulo SP (not permanent). Tel: 55 (11) 2579979.
Languages Portuguese
Established 1978, Sao Paulo, during the 4th General Assembly of the permanent committee of FEBAB.
Major Fields of Interest Social sciences and humanities
Major Goals and Objectives To unite librarians in these fields; to coordinate and standardize their activities; to cooperate with the official organizations throughout the country for the control, organization, and dissemination of the literature in these fields; to promote professional development of librarians in these fields through meetings, courses, seminars, and other activities.
Structure Governed by Executive Board. Affiliations: FEBAB
Sources of Support Membership dues, subsidies from FEBAB and private institutions.
Membership Members are the affiliated groups of the following states: Bahia, Maranhao, Minas Gerais, Pará, and Sao Paulo.
General Assembly Entire membership meets during FEBAB congresses.
Activities Activities focus on developing coordination between the affiliated groups, and the planning of conferences.

134 Federaçao Brasileira de Associaçoes de Bibliotecários - Comissao Brasileira de Documentaçao Jurídica (FEBAB/CBDJ)
(Brazilian Federation of Library Associations - Brazilian Commission of Legal Documentation)

Address Rua Avanhandava 40 - conj. 110, 01306 Sao Paulo (permanent). Tel: 55 (21) 2579979.
Officers Pres: Nylma Thereza de Salles Velloso Amarante; Exec.Secs: Tania Cordeiro Alvarez and Sérgio da Costa Velho

Languages Portuguese
Established 1971, Belo Horizonte, during the VI Congresso Brasileiro de Biblioteconomia e Documentaçao.
Major Fields of Interest Law and legislation documentation, standardization, information, network systems of legal materials, including nonbook materials.
Major Goals and Objectives Organizing Brazilian librarians to establish coordination for solving problems relating to law documentation development in Brazil; adopting the necessary technical processes to accomplish this goal.
Structure Governed by executive officers. Affiliations: FEBAB
Sources of Support Membership dues, sale of publications, private gifts.
Membership Total members: 380+ (individual). Types of membership: Individual, honorary. Requirements: Registration in Regional Librarianship Councils and professional librarians associations.
General Assembly Entire membership meets once a year. Meetings held during annual conferences of FEBAB and other organizations.
Publications *Official journal:* FEBAB/CBDJ Noticias. 1974-. approx.4/yr. Free to members. Address same as Association. Circ: Membership. Portuguese. Other publications: Annual reports, proceedings of annual meetings, seminars, workshops, etc. Publications available for sale. Publications exchange program in effect.
Activities Publication program. Sponsors conferences, workshops, and other continuing education programs. Active in promoting library-related legislation.

**135   Federaçao Brasileira de Associaçoes de Bibliotecários - Comissao Brasileira de Documentaçao Tecnológica (FEBAB/CBDT)
(Brazilian Federation of Library Associations - Brazilian Commission of Technological Documentation)**

Address c/o Instituto Brasileiro de Informaçao em Ciência e Tecnología (IBICT), Ave. W-3N, Quadra 511 - bloco A, Ed. Bittar II, Térreo, 70750 Brasília DF (not permanent).
Officers Pres: Elizabeth María Ramos de Carvalho
Languages Portuguese
Major Fields of Interest Documentation in technology
Major Goals and Objectives To promote and coordinate documentation in technology in Brazil
Structure Governed by executive officers. Affiliations: FEBAB
Sources of Support Membership dues, FEBAB subsidies.
General Assembly Entire membership meets once a year.

**136   Federaçao Brasileira de Associaçoes de Bibliotecários - Comissao Brasileira de Processos Técnicos (FEBAB/CBPT)
(Brazilian Federation ot Library Associations - Brazilian Commission on Technical Processes)**

Address c/o Rua Avanhandava 40 - conj. 110, 01306 Sao Paulo SP (permanent). Tel: 55 (11) 2579979. Fax: 55-11-2830747.
Officers Pres: María Luiza Monteiro da Cunha
Languages Portuguese
Major Fields of Interest Technical proccesses
Structure Governed by executive officers. Affiliations: FEBAB

Brunei Darussalam

137   Persatuan Perpustakaan Kebangsaan
(National Library Association of Brunei)

Address c/o PO Box 1209, Gadong Post Office, Bandar Seri Begawan 3112, Brunei Darussalam. Tel: (2) 43511.

Officers Pres: Nellie Haji Sunny; VP: Raji Abu Bakar Haji Zainal; Sec: Haji Mohd Yusoff Haji Murni; Chair: Haji Hamiddon Mudim Haji Hassan; Treas: Metali Haji Kamis. Exec.Council: 6

Staff None

Languages Malay

Established 1986

Major Fields of Interest Libraries and library services

Major Goals and Objectives To promote the development of library services in Brunei Darussalam; to promote the education and training of professional staff.

Structure Governed by Executive Council.

Sources of Support Membership dues; subsidies

Membership Total members: Approx. 36

General Assembly Entire membership meets once a year

Publications No official journal

Activities To provide a forum for meetings and continuing education.

Bibliography "Brunei," COMLA Newsletter (Dec. 1987):15; "Professional Education in Brunei Darussalam," Focus 20 (1989):28-29.

Bulgaria

138   Sekciya na Bibliotechnite Rabotnitsi pri Centralniya Komitet na Profesionalniya Suyuz na Rabornitsite ot Poligraficheskata Promishlenost i Kulturnite Instituti (Section of Librarians at the Professional Organization of the Workers in the Polygraphic Industry and Cultural Institutions)

Address   c/o Cyril and Methodius National Library, Boulevard Tolbuhin 11, 1504 Sofia. Tel: 359 (2) 882811. Telex: 22432.

Officers   Pres: Stefan Káncev

Languages   Bulgarian

Established   1961, Sofia

Major Fields of Interest   Librarianship and status of librarians and library workers

Major Goals and Objectives   To raise the professional standards of librarians and represent their social welfare, i.e., salaries, benefits, working conditions, vacations.

Structure   Governed by Managing Board meeting monthly. Board includes 7 members representing the various networks within the library system of Bulgaria. This section of the trade union deals with professional problems and aspects of librarianship in Bulgaria. There is no library association as such in Bulgaria as yet, although one is planned for the near future. Officially, Bulgaria is represented in IFLA (since 1957) by the Cyril and Methodius National Library. Coordination of the library activities of governmental departments is effected by the Interdepartmental Coordination Council of the Committee of Culture and Art in Sofia.

Sources of Support   Central Committee of the Trade Union of the Workers in the Polygraphic Industry and Cultural Institutions.

Membership   Total members: 5,000+. Commissions: 2 (research libraries, public libraries). Types of membership: Librarians and library workers from all types of libraries. *Requirements:* Librarians or library personnel. Dues: None.

General Assembly   Entire membership meets once a year in Sofia.

Publications   No official journal. Issues annual reports, and occasional publications jointly with the National Library; contributes to the library journal Bibliotekar and to the bulletin of the Trade Union, Faklonosec.

Activities   Sponsors conferences, seminars and workshops to raise the professional standards of librarians and to represent their social welfare, jointly with the Committee for Culture and Art and the Cyril and Methodius National Library; sponsors awards and contests, usually connected with cultural and historical events in Bulgaria; continues to promote better working conditions for librarians.

Bibliography   Popov, V., "Bulgaria," in ALA World Encyclopedia of Library and Information Services, 2nd ed., pp. 144-146. Chicago: American Library Association, 1986.

Burkina Faso (formerly Upper Volta)

139   Association Voltaïque pour le Développement des Bibliothèques, des Archives et de la Documentation (AVDBAD)
(Voltan Association for the Development of Libraries, Archives and Documentation)

Address   c/o Larba Ali Krissiamba, Chief, Interafrican Committee for Hydraulic Studies (CIEH), Documentation and Information Center, Ouagadougou
Officers   Exec.Sec: Louis Aristide Rouamba
Staff   None
Languages   French
Established   1972, in Ouagadougou, then Upper Volta (since 1960). Country renamed Burkina Faso in 1984.
Major Fields of Interest   Libraries, archives, and documentation centers
Major Goals and Objectives   To further the development of libraries, archives, and documentation centers in the country.
Structure   Governed by Executive Committee. Affiliations: IFLA
Sources of Support   Membership dues, subsidies
Bibliography   Krissiamba, Larba Ali, "Burkina Faso," in ALA World Encyclopedia of Library and Information Services, 2nd ed., p.146. Chicago: American Library Association, 1986.

Cameroon

140   Association des Bibliothécaires, Archivistes, Documentalistes et Muséographes du Cameroun (ABADCAM)
(Cameroon Association of Librarians, Archivists, Documentalists, and Museum Curators)

Address   c/o P.N. Chateh, President, ABADCAM, Bibliothèque Universitaire, BP 1312, Yaoundé. Tel: 220744.
Officers   Pres: Peter Nkangafack Chateh; Sec.Gen: Th. Eno Belinga.
Staff   None
Languages   French, English
Established   1974
Major Fields of Interest   Libraries, archives, documentation centers, and museums
Major Goals and Objectives   To encourage the establishment of libraries at all levels and in all parts of the country; to promote the training of personnel for libraries, archives, museums, and documentation centers.
Structure   Governed by executive officers
Sources of Support   Membership dues, subsidies.
Membership   Total members: 40+.
General Assembly   Entire membership meets irregularly
Publications   Publishes <u>Newsletter</u>.
Activities   Association worked towards recruiting members from the more than 120 eligible librarians in the country; however, activities lapsed in the 1980s (see Chateh's article cited in the Bibliography).
Bibliography   Chateh, Peter Nkangafack, "Cameroon," in <u>ALA World Encyclopedia of Library and Information Services</u>, 2nd ed., pp. 153-155. Chicago: American Library Association, 1986.

Canada

141   Association of Canadian Archivists (ACA)

Address   PO Box 2596, Station D, Ottawa, Ontario K1P SW6 (permanent). Tel: 1 (613) 2323643.
Officers   (elected for 1-yr. term) Pres: Colleen Dempsey; VP: Burton Glendenning; Treas: Catherine Shepard; Sec: Brian Owens; Dir. without Portfolio: Stan Hanson. Exec. Comm: 5.
Staff   1 (paid).
Languages   English.
Established   1975.
Major Fields of Interest   Archivists and all who are concerned with the preservation and use of the records of human experience.
Major Goals and Objectives   To provide an effective agency of communication and professional leadership among all persons who are engaged in the discipline and practice of archival science.
Structure   Governed by the Executive Committee elected by membership. Affiliations: Bureau of Canadian Archivists, Canadian Council of Archives, and regional archival associations.
Sources of Support   Membership dues, government subsidies.
Membership   Total members: 507 (474 individual, 33 institutional). 4 countries represented. Requirements: Interest in archives. Dues (Canadian Dollar): 80+, sustaining; 55, professional; 35, general; 25, student; institutional dues depend on number of employees.
General Assembly   General membership meets once a year. 1987: Hamilton, Ontario, June 1–5; 1988: Windsor, Ontario, June; 1989: Laval, Quebec, June; 1990: Victoria, B.C., June.
Publications   *Official journal:* Archivaria. 1976–. 2/yr. Institutional: (Canadian Dollar) 40 (Canada & US), 45 (foreign); Individual: 30 (Canada & US), 35 (foreign). Same address as Association. Editor: Bruce Wilson. Address: c/o National Archives of Canada, 395 Wellington St., Ottawa, Ontario K1A ON3. English and French. Circ: 900. Indexed in Historical Abstracts, America, History & Life, and Canadian Magazine Index. Also publishes ACA Bulletin (newsletter), and Directory of Canadian Archives. Publications for sale, price lists available.
Activities   Past achievements: Lobbying government for Access to Information, new National Archives legislation; successful yearly conferences, publishing Archivaria. Current: Planning 1988 conference and combined American–Canadian conference in 1992; developing descriptive standards; review of goals and priorities of the Association.
Use of High Technology   Computers (Epson Equity II) for management.
Bibliography   Thompson, T., "Archivaria: A Brief Introduction to the Journal of the Association of Canadian Archivists," American Archivist 51 (1988):132-134.

142   Association of Canadian Map Libraries and Archives (ACML) / Association des Cartothèques et des Archives Canadiennes (formerly Association of Canadian Map Libraries)

Address   c/o Cartographic and Architectural Archives Division, National Archives of Canada, Ottawa, Ontario K1A ON3 (permanent). Tel: 1 (613) 9951077. Telex: 534311. Fax: 1-613-9954451.

Officers   (elected for 1–yr. term) Pres: Cheryl Woods; VP: Brenton MacLeod; Sec (appointed): Cathy Moulder. Past Pres: Lou M. Sebert. Exec.Comm: 3.
Staff   1 (part–time, paid), 7 (volunteers).
Languages   English, French.
Established   1967, as Association of Canadian Map Libraries
Major Fields of Interest   Maps and cartographic librarianship and archives
Major Goals and Objectives   To promote interest in and knowledge of maps and map-related materials; to further the professional knowledge of its members; to encourage high standards in every phase of the organization, administration and development of map libraries.
Structure   Governed by executive officers. Affiliations: IFLA.
Sources of Support   Membership dues, sale of publications. Budget (Canadian Dollar): 1986/87: 17,000. 1987/88: 18,000.
Membership   Total members: 275 (100 individual, 175 institutional). 4 countries represented. Requirements: Affiliation with a map library or map archives. Dues (Canadian Dollar): 25, individual and associate; 30, institutional; honorary membership conferred by Association.
General Assembly   General membership meets once a year. 1988: Peterborough, Ontario; 1989: Regina, Saskatchewan.
Publications   *Official journal:* The Bulletin. 1967–. 4/yr. (Canadian Dollar) 25. Free to members. Address same as Association. Editor: Lorraine Dubrevil. Address: . McGill University, Montreal. English and French. Circ: 300. Other publications: Proceedings of conferences, annual reports, etc. Publications for sale (listed in journal), price lists available. Publications exchange program in effect with other library associations.
Activities   Past achievements: Published three editions of Directory of Canadian Map Collections, two editions of Guide for a Small Map Collection, and 125 facsimiles of historic Canadian maps. Current and Future: Working on additions to the text and map publications. The Association has been active in promoting library–related legislation. Sponsors map exhibits.
Use of High Technology   Computers and databases for management.
Bibliography   Rothstein, S., "Canada," in ALA World Encyclopedia of Library and Information Services, 2nd ed., pp. 155-165. Chicago: American Library Association, 1986.

143   Association of Parliamentary Librarians in Canada / l'Association des Bibliothécaires Parlementaires au Canada (APLIC/ABPAC)

Address   c/o Richard Paré, APLIC Secretary, c/o Library of Parliament, Ottawa, Ontario K1A 0A9 (permanent). Tel: (513)9922427; or c/o Legislative Library of Nova Scotia, PO Box 396, (Province House), Halifax, Nova Scotia B3J 2P8. Tel: 1 (902) 4245932. Fax: 1-902-4245625.
Officers   (elected for 2–yr. term) Pres: Margaret Murphy; Sec: Richard Paré; Past Pres: Marian J. Powell. Exec. Board: 4
Staff   None
Languages   English, French
Established   1975
Major Fields of Interest   Parliamentary libraianship; library services to Parliament
Major Goals and Objectives   Communication among directors of Canadian parliamentary libraries with the goal of bettering service to Canadian parliaments
Structure   Governed by executive officers (informal). Affiliations: IFLA
Sources of Support   No membership dues

Membership Total members: 11 (individual). Requirements: Director of Canadian parliamentary library
General Assembly General membership meets once a year. Biennial program meetings: 1988: Ottawa, Oct.24-27.
Bibliography Rothstein, S., "Canada," in <u>ALA World Encyclopedia of Library and Information Services</u>, 2nd ed., pp. 155-165. Chicago: American Library Association, 1986.

144 Association pour l'Avancement des Sciences et des Techniques de la Documentation (ASTED)
(Association for the Advancement of the Science and Technology of Documentation)

Address 7243 Rue Saint–Denis, Montreal, Quebec H2R 2E3. Tel: 1 (514) 8491889; or, 1030, rue Cherrier, bureau 505, Montreal, Quebec H2L 1H9. Tel: 1 (514) 5227833. Fax: 1-514-5219561.
Officers (elected for 1-yr. term) Pres: Onil Dupuis; VP and Pres.–Elect: Hubert Perron; Past Pres: Carmen Catelli; Treas: Renald Beaumier; Sec: Luc Simard; Exec.Dir. (appointed): J. M. Alain. Exec.Board: 12
Staff 3 (paid)
Languages French
Established 1943, as Association Canadienne des Bibliothécaires de Langue Française (ACBLF) (Association of French Speaking Canadian Librarians); became ASTED, Inc., January 1, 1974.
Major Fields of Interest Concerned with the entire field of library and information science and the technology of documentation.
Major Goals and Objectives To improve the quality of library services and librarianship in libraries and documentation centers; to advocate legislation for the improvement of documentation serving the government; to encourage French–speaking librarians in North America to assume greater roles in their profession.
Structure Governed by general membership and executive officers. Affiliations: IFLA, FID, Canadian Library Association
Sources of Support Membership dues, sale of publications, government subsidies. Budget (Canadian Dollar): 1986/87: 350,000; 1987/88: 280,000
Membership Total members: 744 (551 individual, 193 institutional). Sections: 5. Requirements: To be interested in library and information science and in documentation. Dues (Canadian Dollar): 65–130, individual; 140–760, institutional; 25, student.
General Assembly General membership meets once a year. 1987: Sherbrooke; 1988: Montreal.
Publications *Official journal*: <u>Documentation et Bibliothèques</u>. 1974–. 4/yr. (Canadian Dollar) 32 (36, foreign). Editor: ASTED. French. Other publications: Annual report, <u>Nouvelles ASTED</u>. Publications available for sale.
Activities Past achievements: Promotion of documentation information. Current: Publications, government services, services and communication to members. Future: Increase services to the collective membership; create greater awareness of our national presence. Association has worked on copyright laws and collected statistics on public libraries in the Provinces.
Use of High Technology Computers (Macintosh) and databases for management.
Bibliography Brault, J.R., "Renewed ASTED of a Federation of Associations for Documentation?" <u>Documentation et Bibliothèques</u> 28 (1982):3-13; Rousseau, D. and Perron, H., "L'ASTED, dix ans après: bilan et prospective / ASTED, Ten Years After: Balance Sheet and Perspective," <u>Documentation et Bibliothèques</u> 30 (1984):71-86; Murray-La-

chapelle, R., "International Development and the Focus of ASTED," Canadian Library Journal 42 (1985):211-212; Rothstein, S., "Canada," in ALA World Encyclopedia of Library and Information Services, 2nd ed., pp. 155-165. Chicago: American Library Association, 1986.

145   Bibliographical Society of Canada / La Société Bibliographique du Canada (BSC/SBC)

Address   c/o W. P. Stoneman, Secretary/Treasurer, c/o Department of English, University of Windsor, Windsor, Ontario N9B 3P4 (permanent). Tel: 1 (519) 2534232 ext. 2305
Officers   (elected for 1-yr. term) Pres: Patricia Fleming; Past Pres: Desmond Neill; 1st VP: George Parker; 2nd VP: Apollonia Steele; Sec/Treas: William P. Stoneman; Assoc. Sec: Michel Brisebois.   Exec.Board: 6
Staff   None
Languages   English, French
Established   May, 1946, at an inaugural meeting of librarians, bookmen, and editors, organized by Lorne Pierce.
Major Fields of Interest   Bibliography and bibliographical publications
Major Goals and Objectives   To promote bibliographical publications; to encourage the preservation and extend the knowledge of printed works and manuscripts, particularly those relating to Canada; to facilitate the exchange of information concerning rare Canadiana; to coordinate bibliographical activity and to set standards.
Structure   Governed by executive board according to constitution and by-laws. Affiliations: Canadian Library Association.
Sources of Support   Membership dues, government subsidies.
Membership   Total members: 347 (245 individual, 102 institutional). 7 countries represented. Requirements: Society welcomes as members all who share its aims and wish to support and participate in bibliographical research and publications. Dues (Canadian Dollar): 20, individual; 30, institutional; 10, retirees and students; 500, life member; 75 +, contributing member.
General Assembly   General membership meets once a year. 1987: Vancouver; 1988: Windsor, May 31.
Publications   *Official journal:* Papers/Cahiers. 1962–. 1/yr. Free to members. Editor: Patricia Stone. Address: Canadian Department, North York Public Library, 35 Fairview Mall Dr., Willowdale, Ont., M2J 4S4. Circ: Membership only. English, French. Other publications: Colloquium (series); Bulletin. 1973- (members only); Bibliography of Canadian Bibliographies (new edition in preparation). Price lists available.
Activities   Association considers itself a publishing society, limited in scope only by the amount of money available.

146   Canadian Association for Graduate Education in Library, Archival, and Information Studies / Association Canadienne des Études Supérieures en Bibliothéconomie, Archivistique, et Sciences de l'Information (CAGELAIS/ACESBASI) (formerly Canadian Association of Library Schools/Association Canadienne des Écoles de Bibliothécaires (CALS/ACEB))

Address   c/o Faculty of Library and Information Science, University of Toronto, 140 St. George Street, Toronto, Ontario M5S 1A1 (not permanent). Tel: 1 (416) 9787098
Officers   (elected for 1-yr. term) Pres: Ethel Auster; VP/Pres-Elect: Betty McCamus; Sec/Treas: Joan Cherry; Past Pres: Robert Brundin.   Exec.Board: 4

Staff 12 (volunteers)
Languages English, French
Established 1965, Toronto, after an informal meeting. Officially organized June 19, 1966, at Calgary, Alberta, during CLA annual conference, as Canadian Association of Library Schools/Association Canadienne des Écoles de Bibliothécaires (CALS/ACEB). Present name, reflecting the broader interests, adopted 1987. First President and Vice President: Brian Land and Rev. Edmond Desrochers, SJ.
Major Fields of Interest Education of librarians, information scientists/specialists, archivists
Major Goals and Objectives To promote development and foster improvement in graduate education in library, archival, and information studies; to speak for graduate education for information professionals; to compile and exchange information on education and research for library, archival, and information studies.
Structure Governed by executive officers
Sources of Support Membership dues
Membership Total members: 49 (42 individual, 7 institutional). Requirements: Any person employed in the administrative or instructional staff of a graduate library, archival, or information studies program in a Canadian university who pays the dues. Dues (Canadian Dollar): 5, individual; 25, institutional.
General Assembly Entire membership meets once a year. 1988: Halifax, Nova Scotia, June; 1989: Edmonton, Alberta, June
Publications No official journal. Publishes CAGELAIS/ACESBASI Newsletter, irregular. Address same as the Association. English and French. Annual reports; Membership handbook. All publications for membership only.
Activities Past achievements: Providing a forum for discussion, cooperation, and joint action on topics and issues of mutual interest and concern to members; review of procedure used to accredit member faculties/schools. Current and future: Liaison between faculty members of all Canadian faculties of graduate education in library, archival, and information studies; observer status at Canadian Committee on Cataloguing, National Library of Canada. Association is active in promoting legislation as necessary. Sponsors program at annual meeting.
Use of High Technology Computers (IBM PC) used for management

147 Canadian Association for Information Science / Association Canadienne des Sciences de l'Information (CAIS/ACSI)

Address CAIS/ACSI Secretariat, c/o University of Toronto, 140 St. George Street, Toronto, Ontario M5S 1A1 (permanent). Tel: 1 (415) 9788876
Officers (elected for 1–yr. term, 1989-90) Pres: David Holmes; VP/Pres-Elect: Bryan Getchall; Past Pres: Michael Shepherd; Sec/Treas: Frank Karcich; Directors: Charles T. Meadow, Mary Nash; Ed: Ethel Auster. Exec.Board: 12.
Staff 1 (paid).
Languages English, French.
Established 1970, Ottawa, at University of Ottawa Library School, to represent the specific problems of Canadians in the field of information science.
Major Fields of Interest Transfer of information.
Major Goals and Objectives To provide a forum for dialog and exchange of ideas concerned with the theory and practice of information transfer; to contribute to the advancement of information science in Canada
Structure Governed by Board of Directors. Affiliations: None.
Sources of Support Membership dues, sale of publications, government subsidies.

Membership Total members: 600. Chapters: 6. 5 countries represented. Requirements: Individuals and institutions actively engaged in the gathering, organization and
dissemination of information. Dues (Canadian Dollar): 65, individual; 30, student and
senior citizen; 150, institutional.
General Assembly General membership meets once a year. 1987: London, Ontario;
1988: Ottawa, Ontario.
Publications *Official journal:* Canadian Journal of Information Science/Revue Canadienne des Sciences de l'Information. 1973–. 4/yr. (Canadian Dollar) 95 (110, foreign).
Free to members. Address same as Association. Editor: Ethel Auster. Address: FLIS,
University of Toronto, Toronto, Ont. Circ: 600. English, French. Indexed in Computer
and Control Abstracts, Current Contents, Social and Behavioral Sciences, LISA, Lib.Lit.,
SSCI, Canadian Periodical Index. Other publications for sale: Reports of seminars,
workshops, price list available. Publications exchange program with other library associations.
Activities Activities reflect the diverse membership of individuals and organizations involved in the production, manipulation, storage, retrieval, and dissemination of information in all formats. Members include computer scientists, information scientists and documentation specialists, librarians, journalists, sociologists, psychologists, linguists,
information managers, etc. Activities are carried out by the Chapters, the annual program
meeting and the publication of the journal. Association sponsors exhibits and continuing
education lectures, seminars and workshops.
Use of High Technology Computers (various) and databases for management. QL
systems for electronic mail.
Bibliography Rothstein, S., "Canada," in ALA World Encyclopedia of Library and Information Services, 2nd ed., pp. 155-165. Chicago: American Library Association, 1986;
"Connexions: Linking Mind and Machine; 16th Annual Conference of the Canadian Association for Information Science, University of Ottawa, May 12-14, 1988," Canadian
Journal of Information Science 13 (1988):3-119; "Canadian Association for Information
Science (L'Association Canadienne des Sciences de l'Information)," in The Bowker Annu-
al: Library and Book Trade Almanac, 34th Edition 1989-90, pp. 679-680. New York: R.R.
Bowker, 1989.

148   Canadian Association of Children's Librarians (CACL)
(A Section of the Canadian Association of Public Libraries)

Address c/o Canadian Library Association, 200 Elgin Street, Suite 602, Ottawa, Ontar-
io K2P 1L5 (permanent). Tel: 1 (613) 2329625; Telex: (ENVOY) CLAHQ Fax:
1-613-5639895
Officers (elected for 1–yr. term) Chair: Marie Lynn Bernard; Vice Chair: Judith Buckle;
Sec/Treas: Linda Smith. Exec. Board: 4.
Staff None.
Languages English.
Major Fields of Interest Library services to children.
Major Goals and Objectives To further library services to children in Canada.
Structure Governed by Executive Board. Affiliation: A section of CAPL (Canadian
Association of Public Libraries), which is a division of the Canadian Library Association.
Sources of Support Membership dues drawn from dues paid to the Canadian Library
Association.
General Assembly General membership meets once a year. 1987: Vancouver, B.C.,
June 10–17; 1988: Halifax, Nova Scotia, June; 1989: Edmonton, Alberta, June.

Publications No official journal. CAPL divisional news (of which CACL is a section) appears regularly in <u>Feliciter</u>, the newsletter of the Canadian Library Association. A CLA Publications Committee is in charge of relevant publications for children's librarians. Some of the publications: <u>Storytellers' Encore: More Canadian Stories to Tell to Children</u> (1984); <u>Storytellers' Tape</u> (1986); <u>Subject Index to Canadian Poetry in English for Children and Young People</u> (1986); <u>Library Service to Children</u> (series of pamphlets, 1988); <u>Canadian Films for Children and Young Adults</u> (1987), etc. Publications available through Canadian Library Association.
Activities Carried out through various committees; presentation of two book awards (Book of the Year for Children Award, and Amelia Frances Howard–Gibbon Award).

149   Canadian Association of College and University Libraries / Association Canadienne des Bibliothèques de Collège et d'Université (CACUL/ACBCU)

Address 200 Elgin Street, Suite 602, Ottawa, Ontario K2P 1L5. Tel: (613)2329625; Telex: (ENVOY) CLAHQ. Fax: 1 (613) 5639895
Officers (elected for 1-yr. term, 1989-90) Pres (2-yr.): Pat Appavoo; VP: Richard Greene; Sec/Treas: Barbara Love. Exec.Comm: 6.
Staff None.
Languages English, French.
Established 1963, Winnipeg, Manitoba.
Major Fields of Interest College and university libraries.
Major Goals and Objectives To provide a forum for cooperation and professional development of librarians at colleges and universities; to further the interests of the libraries of those institutions which offer education above the secondary level; to support the highest aims of education and librarianship.
Structure Governed by executive officers who meet four times a year. Affiliation: A division of the Canadian Library Association.
Sources of Support Funds from the parent body (through dues paid to the Canadian Library Association). Budget (Canadian Dollar): Approx. 17,000.
Membership Total members: 1,161 (963 individual, 198 institutional). Sections: 1 (Community and Technical College Libraries/CTCL). Standing Committees: 3 (Academic Status, Library Service, Preservation). Types of membership: Individual, institutional, student. Requirements: Members of Canadian Library Association with concern for and interest in college and university libraries. Dues: Drawn from dues paid to Canadian Library Association.
General Assembly Entire membership meets once a year at the Conference of the Canadian Library Association. 1987: Vancouver, B.C., June; 1988: Halifax, Nova Scotia, June; 1989: Edmonton, Alberta, June.22-24; 1990: Ottawa, June 14-17.
Publications No official journal. <u>CACUL Newsletter/Nouvelles de L'ACBCU</u>. 1963-75. CACUL divisional news now appears in <u>Feliciter</u>, the newsletter of the Canadian Library Association. Other publications: President's annual report; various guidelines (e.g., <u>Guidelines for User Fees in College and University Libraries</u>; <u>Guidelines for the Appointment and Review of University Chief Librarians</u>). Publications for sale, listed in <u>Feliciter</u>.
Activities Survey in Spring of 1986 to obtain data on preservation programs currently in effect in Canadian universities; sponsors conferences, seminars and workshops on relevant topics; provides standards and guidelines; implementation of CACUL's Strategic Plan, especially its continuing education goals through offering provincial/regional workshops.

Bibliography   Rothstein, S., "Canada," ALA World Encyclopedia of Library and Information Services, 2nd ed., pp. 155-165. Chicago: American Library Association, 1986.

150   Canadian Association of Law Libraries / Association Canadienne des Bibliothèques de Droit (CALL/ACBD)

Address   c/o Denis S. Marshall, York University Law Library, 4700 Keele Street, Downsview, Ontario M3J 2R5
Officers   (elected for 2-yr. term) Pres: Joan N. Fraser; Past Pres: Denis Marshall; VP: Maureen McCormick; Sec: Wendy Hearder–Moan; Treas: Patricia Young; Members–at-large: Ann Rae, Paul McKenna. Exec.Board: 7
Staff   None
Languages   English, French
Established   1961, Boston, Massachusetts, at annual meeting of the American Association of Law Libraries.
Major Fields of Interest   Law librarianship
Major Goals and Objectives   To promote law librarianship, develop Canadian law libraries, foster cooperation between them; provide a forum for meetings of persons interested in law librarianship, and cooperate with other associations with similar objectives or interests.
Structure   Governed by executive officers
Sources of Support   Membership dues, sale of publications.
Membership   Total members: 400 (290 individual, 110 institutional). Requirements: Law library or employment in a law library for individual membership. Dues (Canadian Dollar): 100.
General Assembly   General membership meets once a year. 1988: Jasper, Alberta; 1989: Laval, Quebec; 1990: Vancouver, BC
Publications   *Official journal:* Canadian Association of Law Libraries Newsletter/Bulletin de l'Association Canadienne des Bibliothèques de Droit. 1963–. 5/yr. Free to members. Editor: Vicki Whitmell, c/o Osler, Hoskins & Harcourt, 50 First Canadian Place, Toronto, Ont. M5X 1B8. Circ: 400 (membership). English, French. Other publications: Union List of Periodicals in Canadian Law Libraries; membership directory. Publications for sale.
Activities   Association's major purpose is to provide information exchange between members. This is accomplished through conferences, which include workshops and seminars, and through publications program.
Bibliography   Rothstein, Samuel, "Canada," in ALA World Encyclopedia of Library and Information Services, 2nd ed., pp. 155-165. Chicago: American Library Association, 1986; Tearle, B. and Hennessey, J., "CALL of the Wild/Far West: CALL/ACBD Annual Conference [Jasper, Alberta, 15-18 May 1988]," Law Librarian 19 (Aug.1988):64-66.

151   Canadian Association of Music Libraries / Association Canadienne des Bibliothèques Musicales (CAML/ACBM) (A Branch of the International Association of Music Libraries, Archives and Documentation Centres)

Address   c/o Music Division, National Library of Canada, 395 Wellington Street, Ottawa, Ontario K1A ON4 (permanent). Tel: 1 (613) 9963377.
Officers   (elected for 1-yr. term) Pres: Joan Colquhoun; VP: Jane Baldwin; Sec: Anne Fleming; Members–at–Large: Monique Lecavailler, Peter Highham; Past Pres: Alison Hall. (Appointed for 2-yr. term): Treas: Sister Louise Smith; Membership Sec: Debra Begg. Exec. Board: 8.

Staff None.
Languages English, French.
Established 1971.
Major Fields of Interest Music librarianship.
Major Goals and Objectives To foster all aspects of music librarianship in Canada; to encourage the development of music libraries; to initiate and/or participate in projects dealing with music and musical resources; to foster the coming together of individuals or groups with kindred interests or problems; to cooperate with national, international, and other foreign organizations concerned with music in all its aspects; to encourage cooperation between libraries in sharing information about and access to printed music; to issue such publications as the Association deems useful.
Structure Governed by Executive Board. Affiliations: A national branch of the International Association of Music Libraries, Archives and Documentation Centres which is affiliated with IFLA; member of Canadian Library Association, Canadian Music Council and the Canadian Conference of the Arts.
Sources of Support Membership dues, sale of publications. Budget (Canadian Dollar): 1986/87: 8,000; 1987/88: 8,000.
Membership Total members: 149 (102 individual, 47 institutional). Requirements: Interest in music librarianship and the goals of the Association. Dues (Canadian Dollar): 30, individual; 10, student; 55, institutional; 60, sustaining; foreign (for Newsletter subscription only): 10, individual; 15, institutional.
General Assembly General membership meets once a year.
Publications *Official journal:* Newsletter/Nouvelles. 1971–. 3/yr. Price included in membership. Address same as Association. Editor: Kathleen McMorrow. Address: Edward Johnson Music Library, Faculty of Music, University of Toronto, Toronto, Ont. M5S 1A1. Circ: 170. English, French. Other publications: Toomey, K.M.,ed., Musicians in Canada; A Bibliographical Finding List (2nd ed. 1981); Lewis, L.C.,ed., Union List of Music Periodicals in Canadian Libraries (2nd ed. 1981); Parker, C.P.G. and Emerson, D.,eds., Title Index to Canadian Works Listed in "Roll Back the Years"/Indes des titres d'oeuvres canadiennes énumérés dans "En Remontant les Années" by E.K. Moogk (1986). Publications for sale. Publications exchange program with other library associations in effect.
Activities Past achievements: Publications work, expanded the scope and depth of the annual conferences, contributed to international projects (e.g., RILM, RISM, RIdIM), presented programs and workshops for general librarians, participated in the development of national and international standards for cataloging of music materials. Current and future: Continuation of past activities, preparing news publications and brochure. Association sponsors exhibits and continuing education lectures, seminars and workshops.
Bibliography "Canadian Association of Music Libraries," in Encyclopedia of Music in Canada, ed. by H. Kallman, G. Potvin, and K. Winters. Toronto: University of Toronto Press, 1981; Rothstein, S., "Canada," in ALA World Encyclopedia of Library and Information Services, 2nd ed., pp. 155-165. Chicago: American Library Association, 1986.

152   Canadian Association of Public Libraries (CAPL)

Address 21 Elgin Street, Suite 602, Ottawa, Ontario K2P 1L5. Tel: 1 (613) 2329625. Telex: (ENVOY) CLAHQ. Fax: 1-613-5639895
Officers (elected for 1–yr. term) Chair (1989-90): Frances Schwenger; Vice Chair: Barbara Helen Clubb; Sec/Treas: Judy Capes. Exec.Comm: 5.
Staff None.
Languages English.

Established   1973, as a separate division of the Canadian Library Association
Major Fields of Interest   Public libraries.
Major Goals and Objectives   To unite library personnel and other interested groups in
furthering the welfare of public libraries in Canada; to promote and support freedom of
access to public library resources and services, and to augment the ability of all individu-
als to use them.
Structure   Governed by Executive Committee. Affiliations: A division of the Canadian
Library Association.
Sources of Support   Funds from parent body (through membership dues paid to Cana-
dian Library Association).
Membership   Total members: 1,236 (1,032 individual, 204 institutional). Sections: 1.
Requirements: Individuals and institutions belonging to Canadian Library Association
and having interest in and concerns for Canadian public libraries. Dues: Drawn from dues
paid to Canadian Library Association.
General Assembly   General membership meets once a year at the conference of the
Canadian Library Association. 1987: Vancouver, B.C., June 10–17; 1988: Halifax, Nova
Scotia, June; 1989: Edmonton, Alberta, June 22-24; 1990: Ottawa, June 14-17..
Publications   No official journal. CAPL divisional news appear regularly in Feliciter,
the newsletter of the Canadian Library Association. All publications for sale are avail-
able through the Canadian Library Association.
Activities   Carrying out studies, sponsoring workshops and meetings in order to further
the development of Canadian public libraries.
Bibliography   Rothstein, S., "Canada," in ALA World Encyclopedia of Library and Information Services, 2nd ed., pp. 155-165. Chicago: American Library Association, 1986.

**153   Canadian Association of Research Libraries / Association des Bibliothèques
de Recherche du Canada (CARL/ABRC)**

Address   c/o Office of the University Chief Librarian, University of Ottawa, 65 Hastey
Street, Ottawa, Ontario K1N 9A5 (permanent). Tel: 1 (613) 5645864; Telex: 0533338
Officers   (elected for 1–yr. term, renewable for 1 year) Pres (elected for 2–yr. term): G.
Hill; VP: H. Moeller; Sec: W.F. Birdsall; Treas: E. Hoffman; Exec.Dir (appointed): David
McCallum. Exec.Board: 5.
Staff   2 (paid, part–time).
Languages   English, French.
Established   1976, in Regina
Major Fields of Interest   Research libraries and preservation of research library materi-
als.
Major Goals and Objectives   To provide organized leadership for the Canadian re-
search library community; to work toward the realization of a national research library
resource-sharing network.
Structure   Governed by the Board of Directors elected by and from the membership.
Affiliations: AUCC (Association of Universities and Colleges of Canada)
Sources of Support   Membership dues, grants from private corporations.
Membership   Total members: 28 (institutional). Requirements: Institutional membership only and limited to libraries of universities having doctoral graduate programs in the
arts and sciences and to other such institutional libraries as approved by the Board of Di-
rectors. Dues: Not published
General Assembly   General membership meets twice a year.

Publications *Official journal:* Communiqué. 1976–. 12/yr. Price included in membership. Address same as Association. Editor: David McCallum. Circ: 30+ (limited to membership and affiliated organizations). English, French.

Activities Past achievements: Participation in NCIP (North America Collections Inventory Project); User Assistance Project (UAP) funded by grant from GEAC Computers International, Inc. Current and future: NCIP; UAP; support of the National Library of Canada's decentralized networking developments, based on the Open Systems Interconnection (OSI) model. Association has been active in promoting library–related legislation, e.g. Intellectual Freedom and Copyright.

Use of High Technology Computers (GEAC "GOAST" system) for management. Envoy 100 for electronic mail.

Bibliography Steele, C.R., "Conference: Research Libraries in the Online Environment," Australian Academic and Research Libraries 14 (1983):178-181; Rothstein, S., "Canada," in ALA World Encyclopedia of Library and Information Services, 2nd ed., pp. 155-165. Chicago: American Library Association, 1986.

154 Canadian Association of Special Libraries and Information Services (CASLIS)

Address 200 Elgin Street, Suite 602, Ottawa, Ontario K2P 1L5 (pemanent). Tel: 1 (613) 2329624; Telex: (ENVOY) CLAHQ; Fax: 1-613-5639895

Officers (elected for 1–yr. term, 1989-90) Pres: Kathleen Robertson; Past Pres: Sue Patrick; VP: S. Norma Godavari; Treas: Linda Morrison. Exec.Comm: 8.

Staff None.

Languages English.

Established 1969, to replace the Research and Special Libraries Section of the Canadian Library Association.

Major Fields of Interest Special libraries and information sciences.

Major Goals and Objectives (1) Provide a means of communication, cooperation and continuing education programs among information professionals; (2) improve the profile and public image of special librarians and information centers and consultants as essential information specialists.

Structure Governed by Executive Council meeting 3 times a year. Affiliations: A division of the Canadian Library Association.

Sources of Support Membership dues drawn from dues paid to the Canadian Library Association.

Membership Total members: 1,649 (1,337 individual, 312 institutional). Sections: 1. Chapters: 5 (geographic). Types of membership: Individual, institutional. Requirements: Individuals and institutions belonging to the Canadian Library Association and having an interest in special libraries and information services. Dues: Drawn from dues paid to Canadian Library Association.

General Assembly General membership meets once a year at the conference of the Canadian Library Association. 1987: Vancouver, B.C., June 10–17; 1988: Halifax, Nova Scotia, June; 1989: Edmonton, Alberta, June 22-24; 1990: Ottawa, June 14-17.

Publications *Official journal:* AGORA. 1970–75. Divisional news now appear in Feliciter, the newsletter of the Canadian Library Association. A new newsletter was inaugurated in 1989, Special Issues, with the help of outside grants. A Publications Committee is in charge of relevant publications, e.g. the updating of Canadian Business and Economics: A Guide to Sources of Information (ed. B. Brown), and other publications available through the Canadian Library Association

Activities   CASLIS Ottawa Chapter has set up a job bank answering service at CLA headquarters, and there are plans for a national service of this type; workshops and seminars; various activities carried out by geographic chapters, sections (art libraries, health sciences, etc.).
Bibliography   Pandit, J., "CASLIS and SLA Joint Conference a Success," Library Times International 2 (1985):29-30; Rothstein, S., "Canada," in ALA World Encyclopedia of Library and Information Services, 2nd ed., pp. 155-165. Chicago: American Library Association, 1986.

155   Canadian Association of Toy Libraries (CATL)

Address   301 Montrose Avenue, Toronto, Ontario M6G 3G9 (permanent). Tel: 1 (416) 5363394 or 5363395.
Officers   (elected for 3–yr. term) Pres: Judy Howard; Treas: John Gullick; Exec.Dir: Joanna von Levetzow. Exec.Board: 12.
Staff   2 (paid), 6 (volunteer).
Languages   English.
Established   1975, Oakville, Ontario
Major Fields of Interest   Play and toys; toy libraries; child development; parent education.
Major Goals and Objectives   To support the concept of toy libraries by developing a basic philosophy; promoting standards and guidelines; disseminating information and recommending toys, choices of toys and play materials; fostering the understanding of play needs of young children.
Structure   Governed by Volunteer Board. Affiliations: International Association for the Child's Right to Play.
Sources of Support   Membership dues, sale of publications, government subsidies, donations. Budget (Canadian Dollar): 1986/87: 5,000; 1987/88: 5,000 (government subsidies not included).
Membership   Total members: 250 (50 individual, 200 institutional). Requirements: Anyone who supports the aims and objectives of the Association. Dues (Canadian Dollar): 25, Ontario residents; 20, all others and foreign.
General Assembly   General membership meets once a year.
Publications   *Official journal:* Toy Libraries Newsletter. 1975–. 4/yr. Free to members. Address same as Association. Editor: Joanna von Levetzow. Address: 301 Montrose Ave., Toronto, Ont. M6G 3G9. Circ: 300. English. Other publications: Annual report; Toys Help: A Guide to Choosing Toys for Handicapped Children (1981); How to Start and Maintain a Toy Library in Your Community (1986); Westland, C. and Knight, J., Playing, Living, Learning (Venture, PA, 1982). Publications for sale, price lists available.
Activities   Past achievements: Established recognition of the value of toy libraries as support service for families with young children and those with special needs; hosted International Conference of Toy Libraries, May 1987 in Toronto (Conference held very 3 years; 4th one hosted by CATL). Current: Extending Association's network to include Parent/Child Resource Centres. Future: Fundraising for continued activities, publications; compiling a national Directory of Toy Libraries and Parent Centres.
Use of High Technology   Computers (IBM compatible) and databases for management.

156   Canadian Council of Library Schools / Conseil Canadien des Écoles de Bibliothéconomie (CCLS/CCEB)

Address   c/o Mary Dykstra, Chair, c/o School of Library and Information Studies, Dalhousie University, Halifax, Nova Scotia B3H 4H8 (not permanent). Tel: 1 (902) 4243656. Telex: 019-22512.
Officers   (elected for –yr. term) Chair: Mary Dykstra
Staff   None
Languages   English, French
Established   1971, Ottawa, at meeting of Canadian Council of Deans and Directors of Library Schools
Major Fields of Interest   Education for Librarianship
Major Goals and Objectives   To promote the development and foster the improvement of graduate library education in Canada
Structure   Governed by Executive Committee. Affiliations: AUCC (Association of Universities and Colleges of Canada)
Sources of Support   Membership dues
Membership   Total members: 7 library schools. Requirements: Member must be the Dean or Director of a Canadian Library School. Dues (Canadian Dollar): 25
General Assembly   Entire membership meets twice a year.
Publications   No official journal.
Activities   Sponsors joint conferences with relevant associations; involved in evaluation of accreditation process for Canadian library school programs.

157   Canadian Health Libraries Association / Association des Bibliothèques de la Santé du Canada (CHLA/ABSC)

Address   PO Box 434, Station K, Toronto, Ontario M4P 2G9
Languages   French, English
Established   1976
Major Fields of Interest   Health sciences library services
Major Goals and Objectives   To improve health and health care by promoting excellence in access to information; to represent the interests of health libraries on issues involving governmental and private agencies.
Structure   Governed by executive officers
Sources of Support   Membership dues.
Membership   Total members: 400. Local chapters: 14. Requirements: Individuals and institutions supporting the aims of the Association.
General Assembly   General membership meets once a year. 1989: Ottawa, June; 1990: Edmonton, Alberta, June.
Publications   *Official journal:* Bibliotheca Medica Canadiana. 4/yr. Address same as Association. Other publications: Membership directory (annual); CanHealth; occasional papers and course syllabi.
Activities   Sponsors annual meetings with exhibits, and continuing education programs; provides placement service
Use of High Technology   Computers for management: Database, mailing lists, ENVOY 100:CHLA, electronic mail
Bibliography   Groen, F., "Small is Beautiful," Canadian Library Journal 41 (1984):113; Rothstein, S., "Canada," in ALA World Encyclopedia of Library and Information Services, 2nd ed., pp. 155-165. Chicago: American Library Association, 1986; Harrison, C. and Conchelos, M., "Report on the CHLA Membership Survey and Continuing Education Needs Assessment," Bibliotheca Medica Canadiana 8 (1986):54-61.

158   Canadian Libraries in Occupational Safety & Health (CLOSH)

Address   c/o W. Keith McLaughlin, c/o Library Services Branch, Alberta Community and Occupational Health, Seventh Street Plaza, 10030–107 Street, Edmonton, Alberta, T5J 3E4. Tel: (403) 4273530
Officers   Contact person: W. Keith McLaughlin
Staff   None
Languages   English
Established   1980, in Vancouver
Major Fields of Interest   Occupational health and safety
Major Goals and Objectives   Created as a forum to increase communication and re-source sharing among the Canadian libraries which specialize in this broad, multidisciplinary field.
Structure   Informal
Sources of Support   Not applicable.
Membership   Total members: 21 (institutional). Requirements: Heads of individual libraries.
General Assembly   General membership meets irregularly, maximum of one meeting per year.
Publications   No official journal. Publications for sale: <u>Directory of Occupational Health and Safety Libraries and Collections in Canada</u> (4th ed., 1986; regularly updated).
Activities   Development of contacts and resource sharing among member libraries.

159   Canadian Library Association (CLA)

Address   200 Elgin Street, Suite 602, Ottawa, Ontario K2P 1L5. Tel: 1 (613) 2329625; 1-800-2676566; Telex: Envoy CLAHQ; Fax: 1-613-5639895
Officers   (elected for 1–yr. term, 1989-90) Pres: Beth Barlow; 1st VP/Pres-Elect: Ernie Ingles; Treas: Harold Brief; 2nd VP: Jean Dirksen (this office will be eliminated in 1992 according to a 1989 constitutional amendment); Past Pres: Vivienne Monty; Exec. Dir. (appointed): Sharon Henry (1990-; replacing Jane Cooney, 1986-1989). Exec.Board: 10. Council: 18. Both will be combined in an Exec.Council of 14 members in 1992.
Staff   31 (paid).
Languages   English.
Established   1946, in Hamilton; incorporated 1947, in Ottawa as Canadian Library Association/Association Canadienne des Bibliothèques. French title dropped 1968, but bilingual programs kept in order to serve all libraries and librarians in Canada. New Constitution and By-Laws adopted in 1975; amendments passed in 1989.
Major Fields of Interest   Library service in general and type–of–library interests.
Major Goals and Objectives   To improve the quality of library and information services in Canada; to develop higher standards of librarianship; to develop active and meaningful communication among its members; to encourage and support high levels of professional conduct on the part of its members; to promote strong public support for library and information services.
Structure   Governed by Executive Officers, Executive Council and Executive Board. (There is an Executive Council for each of its 5 divisions.) Affiliations: IFLA, ALA, ASTED, COMLA, OLA, and others.
Sources of Support   Membership dues, sale of publications, government subsidies, private gifts, and fees from conferences, meetings and seminars. Budget (Canadian Dollar): 1986/87: Approx. 1,901,700; 1989/90: Approx. 1,900,000.
Membership   Total members: 4,500 (3,600 individual, 900 institutional). Divisions: 5: Canadian Association of College and University Libraries (CACUL): Canadian Associ-

ation of Public Libraries (CAPL): Canadian Association of Special Libraries & Information Services (CASLIS): Canadian Library Trustees Association (CLTA); Canadian School Library Association (CSLA). Chapters: 5. Interest Groups: 20. 18 countries represented. Requirements: Interest in the improvement of library and information services in Canada. Dues (Canadian Dollar): 113-180, individual, scaled according to position and income; institutional, scaled according to organization's budget; 55, unemployed and retired librarians, full–time students; special dues for life membership.

General Assembly   General membership meets once a year. 1987: Vancouver, B.C., June 10–17; 1988: Halifax, Nova Scotia, June 15-20; 1989: Edmonton, Alberta, June 22-24; 1990: Ottawa, June 14-17.

Publications   *Official journal:* Canadian Library Journal. 1947–. 6/yr. (Canadian Dollar) 40 in Canada, 45 in US, 50, foreign. Free to members. Editor: Sheila Nelson. Address same as Association. Circ: 5,457. English. Indexed in Lib.Lit., LISA, Canadian Periodical Index, International Index to Multi–Media Information. Other publications: Proceedings of meetings; Feliciter, newsletter of the CLA. 1956–. 11/yr. Free to members. (Canadian Dollar) 65. Editor: Mary Budziszewski. Circ: 4,502; CM: A Reviewing Journal of Canadian Materials for Young People (6/yr.); Canadian Periodical Index; The Canadian Library Yearbook; England, C., and Evans, K., Disaster Management for Libraries (1988); Hébert, F., Report on Photocopying in Canadian Libraries (1988); Interlibrary Loan Procedures Manual/Le Manuel de Pret entre Bibliothèques (1989); Weihs, J., with Lewis, S., Nonbook Materials: The Organization of Integrated Collections (3rd ed., 1989), and other monographs, microfilm, etc. Publications for sale; catalogs available.

Activities   Active in promoting legislation relating to copyright, postal regulations, pornography, and access to information. Activities are carried out by the divisions and the interest groups dealing with topics of current interest, such as access to government information, action for peace and security, preservation/conservation, technical services, information technology, multilingual services, services for persons with disabilities, online users, prison libraries, services for distance learning, Third World Libraries, literacy, and others. Active in professional issues on copyright and taxation. Association sponsors exhibits and continuing education lectures, seminars and workshops.

Use of High Technology   Computers (PC compatibles, IBM Series 34) for management.

Bibliography   Wedgeworth, R.F., "ALA-CLA - Ties That Bind But Don't Chafe," (Theme speech, CLA Conference, 1981) Canadian Library Journal 38 (1981):301-305; Horrocks, N., "Constant Change: 38th Annual Conference of the Canadian Library Association," Library Journal 108 (1983):1452-53; Havens, S., "At Its 39th Annual Conference, the Canadian Library Association Considered ... Human Values in the Computer Age," Library Journal 109 (1984):1411-14; Rothstein, S., "Canada," in ALA World Encyclopedia of Library and Information Services, 2nd ed., pp. 155-165. Chicago: American Library Association, 1986; "A Membership Development Strategy for the Canadian Library Association," APLA Bulletin 50 (Nov/Dec.1986):1,7; Embey, S., "Canadian Library Association Conference: A Report," Library Times International 4 (1987):20; Miller, B.M.E., "Canadian Library Association," in ALA Yearbook 1988, pp. 90-93. Chicago: American Library Association, 1988; Owen, L., "Canadian Library Association Bites the Bullet in Halifax," American Libraries 19 (1988):563-564; Berry, J.N., "Government, Marketplace, & Association; Report on the June 16-20 Conference of the Canadian Library Association," Library Journal 113 (1988):48-50; Nelson, M.G., "Worrying about the Information Market Place in Halifax," Wilson Library Bulletin 63 (1988):37-39; "CLA '88 [conference]: Resource Sharing Comes of Age," Canadian Library Journal 45

(1988):265-266; Cooney, J., "Canadian Library Association," in <u>ALA Yearbook 1989</u>, pp. 83-84. Chicago: American Library Association, 1989; "Canadian Library Association," in <u>The Bowker Annual: Library and Book Trade Almanac, 34th Edition 1989-90</u>, pp. 680-681. New York: R.R. Bowker, 1989.

160   Canadian Library Exhibitors Association (CLEA)

Address   59-120 Beverly Glen Boulevard, TH 59, Scarborough, Ontario M1W 1W6 (permanent). Tel: 1 (416) 4972416
Officers   (elected for 1-yr. term) Pres: Tom Miller; VP: David Macmillan; Past Pres: Rand Winson; Sec/Treas: Frank Turton; Directors: Henry Kosar, James Chalmers, Carol Peterson; Exec.Sec.(appointed): Therese Hicks. Exec.Comm: 7
Staff   1 (paid); Exec.Comm.(volunteers)
Languages   English
Major Fields of Interest   Exhibits for library conferences
Activities   Association requests that all further inquiries should be addressed to the Executive Director of the Canadian Library Association, 200 Elgin Street, Suite 602, Ottawa, Ontario K2P 1L5.

161   Canadian Library Trustees Association (CLTA)

Address   c/o Canadian Library Association, 200 Elgin Street, Suite 602, Ottawa, Ontario K2P 1L5. Tel: 1 (613) 2329625; Telex: Envoy CLAHQ; Fax: 1-613-5629895
Officers   (elected for 1-yr. term, 1989-90) Pres: Margaret Andrewes (RR 3, Beamsville, Ont. L0R 1B0. Tel: 416-5634639); VP: Agnes Richard; Sec: Stephen Kirincich; Treas: Nicholas Spillios; Past Pres: George Bothwell. Exec.Board: 6.
Staff   None.
Languages   English.
Major Fields of Interest   Library trustees.
Major Goals and Objectives   To work towards the improvement of trustees and trusteeship through sharing ideas and information; promote trusteeship as the ideal form of public library governance.
Structure   Governed by Executive Board meeting 4 times a year. Affiliations: A division of the Canadian Library Association.
Sources of Support   Membership dues drawn from dues paid to the Canadian Library Association.
Membership   Total members: 300 (200 individual, 100 institutional). Requirements: Open to library trustees.
General Assembly   General membership meets once a year at the conference of the Canadian Library Association. 1987: Vancouver, B.C., June 10–17; 1988: Halifax, Nova Scotia, June; 1989: Edmonton, Alberta, June 22-24; 1990: Ottawa, June 14-17.
Publications   *Official journal:* <u>CLTA Newsletter</u>; discontinued 1975. Divisional news now appears in <u>Feliciter</u>, the newsletter of the Canadian Library Association. Publishes <u>Canadian Library Trustees' Handbook</u>, available for sale.
Activities   Helps library trustees to understand the responsibilities that are involved in trusteeship; sponsors workshops; various committees. The task of the division is complex due to the diversity of members, who include trustees of large urban libraries, small rural libraries and other types of library service.

162   Canadian School Library Association (CSLA)

Address   200 Elgin Street, Suite 602, Ottawa, Ontario K2P 1L5 (permanent). Tel: 1 (613) 29625; Telex: Envoy CLAHQ. Fax: 1-613-5639895.

Officers   (elected for 1–yr. term, 1989-90) Pres: Adrienne Betty;   VP:Diane Oberg;   Sec/Treas: Joyce Birch.   Exec.Board: 8.

Staff   None.

Languages   English.

Established   1961, at St.Andrews-by-the-Sea, at the Canadian Library Association Conference

Major Fields of Interest   School librarianship, including standards for school library programs; education for school librarianship; exchange of professional information; continuing education..

Major Goals and Objectives   To support and promote the objectives of the Canadian Library Association; to unite library and media personnel and other interested parties in furthering and improving school library media service throughout Canada; to provide for the exchange of ideas among members; to cooperate with other organizations in the advancement of education and librarianship.

Structure   Governed by an Executive Council. Affiliations: A division of the Canadian Library Association. Member of IASL. Note: A vote to separate from CLA and become an independent organization was narrowly defeated at the annual membership meeting in 1989.

Sources of Support   Membership dues drawn from dues paid to Canadian Library Association.

Membership   Total members: 695 (480 individual, 215 institutional). Requirements: Membership in Canadian Library Association and interest in school librarianship. Dues: Drawn from dues paid to Canadian Library Association.

General Assembly   General membership meets once a year at the conference of the Canadian Library Association. 1987: Vancouver, B.C., June 10–17; 1988: Halifax, Nova Scotia, June; 1989: Edmonton, Alberta, June 22-24; 1990: Ottawa, June 14-17.

Publications   *Official journal:* School Libraries in Canada (SLIC) (formerly Mocassin Telegraph). 1961–. 4/yr. (Canadian Dollar) 5, members; 35, non–members; (US Dollar) 35, outside Canada. Address same as Association. Editor: John Tooth. Address: 88 Queensbury Bay, Winnipeg, Manitoba R2N 3E9. Circ: 854. English, occasionally French. Indexed in Canadian Periodical Index, Canadian Education Index, Canadian Magazine Index, Lib.Lit., etc. Other publications: Annual report, position papers, etc. Publications for sale, price lists available through Canadian Library Association. Publications exchange program in effect.

Activities   Past achievements: Organizing professional development workshops; active awards program; successful conference sessions.   Current: Presents yearly awards (School Library Media Periodical Award, Margaret B. Scott Award of Merit); sponsors professional development workshops; various committees formed for publicity, education for school librarianship and professional development; revision of 1977 standards for school libraries, to be published as a series of position papers. Future: Review of organizational structure and program. Association has been active in lobbying federal government on legislation regarding copyright and pornography.

Use of High Technology   Electronic mail (Envoy 100)

Bibliography   Burdenuk, E. and Hambleton, A.E.L., "CSLA Membership Profile: Fifty North and Forty West (Kipling's Danger Point)," School Libraries in Canada 3 (1982):4-6; Burdenuk, E., "Canadian School Library Association, 1961-1984," School Libraries in Canada 4 (1984):7-10; Neill, D.S., "Final Report of an Investigation of the Professional, Legal and Financial Implications of Forming an Independent National School Library Association (with discussion)," ibid.:13-27; "Canadian School Library Association Will Stay within CLA," School Library Journal 30 (1984):14; Rothstein, S., "Canada," in ALA

World Encyclopedia of Library and Information Services, 2nd ed., pp. 155-165. Chicago: American Library Association, 1986; "A Year in Review [reports given at the 28th Annual General Meeting of the Canadian School Library Association, June 1988]," School Libraries in Canada 8 (1988):36-41.

163   Church Library Association

Address   c/o Dorothy Henderson, Secretary/Treasurer, 302-10 Allanhurst Drive, Islington, Ontario M9A 4J5 (permanent). Tel: 1 (416) 2494017
Officers   Pres: Nettie Friesen; Past Pres. and Founder: Anita Dalton; Sec/Treas: Dorothy Henderson; Membership/Ed: Emma Austin
Languages   English
Established   Oct., 1969
Major Fields of Interest   Church libraries
Major Goals and Objectives   A volunteer association for the promotion and establishment of church libraries.
Structure   Affiliations: Church and Synagogue Library Association
Sources of Support   Membership dues
Membership   Total members: 200 (individual). Dues (Canadian Dollar): $8.
General Assembly   Two seminars held each year in spring and fall.
Publications   *Official journal:* Library Lines. 1977–. 3/yr. Free to members. Editor: Emma Austin. Address: 1202 York Mills Road, #1104, Don Mills, Ont. M3A 1Y2. Circ: 200 +. English.
Activities   Establishment of new church libraries and help to those already in existence.

164   Council of Administrators of Large Urban Public Libraries (CALUPL)

Address   c/o Don Mills, Chairperson, 251 Donald Street, Winnipeg, Manitoba R3P 3P5 (not permanent). Tel: 1 (204) 9866472.
Officers   (elected for 1–yr. term) Chair: Don Mills; Vice Chair: Les Fowlie; Sec/Treas: Bey Grieue. Exec.Board: 3.
Staff   None.
Languages   English.
Major Fields of Interest   Public libraries serving large urban communities
Major Goals and Objectives   Promote public libraries.
Sources of Support   Membership dues.
Membership   Total members: 36 (institutional). Types of membership: Institutional. Requirements: Libraries serving a population of 100,000 +. Dues (Canadian Dollar): 50.
General Assembly   General membership meets once a year. 1987: Vancouver, B.C.; 1988: Halifax, Nova Scotia; 1989: Edmonton, Alberta.
Publications   No official journal. Publishes statistics, etc. Publications available for sale.

165   Council of Federal Libraries/Conseil des Bibliothèques du Gouvernement Fédéral (CFL/CBGF)

Address   c/o Federal Libraries Liaison Office (FLLO), National Library of Canada, 395 Wellington Street, Ottawa, Ontario K1A 0N4 (permanent). Tel: 1 (819) 9979780.
Officers   Chair: National librarian: Marianne Scott; Vice Chair: Director, Canada Institute for Scientific and Technical Information; Sec: Federal Libraries Liaison Officer (ex officio) plus 8 elected members. Exec. Board: 10

Staff   FLLO staff
Languages   English, French
Established   1976, recommendation of the "Federal Government Library Survey"
Major Fields of Interest   Coordination of federal library services
Major Goals and Objectives   To advise and assist the National Librarian in coordinating library services in the Government of Canada and to improve communications among federal librarians.
Structure   Governed by the plenary meeting of members and by the Steering Committee between such plenary meetings.
Sources of Support   Government subsidies
Membership   Total members: 58 (institutional). Requirements: Senior library officer of every department or agency having a centralized library system in the administrative branch of the federal government, and in those departments or agencies not having a centralized library system, the senior officer of each library.
General Assembly   General membership meets twice a year.
Publications   *Official journal:* Liaison. 1976–. 4/yr. Editor: Diane Parsonage, Convener, Editorial Committee. Address same as Association. Circ: 500–750. English, French. Publications for sale: "Training Needs in Federal Government Libraries: Survey Report;" "Federal Government Libraries and Access to Government Documents: Report;" etc.
Activities   Past achievements: Improved the quality of library services in the Government of Canada. Current: The Council has 22 task forces and working groups carrying out a variety of projects in the interest of library services. Future: Conservation of library materials, management information system on federal libraries, exchange of technical information on library automation, etc. The Council has a group monitoring and working on the revision of the Canadian Copyright Act.
Use of High Technology   Computers (PC and appropriate software), Management Information System Database, and electronic mail used in management.

166   Ex Libris Association

Address   c/o School of Library and Information Science, Elborn College, University of Western Ontario, London, Ontario N6G 1H1. Tel: 1 (519) 6613542.
Officers   Pres: E. Stanley Beacock; Sec/Treas: Jannette H. White. Exec.Board: 11.
Staff   None.
Languages   English.
Established   1986.
Major Fields of Interest   History of libraries, oral history, archival material.
Major Goals and Objectives   (1) Provide a forum for interested individuals; (2) provide a vehicle for collection of oral library history; (3) identify and ensure collection of materials relating to library history; (4) encourage identification of holdings of archival history; (5) provide a focus for intellectual and social activities of retired members of the library community.
Structure   Governed by Board of Directors. Affiliations: Ontario Library Association.
Sources of Support   Membership dues, government subsidies (organizational grants).
Membership   Total members: 90 (individual). 2 countries represented. Requirements: Interest in objectives of Association. Dues (Canadian Dollar): 5, individual.
General Assembly   General membership meets once a year.
Publications   *Official journal:* Ex Libris News. 1987–. 3/yr. Free to members. Circ: 200. English.
Activities   Current and future: (1) Oral history of county libraries; (2) archival collections: (a) letters of employment; (b) Institute of Professional Librarians of Ontario

(IPLO) records. Association is still in an early stage of development and hopes to succeed.

167   Indexing and Abstracting Society of Canada/Société Canadienne pour l'Analyse de Documents (IASC/SCAD)

Address   PO Box 744, Station F, Toronto, Ontario M4Y 2N6 (permanent). Tel: 1 (416) 4860239; Electronic mail: ALANET 0880, Envoy 100 Klement.Veaner (Telephone and Electronic mail not permanent, are of current president).
Officers   (elected for 2-yr. term) Pres: Susan Klement; Pres–Elect: Sally Grande; Sec/Treas: Jean Wheeler; Past Pres: Ann Schabas; Assoc. Liaison Off: Peter Grieg; Regional Dirs: Gwendoyn Creelman, Kathleen DeLong, C. Ross Goodwin, Asta Sokov, John Wallner. Exec.Board: 11.
Staff   None.
Languages   English, French.
Established   1977.
Major Fields of Interest   Indexing and abstracting.
Major Goals and Objectives   To encourage the production and use of indexes and abstracts; to promote the recognition of indexers and abstracters; to improve indexing and abstracting techniques; and to provide a means of communication among individual indexers and abstracters in Canada.
Structure   Governed by Executive Board. Affiliations: Society of Indexers (UK), American Society of Indexers, Australian Society of Indexers.
Sources of Support   Membership dues, sale of publications. Budget (Canadian Dollar): Approx. 2,500.
Membership   Total members: 118 (99 individual, 19 institutional). Requirements: Interest in indexing and abstracting. Dues (Canadian Dollar): 25, individual; 45, institutional.
General Assembly   Entire membership meets once a year.
Publications   *Official journal:* IASC/SCAD Bulletin. 1977–. 4/yr. Free to members. Address same as Association. Editor: Christopher Blackburn. Address: 16 Purple Sageway, Willowdale, Ont. M2H 2Z5. Circ: 118 (membership). English, French. Other publications: Reports of seminars, workshops, occasional monographs; So You Want to Index; The Indexer as Entrepreneur; IASC/SCAD Chronology; price list available. Publications listed occasionally in Journal.
Activities   Past achievements: Program meetings, publications. Current: Issuing a register of indexers and abstracters. Future: Publication of the register; promotion of the value of indexing among business people and the general public. Association sponsors continuing education lectures, seminars and workshops.
Use of High Technology   Computers (microcomputer used to produce bulletin and mailing lists).

168   Polish–Canadian Librarians Association

Address   c/o Grace B. Kopec, 103 Avenue Road, Apartment 703, Toronto, Ontario M5R 2G9.

169   Ukrainian Librarians Association of Canada

Address   Ukrainian St. Vladimir Institute, 620 Spadina Avenue, Toronto, Ontario M5S 2H4.

Chile

170 Colegio de Bibliotecarios de Chile A.G.
(Chilean Library Association)

Address Diagonal Paraguay 383, Torre 11, Piso 12, Depto. 122, Casilla 3741, Correo Central, Santiago (permanent). Tel: 56 (2) 2225652.
Officers (elected for 4/yr.term) Pres: Marcia Marinovic Simunovic; Sec: Ms. M.A. Calabecero Jimenez. Exec.Comm: 7
Staff 3 (paid)
Languages Spanish
Established 1969, Santiago (Law decree N 17 161), superseding the Asociación de Bibliotecarios de Chile (established 1953).
Major Fields of Interest Library development, especially public and school libraries
Major Goals and Objectives To represent the interests of the library profession and the librarians of Chile; to further library services through public and school libraries.
Structure Governed by Executive Committee meeting twice a month. Affiliations: Confederación de Colegios Profesionales de Chile, IFLA
Sources of Support Membership dues
Membership Total members: 1,380 (individual). Types of membership: Individual. Requirements: To possess a university degree in library science.
General Assembly Entire membership meets twice a year.
Publications *Official journal:* Boletín. irreg. Noticia Bibliotecarios. 12/yr. Both free to members. Address same as Association. Circ: Membership. Spanish. Other publications: Indices de Publicaciones Periodicas en Bibliotecología (Catalog of Periodical Publications in Librarianship); Micronoticias; Servicio de Alerta; a "Code of Professional Ethics;" "Standards for Chilean Public and School Libraries;" "Chilean Standards for Documentation," and others. Publications issued for sale, price lists available. Has publications exchange program with other associations and libraries.
Activities Development of standards and publications program; protecting the rights of the library profession. Active in promoting library-related legislation.
Bibliography Herrero de Alvarez, M. Teresa, "Chile," in ALA World Encyclopedia of Library and Information Services, 2nd ed., pp.188-190. Chicago: American Library Association, 1986.

China

171   Association of Chinese Archivists

Address   c/o The National Archives, Beijing
Languages   Chinese
Established   Dec., 1981
Major Fields of Interest   Archives
Major Goals and Objectives   To further development of archives in China
Membership   Total members: Approx.400 + .

172   China Society of Library Science (CSLS) / Zhongguo Tushuguan Xuehui

Address   7 Wen Jin Street, Beijing 7 (permanent). Tel: 666331 ext.312. Telex: 0222211 Nlc On
Officers   Pres: Du Ke; VPs: Huang Yusheng, Gu Tinglong, Tan Xiangjin, Zhuang Shojing, Bao Zhengxi; Sec.Gen: Liu Deyuan. Exec.Council: 70 members.
Staff   10 (paid)
Languages   Chinese
Established   July 13, 1979, Beijing
Major Fields of Interest   Libraries and library science
Major Goals and Objectives   To unite librarians from all over the country for the exchange of experiences and the furthering of professional development; to promote the principle of combining theory and practice in education for librarianship; to develop various types of professional activities; to promote the development of libraries and library science; to contribute to the development of socialist materials and culture.
Structure   Governed by the Executive Council. Affiliations: IFLA, FID
Sources of Support   Sale of publications, government subsidies. Budget (Yuan Renminbi): 1986/87: 60,000; 1987/88: 60,000.
Membership   Total members: 5,030 (5,000 individual, 30 institutional). Divisions: 4. Sections: 13. Chapters (Provincial Regional Societies): 30. Requirements: Individuals who qualify in any of the following areas: (1) Teaching instructor, librarian, or similar professional rank; (2) Master Degree or above; (3) Degree in library science with 3 years practical experience or as researcher with demonstrated ability; or, without library science degree, but extensive experience and achievement of equal professional level; (4) Made important contributions to library science or to the cause of library service; (5) Leading cadre who is engaged in organizing libraries and in administrative work, and who actively supports the work of the Society; or a professional from another field, who has made contributions to research and development of library science. Institutional: All library associations of the provincial, municipal, and autonomous regions and specialized libraries are ex officio members. Dues: None.
General Assembly   Entire membership meets every 4 years.
Publications   *Official journal:* Bulletin of Library Science. 1979-. 4/yr. (Yuan Renminbi) 3.20. Address same as Association. Editor: Yuan Yongqiu. Circ: 30,000. Chinese, with English table of contents. Indexed in LISA. Issues various publications. Publications exchange program with other associations, libraries, and other institutions and organizations.
Activities   Active in sponsoring numerous symposia on current topics (26 through 1985, with 1,080 papers presented, and 2,477 participants); edited and published 3 volumes of Abstracts of Scientific Seminars; The Descriptive Cataloguing Rules for Western Lan-

guage Materials; and 5 editions of papers on special subjects. Association strengthened international participation by attending IFLA Congresses and by establishing professional relations with the USA, Great Britain, Australia, the Philippines and Thailand by sending delegations from both sides for the exchange of experiences. Continues preparing for national meetings, such as the 4th Library and Information Science Seminar on Deployment of Documents and Resources. Association has been active in promoting library-related legislation through discussions with government authorities and making appropriate suggestions.

Bibliography   Ding, Zhigang, "China, People's Republic of," in ALA World Encyclopedia of Library and Information Services, 2nd ed., pp.190-192. Chicago: American Library Association, 1986; Khurshid, A., "Library Associations in Asia," Herald of Library Science 28 (1989):3-10; Hu, Wendy Lin, "Current State of Library and Information Science Development in China," Journal of Education for Library and Information Science 30 (1990):183-192.

173   Chinese Society of Scientific and Technical Information (CSSTI) / Zhongguo Kexue Jishu Qingbao Xuehui

Address   PO Box 640, He Ping Li, Beijing (not permanent). Tel: 46-2598. Telex: 20079 Istic Cn

Officers   (elected for 4-yr.term) Chair of CSSTI Council: Wu Heng; Vice Chairs: Lin Zixin, Wang Tingjiong, Li Yongxin, Hu Anqun; Sec.Gen: Liu Zhaodong. Exec.Board: 17

Staff   5 (paid)

Languages   Chinese, English

Established   1978, Suzhou

Major Fields of Interest   Information science of Science and technology

Major Goals and Objectives   To develop information science; to promote information activities and to further the development of science, technology and economy in China

Structure   Governed by Executive Board. Affiliations: FID

Sources of Support   Government subsidies.

Membership   Total members: 10,000. 29 provinces represented. Requirements: Individual: Members are elected; Institutional: Members of Science and Technology Information Associations of the provinces, municipalities, and autonomous regions. Dues: None.

General Assembly   Entire membership meets 3 times a year.

Publications   *Official journal:* Journal of the Chinese Society of Scientific and Technical Information (ISSN 1-000-135). 1982-. 6/yr. (Yuan Renminbi) 1.30. Address same as Association. Editor: Liang Shuchai. Circ: 6,000. Chinese, with English abstracts. Other publications: Proceedings of meetings, reports of seminars, workshops. monographs. Publications for sale, listed in journal. Publications exchange program in effect.

Activities   To carry out the goals and objectives, activities cover the following areas: (1) Domestic and international exchanges; (2) Popularizing basic knowledge of information science; (3) Consultation services for users; (4) Editing and publishing books and periodicals in science and technology information. The Society sponsored over 40 conferences and received over 3,000 papers; offered special short-term training courses and trained over 1,000 students; published over 12 books and many periodicals; active in promoting relevant legislation, such as the "PRC Legislation on Sci-Tech Information." Sponsors ongoing continuing education programs and international conferences.

Use of High Technology   Computers, databases used for management.

Bibliography   "Organization Profile: 7. China Society of Scientific and Technical Information," Journal of Information Science 9 (1984):29-30; Khurshid, A., "Library Associations in Asia," Herald of Library Science 28 (1989):3-10.

174   Chung-kuo t'u-shu-kuan hsüeh-hui / Library Association of China (LAC)

Address   20 Chungshan S. Road, Taipei 10040, Taiwan (not permanent). Tel: 886 (2) 3619132. Fax: 886 (2) 3619144.
Officers   Exec.Dir: Teresa Wang Chang
Staff   2 (volunteers)
Languages   Chinese, English
Established   1953 (incorporated).
Major Fields of Interest   Librarianship
Major Goals and Objectives   To promote Chinese culture; to promote the study of library science; to organize librarians and library personnel and to further their professional development.
Structure   Governed by Executive Board. Affiliations: IFLA.
Sources of Support   Membership dues, government subsidies.
Membership   Total members: Approx.1,300 (1,184 individual, 116 institutional). Divisions: 8. Types of membership: Active, honorary, student, life, emeritus, institutional. Requirements: Open to anyone who has studied library science or is interested in library work. Dues (New Taiwan Dollar): 75, individual; 550-1,100, institutional.
General Assembly   Entire membership meets annually in Taipei in December.
Publications   *Official journal:* Bulletin of the Library Association of China/Chung-kuo t'u-shu-kuan hsüeh-hui hui-pao. 1954-. 1/yr. (New Taiwan Dollar) 40. Address same as Association. Chinese, English. Other publications: Library Association of China Newsletter. 1975-. 6/yr. Chinese; proceedings of conferences, seminars. Publications for sale.
Activities   Sponsorship of continuing education programs, such as summer workshops, seminars; formulation of library standards; working for general improvements of library services. Association is involved in joint library automation projects with the National Central Library, and Chinese language bibliographies.
Bibliography   Wang, Chen-Ku, "China, Republic of (Taiwan)," in ALA World Encyclopedia of Library and Information Services, 2nd ed., pp. 192-194. Chicago: American Library Association, 1986; Khurshid, A., "Library Associations in Asia," Herald of Library Science 28 (1989):3-10.

175   Library Science Society

Address   c/o Department of Library Science, Taiwan University, Roosevelt Road, Section 4, Taipei 10764, Taiwan. Tel: 886 (2) 3510231 ext.2296/2641.
Languages   Chinese
Major Fields of Interest   Library science

Colombia

176   Asociación Colombiana de Archivistas (ACAR) (Association of Colombian Archivists)

Address   Capítulo de Cundinamarca, Apartado Aéreo 49701, Bogotá.
Officers   Pres: Clara Ines Puentes Sarmiento
Staff   None
Languages   Spanish
Major Fields of Interest   Archives
Major Goals and Objectives   To further the development of archives in Colombia
Bibliography   Torres, A., "Colombia," in ALA World Encyclopedia of Library and Information Services, 2nd ed., pp. 213-315. Chicago: American Library Association, 1986.

177   Asociación Colombiana de Bibliotecarios (ASCOLBI) (Colombian Association of Librarians)

Address   Apartado aéreo 30883, Bogota DE. Tel: 57 (1) 2694219
Officers   (elected for 2-yr.term) Pres: Silvia Castrillón de Miranda; Sec: Bertha Nelly Cardona de Gil. Exec.Comm: 6
Staff   9 (volunteers)
Languages   Spanish
Established   1956, at Biblioteca Nacional
Major Fields of Interest   Library profession
Major Goals and Objectives   To contribute to the cultural, economic, and social development of the nation; to promote and make known the objectives of the library profession; to promote relationships between librarians and to improve the status of the members of the Association; to promote research and to provide technical assistance to the public and private sectors.
Structure   Governed by Executive Committee. Affiliations: FID, IFLA
Sources of Support   Membership dues, private gifts, sale of publications.
Membership   Total members: 400 (390 individual, 10 institutional). Chapters: 4. Types of membership: Individual, institutional, student, honorary. Requirements: Individual: Professional librarians, assisting staff, students of library science, teachers of library science, or persons with experience in the library field; Institutions: All legally constituted organizations interested in the promotion of books, libraries, documentation, and information in general. Dues (US Dollar): 30, individual; 40, institutional.
General Assembly   Entire membership meets once a year.
Publications   *Official journal:* Carta al Bibliotecario (supersedes Boletín de la Asociación Colombiana de Bibliotecarios, 1957-79). 1979-. 4/yr. (US Dollar) 10. Free to members. Editors: Moisés Pedraza and Lucy Espinosa. Address same as Association. Circ: 1,200. Spanish.
Activities   Past achievements: A major contribution was the implementation of Law 11, 1978, which recognized the library profession in Colombia, and the exercise of the bylaws of this legislation. Current and future: To improve the financial status of the Association; to improve the official journal; to strengthen the Association's work by creating a network of concerned professionals, and by publishing a national directory. Association continues to be active in promoting library-related legislation and its implementation.
Bibliography   Torres, A., "Colombia," in ALA World Encyclopedia of Library and Information Services, 2nd ed., pp. 213-215. Chicago: American Library Association, 1986.

178   Asociación Nacional de Bibliotecas Públicas
(National Association of Public Libraries)

Address   c/o Biblioteca Nacional de Colombia, Calle 24, No.5-60-4ºpiso, Apartado
Aéreo 27600, Bogotá DE. Tel: (01)414029.
Languages   Spanish
Established   1985, Bogotá, during the Seminario Nacional de Bibliotecas Públicas (National Seminar of Public Libraries)
Major Fields of Interest   Public library service
Major Goals and Objectives   To further public library services; to promote local and
regional networks for eventual national integration of public library services.
Activities   Works in close cooperation and with the support of the Instituto Colombiano
de Cultura (COLCULTURA) for better public library services and to create a network of
public libraries; participated in a National Inventory of Information Resources and Services in Public Libraries.
Bibliography   Torres, A., "Colombia," in ALA World Encyclopedia of Library and Information Services, 2nd ed., pp. 213-215. Chicago: American Library Association, 1986.

179   Bibliotecarios Agrícolas Colombianos
(Agricultural Librarians of Colombia)

Address   c/o Biblioteca de Tibaitatá, Apartado Aéreo 7984, Bogotá DE
Officers   Pres: Julialba Hurtado; VP: Gloria Estrada; Sec: Héctor Galeano; Treas: Ruth
Buitrago, Ernesto Delgado

180   Colegio Colombiano de Bibliotecarios
(Colombian Academy of Librarians)

Address   Apartado Aéreo 1307, Medellin.
Languages   Spanish
Established   Aug. 7, 1968, through a merger of the Colegio de Bibliotecarios Colombianos (CBC) and the Asociación de Egresados de la Escuela Interamericana de Bibliotecología (ASEIB).   No further information available.

Congo

181   Association Congolaise pour le Développement de la Documentation, des Bibliothèques et des Archives (ACDBA)
(Congolese Association for the Development of Documentation, Libraries and Archives)

Address   c/o Bibliothèque Nationale du Congo, Direction des Services de Bibliothèques, d'Archives et de Documentation, BP 1489, Brazzaville (permanent). Tel: 813485.
Languages   French
Established   1984
Major Fields of Interest   Libraries, archives and documentation
Major Goals and Objectives   To further the development of libraries, archives, and documentation centers in the People's Republic of the Congo
Structure   Governed by executive officers.
Sources of Support   Membership dues.
Membership   Total members: Approx. 75 (individual).
General Assembly   Entire membership meets once a year.
Activities   Carried out in accordance with the aims of the Association. Sponsors meetings, seminars, etc.
Bibliography   Wambi, B., "Congo," in <u>ALA Encyclopedia of Library and Information Services</u>, 2nd ed., pp. 216-218. Chicago: American Library Association, 1986.

Costa Rica

182   Asociación Costarricense de Bibliotecarios (ACB)
(Costa Rican Association of Librarians)

Address   Apartado Postal 3308, San José (not permanent)
Officers   Gen.Sec: Nelly Kopper
Staff   None
Languages   Spanish
Established   1949, San José, at Biblioteca Nacional
Major Fields of Interest   Libraries and librarianship
Major Goals and Objectives   To develop librarianship and libraries in Costa Rica; to create a national library system.
Structure   Governed by Executive Board (president, general secretary, second secretary, treasurer, fiscal auditor).
Sources of Support   Membership dues, subsidies.
Membership   Types of membership: Individual (founders, active, honorary). Requirements: Age 18, upon written application and acceptance by membership through secret vote.
General Assembly   Entire membership meets once a year.
Publications   *Official journal:* Boletín de ACB. 1955-. Irreg. Address same as Association. Publishes Anuario bibliográfico costarricense (Yearbook of Costa Rican Bibliography). 1956-.
Activities   Sponsors conferences, meetings in order to promote libraries and professional development. Activities are nonpolitical and nonreligious in keeping with the statutes. Celebrates Library Day each March 19th.
Bibliography   Retana, P., "Costa Rica," in ALA World Encyclopedia of Library and Information Services, 2nd ed., pp. 230-231. Chicago: American Library Association, 1986.

183   Colegio de Bibliotecarios de Costa Rica
(Library Association of Costa Rica)

Address   c/o Lupita Rodríguez Méndez, Encargada de Biblioteca, Instituto de Fomento Asesoria Municipal, San José, or, c/o Efraín Picado, Dir.Gen., Biblioteca Nacional, Apdo 10008, San José.
Languages   Spanish
Established   1971, San José
Major Fields of Interest   Libraries and librarianship
Major Goals and Objectives   To improve professional qualifications of members through courses, seminars, and various programs; to represent and protect professional interests of librarians.
Activities   Association acts as an umbrella organization for librarians in all types of libraries in the country; activities are carried out in accordance with the goals and objectives.
Bibliography   Retana, P., "Costa Rica," in ALA World Encyclopedia of Library and Information Services, 2nd ed., pp. 230-231. Chicago: American Library Association, 1986.

Cuba

184   Library Association of Cuba

Address   c/o Biblioteca Nacional, Plaza de la Revolución, Havana (permanent). Tel: 708277/705092. Telex: 511963.
Officers   Pres: Marta Terry, National Librarian
Staff   (provided by National Library)
Languages   Spanish
Established   1981, Havana
Major Fields of Interest   Libraries and library services
Major Goals and Objectives   To further the development of libraries and librarians in the country
Structure   Governed by executive officers. Affiliations: IFLA (since 1982).
Sources of Support   Government subsidies
Bibliography   Terry, M., "Cuba," in ALA World Encyclopedia of Library and Information Services, 2nd ed., pp. 231-235. Chicago: American Library Association, 1986.

Cyprus

185 Cyprus Association of Professional Librarians (CAPL)

Address   c/o Mr. Savvas Petrides, Secretary, PO Box 3726, Nicosia
Officers   Pres: Andreas Savva; Past Pres: Photis Pittas; VP and COMLA Rep: Charles Glover (The Middle East Library, PO Box 2098, Nicosia); Sec: Savvas Petrides (Inspector of Libraries, Cultural Service, Ministry of Education); Asst.Sec: Bridget Scrivens; Treas: Demetris Nicolaou; Publications: Nicos Palazis; Publicity: Yioula Moniat. Exec.Board: 7
Staff None
Languages   Greek, Turkish, English
Established   1987
Major Fields of Interest   Professional librarianship
Major Goals and Objectives   "To work, with every legal means, for the development and promotion to the highest level, of Librarianship, Archives and Information Science in Cyprus, and to secure and protect by rules the profession of Librarianship."
Structure   Governed by Executive Board. Affiliations: COMLA (since fall 1988, replaces the Cyprus Library Association as official representative of Cyprus)
Sources of Support   Membership dues.
Membership   Requirements: Open not only to those holding recognized degrees or diplomas in librarianship, archives or information science, but also to those holding a position as a librarian, or students enrolled in a course in librarianship (which must be for at least a year). Institutions are also eligible for membership, including companies, legal persons and other organizations which keep or are interested in libraries, archives or information centers.
General Assembly   Entire membership met for the first symposium on March 21, 1987.
Publications   Publications program not yet established.
Activities   Active in establishing the new Cyprus Library Act, which came into force Sept. 1987.
Bibliography   "New Library Association Completes First Year," Library Times International 4 (1986):64, 66; Petrides, S., "A Library Law for Cyprus and a New Professional Body for Librarians," COMLA Newsletter 57 (Sept.1987):5; "Libraries and Librarianship in Cyprus Today," ibid.:12; "Cyprus Library Act Results from COMLA Initiative [new professional association for librarians was also set up recently: Cyprus Association of Professional Librarians]," Library Association Record 89 (1987):498; "Cyprus Association of Professional Librarians Replaces Cyprus Library Association," COMLA Newsletter 62 (Dec.1988):16.

186 Kypriakos Synthesmos Vivliothicarion (Cyprus Library Association) (CLA)

Address   c/o Pedagogical Academy, PO Box 1039, Nicosia (permanent). Tel: 357 (2) 402310
Officers   Pres: Costas D. Stephanou; Sec: Paris G. Rossos. Exec.Comm: 5
Staff None
Languages   Greek, English
Established   1962, as Hellenikos Synthesmos Vivliothikarion Kyprou (Greek Library Association of Cyprus). Present name adopted 1974.
Major Fields of Interest   Librarianship
Major Goals and Objectives   To improve library services in Cyprus.

Structure   Governed by Executive Committee. Affiliations: IFLA, COMLA (founding member; replaced by CAPL as representative member of Cyprus in 1988).
Sources of Support   Membership dues.
Membership   Total Members: 30. Types of membership: Individual, life, emeritus, honorary. Requirements: Open to individuals working in a library.
General Assembly   Entire membership meets annually.
Publications   No publications program.
Activities   Past achievements: Building up library facilities and services that were severely damaged and interrupted during the war of 1974. Current: Sponsoring seminars and workshops, and raising public awareness of libraries and their services in general.
Bibliography   Stephanou, C.D., "Cyprus," in ALA World Encyclopedia of Library and Information Services, 2nd ed., pp. 240-241. Chicago: American Library Association, 1986; Khurshid, A., "Library Associations in Asia," Herald of Library Science 28 (1989):3-10.

Czechoslovakia

187   Ustrední Knihovnická Rada CSR (UKR CSR)
(Central Library Council of the CSR)

Address   c/o The Ministry of Culture of the Czech Socialist Republic, Valdstejnské nám. 4, 11811 Prague 1 (permanent). Tel: 42 (2) 536166/536138.
Officers   (elected for 3-yr.term) Pres: Jirí Kábrt (Head, Dept. of Library and Information Science, Charles University, Prague); Other officers: Karel Kozelek, Miloslava Nepovímová. Exec.Board: 3
Staff   1 (paid), 2 (volunteer)
Languages   Czech
Established   1955
Major Fields of Interest   Library science and bibliographic information
Major Goals and Objectives   To function as an advisory, initiative, and coordinating body of the Ministry of Culture of the CSR; to evaluate the activity of the library systems; to consider their development and long-term plans of activity; to supervise the advancement of political and professional development of library workers, as well as their social appreciation and adequate remuneration.
Structure   Governed by the Ministry of Culture of the CSR. Affiliations: IFLA
Sources of Support   Government
Membership   Total members: 104 (78 individual, 26 institutional). Sections: 7. Requirements: The Council is an advisory and coordinating body whose members are library administrators and experts in the field of library and information science, and include representatives of all library networks. Dues: None
General Assembly   Entire membership meets 3 times a year in Prague (March, June, November).
Publications   No official journal. Council uses the publishing facilities of the State Library of the CSR, as well as other leading libraries. It does not issue its own publications, but participates in the publishing of library science material.
Activities   Past achievements: The Council has significantly contributed to and taken part in all important Czechoslovakian projects, meetings of experts, seminars, as well as in the preparation of all seminal material in the field of library science. Current: Work in the following committees of the Council: For bibliography, normative basis of librarianship, fund raising, processing, work with historical collections, scientific and methodological work, problems of technological and economic development. Future: Development of library and bibliographic services in accordance with the latest technological standards and in coordination with the demands of the state and cultural policy. Council was active in promoting library-related legislation, such as the Library Act, plans for development of library work, directives and methodical instruction for various fields of library work.
Use of High Technology   Computers (EC 1057 and PC Commodore) for management.
Bibliography   Kolárova-Pálkova, H., "Czechoslovakia," in <u>ALA World Encyclopedia of Library and Information Services</u>, 2nd ed., pp. 241-243. Chicago: American Library Association, 1986.
Additional Information   In Slovakia, the same functions are carried out by the Slovak Library Council (Slovenská Kniznicná Rada, Ministerstvo kultúry SSR, 81331 Bratislava, Suvorovová 12).

188   Zväz Slovenskych Knihovníkov a Informatikov (ZSKI)
(Association des Bibliothécaires et Documentalistes Slovaques / Association of Slovak Librarians and Information Workers)

Address   Michalská 1, 81417 Bratislava (permanent). Tel: 42 (7) 330557. Telex: 93255.
Officers   (elected for 4-yr.term) Pres: Elena Sakálová; Past Pres: Vít Rak; VPs: Miroslav Bielik, Ludmila Benetinova, Stefan Kimlicka; Exec.Sec: D. Krausová. Exec.Board: 12; Exec.Comm: 40
Staff   4 (paid)
Languages   Slovak, Russian, English, German
Established   1968, Bratislava
Major Fields of Interest   Library and information science development
Major Goals and Objectives   Maintain progress in librarianship and information science; give aid to librarians and information workers; organize seminars, lectures, etc.
Structure   Governed by Executive Board meeting 2 times a year; Executive Committee meets 6 times a year. Affiliations: IFLA
Sources of Support   Membership dues, government subsidies. Budget (Koruna): 1986/87: 580,000; 1987/88: 500,000.
Membership   Total members: 2,813 (2,762 individual, 51 institutional). Divisions: 3. Regional sections: 3. Chapters: 7. Requirements: Persons employed in librarianship and information science.
General Assembly   Entire membership meets every 4 years.
Publications   *Official journal:* Zväzovy Bulletin. 1969-. 4/yr. Free to members. Editor: Vít Rak. Address same as Association. Circ: 2,900. Slovak. Issues proceedings of meetings, reports of seminars, workshops. No publications exchange program.
Activities   Past achievements: Professional conferences, seminars, 44th IFLA Congress in CSSR, other contributions to IFLA. Current: Sponsors conferences, seminars. Future: Long-term planning of the theoretical and practical work of the Association. Association has been active in promoting library-related legislation and in continuing education offerings.
Bibliography   Kolárová-Pálkova, H., "Czechoslovakia," in ALA World Encyclopedia of Library and Information Services, 2nd ed., pp. 241-243. Chicago: American Library Association, 1986; Kolárová-Pálkova, H., "Das Slowakische Bibliothekswesen," (Slovakian Librarianship) Mitteilungen der Vereinigung Österreichischer Bibliothekare 42 (1989):126-130 (in German).

Denmark

189   Arkivforeningen
(Danish Association of Archivists)

Address   Rigsarkivet (Danish National Archives), Rigsdagsgarden 9, DK-1218 Copenhagen K (permanent). Tel: 45 (1) 923310.
Officers   (elected for indefinite term) Pres: Margit Mogensen; Sec: Poul Olsen
Staff   None
Languages   Danish
Established   1917, Copenhagen
Major Fields of Interest   Archives and archival studies
Major Goals and Objectives   To be the forum for lectures and discussions on archival subjects and other activities of common interest to all employed in archives.
Structure   Governed by Executive Committee.
Sources of Support   Membership dues.
Membership   Total members: 120 (individual). Types of membership: Individual, honorary. Requirements: Open to those whose applications are approved by the Executive Committee. Dues (Danish Krone): 70.
General Assembly   Entire membership meets once a year in June.
Publications   No official journal. Arkivforeningens Publikationer. Irreg. Issues proceedings of seminars, reports, manuals for archivists, and other publications. Price lists available. No publications exchange program.
Activities   Sponsors seminars and conferences.

190   Bibliotekarforbundet (BF)
(The Union of Danish Librarians)

Address   Jagtvej 111, DK-2200 Copenhagen N (permanent). Tel: 45 (31) 852822. Fax: 45-31-852120
Officers   (elected for 1-2-yr.term) Pres: Ole Jamm; Past Pres: Johannes Balslev; VP: Birgit Grosfjeld; Sec: Sren Juel Nielsen. Other officers: Lars Andren, Bodil Holstein, Tage Sorensen. Exec.Comm: 11
Staff   21 (paid)
Languages   Danish
Established   1924, Copenhagen
Major Fields of Interest   Library affairs; cultural matters; union matters.
Major Goals and Objectives   To take care of professional economic, legal and educational interests for the members of the union; to conduct wage and contract negotiations for union members.
Structure   Governed by Executive Committee. Affiliations: IFLA
Sources of Support   Membership dues. Budget (Danish Krone): 1986/87: 24,331,580; 1987/88: 26,274,271.
Membership   Total members: 4,740 (individual). Types of membership: Individual only. Requirements: Librarians educated at the Royal School of Librarianship in Denmark. Dues (Danish Krone): 6,000, which includes unemployment insurance.
General Assembly   Entire membership meets once a year.
Publications   *Official journal:* Bibliotek 70. 1970-. 22/yr. (Danish Krone) 225. Free to members. Address same as Association. Editor: Per Nyeng. Address: Rosenborggade 9, DK-ll30 Copenhagen K. Circ: 6,000. Danish. Indexed in LISA, Library Section Index. Issues various publications on professional issues.

Activities   As a trade union concerned with salaries and working conditions of professional librarians, activities focus on related issues. Past achievements: State employees achieved equal wage requirements as municipal employees; campaign for librarians employed in the private sector; cultural offensive in cooperation with other art and cultural organizations; improved education for librarians; prepared a book collection for a library in Nicaragua. Current: Continuing activities in accordance with the goals and objectives. Future: Reduction of working hours, better wages, more employment opportunities for librarians, more grants for libraries, better continuing education offerings. The Union was active in promoting library-related legislation, e.g., submitted comments on a new law for public libraries to the Danish Parliament
Bibliography   Kirkegaard, P., "Denmark," in ALA World Encyclopedia of Library and Information Services, 2nd ed., pp. 246-248. Chicago: American Library Association, 1986.

**191   Danmarks Biblioteksforening (DB)
(Danish Library Association)**

Address   Trekronergade 15, DK-2500 Valby-Copenhagen (permanent). Tel: 45 (31) 308682. Fax: 45-31-308080.
Officers   (elected for 4-yr.term) Pres: Bent Sorensen; Exec.Dir.(appointed): Flemming Ettrup. Exec.Comm: 24
Staff   10 (paid)
Languages   Danish
Established   1905, Copenhagen
Major Fields of Interest   Public libraries, library policy, public relations.
Major Goals and Objectives   To further the development of libraries and library service in Denmark
Structure   Governed by Executive Committee. Affiliations: IFLA
Sources of Support   Membership dues, sale of publications, government subsidies.
Membership   Total members: 3,000+ (2,700 individual, 300 institutional). Divisions: 4. 3 countries represented. Types of membership: Individual, institutional, student, honorary. Requirements: Individual: Open to all interested persons, no special requirements. Institutional: Libraries and other institutions and associations interested in library development. Dues (Danish Krone): 200, individual; 100, student; institutions according to budget.
General Assembly   Entire membership meets annually.
Publications   *Official journal:* Bogens Verden (Library Journal). 1918-. 8/yr. (Danish Krone) 335. Free to members. Editors: Flemming Ettrup and Erik Skyum-Nielsen. Address same as Association. Circ: 5,000. Danish. Indexed in Lib.Lit., LISA, ISA. Other publications: Vivliorwkaevof (Library Yearbook); Biblioteksvejviser (Library Directory, annual); and others. Publications for sale, price lists available. Publications exchange program in effect with other associations, libraries, and institutions.
Activities   Sponsors seminars, workshops, continuing education offerings; active in promoting library-related legislation; the oldest and main association in Denmark, with active branches in all counties.
Bibliography   Kirkegaard, P., "Denmark," in ALA World Encyclopedia of Library and Information Services, 2nd ed., pp. 246-248. Chicago: American Library Association, 1986; Niegaard, H., "Danmarks Biblioteksforenigings asmode 1985: Konsoliderigens time?" (The Danish Library Association's Annual Meeting 1985: Time to Consolidate?" Bibliotek 70 7 (1986):190-193 (in Danish); "Danmarks Biblioteksforenings arsmode i Nyborg den 19-21 marts 1986," (The Danish Library Association's Annual Meeting in Nyborg,

19-21 March 1986) <u>Bogens Verden</u> (1986):193-244 (special issue, in Danish); Kajberg, L., "The Library of the Future Key Issue at the Annual Conference of the Danish Library Association," <u>Library Times International</u> 4 (1987):20.

192   Danmarks Forskningsbiblioteksforening (DF)
(Danish Research Library Association)

Address   c/o Statsbiblioteket, Universitetsparken, DK-8000 Aarhus C (permanent). Tel: 45 (6) 125759. Telex: 64515
Officers   (elected for 1-yr.term) Chair: Mette Stockmarr; Vice-Chair: Niels Henrik Gylstorff; Treas: Kristian Salling Pedersen; Sec: Mogens Sandfaer. Exec.Board: 12
Staff   1 (half-time, paid)
Languages   Danish
Established   1978
Major Fields of Interest   Research libraries and the library community
Major Goals and Objectives   To further cooperation between research libraries; to promote research libraries and their viewpoints among the general public and the political decision-makers; to support and encourage cooperation with national and international organizations.
Structure   Governed by Executive Board. Affiliations: IFLA (2 memberships, one for each Section)
Sources of Support   Membership dues, government subsidies. Budget (Danish Krone): Approx. 450,000.
Membership   Total members: 661 (540 individual, 121 institutional). The Association consists of 2 independent Sections: (1) Sammenslutningen af Danmarks Forskningsbiblioteker (SDF) (Association of Danish Research Libraries; formerly a group of the Danish Library Association, 1948-1978), and (2) Foreningen af Medarbejdere ved Danmarks Forskningsbiblioteker (FMDF) (Association of Staff Members of Danish Research Libraries; which changed its name to include not only librarians, but all staff of research libraries). Requirements: Membership through the Sections. Dues (Danish Krone): SDF: 74,500; FMDF: 40,000; Associated members: 250.
General Assembly   Entire membership meets once a year.
Publications   *Official journal:* <u>DF-Revy</u>. 1978-. 10/yr. 145 Danish Krone. Free to members. Address: Kristian Salling Pedersen, Statsbiblioteket, Universitetsparken, DK-8000 Arhus C. Editor: Palle Birkelund. Address: Birketinget 6, DK-2300 Copenhagen S. Circ: 800. Scandinavian languages, occasionally English. Indexed in <u>LISA</u>, <u>Nordisk BDI-index</u>.
Activities   Sponsors conferences, seminars, meetings and other continuing education programs. Association has been active in promoting library-related legislation, such as working for a new administrative framework which resulted in the establishment of the new office of National Librarian.
Bibliography   Birkelund, P., "Danish Research Librarianship Organizes Itself into a New Group," <u>Nordinsk Tidskrift for Bok och Biblioteksvasen</u> 67 (1980):19-21 (in Danish); Gregerson, K., "Association of Danish Research Libraries Wants to Keep a Low Profile," <u>Bogens Verden</u> 63 (1981):428-429 (in Danish); Gronbaek, J.H., "Stop the Discord: Danish Research Libraries Association's Renewed Potshots at the Danish Library Association Harms the Entire Library Cause," <u>ibid</u>.:464-466 (in Danish); Kirkegaard, P., "Denmark," in <u>ALA World Encyclopedia of Library and Information Services</u>, 2nd ed., pp. 346-348. Chicago: American Library Association, 1986.

193   Danmarks Skolebibliotekarforening
(Association of Danish School Librarians)

Address   Mariavej 1, Sdr Bjert, DK-6091 Bjert. Tel: 45 (5) 577101.
Languages   Danish
Major Fields of Interest   School libraries and librarians
Major Goals and Objectives   To further school libraries and the professional develop-
ment of school librarians.
Publications   *Official journal:* Skole Biblioteket (The School Library). Address:
Kongshvilebakken 10-12, DK-2800 Lyngby

194   Danmarks Skolebiblioteksforening
(Association of Danish School Libraries)

Address   Norrebrogade 159, DK-2200 Copenhagen N. Tel: 45 (31) 811666.
Officers   Chair: Ib Juul; Exec.Dir: Ove Frank. Exec.Board: 10.
Staff   5 (paid)
Languages   Danish
Established   1933, Copenhagen
Major Fields of Interest   School libraries, educational materials, children's literature,
children and youth culture.
Major Goals and Objectives   To support and coordinate the work done to instill cul-
tural and educational values in children and young people; to encourage cooperation and
exchange of experience and ideas concerning school libraries; to provide a forum to dis-
cuss how to improve contacts between school library users, school library staff and politicians who are responsible for school libraries.
Structure   Governed by Executive Committee. Affiliations: IFLA.
Sources of Support   Membership dues, sale of publications, government subsidies.
Membership   Total members: 375 (30 individual, 345 institutional). Types of membership: Individual, institutional. Requirements: Individuals and institutions involved with
school libraries, especially in Danish boroughs and municipalities. Dues (Danish Krone):
200, individual; 800, institutional.
General Assembly   Entire membership meets once a year.
Publications   *Official journal:* Born og Boger (Children and Books). 1946-. 8/yr. (Danish Krone) 200. Free to members. Editor: Arne Holst. Address same as Association.
Circ: 4,000. Danish. Indexed in LISA. Issues proceedings of conferences, annual report,
and other publications on statistics, audiovisual materials, standards for school libraries in
Denmark, resource material for primary schools, etc. Publications for sale. Has publications exchange program with other associations and nonlibrary institutions.
Activities   Sponsors conferences, workshops, seminars and other activities in accordance
with the Association's goals and objectives; extensive publications program; active in promoting library-related legislation for school libraries.
Bibliography   "The New Laws for the Danish School Libraries Association," Bogens
Verden 64 (1982):332-334 (in Danish); Kirkegaard, P., "Denmark," in ALA World Encyclopedia of Library and Information Services, 2nd ed., pp. 246-248. Chicago: American
Library Association, 1986.

195   Dansk Arkivselskab
(Danish Archives Association)

Address   c/o Secretariat, Bylokken 2, DK-8240 Risskov. Tel: 45 (6) 128533

Languages   Danish
Established   1976
Major Fields of Interest   Archives
Major Goals and Objectives   To further the development of archives in Denmark
Sources of Support   Membership dues
Membership   Total members: 330 (individual). Requirements: Interest in archives.
Publications   Official journal: <u>Arkivnyt</u>. Other publications: <u>Arkivordbog m.v.</u>.
Activities   Sponsors meetings, conferences and other continuing education programs for members.

196   Dansk Musikbiblioteksforening (Danish Association of Music Libraries)

Address   c/o Secretary, Duevej 14-6, DK-2000 Copenhagen F
Languages   Danish
Major Fields of Interest   Music libraries, music librarianship
Major Goals and Objectives   To further the development of music libraries and music librarianship
Structure   Affiliations: Association is the Danish Branch of the International Association of Music Libraries, Archives and Documentation Centres (IAML)
Sources of Support   Membership dues
Membership   Requirements: Interest in music librarianship
Bibliography   Kirkegaard, P., "Denmark," in <u>ALA World Encyclopedia of Library and Information Services</u>, 2nd ed., pp. 246-248. Chicago: American Library Association, 1986.

197   Foreningen af Medarbejdere ved Danmarks Forskningsbiblioteker (FMDF) (Association of Staff Members of Research Libraries in Denmark)

Address   c/o Statsbiblioteket, Universitetsparken, DK-8000 Aarhus C (permanent). Tel: 45 (86) 125759. Telex: 64515. Fax: 45-86-132704.
Officers   (elected for 2-yr.term) Chair: Niels-Henrik Gylstorff; Vice-Chair: Jytte Halling; Treas: Kristian Salling Pedersen; Sec: Grethe Lillelund. Exec.Board: 6
Staff   None
Languages   Danish
Established   1934, as Bibliotekarsammenslutningen for Danmarks Forskningsblioteker (Association of Librarians of Danish Research Libraries). New name adopted in 1978 to broaden its membership to include all categories of staff of research libraries.
Major Fields of Interest   Research library community
Major Goals and Objectives   To further the cooperation of research libraries and to promote the research libraries at an organizational and political level by cooperating with national and international organizations
Structure   Governed by Executive Board. Affiliations: A section of Danmarks Forskningsbiblioteksforening (Danish Research Library Association), IFLA, Nordiska Vetenskapliga Bibliotekariesamfundet (NVBF)
Sources of Support   Membership dues. Budget (Danish Krone): 1986: 95,000; 1987: 105,000.
Membership   Total members: 540 (individual). Association is one of the 2 Sections of Danmarks Forskningsbiblioteksforening (DF) and members are automatically members of DF. Types of membership: Individual. Requirements: Staff member of research library. Dues (Danish Krone): 185.

General Assembly   Entire membership meets once a year.
Publications   No official journal. Association uses publications of DF.
Activities   About half of the activities take place within the scope of DF.
Bibliography   Kirkegaard, P., "Denmark," in <u>ALA World Encyclopedia of Library and Information Services</u>, 2nd ed., pp.246-248. Chicago: American Library Association, 1986.

198   Sammenslutningen af Danmarks Forskningsbiblioteker (SDF) (Association of Danish Research Libraries)

Address   c/o Statsbiblioteket, Universitetsparken, DK-8000 Aarhus C (permanent). Tel: 45 (86) 125759. Telex: 64515. Fax: 45-86-132704.
Officers   (elected for 2-yr.term) Chair: Niels Mark; Past Chair: Mette Stockmarr; Vice-Chair: Torben Nielsen; Treas: Arne Molgaard Frandsen; Sec: Ms. A. Lindahl.
Staff   None
Languages   Danish
Established   1949, Copenhagen
Major Fields of Interest   Research libraries and the library community
Major Goals and Objectives   To further cooperation and coordination between research libraries in Denmark; to promote research libraries at an organizational and political level by cooperating with national and international organizations.
Structure   Governed by Executive Board. Affiliations: A section of Danmarks Forskningsbiblioteksforening (Danish Research Library Association), IFLA
Sources of Support   Membership dues. Budget (Danish Krone): 1986/87: 100,000; 1987/88: 110,000.
Membership   Total members: 121 (institutional). Association is one of the 2 Sections of Danmarks Forskningsbiblioteksforening (DF) and members are automatically members of DF. Types of membership: Institutional. Requirements: Research or professional library. Dues (Danish Krone): From 350 to 4,000, depending on size of library
General Assembly   Entire membership meets once a year.
Publications   No official journal. Association uses publications of DF.
Activities   Active in promoting library-related legislation: Promotion of a new administrative framework resulted in the establishment of the new office of National Librarian. Sponsors general library meetings. Most of the activities take place within the scope of the Danish Research Library Association (DF).
Bibliography   Kirkegaard, P., "Denmark," in <u>ALA World Encyclopedia of Library and Information Services</u>, 2nd ed., pp. 246-248. Chicago: American Library Association, 1986.

Dominican Republic

199   Asociación Dominicana de Bibliotecarios, Inc. (ASODOBI) (Dominican Association of Librarians, Inc.)

Address   c/o Biblioteca Nacional, Plaza de la Cultura, Santo Domingo (permanent). Tel: 1 (809) 6884086.
Officers   (elected for 2-yr.term) Pres: Prospero J. Mella-Chavier; Sec: Ms. V. Regús. Exec.Board: 5
Staff   None
Languages   Spanish
Established   1974, at a Constitutional Assembly related to national libraries.
Major Fields of Interest   Librarianship and librarians
Major Goals and Objectives   To promote the extension of library services throughout the country; to promote the profession of librarianship and protect the professional interests of librarians; to procure the continuous interest of the nation in libraries; to maintain relations with other national and international organizations.
Structure   Governed by Executive Committee and General Assembly. Affiliations: IFLA
Sources of Support   Membership dues
Membership   Total members: 60 (individual). Types of membership: Individual. Requirements: Graduates of library schools, or experience/employment in libraries. Dues (Dominican Peso): 15
General Assembly   Entire membership meets once a year.
Publications   *Official journal:* El Papiro. 1976-. 3/yr. Free to members. Editor: Miriam Michel de Campusano. Address same as Association. Circ: 500. Spanish.
Activities   Sponsors workshops, meetings, continuing education programs, compilation of national bibliography; presents awards for outstanding achievements.
Bibliography   Florén, M., "Dominican Republic," in ALA World Encyclopedia of Library and Information Services, 2nd ed., pp. 252-255. Chicago; American Library Association, 1986 (tr. by E.S. Gleaves)

200   Association of University Libraries

Address   c/o Biblioteca de la Universidad Autónoma de Santo Domingo, Ciudad Universitaria, Apdo 1355, Santo Domingo
Staff   None
Languages   Spanish
Established   1978, by resolution of CONIES (National Council of Institutions of Higher Learning)
Major Fields of Interest   University libraries
Major Goals and Objectives   To coordinate activities of university libraries in developing their collections as well as channels of communication, in order to avoid duplication of efforts.
Bibliography   Florén, M., "Dominican Republic," in ALA World Encyclopedia of Library and Information Services, 2nd ed. pp. 252-255. Chicago: American Library Association, 1986 (tr. by E.S. Gleaves)

Ecuador

201 Asociación Ecuatoriana de Administradores de Documentos y Archivos (Ecuadorian Association of Administrators of Documents and Archives)

Address c/o Archivo-Biblioteca de la Función Legislativa, Palacio Legislativo, Quito
Officers Pres: Lic. Rafael A. Piedra y Solis.

202 Asociación Ecuatoriana de Bibliotecarios (AEB) (Ecuadorian Library Association)

Address c/o Casa de la Cultura Ecuatoriana, Casilla 87, Quito (permanent). Tel: 593 (2) 528840; Headquarters 593 (2) 253474.
Officers (elected for 1-yr.term) Pres: Carmen Carrera Carrillo; VP: Julia de Buchelly; Exec.Sec: Elizabeth Carrion; Treas: Guadalupe Hidaleo. Exec.Comm: 15
Staff None
Languages Spanish
Established 1945, at the Casa de la Cultura Ecuatoriana (Ecuatorian Cultural Center), Quito
Major Fields of Interest Professional training and the establishment of new libraries
Major Goals and Objectives Established as a professional and cultural organization with national and international interests "to promote and improve libraries in Ecuador, to recruit able members to the library profession" (Statutes, arts. 1-2,i,j).
Structure Governed by Executive Council meeting once a month.
Sources of Support Membership dues
Membership Total members: 450 (individual). Types of membership: Individual, honorary. Requirements: Open to any person who works in a library. Dues (Sucre): 80.
General Assembly Entire membership meets annually.
Publications *Official journal*: Unidad Bibliotecaria. 1973-. 3/yr. Free to members. Address same as Association. Circ: 500. Spanish. Publishes Boletín Bibliográfico Ecuatoriano. No other publications program.
Activities After some inactivity, Association was revived in 1965, and is currently very active in sponsoring conferences, continuing education programs, and furthering the development of the profession in the country.
Bibliography Gorman, M., "Ecuador," in ALA World Encyclopedia of Library and Information Services, 2nd ed., pp. 259-260. Chicago: American Library Association, 1986.

Egypt

203   Egyptian Association for Scientific and Technical Libraries and Information Centres

Address   c/o National Information and Documentation Centre, Sh. Al-Tahrir, Dokki, Cairo
Officers   Chair: Ahmed Kabesh; Vice-Chair: Abdel Bassit; Sec.Gen: Adael El-Duweini; Treas: A. El-Bashari; other officers: Hoda El-Sharaway, Omnia Moussa (British Council Librarian), Essam Abdel-Khaffey. Exec.Board: 7
Staff   None
Languages   Arabic
Established   1988, Cairo
Major Fields of Interest   Scientific and technical libraries and information services
Major Goals and Objectives   To serve librarians and information workers in the field of science and technology in Egypt; to promote liaison with other societies in Egypt and abroad.
Structure   Governed by Executive Board
Sources of Support   Membership dues
Membership   Requirements: Scientific/technical libraries or information centers
Activities   The Association was established with the initiative of Chris Harison, Books and Libraries Officer in the British Council, Egypt, and its program of activities and publications is being developed.
Bibliography   "Egyptian Association for Scientific and Technical Libraries Established," Herald of Library Science 38 (1989):142-143.

204   Egyptian Library and Archives Association (ELAA)

Address   c/o Library of Fine Arts, 24 El-Matbaa, Al-Ahlia, Boulac, Cairo
Officers   Pres: S.M. El Shemiti; Exec.Sec: Ahmed M. Mansour.
Staff   None
Languages   Arabic
Established   1946, Cairo, as Cairo Library Association; became Egyptian Library Association in 1952; present name adopted in 1970.
Major Fields of Interest   Library and archive development, education and training
Major Goals and Objectives   To improve professional standards of librarianship and archival science; to further the development of library and archival collections; to increase publications of Arabic library and archives literature.
Structure   Governed by Executive Board
Sources of Support   Membership dues
Membership   Total members: Approx. 600. Requirements: Open to Egyptian librarians and archivists, as well as overseas librarians working in Egyptian libraries and archives. Members include Egyptians, Syrians, Jordanians, Palestinians, and other Arab nationals.
General Assembly   Entire membership meets annually.
Publications   *Official journal:* Alam al-Maktabát (Library World). 1958-1970. 6/yr. Superseded by Sahifat al-Maktabát (Library Journal), published by the Egyptian School Library Association.
Activities   Carried out in accordance with the goals and objectives of the Association, in order to improve development of libraries and archives in Egypt.

Bibliography   Aman, M.M., and Khalifa, Sha'Ban, "Egypt," in <u>ALA World Encyclopedia of Library and Information Services</u>, 2nd ed., pp. 264-265. Chicago: American Library Association, 1986.

205   Egyptian School Library Association (ESLA)

Address   35 Algalaa Street, Cairo (permanent). Tel: (20) 45201
Officers   (elected for 5-yr.term) Pres: Medhat Kazem; VP: M.A. Al-Kabbah; Exec.Sec: M. Salem; Treas: Gamal Shaalan. Exec.Council: 15
Staff   8 (3 paid, 5 volunteers)
Languages   Arabic
Established   1967, Cairo
Major Fields of Interest   School libraries
Major Goals and Objectives   To raise technical standards of members; to develop library service in schools; to work towards increasing the reading ability of pupils in different types of schools; to update technical methods in school libraries.
Structure   Governed by Executive Council.
Sources of Support   Membership dues, private gifts, sale of publications
Membership   1,200 (1,140 individual, 60 institutional). Types of membership: Individual, institutional, student, honorary. Requirements: Open to school librarians in particular and to personnel in public libraries and educational fields.
General Assembly   Entire membership meets annually in Cairo.
Publications   *Official journal:* <u>Sahifat al-Maktabát</u> (Library Journal). 1969-. 3/yr. Free to members. Editor: Mehat Kazem. Address same as Association. Circ: 1,300. Arabic. Other publications: Annual reports, proceedings of conferences, seminars, workshops.
Activities   Association was instrumental in working for a ministerial decree regarding improvement of library services and the status of librarians. Sponsors various continuing education programs and is expanding its publication program to include, for example, a School Library Directory.

El Salvador

206   Asociación de Bibliotecarios de El Salvador (ABES)
(Association of Salvadoran Librarians)

Address   Urbanización Gerado Barrios Polígono, "B" No. 5, San Salvador, C.A. (permanent). Tel: (503) 220409/253471.
Officers   (elected for 2-yr.term) Pres: Raúl Humberto Flores; VP: Ana del Rosario Luna; Sec.Gen: Edgar Antonio Pérez Borja; Treas: José Joaquin Pérez. Exec.Comm: 9
Languages   Spanish, Portuguese, English
Established   1958, at the Biblioteca Nacional, San Salvador
Major Fields of Interest   Libraries and library education
Major Goals and Objectives   To promote the education and economic status of librarians; to establish, organize, and maintain libraries at all levels; to create a school of librarianship and organize a curriculum for library science; to promote a national bibliography, and to maintain the exchange of professional experiences and ideas among the members of the association.
Structure   Governed by Executive Committee. Affiliations: FID
Sources of Support   Membership dues
Membership   100 (43 individual, 57 institutional). Chapters: 3. Divisions: 5. Types of membership: Individual, institutional, life, honorary. Requirements: Open to those with at least two years experience in the library field, and to holders of the degree of Bachelor of Science and Letters, who work in libraries in El Salvador.
General Assembly   Entire membership meets once a year in July at the Biblioteca Nacional in San Salvador.
Publications   *Official journal*: Informa: Boletín Mensual (newsletter). 1973-. 12/yr. Free to members. Editor: Edgar Antonio Pérez Borja. Address same as Association. Spanish, English, Portuguese. Circ: 150. Issues annual reports and other occasional publications.
Activities   Sponsors conferences, meetings and other activities to carry out the goals and objectives of the Association.
Bibliography   Fernández de Criado, Jeannette, "El Salvador," in ALA World Encyclopedia of Library and Information Services, 2nd ed., pp.266-267. Chicago: American Library Association, 1986.

207   Asociación General de Archivistas de El Salvador
(Association of Salvadoran Archivists)

Address   c/o Edificio Sede 8, Calle Oriente 314, San Salvador.

Ethiopia

208   Ethiopian Library Association (ELA) / Ye Ethiopia Betemetsahft Serategnot Mahber

Address   PO Box 30530, Addis Ababa (permanent). Tel: (251) 110844 ext.353.
Officers   (elected for indefinite term) Exec.Sec: Befekadu Debela. Exec.Comm: 4
Staff   None
Languages   Amharic, English
Established   1967, Addis Ababa; official status as a registered society, in 1969.
Major Fields of Interest   Public library service
Major Goals and Objectives   To establish and develop library service throughout Ethiopia; to improve public library facilities; to further education and training of librarians.
Structure   Governed by executive officers. Affiliations: IFLA, AIDBA.
Sources of Support   Membership dues.
Membership   110 (105 individual, 5 institutional). Chapters: 5. Types of membership: Individual, institutional. Requirements: Open to those who work in libraries or in related fields. Dues: Scaled according to salary and institutional income.
General Assembly   Entire membership meets once a year in Addis Ababa.
Publications   *Official journal:* Ethiopian Library Association Bulletin. 1965-. 2/yr. (Ethiopian Birr) 85. Free to members. Editor: Adhana Mengste-Ab. Address same as Association. Amharic, English. Circ: 180. Other publications: Directory of Ethiopian Libraries.
Activities   Promoting the use of libraries to the public through radio, newspapers, etc.; sponsors conferences, seminars, continuing education programs; supports literacy programs; works for development of school libraries.
Bibliography   Mengste-Ab, Adhana, "Ethiopia," in ALA World Encyclopedia of Library and Information Services, 2nd ed., pp. 270-272. Chicago: American Library Association, 1986.

Fiji

209   Fiji Library Association (FLA)

Address   c/o Secretary, Box 2292, Government Buildings, Suva (permanent).
Officers   (elected for 1-yr.term) Pres: Ms. D. Simmons; Past Pres: Narendra Nandan;
VP: Elizabeth Fong; Sec: Ms. I. Kuruvoli: Treas: Kanchan Dayal; other officers: Sue Cumberpatch, Joan Teiawa, Lalita Sudhaker, Louisa Finiasi, Lusi Ravuvu, Joan Yee.
Exec.Board: 8
Staff   None
Languages   English
Established   1972, Suva, at University of the South Pacific.
Major Fields of Interest   Development and improvement of library services and training
Major Goals and Objectives   To encourage and foster development of libraries, librarianship, archives and archivists and other associated activities within Fiji and the
South Pacific; to unite all persons engaged or interested in library work; to promote the
better administration of libraries, and the position and qualifications of library personnel;
to assist in the promotion of legislation affecting libraries; to cooperate with other groups
in promoting these aims.
Structure   Governed by FLA Council. Affiliations: COMLA, IFLA
Sources of Support   Membership dues, sale of publications, fundraising.
Membership   92 (80 individual, 12 institutional). 9 countries represented. Type of membership: Individual, institutional, overseas, life. Requirements: Applicants for membership
accepted under rules prescribed by the Association. Open to any person or institution
maintaining libraries or archives. Dues: According to income.
General Assembly   Entire membership meets annually in Suva, in December.
Publications   *Official journal:* Fiji Library Association Journal (formerly Newsletter).
1973-. irreg. Free to members. Address same as Association. Editor: Sue Oates. Circ:
130+. English. Indexed in LISA. Other publications: Proceedings of meetings, annual reports, Libraries and Archives in Fiji; Selection Guide for General References; Fiji Library Directory, and others. Publications for sale, price lists available. No publications
exchange program in effect, but the Association would consider exchanging with other
national associations; the University of the South Pacific Library buys 40+ copies of the
Journal for exchange purposes.
Activities   Past achievements: Holding annual National Library Week since 1979;
sponsoring workshops funded by the Asia Foundation; organizing an annual Fiji Certificate in Librarianship course for the training of paraprofessionals. Current: Continue professional staff training programs for government librarians; organize programs for National Library Week. Future: Prepare a compendium of community library experiences
and resources in the Pacific countries with COMLA support; publish a collection of children's stories. Sponsors seminars, workshops, and other continuing education programs.
Bibliography   Holdsworth, H., "Fiji," in ALA World Encyclopedia of Library and Information Services, 2nd ed., pp. 278-279. Chicago: American Library Association, 1986.

Finland

210   Arkistoyhdistys r.y. - Arkivföreningen r.f. (AY-AF)
(Archival Association)

Address   c/o Valtionarkisto (National Archives), PO Box 258, SF-00171 Helsinki (permanent). Tel: 358 (0) 176911.
Officers   (elected for 1-yr.term) Chair: Raimo Pohjola; Members of Board: Raija Majamaa, Pekka Pirilä, Kauko Rumpunen; Sec: Lisa Salasmaa. Exec.Board: 5
Staff   None
Languages   Finnish, Swedish
Established   May 24, 1947, first organizational meeting in Helsinki
Major Fields of Interest   Archives and professional development of archivists
Major Goals and Objectives   To establish communication between all archivists and to promote knowledge in all essential questions in the archival field
Structure   Governed by Executive Council
Sources of Support   Membership dues, sale of publications.
Membership   Total members: 190 (individual). Types of membership: Individual. Requirements: Archival staff of the state administration and private archives; research workers and others with professional interest in archival matters. Dues (Markka): 30, individual; 5 (voluntary), retired; no dues for honorary members.
General Assembly   Entire membership meets annually, with informal meetings on special themes 3 to 4 times a year.
Publications   No official journal. Publishes series, <u>Arkisto</u> (Archives) in Finnish, with Swedish summaries.
Activities   Sponsors annual meetings and special meetings; arranges excursions to major archives and other places of interest; continues publication program; sponsors continuing education seminars, workshops.

211   Bibliothecarii Medicinae Fenniae r.y. (BMF)
(Finnish Association of Medical Librarians)

Address   c/o Medical Library, Kuopio University Central Hospital, SF-70210 Kuopio (not permanent). Tel: 358 (71) 173770. Telex: 42218. Fax: 358-71-163410.
Officers   (elected for 2-yr.term) Pres: I. Vakkari; Past Pres: Terttu Soini; VP: Irja-Liisa Öberg; Sec: J. Karppinen. Exec.Board: 7
Staff   None
Languages   Finnish, Swedish
Established   Nov. 14, 1980, constitutive meeting.
Major Fields of Interest   Medical librarianship and librarians
Major Goals and Objectives   To be a connecting link between the personnel in medical libraries in Finland. This is done by developing medical libraries and professional skills of the personnel and making the medical libraries known. On the operational level, these goals are carried out by training, informing and publishing, by arranging meetings, by promoting bills and making statements, and by participating in international cooperative activities.
Structure   Governed by Executive Board. Affiliations: IFLA
Sources of Support   Membership dues, sale of publications, occasional subsidies.
Membership   Total members: 74 (individual). Types of membership: Individual. Requirements: Biomedical librarianship. Dues (Markka): 60, individual, honorary, corresponding.

General Assembly   Entire membership meets twice a year (statutory meetings)
Publications   No official journal, but sends out membership letters. Other publications: Guide books; Pekkarinen, Päivi, and Toivari, Seija, eds., <u>Lääketieteellinen kirjasto: Opaskirja</u>. No publications exchange program.
Activities   In accordance with the stated goals and objectives: Expanding the Association by bringing together medical librarians in Finland; sponsoring information exchanges, publishing, training; participating in activities of international medical librarianship; offering continuing education programs.

212   Finlands Svenska Biblioteksförening r.f.
(The Finnish-Swedish Library Association)

Address   Linvävaregatan 2, SF-10600 Ekenäs (not permanent). Tel: 358 (911) 12361.
Officers   Pres: Kerstin Rosenqvist; Sec: Ms. K. Virtanan.
Staff   None
Languages   Swedish, Finnish
Established   Nov. 13, 1982, through a merger of two regional associations of Swedish-language librarians, Södra Finlands svenska biblioteksförening (for Southern Finland) and Österbottens svenska biblioteksförening (for Ostrobothnia, i.e. west Finland).
Major Fields of Interest   Swedish-language librarianship
Major Goals and Objectives   To promote the interests and professional development of Swedish-language librarians in Finland
Structure   Governed by Executive Council. Affiliations: IFLA (since 1987).
Sources of Support   Membership dues
General Assembly   Entire membership meets annually.
Bibliography   "Finlands Svenska Biblioteksförening," <u>Kirjastolehti</u> 75 (1982):627-628.

213   Kirjastonhoitajien Keskusliitto - Bibliotekariernas Centralföbund (KKL)
(Central Federation of Librarians)

Address   Rautatieläisenkatu 6, SF-00520 Helsinki (permanent). Tel: 358 (90) 1502479.
Officers   Gen.Sec: Marjatta Huuhtanen. Exec.Board: 6
Staff   5 (paid)
Languages   Finnish
Established   1945.
Major Fields of Interest   Coordination between library associations
Major Goals and Objectives   To serve as a central organ of professional librarians to further their social and economic interests. To coordinate the work of the three following associations: (1) Suomen Kirjastonhoitajat-Finlands Bibliotekarier r.y. (Finnish Librarians; 900+ members from public libraries); (2) Kirjastonhoitajat ja Informaatikot-Bibliotekarier och Informatiker r.y. (Association of Research and University Librarians; 300+ members); (3) Kirjastonhoitajien Keskusliiton Helsingin Seudun Osasto r.y. (Division of the librarians in the Helsinki area of KKL)
Structure   Governed by Executive Board. Affiliations: AKAVA r.y. (Finnish Professional Workers' Central Organization)
Sources of Support   Membership dues
Membership   Total members: 1,700+ (individual, = membership of the 3 associations). Requirements: KKL is the librarians' national trade organization and members are mainly employed by local libraries.
General Assembly   Entire membership meets once a year.

Publications   *Official journal:* Kirjastonhoitaja / Bibliotekarien (ISSN-0355 7324). 1973-. Irreg. (Markka) 130. Editor: Riitta Valtonen. Address same as Association. Finnish. Circ: 2,000+.
Activities   Sponsors meetings, seminars and other activities in accordance with the goals and objectives of the Federation.

214   Kirjastotieteen ja Informatiikan Yhdistys r.y.
(Finnish Association of Library and Information Science)

Address   c/o Department of Library and Information Science, University of Tampere, PO Box 607, SF-33101 Tampere 10 (permanent). Tel: 358 (931) 156111. Telex: 22263. Fax: 358-931-134473.
Officers   Pres: Pertti Vakkari; Sec: Juha Hakala; Past Pres: Maria Forsuku; VP: Irmeli Hovi; Treas: Arja Kärkkäinen; Sec: J. Karppinen. Exec.Board: 11
Staff   4 (volunteers)
Languages   Finnish, Swedish
Established   Dec. 1979, Tampere
Major Fields of Interest   Library Science and information research.
Major Goals and Objectives   To promote library science and informatics as a science and as a field of research.
Structure   Governed by Executive Board. Affiliations: IFLA.
Sources of Support   Membership dues, sale of publications, government subsidies. Budget (Markka): 1986/87: 30,000.
Membership   Total members: 180 (175 individual, 5 institutional).
General Assembly   Entire membership meets twice a year.
Publications   *Official journal:* Kirjasstotiede ja Informatiikka. 1981-. 4/yr. 120 Markka. Free to members. Indexed in LISA, ISA. Publications exchange program in effect.
Activities   Past achievements: Annual research seminars for scientists and librarians who are interested in library science and informatics. Current: Publishing the journal; sponsoring research seminars.
Use of High Technology   Computers for management

215   Suomen Kirjastoseura - Finlands Biblioteksförening
(The Finnish Library Association) (FLA)

Address   Museokatu 18A 5, SF-00100 Helsinki (permanent). Tel: 358 (0) 492532.
Officers   (elected for 2-yr.term) Pres: R. Vosukainen; Past Pres: Pentti Lahti-Nuuttila; 1st VP: Liisa Laatu; 2nd VP: Helvi Linna; Sec.Gen (appointed): Tuula Haavisto. Exec.Board: 9
Staff   7 (paid: 6 full-time, 1 part-time)
Languages   Finnish
Established   1910, Helsinki
Major Fields of Interest   Finnish library policy in general, including all types of libraries
Major Goals and Objectives   To promote the development of library services, to make people aware of the libraries' social and academic roles and their cultural significance, and to enhance the professional skills of those involved in the library field.
Structure   Governed by Executive Council. Affiliations: IFLA
Sources of Support   Membership dues, sale of publications, government subsidies, grants from private and public foundations. Budget (Markka): 1986: 2,378,570; 1987: 2,925,505; 1988: 2,962,000.

Membership Total members: 3,035 (2,980 individual, 55 institutional). Divisions: 4. Standing Committees: 6. Requirements: Open to any library supporter, e.g., library staff, library committee members, and library users. Dues (Markka): 100, individual; 50, library students; 200, institutional.

General Assembly Entire membership meets every two years. 1987: Tampere; 1989: Imatra, at a national public library conference.

Publications *Official journal:* Kirjastolehti (Library Journal). 1908-. 12/yr. (including 1 double issue). Address same as Association. (Markka) 170 (195, foreign). Free to members. Sub-Editor: Seppo Verho. Address same as Association. Circ: 7,800. Finnish, Swedish, English, and Swedish abstracts. Indexed in LISA, KATI (includes Finnish articles and monographs); Kirjastokalenteri (Library calendar). Other publications: Professional literature in Finnish; available from Kirjastopalvelu Oy (Library Services Ltd), Särkieniementie 5, SF-00210 Helsinki. Price lists issued in Finnish. Publications exchange program of journal only.

Activities Past achievements: New Public Library Act, 1985; FLA's 75th anniversary with celebrations, 1985; experimental project on the use of ADP 1985-87; starting a national Library Week in 1984 with nomination of the librarian of the year; developing cooperation in the library field, e.g., training of 2 Namibian students in librarianship, starting 1985. Current: Publishing the Journal and other professional publications; organizing training courses; international contacts in different areas; public relations work for the library field; organizing national library meeting in Tampere, 11-13 June, 1987 (with about 1,000 participants); organizing national 500th celebration year of the Finnish Book in 1988. Future: Following up the development of ADP in libraries; following up the effects of the new Public Library Act and the development of state grants to libraries. Association has been active in promoting library-related legislation: The new Public Library Act, which came into force in April 1986, was initiated by FLA, and FLA followed very carefully the reading of the law in Parliament.

Use of High Technology In planning phase

Bibliography "Goals of the Finnish Library Association," Kirjastolehti 74 (1981):271-274 (in Finnish); Hamalainen, S., "Library Organisations Demand a More Developed Library Network," Kirjastolehti 76 (1983):198-200 (in Finnish); "Operational Plan of the Finnish Library Association for 1984," ibid.:201-203 (in Finnish); Koski, P., Suomen kirjastoseura 1910-1985. Helsinki: FLA, 1985 (ISBN 951-9025-40-5, includes English summary); "Suomen Kirjastoseura 1910-1985," Library Times International 2 (Sept. 1985):30; Sievänen-Allen, R., "Finland," in ALA World Encyclopedia of Library and Information Services, 2nd ed., pp. 280-282. Chicago: American Library Association, 1986.

216 Suomen Tieteellinen Kirjastoseura r.y. - Finlands Vetenskapliga Biblioteksamfund r.f.
(Finnish Research Library Association)

Address PO Box 217, SF-00171 Helsinki (permanent). Tel: 358 (921) 654293. Telex: 62301.
Officers (elected for 2-yr.term) Pres: M. Honko; Sec: R. Matilla.
Staff 2 (paid)
Languages Finnish, Swedish
Established 1929, Helsinki
Major Fields of Interest Research libraries and information services

Major Goals and Objectives To promote research and information activities concerning research libraries and information services; to develop the professional skills of its members; to participate in national and international cooperation in the library field.
Structure Governed by Executive Committee. Affiliations: IFLA, NVBF (Nordic Union of Research Librarians).
Sources of Support Membership dues, sale of publications, government subsidies.
Membership Total members: 600 (596 individual, 4 institutional). Sections: 6 (General Service, Interlending, Education, Study Tours, Research and Planning, Periodicals). Requirements: Anyone working in the fields of research libraries and information services or related areas, or anyone interested in furthering the aims of the Association. Dues (Markka): 60, individual; 300, institutional.
General Assembly Entire membership meets twice a year.
Publications *Official journal:* Signum. 1968-. 8/yr. (Markka) 210. Free to members. Address same as Association. Editor: R. Haenninen. Address: Aallonhuippu 12, B19, SF-02320 Espoo. Circ: 1,500. Finnish, Swedish, English abstracts. Other publications: Guide to Research Libraries and Information Services in Finland.
Activities Sponsors conferences, seminars, educational courses, as well as regular monthly meetings on topics of current interest. The 6 sections of the Association also provide a variety of activities. Trips, organized by the Study Tour Section, offer an opportunity for visiting foreign libraries.
Bibliography Sievänen-Allen, R., "Finland," in ALA World Encyclopedia of Library and Information Services, 2nd ed., pp. 280-282. Chicago: American Library Association, 1986.

217 Tietopalveluseura
(Finnish Society for Information Services) (formerly Suomen Kirjallisuuspalvelun Seura, Finnish Association for Documentation)

Address Mannerheimintie 40A 32, SF-00100 Helsinki (permanent). Tel: 358 (0) 408309.
Officers Chair: Merja Kamvalo; Vice-Chairs: Hillevi Iatvmlahti, Annikki Pirnes; Sec (appointed): Hannele Heikkinen. Exec.Board: 11.
Staff 1 (paid); numerous volunteers.
Languages Finnish
Established 1947 as Suomen Kirjallisuuspalvelun Seura (Finnish Association for Documentation); name changed to Tietopalveluseura - Samfundet för Informationsjänst i Finland.
Major Fields of Interest Information services; information resources management.
Major Goals and Objectives To promote information services and act as a bond between individuals and organizations in the information field
Structure Governed by Executive Board. Affiliations: FID, EUSIDIC.
Sources of Support Membership dues.
Membership Total members: 650 (615 individual, 35 institutional). Requirements: Open to individuals, companies and other organizations interested in the aims of the Association. Members work in companies, government and municipal offices, universities, research institutes, and various associations.
General Assembly Entire membership meets annually.
Publications Issues two journals.
Activities Organizes training seminars, handles public relations, and cooperates with national and international organizations in the field; publishes journals, prepares standards, and takes part in document classification.

Bibliography   Sievänen-Allen, R., "Finland," in <u>ALA World Encyclopedia of Library and Information Services</u>, 2nd ed., pp. 280-282. Chicago: American Library Association, 1986.

France

218   Amicale des Directeurs de Bibliothèques Universitaires (ADBU) (Association of Directors of University Libraries)

Address 5 Rue Auguste Vacquerie, F-75116 Paris.
Officers Pres: M. Thoumieux; VPs: M. Brouillard, Ms. Jobert.
Staff None
Languages French
Established 1971. After the university reform of 1968 and the creation of new statutes for university libraries in 1970, directors of university libraries felt the need to organize and cooperate.
Major Fields of Interest Management of university libraries
Major Goals and Objectives (1) To defend university libraries against public authorities, (2) to study problems specific to the organization and administration of university libraries, and (3) to coordinate policies and technical procedures on matters outside the jurisdiction of the library service (e.g., photocopying fees and interlibrary loan).
Structure Governed by Executive Board. Affiliations: IFLA.
Sources of Support Membership dues.
Membership Total members: Approx.100. Members are the directors of all university libraries, plus one section chief per library. No other members admitted.
General Assembly Entire membership meets once a year.
Publications No official journal. Publishes occasional technical reports, such as a "Guide to Interlibrary Lending."
Activities Sponsors conferences, meetings; publications.
Bibliography Chauveinc, M., "France," in ALA World Encyclopedia of Library and Information Services, 2nd ed., pp. 285-292. Chicago: American Library Association, 1986; "Pour une politique documentaire nationale," Documentaliste 23 (1986):155-162 .

219   Association de l'École Nationale Supérieure des Bibliothécaires (AENSB) (Association of the National School of Librarianship)

Address 17-21 Boulevard du 11 Novembre 1918, F-69100 Villeurbanne (permanent). Tel: (33) 78896445.
Officers (elected for 1-yr.term) Pres: Arlette Pailley-Katz; VPs: Jacques Dedeyan, Français Larbre; Treas: Marie-Françoise Bois; Sec: Ms. C. Baryla; Past Pres: Michel Marion. Exec.Board: 8
Staff None
Languages French
Established 1967, Paris, as successor to the Association des Titulaires des Diplômes Supérieures de Bibliothécaires (founded 1960).
Major Fields of Interest Library and information science; professional education; new technology.
Major Goals and Objectives To create and maintain a spirit of cooperation among members; to contribute to the development of the National School of Librarianship; to maintain placement services for library school graduates; to promote research in library science and the professional development of librarians through conferences, publications, and other activities; to establish cooperative relationships with other organizations at a national and international level.
Structure Governed by elected Council of 21 members and executive officers. Affiliations: IFLA.

Sources of Support   Membership dues, sale of publications.
Membership   Total members: 600 (individual). Types of membership: Individual, life, student, emeritus, honorary. Requirements: Diploma of the l'École Nationale Supérieure de Bibliothécaires (ENSB). Dues (French Franc): 70.
General Assembly   Entire membership meets once a year.
Publications   *Official journal:* Bulletin de l'AENSB (supersedes Note d'Information). 1979-. 4/yr. Free to members. Address same as Association. Circ: Membership. French. Issues yearbook (Annuaire de l'Association de l'École Nationale Supérieure des Bibliothécaires). A founding member of Presses de l'ENSB, which publishes professional books in library and information science.
Activities   Making the library profession known and solving professional problems; working with the Library School for educational reform; working for professional recognition and for improving the civil service status of librarians. Association has been active in promoting library-related legislation, such as the reform of national graduate library schools.
Use of High Technology   Computers for management and information dissemination.
Bibliography   Chauveinc, M., "France," in ALA World Encyclopedia of Library and Information Services, 2nd ed., pp. 285-292. Chicago: American Library Association, 1986; "Pour une politique documentaire nationale," Documentaliste 23 (1986):155-162.

220   Association de l'Institut National des Techniques de la Documentation (AINTD)
(Association of the National Institute for Information Science)

Address   6 Rue Henri Barbusse, F-75005 Paris (permanent). Tel: (33) 42735243.
Officers   (elected for 1-yr.term) Pres: Anne-Françoise Pillias; Treas: Marie-Thérése Belaygue; Sec: Annie Buffeteau. Exec.Board: 3
Staff   3 (volunteers)
Languages   French
Established   1953, Paris, as Association des Anciens Elèves de l'INTD; present name adopted in 1970.
Major Fields of Interest   Documentation and information science; promotion of the profession
Major Goals and Objectives   To bring together the alumni and students of the INTD (Institut National des Techniques de la Documentation); to cooperate with other institutions for the improvement of documentation and documentation techniques; to promote the professional development and exchange of information between members through publications and meetings; to represent the professional interests of members; to assist members in public and private employment.
Structure   Governed by Executive Council.
Sources of Support   Membership dues, sale of publications. Budget (French Franc): 1986/87: 40,000.
Membership   Total members: 300 (individual). 10 countries represented. Requirements: To be a student or graduate of the Institute. Dues (French Franc): 120, individual; 50, student.
General Assembly   Entire membership meets once a year in Paris, in December.
Publications   *Official journal:* AINTD - Story. 1983-. 4/yr. Free to members. Address same as Association. Circ: Membership. French. Other publications: Annuaire des anciens élèves de l'INTD (1/yr). No publications exchange program.
Activities   Past and current: Publication of the annual; publication and distribution of documentation on the information scientist from INTD; gives aid to students of library

science and promotes the graduates. Future: To organize conferences on library and information science. Association was active in promoting library-related legislation, such as submitting, with other French associations, statements on the status of librarians to the administrative authorities and ministers.
Bibliography   "Pour une politique documentaire nationale," Documentaliste 23 (1986):155-162.

221   Association des Archivistes Français
(Association of French Archivists)

Address   60 Rue des Francs-Bourgeois, F-75141 Paris, Cedex 03 (permanent). Tel: 33 (1) 42771130
Officers   (elected for 2-yr.term) Pres: Ms. R. Cleyet-Michaud; Secs: Ms. M. P. Arnauld, Ms. E. Gautier-Desuaux. Exec.Board: 12
Staff   6 (volunteers)
Languages   French
Established   1904, Paris
Major Fields of Interest   Archives management, preservation, and research.
Major Goals and Objectives   To promote the development of archives; to improve all aspects of archives management, preservation and research.
Structure   Governed by Executive Board. Affiliations: ICA
Sources of Support   Membership dues.
Membership   Total members: Approx.550. 22 countries represented. Types of membership: Individual, institutional, honorary. Requirements: Interest in aims of Association. Dues (French Franc): 60-100, individual; 350, institutional.
General Assembly   Entire membership meets annually.
Publications   *Official journal:* La Gazette des Archives. 1933-. 4/yr. (French Franc) 180. Free to members. Editor: Gerard Moyse. Address same as Association. Circ: 1,500. French. Publications exchange program with other associations in effect.
Activities   Special issues of the journal on business archives, audiovisual archives, municipal archives, and others.
Bibliography   "Pour une politique documentaire nationale," Documentaliste 23 (1986):155-162.

222   Association des Bibliothécaires Français (ABF)
(Association of French Librarians)

Address   4 Rue Louvois, F-75002 Paris (permanent). Tel: 33 (1) 42975767. Telex: 212614.
Officers   (elected for 3-yr. term) Pres: Françoise Danset; Gen.Sec: Thierry Giappiconi; Treas: Alain Pansu. Exec.Board: 8
Staff   1.5 (paid)
Languages   French
Established   1906, reorganized 1969, new statutes adopted 1972.
Major Fields of Interest   Librarianship and library services
Major Goals and Objectives   To unite those who work in all types of libraries in France; to study all aspects of a scientific, technical, or administrative nature regarding libraries and their personnel; to defend the interests of libraries and of reading; to promote the development of all types of libraries and provide information on new technologies; and to represent French libraries at other national, foreign and international institutions and organizations.

Structure Governed by a National Council of 30 elected members and executive officers. Affiliations: IFLA.
Sources of Support Membership dues, sale of publications, government subsidies.
Membership Total members: 2,000+ (1,700 individual, 300 institutional). Sections: 4 (National Library, Public, Special, University libraries). Regional Groups: 19. Types of membership: Individual, institutional, honorary. Requirements: Open to all those working in libraries or interested in the work of libraries. Dues (French Franc): 50-160, individual, depending on salary; 280, institutional.
General Assembly Entire membership meets once a year.
Publications *Official journal:* Bulletin d'Informations de l'A.B.F.. 1907-. 3/yr. (French Franc) 250. Free to members. Address same as Association. Circ: Membership. French. Indexed in ISA, LISA, Lib.Lit.. Other publications: Note d'Information (supplementary newsnotes to Bulletin), 2/yr.; Annuaire des adhérents (Membership Directory); Lecture publique (published by the Section of Public Libraries); reports of seminars, workshops, and other professional monographs on current issues. Publications for sale; listed in journal; price lists available. Publications exchanged with other library associations.
Activities As the oldest and largest library association in France, the Association represents the profession in a very broad sense. Many activities are carried out by the sections (by types of library) and the 19 regional groups, which have their own governing bodies. Sponsors continuing education programs, workshops, seminars, and annual conferences. Serves as a coordinating body between governmental and private libraries, and between all libraries and the government.
Use of High Technology Computers (Olivetti-LOGABAX) for management.
Bibliography Lethève, J., "On the Occasion of the 75th Anniversary of the French Librarians Association: A Retrospective View," Bulletin d'Information de l'ABF 112 (1981):31-32 (in French); Chauveinc, M., "France," in ALA World Encyclopedia of Library and Information Services, 2nd ed., pp. 285-292. Chicago: American Library Association, 1986; "Pour une politique documentaire nationale," Documentaliste 12 (1986):155-162; Terrac, J.-C., "L'association 'Dialogue entre les cultures'," (The Association 'Dialogue between Cultures') Bulletin d'Informations de l'ABF 132 (1986):36-37 (in French); David, Philippe, "Droits de l'homme, solidarité professionnelle des bibliothécaires et relations internationales: l'activité de la commission de l'ABF," (Human Rights, Professional Solidarity of Librarians and International Relations: The Activity of the French Librarians Association commission), ibid.:48-49 (in French); Gascuel, J., "Assemblée générale: compte rendu d'activité," (The General Assembly: Report of Activities), Bulletin d'Informations de l'ABF 136 (1987):47-48; Antoine, D., "Travail sur le fichier des adhérents de l'ABF," (Analysis of the ABF Membership), ibid.:53-60.

223 Association des Bibliothèques Ecclésiastiques de France (ABEF) (Association of French Theological Libraries)

Address 6 Rue du Regard, F-75006 Paris (permanent)
Officers Exec.Sec: Jean-Marie Barbier
Staff None
Languages French
Established 1963, Paris
Major Fields of Interest Theological libraries
Major Goals and Objectives To further the development of theological libraries through increased cooperation.

Structure Governed by Executive Committee. Affiliations: Conseil International des Associations de Bibliothèques de Théologie (International Council of Theological Library Associations).
Sources of Support Membership dues
Membership Total members: 134. Types of membership: Institutional. Requirements: Libraries of seminaries, monasteries, convents, and other similar institutions. Dues (French Franc): 50.
General Assembly Entire membership meets once a year.
Publications *Official journal:* Bulletin de Liaison de l'ABEF. 1971-. 4/yr. (French Franc) 15. Free to members. Address same as Association. Circ: 160. French.
Activities Commissions on technical services are charged with aiding members in their work; some cooperative activities with International Council of Theological Library Associations.

224 Association des Diplômés de l'École de Bibliothécaires-Documentalistes (ADEBD)
(Association of Graduates of the School of Librarians / Documentalists)

Address c/o Bibliothèque du Saulchoir, 43bis rue de la Glacière, F-75013 Paris (not permanent). Tel: 33 (1) 45870533.
Officers (elected for 3-yr.term) Pres: A. Debert; Sec: A. Salavert. Exec.Board: 12
Staff Volunteers
Languages French
Established 1936, by alumni of the École des Bibliothécaires-Documentalistes of the Catholic Institute in Paris.
Major Fields of Interest Status of librarians and documentalists in France; new fields of library school curriculum.
Major Goals and Objectives To improve communication among members; to provide latest information concerning the profession; to help new graduates of the School find employment; to establish communications with related organizations to promote librarianship.
Structure Governed by Executive Council. Affiliations: IFLA, ADBS, ASLIB, Anciens Elèves de l'Institute Catholique de Paris.
Sources of Support Membership dues.
Membership Total members: 500+ (individual). Types of membership: Individual, honorary. Requirements: Alumni of the École de Bibliothécaires-Documentalistes. Dues (French Franc): 75.
General Assembly Entire membership meets once a year, in or near Paris.
Publications *Official journal:* Bulletin d'Information de l'Association des Diplômés de l'École de Bibliothécaires-Documentalistes. 1971-. 2/yr. Free to members. Editor: Janine Gaillemin. Address same as Association. Circ: 500+. French. Also issues an Annuaire.
Activities Working for improvement of status of librarians; helping members in career placement and professional development; sponsoring meetings, lectures, workshops; providing scholarship aid to students.
Bibliography Chauveinc, M., "France," in ALA World Encyclopedia of Library and Information Services, 2nd ed., pp. 285-292. Chicago: American Library Association, 1986; "Pour une politique documentaire nationale," Documentaliste 23 (1986):155-162.

225 Association Française des Documentalistes et des Bibliothécaires Spécialisés (ADBS)
(French Association of Information Scientists and Special Librarians)

Address 5 Avenue Franco-Russe, F-75007 Paris (permanent). Tel: 33 (1) 45555516. Fax: 33 (1) 45556984.

Officers (elected for 2-yr.term) Pres: Paul-Dominique Pomart; VPs: Andrée Verdiel, Marie-José Dussaud; Gen.Sec: Louis Giraud; Treas: Aline Karczewski. Exec.Board: 27, elected.

Staff 9 (paid)

Languages French

Established 1963, Paris

Major Fields of Interest Information systems; special libraries

Major Goals and Objectives To develop information exchanges among professionals; to improve professional development of members; to promote the status of the profession; to disseminate and develop new technologies

Structure Governed by Council and executive officers. Affiliations: IFLA, WERTID (West European Round Table on Information and Documentation), AIESI (Association Internationale des Écoles en Sciences de l'Information)

Sources of Support Membership dues, grants. Budget (French Franc): Approx. 5 Million.

Membership Total members: 4,000 (individual and institutional). Committees: 3 (˙ Education, Professional Qualifications, Technology of Documentation). Sections: 13 (by subjects, e.g. agriculture, audiovisual, economics, law, medicine, electronics, social sciences, etc.). Regional Groups: 19. 20 countries represented. Types of membership: Individual, institutional, student. Requirements: To be an information specialist or librarian. Dues (French Franc): 305-830, individual, depending on status; 1,700, institutions; dues are slightly higher outside France, 335-890; 1,850.

General Assembly Entire membership meets every 2 years. 1987: Strasbourg, May 13; 1989: Paris, June 21.

Publications *Official journal:* Documentaliste-Sciences de l'Information. 1963-. 5/yr. (French Franc) 360; 420 foreign. Free to members. Director: E. de La Potterie; Chief Editor: Jean-Michel Rauzier. Address same as Association. Circ: 4,200. French. Indexed in LISA, ISA. Journal provides extensive abstracts of French-language professional periodicals and other current information, including latest technology. Issues monthly newsletter, ADBS-Informations. Editor: Paul-Dominique Pomart; annual Membership Directory (e.g., L'Annuaire 89). Extensive publication program on general and specialized topics, e.g., Répertoire des banques de données professionnelles (11th ed., 1989); Michel, Jean and Sutter, Eric, Valeur et compétitivité de l'information documentaire, l'analyse de la valeur en documentation (1988); Recherche en Sciences de l'Information (series); Dictionnaire de Sigles: Electronique-Télécommunications-Informatique (4th ed., 1986); proceedings of congresses, annual reports. Publications issued for sale, price lists available. Publications exchanged with other library associations and libraries.

Activities Since 1974, organized the National Congress on Information and Documentation every 2 years: Le Congrès IDT (information, documentation, transfer des connaissances) with over 1,000 participants from France and abroad. Association acts as a communication link between the public and private sector in information work. Hosted and organized the IFLA Congress in Paris, August 1989. Signed exchange agreement with CSSTI (China Society for Scientific and Technical Information). Extensive system of continuing education courses and specialized offerings.

Use of High Technology 10 microcomputers for management.

Bibliography Kellermann, L., "ADBS and Its Training Activities," Documentaliste 19 (1982):153-156 (in French); "ADBS Activities in the Field of Specialization Training for Documentalists," IAALD Quarterly Bulletin 28 (1983):239-242; Chauveinc, M., "France," in ALA World Encyclopedia of Library and Information Services, 2nd ed., pp. 285-292. Chicago: American Library Association, 1986; "Pour une politique document-aire nationale," Documentaliste 23 (1986):155-162; Robert, L.J., "L'Association Française des Documentalistes et des Bibliothécaires Spécialisés," (French Association of Information Scientists and Special Librarians), Special Libraries 79 (Fall 1988):332-335.

226 Association Générale des Conservateurs des Collections Publiques de France (AGCCPF)
(Association of French Curators of Public Collections)

Address c/o Bibliothèque nationale, 58 Rue de Richelieu, F-75002, Paris, Cedex 2.
Languages French
Major Fields of Interest Public records management
Major Goals and Objectives To promote the management of public records in France
Bibliography "Pour une politique documentaire nationale," Documentaliste 23 (1986):155-162.

227 Association pour la Médiathèque Publique (AMP)
(Association for Public Media Centers)

Address c/o Bibliothèque municipale, 37 Rue St-Georges, F-59400 Cambrai (not per-manent). Tel: 33 (27) 813520.
Officers Pres: Albert Ronsin
Staff None
Languages French
Established 1971, as Association Nationale pour le Développement des Bibliothèques Publiques (ANDBP) (National Association for the Development of Public Libraries)
Major Fields of Interest Media Centers in public libraries
Major Goals and Objectives To promote the development of public media centers
Structure Governed by executive officers
Sources of Support Membership dues
General Assembly Entire membership meets once a year
Publications *Official journal:* Médiathèques Publiques (formerly Lecture et Bi-bliothèque). 1967-. 4/yr. (French Franc) 60. Free to members. Editor: Michel Bouvy. Address same as Association. French. Indexed in LISA.

228 Fédération des Associations de Documentalistes-Bibliothécaires de l'Education Nationale (FADBEN)
(Federation of Associations of Documentalists-Librarians of National Education)

Address 29 Rue d'Ulm, F-75007 Paris.
Officers Pres: Françoise Chapron (25 Rue F. Berat, F-76140 Petit Quevilly)
Staff None
Languages French
Major Fields of Interest Information scientists, librarians
Major Goals and Objectives To further professional development of information scientists/librarians with educational training from public academic institutions
Structure Governed by executive officers

Sources of Support   Membership dues
General Assembly   Entire membership meets annually. 1989: Strasbourg, May 20.
Bibliography   "20.05.89.Strasbourg. Congrès de la FADBEN," <u>ADBS-Informations</u> 232
(June 1989):2

Gabon

229   Gabonese Librarians Association

Address   c/o Archives et bibliothèque nationale, BP 1188, Libreville. Tel: (241) 732543.
Officers   Pres: Amoughe M'Ba Pierre
Staff   None
Languages   French
Established   1981, by Amoughe M'Ba Pierre
Major Fields of Interest   Libraries and archives
Major Goals and Objectives   To promote development of libraries and archives in Gabon
Membership   Total members: 30+ (individual). Requirements: Librarians or archivists.
General Assembly   Entire membership meets once a year.
Publications   No official journal.
Activities   Association still developing its program.
Bibliography   Bouscarle, M.E., "Gabon," in <u>ALA World Encyclopedia of Library and Information Services</u>, 2nd ed., p. 296. Chicago: American Library Association, 1986.

Gambia

230   The Gambia Library Association (GAMLA)

Address   c/o Rosana N'Daw Jallow, President, c/o Gambia National Library, PO Box 552, Banjul, THE GAMBIA, WEST AFRICA
Officers   Pres: Rosana N'Daw Jallow; Sec: Hannah Forster (PO Box 370, Banjul)
Staff   None
Languages   English
Established   March 31, 1989, based on an earlier association formed in 1977.
Major Fields of Interest   Library services
Major Goals and Objectives   To promote libraries in The Gambia
Structure   Governed by executive officers. Affiliations: COMLA
Sources of Support   Membership dues, subsidies
Membership   Total members: 50+.
Activities   Activites reported in COMLA Newsletter.
Bibliography   N'Jie, S.P.C., "Gambia, The," in ALA World Encyclopedia of Library and Information Services, 2nd ed., pp. 296-297. Chicago: American Library Association, 1986; Harris, G., "Branch and Mobile Libraries in The Gambia," COMLA Newsletter 64 (June 1989):6-7; Ferguson, S., "COMLINKS: News and Views from the COMLA Secretariat," COMLA Newsletter 65 (Sept. 1989):2.

German Democratic Republic

231   Bibliotheksverband der Deutschen Demokratischen Republik (BV der DDR) (Library Association of the German Democratic Republic)

Address   Hermann-Matern-Strasse 57, DDR-1040 Berlin (permanent). Tel: 37 (2) 2362845. Telex: 115147 zib dd.
Officers   (elected for 5-yr.term) Pres: Karl-Heinz Jügelt; VP: Norbert Stroscher; Treas: Dieter Schmidmaier; Sec.(appointed): Klaus Plötz; Hon.Pres: Gotthard Rückl.
Exec.Comm: 8. Exec.Board: 40.
Staff   5.5 (paid)
Languages   German
Established   1964, Berlin, at the Deutsche Staatsbibliothek, with delegates from 110 libraries, as Deutscher Bibliotheksverband/DBV; changed to present name in 1974.
Major Fields of Interest   Development of library and information work
Major Goals and Objectives   Promotion of efficiency of libraries and information centers; development of management, technology and cooperation in the library and information fields; promotion of education and research; development of international relations and cooperation.
Structure   Governed by Executive Committee (Präsidium) and Executive Board (Büro des Präsidium). Affiliations: IFLA
Sources of Support   Membership dues, sale of publications. Budget (Mark der DDR): 1986/87: 160,000; 1987/88: 180,000.
Membership   Total members: 2,060 (institutional). Regional groups: 15. Subject sections: 4 (Social Science, Agriculture, Medicine, Technology) and various subsections. Types of membership: Institutional. Requirements: Open to all libraries and information centers. Dues (Mark der DDR): 40-800, depending on size of staff.
General Assembly   Entire membership meets every five years. 1987: Leipzig, Sept.1-4.
Publications   *Official journal:* Bibliotheksverband Aktuell (newsletter, supersedes Informationsblatt des Bibliotheksverbandes der DDR, 1964-74). 1975-. 3/yr. Free to members. Address same as Association. Circ: 2,200. German. Other publications: Jahresbericht (annual report); Das Bibliothekswesen in der Deutschen Demokratischen Republik - Jahresbericht (Librarianship in the German Democratic Republic - Annual Report); proceedings of meetings, reports of seminars, workshops. 20 Jahre Bibliotheksverband der Deutschen Demokratischen Republic: Chronik, Bibliographie und Veröffentlichungen, Statistik, Anschriften der Organe (20 Years Library Association of the German Democratic Republic: Chronology, Bibliography and Publications, Statistics, Addresses of Institutions) (1984). Publications listed in Der Bibliothekar and Zentralblatt für das Bibliothekswesen. Publications for sale. Price lists issued as Bibliotheksverband Aktuell. Publications exchange program in effect.
Activities   Past achievements: Contributed to the preparation of basic documents on the development of library and information work; conferences and recommendations relating to library work with children and in rural areas; exchange of experiences in the application of EDP (Electronic Data Processing). Current: Organizing conferences on: Cultural heritage and libraries; library work in urban working class centers. Future: Statewide integration of library and information work; broader use of modern information and communication technologies; application of new methods of preservation and conservation. Association will continue international activities as representative of the German Democratic Republic, and to work for the implementation of the aims of Unesco. Association has been active in promoting library-related legislation through discussion and com-

ments on legal documents drafted by the government. Sponsors Book Week activities and continuing education seminars and workshops.

Bibliography   Rückl, G., "German Democratic Republic," in <u>ALA World Encyclopedia of Library and Information Services</u>, 2nd ed., pp. 301-306. Chicago: American Library Association, 1986; Rückl, G., "2. Fachtagung des Bibliotheksverbandes der DDR zur sozialistischen Bibliotheksarbeit in ländlichen Bereichen, Schwerin 4.-6.11.1986," (The GDR Library Associations's 2nd Professional Conference on Socialist Library Work in Rural Areas, Schwerin, Nov.4-6, 1986), <u>Bibliothekar</u> 41 (1987):49-54, 97-102 (in German); Rückl, G., "40 Jahre sozialistische Bibliotheksarbeit in der DDR - 25 Jahre Bibliotheksverband," (40 Years of Socialist Librarianship in the GDR - The 25th Anniversary of the Library Association) <u>Bibliothekar</u> 43 (1989):337-341.

232   Internationale Vereinigung der Musikbibliotheken - Ländergruppe Deutsche Demokratische Republik (VMB, Ländergruppe DDR) (International Association of Music Libraries. German Democratic Republic Branch)

Address   c/o Heinz Werner, Director, Franz-Liszt-Hochschule für Musik in der DDR, Platz der Demokratie, DDR-5300 Weimar. Tel: 20780. Telex: (37) 0112757.
Officers   (elected for 3-yr.term) Pres: Heinz Werner. Exec.Board: 5.
Staff None
Languages   German
Established   1959, Berlin
Major Fields of Interest   Music librarianship
Major Goals and Objectives   To promote music librarianship in the country
Structure   Governed by Executive Board (Präsidium). Affiliations: National branch of IAML.
Sources of Support   Membership dues, government subsidies.
Membership   Types of membership: Institutional only. Requirements: Academic music libraries, music departments of public libraries, libraries concerned with music research, and special libraries.
General Assembly   Entire membership meets annually.
Publications   No official journal. <u>Rundschreiben</u>, irreg. newsletter. Members only. Other publications: Reports of conferences, guides to libraries.
Activities   Activities and annual meetings are reported in the <u>Zentralblatt für das Bibliothekswesen</u>, <u>Der Bibliothekar</u>, and <u>Bulletin des Musikrates der DDR</u>. Activities are carried out in accordance with the general objectives of IAML. Sponsors colloquia, seminars and other continuing education programs.
Bibliography   Werner, H., "Zur Arbeit der IVMB - Ländergruppe DDR," (The Work of the IAML - German Democratic Republic's Branch) <u>Zentralblatt für Bibliothekswesen</u> 95 (July 1981):315-318 (in German).

Germany, Federal Republic of

233 Arbeitsgemeinschaft der Archive und Bibliotheken in der Evangelischen Kirche (AABevK)
(Study Group of Archives and Libraries in the Evangelical Church)

Address Veilhofstrasse 28, D-8500 Nuremberg (not permanent). Tel: (0911)550269/550296.
Officers (elected for 6-yr.term) Chair: Helmut Baier; Sec: Eberhard Sperling; Archives Section: Hermann Kuhr; Libraries Section: Isolde Dumke. Exec.Board: 7
Staff None
Languages German
Established 1936, at meeting of church archivists in Eisenach, Thüringen.
Major Fields of Interest Religious/church archives and librarianship
Major Goals and Objectives To function as forum for professional concerns of archives of the Evangelical Church; to assist in basic methods of management; to publish professional material; to give assistance in the evaluation, exchange of experience, and consultation to members for the improvement of their archives; to represent Church archives and librarianship to the public; to communicate and cooperate with similar establishments and organizations; to promote interlending among Church archives and libraries; to establish standards and rules for the classification and cataloging of archival material.
Structure Governed by Executive Committee, under the Evangelical Church. No affiliations.
Sources of Support Sale of publications, support by the Evangelische Kirche in Deutschland (Evangelical Church in Germany). Budget (Deutsche Mark): 1986/87: 44,000; 1987/88: 44,500.
Membership Total members: 82 (1 individual, 81 institutional). Sections: 2 (archives, libraries). Requirements: Archives and research libraries in the Evangelical Church, which are administered by at least 1 full-time worker. No dues.
General Assembly Entire membership meets every 3 years.
Publications *Official journal:* Allgemeine Mitteilungen. 1969-. irreg. Free to members. Editor: Kirchenarchivdirektor Hermann Rückleben. Address: Postfach 2269, Blumenstrasse 1, D-7500 Karlsruhe. Circ: Membership only. German. Other publications: Veröffentlichungen der Arbeitsgemeinschaft der Archive und Bibliotheken in der evangelischen Kirche; Reports of seminars, workshops. Publications for sale. No publications exchange program.
Activities Publication of research in the area of Church archives and librarianship, as well as on Church history. Sponsors continuing education courses, workshops for members working in Church archives and related institutions. Association has been active in promoting library-related legislation for the Evangelical Church in Germany, for regulations as to the use of Church archives and libraries, and others. Sponsors book week activities.
Bibliography Erbacher, H., Zeitschriften-Verzeichnis evangelisch-kirchlicher Bibliotheken (2nd ed., 1980); Bibliotheksführer der evangelischen Kirchen in der Bundesrepublik Deutschland (1982); Handbuch des kirchlichen Archivwesen, Band 1: Die zentralen Archive in der evangelischen Kirche (Handbook of Church Archives, v. 1: The Central Archives of the Evangelical Church) (3rd ed., 1986).

234 Arbeitsgemeinschaft der Bibliotheken und Dokumentationsstellen der Osteuropa-, Südosteuropa- und DDR-Forschung (ABDOSD) (Association of Libraries and Documentation Centers for East-, Southeast- and GDR-Research)

Address   c/o Staatsbibliothek Preussischer Kulturbesitz, Osteuropa-Abteilung, Potsdamer Strasse 33, D-1000 Berlin 30 (not permanent). Tel: 49 (30) 2661. Telex: 183160 staab d
Officers   (elected for 4-yr.term) Chair: Dr. Franz Görner; Sec: Dr. H. v. Chmielewski. Exec.Comm: 1
Staff   None
Languages   German
Established   1970
Major Fields of Interest   Libraries with specialized collections of material on East-, Southeast Europe and the German Democratic Republic (DDR)
Major Goals and Objectives   To provide a forum for exchange of information; to cooperate with other national organizations.
Structure   Governed by chair. Not a registered association. Affiliations: SCONUL-ACOSEEM.
Sources of Support   Conference fees
Membership   Total members: 100 (individual). Requirements: To work in academic or other institutions specializing in research on Eastern Europe, Southeastern Europe, and the German Democratic Republic. No dues.
General Assembly   Entire membership meets once a year. 1987: Ljubljana, Yugoslavia, May 25-27; 1988: Heidelberg, May 9-11; 1989: Munich, May 8-11.
Publications   *Official journal:* ABDOSD-Mitteilungen. 1981-. 4/yr. Free to members. Editor: Dr. Miroslav Novák. Address: TIB Hannover, Welfengarten 1 B, D-300 Hannover 1. Circ: Membership. German, English. Issues proceedings of meetings. Publications exchange program in effect.
Activities   Consist mainly of sponsoring the annual conferences.
Bibliography   Chmielewski, H. von, "Auf Osteuropa bezogene Bibliotheksfragen. ABDOSD - Arbeitstagung 1982 in Kiel," (Library Issues regarding Eastern Europe: ABDOSD Conference in Kiel, 1982) Zeitschrift für Bibliothekswesen und Bibliographie 29 (1982):410-412; Mitteilungsblatt Verband der Bibliotheken des Landes Nordrhein-Westfalen 36 (1986):213-216; 37 (1987):350-354; Steiner, J., "18. Arbeits- und Fortbildungstagung der ABDOSD in München," (18th Continuing Education Conference of ABDOSD in Munich) Mitteilungen der Vereinigung Österreichischer Bibliothekare 42 (1989):24-25 (in German).

235 Arbeitsgemeinschaft der Fachhochschulbibliotheken (Association of Libraries of Polytechnic Institutions)

Address   c/o Fachhochschule für Bibliotheks- und Dokumentationswesen in Köln, Claudiusstrasse 1, D-5000 Cologne (not permanent). Tel: 49 (221) 3386374.
Languages   German
Major Fields of Interest   Libraries of polytechnic institutions
Major Goals and Objectives   To promote the development of polytechnic libraries and provide a forum for the exchange of ideas and cooperation.
Membership   Open to libraries of polytechnic instituions (Fachhochschulen)
General Assembly   Entire membership meets annually.
Activities   Meetings are hosted by a member institution. Some current activities are in the area of library automation, user services, government support, etc.

236   Arbeitsgemeinschaft der Grosstadtbibliotheken
(Association of Metropolitan City Libraries)

Address   c/o Deutsche Bibliothek, Zeppelinallee 4-8, Frankfurt am Main 1 (not permanent). Tel: 49 (59) 75661. Telex: 416643.
Languages   German
Major Fields of Interest   Metropolitan city libraries
Major Goals and Objectives   To provide a forum for cooperation and exchange of information for metropolitan city libraries; to further the development of such libraries.
Membership   Open to libraries serving metropolitan areas
General Assembly   Entire membership meets annually
Activities   Sponsors conferences, seminars, etc. Current issues are union catalogs, collection development, and continuing education.

237   Arbeitsgemeinschaft der Hochschulbibliotheken
(Association of University Libraries)

Address   c/o Universitätsbibliothek Bochum, Universitätsstrasse 150, D-4630 Bochum 1 (not permanent). Tel: 49 (234) 7112350. Telex: 824860.
Languages   German
Major Fields of Interest   Academic libraries at the university level
Major Goals and Objectives   To promote the development of university libraries and to provide a forum for cooperation between members.
Membership   Open to university libraries
General Assembly   Entire membership meets annually
Activities   Sponsors conferences, seminars, and other continuing education programs. Some topics of current interest are: Interlibrary loan, education and training, online information services, etc.

238   Arbeitsgemeinschaft der Kirchlichen Büchereiverbände Deutschlands
(Joint Association of Library Associations of the Churches in Germany)

Address   Wittelsbacherring 9, D-5300 Bonn 1 (permanent). Tel: 49 (228) 631055.
Officers   Exec.Sec.(appointed): Erich Hodick. Exec.Comm: 7
Staff   None
Languages   German
Established   1957, Würzburg
Major Fields of Interest   Public library activities of the Protestant and Catholic churches in the country
Major Goals and Objectives   Pursuit of common interests of the member associations.
Structure   Governed alternatively by one of the presidents of the member associations. They are: (1) Borromäusverein, Wittelsbacherring 9, D-5300 Bonn; (2) Deutscher Verband Evangelischer Büchereien, Bürgerstrasse 2, D-3400 Göttingen; (3) St. Michaelsbund, Herzog-Wilhelm-Strasse 5, D-8000 Munich.
Sources of Support   Subject to special arrangements among member associations.
Membership   Total members: 3 (institutional). Requirements: Library associations of the Churches. Dues: Special arrangements.
General Assembly   Entire membership meets every two years: 1987; 1989; 1991.
Publications   No official journal. Issues reports of seminars, workshops, etc. Publications not available for sale, but distributed free to members and libraries.
Activities   Past achievements: Jointly agreed upon guidelines for public library activities of the Churches in the Federal Republic of Germany. Current: Public relations activities.

Future: Planning joint activities on a local level. Association has been active in promoting library-related legislation, such as counteracting trends of over-centralization. Sponsors Book Week activities; exhibits; continuing education lectures, seminars, workshops and special programs for the education of volunteers in public libraries.

Bibliography   Kirchliche Büchereiarbeit im Gespräch (Discussions about the Work of Church Libraries) (1982); Kirchliche Büchereiarbeit - Dienst für alle (The Work of Church Libraries: Services for All) (1982).

239   Arbeitsgemeinschaft der Kunstbibliotheken (AKB) (Working Group of Art Libraries)

Address   c/o Bernd Evers, Chair, AKB, Kunstbibliothek, Staatliche Museen Preussischer Kulturbesitz, Jebensstrasse 2, D-1000 Berlin 12 (not permanent).
Officers   (elected for indefinite term) Chair: Bernd Evers.
Staff   None
Languages   German
Established   1965, Nuremberg
Major Fields of Interest   Cooperation and bibliographical activities of German art libraries
Major Goals and Objectives   Promotion of research in art history by: (1) increasing the availability of subject literature, and (2) disseminating the literature through catalogs, bibliographies, and documentation.
Structure   Governed by executive officers. Affiliations: ASpB (Arbeitsgemeinschaft der Spezialbiblitheken/Association of Special Libraries).
Sources of Support   Private gifts
Membership   Total members: 9 (institutional). Types of membership: Institutional. Requirements: Art libraries. No dues.
General Assembly   Entire membership meets once a year.
Publications   No official journal.
Activities   Establishing coordinated program of acquisitions for member libraries; publishing reference works on art libraries in the German Democratic Republic; and continuing work on publishing union list and bibliographic tools for art libraries.
Bibliography   For background information see Arbeitsgemeinschaft der Kunstbibliotheken, Deutsche Kunstbibliotheken Berlin, Florenz, Köln, München, Nürnberg, Rom. (Munich: Verlag Dokumentation, 1975).

240   Arbeitsgemeinschaft der Parlaments- und Behördenbibliotheken (APBB) (Association of Parliamentary and Administrative Libraries)

Address   c/o Bibliothek des Deutschen Patentamts, Zweibrückenstrasse 12, D-8000 Munich 2 (permanent). Tel: 49 (89) 21952448. Telex: 0523534.
Officers   (elected for 2-yr.term) Pres: Echard Derday; Sec: Hubert Rothe; Treas: Arnold Dollt. Exec.Board: 10
Staff   4 (volunteers)
Languages   German
Established   1955, Düsseldorf, as Commission of Parliamentary and Administrative Libraries of the Association of German Librarians (Verein Deutscher Bibliothekare).
Major Fields of Interest   All activities of parliamentary and administrative libraries
Major Goals and Objectives   Representation of common interests towards third parties; improvement of cooperation between parliamentary and administrative libraries in the Federal Republic of Germany; counselling of the member libraries and their staff, e.g., with regard to the introduction of electronic data processing in libraries.

Structure   Governed by executive officers.
Sources of Support   Sale of publications
Membership   Total members: 500 (institutional). Types of membership: Institutional. Requirements: Member institutions should be parliamentary or administrative libraries. No dues.
General Assembly   Entire membership meets once a year. 1987: Augsburg; 1988: Berlin.
Publications   *Official journal:* Mitteilungen (news bulletin). 1958-. 2/yr. (Deutsche Mark) 18. Address same as Association. Circ: 600. German. Indexed in Deutsche Bibliographie, Bibliotheksdienst. Issues Arbeitshefte (Working Papers) (annual). No publications exchange program.
Activities   Past achievements: Organizing special lectures on the occasion of the annual Congress of German Librarians (Deutscher Bibliothekartag); setting up specific rules for alphabetic cataloging in parliamentary and administrative libraries; establishing a common classification for the libraries of the chambers of commerce and industry; updating and issuing a new edition of the directory of parliamentary and administrative libraries in the Federal Republic of Germany. Current and future: Counselling the member libraries on electronic data processing in libraries. Association has been active in promoting library-related legislation in connection with preventing the introduction of the importation turnover tax on books.
Use of High Technology   Computers used for management: Names and addresses of member libraries are stored on floppy disks.
Bibliography   Taube, Utz-Friedebert, "25 Jahre Arbeitsgemeinschaft der Parlaments- und Behördenbibliotheken,"(25 Years of APBB) Zeitschrift für Bibliothekswesen und Bibliographie 28(1981):76-79; Dietz, W., Kirchner, H., and Wenicke, K.G., eds., Bibliotheksarbeit für Parlamente und Behörden: Festschrift zum 25-jährigen Bestehen der Arbeitsgemeinschaft der Parlaments- und Behördenbibliotheken (Library Work for Parliaments and Government Agencies: Festschrift for the 25th Anniversary of APBB). Munich: Saur, 1980 (all in German).

241   Arbeitsgemeinschaft der Spezialbibliotheken e.V. (ASpB)
(Association of Special Libraries)

Address   Dr. Marianne Schwarzer, Executive Secretary, c/o Kekulé-Bibliothek, Bayer AG, D-5090 Leverkusen-Bayerwerk (permanent). Tel: 49 (214) 307819. Telex: 85103-0.
Officers   (elected for 3-yr.term) Chair: W. Laux; Sec: Marianne Schwarzer; Treas: Ursula Mende. Exec.Board: 13
Staff   None
Languages   German
Established   1946, Essen
Major Fields of Interest   Cooperation among special libraries
Major Goals and Objectives   To promote the exchange of practical experience and the cooperation between special libraries, particularly with respect to lending and exchange of facilities.
Structure   Governed by Executive Board. Affiliations: IFLA.
Sources of Support   Membership dues, sale of publications.
Membership   Total members: 484 (individual and institutional). Requirements: Open to libraries, documentation centers, institutes, business and lawyers and other interested persons. Dues: None. Members are obligated to purchase conference reports.
General Assembly   Entire membership meets every 2 years. 1987: Kiel, March 25-27.

Publications   Official journal: <u>Inspel: International Journal of Special Libraries</u>. 1966-. 4/yr.; <u>Bericht über die Tagung</u> (Conference report). 1946-. Biennial. Address same as Association. Other publications: Proceedings of meetings, <u>Arbeitshilfen für Spezialbibliotheken</u> (Working aids for special libraries), etc. Publications available for sale.
Activities   Carried out in accordance with the aims of the Association: Sponsoring conferences; publishing guidelines for special libraries; promoting information and documentation facilities in special libraries; training librarians in modern technologies for information management and information services; representing special libraries of the Federal Republic of Germany at international organizations and meetings.
Bibliography   Pflug, Günther and Kaegbein, Paul, "Germany, Federal Republic of," in <u>ALA World Encyclopedia of Library and Information Services</u>, 2nd ed., pp. 306-309. Chicago: American Library Association, 1986.

242   Arbeitsgemeinschaft für Juristisches Bibliotheks- und Dokumentationswesen (AjBD) (Association of Law Libraries and Legal Documentation)

Address   AjBD, Teilbibliothek Recht der Universitätsbibliothek, Eichleitnerstrasse 30, D-8900 Augsburg (not permanent). Tel: 49 (821) 598335.
Officers   (elected for 2-yr.term) Chair: Hans-Burkard Meyer; Vice-Chair: Dietrich Pannier; Sec: Eva Schöppl. Exec.Board: 8
Staff   2 (volunteers)
Languages   German
Established   1971, Cologne
Major Fields of Interest   Law librarianship; legal documentation and information; legal bibliography.
Major Goals and Objectives   To promote law librarianship and documentation; to provide exchange of information and mutual assistance to members.
Structure   Governed by Executive Board. Affiliations: IALL (German Section).
Sources of Support   Sale of publications, membership dues.
Membership   Total members: 128 (9 individual, 119 institutional). 4 countries represented.   Requirements: Libraries with law collections and librarians working there.
General Assembly   Entire membership meets once a year. 1987: Augsburg, June; 1988: Berlin, May/June; 1989: Bonn, May/June.
Publications   *Official journal:* <u>Mitteilungen der AjBD</u>. 1971-. 3/yr. (Deutsche Mark) 30. Editor: Werner von Schaper. Address: c/o Staatsbibliothek Preussischer Kulturbesitz, Postfach 1407, D-1000 Berlin 30. Circ: Membership. German. Indexed in <u>KJB/Karlsruher Juristische Bibliographie</u>. Other publications: <u>Arbeitshefte der AjBD</u>, a numbered series, irreg. Price lists available. No publications exchange program.
Activities   Sponsors continuing education programs (about 1-2 per year); publication of series and journal.
Use of High Technology   Computers (Regnecentralen RC 75o Partner) for management.
Bibliography   Wagner, M., "Jahrestagung 1981 der Arbeitsgemeinschaft für Medizinisches Bibliothekswesen," (Annual Conference 1981) <u>Mitteilungsblatt Verband der Bibliotheken des Landes Nordrhein-Westfalen</u> 32 (1982):287-292 (in German).

243   Arbeitsgemeinschaft für Medizinisches Bibliothekswesen (Association for Medical Librarianship)

Address   c/o Robert Koch-Institut des Bundesgesundheitsamtes Bibliothek, Nordufer 20, D-1000 Berlin 65 (not permanent). Tel: 49 (30) 4503328. Telex: 8579573.

Officers   Pres: K. Gerber
Languages   German
Major Fields of Interest   Medical librarianship
Major Goals and Objectives   To promote medical libraries and medical librarianship
Bibliography   For background information see Horstmann, W. and Hansen, U., Arbeitsgemeinschaft für Medizinisches Bibliothekswesen (Berlin: Deutscher Bibliotheksverband, 1975).

244   Arbeitsgemeinschaft für Regionalbibliotheken im Deutschen Bibliotheksverband
(Association of German Regional Libraries)

Address   Lammstrasse 16, D-7500 Karlsruhe (permanent). Tel: 49 (721) 175200.
Officers   (elected for 4-yr.term) Pres: Gerhard Römer (Leitender Bibliotheksdirektor der Badischen Landesbibliothek in Karlsruhe). Exec.Board: 5
Staff   None
Languages   German
Established   1971, Cologne, through a merger of the Arbeitsgemeinschaft Kommunaler Wissenschaftlichen Bibliotheken (Working Group of Municipal Research Libraries) and the Arbeitsgemeinschaft der Landesbibliotheken (Working Group of State Libraries).
Major Fields of Interest   Regional libraries
Major Goals and Objectives   (1) Promotion of librarianship outside the universities; (2) general exchange of knowledge and experience; (3) solution of problems in regional planning; (4) discussion of common projects; (5) mutual support in representing the interests of individual libraries.
Structure   Governed by Executive Board. Affiliations: VDB.
Sources of Support   Member contributions.
Membership   Total members: 35 (institutional). Types of membership: Institutional. Requirements: Libraries with predominant research collections, or central libraries of individual regions (states, districts, cities).
General Assembly   Entire membership meets once a year.
Publications   No publications program.
Activities   Various activities cover the following areas: Analysis of use structure, common guidelines for acquisition policies, expansion of bibliographic services; maintenance of and access to collections, cooperation with universities and professional schools, cooperation with public libraries, and definition of cultural responsibilities

245   Arbeitsgemeinschaft Katholisch-Theologischer Bibliotheken (AKThB)
(Association of Catholic Theological Libraries)

Address   c/o Studien- und Zentralbibliothek der Franziskaner, Hörsterplatz 5, D-4400 Münster (not permanent). Tel: 49 (0251) 40081.
Officers   Pres: P. Heribald Wenke OFM; VP: Sigmund Benker. Exec.Board: 9
Staff   None
Languages   German
Established   1947, Frankfurt am Main.
Major Fields of Interest   Catholic theological libraries
Major Goals and Objectives   To promote and further theological librarianship and theological libraries within the Catholic Church in German-speaking regions; to promote cooperation among member libraries; to improve theological library collections.
Structure   Governed by Executive Board. Affiliations: Conseil International des Associations de Bibliothèques de Théologie (International Council of Theological Libraries).

Sources of Support   Membership dues.
Membership   Total members: 125 (institutional). Types of membership: Institutional only. 5 countries represented. Requirements: Catholic theological libraries. Dues (Deutsche Mark): 50.
General Assembly   Entire membership meets once a year. 1987: Benediktbeuern; 1988: Cologne; 1989: Würzburg.
Publications   *Official journal:* Mitteilungsblatt der AKThB. 1952-. 1/yr. Membership. Editor: Franz Rudolf Reichert. Address: Postfach 1330, D-5500 Trier. German. Other publications: Newsletter of the President; Reichert, F.R., ed., Handbuch der kirchlichen katholisch-theologischen Bibliotheken (2nd ed., Munich, 1979). Publications for sale. No publications exchange program.
Activities   A major accomplishment was the publication of the Memorandum der Arbeitsgemeinschaft Katholisch-Theologischer Bibliotheken über das wissenschaftliche Bibliothekswesen der Kirche (1983), a position paper on Catholic theological libraries.
Bibliography   "35. Jahrestagung," (35th Annual Meeting) Bibliotheksdienst 8 (1982):693-694; Gilmont, J.-F. and Osborne, T.P. "Les associations de bibliothèques de théologie," Revue théologique de Louvain 15 (1984):73-85 (in French). For background information see Reichert, F.R., "Kooperation im kirchlichen Bibliothekswesen Deutschlands. Die Arbeitsgemeinschaft Katholisch-Theologischer Bibliotheken," (Cooperation between Theological Libraries: The AKThB) Bibliotheksarbeit heute. ZfBB Sonderheft 16 (1973):176-184 (in German)

246   Bundesarbeitsgemeinschaft der Katholisch-Kirchlichen Büchereiarbeit (BAG)
(Federal Working Group of Libraries in the Catholic Church)

Address   Wittelsbacherring 9, D-5300 Bonn 1 (permanent). Tel: (0228)631055.
Officers   Pres: Konrad Welzel (appointed); Sec.Gen: Erich Hodick (appointed).
Staff   Part-time secretarial services
Languages   German
Established   1963, Bonn, at the General Assembly of Catholic Library Institutions
Major Fields of Interest   Libraries in the Catholic Church
Major Goals and Objectives   Pursuit of common interests of the members
Structure   Governed by executive officers.
Sources of Support   Borromäusverein (a Catholic cultural organization), membership dues. Budget (Deutsche Mark): Approx. 1 million.
Membership   Total members: 17 (institutional). Types of membership: Institutional. Requirements: Open to the official institutions of the Roman Catholic Church.
General Assembly   Entire membership meets once a year. 1987: Schloss Hirschberg, June; 1988: Münster, May 16-18; 1989: Freiburg, May 8-11; 1990: Mainz, May 28-30.
Publications   *Official journal:* Informationen. 1963-. Irreg. Free to members. Editor: Erich Hodick. Address same as Association. Circ: 130. German. Also publishes occasional circulars. (Matters of common interest are published in the journals of the members). Other publications: Manuals, recommendations, standards, training courses, lectures. Publications issued for sale, exchanged with other associations and libraries, sent free on request.
Activities   Past achievements: Establishing a training program for 20,000 volunteers in public libraries, on the parochial level. Current: Public relations and outreach activities. Future: Cooperating and linking with other library and adult education programs; participation in multi-media activities, including television educational programs. Active in promoting library-related legislation, such as general cooperative library planning in the pub-

lic library field. Awards a Catholic children's book prize (Katholischer Kinderbuchpreis der Deutschen Bischofskonferenz). Sponsors seminars,workshops. Most of the other activities are undertaken by members on the regional level. Comment: The Association is effective in providing services for about 5,000 small public libraries, and the 20,000 volunteers working in them, attracting about 1.2 million readers, half of them children who otherwise would be without any library services.

247   Bundesvereinigung Deutscher Bibliotheksverbände (BDB) (Federal Federation of German Library Associations)

Address   c/o Deutsches Bibliotheksinstitut, Bundesallee 184-185, D-1000 Berlin 31 (not permanent). Tel: 49 (30) 85050
Officers   (elected for 6-yr. term) Speaker: Elmar Mittler (University Librarian, Heidelberg). Coordinating Committee.
Languages   German
Established   Sept. 20, 1989, by prominent librarians representing institutional and personal library associations of the Federal Republic of Germany, in order to centralize lobbying efforts on behalf of libraries and librarians; replaces the Deutsche Bibliothekskonferenz.
Major Fields of Interest   Library associations; librarianship
Major Goals and Objectives   Improving the representation of the library world to the general public of the Federal Republic of Germany; designing public relations work more effectively; strengthening cooperation among library associations
Structure   Governed by Coordinating Committee.
Sources of Support   Membership dues.
Membership   Total members: 5 associations totalling 8,000+ members: (1) Deutscher Bibliotheksverband (DBV); (2) Verein der Bibliothekare an Öffentlichen Bibliotheken (VBB); (3) Verein Deutscher Bibliothekare (VDB); (4) Verein der Diplom-Bibliothekare an Wissenschaftlichen Bibliotheken (VdDB); (5) Bundesvereinigung der Bibliotheksassistenten und anderer Mitarbeiter in Bibliotheken (BBA) (a recently established Federal Association of Library Assistants and Clerical Staff).
Activities   Carried out according to the aims of the Federation. Issues that are important to at least one member association will be considered.
Bibliography   "Germany: New Structure of Cooperation among Library Associations," Herald of Library Science 28 (1989):290-291; "Federal Federation of German Library Associations Founded," Library Times International 6 (1990):54.

248   Deutsche Bibliothekskonferenz (DBK) (German Library Conference)

Address   c/o Deutsche Bibliothek, Zeppelinallee 4-8, D-6000 Frankfurt am Main 1. Tel: 49 (69) 75661. Telex: 416643.
Officers   Presidents of the 6 member associations serve a 1-yr. term as President of DBK.
Staff   None
Languages   German
Major Fields of Interest   Library associations and national planning
Major Goals and Objectives   To coordinate the development of library systems, library services, and library policy on a national level.
Structure   Governed by the executive officers of the member associations.
Sources of Support   Member associations

Membership   Total members: 6 large library associations of the Federal Republic of Germany.
Activities   The German Library Conference works with the Federal government and the states in all library matters, in order to coordinate and unify German library systems.
Bibliography   Pflug, Günther and Kaegbein, Paul, "Germany, Federal Republic of," in ALA World Encyclopedia of Library and Information Services, 2nd ed., pp. 306-309. Chicago: American Library Association, 1986.
The newly formed (1989) Bundesvereinigung Deutscher Bibliotheksverbände (BDB) replaces this Group, in order to centralize public relations for librarianship in the Federal Republic of Germany and to improve the cooperation among library associations.

249   Deutsche Gesellschaft für Dokumentation e.V. (DGD)
(German Society for Documentation)

Address   Westendstrasse 19, D-6000 Frankfurt am Main 1 (permanent). Tel: 49 (069) 747761
Officers   (elected for 3-yr.term) Pres: Peter Canisius; VP: Hanns Bechtel; Sec: Winfried Schmitz-Esser; Treas: Ulrich Neveling; Scientific Sec: Hilde Strohl-Goebel. Exec.Board: 15
Staff   9 (paid)
Languages   German
Established   1941, Berlin; reorganized 1948, Cologne.
Major Fields of Interest   Advancement of information and documentation in theory and practice.
Major Goals and Objectives   To promote research and organization in the fields of theoretical and practical documentation and information science; to promote cooperation with national and international institutions of information and documentation; to promote continuing and specialized education of professional personnel.
Structure   Governed by Executive Council. Affiliations: IFLA, FID, ASLIB, EUSIDIC, ICR (International Council for Reprography), SVD, ÖGDI.
Sources of Support   Membership dues, government subsidies.
Membership   Total members: 1,124 (910 individual, 214 institutional). 16 countries represented. Requirements: Open to individuals and institutions interested in the aims of the Association. Dues (Deutsche Mark): 110, individual; 300, institutional; 400, sustaining.
General Assembly   Entire membership meets once a year.
Publications   *Official journal:* Nachrichten für Dokumentation (NfD) (Documentation News). 1948-. 6/yr. (Deutsche Mark) 128. Free to members. Address same as Association. Circ: 2,000. German, with English summaries. Indexed in Lib.Lit.,LISA,ISA, etc. (A technical journal for information and documentation with an abstracts service in information science). Other publications: Annual reports, proceedings of conferences, seminars, workshops. Various monographs published in series DGD-Schriftenreihe. Publications issued for sale, price lists available, listed in official journal. Publications exchange program in effect with other library associations, libraries, and other institutions.
Activities   Sponsors seminars, workshops and other continuing education programs for the training of professional personnel. Active in international cooperation. Presents award for best German publication in information and documentation.
Use of High Technology   Computers for management
Bibliography   Keren, C. and Schwuchow, W., "Economic Aspect of Information Services - Report on a Symposium," Journal of Informaion Science 3 (Nov. 1981):249-21; Pflug, Günther and Kaegbein, Paul, "Germany, Federal Republic of," in ALA World Encyclopedia of Library and Information Services, 2nd ed., pp. 306-309. Chicago: American

Library Association, 1986; Schwuchow, W., "Deutsche Gesellschaft für Dokumentation (DGD) Conference (FRG, 1989)," International Forum for Information and Documentation 14, no. 4 (1989):31+.

250   Deutscher Bibliotheksverband e.V. (DBV)
(German Library Association)

Address   Bundesallee 184-185, D-1000 Berlin 31 (permanent). Tel: 49 (3) 8505274. Telex: 184166. Fax: 49-30-8505100.

Officers   (elected for 1989-92) Pres (Vorsitzender): Jürgen Hering; Past Pres: Gustav Rottacker;   Chair (Präsident): Ernst Pappermann; VPs: Christian Bode and Kurt Kreuser; Sec: G. Beyersdorff (appointed). Exec.Board: 7

Staff   7 (volunteers)

Languages   German

Established   1949, Nierstein, as Deutscher Büchereiverband e.V. (DBV); 1961, founding of state library associations in the Federal Republic of Germany; 1973, new name adopted and membership expanded from public libraries to include research libraries.

Major Fields of Interest   Public libraries; research libraries; library services

Major Goals and Objectives   Promotion of library work and professional librarianship

Structure   Governed by Board of Directors. Affiliations: IFLA, ALA, CLA (Canada), LA, Arbeitskreis für Jugendliteratur e.V. (Munich), Deutsche Friedrich Schiller Stiftung e.V. (Darmstadt), etc.

Sources of Support   Membership dues. Budget (Deutsche Mark): Approx. 400,000.

Membership   Total members: 650+ (institutional). Types of membership: Institutional. Requirements: Libraries and their financing institutions. Dues (Deutsche Mark): 8.00 for each 1,000 inhabitants; or 16.00 for each 1,000 volumes.

General Assembly   Entire membership meets once a year. 1989: Dortmund, Aug.31.

Publications   *Official journal:* Bibliotheksdienst (issued jointly with Deutsche Bibliothekskonferenz). 1949-. 12/yr. (Deutsche Mark) 52. (39 for members). Address same as Association. Circ: 3,000. German. Jointly with VBB edits the biennial Handbuch der Öffentlichen Büchereien (Handbook of Public Libraries). Issues annual report, proceedings of annual meetings, and others.

Activities   DBV is the association of reference and lending libraries and other institutions concerned with library work, as well as the legal holders of libraries, such as parishes, boroughs, and other districts in so far as they maintain public libraries and give grants to libraries within their reach. The Association works for improvement of library services according to international standards through collective projects, such as library statistics, standards for classification, bookmobiles, lecture programs, research on hospital libraries, libraries for the blind, periodical indexes, etc. Individual projects include telex network, user studies, budget efficiency, library service with bookmobiles for immigrant workers, etc. Maintains the library foreign office (Bibliothekarische Auslandsstelle), which is responsible for international communications and projects.

Bibliography   Segebrecht, D., "Vorsichtige Betrachtung eines Schrumpfprozesses: DBV-Jahrestagung in Bremen," (Observations of a Process of Shrinking: DBV-Annual Meeting in Bremen) Buch und Bibliothek 34 (1982):29-32; Pflug, G. and Kaegbein, P., "Germany, Federal Republic of," in ALA World Encyclopedia of Library and Information Services, 2nd ed., pp. 306-309. Chicago: American Library Association, 1986; Hundrieser, J., "Schaffen wir das Jahr 2000? DBV und Verband der Bibliotheken NW tagen in Köln," (Do we make it to the year 2000? Joint Conference of the DBV and Association of Libraries in North-Rhine Westphalia, Cologne, 1985), Buch und Bibliothek 37 (Nov/Dec.1985):898+; Lohse, Hartwig, "Die 37. Jahresversammlung des Verbandes und der

Jahrestagung des Deutschen Bibliotheksverbandes vom 2.-4.Okt. 1985 in Köln," (The 37th Annual Meeting of the Association and the Annual Conference of the German Library Association from Oct.2-4, 1985 in Cologne), <u>Mitteilungsblatt Verband der Bibliotheken des Landes Nordrhein-Westfalen</u> 36 (1986):18-19 (in German); "Deutscher Bibliotheksverband. Zur Konzentration der Vereine und Verbände des Bibliothekswesens in der Bundesrepublik," (The German Library Association. On the Concentration of Library Associations and Unions in West Germany) <u>Bibliotheksdienst</u> 21 (1987):269-281 (in German).

251   Deutscher Verband Evangelischer Büchereien e.V. (DVEB)
(German Association of Lutheran Libraries)

Address   Bürgerstrasse 2, D-3400 Göttingen (permanent). Tel: 49 (551) 74917.
Officers   (elected for 4-yr.term) 1st Pres: Hans Wulf; 2nd Pres: Hans-Werner Pohl; Manager: Christine Razum. Exec.Board: 6
Staff   9 (paid)
Languages   German
Established   1951
Major Fields of Interest   Lutheran libraries
Major Goals and Objectives   Support and organization of Lutheran libraries
Structure   Governed by Executive Board.
Sources of Support   Sale of publications, Evangelische Kirche in Deutschland (Lutheran Church)
Membership   Total members: 20 (institutional). Requirements: Libraries of the Lutheran Church. No dues.
General Assembly   Entire membership meets once a year. 1987: Beilgries, Bavaria, June 1-4; 1988: Leinfelden, May 16-19.
Publications   *Official journal:* <u>Der Evangelische Buchberater.</u> 1947-. 4/yr. (Deutsche Mark) 15. Editor: Andreas Schimkus. Address same as Association. Circ: Membership. German. Other publicaions: <u>Buchauswahl für Evangelische Büchereien</u> (annual book review); <u>Handwörterbuch der evangelischen Büchereiarbeit</u> (Handbook for Lutheran Libraries) (1980).
Activities   Developing and organizing Lutheran libraries open to the public. Sponsors Book Week and continuing education programs.

252   Gesellschaft für Bibliothekswesen und Dokumentation des Landbaues (GBDL)
(Association of Librarianship and Documentation in Agriculture)

Address   Paracelsusstrasse 2, D-7000 Stuttgart 70 (permanent). Tel: 49 (711) 45012111
Officers   (elected for 4-yr.term) Pres: W. Laux (Berlin); VP: W. Bartels (Leverkusen); Exec.Sec: Hans-Joachim Friede (Stuttgart); Ed: G.Weiland. Exec.Board: 6
Staff   None
Languages   German
Established   1958, Bad Godesberg
Major Fields of Interest   Agricultural libraries and documentation centers
Major Goals and Objectives   Promotion and development of documentation and information in the field of agricultural sciences in the country; international cooperation with information and documentation centers and libraries; conferences.
Structure   Governed by elected executive officers. Affiliations: IAALD.
Sources of Support   Membership dues, sale of publications.

Membership   Total members: 150 (119 individual, 31 institutional). 8 countries represented. Requirements: Education in documentation or library affairs, agricultural sciences. Dues (Deutsche Mark): 10, individual; 30, institutional; 75, industry.
General Assembly   Entire membership meets every 2 years. 1988: Kiel, April/May.
Publications   *Official journal:* Mitteilungen der Gesellschaft für Bibliothekswesen und Dokumentation des Landbaues. 1958-. 2/yr. (Deutsche Mark) 15. Free to members. Editor: Dr. G. Weiland. Address: TU Berlin, Dokumentationsstelle Obstbau, Albrecht-Thaer-Weg 3, D-1000 Berlin 33. Circ: 170. German. Indexed in Schrifttum zur Informationswissenschaft und -praxis. Conference papers are published in official journal.
Activities   Sponsors conferences, sometimes jointly with other agricultural associations; furthers international cooperation with information and documentation centers and libraries dealing with literature in the agricultural sciences; furthers the development of agricultural information and documentation in the Federal Republic of Germany.
Bibliography   10 Jahre Dachverband wissenschaftlicher Gesellschaften der Agrar-, Forst-, Ernährungs-, Veterinär- und Umweltforschung e.V. Munich, 1983. pp.26-30. (in German)

253   Internationale Vereinigung der Musikbibliotheken, Musikarchive und Musikdokumentationszentren - Gruppe Bundesrepublik Deutschland (IVMB - Deutsche Gruppe/BRD) / International Association of Music Libraries, Archives and Documentation Centres - German Branch/FRG (IAML-FRG)

Address   c/o Prof. Wolfgang Krueger, Fachhochschule für Bibliothekswesen, Wolframstrasse 23, D-7000 Stuttgart 1 (permanent). Tel: 49 (711) 2570613.
Officers   (elected for indefinite term) Pres: Wolfgang Krueger; Gen.Sec: Barbara Delcker-Wirth (Musikbibliothek, Königstorgraben 3, D-8500 Nuremberg 3). Exec.Board: 3
Staff   None
Languages   German, English, French
Established   1976, as a national branch of IAML, to take over the activities of the Arbeitsgemeinschaft der Musikbiblitheken (Working Group of Music Libraries).
Major Fields of Interest   Music librarianship
Major Goals and Objectives   To further the development of music libraries and documentation centers, and to be concerned with their practical problems.
Structure   Governed by executive officers. Affiliations: A national branch of IAML; IFLA,
Sources of Support   Membership dues
Membership   Total members: 250 (100 individual, 150 institutional). Divisions: 4. Requirements: Music libraries and documentation centers or those with music collections and librarians working there.
General Assembly   Entire membership meets once a year in October.
Publications   *Official journal:* Forum Musikbibliothek. 1980-. 4/yr. Address: Deutsches Bibliotheksinstitut, Bundesallee 184-185, D-1000 Berlin 31. Editor: Helmut Rösner. German.
Activities   Sponsors meetings, seminars, workshops.

254   Verband Deutscher Werkbibliotheken e.V.
(Association of German Industrial Libraries)

Address   c/o Christiane Lüderssen, President, c/o BASF AG, Werkbücherei, Carl-Bosch-Strasse, D-6700 Ludwigshafen (not permanent). Tel: 49 (621) 603689.
Officers   (elected for 2-yr.term) Pres: Christiane Lüderssen

Staff 4 (volunteers)
Languages German
Established 1955, as Arbeitsgemeinschaft Werkbüchereien für das Bundesgebiet und Berlin (Working group); became an Association (e.V.), 1962.; present name adopted, 1975.
Major Fields of Interest Special libraries in industries and corporations
Major Goals and Objectives To provide opportunity for exchange of professional knowledge; to provide continuing education programs for members in industrial libraries; to further mutual cooperation and assistance through ideas in the development and establishment of industrial libraries.
Structure Governed by executive officers.
Sources of Support Membership dues
Membership Total members: 180. Regional divisions: 6 (Rheinland/Pfalz; Baden; Nordrhein-Westfalen; Württemberg/Bayern; Niedersachsen; Berlin). Types of membership: Individual, institutional, honorary. Requirements: Industrial libraries and staff members of an industrial library. Dues (Deutsche Mark): 50, individual and institutional.
General Assembly Entire membership meets once a year.
Publications *Official journal:* Werkbücherei. 1964-. Irreg. Address same as Association. Issues annual reports, proceedings of annual meetings, other occasional publications.
Activities Sponsors seminars, workshops; cooperates with other library associations; programs by regional divisions; provides assistance to small and medium-sized industrial libraries.
Bibliography Wolf-Hauschild, R., "Von der Stiftsmühle zum Schloss. 25. Jahrestagung des Verbandes der Werkbibliotheken," (From the Mill to the Castle: 25th Annual Meeting) Buch und Bibliothek 33 (1981):681-682; Kröhner, G., "29. Jahrestagung des Verbandes Deutscher Werkbibliotheken," (29th Annual Meeting), Buch und Bibliothek 37 (1985):606 + .

255   Verein Angehörige des Mittleren und Nichtdiplomierten Bibliotheksdienstes e.V.
(Association of Librarians without Professional Status)

Address Klattenweg 59, Bremen
Officers (elected for 4-yr.term) Chair: Elke Wegener; Sec: Melitta Thomas. Exec.Board: 5
Staff None
Languages German
Established 1971, Bremen, at Staatsbibliothek, as Verein Deutscher Bibliotheksangestellter (VDBA)
Major Fields of Interest Promoting the interests of nonprofessional librarians
Major Goals and Objectives To represent the interests of nonprofessional librarians, especially toward employers and coworkers; to cooperate with other associations of library and information science; to promote continuing education of members.
Structure Governed by executive officers.
Sources of Support Membership dues.
Membership Total members: 170 (individual). Requirements: To have been employed in a library for one year. Dues: Determined by General Assembly.
General Assembly Entire membership meets once a year.
Publications No publications program.
Activities General Assembly only.

256   Verein der Bibliothekare an Öffentlichen Bibliotheken e.V. (VBB) (Association of Librarians in Public Libraries)

Address   Postfach 1324, D-7410 Reutlingen (permanent). Tel: 49 (7121) 36999. Headquarters: Gartenstrasse 18, D-7410 Reutlingen.
Officers   (elected for 3-yr.term) Pres: Birgit Dankert (Solitüder Str. 20, D-2390 Flensburg. Tel: 49 (461) 38224); Sec: Katharina Boulanger. Exec.Board: 5
Staff   2 (paid)
Languages   German
Established   1922, as Verein Deutscher Volksbibliothekare; reactivated 1949, Fulda; present name adopted 1977, Augsburg.
Major Fields of Interest   Public libraries
Major Goals and Objectives   To improve professional conditions; to improve public librarianship; to promote professional and library policy; to promote professional development through continuing education; to represent the interests of members in trade unions, cultural policy and social policy.
Structure   Governed by executive offices. Affiliations: IFLA
Sources of Support   Membership dues. Budget (Deutsche Mark): 1986/87: 500,000; 1987/88: 500,000
Membership   Total members: 3,900 (individual). Divisions: 10. 3 countries represented. Types of membership: Individual, student, emeritus. Requirements: Any professional librarian or student enrolled in library school. Dues vary according to income.
General Assembly   Entire membership meets once a year. 1987: Wiesbaden, June 17-21; 1988: Berlin, May 15-18.
Publications   *Official journal:* Buch und Bibliothek - BuB (Book and Library). 1949-. 10/yr. (Deutsche Mark) 15 (9, student). Free to members. Edited by Association. Circ: Approx.7,000. German, with English abstracts. Other publications: Annual report; proceedings of meetings; reports of seminars, workshops. Price lists available. No publications exchange program.
Activities   As an organization representing personnel of public libraries, activities are carried out accordingly. Past achievements: Library policy against cuts in continuing education. Current and future: Promote continuing education; programs to prevent unemployment of librarians; information dissemination on developments in international public librarianship; library policy against budget cuts; and any other activities in support of the aims of the Association. Sponsors Book Week activities and continuing education lectures, seminars, workshops.
Use of High Technology   Computer (Olivetti PC) for management.
Bibliography   Kersten, H.-H., Rothe, M., and Segebrecht, D., "Literatur braucht Bibliotheken, Bibliotheken brauchen Geld. VBB-Jahrestagung 1982 in Sindelfingen," (Literature Needs Libraries, Libraries Need Money. VBB Annual Meeting, 1982 in Sindelfingen) Buch und Bibliothek 34 (1982):591-605; Kersten, H.-H. et al., "VBB 1985: Zurück zur Natur? Leseförderung und Literaturvermittlung - Auftrag der Bibliotheken," (VBB 1985: Back to Nature? To Promote Reading and Provide Literature - Mission of Libraries), Buch und Bibliothek 37 (1985):576-582 (in German); Harms, G., "Zur Fortbildung der Bibliothekare/innen an Öffentlichen Bibliotheken," (Continuing Education of Librarians at Public Libraries), Buch und Bibliothek 38 (1986):224-227; Pflug, G. and Kaegbein, P., "Germany, Federal Republic of," in ALA World Encyclopedia of Library and Information Services, 2nd ed., pp. 306-309. Chicago: American Library Association, 1986.

257   Verein der Diplom-Bibliothekare an Wissenschaftlichen Bibliotheken e.V. (VdDB)
(Association of Professional Librarians in Academic/Research Libraries)

Address   c/o Niedersächsische Staats- und Universitätsbibliothek, Prinzenstrasse 1, D-3400 Göttingen (not permanent). Tel: 49 (551) 395212
Officers   (elected for 2-yr.term) Chair: H.-J. Kuhlmeyer; Past Chair: Helga Schwarz; Vice-Chairs: Ulla Usemann-Keller, Margit Rützel; Sec: B. Hoffmann; Treas: Bärbel Volle; Publications Officer: Ilse-Lotte Hoffmann. Exec.Board: 5
Staff   None
Languages   German
Established   1948, Hamburg
Major Fields of Interest   Representing interests of professional librarians; promoting academic/research librarianship
Major Goals and Objectives   Association has the duty of asserting the professional interests of its members. It is concerned with education and continuing education, salary and collective bargaining with the bargaining parties, planning and structural questions, and contacts with other associations in the profession.
Structure   Governed by Executive Board. Affiliations: IFLA, DBV (Deutscher Bibliotheksverband), DBK (Deutsche Bibliothekskonferenz)
Sources of Support   Membership dues, sale of publications. Budget (Deutsche Mark): Approx.150,000.
Membership   Total members: 2,300 (individual). Regional divisions: 11. Types of membership: Individual. Requirements: Librarian with a professional degree (Diplom-Bibliothekar). Dues (Deutsche Mark): 40, full-time employed, less for part-time and retired.
General Assembly   Entire membership meets once a year. 1987: Augsburg, June; 1988: Berlin, May; 1989: Bonn.
Publications   *Official journal:* Zeitschrift für Bibliothekswesen und Bibliographie. 1954-. 6/yr. (Deutsche Mark) 86 (48, members). Address: Verlag Vittorio Klostermann, Postfach 900601, D-6000 Frankfurt am Main 90. Editor: Klaus-Dieter Lehmann. Address: Deutsche Bibliothek, Zeppelinallee 4-8, Frankfurt am Main 1. Circ: 1,300+. German. Indexed in LISA, Lib.Lit.; published jointly with the Verein Deutscher Bibliothekare e.V. (VDB). Newsletter: Rundschreiben (VdDB and VDB). 1948-. 4/yr. Free to members. Address same as Association. Editors: Ilse-Lotte Hoffmann and Alexandra Habermann. Circ: 5,000. German. Other publications: Stellenpläne und Personalbedarf an wissenschaftlichen Bibliotheken (Personnel Needs of Research Libraries); Ausgewählte Literatur zu neuen Technologien (Selected Literature on New Technologies); Der Diplom-Bibliothekar an wissenschaftlichen Bibliotheken: Ein Berufsbild (Profile of the Professional Librarian in Research Libraries); Ausbildung im Wandel (Changes in Professional Education), etc. Publications issued for sale, price lists available.
Activities   Sponsors conferences, seminars; planning new training regulations and continuing education programs; improvement of salary classification.
Use of High Technology   Computers for managing members' data and for mailing addresses (Siemens Computer of German Library Institute)
Bibliography   Sobottke, I. and Goth, M., "Protokoll der 33. ordentlichen Mitgliederversammlung am 3. Juni 1982 in Darmstadt," (Minutes of the 33rd Annual Meeting, June 3, 1982 in Darmstadt) Zeitschrift für Bibliothekswesen und Bibliographie 29 (1982):433-437; Sobottke, I., "Jahresbericht 1981/82," (Annual Report 1981/82) ibid.:431-433; Pflug, G. and Kaegbein, P., "Germany, Federal Republic of," ALA World Encyclopedia of Library and Information Services, 2nd ed., pp. 306-309. Chicago: American Library Association,

1986; "Der VdDB stellt sich vor," (The VdDB introduces itself), Auskunft: Mitteilungs-blatt Hamburger Bibliothekare 1 (1986):38-40 (in German).

258 Verein Deutscher Archivare (VdA) (Association of German Archivists)

Address c/o Generaldirektion der Staatlichen Archive Bayerns, Schönfeldstrasse 5, D-8000 Munich 22 (permanent). Tel: 49 (89) 2198484.
Officers (elected for 4-yr.term) Chair: Hermann Rumschöttel; Vice-Chair: Hans Eugen Specker; Treas: Wolfgang Löhr. Exec.Board: 15.
Staff None
Languages German
Established Dec., 1946, at the Constitutional Assembly in Buende, Westphalia.
Major Fields of Interest Archives
Major Goals and Objectives Promotion of German archives and archival science; promotion of education and continuing education of archivists; promotion of exchange of experiences and improvement of cooperation between archives and archivists, and with related disciplines in the information and documentation field at the national and international level.
Structure Governed by executive officers and general assembly.
Sources of Support Membership dues.
Membership Total members: 1,000 (individual). Sections: 8. 7 countries represented. Type of membership: Individual, student, emeritus. Requirements: Trained archivists or staff of archives. Dues (Deutsche Mark): 40, individual (25, without journal).
General Assembly Entire membership meets once a year.
Publications *Official journal:* Der Archivar. 1947-. 4/yr. (Deutsche Mark) 42. Free to members. Address: c/o Nordrhein-Westfälisches Hauptstaatsarchiv, Mauerstrasse 55, D-4000 Düsseldorf 30. Circ: 2,000. German. Issues proceedings of conferences. Also publishes Archive und Archivare (Directory of Archives and Archivists), updated about every 5 years. Publications for sale.
Activities Mainly planning for annual congresses (Deutsche Archivtage); sponsors continuing education programs and workshops on specialized topics. Association has been active in promoting library-related legislation, such as archival legislation (Archivgesetzgebung) in the Federal Republic of Germany.
Bibliography Eckhart, G. F., "Verein deutscher Archivare," Der Archivar 37 (1984):455-460 (in German).

259 Verein Deutscher Bibliothekare e.V. (VDB) (Association of German Librarians)

Address c/o Universitätsbibliothek, Olshausenstrasse 29, D-2300 Kiel 1 (not permanent). Tel: 49 (431) 8802700.
Officers (elected for 2-yr.term) Pres: Engelbert Plassmann; Past Pres: Günther Wiegand; VPs: Yorck A. Haase, Engelbert Plassmann; Sec: K. Peters; Treas: Johannes Marbach. Sec: Gerhard Haass (appointed). Exec.Board: 5.
Staff 5 (volunteer)
Languages German
Established 1900; reactivated 1948, Munich
Major Fields of Interest Development of libraries and library services.
Major Goals and Objectives The Association represents the academic and research librarians of the Federal Republic of Germany and promotes their professional interests,

continuing education and training, and cooperation between librarians on a national and international level.

Structure   Governed by executive officers and Executive Council of 13 members.

Sources of Support   Membership dues; revenues from annual meetings. Budget (Deutsche Mark): Approx.90,000.

Membership   Total members: 1,300 + (individual). Regional associations: 7. Types of membership: Individual. Requirements: Academic and research librarians with university degree. Dues (Deutsche Mark): 40, individual; 20, retired or unemployed; no dues yet for extraordinary membership for members from foreign countries; no dues for honorary members.

General Assembly   Entire membership meets once a year, in the week following Pentecost (Tuesday to Saturday). 1987: Augsburg; 1988: Berlin, May 24-28.

Publications   *Official journal:* Zeitschrift für Bibliothekswesen und Bibliographie. 1954-. 6/yr. (Deutsche Mark) 86 (48 for members). Address: Verlag Vittorio Klostermann, Postfach 900601, D-6000 Frankfurt am Main 90. Editor: Klaus-Dieter Lehmann. Address: Deutsche Bibliothek, Zeppelinallee 4-8, D-6000 Frankfurt am Main 1. Circ: 1,300 +. German. Indexed in LISA, Lib.Lit.; published jointly with Verein der Diplom-Bibliothekare an Wissenschaftlichen Bibliotheken e.V. (VdDB). Other publications for sale: Jahrbuch der Deutschen Bibliotheken (Yearbook of German Libraries), biennial.

Activities   Past achievements: Proposals for the education and training of academic and research librarians (upper level staff), published as Empfehlungen für die Ausbildung des höheren Bibliotheksdienstes (Darmstadt, 1986. 129pp.). Current: To find a better form of cooperation between all German library associations and institutions. Future: Achieving the above mentioned cooperation to establish an effective board of representation of German librarianship; continuing education, especially in the field of new library technology. Association has been active in promoting library-related legislation on photocopying and copyright. Sponsors exhibits; continuing education lectures, seminars, workshops.

Bibliography   Hering, J. and Jopp, R.K., "Bericht über die 34. ordentliche Mitgliederversammlung am 3. Juni 1982 in der Technischen Hochschule Darmstadt," (Report of the 34th Annual Meeting in Darmstadt, June 3, 1982) Zeitschrift für Bibliothekswesen und Bibliographie 29 (1982):412-430 (in German); Bermann, H., "72. Deutscher Bibliothekartag, Darmstadt, 1.-5. Juni 1982," (German Libary Conference, Darmstadt, June 1-5, 1982) Biblos 31 (1982):348-350; Pflug, G. and Kaegbein, P., "Germany, Federal Republic of," in ALA World Encyclopedia of Library and Information Services, 2nd ed., pp. 306-309. Chicago: American Library Association, 1986.

260   Verein Deutscher Dokumentare e.V. (VDD) (Association of German Documentalists)

Address   c/o VDD, Berufsverband Dokumentation, Information, Kommunikation e.V., Postfach 2509, D-5300 Bonn 1

Officers   Chair: Winfried Schmitz-Esser; Vice-Chair: Bernd Habel. Exec.Board: 7

Staff   7 (volunteer)

Languages   German

Established   1961, Bonn

Major Fields of Interest   Information management and documentation

Major Goals and Objectives   Promotion of the profession of information managers and documentalists

Structure   Governed by Executive Council. Affiliations: DGD (Deutsche Gesellschaft für Dokumentation), FID.

Sources of Support   Membership dues

Membership   Total members: 300+ (individual). Requirements: Passing final exams of the LID (Lehrinstitut für Dokumentation), Frankfurt; adequate university examination; or having practical experience in the documentation field. Dues (Deutsche Mark): 30.
General Assembly   Entire membership meets once a year.
Publications   No official journal. Issues VDD Schriftenreihe, an irregular series. Organizational news published in Nachrichten für Dokumentation, the official journal of DGD.
Activities   Sponsoring workshops, seminars and other continuing education programs; carrying out the aims of the Association

261   Verein zur Förderung Bibliothekarischer Berufsperspektiven e.V. (Association for Promoting the Professional Career of Librarians)

Address   c/o Jörg Sämann, Barthelstrasse 52/54, D-5000 Cologne 30. Tel: (0221) 514129; or c/o Gudula Dinkelbach, Luxemburger Strasse 441-443, D-5000 Cologne 41. Tel: (0221) 462604.
Officers   Contact Persons: Jörg Sämann or Gudula Dinkelbach.
Staff   None
Languages   German
Established   Aug. 25, 1988, Cologne. Since late 1987 there had existed a national group, "Initiative Arbeitsloser Bibliothekare/innen" (Initiative of Unemployed Librarians), which assisted unemployed librarians to find a position by functioning as a national placement and referral center, and holding monthly meetings for exchange of experiences (see Töppe/Mertens, Bibliotheksdienst 22, 1988, no.11, pp.1081-85). It was felt, that this group, though helping the individual librarians, did not address the underlying problems and that there was a need to establish a new association.
Major Fields of Interest   Professional development, career of librarianship
Major Goals and Objectives   To study and find solutions for the basic problem of career choices for the professional librarian and the availability of options; to study changes in the areas of library activities and disseminate information; to keep abreast of developments in the field and provide opportunities for continuing education and retraining; to work for the creation of more positions for librarians, and help them to update their competencies accordingly; to address the needs of both unemployed librarians and those in the work force.
Structure   Governed by executive officers.
Sources of Support   Membership dues, private donations.
Membership   Membership drive is underway, so that the Association will have an impact. Dues (Deutsche Mark): 40, individual. Contributions are invited.
General Assembly   Entire membership meets at least once a year.
Publications   No official journal.
Activities   As its first projects, the Association plans to continue a study on the graduates of the Library School at Cologne, and to compile a reader on the various career opportunities for librarians. Furthermore, it plans to prepare information on continuing education and re-training. The Association plans to work jointly with the "Organisation von Fortbildungsveranstaltungen" (Organization of Continuing Education Programs) to expand the job market for librarians by enhancing their skills and competencies. Association makes great efforts to increase its membership, since the success of its goals and objectives depends on a large membership.
Bibliography   Dinkelbach, G., "Verein zur Förderung bibliothekarischer Berufsperspektiven," Mitteilungsblatt des Vereins Nordrhein-Westfalen 39 (1989):355-356 (in German).

Ghana

262 Ghana Library Association

Address PO Box 4105, Accra (permanent). Tel: 76591/5.
Officers (elected for 2-yr.term) Pres: S.A. Afre; Exec.Sec: E. Cabutey-Adodoadji.
Staff None
Languages English
Established 1962, Accra, at the University of Ghana
Major Fields of Interest Development of libraries; advancement of the professional status of librarians
Major Goals and Objectives To unite all professional librarians in Ghana; to promote libraries and library service; to advance the professional status of members.
Structure Governed by executive officers: Affiliations: IFLA, COMLA.
Sources of Support Membership dues, subsidies.
Membership Total members: 100+. Types of membership: Individual, institutional. Requirements: Open to all librarians and institutions having libraries. Dues scaled according to salary.
General Assembly Entire membership meets annually.
Publications *Official journal:* Ghana Library Journal. 1963-. 2/yr. Free to members. Address same as Association. English. Proceedings of annual meeting, workshops, and conferences appear in journal.
Activities Past achievements: Uniting all librarians in Ghana; achieving recognition for librarians from the central government. Current and Future: Working for the improvement of libraries relevant to the needs of Ghana.
Bibliography Dua-Agyemang, H. "Ghana," in ALA World Encyclopedia of Library and Information Services, 2nd ed., pp. 310-312. Chicago: American Library Association, 1986; Agyei-Gyane, L., "The Ghana Library Association: History and Development," Libri 36 (1985):113-118.

Greece

263   Enosis Ellenon Bibliothekarion (EEB)
(Greek Library Association - GLA)

Address   4 Skouleniou Street, GR-10561 Athens (permanent). Tel: 30 (1) 3226625.
Officers   (elected for 2-yr.term) Pres: Ms. N. Skandali; Exec.Sec: D. Karakostas; Secs: Anna Solomou, Sofia Palamiotou, Niko Contopoulou.
Staff   None
Languages   Greek, English
Established   1968, Athens College Library, after a seminar held for librarians
Major Fields of Interest   Libraries and library development in Greece
Major Goals and Objectives   To promote library development in Greece; to promote librarianship as a science; to assist in legislation for better library service; to increase public awareness of the significance of libraries for cultural and technological development; to cooperate with other professional associations abroad.
Structure   Governed by executive officers. Affiliations: IFLA
Sources of Support   Membership dues, government subsidies.
Membership   Total members: 230+. Types of membership: Individual, institutional. Requirements: Library school degree or 6 months in library service.
General Assembly   Entire membership meets annually in Athens.
Publications   *Official journal:* Greek Library Association Bulletin. 1970-. Irregular. Free to members. Address same as Association.
Activities   Various activities carried out by Committees, e.g. Documentation, Cataloging and Classification, Union Catalog of Books, Public Affairs, Communications, etc. Sponsors conferences, seminars, workshops. Participates in international congresses and represents Greek librarianship.
Bibliography   Papademetriou, George C., "Greece," in ALA World Encyclopedia of Library and Information Services, 2nd ed., pp.315-316. Chicago: American Library Association, 1986.

Guatemala

264   Asociación Bibliotecológica de Guatemala
(Library Association of Guatemala)

Address   c/o Susana Prera de Meza, dir. O calle 15-70, zona 15, Colonia El Maestro, Guatemala, Central America
Officers   Pres: Elizabeth Flores; Sec: Susana Prera de Meza.
Staff   None
Languages   Spanish
Established   1972
Major Fields of Interest   Libraries and library services in Guatemala
Major Goals and Objectives   To promote libraries and library services in the country; to further the status of librarians and their professional development.
Structure   Governed by executive officers.
Sources of Support   Membership dues, subsidies.
Membership   Total members: 50 (35 librarians with diploma, 15 other individuals). Type of membership: Individual. Requirements: Librarians with diploma, or others working in libraries.
General Assembly   Entire membership meets once a year.
Publications   *Official journal:* Boletín de la Asociación Bibliotecológica de Guatemala. Irreg.
Activities   Sponsors meetings, seminars, workshops and other continuing education programs for librarians.
Bibliography   Palma R., G., "Guatemala," in ALA World Encyclopedia of Library and Information Services, 2nd ed., pp. 317-318. Chicago: American Library Association, 1986.

Guinea-Bissau

265   Instituto Nacional de Estudos e Pesquisa (INEP)
(National Institute for Studies and Research)

Address   Complexo Escolar "14 de Novembro," Bairro Cobornel-Bissau (permanent). Postal address: Caixa Postal 112, Guinea-Bissau (West Africa). Tel: 211301/214497. Telex: 275 Miplan BI.

Officers   (appointed) General Director: Carlos Lopes; Center of Contemporary History: Carlos Cardoso; Center of Socio-Economic Studies: Daiana Lima Handem; Center of Appropriate Technology: Abdulai Sila. Exec.Board: 4

Staff   32 (paid), 5 (volunteers)

Languages   Portuguese, French, English, German.

Established   Oct. 10, 1984

Major Fields of Interest   Social sciences, natural sciences, archival studies.

Major Goals and Objectives   To conduct research in these fields and produce publications.

Structure   Governed by Board according to a decree of the Council of Ministers. Affiliations: ICA, CODESRIA, IFS, CERDAS, AAPS.

Sources of Support   Government subsidies; consultancy.

Membership   Total members: 32 (individual). Divisions: 4. Sections: 6.

Publications   *Official journal:* Soronda. 1985-. 2/yr. (Guinea-Bissau Peso) 15. Address same as Institute. Portuguese. Publishes annual reports, proceedings of meetings, reports of seminars, workshops. Other publications: Monograph series Kacu Martel; a Socio-Economic Information Bulletin (BISE); a Scientific Technological Information Bulletin. Publications available for sale and exchange.

Activities   Past achievements: Organizing international Colloquium in 1986: "Sobre a Formaçâo da Naçâo;" National and Technical Cooperation Assessments and Practical Programmes for Guinea Bissau. Current and future: Research activities and publications. Institute has been active in library-related legislation, such as Legal Deposit, and National Archives Law. Sponsors continuing education programs.

Use of High Technology   Computers (Olivetti M24, M28) and databases for management.

Bibliography   St-Amant, R., "The Beginnings of the National Institute for Studies and Research in Guinea-Bissau," CAD Information (Paris: International Council on Archives, May, 1987), pp. 9-10 (available in French and English); Cruzeiro, M. M., "Guinea-Bissau," in ALA World Encyclopedia of Library and Information Services, 2nd ed., p. 319. Chicago: American Library Association, 1986.

Guyana

266 Guyana Library Association (GLA)

Address c/o National Library, 76-77 Church and Main Streets, Georgetown. Postal address: PO Box 10240, Georgetown (permanent).
Officers (elected) Pres: Wenda R. Stephenson; VP: Gwyneth Browman; Sec: Alethea John; Treas: Indrowty Dianand. Exec.Board: 11
Staff None
Languages English
Established 1968, at National Library in Georgetown.
Major Fields of Interest Development of libraries; training of library assistants; educating users on the value of libraries; documentation and information services.
Major Goals and Objectives (1) To foster the close association of all persons and organizations in Guyana interested in the promotion of librarianship and related fields; (2) to publicize the role of libraries and librarians in national development and to make recommendations for the promotion of legislation affecting libraries and librarians; (3) to organize meetings, lectures, seminars, training courses, etc. for the purpose of promoting effective library services in Guyana; (4) to promote the recruitment, training and education of librarians and to improve their status; (5) to promote bibliographic activities in Guyana; (6) to advise on the organization of new libraries, the improvement of existing libraries, and to promote a high standard of library services in Guyana; (6) to publish a journal at regular intervals to record the activities of the Association and to publish articles of interest to members.
Structure Governed by Executive Committee. Affiliations: COMLA, ACURIL, Guyana Society
Sources of Support Membership dues, sale of publications, fund raising activities.
Membership Total members: 32 (24 individual, 8 institutional). Sections: 6. Requirements: Open to all librarians regardless of professional rank, archivists, documentalists, and all other persons interested in the goals of the Association. Dues (Guyana Dollar): 50, institutional; 12, 20, 25, individual (part-time to full-time); 10, associate.
General Assembly Entire membership meets 3 times a year.
Publications *Official journal:* Guyana Library Association Bulletin. 1971-. 2/yr. (US Dollar) 10. Free to members. Address same as Association. Editor: K. Sills. English. Other publications: Guide to Library Services in Guyana (revised periodically); Union List of Scientific and Technical Periodicals held in the Libraries of Guyana; Newsbrief. 1985-. Irreg. Publications available for sale, some free.
Activities Past achievements: Publication of Union List; workshop on user education, 1983; Caribbean Cultural Experience Lecture Series sponsored jointly with USIS. Current: Workshop on computers in libraries; updating of Union List; continuing publication of Bulletin. Future: Training of paraprofessionals; assisting in the development of a National Information System for Guyana; promoting bibliographic activities. Sponsors continuing education programs, book sales.
Bibliography Stephenson, Y.V., "Guyana," in ALA World Encyclopedia of Library and Information Services, 2nd ed., pp. 319-321. Chicago: American Library Association, 1986.

Honduras

267   Asociación de Bibliotecarios y Archiveros de Honduras (ABAH)
(Association of Librarians and Archivists of Honduras)

Address   3 Avenidas, 4 y 5 Calles, No. 416 Comayagüela, DC, Tegucigalpa, Honduras, C.A. (permanent)

Officers   (elected for 2-yr.term) Pres: Francisca de Escoto Espinoza; Sec.Gen: Juan Angel Ayes R.

Staff   None

Languages   Spanish

Major Fields of Interest   Libraries and library services in Honduras

Major Goals and Objectives   To improve the organization and services of Honduran libraries; to promote professional development of librarians.

Structure   Governed by executive officers. Affiliations: ACURIL

Sources of Support   Membership dues

Membership   Total members: 55. Requirements: Open to those who have received library training or are engaged in educational and cultural activities.

General Assembly   Entire membership meets monthly.

Publications   *Official journal:* Cátálogo de Préstamo. 12/yr. Address same as Association.

Activities   Sponsors education and training courses; maintains small reference library; organizes meetings.

Bibliography   Barthell, D.W., "Honduras," in ALA World Encyclopedia of Library and Information Services, 2nd ed., pp. 339-340. Chicago: American Library Association, 1986.

Hong Kong

268 Hong Kong Library Association

Address PO Box 10095, General Post Office, Hong Kong (permanent).
Officers (elected for 1-yr.term) Chair: Ms. V.E. Morgan; Past Chair: David S. Yen; Vice-Chair: S.C. Au-Yeung; Hon.Sec: Ms. E. Wu; Hon.Treas: Julia Chan. Exec.Board: 10
Staff None
Languages English
Established 1958, Hong Kong; constitution was revised in 1987, with right to vote and hold office restricted to professionally qualified members.
Major Fields of Interest Library and information science
Major Goals and Objectives To unite all persons engaged in library work or interested in libraries in Hong Kong; to encourage the establishment and development of libraries and information centers in Hong Kong; to encourage professional education and training for librarianship; to organize meetings, conferences, and to cooperate with other international library associations.
Structure Governed by Executive Committee. Affiliations: COMLA, IFLA
Sources of Support Membership dues, sale of publications.
Membership Total members: 438 (413 individual, 25 institutional). Types of membership: Individual (331), student (77), corresponding (2), institutional (25), honorary (3). Requirements: Open to those whose professional activities in library, information, or documentation work qualify them for membership. Dues (Hong Kong Dollar): 25-80, individual; 140, institutional.
General Assembly Entire membership meets once a year, in December, in Hong Kong.
Publications *Official journal:* Journal of the Hong Kong Library Association. 1969-. 1/yr. (US Dollar) 15. Free to members. Address same as Association. Circ: 500+. English and Chinese. Issues Newsletter; Directory of Special Libraries in Hong Kong (1983). Publications for sale. Publications exchange program in effect.
Activities Sponsors annual conferences, continuing education seminars, workshops, lectures, exhibits.
Bibliography Kan, Lai-Bing, "Hong Kong," in ALA World Encyclopedia of Library and Information Services, 2nd ed., pp. 340-341. Chicago: American Library Association, 1986; Kan, Lai-Bing, and Yan, A.S.W., "Libraries in Hong Kong: Growth and Development," Singapore Libraries 18 (1988):65-74; Khurshid, A., "Library Associations in Asia," Herald of Library Science 28 (1989):3-10.

269 Hong Kong Teacher Librarians' Association

Address c/o Dr. Kan Lai-Bing, Director, University of Hong Kong Libraries, Pokfulam Road, Hong Kong (not permanent). Tel: 852 (5) 8592203. Fax: 852-5-479907.
Languages English
Established 1983
Major Fields of Interest Teacher librarians
Major Goals and Objectives To promote schoolwork in support of educational development; to facilitate the exchange of work experience among members who had completed the first In-Service Training Course for School Librarians; to organize recreational activities for members and to look after their general welfare.
Structure Governed by executive officers.

Sources of Support   Membership dues.
Membership   Total members: 63 (individual)
Activities   Carried out to in accordance with the aims of the Association
Bibliography   Kan, Lai-Bing, and Yan, A.S.W., "Libraries in Hong Kong: Growth and Development," Singapore Libraries 18 (1988):65-74.

Hungary

270   Magyar Könyvtárosok Egyesülete (MKE) (Hungarian Library Association / HLA)

Address   Uri u. 54-56, H-1014 Budapest (permanent). Tel: 36 (1) 556857.
Officers   (elected for 4-yr.term) Pres: Ibolya Billédi; Sec-Gen: Ms. G. Poprády.
Exec.Board: 25.
Staff   5 (paid), 30 (volunteers)
Languages   Hungarian
Established   1935, Budapest, as Hungarian Library and Archive Association (HLAA); in 1950 current name adopted; in 1985 membership widened to include archivists again.
Major Fields of Interest   Library policy; representation of professional interests of librarians and archivists; training and continuing education of librarians and archivists
Major Goals and Objectives   To formulate library policy; to represent the professional interests of librarians and archivists; to promote professional development of librarians and archivists through education and continuing education programs; to promote professional recognition; to develop relations with other organizations; to represent Hungarian libraries in IFLA and improve international relations.
Structure   Governed by Executive Board. Affiliations: IFLA.
Sources of Support   Membership dues, sale of publications, government subsidies.
Membership   Total members: 3,760 (3,700 individual, 60 institutional). Divisions: 6. Committees: 6. Affiliated with 19 regional associations in counties. Requirements: Professional qualification in library, information science or archival studies. Dues: Individual, according to salary.
General Assembly   Entire membership meets every 2 years. 1987: Szolnok.
Publications   *Official journal:* Tájékoztató (Bulletin). 1965-. 6/yr. Free to members. Editor: Ibolya Billédi. Address same as Association. Circ: 4,000. Hungarian. Issues annual reports.
Activities   Past achievements: Improvement of members' activities; strengthening of international relations; signed bilateral agreements with foreign library associations, such as the Library Association (UK), in 1985, the year of its 50th anniversary. Association has increased its membership and expanded its field of activities. An independent Section for Archivists was established and regional membership introduced. An international seminar on library school education was held in Budapest in 1986. Current: Continuing education programs for members; support of IFLA core programs. Future: To continue programs and activities according to the Association's policy, that are useful to both institutions and individuals, that will improve libraries, and promote professional development and professional recognition of members.
Bibliography   Ferencné, B., "The Hungarian Library Association," Library Association Record 88 (1986):294; Kiss, J., "Hungary," in ALA World Encyclopedia of Library and Information Services, 2nd ed., pp. 343-346; Slawinski, I., "21. Tagung der Vereinigung der Ungarischen Bibliothekare," (21st Conference of the Hungarian Library Association) Mitteilungen der Vereinigung Österreichischer Bibliothekare 42 (1989):33-34 (in German)

271   MTESZ Tájékoztatási Tudományos Tanács (MTESZ - TTT) (Information Science Council of the Federation of Technical and Scientific Societies)

Address   Kossuth Lajos tér 6-8, H-1055 Budapest (permanent). Postal address: PO Box 240, H-1368 Budapest. Tel: (361) 533333. Telex: 225792 MTESZ-H.
Officers   (elected for 5-yr.term) Pres: Pál Gágyor (Tel: 361-119880; telex: 225262 info-h); Sec: György Reich (Tel: 361-112436). Exec.Board: 8
Staff   1 (paid), 7 (volunteers)
Languages   Hungarian
Established   1970
Major Fields of Interest   Technical and scientific information
Major Goals and Objectives   To coordinate the activities and the network for technical and scientific information in Hungary
Structure   Governed by MTESZ, the Federation of Technical and Scientific Societies (Müszaki és Természettudományi Egyesületek Szövetsége). Affiliations: WIFO, FENTO
Sources of Support   Does not have its own budget, but works as a Council of MTESZ, which has a budget of approx. 400 million Forint.
Membership   Total members: 52 (institutional). Requirements: Members are delegations of the 33 member societies of MTESZ.
General Assembly   Entire membership meets 4 times a year, in Budapest.
Publications   No official journal.
Activities   Centered in those of MTESZ. Is involved in the organization of the Hungarian database of all MTESZ events - about 10,000 a year.
Use of High Technology   Computers (PCs) and databases for management.

Iceland

272   Bókavarðafélag Islands
(Icelandic Library Association)

Address   PO Box 1497, 127 Reykjavik (permanent).
Officers   (elected for 2-yr.term) Pres: Ms. A. Jóhannsdóttir; Past Pres: Thórdis Thor-valdsdóttir; Secs: Ms. P. Héfinsdóttir, Sólveig Thorsteinsdóttir, Asdís Egilsdóttir.
Staff   Volunteers
Languages   Icelandic
Established   1960, at Public Library in Hafnarfjördur.
Major Fields of Interest   Development of libraries and the library profession
Major Goals and Objectives   To further library development in Iceland.
Structure   Governed by Executive Board. Association is a federation of the 3 Icelandic library associations. Affiliations: IFLA
Sources of Support   Membership dues.
Membership   Total members: 300+ (individual). Requirements: Individuals working full-time or part-time as librarians.
General Assembly   Entire membership meets every 2 years in Reykjavik.
Publications   *Official journal:* Fregnir (Newsletter). 1976-. 4/yr. Free to members. Editor: Viggó Gíslason. Address: Bókasafni Alpingis, Vonarstraeti 8, 101 Reykjavik. Icelandic. Published in cooperation with other library associations in Iceland.
Activities   Association works for improvement of library services; represents Icelandic librarians at international bodies, particularly IFLA (since 1966). Active in promoting library-related legislation, such as the Law on Professional Librarians, which defines qualifications for the title of professional librarian (bókasafnsfraedingur), and was passed by the Icelandic Parliament in May 1984.
Bibliography   Harðarson, Hrafn A. and Conaway, C.W., "Iceland," in ALA World Encyclopedia of Library and Information Services, 2nd ed., pp. 349-350. Chicago: American Library Association, 1986.

273   Félag Bókasafnsfraedinga
(Association of Professional Librarians)

Address   PO Box 1167, Reykjavik (permanent). Tel: (354) 40281/27130.
Officers   (elected for 1-yr.term) Pres: Helga Einarsdóttir; VP: Halldóra Porsteinsdóttir; Exec.Sec: Anna Torfardóttir; Treas: Anna Magnusdóttir ; Exec.Board: 6
Staff   6 (volunteers = Exec.Board)
Languages   Icelandic
Established   1973
Major Fields of Interest   Library science
Major Goals and Objectives   To promote library science in Iceland; to promote the professional status of librarians.
Structure   Governed by executive officers.
Sources of Support   Membership dues
Membership   Total members: 100+ (individual). Requirements: Individuals holding a professional university-level degree from the University of Iceland or similar institutions abroad.
General Assembly   Entire membership meets 2 to 4 times a year.
Publications   No official journal.

Activities   Active in promoting library-related legislation, such as the Law on Professional Librarians, passed by the Icelandic Parliament in May 1984. It defines qualifications for the title of professional librarian (bókasafnsfraeðingur).
Bibliography   Harðarson, Hrafn A., and Conaway, C.W., "Iceland," in <u>ALA World Encyclopedia of Library and Information Services</u>, 2nd ed., pp. 349-350. Chicago: American Library Association, 1986.

274   Félag Bókavarða í Rannsóknarbókasöfnum (FBR) (Association of Librarians in Research Libraries)

Address   c/o Hildur G. Eypórsdóttir, Landsbókasafni, Safnahúsinu, v/Hverfisgötu, 101 Reykjavik (not permanent). Tel: (354) 13080.
Officers   (elected for 1-yr.term) Chair: Hildur G. Eypórsdóttir; Treas: Valbor Stefánsdóttir; Sec: Thórir Ragnarsson; Other officers: Audur Gestsdóttir, Lotte Gestsson. Exec.Board: 5
Staff   None
Languages   Icelandic
Established   May 6, 1966, Reykjavik, as a division of Bókavardafélag Islands (Icelandic Library Association).
Major Fields of Interest   Research libraries and librarians
Major Goals and Objectives   To support the cooperation of librarians in research libraries and advance the development of libraries and information services.
Structure   FBR is one of the 3 associations which form the Bókvarðafélag Islands (Icelandic Library Association), which is a federation of library associations in Iceland.
Sources of Support   Membership dues.
Membership   Total members: 97 (87 individual, 10 institutional). Requirements: Anyone interested in libraries and information can become a member. Dues (Iceland Krona): 300.
General Assembly   Entire membership meets 3-4 times a year.
Publications   *Official journal:* <u>Fregnir</u> (published in cooperation with other library associations). 1976-. 4/yr. Free to members. Editor: Viggó Gíslason. Address: Bókasafni Alpingis, Vonarstraeti 8, 101 Reykjavik. Circ: Membership. Icelandic.
Activities   Organizing meetings, seminars, etc., for professional librarians.
Bibliography   Harðarson, Hrafn A., and Conaway, C.W., "Iceland," in <u>ALA World Encyclopedia of Library and Information Service</u>, 2nd ed., pp. 349-350. Chicago: American Library Association, 1986.

India

275   Association of Agricultural Librarians and Documentalists of India

Address   c/o S. Moitra, Secretary, Chief Librarian, Indian Council of Agricultural Research, Krishi Bhawan, Dr. Rajendra Prasad Road, New Delhi 110001 (not permanent)
Officers   Sec: S. Moitra
Major Fields of Interest   Agricultural librarianship and documentation
Major Goals and Objectives   To further the development of agricultural librarianship and documentation in India
Bibliography   Ramachandra, A.R., "Association of Agricultural Librarians and Documentalists of India," Quarterly Bulletin of IAALD 26 (1981):102.

276   Association of Government Librarians and Information Specialists (AGLIS) (formerly Government of India Librarians Association)

Address   c/o DESIDOC, Metcalfe House, Delhi 110054 (not permanent). Tel: (91) 237466/231587. Telex: (31) 5030.
Officers   (elected for 2-yr.term) Pres: S.S. Murthy; Sec: S.N. Mehta; Asst.Sec: R.L. Sharma. Exec.Board: 16
Staff   4 (paid), 8 (volunteers)
Languages   English
Established   1933, as Government of India Librarians Association (GILA); new name adopted 1987.
Major Fields of Interest   Government library and information services; professional development of librarians and information specialists
Major Goals and Objectives   (1) To promote library and information service; (2) to help libraries provide effective and efficient service to planners, policy makers, and administrators; (3) to evolve methods and techniques for the continuing education of library personnel and continuous quality of information and documentation services; (4) to foster mutual cooperation and assistance between various libraries and library personnel in India.
Structure   Governed by executive officers. Affiliations: IFLA.
Sources of Support   Membership dues, sale of publications, government subsidies. Budget (Indian Rupee): Approx. 150,000.
Membership   Total members: 600 (300 individual, 300 institutional). Divisions: 2. Requirements: Any person working in a library or any other institution concerned with information and documentation services. Dues (Indian Rupee): 10, individual; 100, life; 50, nonprofit institution; 100, profit-making institution.
General Assembly   Entire membership meets once a year.
Publications   *Official journal:* GILA Bulletin. 1982-. 4/yr. Free to members. Address same as Association. Editor: V.K. Jai. Address: Chief Librarian, Ministry of External Affairs, Patialo House, New Delhi. Circ: 700. English. Indexed in several journals. Other publications: Annual reports, proceedings of meetings; Directory of Government of India Libraries in Delhi.
Activities   In accordance with the goals and objectives, the major areas of activities are: (1) seminars, conferences, meetings; (2) refresher courses and workshops in the field of library and information services, including computers; (3) publication of directories, etc. Past and current: Conducted tour of librarians to visit libraries, information/documentation centers of South East Asia, i.e. Thailand, Malaysia and Singapore. Held All-India Li-

brary Convention; sponsors continuing education programs. Future: Workshops on computer applications in libraries, and other topics of interest. Association has been active in promoting library-related legislation.
Use of High Technology Databases used for management.
Bibliography 50 Years of Government of India Librarians Association (1983); Purkayastha, P.D., "National Library Associations: The Indian Scene," International Library Movement 7 (1985):61-69; "Annual General Body Meeting of Association of Government Libraians and Information Specialists (AGLIS)," Herald of Library Science 28 (1989):278; Khurshid, A., "Library Associations in Asia," Herald of Library Science 28 (1989):3-10.

277   Association of Indian Archivists

Address c/o National Archives of India, Janpath, New Delhi 110001 (permanent). Tel: (91) 383436/388557.
Officers (elected for 2-yr.term) Pres: R.K. Perti; VP: R. Muniswamy; Sec: M.L. Kachroo; Joint Sec: Ms.V.Lalitha; Treas: V.V. Talwar. National Exec. Board: 15
Staff 8 (volunteers)
Languages Mostly English, occasionally Hindi
Established 1976
Major Fields of Interest Archival science, archival management
Major Goals and Objectives To promote the preservation and utilization of the cultural heritage of the nation in the form of records and other recorded materials; to promote and advance the profession of archives administration, and to arouse public interest and enlighten public opinion on matters affecting records; to disseminate professional knowledge and techniques concerning archives and related fields of endeavour through international sharing of experience; to promote access to archives for the purpose of bonafide research; and to promote principles of sound archival economy.
Structure Governed by executive officers. Affiliation: International Council on Archives
Sources of Support Membership dues.
Membership Total members: 352 (320 individual, 32 institutional). All the States of the Indian Union represented. Requirements: Any individual who is working in an archival institution, library, museum, record management organization, or institutions engaged in the preservation and utilization of records/archives. Dues (Indian Rupee): 10, individual; 100, life; 100, institutional.
General Assembly Entire membership meets every 2 years, usually in April/May.
Publications *Official journal:* News Bulletin. 1986-. 4/yr. Free to members. Address same as Association. Editor: M. L. Kachroo, Hon.Sec. Circ: 500. English. Issues annual report, proceedings of meetings. Publications not for sale.
Activities Past achievements: Since its founding, the Association has directed its efforts towards the proper management, preservation, and utilization of archives, whether in public or private custody. It has also made special efforts to arouse public opinion to preserve and save archives for posterity and historic research. As a result, records management programs have been taken up at universities and banking institutions, with promising results. Current: The Association is endeavouring to ensure that private and semi-government institutions assume the management and preservation of records in their custody and their utilization for bonafide research. Future: The Association is striving to induce business establishments in the country to avail themselves of the services of the Association in order to ensure proper preservation of their archives. Accordingly, the Association sponsored a seminar on "The Mission of the Archivist." Association sponsors

exhibits, workshops, seminars and other continuing educaton programs on current topics, such as records management in universities, in banking institutions in India, etc.

278   Federation of Indian Library Associations (FILA)

Address   Misri Bazar, Patiala, Punjab (permanent). Address of Secretary: K.S. Pareek, Marwari Public Library, Chandni Chowk, Delhi 6.
Officers   (elected) Pres: P.N. Kaula; VP: S. Bashiruddin; Exec.Sec: R.N. Kaul, Sec: K.S. Pareek; Treas: M.S. Tyadi. Exec.Council: 35
Staff   3 (volunteer)
Languages   English
Established   1966, Chandigarh, at the All India Congress. Founder: P.N. Kaula.
Major Fields of Interest   Library science; information service; library organization; book production.
Major Goals and Objectives   To promote library movements; to coordinate library activities of various associations; to act as the unifying body for library associations in India.
Structure   Governed by Executive Council meeting with the National Council of Indian Library Associations (NACILA) every two months.
Sources of Support   Membership dues, paid through state and regional associations.
Membership   Total members: 1,500 (individual). Types of membership: Associate. Requirements: Open to any member of professional bodies, state and regional associations.
Publications   No official journal.
Activities   Participating in All Indian Library Convention, sponsored by NACILA.
Bibliography   Das Gupta, R.K., "India," ALA World Encyclopedia of Library and Information Services, 2nd ed., pp. 350-353. Chicago: American Library Association, 1986; Khurshid, A., "Library Associations in Asia," Herald of Library Science 28 (1989):3-10.

279   Indian Association of Academic Librarians (INDAAL)

Address   c/o Dr. Zakir Husein Library, Jamia Milia Islamia University, Jamia Milia, Okhla, New Delhi (not permanent). Tel: 01 (11) 632360.
Officers   Pres: Girja Kumar; Sec: M.M. Kashyap
Established   1978
Major Fields of Interest   Academic librarianship
Major Goals and Objectives   To further professional development and status of academic librarians; to represent the interests of college and university libraries
Publications   Publishes Newsletter.
Bibliography   Khurshid, A., "Library Associations in Asia," Herald of Library Science 28 (1989):3-10; Inamder, N.B., and Ramaiah, L.S., eds., National Policy for University Libraries in India: Problems and Perspectives (New Delhi: Concept Publishing, 1989).

280   Indian Association of Special Libraries and Information Centres (IASLIC)

Address   P. 291 CIT Scheme no. 6M, PO Kankurgachi, Calcutta 700054 (permanent). Tel: 91 (33) 359651.
Officers   (elected for 3-yr.term) Pres: Sankar Sen; Past Pres: B.P. Adhikari; Sec: S.M. Ganguly. Exec.Board: 11
Staff   21 (7 paid, 14 volunteers)
Languages   English
Established   1955, Calcutta
Major Fields of Interest   Special librarianship; documentation and information services; translating and abstracting; reprography; management techniques.

Major Goals and Objectives   To promote library and information service; to coordinate activities and forst mutual cooperation among special libraries; to imprve technical efficiency and professional welfare; to act as a center of research and study.

Structure   Governed by Executive Council. Affiliations: FID, IFLA, National Commission for Unesco in India.

Sources of Support   Membership dues, sale of publications, government subsidies.

Membership   Total members: 900 (520 individual, 380 institutional). Divisions: 5. Chapters: 5. 6 countries represented. Types of membership: Individual, institutional, life, honorary. Requirements: Individuals admitted on receipt of subscription, into different categories. Institutions, both profit and nonprofit, admitted on receipt of subscription. Dues (Indian Rupee); 25, individual; 20 - 150, institutional; 250, life; 1,000 +, donor.

General Assembly   Entire membership meets once a year. 1988: Calcutta, Dec.20-23.

Publications   *Official journal:* IASLIC Bulletin. 1956-. 4/yr. 70 Indian Rupee. Free to members. Editor: S.K. Kapoor. Address same as Association; Circ: 1,200. English. Indexed in ILSA (Indian Library Science Abstracts). Other publications: Annual reports, proceedings of seminars, conferences, workshops; IASLIC Newsletter. 1966-. 12/yr; Indian Library Science Abstracts. 1967-. 4/yr; Directory of Special and Research Libraries in India, and many other monographs. Publications for sale, price lists available. Publications exchanged with other associations.

Activities   Major activities are the organizing of seminars and publication of papers. The 13th National Seminar of IASLIC was jointly held with the 34th All India Conference of ILA at Calcutta, December 1988, and dealt with "Narketing of Library and Information Services in India." Activities are carried out by the various Special Interest Groups and the IASLIC Study Circle (which was started in 1965 and had great impact on the development of the Association). Association organized a postgraduate post-diploma course in "Special Librarianship and Documentation" in 1967, and has offered continuing education programs since then.

Bibliography   Das Gupta, R.K., "India," in ALA World Encyclopedia of Library and Information Services, 2nd ed., pp. 350-353. Chicago: American Library Association, 1986; Subba Rao, C.V., "Professional Associations of India: IASLIC's Record of Service and Achievements," Herald of Library Science 26 (1987):192-201; Khurshid, A., "Library Associations in Asia," Herald of Library Science 28 (1989):3-10; Singh, Sewa, "Joint ILA/IASLIC Conference," ibid.:86-90; Kaula, P.N., "13th National Seminar of IASLIC," ibid.:107-108; Subba Rao, G.V., "Some Obsevations on the Joint Conference of ILA and IASLIC at Calcutta," ibid.:212-218; Kaula, P.N., "Joint ILA and IASLIC Conference: Resolutions," ibid.:256-257.

281   Indian Association of Teachers of Library and Information Science (IATLIS)

Address   Department of Library Science, Banaras Hindu University, Varanasi 221005(UP) (permanent). Tel: (91) 54291/212

Officers   (elected for 6-yr.term) Pres: Krishan Kumar (Professor, Delhi University); Past Pres: P.N. Kaula; VP: P.S.G. Kumar (Head, Department of Library and Information Science, Nagpur University); Exec.Sec: A. Tejomurty; Treas: S. Kumar. Exec.Board: 15

Staff   1 (volunteer)

Languages   English

Established   1969, at Documentation Research and Training Centre, Bangalore.

Major Fields of Interest   Library and information science education

Major Goals and Objectives   To promote library and information science education and research; to protect the interests and status of teachers of library science.

Structure   Governed by Executive Committee.

Sources of Support   Membership dues, private donations.
Membership   Total members: 105 (88 individual, 17 institutional). Divisions: 3. Chapters: 2. Types of membership: Individual, institutional, life. Requirements: Payment of annual dues, professional status. Dues (Indian Rupee): 15, individual; 40, institutional; 250, life.
General Assembly   Entire membership meets annually.
Publications   *Official journal:* IATLIS Newsletter. 1975-. 6/yr. 25 Indian Rupee. Free to members. Editor: P.S.G. Kumar. Address same as Association. Circ: 500. English. Issues annual report. Publications exchanged with other associations.
Activities   Publication of Directory of Library and Information Schools; promoting research in schools of library and information studies. Active in sponsoring library-related legislation; organizing continuing education programs; furthering the professional development and status of teachers of library and information science. At the 6th IATLIS National Seminar on Education for Academic Librarianship (Gulbarga University, Nov. 21-23, 1988), some of the priorities identified were the need for standards in professional library and information science education, and the establishment of a National Institute of Library and Information Science.
Bibliography   Kumar, P.S.G., "Indian Association of Teachers of Library Science," Herald of Library Science 25 (1986):83-86; Khurshid, A., "Library Associations in Asia," Herald of Library Science 28 (1989):3-10; Kumar, Sudhir, "Sixth IATLIS National Seminar on Education for Academic Librarianship," ibid.:91-95.

282   Indian College Library Association (ICLA)

Address   66 Ranjan Colony, Hyderabad 500253 (not permanent). Tel: (842)525282; or, 19-2-81 Ranjan Colony, Nawab Saheb Kunta, Jahanuma, Hyderabad 500001; or, 25 Bahadurpura Colony, Hyderabad 500264, Andhra Pradesh. Tel: (91) 45282.
Officers   (elected for 2-yr.term) Pres: A.P. Jain; VP: B.V. Kripanithi; Exec.Sec: Ms. B.V.L. Reddy; Treas: T. Bhasker. Exec.Board: 25
Staff   None
Languages   English
Established   1967, Hyderabad
Major Fields of Interest   College library management
Major Goals and Objectives   Administration and organization of effective library services; promotion of the ethical, social, economic, and academic aspects of members.
Structure   Governed by the Executive Committee.
Sources of Support   Membership dues, private donations.
Membership   Total members: 1,000+ (individual). Types of membership: Individual, honorary. Requirements: Support of the aims of the Association and payment of dues. Members are mostly professional librarians. Dues (Indian Rupee): 5.
General Assembly   Entire membership meets twice a year.
Publications   No publications program
Activities   Works for adjustments in pay equity for college librarians; for vacation leave; and the removal of personal payment by librarians for book losses; sponsors meetings, conferences, seminars.
Bibliography   Khurshid, A., "Library Associations in Asia," Herald of Library Science 28 (1989):3-10.

283   Indian Library Association (ILA)

Address   A/40-41, Flat no. 201, Ansal Buildings, Dr.Mukerjee Nagar, Delhi 110009 (permanent). Tel: 91 (11) 7117743.

Officers   (elected for 2-yr.term) Pres: Krishan Kumar; Hon.Sec: C.P. Vashishth; 6 Vice
Presidents. Exec.Board: 8; Exec.Council: 26; Sectional Comm.Chairs: 10.
Staff   5 (paid), 6 (volunteers)
Languages   English, Hindi
Established   1933, Calcutta
Major Fields of Interest   Library and information science
Major Goals and Objectives   To promote the library movement, library service, library
science and the library profession in India; to promote bibliographic study and research in
library science; to improve library training status and conditions of service of librarians;
to affiliate with state and other library associations; to cooperate with international orga-
nizations having similar objectives; to promote library legislation; to promote the establishment of documentation and information centers.
Structure   Governed by executive officers and Executive Council. Affiliations: IFLA,
COMLA.
Sources of Support   Membership dues, sale of publications, consultative projects. Bud-
get (Indian Rupee): Approx. 3.5 million.
Membership   Total members: 1,600 (1,300 individual, 300 institutional). Sections: 11.
Types of membership: Individual, institutional, honorary, life. Requirements: All those
who subscribe to the objectives of the Association. Dues (Indian Rupee): 25, individual;
100, institutional; 300, life.
General Assembly   Entire membership meets once a year. 1987: Tiruchirapalli, Tamil
Nadu; 1988: Calcutta, Dec.20-23 (34th All India Conference).
Publications   *Official journal:* ILA Bulletin. 1964-. 4/yr. (Indian Rupee) 200. Free to
members. Address same as Association. Editor: Krishan Kumar. Address: Department of
Library and Information Science, University of Delhi, Delhi 110007. Circ: 2,000. English.
Indexed in LISA, ILSA (Indian Library Science Abstracts). Other publications: Annual
reports, proceedings of meetings, reports of seminars, workshops, directories, Indian Library Directory, Subject Headings in Hindi, etc. Publications available for sale, listed in
journal. Publications exchange program in effect.
Activities   Annual conferences; several seminars; international conferences (e.g., on
Ranganathan's Philosophy, in New Delhi, Nov. 11-14, 1985); continuing education workshops; publication program; promoting interest in library profession, library development
and services in India. Association has been active in promoting library-related legislation,
such as efforts to formulate a National Library Policy. This resulted in the National
Policy on Library and Information System Document, May 1986, as a first step for national planning by the Government.
Bibliography   Trehan, G.L., "Unity of Librarians and ILA," Indian Librarian 36
(1981):24-26; Grover, D.R. and Bhagi, S.A., "Future Role of Indian Library Association," International Library Movement 5 (1983):152-156; Kumar, Girja, "Indian Library
Association: Retrospect and Prospect," Library Times International 1 (1985):77-78; "ILA
to Host an International Confeence on Ranganathan," ibid. (1985):81-82; Das Gupta,
R.K., "India," in ALA World Encyclopedia of Library and Information Services, 2nd ed.,
pp. 550-553. Chicago: American Library Association, 1986; Khurshid, A., "Library Associations in Asia," Herald of Library Science 28 (1989):3-10; Subba Rao, C.V., "Some Observations on the Joint Conference of ILA and IASLIC at Calcutta," ibid.:212-218; Kaula, P.N., "Joint ILA and IASLIC Conference: Resolutions," ibid.:256-257.
Additional Information   Medical and other specialized librarians of India have formed
their own associations. See C.V. Subba Rao, "Professional Associations of India," Herald
of Library Science 26 (1987):200.

284   Indian Society for Information Science (ISIS)

Address   c/o Documentation Research and Training Centre, Indian Statistical Institute, 8th Mile, Mysore Road, R.V. College P.O. Bangalore 560059 (not permanent). Tel: 91 (812) 604648. Telex: 8458376.

Indonesia

285   Ikatan Pustakawan Indonesia (IPI)
(Indonesian Library Association)

Address   Jalan Salemba Raya no. 28A, PO Box 3624, Jakarta 10002 (permanent). Tel: 62 (21) 3101411.
Officers   (elected for 3-yr.term) Pres: Prabowo Tjitroprawiro; Sec.Gen: Nurhadi Sudarno. Exec.Board: 7
Staff   2 (paid)
Languages   Indonesian, English
Established   1974, Ciawi-Bogor, through a merger of the existing library associations: Indonesian Association of Special Libraries (1969), and the Indonesian Library, Archive and Documentation Association. Before that, there was an Indonesian Library Association, founded in 1954.
Major Fields of Interest   All types of libraries; education for librarianship; all aspects of information studies and development.
Major Goals and Objectives   (1) To improve the status of librarians; (2) to enhance library activities in national development; (3) to develop, promote, and apply the principles of library science to further education, science, and social welfare; (4) to develop the professional qualities of librarians.
Structure   Governed by executive officers. Affiliations: IFLA, CONSAL.
Sources of Support   Membership dues, sale of publications, government subsidies. Budget (Rupiah): Approx. 40,000.
Membership   Total members: 3,600 (2,440 individual, 160 institutional). 6 countries represented. Types of membership: Individual, institutional, student, honorary. Requirements: Individuals must have a diploma in librarianship and interest in librarianship, libraries, documentation. Institutions must have an interest in library information development. Dues (Rupiah): 1,200, individual; 2,500, institutional.
General Assembly   Entire membership meets every 3 years.
Publications   *Official journal:* Majalah Ikatan Pustakawan Indonesia (Journal of the Indonesian Library Association). 1974-. 4/yr. (Rupiah) 2,000. Free to members. Editor: K. Sukarman. Address same as Association. Circ: 3,600 +. Indonesian. Indexed in Indonesian Learned Periodicals Index. Other publications: Berita Ikatan Pustakawan Indonesia (IPI) (Indonesia Library Association News); annual reports, proceedings of seminars, workshops, conferences, monographs. Publications available for sale. Publications exchange programs with other associations, libraries, and nonlibrary institutions.
Activities   Promoting the development and establishment of libraries, including a National Library and rural libraries; publications program, especially library manuals; sponsors continuing education workshops, seminars.
Bibliography   Pringgoadisurjo, Luwarsih, "Indonesia," in ALA World Encyclopedia of Library and Information Services, 2nd ed., pp. 353-354. Chicago: American Library Association, 1986; Khurshid, A., "Library Associations in Asia," Herald of Library Science 28 (1989):3-10.

Iran

286   Anjoman-e Ketabdaran-e Iran / Iranian Library Association (ILA)

Address   PO Box 11-1391, Tehran (permanent). Tel: 98 (21) 662768-228.
Officers   Exec.Sec: M. Nikham Vazifeh
Staff   None
Languages   Persian
Established   1966, Tehran
Major Fields of Interest   Library and information science; books; reading; education.
Major Goals and Objectives   To develop the essence and principles of modern library science in Iran; to make known to the people the importance of the library professions; to protect the rights of librarians and to increase their professional status.
Structure   Governed by executive officers. Affiliations: IFLA.
Sources of Support   Membership dues, sale of publications, government subsidies.
Membership   Total members: Approx. 949 (914 individual, 35 institutional). Types of membership: Individual, institutional, student, honorary. Requirements: Professional or nonprofessional librarian status or a love for books and an interest in the aims and work of the organization.
General Assembly   Entire membership meets annually.
Publications   *Official journal:* ILA Bulletin (in Persian). 1970-?. 4/yr. No information, whether the journal is still being published.
Bibliography   Sharify, Nasser, and Sharify, Homayoun Gloria, "Iran," in ALA World Encyclopedia of Library and Information Services, 2nd ed., pp. 386-387. Chicago: American Library Association, 1986; Khurshid, A., "Library Associations in Asia," Herald of Library Science 28 (1989):3-10.

Iraq

287 Iraqi Library Association

Address PO Box 4081, Baghad-Adhamya (not permanent). Tel: 964 (1) 27077
Officers Exec.Sec: N. Kamal-al-Deen
Staff None
Languages Arabic
Established 1968, Baghdad
Major Fields of Interest Library and information science
Major Goals and Objectives To promote libraries and library services in the country; to promote the status and professional development of librarians.
Structure Governed by executive officers
Sources of Support Membership dues.
Membership Total members: Approx. 300 (individual).
General Assembly Entire membership meets annually.
Publications No official journal. Published: Kindilchie, Amer Ibrahim, Guide to Iraqi Libraries (1981; in Arabic).
Activities Sponsors meetings, seminars, continuing education programs, book fairs.
Bibliography Kindilchie, Amer Ibrahim, "Iraq," in ALA World Encyclopedia of Library and Information Services, 2nd ed., pp. 387-389. Chicago: American Library Association, 1986; Khurshid, A., "Library Associations in Asia," Herald of Library Science 28 (1989):3-10.

Ireland

288   Central Catholic Library Association, Inc. (CCL)

Address   74 Merrion Square, Dublin 2 (permanent). Tel: 353 (1) 761264
Officers   Librarian: Maurice Curtis; Hon.Librarian: Ms. M. O'Broin. Exec.Board: 20
Staff   3 (paid), 60 (volunteers)
Languages   English
Established   1922
Major Fields of Interest   Information services in the Catholic religion
Major Goals and Objectives   The promotion of knowledge and appreciation of Catholicism
Structure   Governed by Council. Affiliations: IFLA
Sources of Support   Membership dues, donations
Membership   Total members: 600 (individual). Types of membership: Individual. Requirements: No strict requirements. Dues (Irish Pound): 5.
General Assembly   Entire membership meets once a year, in Dublin.
Publications   No publications program
Activities   Past achievements: Increased the number of users of lending and reference services. Current: Provision of greater lending and reference facilities. Future: Holding exhibitions relative to CCL's functions; increasing people's awareness of CCL and its facilities; improving efficiency of operations; and recognizing members' needs.

289   Cumann Leabharlann na h-Éireann / The Library Association of Ireland (LAI)

Address   53 Upper Mount Street, Dublin 2 (permanent). Tel: 353 (1) 619000. Fax: 353-1-761628.
Officers   (elected for 1-yr.term) Pres: N. Hughes; Past Pres: Ms. N. Hardiman; Hon.Sec: Ms. F. Hanrahan; Hon.Treas: D. O'Gorman. Exec.Board: 24
Staff   1 (part-time); Hon.officers and officers of sections and groups are volunteers
Languages   English, Irish
Established   1928, at meeting held to re-establish the earlier, defunct Cumann na Leabharlann. Incorporated in 1952.
Major Fields of Interest   Librarianship in all its aspects, and information work.
Major Goals and Objectives   To promote and develop high standards of librarianship and of library and information services in Ireland; to maintain the profession of librarianship in an appropriate status among the learned and technical professions.
Structure   Governed by Executive Board and honorary officers. Affiliations: IFLA; The Library Association, Northern Ireland Branch/LANI (with LANI joint annual conference, and joint publication of journal).
Sources of Support   Membership dues, sale of publications, fees from conferences and seminars. Budget (Irish Pound): 1986/87: 9,000; 1987/88: 10,000.
Membership   Total members: 595 (520 individual, 75 institutional). Sections: 11. 3 countries represented. Types of membership: Individual, institutional, life. Requirements: Open to those employed in libraries and/or information services, and to those interested in the welfare and progress of libraries and information services. Dues (Irish Pound): 10-25, individual; 40, institutional.
General Assembly   Entire membership meets once a year, and at the Annual Joint Conference with the Library Association, Northern Ireland Branch.
Publications   *Official journal:* <u>An Leabharlann. The Irish Library</u>. 1930-. 4/yr. (Irish Pound) 15. Free to members. Published jointly with the Northern Ireland Branch of the

Library Association: Editor: Peter Fox. Address: Trinity College Library, College Street, Dublin 2; and, Editor: Andrew Morrow. Address: Southern Education and Library Board, 1 Markethill Road, Armogh, Northern Ireland BT60 INR. Circ: 750. English. Indexed in LISA. Other publications: Annual reports, reports of seminars, workshops, Directory of Irish Libraries.
Activities   Past achievements: Maintaining close liaison with the Northern Ireland Branch of The Library Association; developing new special interest groups and sections within the Association; establishing Children's Book Week in the Republic of Ireland (through the Youth Library Group). Current: Campaigning for: (a) removal of charges for admission to public libraries; (b) acceptance of post-graduate professional qualification as the norm in Irish libraries; (c) improvement and extension of school library services. Association is working on a membership survey as a basis for planning future activity; preparing a new edition of the Directory. Future: Implementation of a nation-wide distance learning staff training scheme for libraries and information services; the provision of more and better opportunities and facilities for members to improve and extend their professional interests and expertise. Association has been active in promoting library-related legislation, such as the Public Libraries Act 1947. Currently involved in promoting new legislation for public libraries in Ireland. Sponsors Book Week activities, exhibits, continuing education programs.
Use of High Technology   Microcomputers for management.
Bibliography   Ellis-King, D., "Ireland" in ALA World Encyclopedia of Library and Information Services, 2nd ed., pp. 389-391. Chicago: American Library Association, 1986; Shorley, D., "'Free for All, Fee for All': Belfast 1988; the Joint Conference of the Northern Ireland Branch of the Library Association and the Library Association of Ireland: View from the Chair," Library Association Record 90 (May 1988):289.

290   Cumann Leabharlannaithe Scoile (CLS) / Irish Association of School Librarians

Address   c/o The Library, University College Dublin, Belfield, Dublin 4 (permanent Headquarters). Tel: 353 (1) 693244. Telex: 93207 Ei.
Officers   Exec.Sec: Sister Mary Columban (Loreto Convent, Foxrock Co., Dublin); Sister Monaghan. Exec.Comm: 14
Staff   None
Languages   English
Established   1962, at University College, Dublin.
Major Fields of Interest   School libraries
Major Goals and Objectives   To promote the establishment, development, and use of school libraries in Ireland as instruments of education, both formal and informal; to provide school librarians with opportunities for mutual assistance and further education.
Structure   Governed by Executive Council.
Sources of Support   Membership dues.
Membership   Total members: 160 (individual). Chapter: 1. Types of membership: Individual. Requirements: Interest in school libraries. Dues (Irish Pound): 5.
General Assembly   Entire membership meets annually.
Publications   Official journal: C.L.S. Bulletin. 1962-. 1/yr. Free to members. Address same as Association.
Activities   Sponsors summer courses for school librarians and other continuing education programs; active in obtaining official support for secondary school libraries from national and local government funds.

Bibliography   Ellis-King, D., "Ireland," in <u>ALA World Encyclopedia of Library and Information Services</u>, 2nd ed., pp. 389-391. Chicago: American Library Association, 1986.

291   Institute of Information Scientists. Irish Branch (IIS-Irish Branch)

Address   c/o National Board for Science and Technology, Shelbourne House, Dublin 4 (permanent).
Additional Information   This is the Irish Branch of the Institute of Information Scientists (IIS) of the United Kingdom, and generally follows the goals, objectives, and activities of that organization adapted to national needs.

292   Irish Society for Archives (ISA)

Address   c/o Dublin Diocesan Archives, Archbishop's House, Drumcondra, Dublin 9 (not permanent). Tel: 353 (1) 379253.
Officers   (elected for 1-yr.term) Chair: Kevin B. Nowlan; Hon.Sec: David C. Sheehy; Hon.Treas: Brian Donnelly; Hon.Ed: Ailsa C. Holland. Exec.Board: 11
Staff   None
Languages   English, Irish
Established   1971, at the University College, Dublin
Major Fields of Interest   Promotion and preservation of archives
Major Goals and Objectives   To further the establishment and development of archives in Ireland; to promote the professional development of archivists. Specific objectives are: (1) To promote the preservation of archives and to aid in the rescue of material from destruction, neglect, or loss; (2) to increase public interest in archives and to promote greater use of and access to archives; (3) to coordinate the work of all authorities, institutions, and individuals concerned or interested in the custody, study, or publication of records; (4) to provide a center for the collection and dissemination of technical information of value to those engaged or interested in archives; (5) to publish informal news sheets of archival interest and to arrange for lectures on this and related subjects.
Structure   Governed by executive officers. Affiliations: ICA
Sources of Support   Membership dues, sale of publications, government subsidies.
Membership   Total members: 110 (80 individual, 30 institutional). Requirements: Archivists and those interested in archives; archival institutions. Dues (Irish Pound): 7, individual; 15, institutional.
General Assembly   Entire membership meets 7 times a year.
Publications   *Official journal:* <u>Irish Archives Bulletin</u>. 1971-. 1/yr. (Irish Pound) 4.50. Address same as Association. Editor: Ailsa C. Holland. Address: Department of Archives, University College Dublin, Belfield, Dublin. Circ: Membership. English, Irish.
Activities   Sponsors meetings, conferences, workshops for the members, who are archivists, librarians, public servants, and professional and amateur historians.
Bibliography   Ellis-King, D., "Ireland," in <u>ALA World Encyclopedia of Library and Information Services</u>, 2nd ed., pp. 389-391. Chicago: American Library Association, 1986.

Israel

293   Information Processing Association of Israel (IPA)

Address   PO Box 13009, Jerusalem 91130 (permanent). Tel: 972 (2) 521930.
Officers   (elected for 1-yr.term) Pres: Dov Chevion; Sec: Tuvia Saks (appointed); Treas: M. Halbort
Staff   5 (paid)
Languages   English, Hebrew
Established   1956; originally founded as the Association of the Users of Unit-Record Equipment, new name adopted 1964.
Major Fields of Interest   Information processing and technology
Major Goals and Objectives   Advancement of information processing in all areas; raising and advancing the professional level of all people connected with information processing; development of public consciousness of the field of information processing.
Structure   Governed by Executive Council composed of 27 members. The Council in turn elects an Executive Board of 7 members. Affiliations: IFLA
Sources of Support   Membership dues.
Membership   Total members: 1,500+. Divisions: 1. Study Groups: 10 (by specific subjects). Types of membership: Individual. Requirements: Open to anyone who has had at least 1 year of experience in data processing. Dues (Shekel): 20.
General Assembly   Entire membership meets annually.
Publications   *Official journal:* Ma'ase Cho-shev (Action and Thought). 1972-. 6/yr. Membership only. Address same as Association. Hebrew, with some English translations. Other publications: Annual reports, proceedings of meetings, seminars, conferences, and others. Publications available for sale. Publications exchange program in effect.
Activities   Sponsors seminars, workshops, and other continuing education offerings; promotes the exchange and sharing of information on a broad international scale; promotes staff exchanges and studies abroad of Israeli professionals.
Bibliography   Khurshid, A., "Library Associations in Asia," Herald of Library Science 28 (1989):3-10.

294   Irgun Saferane Israel / Israel Library Association (ILA)

Address   PO Box 303, Tel Aviv 61002 (permanent)
Officers   (elected) Pres: I. Shapira; Past Pres: A. Vilner; Sec: Ms. N. Ravid.
Staff   37 (volunteers)
Languages   Hebrew
Established   1952, Jerusalem, at the National Library
Major Fields of Interest   Development of libraries and the library profession
Major Goals and Objectives   To promote the development of libraries, archives, and information services in Israel; to promote the professional development of personnel.
Structure   Governed by Executive Council. Affiliations: IFLA, Aslib.
Sources of Support   Membership dues, subsidies
Membership   Total members: 2,000+ (individual). Divisions: 7 (Public, School, University, Rabbinic, Special, and Kibbutzim Libraries; Archives). Types of membership: Individual, honorary, life. Requirements: Librarian's diploma. Dues (Shekel): 20.
General Assembly   Entire membership meets annually.
Publications   *Official journal:* Yad La-Koré (The Reader's Aid: Israel's Journal for Libraries and Archives). 1946-.4/yr. Address: The Centre for Public Libraries, PO Box 242,

Jerusalem 91002. Editor: Irene Sever. Circ: 1,500. Hebrew, with English summaries. Indexed in LISA, etc. Issues proceedings of annual meetings, bibliographies, and other occasional publications.
Activities   Works for improvement of professional education and promotion and improvement of library services. Sponsors continuing education seminars, workshops, and other programs. Works for better standards at all levels of librarianship.
Bibliography   Sever, S., "Israel," in ALA World Encyclopedia of Library and Information Services, 2nd ed., pp. 393-398. Chicago: American Library Association, 1986; Khurshid, A., "Library Associations in Asia," Herald of Library Science 28 (1989):3-10.

295   Israel Archives Association

Address   c/o The Central Zionist Archives, PO Box 92, Jerusalem 91920, or, c/o The Central Archives for the History of the Jewish People, Jerusalem University Campus, Sprinzak Building, PO Box 1149, Jerusalem.
Languages   Hebrew
Established   1956
Major Fields of Interest   Archives
Major Goals and Objectives   To promote the development of archives in Israel
Structure   Governed by executive officers
Sources of Support   Membership dues
Membership   Total members 208 (180 individual, 28 institutional).
General Assembly   Entire membership meets once a year.
Publications   *Official journal:* Yad-La-Koré, published jointly with Israel Library Association and The Centre for Public Libraries. The publication of an independent journal devoted to archival studies only is being planned. Issues reports of conferences and occasional papers.
Activities   Sponsors continuing education programs for qualified archivists; sponsors adaptation of archival terminology to Hebrew.
Bibliography   Sever, S., "Israel," in ALA World Encyclopedia of Library and Information Services, 2nd ed., pp. 393-398. Chicago: American Library Association, 1986.

296   Israel Society of Special Libraries and Information Centres (ISLIC)

Address   PO Box 20125, Tel Aviv 61200 (permanent). Tel: 972 (3) 297781. Headquarters: 84 Ha-Hashmonaim Street, Tel Aviv 61200.
Officers   (elected for 3-yr.term) Hon.Sec: S. Langermann. Exec.Board: 7
Staff   2 (paid), 7 (volunteers)
Languages   Hebrew, English
Established   1966
Major Fields of Interest   Special libraries; information work
Major Goals and Objectives   To encourage and promote the utilization of knowledge through special libraries and information centers; to undertake any projects serving this purpose; to promote professional standards; to facilitate oral and written communication among members; to promote professional training of members and of those wishing to join the profession by setting standards of professional education and initiating or administering professional examinations; to cooperate and affiliate with other bodies having similar or allied interests in Israel or abroad.
Structure   Governed by Executive Committee and officers. Affiliations: FID (through Israel's national membership), IFLA.
Sources of Support   Membership dues, sale of publications, government subsidies.

Membership   Total members: 600. Chapters: 4. Types of membership: Full, associate, institutional, student, honorary, supporting. Requirements: Education in librarianship and/or information work, and actual employment in one of these fields. Dues fixed annually by the General Assembly.

General Assembly   Entire membership meets once a year.

Publications   *Official journal:* ISLIC Bulletin. 1966-. 2/yr. Free to members. Editor: L. Eisenberg. Address same as Association. Circ: 600. Hebrew, English. Indexed in LISA. Other publications: Contributions to Information Science (irreg.); annual reports, proceedings of seminars, meetings, and other occasional publications. Price lists available. Publications exchange program in effect.

Activities   Sponsors courses, seminars, continuing education programs in library and information science.

Bibliography   Sever, S., "Israel," in ALA World Encyclopedia of Library and Information Services, 2nd ed., pp. 393-398. Chicago: American Library Association, 1986.

Italy

297   Associazione Archivistica Ecclesiastica (AAE)
(Ecclesiastical Archivists Association)

Address   Piazza S. Calisto, 16, I-00153 Rome (permanent). Tel: 39 (6) 6701228
Officers   (elected for 2-yr.term) Pres: P. Vincenzo Monachino; VP: Salvatore Palese;
Sec: P. Emanuele Boaga; Treas: Sr. Eladia De Meer; Councilors: Mons. Antonio Arcolin,
Filippo R. De Luca, Guido De Lucia, Piergiorgio Figini, P. Jesus Torres, plus 4 more.
Exec.Board: 13.
Staff   All volunteers
Languages   Italian, occasionally French, Spanish, English
Established   Feb. 4, 1956, to help the ecclesiastical authorities and ecclesiastical archivists.
Major Fields of Interest   All types of archives of the Catholic Church: Diocesan, Parochial, Cathedral Chapters (Capitoli Cattedrali), Houses of Religious Orders and Congregations, various ecclesiastical associations, Catholic laypersons' associations.
Major Goals and Objectives   To promote the development and effective management
of ecclesiastical archives of all types.
Structure   Governed by Executive Council, elected every 2 years.
Sources of Support   Membership dues, sale of publications, government subsidies, occasional donations.
Membership   Total members: Approx. 270 (260 individual, 10 institutional). 10 countries represented. Requirements: Archivist in some ecclesiastical institution or scholar of
archival studies.   Dues (Italian Lira): 15,000; no dues for honorary members; special rates
for retired members.
General Assembly   Entire membership meets every 2 years. 1987: Rome, Oct.
Publications   *Official journal:* Archiva Ecclesiae. 1958-. Biennial. Price depends on
number of pages. Editor: President of Association. Address same as Association. Italian.
Other occasional publications.
Activities   Promoting good management of ecclesiastical archives, good reference services, and cooperation of members. Sponsored meetings in Brescia 1980, in Rome 1982,
in Loreto 1984; publication of proceedings; continuing the journal, with one volume commemorating the 25 years of the Association (1982); beginning of a Guida degli Archivi
Diocesani d'Italia (Guide to Diocesan Archives in Italy).
Bibliography   References to the Association's activities and achievements may be found
in the Guida Monaci for many years; in the Bibliography of Archivum Historiae Pontificiae since 1980, and in L'Osservatore Romano in the years of meetings or publication of
the volumes of Archiva Ecclesiae.

298   Associazione Italiana Biblioteche (AIB)
(Italian Libraries Association)

Address   Presso Instituto Centrale per il Catalogo Unico e le Informazioni Bibliografiche, Rome. Postal address: Casella Postale 2461, I-00100 Rome A-D (not permanent).
Tel: 39 (6) 493532.
Officers   (elected for 3-yr.term) Pres: G. Solimine; Past Pres: Luigi Crocetti; VP: Maria
Carla Cavagnis Sotgiu; National Sec: Giovanni Lazzari (appointed, 1983-). Exec.Board: 5
Staff   4 (volunteers)
Languages   Italian

Established   1930, Rome, at the First International Congress of Libraries and Bibliography; reorganized 1951.
Major Fields of Interest   Library policy, library science, library education.
Major Goals and Objectives   Development of library services; raising the status of librarians; promote library education and training; cooperation with other cultural institutions in Italy and internationally.
Structure   Governed by national and regional executive presidential councils and committees. Affiliations: IFLA, FID
Sources of Support   Membership dues, sale of publications, government subsidies. Budget (Italian Lira): 1986/87: Approx.120 million; 1987/88: Approx.130 million.
Membership   Total members: 2,600 (1,800 individual, 800 institutional). Sections: 17. Types of membership: Individual, institutional, honorary. Requirements: Librarians, libraries and interested institutions. Dues (Italian Lira): 35,000, individual; 50,000-100,000, institutional.
General Assembly   Entire membership meets once a year.
Publications   *Official journal:* Bollettino d'Informazioni. 1961-. 3/yr. (Italian Lira) 60,000 (70,000, foreign). Address same as Association. Circ: 3,000. Italian, with English abstracts. Indexed in LISA. Other publications: Proceedings of meetings; reports of seminars, workshops. Publications available for sale. Publications exchange program in effect.
Activities   Past achievements: Contributed to regional legislation; to the dissemination of information cataloging rules and to the professional education of librarians. Current: National Commissions on special, public, and university libraries; on cataloging and information technology; Study Groups on the profession and library legislation. Future: Improve the coordination of library policies in Italy; propose further rules on cataloging; redefine professional status of librarians in Government service. Association has been active in promoting library-related legislation, such as participation in the passage of regional legislation, and in Parliament on laws regarding cultural property, school libraries, and university librarians.
Bibliography   Solimine, G., "Lo sviluppo dell'Associazione, le sue strutture, la sua organizzazione," (The Association's Growth, Its Composition, Its Organization), Bollettino d'Informazioni 25 (1985):435-441 (in Italian); Sotgiu, M.C.C., "The Association and Its Questioners," ibid.:527-530 (in Italian); Revelli, Carlo, "Considerazione tra un congresso e l'altro," (Some Reflections between Two Congresses), Bollettino d'Informazioni 26 (1986):421-429; Carpenter, Ray L., "Italy," in ALA World Encyclopedia of Library and Information Services, 2nd ed., pp. 398-400. Chicago: American Library Association, 1986; Mandillo, A.M., "Il gruppo nazionale sulla professione dell'AIB," (AIB's National Group on the Profession), Bollettino d'Informazioni 28 (1988):37-39; "Le interviste di Erasmus: un presidente allo specchio," (Erasmus' Interviews: A President in the Mirror), Biblioteche Oggi 6 (1988):33-41 (in Italian).

299   Associazione Italiana per la Documentazione Avanzata (AIDA) (Italian Association for Advanced Documentation)

Address   c/o ISRDS-CNR, Via Cesare De Lollis 12, I-00185 Rome (not permanent). Tel: 39 (6) 495-2351.
Officers   Pres: Paolo Bisogno
Staff   None
Languages   Italian, English (for correspondence)
Established   1980
Major Fields of Interest   Advanced documentation and information services.

Major Goals and Objectives   To promote more efficient use of specialized knowledge; to promote the documentalist profession; to develop information services and activities.
Structure   Governed by executive officers
Sources of Support   Membership dues.
Membership   Total members: 265. Local Chapters: 5.
General Assembly   Entire membership meets every two years. 1988, 1990, 1992.
Publications   *Official journal:* AIDA Informazioni (newsletter). Irreg. Free to members. Address same as Association. Italian. Issues proceedings of conferences and other occasional publications.
Activities   Promoting the profession of documentalist; sponsoring workshops, seminars, meetings to give members opportunity for exchange of information and continuing education in the area of documentation.

300   Associazione Nazionale Archivistica Italiana (ANAI) (National Association of Italian Archivists)

Address   Via Guido D'Arezzo, 18, I-00198 Rome (not permanent)
Officers   (elected for 2-yr.term) Sec: Enrica Ormanni (appointed)
Staff   8 (volunteers)
Languages   Italian, French
Established   1949, Orvieto
Major Fields of Interest   Archival collections
Major Goals and Objectives   To study problems concerning public and private archives; to contribute to the preservation and utilization of the holdings of Italian archives; to encourage cooperation between Italian and foreign archivists; to promote scientific and technical activities of archivists; to improve the standards of archive personnel and to protect their interests.
Structure   Governed by Executive Board. Affiliations: ICA
Sources of Support   Membership dues, government subsidies, private gifts
Membership   Total members: 450 (individual). Divisions: 2 (General Affairs, Scientific Research). Types of membership: Individual, honorary. Requirements: Open to archivists, students, other interested persons. Dues (Italian Lira): 2,300, individual.
General Assembly   Entire membership meets annually or biennially.
Publications   *Official journal:* Archivi e Cultura (Archives and Culture). 1967-. 2/yr. (Italian Lira) 2,300. Free to members. Address same as Association. Circ: 2,400+. Italian. Other publications: Annual report, proceedings of workshops, seminars, conferences, and monographs. Publications for sale. Publications exchange program in effect with foreign countries.
Activities   Sponsors conferences, workshops, seminars, and other continuing education programs; works for greater political and cultural unity in matters of scientific research and greater economic assistance for archival activities.

301   Ente Nazionale per le Biblioteche Popolari e Scolastiche (National Group for Public and School Libraries)

Address   c/o Via Michele Mercati 4, Rome
Languages   Italian
Major Fields of Interest   Public libraries; school libraries
Major Goals and Objectives   To further the establishment and development of public and school libraries in Italy
Sources of Support   Membership dues

Publications   *Official journal*: La Parola e il Libro (The Word and the Book). 1917-.
12/yr. (Italian Lira) 1,200. Free to members. Editor: Ettore Apolloni. Address same as
Association. Circ: 25,000. Indexed in LISA, etc. Italian.

302   Federazione Italiana delle Biblioteche Popolari (FIBP)
(Italian Federation of Public Libraries)

Address   c/o la "Società Umanitaria," Via Daverio 7, I-20122 Milan (permanent)
Languages   Italian
Major Fields of Interest   Public libraries

303   Gruppo Italiana - IAML
(International Association of Music Libraries, Archives and Documentation
Centres - Italian Branch) (IAML - Italian Branch)

Address   c/o Dr. Mariangela Donà, Via S. Marco 22/A, I-20121 Milan (permanent).
Tel: 39 (2) 653619.
Officers   (elected for indefinite term) Pres: Mariangela Donà; Sec: Agostina Zecca Lat-
erza. Exec.Board: 2
Staff   None
Languages   Italian, English, German, French
Major Fields of Interest   Music bibliography and librarianship
Major Goals and Objectives   To represent Italy within the IAML and to coordinate the
activities of Italian IAML members.
Structure   Governed by executive officers. Affiliations: A national branch of IAML
(Association does not have its own constitution).
Sources of Support   Membership dues.
Membership   Total members: 72 (22 national, 50 institutional).
Publications   No publications program.
Activities   Association has participated in some IAML activities, especially in RISM,
RILM, RIdIM and RIPMXIX. In 1984, organized the annual meeting of IAML in Como.
In cooperation with the Ufficio Ricerca Fondi Musicali (Milan), Association established
the rules for cataloging printed and manuscript music.

304   Società Italiana di Documentazione e d'Informazione
(Italian Association for Documentation and Information)

Address   Via Vittoria Colunna 39, I-00139 Rome. Tel: 39 (6) 3604841
Officers   Vice-Pres: Carlo Cya.
Languages   Italian
Major Fields of Interest   Documentation and information services
Publications   *Official journal*: Documentazione e Informazione. 1/yr. Free to members.
Address same as Association. Italian.

Ivory Coast

305   Association pour le Développement de la Documentation, des Bibliothèques et Archives de la Côte d'Ivoire (ADBACI)
(Association for the Development of Documentation, Libraries and Archives of the Ivory Coast)

Address   c/o Bibliothèque Nationale, BPV 180, Abidjan
Officers   Sec.Gen: Cangah Guy
Languages   French
Major Fields of Interest   Libraries, archives and documentation centers
Major Goals and Objectives   To further the establishment and development of libraries, archives and documentation centers in the country; to promote professional education and training of personnel.
Structure   Affiliations: IFLA (since 1975)
Sources of Support   Membership dues, government subsidies
Activities   The National Library provides the headquarters of the Association and support for activities, such as meetings and training workshops.
Bibliography   Handloff, R.E., and Gueye, S., "Ivory Coast," in <u>ALA World Encyclopedia of Library and Information Services</u>, 2nd ed., pp. 400-401. Chicago: American Library Association, 1986.

Jamaica

306   Jamaica Library Association (JLA)

Address   PO Box 58, Kingston 5 (permanent). Headquarters: c/o The Professional Centre 2, 3/4 Ruthven Road, Kingston 10. Tel: 62434.
Officers   Pres: Albertina Jefferson; Past Pres: Norma Amenu-Kpodo; Hon.Treas: Laura-Ann Munro; Hon.Sec: Ms. A. Chambers. Exec.Comm: 14
Staff   None
Languages   English
Established   1950, Kingston, at Institute of Jamaica.
Major Fields of Interest   Library profession and library development.
Major Goals and Objectives   (1) To unite all persons engaged in or interested in library work in Jamaica, and to provide opportunities for their meeting together to discuss matters relating to libraries; (2) to encourage cooperation among libraries and to promote the active development and maintenance of libraries throughout Jamaica; (3) to promote a high standard of education and training of library staff and whatever may improve the status of librarians; (4) to promote a wide knowledge of library work and to form an educated public opinion on libraries.
Structure   Governed by Executive Council. Affiliations: COMLA, ACURIL, IFLA, ALA, LA.
Sources of Support   Financed by membership dues.
Membership   Total members: 330. Types of membership: Individual, institutional, honorary, student. Requirements: Open to all library staff members, and to those having an interest in libraries and library work. Dues (Jamaican Dollar): 20.
General Assembly   Entire membership meets once a year.
Publications   *Official journal:* Jamaica Library Association Bulletin. 1950-. Annual. (Jamaican Dollar) 4. Address same as Association. Other publications: JLA News. 4/yr.; occasional bibliographies and monographs, Directory of Jamaican Libraries, Brown, Hyacinth, ed., Disaster Planning in Jamaica. Safeguarding documents and vital data (1989).
Activities   Sponsors conferences, seminars, and other continuing education programs. The School Library Section and the Special Library Section carry out various activities, some jointly with the Department of Library Studies of the University of the West Indies. Association was greatly involved in relief efforts for Jamaican libraries devastated by Hurricane Gilbert in September 1988.
Bibliography   Iton, S.M., "Jamaica," in ALA World Encyclopedia of Library and Information Services, 2nd ed., pp. 402-403. Chicago: American Library Association, 1986; "Caribbean Generosity," COMLA Newsletter 66 (Dec. 1989):6.

Japan

307 FLINT: Josei to Toshokan Nettowaku
(FLINT: Feminist Librarians Network)

Address 3-7-9 II-104, Toyosaki, Oyodo-ku, Osaka 531 (not permanent). Tel: 81 (6) 3763950.
Officers Contact persons: Reiko Bungo (address same as Association); Yoko Taguchi (c/o Kyoto Seika University, 137 Kino, Isakura, Sakyo-ku, Kyoto 606. Tel: 81-75-7223384, home; 81-75-7916131, work)
Staff 1 (volunteer)
Languages Japanese
Established 1984
Major Fields of Interest Women's rights and librarianship
Major Goals and Objectives Facilitate the communication among people interested in issues related to women's rights and librarianship.
Structure Governed by members.
Sources of Support Membership dues. Budget (Yen): 1986/87: 104,546; 1987/88: 100,000.
Membership Total members: 60 (individual). Types of membership: Individual. Requirements: Interest in women's rights and librarianship. Dues (Yen): 1,000, initial fee; 2,000 regular.
General Assembly Entire membership meets once a year,
Publications *Official journal:* FLINT Nyusu (Newsletter). 1984-. 5/yr, Free to members. Editors: Mitsuko Hirata and Noriko Nakai. Address same as Association. Circ: 80-90. Japanese. Indexed in Toshokan Zasshi (Library Journal) (occasionally).
Activities Past achievements: Established network and created visibility in the library world; assisted in editing the special issue of Genday no Toshokan on women librarians. Current: A survey research project on the status of male and female librarians in Japan.
Bibliography Toshokan Nennkan 1985 (Library Annual); Taguchi, Y.,"FLINT: A Network for Women and Libraries," Toshokan Zasshi (Library Journal) 79 (1985):149; Kitano, Y., "FLINT," Gendai no Toshokan (Today's Library) 24 (1986):224-225 (text of all in Japanese).

308 Houritsu Toshokan Renrakukai
(The Council of Law Libraries)

Address c/o Statutes on the Parliamentary Documents Research Service, Research and Legislative Reference Bureau, National Diet Library, 1-10-1 Nagata-cho, Chiyoda-ku, Tokyo 100. Tel: 81 (3) 5812331.
Languages Japanese
Established 1955
Major Fields of Interest Law librarianship
Major Goals and Objectives To promote law librarianship; to provide exchange of documents, publications and other information between member libraries; to sponsor workshops and cooperative projects.
Structure Governed by executive officers.
Sources of Support Membership dues.
Membership Total members: 37 institutions.
General Assembly Entire membership meets annually.

Publications *Official journal:* Hotoren Tsushin (Newsletter of the Council of Law Libraries). 1/yr. Address same as Association. Japanese. Other publications: Annual reports, proceedings of conferences, seminars, etc.
Activities Sponsors conferences, seminars, workshops, and other continuing education programs. Compiles a union catalog.
Bibliography Kon, Madoko, "Japan," in ALA World Encyclopedia of Library and Information Services, 2nd ed., pp. 403-408. Chicago: American Library Association, 1986; Librarianship in Japan, ed. by Editorial Committee, Japan Organizing Committee of IFLA Tokyo, Aug. 1986, p.71.

309 IAML Nihon Shibu (Kokusai Ongaku Bunken- Kyokai Nihon Shibu) (International Association of Music Libraries, Archives and Documentation Centers - Japanese Branch)

Address 5-30-16 Seijo, Setagaya-ku, Tokyo 157. Tel: 81 (3) 4820287.
Officers Exec.Sec: Noriko Murai
Staff None
Languages Japanese, English
Established 1979, Tokyo
Major Fields of Interest Music libraries, archives, and documentation.
Major Goals and Objectives To accomplish within a national framework all the tasks IAML undertakes on an international scale, and to collaborate in all of the fields the Association deems necessary.
Structure Governed by executive officers. Affiliations: IMC Japanese Committee.
Sources of Support Membership dues.
Membership Total members: Approx. 70 (individual, institutional). Requirements: Payment of dues.
General Assembly Entire membership meets once a year in Tokyo, May or June.
Publications No official journal. Publishes newsletter.
Activities Sponsors conferences, seminars, workshops, and other continuing education programs.
Bibliography Kon, Madoko,"Japan," in ALA World Encyclopedia of Library and Information Services, 2nd ed., pp.403-408. Chicago: American Library Association, 1986.

310 Japan Orientalist Librarians Group (JOLG)

Address 100 Makigahara, Asahi-ku, Yokohama 241.
Officers Exec.Dir: Kazushige Kaneko; Manag.Dir: Kanenobu Watanabe
Staff None
Languages Japanese
Established 1981
Major Fields of Interest Asian studies
Major Goals and Objectives To exchange information on Asian area studies among members; to promote acquisition processing of Asian materials; to promote the use of Asian materials in Japan by mutual understanding and cooperation of members; to sponsor bibliographical projects on Asian materials and their publication; to sponsor workshops and other training programs for area study librarians; to strengthen the interrelations with Asian peoples and exchange necessary information with Asian countries.
Structure Governed by executive officers.
Sources of Support Membership dues, sale of publications, private subsidies.
Membership Total members: No information available. Subject Groups of Area Study: 5 (China, Korea, Southeast Asia, South Asia, West Asia).

General Assembly   Entire membership meets annually.
Publications   *Official journal:* JOLG Newsletter. 4/yr. (ISSN 0288-061X). Edited by
Editorial Committee. Address same as Association. Japanese. Foreign contributions are
invited. Other publications: Annual reports, proceedings of conferences, seminars, etc.
Bibliography on Southeast Asian Materials in the Japanese language, 1946-1983 (1985;
distr. Kinokuniya Book Co.)
Activities   Publication program: Continuing the Bibliography on Southeast Asian Mate-
rials, covering materials published before 1945 (with grant from Toyota Foundation).
Holds regular Area Study Workshops for people interested in Asian materials, such as
scholars, researchers, librarians. Sponsors conferences, workshops, and other continuing
education programs, e.g. seminars for training area study librarians. Sponsors exhibits of
Asian books, to make the Japanese people aware of Asian materials (1987).
Bibliography   Kon, Madoko,"Japan," in ALA World Encyclopedia of Library and Information Services, 2nd ed., pp. 403-408. Chicago: American Library Association, 1986.

311   Jidou Toshokan Kenkyukai (JITOKEN)
(Society for Children's Libraries)

Address   c/o Japan Library Association, 1-1-10 Taishido, Setagaya-ku, Tokyo 154 (per-
manent). Tel: (81 (3) 4106411.
Officers   (elected for 1-yr.term) Hon.Pres: Yoshiko Kogouchi; Pres: Yasuko Nakata;
VPs: Yoshiyuki Tatsumi, Ryoko Sato; Dir: Reiko Okura. Exec.Comm: 6
Staff   1 (volunteer)
Languages   Japanese, English
Established   Oct. 23, 1953.
Major Fields of Interest   Children's libraries in Japan
Major Goals and Objectives   To promote research and studies of children's librarian-
ship; to strive for improvement and expansion of children's libraries in Japan.
Structure   Governed by Executive Committee. Affiliations: IFLA, Japan Library Associ-
ation (JLA); Japan Board of Books for the Young (JBBY), and other associations in Japan.
Sources of Support   Membership dues, sale of publications. Budget (Yen): 1986/87:
4,320,210; 1987/88: 5,451,472.
Membership   Total members: 763 (670 individual, 93 institutional). Chapters: 6. 5 countries represented. Requirements: Anyone supporting the goals and objectives of the Association. Individual membership: Librarians, Bunko-librarians, teachers, kindergarten
teachers, publishers, editors, booksellers, etc. Institutional membership: Various libraries,
publishing houses and bookshops.
General Assembly   Entire membership meets once a year.
Publications   *Official journal:* Kodomo no Toshyokan (Children's Library). 1954-. 12/yr.
(Yen) 5,000. Free to members. Address same as Association. Circ: 800. Japanese. Other
publications: Annual reports, proceedings of conferences, seminars, etc. Publications
available for sale.
Activities   Past achievements: Publishing Journal; editing annual reports; 9th Annual
Storytelling Workshop at the University of Washington, USA; workshop on "Sign and Exhibition at Children's Library;" seminar for middle level librarians; editing of various
publications, such as "Storytelling: Nowaday Stories," "Booklist: Science Picture Books,"
and of a picture book, "Library." Current and future: Participating in national and international conferences; continuing publishing program, such as the "Booklists." Sponsors
conferences, seminars, workshops, and other continuing education programs, dealing with
management of children's libraries and recommendations for children's readings. Associ-

ation has been active in promoting library-related legislation, such as, with other organizations, the Declaration of "Intellectual Freedom of Libraries" (1979), and Professional Code for Librarians (1980). Sponsors Book Week and the movement for supporting "Freedom to Read."

Bibliography Kon, Madoko,"Japan," in <u>ALA World Encyclopedia of Library and Information Services</u>, 2nd ed., pp. 403-408. Chicago: American Library Association, 1986; <u>Librarianship in Japan</u>, ed. by Editorial Committee of Librarianship in Japan, Japan Organizing Committee of IFLA Tokyo, August 1986, p. 75.

312 Jouhou Kagaku Gijutsu Kyokai (Information Science and Technology Association) (INFOSTA)

Address Sasaki Building, 2-5-7 Koisikawa, Bunkyo-ku, Tokyo 112. Tel: 81 (3) 8133791.
Officers Pres: Y. Nakamura
Languages Japanese, English
Established 1950. Originally founded as the Japan Society for Universal Decimal Classification (UDC).
Major Fields of Interest Information science and technology; documentation.
Major Goals and Objectives To promote research on the theory and application of documentation; to promote dissemination of knowledge about the UDC system in Japan; to collect materials on documentation and its usage; to sponsor lectures, symposia and training courses.
Structure Governed by executive officers. Affiliations: FID
Sources of Support Membership dues, sale of publications, private subsidies.
Membership Total members: 1,174 (883 individual, 291 institutional).
General Assembly Entire membership meets annually.
Publications *Official journal:* <u>Dokumenteshon Kenkyu</u> (Journal of Information Science and Technology Association). 12/yr. Free to members. Address same as Association. Japanese. Other publications: <u>Infomanto</u> (Informant). 2/yr.; annual reports, proceedings of conferences, seminars, etc.
Activities Sponsors conferences, seminars, workshops, and other continuing education programs.
Bibliography Kon, Madoko,"Japan," in <u>ALA World Encyclopedia of Library and Information Services</u>, 2nd ed., pp. 403-408. Chicago: American Library Association, 1986; <u>Librarianship in Japan</u>, ed. by Editorial Committee of Librarianship in Japan, Japan Organizing Committee of IFLA Tokyo, August 1986, p. 71.

313 Kokuritsu Daigaku Toshokan Kyogikai (Council on National University Libraries)

Address c/o General Library, University of Tokyo Library System, 7-3-1 Hongo, Bunkyo-ku, Tokyo 113 (permanent). Tel: 81 (3) 8122111. Telex: UNITOKYO J25510.
Officers (elected for 1-yr.term) Pres: Hiro Yamasaki; Sec.Gen: Hisafumi Tanaka. Exec.Comm: 5
Staff 5 (volunteers)
Languages Japanese
Established 1954
Major Fields of Interest Academic and research library and information services
Major Goals and Objectives To promote the advancement of library and information services in Japan through close cooperation between national academic and research institutions.

Structure Governed by Executive Committee. Affiliations: Japanese University Libraries International Liaison Committee; Joint Committee for Library Cooperation of National, Public and Private Universities; Japan Library Association (JLA).
Sources of Support Membership dues. Budget (Yen): 1986/87: 2,503,153; 1987/88: 3,422,954.
Membership Total members: 96 (institutional). Type of membership: Institutional. Requirements: Libraries of academic institutions fully supported by the Japanese National Government. Dues (Yen): 30,000.
General Assembly Entire membership meets annually.
Publications *Official journal:* Daigaku Toshokan Kenkyu (Journal of College and University Libraries).1972-. 2/yr. (Yen) 5,800. Published by the Joint Committee for Library Cooperation of National, Public and Private Universities. Editor: Eiichi Kurahashi. Address: Tokyo Institute of Technology Library, 2-12-1 Oukayama, Meguro-ku, Tokyo 152. Circ: 950. Japanese. Indexed in LISA. Other publications: Annual reports, proceedings of conferences, seminars, etc.
Activities Past achievements: (1) Worked out a policy guideline for public access to a National University Library (NUL); (2) appealed to the National Government for augmenting book funds of NULs and for promoting expansion of the Library Information Network. Current and future: (1) Survey measures for recruiting staff at NULs and propose improvements to current system of the National Personnel Authority; (2) prepare "Guidelines for a Computerization System at a Small Library;" (3) investigate measures for enhancing inter-library lending procedures among NULs. Sponsors conferences, seminars, workshops, and other continuing education programs. Investigation and research activities carried out by various Committees and Groups.
Use of High Technology Computers (HITAC M260-D) used for management.
Bibliography Kon, Madoko,"Japan," in ALA World Encyclopedia of Library and Information Services, 2nd ed., pp. 403-408. Chicago: American Library Association, 1986; Librarianship in Japan, ed. by Editorial Committee of Librarianship in Japan, Japan Organizing Committee of IFLA Tokyo, August 1986, p. 71; Khurshid, A., "Library Associations in Asia," Herald of Library Science 28 (1989):3-10.

314 Kouritsu Daigaku Kyokai Toshokan Kyogikai (KODAIKYO) (Public University Library Association)

Address c/o Library, Fukuoka Women's University, 1-1-1 Kasumigaoka, Higashi-ku, Fukuoka-shi 813. Tel: 81 (92) 6612411.
Languages Japanese
Established 1969
Major Fields of Interest Public university libraries
Major Goals and Objectives To promote research and cooperation between public university libraries in Japan.
Structure Governed by executive officers.
Sources of Support Membership dues, sale of publications, government subsidies.
Membership Total members: 36 (institutional). Requirements: Library of public university in Japan.
General Assembly Entire membership meets annually.
Publications *Official journal:* Kouritsu Daigaku Kyokai Toshokan Kyogikai Kaihou (KODAIKYO Bulletin). 1/yr.; Kouritsu Daigaku Toshokan Gaiyou (Public University Library Annual). 1/yr.; Kouritsu Daigaku Jittai Chosa, Fuzoku Toshokanhen (Public University States Report. Library Division). 1/yr.; Koudaikyo Toshokan Kyogikai Kenshu Houkokusho (KODAIKYO Study Report). 1/yr. Daigaku Toshokan Kenkyu (Journal of

College and University Libraries). 1972-. 2/yr. (Yen) 5,800. Published by Joint Committee for Library Cooperation of National, Public and Private Universities. Editor: Eiichi Kurahashi. Address: Tokyo Institute of Technology Library, 2-12-1 Okayama, Meguro-ku, Tokyo 152. Circ: 950. Japanese. Indexed in LISA. Other publications: Annual reports, proceedings of conferences, seminars, etc.
Activities Sponsors conferences, seminars, workshops, and other continuing education programs.
Bibliography Kon, Madoko,"Japan," in ALA World Encyclopedia of Library and Information Services, 2nd ed., pp. 403-408. Chicago: American Library Association, 1986; Librarianship in Japan, ed. by Editorial Committee of Librarianship in Japan, Japan Organizing Committee of IFLA Tokyo, August 1986, p. 75.

315   Kouritsu Tanki Daigaku Toshokan Kyogikai (KOTANTOKYO) (Association of Prefectural and Municipal College Libraries)

Address c/o Library, The Maebashi City College of Technology, 460 Kamisadori-machi, Maebashi, Gumma-ken 371. Tel: 81 (272) 650111
Languages Japanese
Established 1971
Major Fields of Interest Academic libraries.
Major Goals and Objectives To promote cooperation between member institutional libraries; to promote the professional training of librarians; to improve library services of member libraries.
Structure Governed by Executive Committee.
Sources of Support Membership dues.
Membership Total members: 49 (institutional). Requirements: Libraries of prefectural and municipal colleges.
General Assembly Entire membership meets annually.
Publications No official journal. Other publications: Kouritsu Tanki Daigaku Toshokan Kiteishu (KOTANTOKYO Rules) (1981).
Activities Sponsors conferences, seminars, workshops, and other continuing education programs.
Bibliography Kon, Madoko,"Japan," in ALA World Encyclopedia of Library and Information Services, 2nd ed., pp. 403-408. Chicago: American Library Association, 1986; Librarianship in Japan, ed. by Editorial Committee of Librarianship in Japan, Japan Organizing Committee of IFLA Tokyo, August 1986, p. 70.

316   Mita Toshokan Joho Gakkai (Mita Society for Library and Information Science)

Address c/o School of Library and Information Science, Keio University, 2-15-45 Mita, Minato-ku, Tokyo 108 (permanent). Tel: 81 (3) 4533920.
Officers (elected) Pres: Takahisa Sawamoto; Sec: Shuichi Ueda.
Staff 1 (paid)
Languages Japanese, English
Established 1963, Tokyo
Major Fields of Interest Library and information science
Major Goals and Objectives To develop library and information science, and promote librarianship and information activities.
Structure Governed by Executive Committee.
Sources of Support Membership dues, sale of publications. Budget (Yen): 1986/87: 10,987,000; 1987/88: 7,239,000.

Membership Total members: 1,370 (1,050 individual, 320 institutional). Divisions: 2.
Requirements: Open to librarians and other interested persons and institutions.
General Assembly Entire membership meets annually.
Publications *Official journal:* Library and Information Science. 1963-. 1/yr. (Yen) 3,000
(or 17 US Dollar). Address same as Association. Circ: 1,750. Japanese, English. Indexed
in Lib.Lit., LISA. Other publications: Annual reports, proceedings of conferences (pre-
prints), seminars, etc.
Activities Sponsors conferences, seminars, workshops, and other continuing education
programs.
Bibliography Kon, Madoko,"Japan," in ALA World Encyclopedia of Library and Information Services, 2nd ed., pp. 403-408. Chicago: American Library Association, 1986; Librarianship in Japan, ed. by Editorial Committee of Librarianship in Japan, Japan Organizing Committee of IFLA Tokyo, August 1986, p. 74.

317   Nihon Igaku Toshokan Kyokai
(Japan Medical Library Association) (JMLA)

Address c/o Gakkai Center Building 5F, 2-4-16 Yayoi, Bunkyo-ku, Tokyo 113 (perma-
nent). Tel: 81 (3) 8151942. Fax: 81-3-8151608.
Officers (elected for 2-yr.term) Pres: Yoshio Kurosu; Past Pres: Takeshi Yokota;
Sec.Gen: Yasuo Okubo; Sec: Hidetaro Miyata; Dir. of Finance: Takayuki Yokota; Dir. of
Public Affairs: Shigeharu Kosai; Dir. of Constitutional Affairs: Eishin Inoue. Exec.Comm:
11
Staff 2 (paid)
Languages Japanese
Established 1927
Major Fields of Interest Library and information science for medicine and dentistry.
Major Goals and Objectives (1) To promote the progress of medicine through the var-
ious activities of medical libraries; (2) to fulfill this mission, the Association carries out
the following programs: (a) Research in medical library administration and management
of information systems, (b) interlibrary loan and document supply services, (c) training
and education of medical librarians, and (d) a variety of other activities.
Structure Governed by Executive Committee. Affiliations: IFLA, Japan Library Association (JLA).
Sources of Support Membership dues, sale of publications, documents supplied from
abroad to member libraries. Budget (Yen): 1986/87: 67,813,179; 1987/88: 59,192,927.
Membership Total members: 102 (institutional). Chapters: 8. Requirements: Libraries
attached to non-profit institutions, which possess a certain amount of holdings as provided in the Constitution and Bylaws. Dues (Yen): 70,000, regular member; 50,000 +, sustaining member; 70,000, emeritus member.
General Assembly Entire membership meets once a year. 1987: Tokyo; 1988: Osaka;
1989: Tokyo; 1990: Nagoya.
Publications *Official journal:* Igaku Toshokan (Medical Library). 1954-. 4/yr. (Yen)
70,000. Free to members. Address same as Association. Editor: Terumichi Kawai. Address: c/o Dokkyo University School of Medicine Library, 880 Kitakobayashi, Nibu-ma-
chi, Tochigi-ken. Circ: 1,560. Japanese, with English abstracts. Other publications: Annual reports, proceedings of conferences, seminars, etc. Kaiho. 6/yr.; Genko Igaku Zasshi
Shozai Mokuroku (Union List of Current Periodicals Acquired by the Japanese Medical,
Dental and Pharmaceutical Libraries). 1/yr.; Igaku Yousho Sougou Mokuroku (Union
Catalog of Foreign Medical Books). 4/yr., annual cumulation. Publications listed in journal; available for sale.

Activities   Past achievements: Changed the Association's fiscal year to the present system (beginning April and ending March); revised rules for regular membership and abolished associate membership in order to unify members. Current and future: Building an integrated network for supporting the nation's 1,000 hospital libraries in their activities and document supply. Sponsors conferences, seminars, workshops, and other continuing education programs.
Use of High Technology   Computer (word processor for Japanese language) for management.
Bibliography   Tonosaki, M., "The Activities of the Japan Medical Library Association," Az Orvosi Konyvtaros 25 (1985):223-235; Kon, Madoko,"Japan," in ALA World Encyclopedia of Library and Information Services, 2nd ed., pp. 403-408. Chicago: American Library Association, 1986; Librarianship in Japan, ed. by Editorial Committee of Librarianship in Japan, Japan Organizing Committee of IFLA Tokyo, August 1986, p. 72; Khurshid, A., "Library Associations in Asia," Herald of Library Science 28 (1989):3-10.

318   Nihon Nougaku Toshokan Kyogikai (NOTOKYO)
(Japan Association of Agricultural Librarians and Documentalists) (JAALD)

Address   Taiyo Seimei Building, 2-17-2 Shibuya, Shibuya-ku, Tokyo 150 (permanent). Tel: 81 (3) 4090722.
Officers   (elected for 2-yr.term) Pres: Takahisa Sawamoto; Sec: Ms. Shukuko Kamiya. Exec.Board: 10.
Staff   3 (paid), 17 (volunteers)
Languages   Japanese
Established   1966, Tokyo
Major Fields of Interest   Agricultural librarianship and documentation (including forestry, fisheries, and veterinary science).
Major Goals and Objectives   To promote agriculture, forestry, fisheries, and veterinary science, and to contribute to research and development in these fields.
Structure   Governed by Board of Directors. Affiliations: IAALD.
Sources of Support   Membership dues, sale of publications, translations (from Japanese to English), indexing and abstracting services. Budget (Yen): 1986/87: 14,990,000; 1987/88: Approx.15 million.
Membership   Total members: 174 (17 individual, 157 institutional). Requirements: To be approved by the Executive Board of JAALD and pay the required dues. Dues (Yen): 3,000, individual; 18,000, regular institutional member; 30,000, special institutional member.
General Assembly   Entire membership meets once a year in Tokyo.
Publications   *Official journal:* Nihon Nougaku Toshokan Kyogikai Kaiho (Bulletin of JAALD). 1966-. 4/yr. Free to members. Editor: Shin-ichi Makiyama. Address same as Association. Circ: Membership. Japanese. Indexed in Dokumenteshon Kenkyu; Japanese Agricultural Sciences Index (JASI). Other publications: Annual reports, proceedings of conferences, seminars, etc. JAALD Sirizu (JAALD Series). Irreg. Publications for sale. No publications exchange program in effect.
Activities   Past achievements: Publication of the translations of four papers in International Agricultural Librarianship (1981); translation of Primer for Agricultural Libraries by O. Lendray (1983); translation of CAB/CAIN Evaluation Project by S. Harvey (1984). Current and future: Compilation of a Bibliography of Japanese Agricultural Bibliographies; publication of "How to Search for Information in the Agricultural Sciences." Sponsors conferences, seminars, workshops, and other continuing education programs.

Bibliography   Makiyama, Shin-ichi, "Japan Association of Agricultural Librarians and Documentalists (JAALD)," Quarterly Bulletin of IAALD 26 (1983):100-101; Makiyama, Shin-ichi, "Japan Association of Agricultural Librarians and Documentalists," Igaku Toshokan 31 (June 1984):105-111 (in Japanese); Kon, Madoko,"Japan," in ALA World Encyclopedia of Library and Information Services, 2nd ed., pp. 403-408. Chicago: American Library Association, 1986; Librarianship in Japan, ed. by Editorial Committee of Librarianship in Japan, Japan Organizing Committee of IFLA Tokyo, August 1986, p. 71-72; Khurshid, A., "Library Associations in Asia," Herald of Library Science 28 (1989):3-10.

319   Nihon Toshokan Gakkai
(Japan Society of Library Science)

Address   c/o Japan Library Association, 1-1-10 Taishido, Setagaya-ku, Tokyo 154 (permanent). Tel: 81 (3) 4106411.
Officers   (elected for 2-yr.term) Pres: Takeo Urata; VP: Toshio Iwasaru; Sec: Hiroshi Kawai; Exec.Sec: Yasuo Iwabuchi; other Exec.Board members: Kimio Hosono, Hiroshi Ishiyama, Takaaki Kuroiwa, Masao Nagasawa, Yoshihiko Shibuya. Exec.Board: 8.
Staff   1 (volunteer)
Languages   Japanese
Established   1953, Tokyo.
Major Fields of Interest   Library and information science
Major Goals and Objectives   To contribute to the development of library and information science.
Structure   Governed by Executive Board.
Sources of Support   Membership dues, sale of publications, government subsidies. Budget (Yen): Approx. 5 million.
Membership   Total members: 559 (505 individual, 54 institutional). Requirements: Those who are engaged and/or interested in the study and/or duty of library science and library service. Dues (Yen): 4,000, individual; 2,000, student; 6,500, institutional; 10,000 sustaining.
General Assembly   Entire membership meets once a year.
Publications   *Official journal:* Toshokan Gakkai Nempou (Annals of the Japan Society of Library Science). 1954-. 4/yr. (Yen) 6,000. Free to members. Editor: Takaaki Kuroiwa. Address same as Association. Circ: 600+. Japanese, English. Other publications: Annual reports, proceedings of conferences, seminars; Toshokangaku Nenji Bunken Mokuroku (Annual Bibliography of Library Science). 1/yr.; Ronshu: Toshokangaku no Ayumi (Monograph Series: Development of Library Science). 4/yr. Publisher: Nichigai Associates. Publications exchange program in effect.
Activities   Sponsors symposia on major topics of library science at the annual meetings and publication of papers presented; extensive publications program, which contributes to research in library and information science. Sponsors conferences, monthly seminars, workshops, and other continuing education programs.
Bibliography   Kon, Madoko,"Japan," in ALA World Encyclopedia of Library and Information Services, 2nd ed., pp. 403-408. Chicago: American Library Association, 1986; Librarianship in Japan, ed. by Editorial Committee of Librarianship in Japan, Japan Organizing Committee of IFLA Tokyo, August 1986, p. 73.

320   Nihon Toshokan Kenkyukai (NITTOKEN)
(Nippon Association for Librarianship) (NAL)

Address   3-8-5-104 Toyosaki, Ouyodo-ku, Osaka 531. Tel: 81 (6) 3763950.

Languages Japanese
Established 1946
Major Fields of Interest Library science
Major Goals and Objectives To promote library studies; to facilitate cooperation between members; to offer guidance on library management.
Structure Governed by Executive Board.
Sources of Support Membership dues, sale of publications.
Membership Total members: 1,600 (1,100 individual, 500 institutional). Requirements: Interested in goals and objectives of Association.
General Assembly Entire membership meets annually.
Publications *Official journal:* Toshokankai (Library World). 6/yr. Other publications: Daigakusei to Toshokan (College Student and Library) (1981); annual reports, proceedings of conferences, seminars, etc.
Activities Supports library studies; sponsors conferences, seminars, workshops, and other continuing education programs.
Bibliography Kon, Madoko,"Japan," in ALA World Encyclopedia of Library and Information Services, 2nd ed., pp. 403-408. Chicago: American Library Association, 1986; Librarianship in Japan, ed. by Editorial Committee of Librarianship in Japan, Japan Organizing Committee of IFLA Tokyo, August 1986, p. 75.

**321 Nihon Toshokan Kyokai (NITOKYO)
(Japan Library Association) (JLA)**

Address 1-1-10 Taishido, Setagaya-ku, Tokyo 154 (permanent). Tel: 81 (3) 4106411.
Officers Pres: M. Nagai; Sec: Hitoshi Kurihara (appointed). Exec.Board: 30.
Staff 27 (paid)
Languages Japanese
Established 1892, Tokyo, as Nihon Bunko Kyokai.
Major Fields of Interest Libraries and librarianship
Major Goals and Objectives To foster the development of libraries in Japan by acting as a liaison and encouraging cooperation among various types of libraries and reading facilities; to contribute to the cultural development of the nation; to improve the professional status of librarians; to promote reading campaigns; to represent Japanese librarianship abroad by serving as a liaison with overseas libraries and library associations.
Structure Governed by Executive Board. Affiliations: IFLA
Sources of Support Membership dues, sale of publications, government subsidies.
Membership Total members: 7,461 (5,521 individual, 1,940 institutional). Divisions: 8 (by types of library). Committees: 24. Types of membership: Individual, institutional, student, patron. Requirements: Open to librarians and any other interested persons. Dues (Yen): 4,000, individual; 6,000-12,000, institutional (3 categories); 3,000, student; 12,000 sustaining.
General Assembly Entire membership meets annually at the All Japan Library Conference.
Publications *Official journal:* Toshokan Zasshi (Library Journal). 1907-. 12/yr. (Yen) 700. Free to members. Address same as Association. Circ: 8,000. Japanese. Other publications: Toshokan Nenkan (Library Yearbook), 1/yr.; Gendai no Toshokan (Libraries Today), 4/yr.; Nihon no Toshokan (Statistics on Libraries in Japan), 4/yr.; Nihon no Sankou Tosho Shiki-ban (Quarterly Guide to Japanese Reference Books), 4/yr.; Nihon no Sankou Tosho (Japanese Reference Books); Toshokan Handobukku (Library Handbook); Nihon Mokuroku Kisoku (Nippon Cataloging Rules); Nihon Jusshin Bunrui-hou (Nippon Decimal Classification); Kohon Kemmei Hyomoku (Basic Subject Headings); annual re-

ports, proceedings of conferences, seminars, etc. Publications for sale. Publications exchange program in effect with other library associations, libraries, and nonlibrary groups.
Activities   As the only general association of Japan covering all types of libraries and subjects, activities span a wide range of areas. Acts as the representative association for Japanese librarianship at national and international library associations. Association expanded international library relations and sponsored the IFLA Congress in Tokyo, August 1986.   Promotes the development of libraries in Japan by acting as a liaison and encouraging cooperation between various types of libraries and reading facilities. Works for improving the status of librarians. Promotes reading campaigns. Sponsors conferences, seminars, workshops, and other continuing education programs.
Bibliography   Kon, Madoko,"Japan," in ALA World Encyclopedia of Library and Information Services, 2nd ed., pp. 403-408. Chicago: American Library Association, 1986; Librarianship in Japan, ed. by Editorial Committee of Librarianship in Japan, Japan Organizing Committee of IFLA Tokyo, August 1986, p. 70; Khurshid, A., "Library Associations in Asia," Herald of Library Science 28 (1989):3-10.

322   Nihon Yakugaku Toshokan Kyogikai (YAKUTOKYO) (Japan Pharmaceutical Library Association) (JPLA)

Address   c/o Pharmaceutical Library, Pharmaceutical Sciences, University of Tokyo, 7-3-1 Hongo, Bunkyo-ku, Tokyo 113. Tel: 81 (3) 8122111 ext.4705.
Officers   Exec.Sec: Yajima Hideo. Exec.Comm: 7.
Staff   1 (paid), 3 (volunteers)
Languages   Japanese
Established   1955, Tokyo
Major Fields of Interest   Library services and documentation in the field of pharmacy and pharmaceutical sciences.
Major Goals and Objectives   To develop pharmaceutical libraries and fulfill the library's mission as the special information center for research and education in the pharmaceutical sciences; to conduct research on the management, operation and technologies of pharmaceutical libraries; to facilitate cooperation between member libraries as well as other associations with similar interests.
Structure   Governed by Executive Committee. Affiliations: Pharmaceutical Society of Japan.
Sources of Support   Membership dues, sale of publications.
Membership   Total members: 225 (130 individual, 95 institutional). Requirements: Open to libraries and librarians of pharmaceutical colleges and pharmaceutical firms.
General Assembly   Entire membership meets once a year, in Tokyo.
Publications   *Official journal:* Yakugaku Toshokan (Pharmaceutical Library Bulletin). 1956-. 4/yr. Free to members. Address same as Association. Circ: 280. Japanese. Indexed in Dokumenteshon Kenkyu. Other publications: Annual reports, proceedings of conferences, seminars, Union List of Periodicals of Pharmaceutical Libraries (1980), and other monographs. Publications for sale.   Publications exchange program in effect with other associations.
Activities   In accordance with the goals and objectives, encourages cooperation among members in such areas as expanding interlibrary loan, compilation of union catalogs, etc. Sponsors exhibits, conferences, seminars, workshops, and other continuing education programs.
Bibliography   Kon, Madoko,"Japan," in ALA World Encyclopedia of Library and Information Services, 2nd ed., pp. 403-408. Chicago: American Library Association, 1986; Librarianship in Japan, ed. by Editorial Committee of Librarianship in Japan, Japan Orga-

nizing Committee of IFLA Tokyo, August 1986, p. 72; Khurshid, A., "Library Associations in Asia," Herald of Library Science 28 (1989):3-10.

323   Ongaku Toshokan Kyogikai (ONTOKYO) (Music Library Association of Japan) (MLAJ)

Address   c/o Library, Kunitachi College of Music, 5-5-1 Kashiwa-machi, Kunitachi-shi, Tokyo 190. Tel: 81 (425) 360321.
Languages   Japanese
Established   1971
Major Fields of Interest   Music librarianship
Major Goals and Objectives   To serve as a resource sharing organization for music materials in Japan; to encourage the collection and organization of music materials in Japan.
Structure   Governed by Executive Committee.
Sources of Support   Membership dues, sale of publications.
Membership   Total members: 32 (5 individual; 27 institutional)
General Assembly   Entire membership meets annually.
Publications   *Official journal:* MLAJ Newsletter. 6/yr. Free to members. Address same as Association. Other publications: Ongaku Kankei Chikuji Kankobutsu Shozai Mokuroku (Union List of Periodicals in Music); Sakkyokuka Zenshu, Gakufu Sosho Shozai Mokuroku (Union Catalog of Selected and Complete Works of Music in Japanese Music Libraries) (1983); annual reports, proceedings of conferences, seminars, etc.
Activities   Sponsors conferences, seminars, workshops, and other continuing education programs.
Bibliography   Kon, Madoko,"Japan," in ALA World Encyclopedia of Library and Information Services, 2nd ed., pp. 403-408. Chicago: American Library Association, 1986; Librarianship in Japan, ed. by Editorial Committee of Librarianship in Japan, Japan Organizing Committee of IFLA Tokyo, August 1986, p. 74.

324   Senmon Toshokan Kyogikai (SENTOKYO) (Japan Special Libraries Association /JSLA)

Address   c/o National Diet Library, 1-10-1 Nagatacho, Chiyoda-ku, Tokyo 100 (permanent). Tel: 81 (3) 5812331. Fax: 81-3-5810989
Officers   (elected for 1-yr.term) Pres: Rokuro Ishikawa; Past Pres: Noboru Goto; VPs: Goro Ishii and others; Exec.Dir: Atsumi Kumata; Treas: Kenkichi Masui. Exec.Council: 62.
Staff   1 (paid)
Languages   Japanese
Established   1953, Tokyo
Major Fields of Interest   Special libraries
Major Goals and Objectives   To promote cooperative activities between government libraries, local assembly libraries, nongovernmental organizations, research and other institutions, in order to stimulate their growth and development.
Structure   Governed by Executive Council. Affiliations: IFLA.
Sources of Support   Membership dues, sale of publications. Budget (Yen): 1986/87: 16,273,672; 1987/88: 17,604,542.
Membership   Total members: 630 (institutional). Districts: 7 (geographical). Committees: 8 (Editorial and Publishing, Education and Training, Research and Statistics, Research Projects, National Plan, Copyright, International Liaison, Awards). Types of mem-

bership: Institutional. Requirements: Open to all institutions having a library and interested in the work of the Association. Dues (Yen): 30,000, institutional.
General Assembly   Entire membership meets once a year.
Publications   *Official journal:* <u>Senmon Toshokan</u> (Bulletin of the Japan Special Libraries Association). 1960-. 5/yr. (Yen) 7,000. Free to members. Editor: Editorial Committee. Address same as Association. Circ: 1,500. Japanese.   Other publications: <u>Senmon Joho Kikan Soran</u> (Directory of Special Libraries in Japan); <u>Directory of Information Sources in Japan</u> (in English, every 3 years); <u>Guide to Japanese Government Publications</u>; annual reports, proceedings of conferences, seminars, JSLA Research Papers, etc.
Activities   (1) Publishing program; (2) establishing government publication centers; (3) organizing general conferences and workshops; (4) compiling bibliographies and other technical documents; (5) promoting interlibrary loan among member institutions and exchange of information; (6) functioning as Clearing House of library materials; (7) exchange of printed information and other cooperative activities with overseas associations and institutions. Association organizes delegates' observation tours of libraries abroad. Sponsors exhibits, conferences, seminars, workshops, and other continuing education programs.
Bibliography   Kon, Madoko,"Japan," in <u>ALA World Encyclopedia of Library and Information Services</u>, 2nd ed., pp. 403-408. Chicago: American Library Association, 1986; <u>Librarianship in Japan</u>, ed. by Editorial Committee of Librarianship in Japan, Japan Organizing Committee of IFLA Tokyo, August 1986, p. 73; Khurshid, A., "Library Associations in Asia," <u>Herald of Library Science</u> 28 (1989):3-10.

325   Shiritsu Daigaku Toshokan Kyokai
(Japan Association of Private University Libraries) (JASPUL)

Address   c/o Kwansei Gakuin University Library, 1-1-155 Bancho, Uegahara, Nishinomiya 662 (not permanent). Tel: 81 (798) 53611. Fax: 81-798-510911
Officers   (elected for 2-yr.term) Pres: K. Sugita; Past Pres: Seiji Kaneko; Sec: Z. Nagaya. Exec.Board: 17.
Staff   None
Languages   Japanese
Established   1938
Major Fields of Interest   Libraries of private universities
Major Goals and Objectives   To promote the development of university libraries through (1) research and study of university libraries and their publications, (2) organizing conferences and lectures on research, (3) publishing an official journal, (4) liaison activities.
Structure   Governed by general meetings, Board of Directors, and District Conference. Affiliations: IFLA, Kokkosiritu Daigaku Toshokan Kyoryoku Iinkai (Joint Committee for Library Cooperation of National, Public and Private Universities), Daigaku Toshokan Kokusai Renraku Iinkai (International Liaison Committee of University Libraries), Nihon Toshokan Kyokai (Japan Library Association).
Sources of Support   Membership dues, sale of publications. Budget (Yen): Approx. 19 million.
Membership   Total members: 280 (institutional). Requirements: 4-year private university libraries in Japan. Dues (Yen): 22,000 basic dues, plus 5,000 to 20,000, according to number of students.
General Assembly   Entire membership meets once a year.
Publications   *Official journal:* <u>Shiritsu Daigaku Toshokan Kyokai Kaihou</u> (Bulletin of the Japan Association of Private University Libraries). 1952-. 2/yr. 2,000 Yen. Free to

members. Address same as Association. Editorial address: Kyoto University Library of Foreign Studies, 6, Saiinkasame-cho, Ukyo-ku, Kyoto 615. Circ: 500. Japanese. Other publications: Annual reports, proceedings of conferences, seminars, etc. Official journal for sale.

Activities Organizes annual general and research meetings on various themes concerning the private university library, such as the effects of computerization, the new media, the future, etc. Participated in the IFLA Tokyo Convention (1986). Sponsors conferences, seminars, workshops, and other continuing education programs.

Bibliography Kon, Madoko,"Japan," in ALA World Encyclopedia of Library and Information Services, 2nd ed., pp. 403-408. Chicago: American Library Association, 1986; Librarianship in Japan, ed. by Editorial Committee of Librarianship in Japan, Japan Organizing Committee of IFLA Tokyo, August 1986, p. 72; Khurshid, A., "Library Associations in Asia," Herald of Library Science 28 (1989):3-10.

326 Shiritsu Tanki Daigaku Toshokan Kyogikai (SHITANTOKYO) (Junior College Library Association)

Address c/o Library, Tokyo Women's Christian University Junior College, 4-3-1 Mure, Mitaka-shi, Tokyo 181. Tel: 81 (422) 454145 ext.234.
Officers Pres: A. Arioka; Sec: T. Watanabe.
Languages Japanese
Established 1977
Major Fields of Interest Junior college libraries
Major Goals and Objectives To promote the development of junior college libraries; to conduct research on junior college libraries.
Structure Governed by Executive Board. Affiliations: IFLA.
Sources of Support Membership dues, sale of publications.
Membership Total members: 255 (institutional). Requirements: Libraries of junior colleges in Japan.
General Assembly Entire membership meets annually.
Publications *Official journal:* Tanki Daigaku Toshokan Kenkyu (Journal of Junior College Libraries). 1/yr.; Shiritsu Tanki Daigaku Toshokan Kyogikai Kaihou (Bulletin of the Junior College Library Association). 2/yr. Other publications: Annual reports, proceedings of conferences, seminars, etc.
Activities Conducts research on junior college libraries. Sponsors conferences, seminars, workshops, and other continuing education programs.
Bibliography Kon, Madoko,"Japan," in ALA World Encyclopedia of Library and Information Services, 2nd ed., pp. 403-408. Chicago: American Library Association, 1986; Librarianship in Japan, ed. by Editorial Committee of Librarianship in Japan, Japan Organizing Committee of IFLA Tokyo, August 1986, p. 74; Khurshid, A., "Library Associations in Asia," Herald of Library Science 28 (1989):3-10.

327 Toshokan Mondai Kenkyukai (TOMONKEN) (Society for the Study of Library Issues, Japan)

Address c/o Kyoiku Shiryo Shuppankai, Shin-Kanda Building 4F, 1-4-13 Nishi-Kanda, Chiyoda-ku, Tokyo 101. Tel: 81 (63) 2930316.
Languages Japanese
Established 1955
Major Fields of Interest Library services
Major Goals and Objectives To study and conduct research for the improvement of library services in Japan.

Structure   Governed by Executive Board.
Sources of Support   Membership dues, sale of publications.
Membership   Total members: 1,707 (individual). Requirements: Interested in aims of Association.
General Assembly   Entire membership meets annually.
Publications   *Official journal:* Minna no Toshokan (People's Library). 12/yr.; Toshokan Hyoron (Library Review). 1/yr. Other publications: Toshokan Yougo Jiten (Library Glossary) (1982); annual reports, proceedings of conferences, seminars, etc.
Activities   Sponsors conferences, seminars, workshops, and other continuing education programs.
Bibliography   Kon, Madoko, "Japan," in ALA World Encyclopedia of Library and Information Services, 2nd ed., pp. 403-408. Chicago: American Library Association, 1986; Librarianship in Japan, ed. by Editorial Committee of Librarianship in Japan, Japan Organizing Committee of IFLA Tokyo, August 1986, pp. 75-76.

328   Zenkoku Gakkou Kouritsu Toshokan Kyougikai (ZENKOKU SLA) (Japan School Library Association) (JSLA)

Address   2-2-7 Kasuga, Bunkyo-ku, Tokyo 112. Tel: 81 (3) 8144317. Fax: 81-3-8141790.
Officers   (elected for 2-yr.term) Pres: Y. Sakai; Exec.Dir: T. Sano. Exec.Board: 18.
Staff   14 (paid), 11 (volunteer councilors, working as teachers or librarians)
Languages   Japanese
Established   1950
Major Fields of Interest   School libraries
Major Goals and Objectives   To promote communication among prefectural school library associations; to promote the development of school libraries through seminars, surveys and research.
Structure   Governed by Executive Committee. Affiliations: IFLA.
Sources of Support   Membership dues, sale of publications. Budget (Yen): 1986/87: 276,000,000; 1987/88: 276,000,000.
Membership   Total members: 60 (prefectural school library associations). Divisions: 7. Sections: 5. Requirements: (1) Being a prefectural school library association; (2) Obtaining approval by the Board of Directors; (3) Paying membership dues. Dues: Amount decided on basis of scale of prefectural school library association.
General Assembly   Entire membership meets once a year, with national and regional conferences alternating.
Publications   *Official journal:* Gakkou Toshokan (School Library). 1950-. 12/yr. (Yen) 9,000. Free to members. Editor: Yoshiro Kasahara. Address same as Association. Circ: 21,000. Japanese; Gakkou Toshokan Sokuhou-ban (School Library Newsletter). 1954-. every 10 days. Free to members. Address same as Association. Circ: 21,000. Japanese. Other publications: Gakkou Toshokan Kihon Tosho Mokuroku (Masterpieces for the School Library). 1/yr.; Subject Headings for School Libraries; An Outline of Library Science; annual reports, proceedings of conferences, seminars, etc. Publications for sale; price lists available. Publications exchange program in effect.
Activities   Past achievements: To hold National Conference of JSLA; publication of proposal "In Pursuit of Education from the Learner's Point of View;" awarding "School Library Prizes" to outstanding practitioners. Current: Awarding "The Japan Picture Book Prize;" organizing workshops and assemblies for each category of library employees; examining standards for selecting comic books for school libraries. Future: Examination of standards for school library facilities; publication of "School Library White Paper." Association has been active in promoting library-related legislation: The School Library Law

was enacted in 1953. JSLA has been taking a leading role in the movement for a revision
of this law. Sponsors exhibits, conferences, seminars, workshops, and other continuing
education programs.
Use of High Technology   Computers (PCs) for management.
Bibliography   Kon, Madoko,"Japan," in ALA World Encyclopedia of Library and Information Services, 2nd ed., pp. 403-408. Chicago: American Library Association, 1986; Librarianship in Japan, ed. by Editorial Committee of Librarianship in Japan, Japan Organizing Committee of IFLA Tokyo, August 1986, p. 73; Khurshid, A., "Library
Associations in Asia," Herald of Library Science 28 (1989):3-10.

329   Zenkoku Koritsu Toshokan Kyogikai (ZENKOTO) (National Council of Public Libraries)

Address   c/o Tokyo Metropolitan Central Library, 5-7-13 Minami-Azabu, Minato-ku,
Tokyo 106. Tel: 81 (3) 4428451. Fax: 81-3-4478924.
Officers   Pres: Shuichi Kato; Sec: Masataka Ogura.
Languages   Japanese
Established   1970
Major Fields of Interest   Public libraries
Major Goals and Objectives   To develop public libraries in Japan; to coordinate their
activities and provide a forum for information exchange; to provide assistance to member
libraries; to promote research and studies of public libraries.
Structure   Governed by Executive Board. Affiliations: IFLA.
Sources of Support   Membership dues.
Membership   Total members: 1,633 (institutional). Requirements: Membership open to
public libraries in Japan.
General Assembly   Entire membership meets annually.
Publications   No official journal; Toshokan Zenkoku Keikaku no Tame no Kiso Shiryoshu (Databook for a National Library Plan) (4 vols., 1979-84); annual reports, proceedings of conferences, seminars, etc.
Activities   Conducts research on public libraries (their administration, finance and activities). Collects material and encourages exchange of information between member libraries in order to assist in their work. Sponsors conferences, seminars, workshops, and
other continuing education programs.
Bibliography   Kon, Madoko,"Japan," in ALA World Encyclopedia of Library and Information Services, 2nd ed., pp. 403-408. Chicago: American Library Association, 1986; Librarianship in Japan, ed. by Editorial Committee of Librarianship in Japan, Japan Organizing Committee of IFLA Tokyo, August 1986, p. 74; Khurshid, A., "Library
Associations in Asia," Herald of Library Science 28 (1989):3-10.

Jordan

330   Jordan Library Association (JLA)

Address   PO Box 6289, Amman (permanent). Tel: 962 (6) 629412.
Officers   (elected) Pres: Farouk Mo'az; VP: Izat Zahdi; Sec: Medhat Mar'ei; Treas: Ali
Turki; Other members: Hani Al Amad, Nayef Khalifa, Yousef Qandeal. Exec.Comm: 7
Staff   3 (paid), 25 (volunteers)
Languages   Arabic, English
Established   1963, Amman
Major Fields of Interest   Librarianship, documentation, information, archives.
Major Goals and Objectives   (1) To unite the efforts of Jordanian librarians to pro-
mote library services in Jordan; (2) to promote and develop library services in the Arab
countries; (3) to collect and publish studies in library science, information and documen-
tation; (4) to encourage the public and private sectors to establish libraries in Jordan; (5)
to provide training of personnel in order to establish and improve library services in Jordan and the Arab countries.
Structure   Governed by Executive Committee. Affiliations: IFLA; Ministry of Culture
and Youth.
Sources of Support   Membership dues, sale of publications, social activities, fees from
training courses. Budget (Jordanian Dinar): Approx. 39,310.
Membership   Total members: 543 (368 individual, 175 institutional). 20 countries represented. Types of membership: Individual, institutional, honorary, supporter. Requirements: (1) Academic degree in library science; (2) academic degree in the arts and
sciences plus 5 years experience in libraries; (3) high school certificate plus 10 years experience. Dues (Jordanian Dinar): 3.5, active (employed); contributions from supporters; no
dues, honorary.
General Assembly   Entire membership meets once a year.
Publications   *Official journal:* Rissalat al-Maktaba (The Message of the Library). 1964-.
4/yr. Free to members. Editor: Farouk Mo'az. Address same as Association. Circ: 1,000.
Arabic, with English abstracts. Other publications: Annual reports, proceedings of meetings; Jordanian National Bibliography; Directory of Libraries and Librarians in Jordan
(bilingual; updated every few years); various directories of libraries and periodicals in Jordan; publications related to library science practices. Price lists issued, publications listed
in official journal.
Activities   Offering courses in library science (over 25 in last 5 years); participating in
many cultural and social activities in Jordan and other countries; translating Dewey Decimal Classification, the Anglo-American Cataloging Rules, and numerous books in library
science; participating in Book Fairs. Association offers continuing education programs;
sponsors the Jordanian National Bibliography and Cataloging in Publication Data.
Bibliography   Nimer, R.E. and Akrush, A., "Jordan Library Association in Twenty Years
1963-1983," Rissalat-Al Maktaba 18 (Dec. 1983):3-7 (in English and Arabic); "The JLA
Administrative Report for the Year 1984," Rissalat-Al Mataba 20 (1985):45-54 (in Arabic); El Hadi, Mohamed M., "Jordan," in ALA World Encyclopedia of Library and Information Service, 2nd ed., p. 415. Chicago: American Library Association, 1986.

Kenya

331 Kenya Library Association

Address PO Box 46031, Nairobi (permanent). Tel: 254 (2) 566073/569791. Telex: 22035.
Officers (elected for 1-yr.term) Chair: J. Lilech; Past Chair: Matthews J. Ong'any; Vice-Chair: Michael Gathua; Sec: Lily Nyariki; Asst.Sec: Ms. I. Wanyaga; Treas: Peter Weche; Asst.Treas: George King'ori; Ed: Hudson Liyai; Asst.Ed: Arthur Otieno-Rabare; Registrar: Patrick Wanyama. Exec.Board: 10.
Staff None
Languages English
Established 1956, Nairobi, as a branch of the East African Library Association (EALA), until it was dissolved late 1972. In 1973, the Kenya Library Association was established as an independent organization.
Major Fields of Interest Library development and the library profession.
Major Goals and Objectives To encourage the promotion, establishment, and improvement of libraries, library services, books, and book production in East Africa; to improve the standard of librarianship and the status of the library profession; to bring together all who are interested in libraries and librarianship.
Structure Governed by Executive Council. Affiliations: IFLA.
Sources of Support Membership dues, government subsidies.
Membership Total members: 220 (individual and institutional). Requirements: Librarians and those working in libraries; libraries and related institutions. Only professional librarians can vote. Dues (Kenyan Shilling): Individual, scaled according to income; institutional, varies.
General Assembly Entire membership meets once a year.
Publications *Official journal:* Maktaba (Libraries [in Kiswahili]). 1972-. 2/yr. Address same as Association. Editor: Johnston L. Abukutsa. English, Kiswahili. Newsletter: Kelias News, 6/yr. Other publications: Annual reports, proceedings of conferences.
Activities New constitution adopted in 1982 to strengthen the professional nature of the Association, in order to improve professional standards and professional development of librarians. Hosted the IFLA Congress in 1984 in Nairobi. Sponsors continuing education programs and works towards improving educational programs and training facilities for librarians.
Bibliography Howe, V., "International Conference on Education and Training for Agricultural Library and Information Work, Nairobi, March 1983," Quarterly Bulletin of IAALD 28 (1983):19-23; Ndegwa, J., "Kenya," in ALA World Encyclopedia of Library and Information Services, 2nd ed., pp.416-417. Chicago: American Library Association, 1986.

Korea, Democratic People's Republic of

332   Library Association of the Democratic People's Republic of Korea

Address   The Grand People's Study House of the Democratic People's Republic of Korea, PO Box 200, Pyongyang, Central District (permanent). Tel: 3-4066.
Officers   Pres: Li Yeng Chang; Sec: Li Geug
Languages   Korean
Established   1953, Pyongyang
Major Fields of Interest   Library development and library services
Major Goals and Objectives   To promote the development of libraries and library services in the country; to further the professional development of librarians.
Structure   Affiliations: IFLA
Bibliography   Lee, Pongsoon, "Korea, Democratic People's Republic of," in <u>ALA World Encyclopedia of Library and Information Services</u>, 2nd ed., pp. 421-422. Chicago: American Library Association, 1986; Khurshid, A., "Library Associations in Asia," <u>Herald of Library Science</u> 28 (1989):3-10.

Korea, Republic of

333   Hanguk Seoji Hakhoe / Korean Bibliographical Society

Address   c/o National Assembly Library, Yoi-dong 1, Yeongdeungpo-gu, Seoul 150. Tel: 82 (2) 7882271.
Languages   Korean
Established   1968, Seoul
Major Fields of Interest   Bibliography and bibliographical services
Major Goals and Objectives   To promote bibliographical services in Korea.
Structure   Governed by executive officers
Sources of Support   Membership dues, sale of publications.
Publications   *Official journal:* Sujihak (Bibliographical Studies). Address same as Association. Korean.
Activities   Sponsors seminars and lectures for librarians and scholars interested in bibliographical studies and services.
Bibliography   Lee, Pongsoon, "Korea, Republic of," in ALA World Encyclopedia of Library and Information Services, 2nd ed., pp. 422-424. Chicago: American Library Association, 1986.

334   Hanguk Tosogwan Hakhoe / Korean Library Science Society (KLSS)

Address   c/o Department of Library Science, Sung Kyun Kwan University, 53, 3-ka, Myonglyun-dong, Chongno-ku, Seoul 110 (permanent). Tel: 82 (762) 5020 ext.189.
Officers   (elected for 2-yr.term) Pres: Choon-Hee Lee; Exec.Sec: Sung-Chin Choi; Treas: Ja-Young Ku. Exec.Comm: 5
Staff   2 (volunteers)
Languages   Korean
Established   1970, Seoul, at meeting at Ewha Woman's University Library, through sponsorship of the Asia Foundation and leading librarians.
Major Fields of Interest   All aspects of library and information services in Korea
Major Goals and Objectives   To exchange results of research and development in librarianship and information science carried out by members.
Structure   Governed by Executive Committee.
Sources of Support   Membership dues
Membership   Total members: 120 (individual). Types of membership: Individual. Requirements: Open to any professional librarian or to any interested person recommended for membership by any two members.
General Assembly   Entire membership meets once a year in Seoul.
Publications   *Official journal:* Tosogwan Hak (Studies in Library Science). 1970-. Annual. Free to members. Circ: 600. Korean, with English abstracts. Address: c/o Ewha Woman's University Library, 11-1 Dachyun-dong, Sudaemun-ku, Seoul 120. Other publications: Proceedings of seminars, conferences, workshops. Publications exchange program in effect with libraries.
Activities   Sponsors seminars on development of library school curricula and other relevant topics in librarianship and information science. Offers continuing education programs.
Bibliography   Lee, Pongsoon, "Korea, Republic of," in ALA World Encyclopedia of Library and Information Services, 2nd ed., pp. 422-424. Chicago: American Library Association, 1986; Khurshid, A., "Library Associations in Asia," Herald of Library Science 28 (1989):3-10.

335   Hanguk Tosogwan Hyophoe (TOHYOP) / Korean Library Association (KLA)

Address   No. 60-1, Panpo-2 Dong, Seochu-ku, CPO Box 2041, Seoul (permanent). Tel: 82 (2) 5354868/5355616
Officers   (elected for 2-yr.term) Pres: Choon-Hee Lee (Prof. of Library Science, Sung Kyun Kwan University, 53, 3-ka, Myonglyun-dong, Chongno-ku, Seoul); Exec.Dir: Dae-Kwon Park (appointed); Sec: Kyung-Il Kim.
Staff   7 (paid)
Languages   Korean
Established   1945, Seoul, as Chosun Library Association; renamed 1955.
Major Fields of Interest   Library services
Major Goals and Objectives   To promote and improve library services and facilities in Korea through mutual exchanges and cooperation among domestic and foreign libraries and librarians, with the ultimate purpose of contributing to the cultural and economic development of the Republic of Korea.
Structure   Governed by Board of Directors. Affiliations: IFLA .
Sources of Support   Membership dues, government subsidies, private donations.
Membership   Total members: 1,335 (700 individual, 635 institutional). 4 countries represented. Committees: 8 (Administration and International Relations, Training and Research, Classification, Cataloging, Publications, Terminology, Bibliography, Automation). Divisions: 4 (Public Library, College and University Library, School Library, Special Library). Requirements and types of membership: (1) Institutional: Libraries, schools, and other organizations that provide library services; (2) Individual: Employees of libraries and other organizations that provide library services; (3) Supporting: Individuals or groups that support the principles and objectives of the Association; (4) Honorary: Those who have made contributions to the development of the Association, and are recommended by the Board of Directors. Dues (Won): 800, individual; 3,000 to 30,000, institutional.
General Assembly   Entire membership meets annually at the National Library Convention.
Publications   *Official journal:* Tohyop Wolbo (KLA Bulletin). 1969-. 12/yr. (Won) 130. Free to members. Address same as Association. Korean. Other publications: Annual reports, bibliographies, proceedings of seminars, conferences; Library Research. 6/yr; Statistics on Libraries in Korea. 1965-, 1/yr; List of Selected Korean Books. 1964-; Korean Cataloging Rules, etc. Price lists available.
Activities   As the oldest library association in the country, KLA has been representing Korean libraries at international conferences, particularly at IFLA; sponsors workshops, seminars, conferences, Book Week, Library Week and numerous continuing education programs; and continues the extensive publication program of practical library tools and other reference works.
Bibliography   Lee, Pongsoon, "Korea, Republic of," in ALA World Encyclopedia of Library and Information Science, 2nd ed., pp. 422-424. Chicago: American Library Association, 1986; Khurshid, A., "Library Associations in Asia," Herald of Library Science 28 (1989):3-10.

336   Korean Micro-Library Association

Address   c/o Central National Library Building, 100-177 Hoehyun-dong 1-ka, Chung-ku, Seoul 100
Languages   Korean
Established   1961

Major Fields of Interest   Rural library services
Major Goals and Objectives   To provide effective library services at the village and farm level
Structure   The Association was first under the direction of the Ministry of Education, but is now under the Ministry of Home Affairs.
Sources of Support   Membership and government subsidies.
Membership   Total members: Approx. 35,025 libraries under the Ministry of Home Affairs.
Publications   *Official journal:* Saemaul Mungo (New Village Micro Library).   12/yr.
Activities   The Association "is a grass-roots effort to reach individuals at the village and farm level and is a part of the New Village Movement, a unique Korean community movement for better living in the rural areas. Each Saemaul Mungo (New Village Micro Library) of approx. 60 titles is self-contained in a wooden bookcase that holds upward of 300 volumes." (Pongsoon Lee). Selection of titles is according to needs and interests. Each recipient is expected to add new volumes. A Village Reading Club is in charge of each library and books are lent free of charge.
Bibliography   Lee, Pongsoon, "Korea, Republic of," in ALA World Encyclopedia of Library and Information Services, 2nd ed., pp. 422-424. Chicago: American Library Association, 1986; Khurshid, A., "Library Associations in Asia," Herald of Library Science 28 (1989):3-10.

337   Korean Research and Development Library Association (KORDELA)

Address   Room 0411, KIST Library, PO Box 131, Chong-Ryang, Seoul. Tel: 82 (2) 9628801. Telex: 27380. Fax: 82-2-9634013.
Officers   Pres: Ke-Hong Park (Korea Advanced Institute of Science and Technology, PO Box 131, Chong Ryang, Seoul); Sec: Keon Tak Oh.
Languages   Korean
Established   1979
Major Fields of Interest   Library research and development
Major Goals and Objectives   To promote research in library science; to promote the development of library science
Structure   Governed by executive officers. Affiliations: IFLA (since 1980).
Sources of Support   Membership dues
Bibliography   Khurshid, A., "Library Associations in Asia," Herald of Library Science 28 (1989):3-10.

Laos

338 Association des Bibliothécaires Laotiens
(The Lao Library Association)

Address   c/o Direction de la Bibliothèque Nationale, Ministry of Education, BP 704, Vientiane.
Languages   Lao (official), French
Major Fields of Interest   Libraries and library services
Major Goals and Objectives   To promote library services in Laos
Bibliography   Poole, P.A., "Laos," in ALA World Encyclopedia of Library and Information Services, 2nd ed., pp. 429-430. Chicago: American Library Association, 1986.

Lebanon

339   The Lebanese Library Association / Association des Bibliothèques Libanaises (LLA/ABL)

Address   c/o American University of Beirut, University Library, Beirut. Tel: 340740 ext. 28354. Telex: 20801.
Officers   (elected for 1-yr.term) Pres: M.F. Rafeh; Sec: Ms. L. Sadaka. Exec.Board: 10
Staff   None
Languages   Arabic (some French, Armenian, English)
Established   1960, Beirut.
Major Fields of Interest   Development of libraries and professional standards for librarians
Major Goals and Objectives   To raise the standards of libraries and librarians in Lebanon; to develop bibliographic research and facilitate cooperation in national and international fields; to urge the authorities concerned to organize courses in library science; to work for the formation of a union of Arab library associations.
Structure   Governed by Executive Board. Affiliations: IFLA
Sources of Support   Membership dues
Membership   Total members: 97 (95 individual, 2 institutional)
General Assembly   Entire membership meets once a year, in December, in Beirut.
Publications   *Official journal:* Newsletter of the Lebanese Library Association. 1975-. 4/yr. Free to members. Editor: Samira Meghdessian. Address: Beirut University College Library, P.O. Box 4080, Beirut. Tel. 25290/22. Circ: 150. Arabic. Other publications: Annual report.
Activities   Participation in IFLA; sponsors continuing education workshops, seminars, conferences; instrumental in developing a library science program at the Lebanese University.
Bibliography   Hanhan, L.M., "Lebanese Library Association: Past and Present," Library Times International 1 (1984):13-14; Hafez, Aida Kassantini, "Lebanon," in ALA World Encyclopedia of Library and Information Services, 2nd ed., pp. 446-447. Chicago: American Library Association, 1986; Khurshid, A., "Library Associations in Asia," Herald of Library Science 28 (1989):3-10.

Lesotho

340 Lesotho Library Association

Address Private Bag A26, Maseru 100. Telegrams: LELIA. Headquarters address: c/o National Library, PO Box 985, Maseru 100. Tel: 22592.
Officers Chair: M.M. Moshoeshoe; Sec: S.M. Mohai.
Staff None
Languages English, Sesotho
Established 1978
Major Fields of Interest Library development
Major Goals and Objectives To promote, safeguard and encourage the establishment and improvement of libraries and the professional interests of librarians in Lesotho.
Structure Governed by executive officers. Affiliations: IFLA
Sources of Support Membership dues, government subsidies.
Membership Total members: 72+ (10 professional librarians, 16 institutions, 46 other individuals). Committees: 6. Requirements: Professional librarian, or working in library; institution with library.
General Assembly Entire membership meets once a year.
Publications *Official journal:* Lesotho Books and Libraries. 1/yr. Other publications: Annual reports, proceedings of conferences, e.g. Proceedings of SCECSAL (1980).
Activities Assisted in drafting of deposit law for Lesotho; active in areas of public, school, and special libraries, information services, and education and training. Sponsors continuing education workshops and seminars.
Bibliography Lebotsa, M.M., "Lesotho Library Association Annual General Meeting - Hlotse High School, 19th March, 1983," Lesotho Books and Libraries 3 (1982/83):1-9; Forshaw, V., "Lesotho," in ALA World Encyclopedia of Library and Information Services, 2nd ed., pp. 451-452. Chicago: American Library Association, 1986.

Liberia

341   Liberian Library Association (LLA)

Address   c/o C. Wesley Armstrong, Vice President for Academic Affairs and former Director of Libraries, University of Liberia, Monrovia
Languages   English
Established   1977
Major Fields of Interest   Library development and library services
Major Goals and Objectives   To develop and improve library services and librarianship throughout the country.
Structure   Governed by executive officers.
Sources of Support   Membership dues
Membership   Open to professionally trained librarians and to any individual working in a library.
Activities   Sponsors workshops and other continuing education offerings.
Bibliography   Armstrong, C. W., "Liberia," in <u>ALA World Encyclopedia of Library and Information Services</u>, 2nd ed., pp. 452-453. Chicago: American Library Association, 1986.

Madagascar

342   Office du Livre Malagasy (OLM)
(Malagasy Book Office)

Address   BP 617, Tananarive (permanent). Tel: (2) 24449
Officers   (elected for 1-yr.term) Pres: Juliette Ratsimandrava; Exec.Sec: Lydia Rajona; Treas: Louis Ralaisaholimanana. Exec.Comm: 7
Staff   3 (paid), 8 (volunteers)
Languages   Malagasy, French
Established   1971, Tananarive, at the National Library.
Major Fields of Interest   Publishing books in the Malagasy language; providing book services to all residents
Major Goals and Objectives   To publish and disseminate works useful for the development of literary tastes of Malagasian citizens; to provide a national policy for book standards; to serve as a center of information on questions related to books and to information about authors and writers.
Structure   Governed by Executive Committee. Affiliations: AIDBA.
Sources of Support   Membership dues, sale of publications, government subsidies, private gifts. Budget (Malagasy Franc): Approx. 25 million.
Membership   Types of membership: Individual. Requirements: Open to all librarians, editors, and authors.
General Assembly   Entire membership meets annually in Tananarive, in August or September.
Publications   *Official journal:* Ny Boky loharanom-pandrosoana/Le Livre Source du Progrès. 1966-. Irreg. (Malagasy Franc) 700. Free to members. Address same as Association. Malagasy, French. Circ: 600. Indexed in Lib.Lit. Other publications: Annual reports, proceedings of meetings. Price lists available. Publications exchange program in effect with other associations and libraries.
Activities   Past achievements: Publications program and sale of Malagasy books in the different cities in the provinces; conferences held at the universities in the provinces. Current and future: Publications program and promotion of books in Madagascar; translation program of foreign publications, books for children; sponsors traveling book exhibits to promote books in localities lacking books and libraries. Active in sponsoring library-related legislation. Association has been involved in the acquisition of historical material for the completion of a national bibliography; has been collaborating with other groups in book services to promote legislation for the construction of a national library. Sponsors book exhibits and seminars.
Bibliography   Ratsimandrava, J., "Madagascar," in ALA World Encyclopedia of Library and Information Services, 2nd ed., pp. 508-509. Chicago: American Library Association, 1986.

343   Tiraisan'ny Mpikajy ny Harentsain'ny Tirenena / Association Nationale des Archivistes, Bibliothécaires, Documentalistes et Muséographes de Madagascar
(Association of Archivists, Librarians, Documentalists and Museologists of Madagascar)

Address   c/o Bibliothèque nationale, BP 257, Anosy, Tananarive. Tel: (2) 25872.
Languages   Malagasy, French
Established   1976

Major Fields of Interest   Archives, libraries, information centers, museum studies; professional development
Major Goals and Objectives   To further the professional development of archivists, librarians, documentalists and museologists, and represent their interests.
Structure   Governed by executive officers
Sources of Support   Membership dues
Bibliography   Ratsimandrava, J., "Madagascar," in <u>ALA World Encyclopedia of Library and Information Services</u>, 2nd ed., pp. 508-509. Chicago: American Library Association, 1986.

Malawi

344 Malawi Library Association (MALA)

Address PO Box 429, Zomba (permanent). Tel: (265) 522222.
Officers (elected for 3-yr.term) Chair: R. Masanjika; Past Chair: Joseph J. Uta; Sec:
Ms. F. Matenje; Treas: Cynthia Nyirenda; Ed: Foster G. Howse. Exec.Comm: 8
Staff Volunteers
Languages English
Established 1977, at Chancellor College, Zomba.
Major Fields of Interest Library training; library planning and research
Major Goals and Objectives To unite all persons and organizations engaged in library,
archives, documentation and information work or interested in the promotion of these
services; to promote national development of library services, and engage in bibliographi-
cal work and related research.
Structure Governed by Executive Committee. Affiliations: IFLA; COMLA; Standing
Conference of Eastern, Central and Southern African Librarians (SCECSAL).
Sources of Support Membership dues, sale of publications, government subsidies.
Budget (Kwacha): 1986/87: 21,000; 1987/88: 32,000.
Membership Total members: 150 (126 individual, 24 institutional). Chapters: 2. Re-
quirements: Open to all working in library and information services. Dues (Kwacha):
2.50-15.00, individual, according to salary; 40, institutional.
General Assembly Entire membership meets once a year. 1988: Zomba, March 11.
Publications *Official journal:* MALA Bulletin. 1978-. 1/yr. (Kwacha) 10. Free to members. Address same as Association. Editor: Foster G. Howse. Address: Chancellor College, PO Box 280, Zomba. Circ: 200. English. Other publications: Annual reports, proceedings of meetings, reports of seminars, workshops; Libraries in Malawi: A Textbook
for Library Assistants (1985); Manual for Small Libraries.
Activities Past and current: Bibliographical work and research; training of library assistants at certificate level by offering an 8-month certificate course (so far over 150
trained); government recognition of the Malawi Library Assistants Certificate; conducting
national and international seminars and workshops on special themes in library and information services, such as, user education, school library development, etc. Worked for the
establishment of a non-graduate diploma in library and information studies at the University of Malawi in 1988. Future: Harmonization of national bibliographical control activities. Association has been active in promoting library-related legislation, such as the creation of a National Information Policy, and a Legal Deposit Law. Sponsors seminars,
workshops and other continuing education offerings on various topics, such as, standardization of bibliographic control of Malawiana, cataloging, rural services, etc. Association
offers professional advice to organizations in the country on setting up and managing libraries.
Bibliography Mwiyeriwa, S.S., "Malawi," in ALA World Encyclopedia of Library and
Information Services, 2nd ed., pp. 510-511. Chicago: American Library Association, 1986;
Mabomba, R.S., "From Malawi: News on Information Developments," COMLA Newsletter 63 (Mar. 1989):13, 16.

Malaysia

345 Persatuan Perpustakaan Malaysia (PPM) / Library Association of Malaysia

Address Peti Surat 1245, 50782 Kuala Lumpur (permanent).
Officers (elected for 1-yr.term) Pres: Mariam Abdul Kadir; Past Pres: Rugayah Abdul Rashid; Hon.Sec: Raslin Bin Abu Bakar.
Staff 1 (paid)
Languages Malay, English
Established 1955, Singapore, as the Malayan Library Group; reorganized 1958, as the Library Association of Malaya and Singapore. When Singapore became an independent republic in 1965, the library association changed into two separate organizations (1966), the Library Association of Singapore and the present Library Association of Malaysia.
Major Fields of Interest Development of libraries and the library profession
Major Goals and Objectives (1) To unite all persons engaged in library work or interested in libraries; (2) to promote better administration of libraries; (3) to encourage the establishment, development, and use of libraries in Malaysia; (4) to encourage professional education and training for librarianship; (5) to publish information of service to members; (6) to undertake such activities, including the holding of meetings and conferences, as are appropriate to the attainment of the above objectives.
Structure Governed by an Executive Council. Affiliations: IFLA, CONSAL; maintains close cooperation with the Library Association of Singapore through a permanent Joint Liaison Council.
Sources of Support Membership dues, government and private subsidies.
Membership Total members: 238 (individual and institutional). Standing Committees: 5. Requirements: Open to persons or institutions interested in libraries in Malaysia.
General Assembly Entire membership meets annually in Kuala Lumpur in March.
Publications *Official journal:* Majallah Perpustakaan Malaysia. 1971-. 2/yr. Membership. Address same as Association. Circ: 500. Malay and English. Other publications: Berita PPM. 6/yr; Sumer Pustaka, newsletters, Malay and English. Issues annual reports, proceedings of meetings, workshops, seminars, in Malay and English. Publications available for sale.
Activities Sponsored national and international conferences; offers continuing education workshops, seminars, etc. Worked for the establishment of a School of Library and Information Studies at Mara Institute of Technology. Cooperates with Library Association of Singapore on committees, such as Committee on Bibliographical and Library Cooperation (BILCO), Sub-committee on Cataloguing and Classification (SCAC), etc.
Bibliography Osman, Z.B., The Role of the Library Association of Malaysia in Providing Professional Leadership in Malaysia. Loughborough, England: Loughborough University of Technology, 1981; Wijasuriya, D.E.K., "Malaysia," in ALA World Encyclopedia of Library and Information Services, 2nd ed., pp. 510-512. Chicago: American Library Association, 1986; Khurshid, A., "Library Associations in Asia," Herald of Library Science 28 (1989):3-10.

Maldives

346   Maldives Library Association

Address   c/o National Library, Biloorijehige, Majeedee Magu 20-04, Male', Republic of Maldives (permanent). Tel: 3485.
Officers   (elected for 1-yr.term) Pres: Habeeba Hussain Habeeb; VP: Vaseema Mohamed; Sec: Janet Fleming; Asst.Sec: Zulfa Mohamed; Training Officer: Alastair MacLeod; Pub.Off: Ibrahim Sabir. Exec.Board: 6
Staff   6 (volunteers)
Languages   Dhivehi, English
Established   Feb. 22, 1987, first inaugural meeting
Major Fields of Interest   Library development; library education; promotion of library use.
Major Goals and Objectives   To upgrade all libraries in the Maldives, to have training courses and workshops for staff, and to promote library use.
Structure   Governed by executive officers and National Library.
Sources of Support   Membership dues; National Library (included in budget).
Membership   12 (individual and institutional). Requirements: Interest in library work. Dues (Ruliyea): 26.
General Assembly   Entire membership meets 3 times a year.
Publications   No official journal; publishes newsletter. No publications exchange program.
Activities   Past achievements: Establishment of the library association in order to improve and upgrade libraries, which are in the early stages of development. Current: Organizing meetings to discuss common problems. Future: Invite experts from overseas to advise on particular problems and to run workshops. Active in promoting library-related legislation, such as a constitutional law for the library association. Plans a series of films for local television.

Mali

347   Association Malienne des Bibliothécaires, Archivistes et Documentalistes (AMBAD)
(Association of Librarians, Archivists and Documentalists of Mali)

Address   Rue Kassé Keîta, Bibliothèque Nationale, Bamako. Postal address: BP 2529, Bamako.
Languages   French
Established   1978
Major Fields of Interest   Archives, libraries, information services
Major Goals and Objectives   To promote development of archives, libraries and documentation services in Mali.
Sources of Support   Membership dues
Membership   Total members: 87 (individual)
Publications   No official journal; some occasional publications.
Activities   Organizes seminars, conferences, exhibits; has contact with other national and international related organizations.
Bibliography   Koita, Al Hadi, "Mali," in <u>ALA World Encyclopedia of Library and Information Services</u>, 2nd ed., pp. 513-514. Chicago: American Library Association, 1986.

Malta

348   Ghaqda Bibljotekarji (GH.B) / Library Association (LA)
(formerly Malta Library Association)

Address   c/o "Din L-Art Helwa," 133 Melita Street, Valletta (permanent). Tel: 227075 / 486992. Postal address: c/o Public Library, Beltissebh.
Officers   (elected for 1-yr.term, 1989-90) Chair: Paul Xuereb (University of Malta Library, Msida, Malta. Fax: 356-314306); Vice-Chair: Joseph Grima (Central Bank Library); Sec: Joseph Boffa (c/o Public Library, Beltissebh); Treas: Marie Thérèse Baluci; Asst.Sec: Joseph Debattista; Past Chair: Rev. Anthony F. Sapienza. Exec.Council: 9
Staff   1 (volunteer)
Languages   Maltese, English
Established   1969
Major Fields of Interest   Library education and library development in Malta and the Mediterranean.
Major Goals and Objectives   To unite all persons engaged or interested in library work; to assist in improving the status, salaries, and qualifications of librarians; to focus national attention on library work; to encourage the establishment, promotion and use of libraries in Malta and Gozo; to promote, encourage and assist bibliographic studies and research; to hold courses and examinations in librarianship; to maintain a register of qualified librarians.
Structure   Governed by Executive Council. Affiliations: IFLA, COMLA.
Sources of Support   Membership dues, sale of publications.
Membership   Total members: 81 (individual). 4 countries represented. Requirements: Professional librarian; library trainee; working in library or archive. Dues (Maltese Lira): 2, individual; 30, life; no dues, honorary (elected by Council).
General Assembly   Entire membership meets once a year in Valletta.
Publications   *Official journal:* GH.B./L.A. Newsletter. 1969-. 4/yr. Free to members. Editor: Anthony F. Sapienza. Address: 226 St. Paul Street, Valletta. Circ: 100. English. The Yearbook (2/yr.) ceased publication in 1979 due to rising printing costs. Other publications: Annual reports, reports of seminars, workshops, occasional papers. Xuereb, P., ed., Papers and Proceedings of a COMLA Regional Workshop, Malta, 13-16 November 1984 (1985)
Activities   Past achievements: First register of practicing qualified librarians opened in 1988, with 16 professionals. Worked for the improvement of Maltese librarians' salaries, status and working conditions; achieved recognition of teacher librarians by the Department of Education; promoted staff development and training; created public awareness of the need for library and information services and the necessary financial support; promoted a national information policy and the establishment of a National Council for Libraries, Archives and Documentation Centres; promoted a public library system, with the inauguration of the Public Library at Beltissebh in 1974; sponsored the establishment of a National Archives in 1987. Sponsored international conferences, such as, Conference of Mediterranean Librarians, 1983; COMLA Regional Workshop on Bibliography, 1984; COMLA Regional Council for Europe Meeting, 1984, etc. Current and Future: Diploma course in Library and Information Studies, Faculty of Education, University of Malta; editing, designing and distributing COMLA Newsletter since 1986. A major achievement has been the production of the Malta National Bibliography since 1984, which is compiled cooperatively by Association members. Association has been active in promoting

library-related legislation through the work of the National Librarian. Sponsors annual
Book Week and continuing education programs.

Bibliography   "Malta's LA (renamed)," <u>Library Association Record</u> 84 (1982):376; Sapienza, A.F., "Conference of Mediterranean Librarians, 8-9, April 1983," <u>IFLA Journal</u> 9
(1983):259-262; Xuereb, P., "Maltese Libraries through the Ages," in <u>The Year Book of
Malta 1984</u> (Malta: De la Salle Brothers, 1985); Sultana, J.B., "Malta," in <u>ALA World
Encyclopedia of Library and Information Services</u>, 2nd ed., pp. 514-516. Chicago: American Library Association, 1986; Xuereb, P., "The Ghaqda Bibljotekarji: Twenty Years After," <u>COMLA Newsletter</u> 63 (Mar. 1989):8-9,12.

Mauritania

349   Association Mauritanienne des Bibliothécaires, des Archivistes et des Documentalistes (AMBAD)
(Mauritanian Association of Librarians, Archivists, and Documentalists)

Address   BP 20, Nouakchott (permanent). Headquarters: Bibliothèque Nationale, Nouakchott. Tel: 2435.
Officers   Pres: Oumar Diouwara, Director, National Library; Sec: Sid'Ahmed Fall dit Dah. The Director of the National Library serves as President.
Staff   National Library
Languages   Arabic, French
Established   1979, to replace the Section Mauritanienne de l'Association Internationale pour le Développement de la Documentation, des Bibliothèques et des Archives en Afrique (AIDBA).
Major Fields of Interest   Libraries, archives, documentation centers
Major Goals and Objectives   To promote the development and effective administration of libraries, documentation centers, and archives; to organize the promotion of public libraries.
Structure   Governed by executive officers. Affiliations: IFLA
Sources of Support   Membership dues, government subsidies
Membership   Total members: 80 (individual).
General Assembly   Entire membership meets at least once a year.
Publications   *Official journal:* Liaison - AMBAD. 3/yr. Address same as Association. Circ: Membership. French, Arabic. Revue mauritanienne des sciences de l'information.
Activities   Sponsors conferences, workshops, continuing education offerings.
Bibliography   Diouwara, O., "Mauritania," in ALA World Encyclopedia of Library and Information Services, 2nd ed., p. 520. Chicago: American Library Association, 1986.

Mauritius

350   Mauritius Library Association

Address   c/o The British Council Library, Royal Road, Rose Hill. Tel: 541601. Fax: 549553.
Officers   Pres: K. Appadoo; Sec: Ms. C. Nepaul.
Staff   None
Languages   English
Established   1973
Major Fields of Interest   Library development
Major Goals and Objectives   To promote the establishment and improvement of libraries in Mauritius; to raise the standard of libraries and the status of librarians; to unite all those who are interested in books.
Structure   Governed by executive officers. Affiliations: IFLA
Sources of Support   Membership dues.
Membership   Total members: Approx. 50 (individual). Requirements: Librarians and those interested in the aims of the Association. Members include about 15 professional librarians, library personnel, and booksellers.
General Assembly   Entire membership meets once a year.
Publications   *Official journal:* Mauritius Library Association Newsletter. 4/yr. Address same as Association. English.
Activities   Sponsors conferences, workshops, seminars.
Bibliography   Jean-François, S., "Mauritius," in ALA World Encyclopedia of Library and Information Services, 2nd ed., pp.521-522. Chicago: American Library Association, 1986.

Mexico

351 Asociación de Bibliotecarios en Instituciónes de Enseñanza Superior e Investigación (ABIESI)
(Association of Librarians in Academic and Research Institutions)

Address Apartado postal 5-611, 06500 Mexico 5, DF (not permanent). Tel: 52 (5) 5505024.
Officers (elected for 2-yr.term) Pres: Nahúm Pérez Paz; Sec: Alejandro Ramírez E; Treas: Fabiola Mendez; Past Pres: Elsa Barberena B. Exec.Board: 6
Staff 6 (volunteers)
Languages Spanish
Established 1957, at San Luis Potósi, S.L.P. Mexico.
Major Fields of Interest College, university and research libraries; documentation centers
Major Goals and Objectives To improve library services; to contribute to the professional development of members; to collaborate in library development.
Structure Governed by executive officers in Executive Council. Affiliations: FID. ABIESI is an affiliate of AMBAC, the Mexican Association of Librarians.
Sources of Support Membership dues. Budget (Mexican Peso): Approx. 500,000.
Membership Total members: 180 (120 individual, 60 institutional). 2 countries represented. Types of membership: Individual, institutional. Requirements: To work in college, university, or research library or documentation center. Dues (Mexican Peso): 3% of monthly salary, individual; 1,500 Peso, institutional.
General Assembly Entire membership meets twice a year.
Publications No official journal. Publishes 2 irregular series, Cuadernos de ABIESI, and Archivos de ABIESI; issues Boletín de ABIESI (irreg.); annual reports, proceedings of conferences, etc. Publications for sale.
Activities Sponsors conferences, seminars, workshops, and other continuing education programs; sponsors scholarship aid to students in library and information science.
Bibliography Magaloni de Bustamente, Ana María, "Mexico," in ALA World Encyclopedia of Library and Information Services, 2nd ed., pp. 546-548. Chicago: American Library Association, 1986.

352 Asociación Mexicana de Bibliotecarios, A.C. (Asociación Civil) (AMBAC)
(Mexican Association of Librarians)

Address Angel Urraza No. 817-A, Col. del Valle, CP 03100, Mexico, DF. Headquarters: Apartado Postal 27-651, Administración de Correos 27, 06760 Mexico, D.F. Tel: 52 (5) 5751135.
Officers (elected for 2-yr.term) Pres: Roberto A. Gordillo; Past Pres: Rosa Maria Fernández de Zamora; VP: Estela Morales Campos; Secs: Elsa Barberena Blasquez, Rosalba Cruz; Treas: Enrique Molina León; Pro-Treas: Oscar Zambrano. Exec.Board: 6
Staff Volunteers
Languages Spanish
Established 1924, as Asociación de Bibliotecarios Mexicanos; reactivated in 1954 under present name.
Major Fields of Interest Librarianship and information science
Major Goals and Objectives To promote libraries, library service, and librarianship in Mexico; to further the professional education and development of members, and to improve their status.

Structure   Governed by directive body and Technical Council. Affiliations: IFLA. ABIESI is an affiliate of AMBAC.
Sources of Support   Membership dues, sale of publications.
Membership   Total members: 427 (404 individual, 23 institutional). Sections: 5. Requirements: Professional librarian; student of library science; working in some area of librarianship. Dues: 3% of one month's salary, individual; 5 days of monthly salary, institutional.
General Assembly   Entire membership meets once a year. 1987: Mexico; 1988: Tabasco, Villahermosa; 1989: XX Jornadas Mexicanas de Biblioteconomía, Coahuila, Coahuila.
Publications   *Official journal:* Noticiero de la AMBAC (News of AMBAC). 1956-. 4/yr. Editor: Estela Morales Campos. Address: Angel Urraza No. 817-A, Col. del Valle, CP 03100, Mexico, DF. Tel: 5434339. Circ: 600. Spanish. Indexed in Fichero Bibliográfico Hispanoamericano. Other publications: Proceedings of meetings and occasional papers. Publications available for sale. Publications exchange program in effect.
Activities   Past and current: Organizing annual National Congresses; sponsoring continuing education courses, training workshops for new members, seminars. Association has been active in promoting library-related legislation as an advisor on the General Libraries Law.
Bibliography   Fernandez de Zamora, R.M., "39th Anniversary of the Mexican Library Association (AMBAC)," Library Times International 1 (May 1985):88; Bustamente, Ana María Magaloni de, "Mexico," in ALA World Encyclopedia of Library and Information Services, 2nd ed., pp.546-548. Chicago: American Library Association, 1986.

353   Sociedad Mexicana de Archivistas, A.C.
(Mexican Society of Archivists)

Address   Headquarters: Antillas No. 811, Col. Portales, Delegación Benito Juarez, 03300 Mexico, DF. Tel: 52 (5) 5323211. Postal address: Apartado Postal 73-010, 03300 Mexico, DF.
Officers   Pres: Norberto Ramírez Monroy.
Staff   None
Languages   Spanish
Established   1955
Major Fields of Interest   Archives management
Major Goals and Objectives   To promote development of archives in Mexico; to further the organization and administration of archives of government or private institutions; to sponsor conferences, seminars, and other meetings on topics of current interest; to promote archival studies.
Structure   Governed by executive officers. Affiliations: ICA, Unesco.
Sources of Support   Membership dues
Membership   Total members: 75
General Assembly   Entire membership meets once a year.
Activities   Sponsors annual meetings, continuing education programs on topics of current interest for members, such as classification, methods of record management, preservation of documents, national and international activities in archival studies.

Morocco

354   Association Nationale des Informatistes
(National Association of Information Specialists)

Address   BP 616, Rabat-Chellah. Tel: 212 (1) 74944/73131. Telex: 31052. Headquarters: Siège du Centre National de Coordination et de Planification de la Recherche Scientifique et Technique, 52 Charia Omar Ibn Al-Khattab Agdal, Rabat.
Officers   Pres: Ms. L. Bachr
Languages   Arabic, French
Established   1972
Major Fields of Interest   Librarianship; information services; information studies; archival studies; professional development.
Major Goals and Objectives   To unite information scientists and specialists; to improve the level of information science in Morocco through conferences, round tables, seminars, and continuing education programs; to represent the interests of librarians, archivists and information specialists.
Structure   Governed by executive officers. Affiliations: IFLA
Sources of Support   Membership dues; government subsidies
Membership   Total members: 221 (205 professional librarians, 16 other individuals). Types of membership: Individual.
General Assembly   Entire membership meets once a year.
Publications   *Official journal:* Bulletin de l'Informatiste. 12/yr. Circ: Membership. Address same as Association. French. L'Informatiste. 2/yr.
Activities   Carried out in accordance with goals and objectives.
Bibliography   Hariki, G. and Lekbir, B., "Morocco," in ALA World Encyclopedia of Library and Information Services, 2nd ed., pp. 565-566. Chicago: American Library Association, 1986.

Namibia

355   South African Institute of Librarianship and Information Science. South West Africa/Namibia Branch (SAILIS-SWA/Namibia Branch)

Address   PO Box 1203, Windhoek 9000, Namibia (South West Africa) (not permanent). Tel: 293336
Officers   (elected for 2-yr.term) Chair: T.M. Geyser; Vice-Chair: J.J. Marais; Sec: T.B. Serpontein; Treas: Ms. M. Wassermann. Exec.Comm: 8
Staff   Volunteers (Executive Committee)
Languages   Afrikaans, English
Established   1979, founding of SAILIS
Major Fields of Interest   Librarianship, and library and information services
Major Goals and Objectives   To further the development of library and information services in Namibia.
Structure   Governed by executive officers
Sources of Support   Membership dues
Membership   Total members: 50 (individual)
General Assembly   Entire membership meets annually.
Publications   No official journal. Publishes newsletter, 4/yr.
Activities   The Association is expected to undergo changes in view of the country's independence in 1990.
Bibliography   Pieterse, P.B. and Viljoen, M.M., "Namibia," in <u>ALA World Encyclopedia of Library and Information Services</u>, 2nd ed., pp. 573-575. Chicago: American Library Association, 1986.

Netherlands

356   Federatie van Organisaties op het Gebied van het Bibliotheek-, Informatie-en Documentatiewezen (FOBID)
(Federation of Organizations in the Fields of Library, Information, and Documentation Services)

Address   Taco Scheltemastraat 5, NL-2597 BH The Hague. Tel: 31 (70) 3141541. Postal address: Postbus 93054, NL-2509 AB The Hague (permanent). Tel: 31 (70) 3141500.
Officers   Pres: P.J.Th. Schoots; Coord.Officer: Ms. F. Droogh. Exec.Board: 5
Staff   1 (paid)
Languages   Dutch
Established   1974, to serve the common interests of the members of NVB and NBLC
Major Fields of Interest   Professional associations in library, information, and documentation services
Major Goals and Objectives   To coordinate the work of the professional associations in library, information, and documentation services in the Netherlands, to be a focal point for the whole profession, to have a framework for cooperation where desirable, and to unite the various fields of librarianship.
Structure   Governed by Executive Board. Affiliations: IFLA
Sources of Support   Membership dues, government subsidies.
Membership   Three Dutch associations in library, information, and documentation services: NVB, NBLC, and UKB. Regional Groups: 8
Publications   *Official journal:* Open: Vaktijdschrift voor Bibliothecarissen, Literatuuronderzoekers, Bedrijfsarchivarissen en Documentalisten. 1969-. 11/yr. (Published jointly with the other library associations in the Netherlands). Publishing Committee: Chair: A.H.H.M. Mathijsen; Sec: F.J. Schuitemaker-Vinkenborg. Address: Kerklaan 72, NL-2451 CH Leimuiden. Tel: 31 (1721) 9251. Editorial Committee: Chair: J. van Goinga-van Driel; Sec: C.E. van Schendel. Address: Keizersgracht 802, NL-1017 ED Amsterdam. Tel: 31 (20) 224322. Other publications: Netherlands Library and Documentation Guide (in Dutch, 1987; regularly revised); series of cataloging rules according to ISBD, etc.
Activities   Providing coordination and unity among the associations in the Netherlands. Federation carries out tasks on behalf of the member associations, such as organizing the annual library congress, professional projects in the field of normalization, unification of cataloging rules according to ISBD, and publication of directories.
Bibliography   Mathijsen, A.H.H.M., "Netherlands," in ALA World Encyclopedia of Library and Information Services, 2nd ed., pp. 596-599. Chicago: American Library Association, 1986; Mathijsen, A.H.H.M., "Professional Organizations," in Libraries and Documentation Centres in the Netherlands, ed. E.Z.R. Cohen et al., pp.15-20. The Hague, Nederlands Bibliotheek en Lektuur Centrum, 1987.

357   Nederlands Bibliotheek en Lektuur Centrum (NBLC)
(Dutch Centre for Public Libraries and Literature)

Address   Taco Scheltemastraat 5, NL-2597 CP The Hague. Postal address: Postbus 93054, NL-2509 AB The Hague (permanent). Tel: 31 (70) 3141500. Telex: 32102. Fax: 31-70-3141600.
Officers   (elected) Pres: E.M. d'Hondt; Exec.Dir: D. Reumer (R. v.d. Velde, Oct.1, 1990-); Sec: H. Middelveld. Exec.Board: 19
Staff   241 (paid)

Languages Dutch, English

Established 1972, Amsterdam; based on The Central Association for Public Libraries, founded 1908, and combining denominational public library groups, such as the Katholiek Lectuur Centrum (KLC) (Catholic Centre for Libraries and Literature) and the Christelijk Lektuur Centrum (CLC) (Christian Centre for Literature), into one unified national organization of public library work.

Major Fields of Interest Public library work; ethnic minorities; education; technical innovations in library work; literacy and reading promotion.

Major Goals and Objectives To promote optimal functioning of public librarianship; to cooperate with other organizations and institutions active in the field of books and information; to establish contact with organizations concerned with education and training.

Structure Governed by the Executive Board. Affiliations: IFLA, NVB, ROTNAC, VBC (Flemish Library Centre).

Sources of Support Membership dues, sale of publications, government subsidies; Central Services. Budget (Dutch Guilder): 1988: 27 million; 1989: 29 million.

Membership Total members: 625 (institutional). Sections: 3 (Music and Record Libraries, Children's Library Work, Library Work for the Aged, the Sick and the Handicapped). Working Groups and Committees. Requirements for membership in association: Public library; for membership in section: Working in public library. Dues (Dutch Guilder): Depending on number of inhabitants, 66.75 per 1,000 inhabitants. No section dues.

General Assembly Entire membership meets twice a year. 1989: June 6, Dec. 21; 1990: June 21, Dec. 20.

Publications *Official journal:* Bibliotheek en Samenleving (Library and Society). 1972-. 12/yr. (Dutch Guilder) 47.40. Free to members. Editor: Frans Stein. Address same as Association. Circ: 6,500. Dutch, with English summaries. Publishes professional publications on various subjects, for specific readers' groups, including adult education and minorities. Price lists available. Publications listed in a weekly Information Bulletin.

Activities Past achievements: Library work for ethnic minorities, mentally handicapped and adult education integrated into Association's activities and in many public libraries. Current: Information technology; user friendly library work; promotion of reading. Future: Development of local community centers in public libraries, and continuing current activities. Association has been active in promoting library-related legislation, e.g. a draft Library Act was made when the present one was abolished, but without success, and library work is now regulated by the Welfare Act, but rather poorly. Association receives occasional grants from government for special activities, apart from regular subsidies. Association participates in the 'Nederlandse Bibliotheek Dienst' (Netherlands Library Service), which supplies public libraries with already processed and bound Dutch publications. Various working groups are concerned with library building, mobile libraries, standards, automation, Literature Information Service, etc.

Use of High Technology Electronic publisher (CD-ROM and WORM), host for profit and non-profit organizations, front-end system with uniformed interface to databases with different retrieval languages, gateway to other databases of other host organizations by means of above mentioned front-end system. Attached to the Association is a commercial firm dealing with (1) library design and furniture and (2) hard- and software especially designed for libraries.

Bibliography Spruit, E.M., "National Service to Public Libraries in the Field of Audiovisual Media: The Situation in the Netherlands," INSPEL 16 (1982):103-109; Hersch-van-der Stoel, F., "The 10th Anniversary of the Dutch Centre for Libraries and Literature," Bibliotheek en Samenleving 10 (1982):39-42 (in Dutch); Mathijsen, A.H.H.M., "Netherlands," in ALA World Encyclopedia of Library and Information Services, 2nd ed., pp. 596-599. Chicago: American Library Association, 1986; Riesthuis-Groenland, M.-L., "Het NBLC: structuur en taken," (The NBLC: Its Structure and Services), Open 18 (1986):291-298 (in Dutch); Mathijsen, A.H.H.M., "Professional Organizations," in Libraries and Documentation Centres in the Netherlands, ed. E.Z.R. Cohen et al., pp. 15-20, The Hague: NBLC, 1987; Boulogne, G., "Structuurwijziging van het NBLC: vergroting van de slagvaardigheid met behoud van een gewaarborgde beroepsinhoudelijke inbreng," (Structural Reform of the NBLC: Increasing the Effectiveness while Retaining the Guaranteed Professional Contribution), Bibliotheek en Samenleving 15 (1987):323-324; Riesthuis-Groenland, M.-L., "Hoe en waarom een nieuwe NBLC-structuur?: Enkele antwoorden op eerste reacties," (How and Why a New NBLC Structure?: Some Comments on the First Reactions), ibid.:337-338; "Literatuurlijst structuur NBLC," (Bibliography on the Reform of the NBLC), ibid.:341-342.

358   Nederlandse Stichting voor Classificatie en Andere Ontsluitingsmethoden (NCS) (Netherlands Foundation for Classification and Indexing)

Address   Secretariat: c/o Gemeente Hellendoorn, Willem Alexanderstraat 7, NL-7442 MA Nijverdal (not permanent). Tel: 31 (5486) 13363.
Officers   Pres: G.J. Wijnands; Sec-Treas: A. Hartkamp
Languages   Dutch
Established   1980
Major Fields of Interest   Classification and indexing
Major Goals and Objectives   The study, maintenance, and use of all indexing and classification systems.
Structure   Governed by Executive Board, on which all interested and contributing parties are represented, e.g., NVB, NVBA (Association of Industrial Archivists), SOD (Association for Documentation and Administrative Organization), etc.
Sources of Support   Membership dues, sale of publications.
Activities   Four divisions are concerned with the following activities: (1) Universal Decimal Classification; (2) foundations of classification and classification research; (3) thesauri and other word systems; (4) rules for alphabetizing.
Bibliography   Mathijsen, A.H.H.M., "Professional Organizations," in Libraries and Documentation Centres in the Netherlands, ed. E.Z.R. Cohen et al., pp. 15-20. The Hague, NBLC, 1987.

359   Nederlandse Vereniging van Bedrijfsarchivarissen (NVBA) (Netherlands Association of Industrial Archivists)

Address   c/o Secretariat, Schanswal 30, NL-9407 AB Assen (permanent). Tel: 31 (5920) 44007.
Officers   Chair: D. R. Bouhuijs; Vice-Chair: F.L.J.M. Versteden; Sec: A.M.J. Kremer; Treas: W.R. de Road. Exec.Board: 9
Staff   4 (volunteer)
Languages   Dutch
Established   1947, The Hague, as Nederlandse Documentalistenkring (NDK).
Major Fields of Interest   Archival studies; records management; library and office automation.
Major Goals and Objectives   (1) To promote the professional skills of members; (2) to provide professional contacts and promote cooperation among members; (3) to represent the members' interests regarding their profession.
Structure   Governed by executive officers.

Sources of Support   Membership dues, private subsidies. Budget (Dutch Guilder): 1986/87: 23,450; 1987/88: 25,000.
Membership   Total members: 350 (individual). Types of membership: Individual. Requirements: Active in archives/documentation. Dues (Dutch Guilder): 75.
General Assembly   Entire membership meets twice a year, usually in May/June and November/December.
Publications   *Official journal:* Repeat. 1987-. 11/yr. (Dutch Guilder) 75. Free to members. Editor: Johan Janssen B.V. Address: Postbus 240, 5060 AE Oisterwijk. Tel: 31 (4242) 16923. Circ: 400+. Dutch. Other publications: Bewaartermijnerlijst in een Bedrijfsarchief (1986), etc.
Activities   Past achievements: Information exchanges concerning office automation. Current: The place of a company/business archive in today's offices. Future: Protect the name of company/business archives as related to Records Management.

360   Nederlandse Vereniging van Bibliothecarissen, Documentalisten en Literatuuronderzoekers (NVB)
(Netherlands Association of Librarians, Documentalists and Information Officers)

Address   c/o Secretary, Nolweg 13d, NL-4209 AW Schelluinen (permanent). Tel: 31 (1830) 23386.
Officers   (elected for 3-yr.term) Pres: G.A.J.S. van Marle; Sec: G. Koers. Exec.Board: 5
Staff   1 (part-time, 0.6 FTE, paid)
Languages   Dutch
Established   1912, as Nederlandse Vereniging van Bibliothecarissen; new name adopted in 1974, reflecting the expansion of membership to include documentalists and information specialists.
Major Fields of Interest   Research libraries; special libraries; public libraries; professional staff.
Major Goals and Objectives   To stimulate library and information science and documentation research; to promote the status and represent the interests of members.
Structure   Governed by Executive Board. Affiliations: IFLA.
Sources of Support   Membership dues; donations.
Membership   Total members: 2,000 (1,500 individual, 500 institutional). Sections: 7. Requirements: Individuals and institutions engaged in library, documentation or information work outside the public library field.
General Assembly   Entire membership meets twice a year.
Publications   *Official journal:* NVB Nieuwsbrief. 1985-. 6/yr. Free to members. Secretary of Association serves as editor. Address same as Association. Circ: Membership. Dutch. Other publications: Open (published jointly with other Dutch library associations; see FOBID entry); annual reports, proceedings of meetings. Publications available for sale, listed in Open.
Activities   Various activities according to the goals and objectives of the Association. Activities carried out by the various sections within the Association in the areas of public libraries, research libraries, vocational college libraries, and for information specialists, law librarians and medical librarians. A number of working groups are concerned with special topics, e.g. automation, public relations, subject cataloging, information services in the fields of economics and philosophy, school libraries, collection development, user education, access to legal information, etc., and some publish their own newsletters. Four standing advisory committees aid the Executive Board: For educational matters, for professional policy matters, for personnel employment matters, and the council of the sections for internal policy and coordination matters.

Bibliography Mathijsen, A.H.H.M., "Netherlands," in ALA World Encyclopedia of Library and Information Services, 2nd. ed., pp. 396-399. Chicago: American Library Association, 1986; Mathijsen, A.H.H.M., "Professional Organizations," in Libraries and Documentation Centres in the Netherlands, ed. E.Z.R. Cohen et al., pp.15-20, The Hague: Nederlands Bibliotheek en Lektuur Centrum, 1987; Van Swigchem, P.J., "Vijf en zeventig jaar NVB," (75 Years of NVB), Bibliotheek en Samenleving 15 (1987):192-193; Wijnstroom, M., "Nederlanders op het internationale bibliotheek vinkentouw," (The Dutch at the International Library Helm), Open 19 (1987):409-413; "De NVB een huis voor velen," (The NVB as a House for Many; Conference to Celebrate the 57th Anniversary of the NVB; special issue), ibid.:381-413 (in Dutch).

361 Nederlandse Vereniging van Gebruikers van Online Informatiesystemen (VOGIN)
(Netherlands Association of Users of Online Information Systems)

Address VOGIN-Secretariaat: H. Schrik, c/o SWIDOC, Herengracht 410-412, 1017 BX Amsterdam (not permanent). Tel: 31 (20) 225061. Fax: 31-20-238374.
Officers (elected for 4-yr.term) Chair: K. R. G. Kuipers (Kluwer Datalex, Postbus 23, 7400 GA Deventer. Tel: 31 (5700) 47141. Fax: 31-5700-34740); Treas: J. A. Agasi; Sec: H. Schrik. Exec.Board: 9
Staff 9 (volunteers)
Languages Dutch, English
Established 1977, Delft
Major Fields of Interest Online information systems.
Major Goals and Objectives To increase the knowledge of its members about computer readable databases and to foster the use of these; to collect and exchange experiences in this field; to cooperate with other related organizations, both in the Netherlands and abroad; to influence policy-making bodies in this field.
Structure Governed by Executive Board. Affiliations: EUSIDIC.
Sources of Support Membership dues, government subsidies.
Membership Total members: 500 (300 individual, 200 institutional). Requirements: Individuals and institutions engaged in online work or interested in the topic.
General Assembly Entire membership meets twice a year.
Publications Official journal: LOGIN. 1977-. 4/yr. Free to members. Editor: I. V. Veerman. Address: c/o PUDOC, Postbus 4, 6700 AA Wageningen. Circ: Membership. Dutch. Published textbook on online work in 1983.
Activities Past achievements: Seminars on special subjects; sponsoring biannual National Online Conference; sponsoring online training activities. Current: Activities carried out in Working Groups. Sponsors training and continuing education courses for members.
Bibliography Mathijsen, A.H.H.M., "Netherlands," in ALA World Encyclopedia of Library and Information Services, 2nd ed., pp. 596-599. Chicago: American Library Association, 1986; Mathijsen, A.H.H.M., "Professional Organizations," in Libraries and Documentation Centres in the Netherlands, ed. E.Z.R. Cohen et al., pp.15-20, The Hague: Nederlands Bibliotheek en Lektuur Centrum, 1987.

362 UKB (Samenwerkingsverband van de Universiteitsbibliotheken, de Koninklijke Bibliotheek en de Bibliotheek van de Koninklijke Nederlandse Akademie van Wetenschappen)
(Association of the University Libraries, the Royal Library and the Library of the Royal Netherlands Academy of Arts and Sciences)

Address c/o Bibliotheek der Rijksuniversiteit Limburg, Postbus 616, NL-6200 MD Maastricht (not permanent). Tel: 31 (43) 888427. Telex: 56726. Fax: 31-43-252195.
Officers (elected for 3 yr.-term) Pres: Rolf L. Schuursma; VP: Johan Stellingwerff; Sec: Joop L.M. van Dijk. Exec.Board: 3
Staff 1 (volunteer)
Languages Dutch
Established 1977, as successor to the Rijkscommissie van Advies inzake het Biblio-theekwezen (Advisory Council on Library Affairs), abolished in 1975.
Major Fields of Interest Library cooperation
Major Goals and Objectives Promote mutual consultation and cooperation among member libraries; coordination of inter-library loan, collection development, subject ac-cessing, preservation or library material, etc.
Structure Governed by Executive Board. Affiliations: IFLA
Sources of Support Membership dues. Budget (Dutch Guilder): 1986/87: 31,500; 1987/88: 31,500.
Membership Total members: 15 (institutional). Types of membership: Institutions. Re-quirements: Members are represented by chief librarians of the institutions (university li-braries and national library).
General Assembly Entire membership meets 5 or 6 times a year.
Publications No official journal. Occasional publications.
Activities Past achievements: Coordinatie van de Collectievorming (UKB Report on Collection Development), published in 1987. Current: Coordination between UKB and the PICA National Database in the areas of collection development and subject access-ing. Involved in areas of interlending, statistics, preservation, among others. Future: Dis-cussion and cooperative application of new developments in the library and information field. Association has been active in promoting library-related legislation, such as the law regarding university education (Wet op het Wetenschappelijk onderwijs).
Use of High Technology Computer (word processor) for management.
Bibliography Brak, J.A.W., "Library Consortia," in Libraries and Documentation Centres in the Netherlands, ed. E.Z.R. Cohen et al., pp. 21-30, The Hague: NBLC, 1987.

363 Vereniging van Archivarissen in Nederland (VAN)
(Association of Archivists in the Netherlands)

Address Postbus 11645, NL-2502 AP The Hague (not permanent). Tel: 31 (70) 814381 ext.331.
Officers (elected for 5-yr.term) Pres: I.W.L.A. Caminada; VP: J.N.T. van Albada; Exec.Sec: J.A.M.Y. Bos-Rops; Treas: W. Veerman. Exec.Board: 7
Staff 1 (paid)
Languages Dutch
Established 1891, Haarlem
Major Fields of Interest Archives and records management.
Major Goals and Objectives To promote the development of archives and records management in the Netherlands.
Structure Governed by executive officers. Affiliations: ICA

Sources of Support   Membership dues.
Membership   Total members: Approx. 800 (individual). Types of membership: Individual. Requirements: Certificate of the Rijksarchiefschool (Archivist training school), or working in archives for more than one year.
General Assembly   Entire membership meets twice a year.
Publications   *Official journal:* Nederlands Archievenblad. 1892-. 4/yr. Free to members. Editor: P. Brood. Address: Rijksarchief Drenthe, Postbus 595, NL-9400 AN Assen. Circ: Membership. Dutch, with English summaries. Other publications: Nieuwe van Archieven (Archives News).
Activities   Sponsors meetings, continuing education programs, publication of journal, etc.
Use of High Technology   Computer (IBM-PC) for management.

364   Vereniging van Pers- en Omroepdocumentalisten (Association of Press and Broadcasting Documentalists)

Address   Secretariat, H. Cleyndertweg 497, NL-1025 DV Amsterdam (not permanent). Tel: 31 (20) 5674475.
Officers   Chair: F. P. Jonkman; Sec: Ms. Y.J. van der Krol
Languages   Dutch
Major Fields of Interest   Press and broadcasting documentation

365   Vereniging voor het Theologisch Bibliothecariaat (VTB) (Theological Library Association)

Address   c/o Secretariat, Postbus 289, NL-6500 AG Nijmegen. Tel: 31 (80) 228467/515478/512162.
Officers   Pres: J.N. Ijkel; Treas: H. Rutten; Sec: P.J.A. Nissen.
Staff   None
Languages   Dutch
Established   1947, Tilburg, as Vereniging voor het Godsdienstig-wetenschappelijk Bibliothecariaat (VSKB) (Association for Seminary and Monastery Libraries); new name adopted 1973 and membership no longer restricted to Catholic institutions.
Major Fields of Interest   Theology and auxiliary sciences.
Major Goals and Objectives   To promote librarianship in the fields of the theological sciences.
Structure   Governed by executive officers. Affiliations: Conseil Interational des Associations des Bibliothèques de Théologie.
Sources of Support   Membership dues, private subsidies.
Membership   Total members: Approx.100 (individual). Requirements: To subscribe to the aims of the Association and to be admitted by the governing authorities. Dues (Dutch Guilder): 50.
General Assembly   Entire membership meets annually.
Publications   *Official journal:* Medelingen van de VTB (Communications of the VTB) (supersedes Medelingen van de VSKB, 1948-73). 1973-. 4/yr. (Dutch Guilder) 25. Free to members. Editor: N. Versluis. Address same as Association. Circ: 150. Dutch. Issues Lijst van Lopende Periodieken in de Nederlandse Theologische Instituten (Union List of Current Periodicals in Dutch Theological Libraries); Bibliografie Doctorale Scripties Theologie (Bibliography of Doctoral Theses in Theology). 1978-. 1/yr.; Guide to Theological Libraries (1983), etc..
Activities   Cooperation among theological research libraries. When founded, the organization was intended for Catholics only, but now has effectively expanded to include li-

brarians of all denominations in the field of theology. Activities carried out through several working groups.
Bibliography Mathijsen, A.H.H.M., "Professional Organizations," in Libraries and Documentation Centres in the Netherlands, ed. E.Z.R. Cohen et al., pp.15-20, The Hague: Nederlands Bibliotheek en Lektuur Centrum, 1987.

366 Vereniging/Werkgemeenschap Octrooi-Informatie Nederland (WON) (Association/Working Group for Patent Information in the Netherlands)

Address Secretariat: c/o G.K.F. van der Woud, PTT Nederland N.V., Juridische Zaken/GIE, Postbus 95321, NL-2509 CH, The Hague. Tel: 31 (70) 3325835.
Officers Chair: W.G. Vijvers; Sec: G.K.F. van der Woud.
Languages Dutch
Established 1976, as a working group by patent information specialists; registered as an association in 1977.
Major Fields of Interest Patents
Major Goals and Objectives To exchange information; to study the developments in the field; and to stimulate improvements in providing patent information.
Structure Governed by executive officers.
Membership Requirements: Individuals and institutions interested in patent information. Dues (Dutch Guilders): 150.
Publications An irregular newsletter, approx. 4/yr.
Activities Acts as national focus for contacts with similar organizations in other countries and in the Netherlands. Sponsors conferences, seminars, workshops, and other continuing education programs.
Bibliography Mathijsen, A.H.H.M., "Professional Organizations," in Libraries and Documentation Centres in the Netherlands, ed. E.Z.R. Cohen et al., pp. 15-20, The Hague: NBLC, 1987.

367 Werkgroep Kaartbeheer van de Nederlandse Vereniging voor Kartografie (WKB) (Working Group for Map Curatorship of the Dutch Cartographic Society)

Address c/o Office for Maps, Koninklijke Bibliotheek, PO Box 90.407, NL-2509 LK The Hague (permanent). Tel: 31 (70) 3140241
Officers Chair: Jan Smits
Staff None
Languages Dutch, English
Established May 2, 1975, to organize Keepers of Map Collections, whose positions developed since the early 1970s.
Major Fields of Interest Map collections in libraries, archives, museums, and map-producing agencies; map curators.
Major Goals and Objectives Promotion of good map keeping (e.g. conservation, accessibility, schooling of map curators), and of the position of Keepers of Map Collections.
Structure One of a number of working groups of the Dutch Cartographic Society
Sources of Support Registration fees for study-days and courses.
Membership No separate membership. Open to all members of the Dutch Cartographic Society and to all institutions concerned with map curatorship.
Publications *Official journal:* Kartografisch Tijdschrift. Other publications: Guide to Map Collections in the Netherlands (1980); Report on summercourse 1982, title-description for cartographic materials (1983); List of Recommended Abbreviations (1984); Report on summercourse 1989, description of cartographic materials (forthcoming).

Activities   Through 2 study-days a year, summercourses, etc., encourages the cataloging/ archiving of maps according to ISBD (CM) (Cartographic Material), encourages the use of and participation in automated accessing systems, in particular the Dutch Union Catalogue of Maps; acquaints map curators with new technologies in map-producing and -processing; initiates and supports officially recognized continuing education programs.

Bibliography   Waal, E.H. van der, "Backgrounds and Developments at the 10th Anniversary of the Workinggroup for Map Curatorship," Kartografisch Tijdschrift 11 (1985):31-34; Mathiejsen, A.H.H.M., "Professional Organizations," in Libraries and Documentation Centres in the Netherlands, ed. E.Z.R. Cohen et al., pp. 15-20, The Hague, NBLC, 1987.

Netherlands Antilles

368   Antillian Public Library Association

Address   c/o Openbare Bibliotheek Curaçao, Abraham Mendes Chumaceiro Bulevar
z/n Willemstad, Curaçao. Tel: 599 (9) 617565.
Officers   Pres: R. Colastica; Sec: Ms. Marvis Amerikaan
Languages   Dutch, English
Established   This Association was preceded by the Asociation di Biblioteka i Archivo
di Korsow (ABAK) (Association of Libraries and Archives), whose President was Maritza
F. Eustatia, and which existed from 1972 to 1978.
Major Fields of Interest   Public libraries
Major Goals and Objectives   To develop public libraries in the Netherland Antilles
Structure   Affiliations: IFLA (since 1983).
Bibliography   Foster, B., "Netherlands Antilles," in <u>ALA World Encyclopedia of Li-
brary and Information Services</u>, 2nd ed., pp. 599-600. Chicago: American Library Associ-
ation, 1986.

New Zealand

369   Archives and Records Association of New Zealand, Inc. (ARANZ)

Address   PO Box 11-553, Manners Street, Wellington (permanent). Tel: 64 (4) 848109/8
Officers   (elected) Pres: Stuart Strachar; VPs: Brad Patterson, Mary Red; Sec: Michael E. Hoare; Treas: Marlene Sayers. Exec.Board: 13
Staff   5 (volunteer)
Languages   English
Established   1976, Wellington
Major Fields of Interest   Archives; records management; history; professional and lay education; preservation; journal production and reviews
Major Goals and Objectives   Preservation of archives and records in New Zealand; training of archival personnel; management and promotion of archives.
Structure   Governed by Council. Affiliations: Genealogical Society of New Zealand; ICA.
Sources of Support   Membership dues; trusts. Budget (New Zealand Dollar): Approx. 25,000+.
Membership   Total members: 550 (500 individual, 50 institutional). Divisions: 5. Sections: 10. 25 countries represented. Requirements: Interest in the aims of the Association. Dues (New Zealand Dollar) : 17, individual; 25, institutional.
General Assembly   Entire membership meets once a year.
Publications   *Official journal:* Archifacts. 1974-. 4/yr. (New Zealand Dollar) 17. Free to members. Editor: Cathy Marr. Address same as Association. Circ: 600. English. Other publications: Annual reports, proceedings of meetings, reports of seminars, workshops. Publications available for sale. Publications exchange program in effect.
Activities   Past achievements: Training improved for lay and professional personnel; standards improved in major and minor institutions; successful conferences; raising of archives awareness; political lobbying. Current: Organizing conferences and seminars; continuing lobbying efforts. Future: Work for legislation for archives; professional training within New Zealand. Association has been active in supporting library-related legislation, such as the New Archives Act for New Zealand. Sponsors continuing education offerings, workshops, and seminars dealing with topics in history.
Use of High Technology   Databases for management.
Bibliography   Patterson, B., "The Anatomy of an Interest Group," Archifacts 2 (June 1986):1-5.

370   Health Information Association of New Zealand (HIANZ)

Address   c/o NZLA, 20 Brandon Street, PO Box 12-212, Wellington 1. Tel: 64 (4) 735834.
Languages   English
Established   June 15, 1989, inaugural meeting; Nov. 15, first annual meeting. Formerly, the Health Libraries Section of NZLA. Members decided to form a separate Association to preserve and enhance the section's work and projects.
Major Fields of Interest   Health sciences
Major Goals and Objectives   To further the work of health sciences information services in New Zealand
Membership   Requirements: Interest in health sciences information.

Bibliography   "Health Information Association of New Zealand (HIANZ)," Library Times International 6 (Jan. 1990):55.

371   International Association of Music Libraries, Archives and Documentation Centres, New Zealand Branch, Incorporated (IAML-NZ)

Address   c/o Secretary, 10/2 Burdendale Grove, Wellington (not permanent). Tel: 64 (4) 780187.
Officers   (elected for 1-yr.term) Pres: Dorothy Freed; VP: Gerald Seaman; Sec: Jill Palmer; Treas: A.W.J. Roberts. Exec.Board: 11
Staff   11 (volunteers)
Languages   English
Established   1970, IAML - Australia and New Zealand formed in Australia; 1974, New Zealand Division formed; 1982, IAML - New Zealand Branch formed.
Major Fields of Interest   Music bibliography; music librarianship
Major Goals and Objectives   To bring together people and music (literature, scores, recordings and music information) through the library system or other suitable channels in New Zealand; and to establish and maintain international links through the parent body, the International Association of Music Libraries, Archives and Documentation Centres (IAML).
Structure   Governed by executive officers under the parent body, the International Association of Music Libraries, Archives and Documentation Centres (IAML). Affiliations: IFLA, National Music Council of New Zealand, New Zealand Library Association.
Sources of Support   Membership dues, sale of publications, private grants. Budget (New Zealand Dollar): 1986/87: 700,000; 1987/88: 800,000.
Membership   Total members: 41 (23 individual, 18 institutional). Requirements: Interest in goals of the Association. Complete a dues form and pay subscription to become a member of the International Association and a member of the New Zealand Branch. Dues (New Zealand Dollar): 70, institutional; 45, individual; 5, student; free for honorary. 80% of dues sent to IAML.
General Assembly   Entire membership meets once a year in February.
Publications   *Official journal:* Crescendo. 1982-. 3/yr. (New Zealand Dollar) 15. Free to members. Editor: Brian Pritchard. Address: Music Department, University of Canterbury, P.B. Christchurch. Circ: 46. English. Indexed in RILM Abstracts; Index to New Zealand Periodicals. Other publications: Freed, Dorothy, and Seaman, Gerald, comps., Orchestral Scores: A Finding List of Performing Editions with Parts, Available on Loan or Hire from Some New Zealand Musical Societies and Libraries (2nd ed. rev., Wellington: NZ Library Association, 1984); Pritchard, Brian W., comp., Sing! A Catalogue of Choral Scores in Multiple Copies Held by New Zealand Musical Societies and Libraries (Wellington: NZLA, 1981); Freed, Dorothy, comp., Directory of New Zealand Music Organisations (Wellington: National Music Council of NZ, 1983); Harvey, D.R., Bibliography of Writings about New Zealand Music Published to the End of 1983 (Wellington: Victoria University Press, 1985). Publications available for sale.
Activities   Major accomplishments of the Association are the publications. Association has been active in promoting library-related legislation, such as Submission on the New Zealand Copyright Act.
Use of High Technology   Computer (word processor) for management.
Bibliography   Freed, D., "Music in New Zealand," New Zealand Libraries 43 (1982):184-185.

372   New Zealand Library Association (NZLA)

Address   20 Brandon Street, PO Box 12-212, Wellington 1 (permanent). Tel: 64 (4) 735834
Officers   (elected for 1-yr.term) Pres: G. Chamberlain; Past Pres: Janet Caudwell (National Library of New Zealand); Gen.Sec: Lydia Klimovitch. Exec.Board: 14
Staff   4 (paid)
Languages   English
Established   March 25-28, 1910, at first conference of representatives from public libraries of New Zealand, as Libraries Association of New Zealand; reconstituted in 1935 under present name to broaden its membership to include personal members.
Major Fields of Interest   Librarianship and information services
Major Goals and Objectives   To unite all persons engaged or interested in matters affecting libraries; to promote better management of libraries; to improve the status and qualifications of librarians; to promote the establishment of libraries; to watch legislation affecting libraries; to publish information of service or of interest to members.
Structure   Governed by Council. Affiliations: IFLA
Sources of Support   Membership dues, sale of publications, sale of commodities, advertising in regular publications.
Membership   Total members: 1,700 (1,300 individual, 400 institutional). Divisions: 2. Sections: 5. Chapters: 5. Requirements: Interest in libraries. Dues (New Zealand Dollar): 36+, individual, scaled; 50+, institutional, scaled.
General Assembly   Entire membership meets once a year: 1987: Wellington, Feb 12; 1988: Hamilton, Feb.11; 1989: Christchurch, Feb.15; 1990: New Plymouth, Feb.13-15.
Publications   *Official journal:* New Zealand Libraries. 1932-. 4/yr. (New Zealand Dollar) 22. Free to members. Address same as Association. Editor: Kenneth Porter. Address: University of Auckland Library, Private Bag, Auckland. Circ: 2,000. English. Indexed in Lib.Lit., LISA, Index to New Zeland Periodicals. Other publications: Library Life (newsletter). 11/yr.; DISLIC (Directory of Special Libraries and Information Centres in New Zealand); Public Libraries of New Zealand (1985); Standards for Special Libraries in New Zealand; Who's Who in New Zealand Libraries (1986); annual reports; proceedings of conferences, seminars, workshops, etc. Publications for sale.
Activities   Current: Concentration on providing a voice for librarianship and providing membership with practical benefits. Future: Several specific projects, e.g., higher media profile; group benefits for members; continuing education programs, etc. Association has been active in promoting library-related legislation, e.g., many submissions on issues, and played a role in establishing positions of teacher librarians in schools. The Association was able to resolve a severe financial crisis in 1989.
Bibliography   Porter, K., "Dunedin Conference Marks 75th Anniversary of New Zealand Library Association," Library Times International 2 (1985):44-45; McKeon, B., "New Zealand," ALA World Encyclopedia in Library and Information Services, 2nd ed., pp. 600-603. Chicago: American Library Association, 1986; "NZLA Splashes Out on Libraries Promotion Campaign," Library Times International 3 (1987):71-72; Wooliscroft, M., "Libraries in the Marketplace: The New Zealand Library Association Conference, February 1988," COMLA Newsletter 60 (June 1988):7; Thompson, J. et al., "Price Waterhouse Report: New Zealand Library Association Submission," New Zealand Libraries 45 (1988):211-214; Johnston, S., "Education for Librarianship," ibid.:226-230; Caudwell, J., "1989 Presidential Address: Winners and Losers," New Zealand Libraries 46 (1989):3,5; "NZ Library Group in Financial Crisis," Library Times International 6 (1989):39; "NZLA Survives Liquidation Threat," COMLA Newsletter 66 (Dec. 1989):2.

Nicaragua

373   Asociación de Bibliotecas Universitarias y Especializadas de Nicaragua (ABUEN)
(Association of University and Special Libraries of Nicaragua)

Address   c/o Biblioteca Central, Universidad Nacional Autónoma de Nicaragua, Apartado No. 68, León (permanent). Tel: (505) 2613.
Officers   (elected for 1-yr.term): Pres: Orfa Báez Reinoso; Sec: Cecilie Aguilar Briceño.
Staff   None
Languages   Spanish
Established   1969, Managua, at Banco Central de Nicaragua.
Major Fields of Interest   University and special libraries
Major Goals and Objectives   (1) To bring together all university and special libraries in Nicaragua; (2) to improve the library service of library participants; (3) to improve the study and practice of library science.
Structure   Governed by executive officers.
Sources of Support   Membership dues, private gifts.
Membership   Total members: Approx. 65 (45 individual, 20 institutional). Types of membership: Individual, institutional. Requirements: Individuals and institutions must file an application for membership for approval by the Executive Board and General Assembly.
General Assembly   Entire membership meets 3 times a year.
Publications   *Official journal:* Boletín de la ABUEN. 1971-. 1/yr. Free to members. Address same as Association. Circ: 400. Spanish.
Activities   Sponsors conferences and continuing education programs.
Bibliography   Cárdenas Perez, L., "Nicaragua," in ALA World Encyclopedia of Library and Information Services, 2nd ed., p. 603. Chicago: American Library Association, 1986.

374   Asociación Nicaragüense de Bibliotecarios y Profesionales Afines (ANIBIPA)
(Nicaraguan Association of Librarians and Related Professionals)

Address   Apartado Postal 3257, Managua
Officers   Exec.Sec: Susana Morales Hernández
Languages   Spanish
Established   1965, as Asociación Nicaragüense de Bibliotecarios (ASNIBI).
Major Fields of Interest   Librarians; professional development
Major Goals and Objectives   To improve libraries and the status and professional development of librarians in Nicaragua.
Structure   Governed by executive officers. Affiliations: IFLA (since 1974)
Sources of Support   Membership dues, government subsidies.
General Assembly   Entire membership meets once a year
Publications   No official journal. Publishes newsletter, Novedades.
Activities   Sponsors conferences, workshops, and other continuing education programs.
Bibliography   Cárdenas Perez, L., "Nicaragua," in ALA World Encyclopedia of Library and Information Services, 2nd ed., p. 603. Chicago: American Library Association, 1986.

Nigeria

375   Anambra State School Libraries Association (ASSLA)

Address   c/o Enugu Campus Library, University of Nigeria, Enugu (permanent). Tel: 234 (42) 332091 ext.5. Telex: Nigersity Library Enugu.
Officers   (elected for 2-yr.term) Chair: E.O. Odukwe; Vice-Chair: E.N.Ezeh; Sec/Treas: Dorothy S. Obi; Ed: Virginia W. Dike; 5 local representatives. Exec.Comm: 10.
Staff   1 (volunteer)
Languages   English
Established   1963, as the Eastern Nigeria School Libraries Association (ENSLA), the School Libraries Section, Eastern Nigeria Division, Nigerian Library Association; inactive from 1967 on; reconstituted 1971 as East Central State School Libraries Association; 1976, name changed to Anambra/Imo States School Libraries Association (AISSLA); 1980, present name adopted, when the Anambra State and Imo State School Libraries Associations became independent State units.
Major Fields of Interest   School libraries; training of school librarians
Major Goals and Objectives   (1) To improve school libraries in Nigeria; (2) to improve the competence of school librarians; (3) to serve as pressure group for better standards in school libraries and better conditions of service for teacher librarians.
Structure   Governed by Executive Committee. Affiliations: A Section of the Nigerian Library Association, IFLA, IASL.
Sources of Support   Membership dues, sale of publications. Budget (Naira): 1986/87: 2,000; 1987/88: 2,000.
Membership   Total members: 170 (20 individual, 150 institutional). Chapters: 5. Requirements: Interest in school libraries. Dues (Naira): 4 for each 1,000 in salary, individual; 35, institutional. Membership dues are same as Nigerian Library Association, to which 50% of all dues are paid.
General Assembly   Entire membership meets twice a year, in February and November.
Publications   *Official journal:* School Libraries Bulletin. 1964-. 2/yr. (Naira) 15. Free to members. Editors: Ms. Virginia W. Dike. Address: Department of Library Studies, University of Nigeria, Nsukka; Dorothy S. Obi. Address same as Association. Circ: 300. English. Indexed in LISA. Other publications: Manual for School Libraries on Small Budgets, etc. Publications available for sale.
Activities   Past achievements: (1) Introduction of library studies programs in Teacher Training Colleges in Anambra State; (2) annual refresher courses for teacher librarians; (3) competition for best primary school libraries in Anambra State. Current and future: (1) Publication of School Libraries Bulletin; (2) organization of annual refresher course for teacher librarians; (3) annual competition for best school library. Association has been active in promoting library-related legislation, such as adoption of standards for school libraries by the Ministry of Education. Sponsors continuing education offerings. Association is officially recognized by the Anambra State Ministry of Education, and works in close cooperation with the Anambra State Library Board, the British Council, and the University of Nigeria.
Bibliography   Dosunmu, J.A., "Nigeria," in ALA World Encyclopedia of Library and Information Services, 2nd ed., pp. 605-606. Chicago: American Library Association, 1986; Obi, D.S., "Promoting School Libraries in Eastern Nigeria: 25 Years of the Eastern Nigeria School Libraries Association," COMLA Newsletter 60 (June 1988):8-9,15.

376   Nigerian Association of Agricultural Librarians and Documentalists (NAALD)

Address   c/o Library & Business Information Centre, Lagos Chamber of Commerce & Industry, Commerce House, 1 Idowu Taylor Street, Victoria Island, Lagos. Tel: 234 (1) 613902/613906/613911.
Officers   Exec.Sec: S.B. Akande
Languages   English
Established   1976
Major Fields of Interest   Agricultural libraries and information services
Major Goals and Objectives   To promote agricultural librarianship and documentation in Nigeria
Structure   Governed by executive officers. Affiliations: IAALD.
Sources of Support   Membership dues, government subsidies

377   Nigerian Library Association (NLA)

Address   c/o The National Library of Nigeria, PMB 12626, Lagos. Tel: 234 (1) 634704. Telex: 20117.
Officers   (elected for 2-yr.term) Pres: J.O. Fasanya; Past Pres: John Adetundi Dosunmu; Sec: L.I. Ehigiator; Treas: J.B. Falode. Exec.Board: 3. Council: 40.
Staff   None
Languages   English
Established   1962
Major Fields of Interest   College, university, public, and special libraries.
Major Goals and Objectives   To unite all practitioners in the field of library and information science and to maintain high standards of library practice in Nigeria.
Structure   Governed by Council. Affiliations: IFLA.
Sources of Support   Membership dues, sale of publications, government subsidies. Budget (Naira): 1986/87: 20,000; 1987/88: 22,000.
Membership   Total members: 3,000 (2,500 individual, 500 institutional). Divisions: 6. Sections: 7. Chapters: 19. Requirements: Must be a qualified librarian, paraprofessional or library student. Dues (Naira): 12, student; 24 to 52, individual, according to income.
General Assembly   Entire membership meets once a year.
Publications   *Official journal:* Nigerian Libraries. 1964-. 2/yr. (US Dollar) 40, other countries. Free to members. Editor: A.O. Banjo. Address: Nigerian Institute of International Affairs, Victoria Island, Lagos. Circ: 3,500. English. Indexed in Lib.Lit.; LISA. Other publications: Proceedings of meetings, reports of seminars, workshops, etc. Publications available for sale through Mrs. O. Jegede, Librarian, Institute of Advanced Legal Studies, University of Lagos, Lagos. No publications exchange program.
Activities   Past and current: Workshops and seminars on special subjects of interest to members. Future: Planning and constructing a permanent secretariat; appointment of fulltime paid staff for the secretariat. Association has been active in promoting library-related legislation, such as the State Library Board in Bendel, Benue, Anambra, Imo, Cross River, Rivers. Sponsors Book Week, exhibits, continuing education programs, and a literacy campaign to promote adult readership.
Bibliography   Dosunmu, J.A., "Nigeria," in ALA World Encyclopedia of Library and Information Services, 2nd ed., pp. 605-606. Chicago: American Library Association, 1986; Dosunmu, J.A., "Preservation and Conservation of Library Materials in Nigeria: A New Awareness," COMLA Newsletter 64 (June 1989):3-4.

Northern Ireland

378   The Library Association, Northern Ireland Branch / LA (NI)

Address   c/o Linda Y. Houston, Honorary Secretary, North Eastern Education and Library Board HQ, Area Library, Demesne Avenue, Ballymena BT43 7BG, Northern Ireland, United Kingdom (not permanent). Tel: 44 (232) 245133.
Officers   (elected for 1-yr.term) Chair: A. Morrow (Southern Education and Library Board); Past Chair: Deborah H. Shorley (University of Ulster); Vice-Chair: Linda Houston; Sec: David Clow; Treas: Sam McDowell. Exec.Comm: 12.
Staff None
Languages   English
Major Fields of Interest   All library matters in Northern Ireland
Major Goals and Objectives   To promote libraries and librarianship in Northern Ireland
Structure   Governed by executive officers as a Branch of the Library Association. All activities are carried out according to the overall goals and objectives of the Library Association (LA).
Sources of Support   Library Association membership dues
General Assembly   Entire membership meets annually at the Library Association conference.
Publications   Newsletter, Matters Arising. Address same as Association.
Bibliography   Shorley, D., "'Free for All, Fee for All': Belfast 1988; the Joint Conference of the Northern Ireland Branch of the Library Association of Ireland: View from the Chair," Library Association Record 90 (1988):289.

Norway

379 Arkivarforeningen
(Association of Archivists)

Address Postboks 10, Kringsjå, N-0807 Oslo 8 (permanent)
Officers (elected for 2-yr.term) Pres: Torbjorn Låg; Sec: Liv Marthinsen. Exec.Board: 5.
Staff None
Languages Norwegian
Established 1936, Oslo.
Major Fields of Interest Archives and archival personnel
Major Goals and Objectives To improve the professional and economic standards of members, such as wages, working conditions, and professional development.
Structure Governed by Executive Board. Affiliations: ICA, Norsk Forskerforbund, Akademikernes Fellesorganisasjon.
Sources of Support Membership dues.
Membership Total members: 55 (individual). Types of membership: Individual. Requirements: Position and qualifications as an archivist within the state archival system. Dues (Norwegian Krone): 300, individual.
General Assembly Entire membership meets every 2 years
Publications *Official journal:* Norsk Arkivforum. 1980-. Biennial. (Norwegian Krone) 60. Free to members. Address same as Association. Circ: 300-400. Norwegian.
Activities Past achievements: Significant improvements in the wage level and some improvements regarding working conditions of members. Current and future: Continue working for better wages, working conditions, and opportunities for professional development of members.

380 ARLIS/Norge. Forening for Kunstbibliotekarbeid
(Norwegian Art Library Association)

Address c/o Riksantikvarens Bibliotek, Akershus festning, Bygning 18, Oslo Mil., N-0015 Oslo 1. Tel: 47 (2) 419600.
Languages Norwegian
Established 1983, Oslo
Major Fields of Interest Art libraries and librarianship
Major Goals and Objectives To promote art librarianship in Norway.
Structure Governed by executive officers. Affiliations: IFLA .
Sources of Support Membership dues
Membership Total members: 60+ (40 individual, 20 institutional). Requirements: Individual: Librarians working in art libraries or with art collections; institutional: Art libraries and other libraries with art collections.
General Assembly Entire membership meets annually.
Publications *Official journal:* ARLIS-Nytt (News from ARLIS/Norge). 1983-. 4/yr. Free to members. Address same as Association. Norwegian.
Activities Organizing annual meetings and conferences on special topics, such as the new Norwegian Art Bibliography, new media, especially video and microfiche, etc. Sponsors continuing education programs.
Bibliography Rabben, A.L. and Bonafede, C.W., "ARLIS/Norge: Art Librarianship in Norway and the Literature of Norwegian Art," Art Libraries Journal 11(1986):25-27. Text of paper presented to the IFLA Section of Art Libraries at the IFLA Conference, Chicago, August 1985.

381   Kommunale Bibliotekarbeideres Forening (KBF)
(Association of Public Library Employees)

Address   c/o Bjoern Bringsvaerd, Skien Bibliotek, Postboks 349, N-3700 Skien (not permanent).
Officers   (elected for 3-yr.term) Pres: Bjoern Bringsvaerd. Exec.Comm: 5
Staff   None
Languages   Norwegian
Established   1957, Oslo, as Kommunale Bibliotekarers Forening.
Major Fields of Interest   Library personnel (wages, education), library legislation
Major Goals and Objectives   Established with the purpose of raising salaries and improving working conditions of librarians, and promoting the qualifications of librarians.
Structure   Governed by Executive Committee. Affiliations: NBF (Norsk Bibliotekforening)
Sources of Support   Membership dues.
Membership   Total members: 650+ (individual). Types of membership: Individual, student. Requirements: Open to those working in libraries and/or members of the local trade union. Dues (Norwegian Krone): 70, individual; 25, student.
General Assembly   Entire membership meets every two years.
Publications   *Official journal:* Kontakten. 1957-. 5/yr. Address same as Association. Circ: Membership. Norwegian.
Activities   Sponsors conferences, seminars, and other continuing education programs; works for improving the quality of libraries, strives for higher education standards, and better salaries for library personnel. Functions as a trade union.
Bibliography   Granheim, E., "Norway," in ALA World Encyclopedia of Library and Information Services, 2nd ed., pp. 608-609. Chicago: American Library Association, 1986.

382   Norsk Bibliotekforening (NBF)
(Norwegian Library Association)

Address   Malerhaugveien 20, N-0661 Oslo 6 (permanent). Tel: 47 (2) 688576
Officers   (elected for 4-yr.term) Pres (2-yr.term): Per Morten Bryhn; Sec/Treas: Ms. Gro Langeland. Exec.Board: 9
Staff   4 (paid)
Languages   Norwegian
Established   1913
Major Fields of Interest   All topics of interest to libraries and librarians
Major Goals and Objectives   To promote the development of the Norwegian library community
Structure   Governed by Executive Board. Affiliations: IFLA. There are 20 regional associations and 8 associations for specific topics within the Association.
Sources of Support   Membership dues, sale of publications. Budget (Norwegian Krone): Approx. 2 million.
Membership   Total members: 3,700 (2,800 individual, 900 institutional). Sections for various types of libraries and types of librarians. Requirements: Open to all, no special requirements. Dues (Norwegian Krone): 220, individual; scaled according to size, institutional.
General Assembly   Entire membership meets every 2 years. 1988: Oslo, Sept.21-25.
Publications   *Official journal:* Internkontakt. 1975-. Approx.9/yr. (Norwegian Krone) 55. Free to members. Editor: Gro Langeland, Sec./Treas. Address same as Association. Circ: Membership. Norwegian. Other publications: Annual reports, proceedings of meet-

ings; The Norwegian Cataloguing Rules; Dewey Decimal Classification, etc. Publications for sale.
Activities Sponsors meetings, conferences and continuing education programs; participates in international activities.
Use of High Technology Computers (PC) for management.
Bibliography Granheim, E., "Norway," in ALA World Encyclopedia of Library and Information Services, 2nd ed., pp. 608-609. Chicago: American Library Association, 1986; Granheim, E., "NLA Conference Report: Libraries for the Future Discussed," (1986 Meeting in Stavanger, Norway) Library Times International 3 (1986):32.

383 Norsk Dokumentasjonsgruppe (Norwegian Dokumentation Society)

Address c/o Brodd, Dahlenenggt. 26, Oslo 4
Officers Pres: Siv Hunstad
Languages Norwegian
Major Fields of Interest Documentation and information services
Major Goals and Objectives To promote documentation and information services in Norway

384 Norsk Fagbibliotekforening (NFF) (Norwegian Association of Special Libraries)

Address Malerhaugveien 20, N-0661 Oslo 6 (permanent). Tel: 47 (2) 688576.
Officers (elected for 2-yr.term) Chair: Else-Margrethe Bredland; Past Chair: Hans Martin Fagerli; Sec: Ms. A. Stefansen. Exec.Board: 6
Staff None
Languages Norwegian
Established 1948; merged with Norske Forskningsbibliotekarers Forening (NFF) (Association of Norwegian Research Librarians).
Major Fields of Interest Special and academic libraries, especially in areas of automation and cooperation.
Major Goals and Objectives To arrange meetings, seminars and courses for the purpose of developing Norwegian special and academic libraries and their personnel; to promote discussion about topics of common interest.
Structure Governed by Executive Board. Affiliations: IFLA, NBF.
Sources of Support Membership dues. Budget (Norwegian Krone): Approx. 250,000.
Membership Total members: 820 (785 individual, 35 institutional). Requirements: Employee of a special library; special library. Dues (Norwegian Krone): 180, individual; 750, institutional, with less than 3 employees; 1,250, institutional, with more than 3 employees.
General Assembly Entire membership meets once a year.
Publications *Official journal:* NFF-Informasjon. 4/yr. Free to members. Editor: Hans Martin Fagerli. Address: Universitetsbiblioteket i Oslo, Planardelingen, Drammensveien 42, N-0255 Oslo 2. Circ: 900. Norwegian. Other publications: Reports of seminars, workshops; NFF-Skrifter, occasional series.
Activities Sponsoring seminars, courses, meetings, newspaper articles; promoting library automation and planning a seminar on automation in special and academic libraries; studying other library interest groups to find a possible common platform; working for the establishment of a national library.
Use of High Technology Computers (VAX/Multitech) for management.
Bibliography Granheim, E., "Norway," in ALA World Encyclopedia of Library and Information Services, 2nd ed., pp. 608-609. Chicago: American Library Association, 1986.

385   Norwegian Association of Blind Library Service

Address   PO Box 6900, Hegdehaugen, N-0308 Oslo 3. Tel: 47 (2) 466990. Telex: 77774.
Languages   Norwegian
Major Fields of Interest   Library services to the blind
Major Goals and Objectives   To promote library services to the blind
Structure   Affiliations: IFLA

Pakistan

386   Library Promotion Bureau (LPB)

Address   PO Box 8421, Karachi University Campus, Karachi 32 (permanent). Tel: (92) 681959.
Officers   (elected for 5-yr.term) Dir: M. Adil Usmani; Sec.Gen: G.A. Sabzwari; Publicity Sec: Rais Ahmed Samdani; Sec./Ed.,Urdu Section: Ms. Nasim Fatima; Treas: Wasil Usmani. Board of Directors: 5
Staff   2 (paid), 5 (volunteers)
Languages   English, Urdu
Established   1965, Karachi
Major Fields of Interest   Library and information science
Major Goals and Objectives   (1) To promote librarianship in Pakistan; (2) to coordinate with all other organizations engaged in promotional activities; (3) to publish reference books, bibliographies, directories, and text books in library science.
Structure   Governed by Board of Directors.
Sources of Support   Membership dues, sale of publications, private donations.
Membership   Total members: 150 (100 individual, 50 institutional). 10 countries represented. Types of membership: Individual, institutional, student. Requirements: Individual: Professional librarians, library science students, friends of the library; Institutional: Libraries, government and research organizations. Dues (Pakistan Rupee): 60.
General Assembly   Entire membership meets once a year.
Publications   *Official journal:* Pakistan Library Bulletin. 1968-. 4/yr. (US Dollar) 60. Free to members. Chief Editor: M. Adil Usmani. Editors: G.A. Sabzwari, Akhtar Hanif, Nasim Fatima, Rais Ahmad Samdani. Address same as Association. Circ: 300. English, Urdu. Indexed in Readers' Guide, LISA, Historical Abstracts, etc. Other publications: Reports of seminars, workshops; Sabzwari, G.A., Who's Who in Library & Information Science in Pakistan (2nd ed.); Fatima, Nasim, Secondary School Library Resources Services in Pakistan; Usmani, M. Adil, Bibliographical Services throughout Pakistan (2nd ed.); Siddiqui, Akthar H., Documents Procurement Service; Libraries in Pakistan; Hanif, Akthrar, and Fatima, Nasim, University Librarianship in Pakistan, etc. Publications listed in official journal. Price lists available. Publications exchange program in effect. The Pakistan Library Bulletin is the only journal in the field of library and information science in Pakistan. The Bureau has published over 30 books.
Activities   Past achievements: Extensive publications program. Current: To publish journal regularly and also to publish books on library and information science, e.g. Pakistan World of Learning and Research (ed. R.A. Samdani). Future: Further reference publications, e.g., A Manual on the Library of Congress Classification Scheme (by G.A. Sabzwari); Cataloging (by Akhtar Hanif), and others. The Bureau has been active in promoting library-related legislation.
Bibliography   Khurshid, A., The State of Library Resources in Pakistan (1982); Khurshid, A., "Pakistan," in ALA World Encyclopedia of Library and Information Services, 2nd ed., pp. 629-633. Chicago: American Library Association, 1986.

387   Library Writers' Bureau, Pakistan

Address   c/o Fida Mohammad Khan, President, Lecturer, Department of Library and Information Science, University of Peshawar (not permanent)
Officers   Pres: Fida Mohammad Khan; Sr.VP: Hamid Rehman; VP: Ms. Bint-e-Zehra; Sec: Sheen Shaukat (Librarian, Nishtar Municipal Public Library, Peshawar)

Languages English, Urdu
Established October 1986, Peshawar
Major Fields of Interest Professional development
Major Goals and Objectives To promote professional development of librarians
Publications Bibliophile (newsletter).
Bibliography "Library Writers' Bureau Pakistan, Peshawar," News and Views 3 (July-Sept. 1987):4-5.

388   Pakistan Bibliographical Working Group (PBWG)

Address c/o Department of Libraries (Regional Office), Ministry of Education, Government of Pakistan, Liaquat Memorial Library Building, Stadium Road, Karachi 5 (permanent). Tel: (92) 417675
Officers (elected for 5-yr.term) Pres: Anwarul Haq Hashmi; Sec: Rais Ahmed Samdani; Treas: Ms. Rukhsana Khatoon; Joint Sec: Latif Ahmed Anwar. Exec.Board: 4.
Staff 2 (paid), 4 (volunteers)
Languages English, Urdu
Established 1957
Major Fields of Interest Bibliography and indexing; library and information science.
Major Goals and Objectives "A professional organization formed by librarians, educators, writers, journalists, intellectuals, and prominent citizens to promote bibliographical studies and services in Pakistan."
Structure Governed by executive officers.
Sources of Support Sale of publications, course fees. Budget (Pakistan Rupee): Approx. 25,000.
Membership Total members: 500 (individual). Type of membership: Individual, life. Requirements: Interest in aims of Association.
General Assembly Entire membership meets once a year
Publications No official journal. The Pakistan National Bibliography (1947-1961) is the most important contribution in publishing. The Secretary, Rais Ahmed Samdani, edits yearly publications. Publications exchange program in effect.
Activities Past achievements: The Group established a "School of Librarianship" in 1958, and introduced an undergraduate certificate course in library science. The purpose of this course is to prepare students to obtain a sound knowledge of library operations and systems used in school, college, special, and public libraries. Current: The Retrospective Pakistan National Bibliography (1947-1961). Future: Certificate course in library science. Sponsors Book Week, exhibits, and continuing education programs.
Bibliography Khurshid, A., "Pakistan," in ALA World Encyclopedia of Library and Information Services, 2nd ed., pp. 629-633. Chicago: American Library Association, 1986; Khurshid, A., "Library Associations in Asia," Herald of Library Science 28 (1989):3-10.

389   Pakistan Library Association (PLA)

Address c/o Pakistan Institute of Development Economics, University Campus, PO Box 1091, Islamabad (not permanent).
Officers (elected for 2-yr.term) Pres: Mahmud Husain; Exec.Sec: A.H. Siddiqui
Staff 2 (volunteers)
Languages English, Urdu
Established 1958. The former East Pakistan Library Association was affiliated with PLA until 1971, when East Pakistan became the independent Bangladesh.
Major Fields of Interest Library development and the library profession.

Major Goals and Objectives   To work for the establishment of comprehensive library service throughout Pakistan; to promote better organization of libraries; to promote study and research in library science and dissemination of information; to improve the status and professional standing of library workers and to safeguard their interests.
Structure   Governed by Executive Council. Affiliations: IFLA.
Sources of Support   Membership dues, subsidies.
Membership   Total members: 650+ (individual and institutional). Divisions: 5 (Public Libraries, College & University Libraries, Special Libraries and Documentation, Library Services for Children and Young People, Library Education).
General Assembly   Entire membership meets once a year.
Publications   *Official journal:* PLA Newsletter. 12/yr. Circ: Membership. Address same as Association. Other publications: Code of Ethics for Librarians (1982); Public Library Facilities in Pakistan; Standards of College Libraries in Pakistan (1983); Standards of Special Libraries; Standards of University Libraries, etc. Publications available for sale.
Activities   As the representative body of librarians in Pakistan, the Association aims to look after the interests of professional librarians and to work for the development and improvement of libraries in education and research. The rotation of headquarters every two years has been creating problems in carrying out activities effectively, and the Association hopes that eventually a permanent headquarters with a permanent secretariat can be established in Islamabad, Lahore, or Karachi, with government help, so that its financial situation can be improved. Immediate and future professional goals for activities are in the areas of library legislation, a national library system, professional status of librarians in all types of libraries, library standards, a national cataloging code, a uniform classification system, a national union catalog, bibliographical and information control, etc. A strong membership campaign is being planned, and an expanded publications program. Active in promoting library-related legislation, such as lobbying for the recognition of the library movement in the country, and increasing public awareness of the benefits of library services. Association has been seeking more financial support from governmental authorities for the development of libraries.
Bibliography   Khurshid, A., "Pakistan," in ALA World Encyclopedia of Library and Information Services, 2nd ed., pp. 629-633. Chicago: American Library Association, 1986; Sabzwari, G.A., "Pakistan Library Association," Pakistan Library Bulletin 19 (Dec.1988):i-v; Khurshid, A., "Library Associations in Asia," Herald of Library Science 28 (1989):3-10.

390   Society for the Promotion and Improvement of Libraries (SPIL)

Address   Al-Majid, Hamdard Centre, Nazimabad, Karachi 18 (permanent). Tel: (92) 616001.
Officers   (elected for 1-yr.term) Pres: Hakim Mohammed Said; Sec: Mohammed Arifuddin; Treas: Ashfaq Husain Qadri; Jr.Sec: Rais A. Samdani. Exec.Board: 15
Staff   1 (paid), 5 (volunteers)
Languages   English, Urdu
Established   1960, Karachi
Major Fields of Interest   Libraries and librarianship
Major Goals and Objectives   (1) To improve existing library facilities in Pakistan; (2) to improve and promote cooperation among libraries in Pakistan; (3) to provide for adult education through libraries.
Structure   Governed by Board of Directors.
Sources of Support   Membership dues, sale of publications, donations from other organizations. Budget (Pakistan Rupee): Approx.30,000

Membership   Total members: 100. Chapters: 4. Requirements: Interest in library development.

General Assembly   Entire membership meets once a year.

Publications   *Official journal:* News and Views. 4/yr. Editor: Amjad Ali. Address same as Association. Circ: 1000. English. Other publications: Proceedings of meetings, reports of seminars, workshops; Islamic Studies: Basic Books for School & Public Libraries (1985); Sabzwari, G.A., Who's Who in Library and Information Science in Pakistan (2nd ed., 1987); etc. Publications available for sale. No publications exchange program.

Activities   Past achievements: Publications in library and information science. Current: Regular publication of the newsletter; conducts seminars, conferences, Library Week, book exhibits, discussions, radio talks, etc. Future: Publish reference books and hold seminars. Association has been active in promoting library-related legislation and was instrumental in creating library awareness in the country.

Use of High Technology   Electronic publishing for management.

Bibliography   Khurshid, A., "Pakistan," in ALA World Encyclopedia of Library and Information Services, 2nd ed., pp. 629-633. Chicago: American Library Association, 1986; The Role of the Society for the Promotion and Improvement of Libraries. Karachi: The Society, 1987; Khurshid, A., "Library Associations in Asia," Herald of Library Science 28 (1989):3-10.

Additional Information   Some new associations have been reported: Pakistan College Library Association (1986), Pakistan Medical Library Association (1986), Association of Pakistan Library Schools (1987), and the Pakistan Association of Special Libraries (PAS-LIB) (originally founded in 1968, disbanded in 1969, and revived in 1988).

Panama

391 Asociación de Bibliotecarios Graduados del Istmo de Panamá (Association of Graduate Librarians of the Isthmus of Panama) (AGLIP)

Address c/o Director de la Biblioteca Bio-Médica des Laboratorio Conmemorativo Gorgas, Apartado 6991, Panama 5 (not permanent). Tel: (507) 274111.
Officers Pres: Manuel Víctor De Las Casas; Sec: Iris de Espinosa.
Languages Spanish, English
Established 1955, Panama
Major Fields of Interest The library profession; library service in Panama.
Major Goals and Objectives To unite professional librarians and represent their interests; to promote professional development of librarians; to further and improve library services in the country.
Structure Governed by Executive Committee.
Sources of Support Membership dues
Membership Total members: 40 (individual). Types of membership: Individual. Requirements: To have earned a library science degree. Dues (US Dollar): 10.
General Assembly Entire membership meets irregularly.
Publications No publications program.
Activities Association still holds occasional meetings, but is mainly inactive

392 Asociación Panameña de Bibliotecarios (Panamenian Association of Librarians)

Address c/o Estafeta Universitaria, Apartado 10808, Panama (not permanent)
Officers Pres: Amelia L. de Barakat; Past Pres: Bexie Rodríguez De León.
Languages Spanish
Established 1951
Major Fields of Interest Libraries and library profession
Major Goals and Objectives To improve the professional status of librarians; to promote library services in Panama.
Structure Governed by executive officers.
Sources of Support Membership dues
Publications *Official journal:* Boletín. 1/yr. Other occasional publications: A bibliography of literature by Panamanian women.
Activities Sponsors conferences, seminars and other continuing education programs; works on recognition of professional status for librarians according to a law of 1956.
Bibliography Mendieta Ortiz, Victor U., "Panama," in ALA World Encyclopedia of Library and Information Services, 2nd ed., pp. 633-634. Chicago: American Library Association, 1986.

Papua New Guinea

393   Papua New Guinea Library Association (PNGLA)

Address   PO Box 5368, Boroko (permanent). Tel: 675 (24) 3900 ext.2252.
Officers   (elected for 1-yr.term) Pres: Margaret J. Obi; VP: Ursula Pawe; Sec: Haro
Raka; Treas; Lewsi Kusso-Aless; Publications Manager: Maria Teka. Exec.Board: 9
Staff   None
Languages   English, Tok Pisin
Established   1973 as an independent association; formerly, Papua New Guinea Branch
of the Library Association of Australia (founded 1967).
Major Fields of Interest   Libraries and librarianship
Major Goals and Objectives   To promote libraries and librarianship in Papua New
Guinea.
Structure   Governed by executive officers. Affiliations: COMLA, IFLA, SCOPAL.
Sources of Support   Membership dues, sale of publications.
Membership   Total members: 150 (individual). 2 countries represented. Requirements:
Interest in the development of libraries in Papua New Guinea. Dues (Kina): 0 to 15, indi-
vidual, according to income; 15, institutional.
General Assembly   Entire membership meets once a year, at Port Moresby.
Publications   *Official journal:* Tok Tok Bilong Haus Buk (Journal of the PNGLA).
1976-. 4/yr. (Kina) 10. Free to members. Editor: Maria Teka. Address same as Association. Circ: Membership. English. Other publications: PNGLA Nius (PNGLA News-
sheets); annual reports, proceedings of annual meetings; Directory of Libraries in Papua
New Guinea; Library and Information Services for the Public, etc. Publications available
for sale. Publications exchange program in effect with other associations and libraries.
Activities   Reactivated Port Moresby Branch in 1988. Sponsors annual conference,
workshops, etc.; works for improving public library services in Papua New Guinea. Active
in sponsoring library-related legislation, such as copyright and legal deposit, and forma-
tion of a National Library Service. Participates in international activities.
Bibliography   Jackson, M.M., "Library and Information Services in the Pacific Islands,"
International Library Review (1981); Bagita, S., "PNGLA: Past, Present and Future, Tok
Tok Bilong Haus Buk 35 (Sept. 1984):11-15 (Report on the 1983 Conference); Baker,
L.R., "Papua New Guinea," in ALA World Encyclopedia of Library and Information Ser-
vices, 2nd ed., pp. 636-637. Chicago: American Library Association, 1986; Evans, J. and
Temu, D., "The Library Council of Papua New Guinea: Summary of History and Activi-
ties," COMLA Newsletter 66 (Dec. 1989):8-12; "Welcome Revival in PNG," ibid.:6.
Additional Information   The School Library Association of Papua New Guinea
(SLAPNG), founded in 1971, in Port Moresby, with some 40 members, is currently inactive.

Paraguay

394   Asociación de Bibliotecarios del Paraguay (ABIPAR)
(Association of Paraguayan Librarians)

Address   Casilla de Correo 1505, Asunción (permanent).
Officers   Sec: Mafalda Cabrerar. Exec.Comm: 9.
Staff   None
Languages   Spanish
Established   1961, Asunción
Major Fields of Interest   Status of librarians; national bibliography; library education
Major Goals and Objectives   To promote the library profession and the national bibliography; to establish a school of library science and a professional journal of librarianship.
Structure   Governed by Executive Committee.
Sources of Support   Membership dues, sale of publications, private donations.
Membership   Total members: 65+. Types of membership: Individual, institutional, student, honorary. Requirements: Open to all library employees and to those who have studied library science.
General Assembly   Entire membership meets once a year.
Publications   *Official journal:* Revista de Bibliotecología y Documentación Paraguaya (Review of Library Science and Documentation in Paraguay). 1972-. 1/yr. Address same as Association. Circ: 200. Spanish. Other publications: Annual reports, proceedings of meetings, workshops.
Activities   Works to improve the status of librarians; publication of journal; to design and carry out research projects. Active in promoting library-related legislation, such as a law to improve library services and the status of librarians.
Bibliography   Freundorfer, Yoshiko Moriya de (tr. by E.S. Gleaves), "Paraguay," in ALA World Encyclopedia of Library and Information Services, 2nd ed., pp. 637-640. Chicago: American Library Association, 1986.

395   Asociación de Bibliotecarios Universitarios del Paraguay (ABUP)
(Paraguayan Association of University Librarians)

Address   c/o Zayda Caballero, Escuela de Bibliotecología, Universidad Nacional de Asunción, Casilla de Correo 1408, Asunción (not permanent)
Officers   Pres: Gloria Ondina Ortiz C; Sec: Celia Villamayor de Díaz.
Staff   None
Languages   Spanish
Established   1974, Asunción, at the Escuela de Bibliotecología, by 17 graduates.
Major Fields of Interest   Professional librarianship; library education; university librarians
Major Goals and Objectives   To promote cooperation among libraries; to represent professional interests of members; to further intellectual and technical training of members; to raise the professional status of librarians in society.
Structure   Governed by executive officers.
Sources of Support   Membership dues.
Membership   Total members: 90+ (individuals). Type of membership: Individual. Requirements: Librarians with a university degree.
General Assembly   Entire membership meets once a year.

Publications *Official journal:* Páginas de Contenido; newsletter: ABUP Informaciones.
Activities Publication of journal and newsletter; sponsoring of meetings and other continuing education programs.
Bibliography Freundorfer, Yoshio Moriya de (tr. by E.S. Gleaves), "Paraguay," in ALA Encyclopedia of Library and Information Services, 2nd ed., pp. 637-640. Chicago: American Library Association, 1986.

Peru

396 Agrupación de Bibliotecas para la Integración de la Información
Socio-Económica (ABIISE)
(Library Group for the Integration of Socio-Economic Information)

Address Apartado 2874, Lima 100 (permanent). Tel: 51 (14) 351760.
Officers Officers are not elected. The Executive Committee of four appointed members serves in this capacity. Dir: Betty Chiriboga de Cussato.
Staff Volunteers
Languages Spanish
Established 1969, by a group representing 15 special libraries, invited by the library of ESAN (Escuela de Administración de Negocios para Graduados / Graduate School of Business Administration), to discuss the integration of socio-economic information. The outcome of this initial meeting was the inclusion of all the libraries in the socio-economic area for such cooperation as interlibrary loan, planned acquisitions, and other activities.
Major Fields of Interest Socio-economic information, and local and international cooperation.
Major Goals and Objectives (1) To accomplish research and cooperative technical works that contribute to the areas of specialization; (2) to encourage interlibrary loan in accordance with existing agreements; (3) to plan the acquisition of bibliographic and documentary materials and to promote the exchange of such publications; (4) to adopt technical and professional standards for the integration of information in coordination with appropriate organizations; (5) to foster other forms of cooperation.
Structure Governed by Executive Committee that meets twice a month.
Sources of Support Private donations, sale of publications.
Membership Total members: 32 institutions. Types of membership: Institutional. Requirements: (1) To be in the field of economic and social development; (2) to fulfill the requirements for a special library.
General Assembly Entire membership meets once a month in Lima, in a member library.
Publications No official journal. Other publications: Directorio de Bibliotecas Especializadas del Perú (Directory of Special Libraries of Peru), etc. Publications available for sale.
Activities The first specialized group in the library field in Peru. Works for standardization of terminology, abbreviations, titles of periodicals, statistics. Sponsors workshops. Plans a union catalog of the holdings of the 32 member libraries.
Bibliography Gorman, M., "Peru," in ALA World Encyclopedia of Library and Information Services, 2nd ed., pp. 642-644. Chicago: American Library Association, 1986.

397 Asociación de Bibliotecarios y Documentalistas Agrícolas del Perú
(ABYDAP) (Filial de AIBDA)
(Association of Agricultural Librarians and Documentalists of Peru) (Branch of AIBDA)

Address Headquarters: c/o Universidad Nacional Agraria, Biblioteca Agrícola Nacional, Avenida de la Universidad, Lima. Tel: 51 (14) 352035. Postal address: Apartado 456, Lima.
Languages Spanish
Established 1966

Major Fields of Interest   Agricultural libraries and information services
Major Goals and Objectives   To promote the cooperation of librarians, documentalists, and information specialists in the field of agriculture of Peru; to organize technical conferences, continuing education courses, workshops, and seminars; to promote professional development and improve the status of members; to further the development and improvement of agricultural information and studies in libraries and documentation centers, and promote their importance.
Structure   Governed by executive officers. Affiliations: Branch of AIBDA.
Sources of Support   Membership dues
Membership   Total members: 66 (individual)
General Assembly   Entire membership meets at least once a year.
Publications   *Official journal:* Boletín Técnico. Irreg. Free to members. Address same as Association. Circ: Membership. Spanish. Other publications: ABYDAP Informa (irregular newsletter); membership directories; Bibliografía sobre Ciencias de la Información (1986), etc.
Activities   Activities carried out according to the goals and objectives of the Association.

398   Asociación Peruana de Archiveros (APA)
(Association of Peruvian Archivists)

Address   C. Manuel Cuadros s/n, Palacio de Justicia, Casilla 3124, Lima 100. Tel: 51 (14) 275930.
Officers   Pres: C. Manuel Cuadros
Staff   None
Languages   Spanish
Established   1961
Major Fields of Interest   Archives and records management
Major Goals and Objectives   To promote the development and organization of archives in Peru; to organize training courses and seminars for archivists; to promote the professional status of archivists; to publish material of interest to members; to encourage cooperation among members and provide opportunities for meetings and exchange of information; to participate in international activities.
Structure   Governed by executive officers. Affiliations: ICA.
Sources of Support   Membership dues.
Membership   Total members: 200 + (individual). Types of membership: Individual. Requirements: Archivists, records managers, and others performing archival work.
General Assembly   Entire membership meets once a year.
Publications   *Official journal:* Hoja Archivera (information bulletin). 12/yr. Free to members. Address same as Association. Circ: Membership. Spanish.
Activities   Sponsors conferences, workshops, seminars, in accordance with the goals and objectives of the Association.

399   Asociación Peruviana de Bibliotecarios (APB)
(Peruvian Library Association)

Address   Bellavista 561, Miraflores, Apartado postal 3760, Lima 18 (permanent). Tel: 51 (14) 474869.
Officers   Pres: Ms. D. Samanez Alzamora; Sec: Ms. C. Barrenechea de Castro.
Staff   None
Languages   Spanish

Established   1945
Major Fields of Interest   Library and information science
Major Goals and Objectives   To unite librarians in Peru; to promote their professional development and professional status; to further library and information services in Peru.
Structure   Governed by executive officers. Affiliations: IFLA (since 1981).
Sources of Support   Membership dues.
Membership   Total members: 300 (individual). Types of membership: Individual. Requirements: Librarian with professional degree.
General Assembly   Entire membership meets once a year in Lima.
Publications   *Official journal:* Carta Informativa. 6/yr. Publishes irregular series, Eventos.
Activities   Sponsors conferences, seminars, and other activities according to the aims of the Association.
Bibliography   Gorman, M., "Peru," in ALA World Encyclopedia of Library and Information Services, 2nd ed., pp. 642-644. Chicago: American Library Association, 1986.

Philippines

400   Agricultural Libraries Association of the Philippines (ALAP)

Address   c/o AIBA/SEARCA, College, Laguna 3720
Languages   Pilipino, English
Established   1972, by librarians from the Association of Colleges of Agriculture in the Philippines (ACAP) as a national association for all types of agricultural librarians.
Major Fields of Interest   Agricultural libraries and information services
Major Goals and Objectives   (1) To promote understanding the nature, scope and importance of agricultural research libraries, (2) to promote better cooperation and coordination among member libraries, (3) to encourage professional interests and growth of agricultural librarianship, (4) to actively encourage the establishment and development of agricultural libraries and the improvement of their services, and (5) to enhance and uphold the dignity of the library profession and to observe professional ethics at all times.
Structure   Governed by executive officers. Affiliations: IAALD.
Sources of Support   Membership dues
Publications   No official journal. Publishes newsletter, ALAP News. Irreg.
Activities   ALAP has a Standing Committee on Conferences and Workshops, which organizes meetings and continuing education programs. Hosted the World Congress of Agricultural Librarians and Documentalists in Manila in 1980.
Bibliography   Sacchanand, C., "Training Programs of Library Associations in the Philippines," Journal of Philippine Librarianship 7 (1983):11-26; "Agricultural Libraries Association of the Philippines," Bulletin of the PLAI 16 (New Series) (1984):138a-138f; Quiason, S., "Philippines," in ALA World Encyclopedia of Library and Information Services, 2nd ed., pp. 645-647. Chicago: American Library Association, 1986; Khurshid, A., "Library Associations in Asia," Herald of Library Science 28 (1989):3-10.

401   Association of Special Libraries of the Philippines (ASLP)

Address   c/o The National Library, Room 301, T.M. Kalaw Street, Manila 2801. Postal address: PO Box 4118, Manila (permanent). Tel: 63 (2) 590177.
Officers   Pres: Victoria S. Mercado; Past Pres: Jesusa C. Manhit.
Staff   21 (1 paid, 20 volunteers)
Languages   Pilipino, English
Established   1954, Manila.
Major Fields of Interest   Special libraries
Major Goals and Objectives   (1) To promote understanding the nature, scope and importance of the work of special libraries, (2) to foster closer relations, cooperation, and vigorous and wholesome fellowship among members, (3) to encourage the establishment of special libraries in the country as well as to help librarians improve their services, (4) to stimulate professional interest and growth of members, and (5) to enhance and uphold the dignity of the library profession and to observe professional ethics at all times.
Structure   Governed by Executive Council. Affiliations: PLAI (Philippine Library Association, Inc.).
Sources of Support   Membership dues, sale of publications, donations.
Membership   Total members: 270+ (individual). Requirements: Open to those actually engaged and/or professionally trained in library, statistical or research work.
General Assembly   Entire membership meets once a year in Manila.
Publications   *Official journal:* ASLP Bulletin. 1954-. 4/yr. Free to members. Address same as Association. Editor: Angelica A. Cabanero. Circ: 500. English. Indexed in LISA.

Other publications: Annual reports, proceedings of conferences; Directory of Special Library Resources and Research Facilities in the Philippines, etc. Publications available for sale.

Activities Sponsors seminars, conferences, workshops and other regular continuing education programs, as well as other activities involving dissemination of information on special libraries; expansion of publication program.

Bibliography Sacchanand, C., "Training Programs of Library Associations in the Philippines," Journal of Philippine Librarianship 7 (1983):11-26; "Association of Special Libraries of the Philippines," Bulletin of the PLAI 16 (New Series) (1984):80-87; Quiason, S., "Philippines," in ALA World Encyclopedia of Library and Information Services, 2nd ed., pp. 645-647. Chicago: American Library Association, 1986; Khurshid, A., "Library Associations in Asia," Herald of Library Science 28 (1989):3-10.

402 Bibliographical Society of the Philippines (BSP)

Address c/o National Archives, National Library Building, T. M. Kalaw Street, Ermita, Manila (not permanent). Tel: 63 (2) 491114.
Officers Sec-Treas: Leticia R. Maloles.
Languages English
Established 1952, Manila
Major Fields of Interest Bibliographical services, book publishing, history.
Major Goals and Objectives To promote bibliographical research and services in the Philippines; to cooperate in international and regional bibliographical activities; to issue bibliographical publications.
Structure Governed by executive officers.
Sources of Support Membership dues.
Membership Total members: 85+ (individual). Requirements: Any person or institution interested in the objectives of the Association may become a member on payment of dues provided for in the bylaws.
General Assembly Entire membership meets once a year in Manila.
Publications *Official journal:* Newsletter of the Bibliographical Society of the Philippines. 1958-72. New series, 1973-. Irreg. Free to members. Address same as Association. Circ: Membership. English. Other publications: Proceedings of conferences, seminars, and occasional monographs. Publications for sale.
Activities Bibliographical publications; surveying bibliographical activities of libraries, institutions, and individuals to assess the state of bibliographical activities in the Philippines; coordinating and improving bibliographical services; expanding publications program.

403 Philippine Association of Academic and Research Libraries (PAARL)

Address c/o PLAI Headquarters, The National Library, T.M. Kalaw Street, Manila (permanent). Tel: 63 (2) 590177
Officers Exec.Sec: Emelinda de Jesus. Exec.Board: 10
Staff Volunteers
Languages English
Established 1972, Manila
Major Fields of Interest Academic and research libraries
Major Goals and Objectives PAARL represents the libraries of institutions supporting scholarly research and/or formal education on the college level and above. The Association's objectives are: (1) to encourage and promote the collection, organization, and dis-

semination of information on research and academic library work; (2) to develop the usefulness and efficiency of these types of library services and librarianship; (3) to promote
the professional welfare and mutual aid among its members; (4) to cooperate with other
organizations having similar aims.
Structure   Governed by Board of Directors. Affiliations: PLAI (Philippine Library Association, Inc.).
Sources of Support   Membership dues, fund raising. Budget (Philippine Peso): Ap-
prox.14,000.
Membership   Total members: 140. Types of membership: Individual, institutional. Requirements: Individual: Librarian of an academic or research library; Institutional: Academic or research institution. Dues (Philippine Peso): 50, individual; 200, institutional.
General Assembly   Entire membership meets once a year.
Publications   *Official journal:* PAARL Newsletter. 1973-. 4/yr. Free to members. Address same as Association. Circ: Membership. English. Indexed in Index to Philippine Periodicals. Other publications: Annual reports, proceedings of conferences, workshops,
seminars; PAARL Directory, etc. Publications available for sale. Publications exchange
program in effect with libraries.
Activities   Carried out under the guidance of a Committee on Programs and Projects.
Sponsors workshops on current topics; publication program. Active in promoting library-
related legislation in library cooperation. Sponsors Book Week and regular continuing
education programs.
Bibliography   Sacchanand, C., "Training Programs of Library Associations in the Philippines," Journal of Philippine Librarianship 7 (1983):11-26; "Philippine Association of
Academic and Research Libraries," Bulletin of the PLAI 16 (New Series)
(1984):124-126; Quiason, S., "Philippines," in ALA World Encyclopedia of Library and
Information Services, 2nd ed., pp. 645-647. Chicago: American Library Association, 1986;
Khurshid, A., "Library Associations in Asia," Herald of Library Science 28 (1989):3-10.

404   Philippine Association of School Librarians (PASL)

Address   c/o DCS Library, 4th Floor, City Hall, Manila (permanent). Tel: 63 (2)
402011, local 157.
Officers   Pres: Pilar R. Perez; Exec.Sec: Esperanza Nasol. Exec.Comm: 15.
Staff   3 (volunteers)
Languages   English
Established   1977, Quezon City, at the Thomas Jefferson Cultural Center, at the end of
a seminar on current trends in school librarianship.
Major Fields of Interest   School librarianship
Major Goals and Objectives   The Association aims to help school librarians maintain
a high degree of professional dignity and services through seminars, discussions, and library cooperation and coordination. Specifically, the objectives are as follows: (1) To
uphold the dignity and ethics of the library profession; (2) to encourage the creation of
school libraries throughout the country, especially in rural areas; (3) to safeguard the professional interest of its members; (4) to foster and maintain among its members high
ideals of integrity, learning, professional competence, public service and conduct; (5) to
cultivate among its members a spirit of cordiality and fellowship; (6) to encourage and
cultivate library cooperation and establish professional contact with school librarians and
their associations in other countries; (7) to encourage and foster a continuing program of
library education and research and make reports and recommendations thereon; (8) to
provide a forum for the discussion of school librarianship, library reform and the relation

of librarians with other professionals and the public, and publish information in relation thereto.
Structure Governed by Executive Committee.
Sources of Support Membership dues, private donations.
Membership Total members: 190+. Chapters: 4. Requirements: Individual: College degree with credits in library science and/or working in a school library; Institutional: Firms, agencies, and/or institutions interested in school librarianship. Dues (Philippine Peso): 20, individual; 40, institutional; 10, associate.
General Assembly Entire membership meets once a year in May.
Publications No publications program.
Activities Carried out under the guidance of a Committee on Professional Development. Sponsors seminars, conferences, workshops and other continuing education programs, as well as in-service training to upgrade skills of school librarians and to make them aware of current trends in school librarianship; organizing of regional chapters (10 possible regions). Active in promoting library-related legislation. Sponsors Book Week, exhibits.
Bibliography Sacchanand, C., "Training Programs of Library Associations in the Philippines," Journal of Philippine Librarianship 7 (1983):11-26.

405 Philippine Association of Teachers of Library Science (PATLS)

Address c/o PLAI Headquarters, Room 301, The National Library, T. M. Kalaw Street, Manila (permanent). Tel: 63 (2) 590177.
Officers (elected for 1-yr.term) Pres: Trinidad M. Albarracin; VP: Angelina Tamesis; Sec: Maria A. Orendain; Treas: Gloria M. Andrade; Pub.Rel.Off: Juan C. Buenrostro, Jr.; Auditor: Manual Camilo. Exec.Board: 10.
Staff 1 (paid), 10 (volunteers)
Languages English
Established 1964, Manila
Major Fields of Interest Library and information science education; teaching and training.
Major Goals and Objectives To improve library education in the Philippines; to initiate and promote cooperative programs in education for librarianship among schools in the Philippines; to plan and implement a program for the accreditation of library schools; to provide a forum for discussion and publication of issues, trends, and other matters in library education.
Structure Governed by Executive Board. Affiliations: PLAI
Sources of Support Membership dues, sale of publications, income from training seminars and other fund-raising activities. Budget (Philippine Peso): 1986/87: 40,000; 1987/88: 50,000.
Membership Total members: 80 (individual). Types of membership: Individual. Requirements: Any librarian or other professional who is teaching or has taught library and information science. Dues (Philippine Peso): 50.
General Assembly Entire membership meets once a year.
Publications *Official journal:* PATLS Newsletter. 1976-. Irreg. Free to members. Editor: Juan C. Buenrostro, Jr. Address: Institute of Library Science, University of the Philippines, Diliman, Quezon City. Circ: Membership. English. Other publications: The Annual National Book Week Program.
Activities Past achievements: (1) Seminars and workshops on new trends and techniques in teaching library science courses; (2) Participation in the IFLA Working Committees during IFLA Conference held in Manila, 1980; (3) Revision of the undergraduate li-

brary science curriculum and publication of <u>Syllabi of Library Science Courses</u> for use by all library science schools in the Philippines; (4) Publication of <u>Directory of Teachers of Library Science</u>; (5) Organized CONSAL VII in the Philippines in 1987. Current: Seminar on methods and techniques in teaching cataloging and reference; attracting more library science education students. Future: To actively participate in the library networking activities of the Philippine Library Association, Inc. Association has been active in promoting library-related legislation; it co-sponsored the proposed legislation for the professional status of librarians in the country. Sponsors Book Week, exhibits, continuing education programs, and standardization of the library science curriculum for undergraduate programs.

Bibliography   Retrospective sources: Agcaoili, C., "The Philippine Association of Teachers of Library Science and Its Objectives," <u>Bulletin of the PLAI</u> 1 (June 1965); Mercado-Tan, F., "Philippine Librarianship: The Present and the Future," <u>Bulletin of the PLAI</u> 12 (1978-79): Nos.1-4; "Philippine Association of Teachers of Library Science," <u>Bulletin of the PLAI</u> 16 (New Series) (1984):126-130; Khurshid, A., "Library Associations in Asia," <u>Herald of Library Science</u> 28 (1989):3-10.

406   Philippine Library Association, Inc. (PLAI)

Address   Headquarters: c/o The National Library, T. M. Kalaw Street, Manila 2801 (permanent). Tel: 63 (2) 590177.

Officers   (elected for 1-yr.term) Pres: Ms. L.M. Seria; Past Pres: Carmencita E. Sta Cruz; Sec: Ms. M.L.C. Moral. Exec.Board: 11.

Staff   1 (paid)

Languages   English

Established   1923, by 32 librarians, in Manila

Major Fields of Interest   Library and information services.

Major Goals and Objectives   To uphold the dignity and ethics of the library profession as well as of library service at high professional levels; to promote the establishment of libraries throughout the country; to promote cooperation, cordiality and fellowship among librarians; to encourage continuing programs of library education and research; to establish and encourage professional contacts among librarians in the Philippines and with other countries.

Structure   Governed by a House of Delegates, representing 25 sectoral and local library associations. Affiliations: IFLA, CONSAL.

Sources of Support   Membership dues

Membership   Total members: Approx. 1,000. Chapters (associations): 25. Types of membership: Through chapters.

General Assembly   Entire membership meets once a year.

Publications   *Official journal:* <u>Bulletin of the Philippine Library Association, Inc.</u>. 4/yr. (Philippine Peso) 150. (50 US Dollar, foreign). Free to members. Editor: Conrado D. David. Address same as Association. Circ: 1,000 (membership). English. Indexed in <u>Ind.Phil.Per.</u>. Other publications: <u>Newsletter</u>; annual reports, proceedings of meetings, etc.

Activities   The PLAI functions as umbrella organization for all professional library associations in the country (about 28), and represents Philippine librarianship at IFLA (sponsored the 1980 IFLA Conference in Manila). Association plays an important role in organizing and conducting regular training programs, seminars, workshops, conferences, etc., at the local, regional and national levels, and is instrumental in promoting and developing library science and librarianship throughout the country.

Bibliography Sacchanand, C., "Training Programs of Library Associations in the Philippines," Journal of Philippine Librarianship 7 (1983):11-16; Vallejo, R.M., ed., "The PLAI: Its Involvement and Commitment. Diamond Anniversary Issue, 1923-1983," Bulletin of the Philippine Library Association, Inc. 16 (New Series) (1984) Nos.1-2; Quiason, S.D., "Philippines," in ALA World Encyclopedia of Library and Information Services, 2nd ed., pp. 645-647. Chicago: American Library Association, 1986; Khurshid, A., "Library Associations in Asia," Herald of Library Science 28 (1989):3-10.

407 Public Libraries Association of the Philippines (PLAP)

Address c/o PLAI Headquarters, The National Library, T. M. Kalaw Street, Manila (permanent). Tel: 63 (2) 590177.
Languages English
Established 1959, at the Bureau of Public Libraries, Manila, by Laureana Villanueva, Chief of the Extension Division of the National Library
Major Fields of Interest Public library services
Major Goals and Objectives To promote public library services, to promote unity and cooperation among public librarians, to know and understand their library problems, and to provide for a meaningful interchange of ideas among members.
Membership Public librarians (civil servants) at all levels.
General Assembly Entire membership meets once a year.
Publications No publications program.
Activities Conducts Librarians' Conference-Workshops with the National Library every 2 years.
Bibliography Sacchanand, C., "Training Programs of Library Associations in the Philippines," Journal of Philippine Librarianship 7 (1983):11-26; "Public Libraries Association of the Philippines," Bulletin of the PLAI 16 (New Series) (1984):130-134; Khurshid, A., "Library Associations in Asia," Herald of Library Science 28 (1989):3-10.

Poland

408   Stowarzyszenie Archivistów Polskich (SAP)
(Association of Polish Archivists)

Address   ulica Niepodleglosci 162, PL-02443, Warsaw. Tel: 48 (22) 495007.
Languages   Polish
Established   1965
Major Fields of Interest   Archives and records management
Major Goals and Objectives   To promote the development of archives in Poland; to promote the profession of archivists; to represent the professional interests of archivists.
Structure   Governed by executive officers
Sources of Support   Membership dues
Membership   Total members: Approx.800
General Assembly   Entire membership meets once a year.
Publications   *Official journal:* Archiwista. Free to members. Address same as Association. Circ: Membership. Polish. Other publications: Materialy Szkoleniowe.
Activities   Sponsors conferences, workshops, continuing education programs.

409   Stowarzyszenie Bibliotekarzy Polskich (SBP)
(Polish Librarians Association) (PLA)

Address   c/o Zarzad Glówny, ulica Konopczynskiego 5/7, PL-00953 Warsaw (permanent). Tel: 48 (22) 275296 / 270847. Telex: 815360.
Officers   (elected for 4-yr.term) Pres: S. Czajka; Past Pres: Stefan Kubów; Gen.Sec: J. Waluszewski. Exec.Board: 9. Exec.Council: 26
Staff   13 (paid)
Languages   Polish, English, Russian
Established   1917, Warsaw, as Union of Polish Librarians and Archivists; present name adopted 1953.
Major Fields of Interest   Library and information services
Major Goals and Objectives   To promote the interests of libraries within society; to promote library science; to promote library education; to exert influence on book production; to influence national library and information policy.
Structure   Governed by Executive Council and Executive Board. A Conference of Delegates meets every 4 years. Affiliations: IFLA.
Sources of Support   Membership dues, sale of publications; government subsidies only when needed.
Membership   Total members: 12,500 (individual). Sections: 13. Types of membership: Individual, emeritus. Requirements: Employment in library or information center; employment in library school or in offices connected with librarianship. Dues: Individual, scaled according to salary; supporting membership for institutions or organizations.
General Assembly   Entire membership meets every 4 years. 1989: Gdansk, May 15-17; 1993.
Publications   *Official journal:* Przeglad Biblioteczny (Library Review). 1927-. 4/yr. (Zloty) 560. Free to members. Editor: Barbara Sordylawa. Address: Palac Kultury i Nauki, PL-00901 Warsaw. Circ: 13,000 + . Polish, with English summaries. Indexed in LISA, Przeglad Pismiennictwa Informacji Naukowej. Other publications: Bibliotekarz (The Librarian), 1934-. 12/yr.; Poradnik Bibliotekarza (Librarian's Advisor), 12/yr.; Informator Bibliotekarza i Ksiegarza (Guide for Librarians and Booksellers), 1/yr.; Literatura Pie-

kna. Bibliografia adnotowana (Fiction. Annotated Bibliography), 1/yr.; Biblioteka Muzyczna (Music Library), irreg; Kolodziejska, J. Bibliotekarstwo - miedzy teoria a praktyka (1986), etc. Publications for sale.

Activities   Past achievements: Organizing conferences: "Libraries and their role in cultural, scientific and educational policy," 1986; Conference of librarians-councillors to local councils, 1984; introduction of CPI, 1987; initiative in foundation of Library Service Bureau "Ksiaznica," 1987. Current: Modernizing curricula of library education; updating and revising Library Act; preparing conference on state library and information policy until 2,000, "Polish Librarianship Today and Tomorrow."   Future: Promotion of library automation; promotion of cultural work of public libraries; development of book conservation programs.   Active in promoting library-related legislation, such as Library Act (1968), Act on Dissemination of Culture (1984). Sponsors continuing education lectures, seminars, workshops.

Bibliography   Mazurkiewicz, M., "Proposals for Organizational Changes within the Polish Librarians Association," Bibliotekarz 48 (1981):9-10 (in Polish); Mazurkiewicz, M., "Is There Really a Crisis in the Polish Library Association?" ibid.:53-54 (in Polish); Bowden, R., "Poland: A Visit," Focus on International and Comparative Librarianship 13 (1982):14-16; Baumgart, J., Bibliotekarstwo. Biblioteki. Bibliotekarze (Warsaw, 1983); Kubów, S., "Stowarzyszenie Bibliotekarzy Polskich - organizacja zawodowa bibliotekarzy i pracowników informacji naukowe," Aktualne Problemy Informacji i Dokumentacji 3 (1984):3-6; Wolosz, J., "The Convocation of the PLA (May 13-15, 1985)," Library Times International 2 (1985):32; Bobinski, G.S., "Poland," in ALA World Encyclopedia of Library and Information Services, 2nd ed., pp. 649-650. Chicago: American Library Association, 1986.

Portugal

410   Associaçâo Portuguesa de Bibliotecários, Arquivistas e Documentalistas (BAD)
(Portuguese Association of Librarians, Archivists and Documentalists)

Address   Edificio de Biblioteca Nacional, Campo Grande 83, 1700 Lisbon (permanent).
Tel: 351 (19) 767862.
Officers   Pres: Luis Filipe de Abreu Nunes; Past Pres: Ms. M. J. Moura; Secs: Ms. A.
Gonçalves Gordo, Jorge Resende, Maria Isabel Carneiro. Exec.Comm: 5.
Staff   2 (paid), 16 (volunteers)
Languages   Portuguese, English, French
Established   1973, Coimbra.
Major Fields of Interest   Librarianship, archives, documentation
Major Goals and Objectives   To promote the development of libraries, archives, and
documentation centers in Portugal; to represent the members and promote their status
and professional development.
Structure   Governed by executive officers. Affiliations: IFLA, FID, ICA.
Sources of Support   Membership dues, sale of publications, grants for training pro-
grams.
Membership   Total members: 600. Types of membership: Individual, institutional, extraordinary. Requirements: A university degree in information science.
General Assembly   Entire membership meets twice a year.
Publications   *Official journal:* Cadernos de Biblioteconomia, Arquivística e Documentaçâo (Library Management, Archives and Documentation). 2/yr. Free to members. Address same as Association. Portuguese, with English summaries. Newsletter: Notícia BAD.
1973-. 4/yr. Other publications: Proceedings of meetings, seminars, workshops, etc. Publications for sale.
Activities   Extensive training programs and continuing education offerings; establishing
an information network for a national information system.
Bibliography   Cruzeiro, M.M., "Portugal," in ALA World Encyclopedia of Library and
Information Services, 2nd ed., pp. 653-654. Chicago: American Library Association, 1986.

Puerto Rico

411   Sociedad de Bibliotecarios de Puerto Rico (SBPR)
(Puerto Rico Librarians Society)

Address   Apartado 22898, Universidad de Puerto Rico, Rio Piedras, P.R. 00931. Tel: (809) 7640000, ext.2122.
Officers   Pres: Digan Cruz de Escalera (-May 1990); Past Pres: Sylvia Muniz de Olmos; Exec.Sec: Ms. E. Rodríguez.
Staff   None
Languages   Spanish, English
Established   1961, at the University of Puerto Rico by a group of librarians interested in problems related to the profession.
Major Fields of Interest   Librarianship, information science
Major Goals and Objectives   To advance the cause of librarians in Puerto Rico; to gain recognition for the profession; to improve qualifications of members; to recruit the best talent available for the profession; to provide opportunities for professional development of individual members.
Structure   Governed by executive officers. Affiliations: ACURIL, ALA, IFLA.
Sources of Support   Membership dues.
Membership   Total members: 350 (individual). Types of membership: Individual, student, honorary. Requirements: Master or Bachelor degree in Library/Information Science, employed in a professional position, or full-time library science students. Dues (US Dollar): 25, individual; 15, student.
General Assembly   Entire membership meets twice a year in San Juan.
Publications   *Official journal:* Boletín de la SBPR. 1961-. Irreg. Free to members. Address same as Association. Circ: 400. Spanish, English. Indexed in Lib.Lit. Newsletter: Informa, irregular. Other publications: Cuadernos Bibliotecologicos; Cuadernos Bibliograficos, etc. Publications for sale. Publications exchange program in effect with other library associations and libraries.
Activities   Was instrumental in the establishment of the Graduate School of Librarianship at the University of Puerto Rico. Continues working for the improvement of library and information services in Puerto Rico. Active in promoting library-related legislation. Sponsors conferences, seminars, and other continuing education programs.
Bibliography   Ortiz, O.R., and Delgado, R.R., "Puerto Rico," in ALA World Encyclopedia of Library and Information Services, 2nd ed., pp. 685-687. Chicago: American Library Association, 1986.

Romania

412   Asociatia bibliotecarilor din Republica Socialistâ România / Association des Bibliothécaires de la République Socialiste de Roumanie (Librarians' Association of Romania)

Address   Biblioteca Centrala Universitara "Mihail Eminescu," 4 Pacurari Strada, R-6600 Iasi (not permanent). Tel: 40 (981) 40709.
Officers   Pres: C. Stefanache; Exec.Sec: St. Gruia
Staff   None
Languages   Romanian
Established   1956
Major Fields of Interest   Library profession and status of library workers.
Major Goals and Objectives   To promote libraries and library services in Romania; to further the professional development of librarians.
Structure   Governed by executive officers. Affiliations: IFLA.
Sources of Support   Membership dues, government subsidies.
Membership   Total members: Approx. 600 (individual). Regional branches; various committees (university libraries, public libraries, children's libraries, cataloging, union catalog, standards and statistics, library education, buildings, personnel). Types of membership: Individual.
General Assembly   Entire membership meets once a year.
Publications   *Official journal:* Revista Bibliotecilor (Library Review). 1947-. 12/yr. Free to members. Address same as Association. Other publications: Proceedings of conferences, seminars, and other professional monographs. Publications for sale.
Activities   Sponsors conferences, seminars and other continuing education programs. Active in promoting library-related legislation. Represents Romanian librarians at international activities.
Bibliography   Popescu-Brädiceni, A., "Romania," in ALA World Encyclopedia of Library and Information Services, 2nd ed., pp. 711-714. Chicago: American Library Association, 1986.

Scotland

413   Association of Scottish Health Sciences Librarians

Address   c/o Sandra Watson, Librarian, Borders Health Board, Thornfield, Selkirk TD7 4DT, Scotland, United Kingdom (not permanent). Tel: 44 (Selkirk) 20212..
Officers   Pres: Ms. E.A. Ferro; Hon.Sec: Sandra Watson Exec.Comm: 7
Staff   None
Languages   English
Established   1975, Edinburgh
Major Fields of Interest   Health sciences librarianship
Major Goals and Objectives   To promote consideration of matters concerning health sciences libraries and afford a channel for expression of members' views; to identify problems concerned with the development of library services in health sciences and take appropriate action; to provide opportunity for discussions and conferences.
Structure   Governed by executive officers. Affiliations: The Library Association.
Sources of Support   Membership dues
Membership   Total members: 70 (66 individual, 4 institutional). Types of membership: Individual, institutional, associate. Requirements: Open to all health sciences librarians and libraries in Scotland. Dues (Pound Sterling): 5, individual; 4, institutional; 2, associate.
General Assembly   Entire membership meets twice a year, in March and November.
Publications   *Official journal:* Interim. 1977-. 2/yr. Free to members. Address same as Association. Circ: Membership. English.
Activities   Providing opportunities for members to meet for continuing education (some members often isolated); participating in surveys, etc., in an ongoing attempt to improve services in facilities. Active in promoting library-related legislation. Association is represented at the Library Association's consultative meetings on the document "Guidelines for Library Provisions in the Health Service" and gives guidance on the differences between the Scottish Health Service and that for England and Wales. Sponsors, seminars, workshops and other continuing education programs.

414   School Library Association in Scotland

Address   c/o Menzieshill High School, Dundee, Scotland, United Kingdom
Officers   Sec: Ms. E. Scott
Languages   English
Major Fields of Interest   School libraries
Major Goals and Objectives   To promote the establishment and improvement of school libraries in Scotland

415   Scottish Library Association (SLA)

Address   c/o R. Craig, Executive Secretary, Motherwell Business Centre, Coursington Road, Motherwell ML1 1PW, Scotland, United Kingdom (permanent). Tel: 44 (698) 52526/52057. Fax: 44-698-52057.
Officers   (elected for 1-yr.term) Pres: A.R. McElroy (Napier College, Edinburgh); VP: H.J. Heaney; Past Pres: Ms. A. Mackenzie; Treas: G.N. Drummond; Exec.Sec (appointed): Robert Craig. Exec.Comm: 35
Staff   1.5 (paid)

Languages English
Established 1908, Edinburgh
Major Fields of Interest Librarianship and information science
Major Goals and Objectives To unite all persons engaged in or interested in library work throughout Scotland by holding conferences and meetings; to promote whatever may tend to the improvement of library administration and the status and qualifications of librarians in Scotland; to provide opportunities for social intercourse among members.
Structure Governed by Council elected by membership. Affiliations: The Library Association (UK)
Sources of Support Membership dues, sale of publications, conferences and courses.
Membership Total members: 2,300 (2,245 individual, 55 institutional). Requirements: Member of the Library Association and living or working in Scotland. Dues scaled according to income.
General Assembly Entire membership meets once a year in May or June.
Publications *Official journal:* Scottish Libraries (formerly SLA News). 1950-. 6/yr. (Pound Sterling) 16 (17, overseas). Free to members. Address same as Association. Editor: Alan R. Fulton. Circ: 3,000. English. Indexed in LISA, Lib.Lit, etc. Other publications: Annual reports, proceedings of conferences, seminars, and Scottish Library Studies Series, e.g., Sweeney, P.J., ed., The Coinage of Scotland: A Select Bibliography (1983); Scottish Library and Information Resources 1987-1988 (1987); In Search of Excellence: Proceedings of the 72nd Annual Conference of the Scottish Library Association, Peebles 1986, ed. A.F. Taylor (1987), etc. Publications for sale, price lists available. Publications exchange program in effect.
Activities Past achievements: Established standards for public and school library services. Current: Promotion of public and school library standards; supporting the development of policies relative to the provision of information and library services at the national and local level. Future: Establishment of a Scottish Library Council. Association has been active in promoting library-related legislation, such as public library legislation for Scotland. Sponsors Book Week activities, exhibits, and continuing education programs.
Bibliography Craig, R., "Pace of Change: SLA 1908-1983," SLA News 177 (Sept/Oct. 1983):7+; "Council Capers," SLA News 178 (Nov/Dec. 1983):5+; "Robert Craig," (Executive Secretary to the SLA) SLA News 187 (May/June 1985):21-22.

Senegal

416   Association Nationale des Bibliothécaires, Archivistes et Documentalistes Sénégalaises (ANABADS)
(National Association of Librarians, Archivists and Documentalists of Senegal)

Address   EBAD (École de Bibliothécaires, Archivistes et Documentalistes de Dakar), BP 3252, Dakar (permanent). Tel: (221) 230739.
Officers   (elected for 2-yr.term) Pres: Mariétou Diongue Diop; Past Pres: Omar Diallo; Exec.Sec: Mamadou Lamine Ndoye. Exec.Comm: 23
Staff   5 (volunteers)
Languages   French
Established   1973
Major Fields of Interest   Libraries, archives, documentation services
Major Goals and Objectives   To promote the development of libraries, archives, and documentation centers in Senegal; to advance the professional status of members.
Structure   Governed by executive officers. Affiliations: CIA, FID, IFLA.
Sources of Support   Membership dues. Budget (CFA Franc BCEAO): Approx. 190,000.
Membership   Total members: 100+ (individual). Divisions: 3. Requirements: All persons working in institutions concerned with archives, libraries and documentation. Dues (CFA Franc BCEAO): 1,000.
General Assembly   Entire membership meets once a year.
Publications   No official journal.
Activities   Past achievements: Published studies on regional archives and on documentation in Senegal. Worked for a merger of the 2 national professional associations concerned with libraries/archives/documentation (see ASBAD). Current: Publish studies about the status and professional training of librarians and archivists. Future: To hold a national seminar on the latest information technologies, and the transfer of information in all regions. ANABADS played an important role in the passage of laws pertaining to the status of librarians, since 1975. Sponsored continuing education programs.
Additional Information   The Association states that "the lack of financial means and lack of contact with associations in other countries are the reasons for our difficulties in promoting our actions." However, on July 9, 1988, the two library associations in Senegal, ANABADS and ASDBAM, were unified into one national association, l'Association Sénégalaise des Bibliothécaires, Archivistes et Documentalistes (ASBAD), which now represents Senegal internationally, and both ANABADS and ASDBAM ceased to exist as separate associations.
Bibliography   Ndaye, Waly (tr. by M.N. Maack), "Senegal," in ALA World Encyclopedia of Library and Information Services, 2nd ed. pp.755-756. Chicago: American Library Association, 1986.

417   Association Sénégalaise des Bibliothécaires, Archivistes et Documentalistes (ASBAD)
(Senegal Association of Librarians, Archivists and Documentalists)

Address   Headquarters: c/o EBAD (École de Bibliothécaires, Archivistes et Documentalistes de Dakar), BP 3253, Dakar (not permanent). Tel: (221) 230739.
Officers   (elected, 1988-) Pres: Mariétou Diongue Diop; 1st VP: Amadou Lamine Gueye; 2nd VP: Alioune Thioune; Gen.Sec: Mamadou Lamine Ndoye; Asst.Sec: Ousseynou Niang; Exec.Sec: Cheikh Faye; Asst.Exec.Sec: Mamadou Diop; Treas: Ngoné Fall; Asst.Treas: Habibou Niang. Exec.Board: 6. National Council: 22.

Languages French
Established July 9, 1988. Dakar, at EBAD, through the merger of 2 professional associations in Senegal, ANABADS and ASDBAM.
Major Fields of Interest Libraries, archives, and documentation services
Major Goals and Objectives (1) To unify librarians, archivists and documentalists and all those interested in libraries, archives and other centers of documentation; (2) to study all questions of a scientific, technical or administrative nature concerning libraries, archives, documentation centers and their staff; (3) to promote the development of libraries, archives and documentation centers; (4) to encourage scientific research
Structure Governed by Congress and National Council, consisting of Executive Board and representatives of the Regional Branches and Committees. Affiliations: IFLA
Sources of Support Membership dues, various subsidies
Membership Members are the combined membership of the former associations ANABADS and ASDBAM. Regional Branches. Committees: 7 (Archives, Libraries, Documentation, Statutes and Education, Social and Cultural Affairs, Finance, Public Information). Types of membership: Individual, associate, honorary, institutional. Requirements: Individual: Persons engaged in professional work in libraries, archives, or documentation centers; Associate: Persons interested in the development of libraries, archives, and documentation centers, and in the promotion of reading and culture; Institutional: Any institution supporting the goals and objectives of the Association. All subject to payment of membership dues, which are regularly set by Council. No dues for honorary members, who are elected by the Congress.
General Assembly Entire membership meets twice a year.
Publications Publications program being developed.
Activities By unifying the financial and personnel resources in the country, the Association hopes to become a strong national voice for the improvement of libraries, archives and documentation centers. It recognized the contributions of the following professionals by electing them to honorary membership at the constitutional congress in 1988: Amadou Mactar Mbow (Honorary President), Amadou Bousso, Samba Ndoucoumane Gueye, Emmanuel Dadzie, Raphaël Ndiaye, Saliou Mbaye, Théodore Ndiaye. The Association functions as the single representative of Senegal at IFLA.
Bibliography "Procès Verbal du Congrès Constitutif de l'Association Sénégalaise des Bibliothécaires, Archivistes et Documentalistes (ASBAD), tenu à Dakar le 9 Juillet 1988." 3 pp. Typescript; ASBAD, "Statuts." Dakar, 9 July 1988. 5 pp. Typescript.

418   Commission des Bibliothèques de l'ASDBAM, Association Sénégalaise pour le Développement de la Documentation, des Bibliothèques, des Archives et des Musées (ASDBAM. Commission des Bibliothèques)
(Senegal Association for the Development of Documentation, Libraries, Archives and Museums. Commission of Libraries)

Address BP 375, Dakar. Tel: (221) 210954.
Officers Pres: S.Nd. Gueye; Sec.Gen: E.K.W. Dadzie
Languages French
Established 1957
Major Fields of Interest Libraries, archives, documentation, museums
Major Goals and Objectives To promote the development of libraries, archives, and documentation centers in Senegal.
Structure Affiliations: IFLA
Activities On July 9, 1988, the Association merged with ANABADS to create a new national association, l'Association Sénégalaise des Bibliothécaires, Archivistes et Documentalistes (ASBAD), which represents Senegal internationally.

Sierra Leone

419   Sierra Leone Association of Archivists, Librarians and Information Scientists (SLAALIS)

Address   c/o Sierra Leone Library Board, PO Box 326, Freetown (permanent). Tel: 23848.
Officers   (elected for 2-yr.term) Pres: Ms. Abator Thomas; Sec: Peter K. Kargbo. Exec.Comm: 13
Staff   None
Languages   English
Established   1970, as Sierra Leone Library Association (SLLA); present name adopted to reflect the expansion in membership and fields of interest.
Major Fields of Interest   Libraries, archives, and information centers
Major Goals and Objectives   To promote the development of libraries, archives and information services in Sierra Leone; to represent the interests of members and further their professional development.
Structure   Governed by Executive Council. Affiliations: COMLA, IFLA.
Sources of Support   Membership dues, sale of publications, government subsidies.
Membership   Total members: Approx.100, mainly individual. Types of membership: Individual, institutional, honorary. Requirements: An interest in libraries, archives, and information science.
General Assembly   Entire membership meets 3 times a year.
Publications   *Official journal:* Sierra Leone Library Journal. 1974-. 2/yr. (Leone) 1.50. Free to members. Address same as Association. Editor: Ms. A.M. Thomas. Address: Milton Margai Teachers College, Private Mail Bag, Goderich near Freetown). Circ: 200. English. Indexed in LISA. Other publications: Directory of Libraries and Information Services; annual reports, proceedings of meetings, seminars. Publications for sale.
Activities   Works for the improvement and development of libraries, archives, and information services in Sierra Leone, concentrating on rural libraries and resource centers. Sponsors continuing education workshops, seminars, etc.
Bibliography   Jusu-Sheriff, G.M., "Sierra Leone," in ALA World Encyclopedia of Library and Information Services, 2nd ed., pp. 764-765. Chicago: American Library Association, 1986.

420   Sierra Leone School Library Association

Address   c/o Sierra Leone Library Board, PO Box 326, Freetown. Tel: 23848.
Languages   English
Established   1975
Major Fields of Interest   School librarianship
Major Goals and Objectives   To promote the establishment of school libraries in Sierra Leone.
Membership   Regional branches: 4
Bibliography   Jusu-Sheriff, G.M., "Sierra Leone," in ALA World Encyclopedia of Library and Information Services, 2nd ed., pp. 764-765. Chicago: American Library Association, 1986.

Singapore

421   Library Association of Singapore (LAS)

Address   Headquarters: c/o The National Library, Stamford Road, Singapore 0617
(permanent). Tel: (65) 3377355.   Postal address: c/o NBDCS Secretariat, Bukit Merah
Branch Library, Bukit Merah Central, Singapore 0315.
Officers   (elected for 1-yr.term, 1989-90) Pres: Jenny Neo; Hon.Sec: Glenda Gwee;
Asst.Hon.Sec: Ms. Hermin Pereira; Hon.Treas: Ms. Chan Mee Lee. Past Pres: R. Rama-
chandran. Exec.Comm: 11
Staff   None
Languages   English, Chinese, Malay
Established   1955, as the Malayan Library Group; when Singapore became an inde-
pendent republic in 1965, it divided into two associations, the Library Association of Ma-
laysia, and the Library Association of Singapore; in 1972, the English name was adopted
as the official one.
Major Fields of Interest   Librarianship and library development, education for librarianship, professional conduct and ethics.
Major Goals and Objectives   To unite and promote the interests of all those interested
in Singapore libraries and those actively engaged in library work; to encourage the estab- ·
lishment and development of libraries, library administration, and the professional education of librarians; to publish information that will prove of service to members.
Structure   Governed by Executive Council. Affiliations: COMLA, CONSAL, IFLA.
Sources of Support   Membership dues, sale of publications.
Membership   Total members: 405. Types of membership: Individual, institutional, life,
honorary, associate, teacher-librarian. Requirements: Open to professional librarians,
those engaged in full-time library work, teacher librarians, interested persons not in the
library field, libraries, and institutions interested in the aims of the Association. Dues
(Singapore Dollar): 15, individual; 30, institutional; 15-20, others.
General Assembly   Entire membership meets annually in Singapore, in March.
Publications   *Official journal:* Singapore Libraries. 1971-. 1/yr. (Singapore Dollar) 18.
Free to members. Editor: Bruce Royan. Address same as Association. Circ: 550. English,
occasionally Chinese, Malay. Indexed in LISA, Lib.Lit. Other publications: LAS Newslet-
ter, 4/yr; Directory of Libraries in Singapore; Standards for Bibliographical Compila-
tions; annual reports, proceedings of conferences, and other occasional publications.
Price lists available. Publications exchanged with other associations.
Activities   Past achievements: Instrumental in founding of CONSAL; revision of copyright legislation; Registration of Professional Librarians Act; organized basic part-time
Postgraduate Course in Library and Information Science with the National Library in
1982. Current and future: Sponsors seminars, celebration of Book Week, exhibits, regular
continuing education programs (together with the National Library). Works closely with
the Library Association of Malaysia (PPM) and maintains a joint liaison council for various bibliographical projects. Association is seeking support from the Government to establish a School of Information Studies, and prepared a curriculum with an emphasis on
information technology and management.
Bibliography   Wee, J.G., "Library Association of Singapore on the Move," Singapore
Libraries 11 (1981):3-9; Seng, C.T., "Point of View: IFLA and LAS," Singapore Libraries
15 (1985):39-44; Anuar, H., "Singapore," in ALA World Encyclopedia of Library and Information Services, 2nd. ed., pp. 365-367. Chicago: American Library Association, 1986;
Zaiton, O., "The Role of the Professional Association in Preparing Its Members for New

Trends," in <u>Singapore-Malaysia Congress of Librarians and Information Scientists [1986: Singapore]. The New Information Professionals,</u> pp. 32-45. Gower, 1987; Khurshid, A., "Library Associations in Asia," <u>Herald of Library Science</u> 28 (1989):3-10; Thuraisingham, A., "Library Association of Singapore," <u>COMLA Newsletter</u> 65 (Sept. 1989):13-14.

South Africa

422   African Library Association of South Africa (ALASA)

Address   c/o Library, University of the North, Private Bag X 5090, Pietersburg 0700.
Tel: Sovenga 33. Telex: 30808.
Officers   Sec/Treas: Ms. A. N. Kambule; Hon.Sec: G.K. Motshologane (Private Bag X
1112, Sovenga 0727)
Staff   None
Languages   English, Afrikaans
Established   1964, in Mamelodi African Township, as Bantu Library Association of
South Africa (BLASA).
Major Fields of Interest   Library services
Major Goals and Objectives   To improve library services for the African population in
South Africa.
Structure   Governed by Executive Council. Affiliations: SAILIS
Sources of Support   Membership dues
Membership   Total members: Approx. 300. Has various branches. Types of member-
ship: Individual, institutional. Requirements: Open to all persons interested in the aims of
the Association.
General Assembly   Entire membership meets every 2 years.
Publications   *Official journal:* ALASA Newsletter (formerly BLASA Newsletter). 1967-.
4/yr. Free to members. Address same as Association.
Activities   Sponsors conferences, seminars, and other continuing education programs.
Many activities are carried out by the branches, e.g. the Zululand Branch (c/o University
Library, University of Zululand, Private Bag X 1001, Kwa-Dlangezwa 3886, Zululand).
Although the reorganization of the South African Library Association into SAILIS in
1980 made separate associations for ethnic groups no longer necessary, this Association
has continued to work effectively for its stated goals.
Bibliography   Musiker, R. Companion to South African Libraries (Johannesburg,
1985); Musiker, R., "South Africa," in ALA World Encyclopedia of Library and Information Services, 2nd. ed., pp. 768-770. Chicago: American Library Association, 1986.

423   Bophuthatswana Library Association (BLA)

Address   PO Box 5002, Mmabatho, Bophuthatswana 8681, Southern Africa (perma-
nent). Tel: 27 (1401)292372
Officers   (elected for 1-yr. term) Chair: Andrew Khutsoane; Hon.Sec: Victor Ndaba;
Hon.Treas: June Smith. Exec.Board: 7
Staff   None
Languages   English
Established   Sept. 21, 1985.
Major Fields of Interest   Libraries and librarianship
Major Goals and Objectives   To stimulate and encourage an awareness of the impor-
tance of libraries in the development of a new, independent (1977), and educationally dis-
advantaged nation, and of the need to support professional development.
Structure   Governed by Executive Board. Affiliations: None as yet.
Sources of Support   Membership dues, sale of publications (a minor source).
Membership   Requirements: Professional qualification, involvement in library work, or
interest in the development of libraries and dissemination of information. Dues (South
African Rand): 15, institutional; 10, individual (both professional and non-professional)

General Assembly   Entire membership meets once a year
Publications   *Official journal:* B.L.A. Newsletter. 1986-. 2/yr. (South African Rand) 1.50 per issue. Free to members. Address same as Association. Editor: J. Phehane. Address: University of Bophuthatswana, Private Bag X 2104, Mafikeng 8670. Circ: 100+. English. Issues annual reports.
Activities   Past achievements: First annual conference, 20-21 Sept. 1986, with theme "The Impact of Libraries on the Educational Process." Current and future: Expanding membership; organizing interesting and stimulating meetings for members; planning Book Exhibit by 8 publishers (Southern African and overseas publishers represented in Southern Africa), with facilities for on-the-spot ordering, aimed at teacher training college level.

424   Library Association of Transkei (LATRA)

Address   c/o University of Transkei Library, Private Bag X2, UNITRA, Umtata, Republic of Transkei, Southern Africa (permanent). Tel: 27 (471) 26811. Telex: 754 TT.
Officers   (elected for 1-yr.term) Chair: S.A. Brink; Hon.Sec: I.E. Nhlapo; Hon.Treas: R. Moropa. Exec.Comm: 10.
Staff   3 (volunteers)
Languages   English
Established   Nov. 11, 1981, at a meeting of interested persons.
Major Fields of Interest   School librarianship; librarianship and information science
Major Goals and Objectives   To promote librarianship and information science in Transkei; to further education and training of librarians and information specialists.
Structure   Governed by Executive Committee. Affiliations: SAILIS
Sources of Support   Membership dues, sale of publications, private donations. Budget (Rand): Approx. 3,000.
Membership   Total members: 60 (58 individual, 2 institutional). 3 countries represented. Requirements: Interest in library work or librarianship.
General Assembly   Entire membership meets once a year, usually on last Thursday in July
Publications   *Official journal:* INQILO (Newsletter). 1987-. Irreg. Free to members. Address same as Association. Circ: Membership. English. Other publications: How to Run Your School Library: A Library Manual for Transkei Schools. Publications program still in planning stage.
Activities   Publishing program; regular radio reviews of Xhosa books for children; organizing exhibitions of children's books (some in conjunction with the Department of Library and Information Science at the University of Transkei); holding a regional conference on Black librarianship in 1988. Sponsors Book Week, lectures, seminars, workshops, and other continuing education programs.
Bibliography   Tötemeyer, A.J., "The State of Libraries and Librarianship in Transkei," South African Journal of Library and Information Science 53 (1985):59-64.

425   South African Institute of Librarianship and Information Science / Suid-Afrikaanse Instituut vir Biblioteek en Inligtingwese (SAILIS/SAIBI)

Address   PO Box 36575, Menlo Park, Pretoria 0102 (permanent). Tel: 27 (12) 464967.
Officers   (elected for 2-yr.term) Pres: Seth Manaka; Past Pres: Ms. S.S. Wallis; Hon.Sec: W.W. Duminy. Exec.Comm: 8.
Staff   2 (paid)
Languages   English, Afrikaans

Established 1930, as South African Library Association. The new name and Constitution were adopted in 1980 to make the Association into a multiracial organization that would include the "segregated library associations for Blacks, Indians, and Coloureds" (R. Musiker, p.770 below).

Major Fields of Interest Librarianship and information science

Major Goals and Objectives Promotion of library science and information science amongst all population groups in South Africa and to ensure that library and information services of a high standard are rendered.

Structure Governed by Council and Executive Committee.

Sources of Support Membership dues. Budget (Rand): Approx. 80,000.

Membership Total members: 2,530 (2,260 individual, 270 institutional). Branches (geographical): 8. Types of membership: Individual, institutional, honorary, fellows, professional associates, affiliated members. Requirements: Varied, according to type of membership, from professional librarian with diploma to an interest in the goals of the Association, for individuals, and any institutions rendering library and information services. Dues (Rand): 30-75, individual; 25, associate; 10, students; 40-60, institutional.

General Assembly Entire membership meets once a year.

Publications *Official journal:* South African Journal of Library and Information Science / Suid-Afrikaanse Tydskrif vir Biblioteek- en Inligtingkunde (formerly South African Libraries / Suid-Afrikaanse Biblioteke; incorporating the South African Journal for Librarianship and Information Science). 1930-. 4/yr. (Rand) 50. Free to members. Editor: Magda Bornman. Address: Bureau for Scientific Publications, PO Box 1748, Pretoria 0001. Circ: Approx. 2,600. English, Afrikaans. Indexed in Lib.Lit., LISA, INSPEC-Computer and Control Abstracts. Journal published jointly with Bureau for Scientific Publications. Other publications: SAIBI/SAILIS Nuusbrief/Newsletter. 1947-. 12/yr. (Rand) 7.50, free to members; annual reports, proceedings of conferences, seminars, etc. Publications for sale.

Activities Activities are carried out by the geographical branches, and by a subject division for law, coordinated by an Administrative Council. Organizes conferences, seminars, and other continuing education programs. In accordance with the stated goals and objectives of the Association representing all racial groups in South Africa, an African President was elected in 1989.

Bibliography Hooper, A.S.C., "SAILIS: Where is It Going?" South African Journal of Librarianship and Information Science 51 (1983):11-17; Musiker, R., Companion for South African Libraries (Johannesburg, 1985); Musiker, R., "South Africa," in ALA World Encyclopedia of Library and Information Services, 2nd. ed., pp. 768-770. Chicago: American Library Association, 1986; Hooper, A.S.C., "SAILIS: Possible Future Directions," Wits Journal of Librarianship & Information Science 4 (1986):19-32; Lessing, C.J.H., "Die Suid-Afrikaanse Biblioteekvereniging en biblioteekopleiding in Suid-Afrika," (The South African Library Association and Library Training in South Africa), South African Journal of Library and Information Science 55 (1987):277-289, Afrikaans, with English summary; Louw, Anna, "South African Librarianship: The Position of SAILIS," New Library World 88 (1987):144-146; "South African Librarians Speak Against Censorship," American Libraries 18 (1987):887.

426 Transvaal School Media Association / Transvaalse Skoolmediavereniging (TSMA/TSMV)

Address Private Bag X 290, Pretoria 0001 (permanent). Tel: (12) 3231274/5/6/7

Officers (elected for 2-yr.term) Chair: Ms. C.F.M. van Wyk; Vice-Chair: J.E. Schutte; Hon.Sec: Ms. R. Reitsma. Exec.Comm: 12

Staff   3 (volunteers)
Languages   English, Afrikaans
Established   1958
Major Fields of Interest   School media centers and the use of media in education; guidance to teacher librarians on all aspects of media use; school and educational library and audiovisual services.
Major Goals and Objectives   To promote and extend media use in education; to stimulate interest in literature for children and young adults; to promote interest in and use of all educational media through purposeful development of skills in the use of media; to organize conferences, symposia and seminars in order to meet specific needs.
Structure   Governed by Executive Committee under the auspices of the Transvaal Educational Media Service.
Sources of Support   Membership dues, sale of publications. Budget (Rand): Approx. 390,000.
Membership   Total members: 835 (335 individual, 500 institutional). Requirements: Individuals who teach or who are concerned with the use of educational media, educational institutions which subscribe to the objectives of the Association.
General Assembly   Entire membership meets once a year.
Publications   *Official journal:* School Media Centre / Skoolmediasentrum. 1969-. 2/yr. (Rand) 10 (12.50, overseas). Free to members. Editor: Ms. C.F.M. van Wyk. Address same as Association. Circ: 2,000. English, Afrikaans. Other publications: Annual reports, proceedings of conferences, School Media Centre, Special edition, 1984 (with selected articles from journal).
Activities   Past achievements: Revising Constitution of the Association; drawing up criteria for the evaluation of ready reference and non-fiction books; organizing a symposium on the use of educational media, and establishing working groups to promote the use of educational media; publishing a series of articles on South African illustrators of children's books. Current: Publishing journal; arranging branch meetings where topical matters are discussed; promoting children's books; exchanging ideas among teacher librarians and classroom teachers on integration of educational media with the school program; organizing symposia, seminars, etc. Future: Expanding membership with a view to establish a national association. Sponsors continuing education programs, exhibits.
Use of High Technology   Computers (IBM PC) used for management.

Spain

427 Asociación Española de Archiveros, Bibliotecarios, Museólogos y Documentalistas (ANABAD)
(Spanish Association of Archivists, Librarians, Museologists and Documentalists)

Address Paseo de Calvo Sotelo 22, Madrid 1 (permanent). Tel: 34 (1) 2756800.
Officers Pres: J.G. Morales; Sec: Ms. C. Iníguez Galíndez. Exec.Comm: 13
Staff 1 (paid)
Languages Spanish
Established 1949, Madrid, as Asociación Nacional de Bibliotecarios, Archiveros y Arqueólogos (ANABA); 1978, new statutes and new name, Asociación Nacional de Bibliotecarios, Archiveros, Arqueólogos y Documentalistas, to expand membership to documentalists, and later to museum curators.
Major Fields of Interest Libraries, archives, museums, documentation.
Major Goals and Objectives To improve the services of libraries, archives, museums, and documentation centers by means of professional personnel; to produce research studies and projects especially related to the practices of librarianship; to issue professional publications, catalogs, bibliographies; to maintain an information center; to cooperate with other organizations of a similar nature, particularly those in Latin American countries.
Structure Governed by Executive Council. Affiliations: FESABID, IFLA (through FESABID).
Sources of Support Membership dues, sale of publications, government and private subsidies.
Membership Total members: 1,500 (individual). Committees: 3 (Public Relations, Education, Publications). Working Groups: 6 (Municipal Archives, Methods of Education and Training, Public Libraries, Historical Archives, Diplomacy, Information Studies). Types of membership: Individual. Requirements: University graduates working in a library, archive, museum or documentation center.
General Assembly Entire membership meets annually in Madrid.
Publications *Official journal:* Boletín de la ANABAD. 1949-. 3/yr. (Spanish Peseta) 400. Free to members. Address same as Association. Circ: 2,000. Spanish. Other publications: Annual reports, proceedings of conferences; series of monographs on special topics of current professional interest. Publications for sale.
Activities Publication of Bulletin and other professional monographs; organizing the national conferences; establishing committees concerned with certain special professional problems; professional education, both basic education and continuing education programs for members; cooperation with other institutions and organizations sharing common interests. Representation of the professions at the international level has been assumed by FESABID since 1989.
Bibliography Escolar-Sobrino, H., "Spain," in ALA World Encyclopedia of Library and Information Services, 2nd.ed., pp. 770-772. Chicago: American Library Association, 1986.

428 Federación Española de Sociedades de Archivística, Biblioteconomía, Documentación y Museística (FESABID)
(Federation of Spanish Archival, Library, Documentation, and Museum Associations)

Address c/o Calle Joaquín Costa, 22, 28020 Madrid (not permanent).

Officers Executive Board consists of President, Secretary/Archivist, and Treasurer.
Languages Spanish
Established 1988, Madrid. Statutes signed by 4 associations: (1) La Asociación Andaluza de Bibliotecarios (AAB) (Andalusian Library Association), (2) La Asociación Española de Archiveros, Bibliotecarios, Museólogos y Documentalistas (ANABAD) (Spanish Association of Archivists, Librarians, Museologists and Documentalists), (3) La Sociedad Española de Documentación e Información Científica (SEDIC) (Spanish Society for Scientific Information and Documentation), and (4) La Societat Catalana de Documentació i Informació (SOCADI) (Catalanian Society for Documentation and Information).
Major Fields of Interest Professional organizations in the fields of archives, libraries, documentation centers, and museums
Major Goals and Objectives (1) Promote and develop professional activities in Spain, and contribute to the improvement of conditions for member associations to carry out their activities; (2) promote the cooperation between member associations and facilitate the exchange of information about their respective activities, as well as their expertise and experiences; (3) publicize the functions and further the professional image and status of those who work in the fields with which the Federation is concerned.
Structure Governed by General Assembly consisting of representatives of member associations, and Executive Board. Affiliations: IFLA
Sources of Support Membership dues, government subsidy.
Membership Total members: Founding members are the 4 associations who signed the Statutes. Each member made an initial contribution of 10,000 Spanish Pesetas. Membership dues will be calculated for each member according to situation.
General Assembly Entire membership meets twice a year.
Activities The Federation aims to strengthen Spanish professional activities in these fields and will act as a unified body representing the Spanish professions at the international level.

429 Sociedad Española de Documentación e Información Científica (SEDIC) (Spanish Society for Scientific Information and Documentation)

Address c/o Facultad de Ciencias, Universidad Autónoma de Madrid, Canto Blanco, 28049 Madrid (permanent). Tel: 34 (1) 7340116. ext.1792. Telex: 27810.
Officers (elected for 4-yr.term) Pres: Emilia Currás Puente; VP: Paloma Postela; Sec: Ricardo Lucas; Treas: María del Mar Zulueta; Vice-Sec: Concepción Borreguero. Exec.Board: 5
Staff 1 (paid), 6 (volunteers)
Languages Spanish
Established 1976, Madrid; first Assembly, June 28, 1977
Major Fields of Interest Information science, librarianship, archival studies
Major Goals and Objectives To further education, training and professional development of information scientists, librarians and archivists
Structure Governed by General Assembly and Executive Council. Affiliations: FESABID, IFLA (through FESABID).
Sources of Support Membership dues, sale of publications. Budget (Spanish Peseta): 1986/87: 600,000; 1987/88: 800,000.
Membership Total members: 250 (individual). Divisions: 4. Requirements: To be a professional information scientist, librarian, or archivist; students and interested persons as associate members. Dues (Spanish Peseta): 3,500.
General Assembly Entire membership meets once a year.

Publications   *Official journal:* Boletín de Noticias de SEDIC. 1977-. 3/yr. Address same as Association. Circ: Membership. Spanish.

Activities   The Association is active in the following areas: (1) Education and training: Organization of formal professional studies in documentation, and continuing education seminars, etc.; (2) Publications: Professional journal and expanding professional publications program; (3) National and international relations: Collaboration with all Spanish organizations concerned with documentation, particularly in the field of application of new technologies; collaborating with Portuguese organizations in sponsoring a congress on scientific and technical information in Salamanca in 1988; (4) Research and studies: Supporting various projects, such as survey of the current situation of documentalists in Spain; and a study of the needs in documentation in Spain; (5) Relations with members: Organizing conferences, study visits, seminars and various continuing education programs; expanding membership.

Sri Lanka

430   Sri Lanka Library Association (SLLA)

Address   Organisation of Professional Associations (OPA) Centre, 275/75 Bauddhaloka Mawatha, Colombo 7 (permanent). Tel: 94 (1) 589103.
Officers   (elected for 1-yr.term, 1989-90) Pres: Ms. C.L.M. Nethsingha (Ceylon Institute of Scientific & Industrial Research); VP: J. Lankage (Univ. of Kelaniya); Gen.Sec: M.F. Hamid (Central Bank); Asst.Sec: G.M. Punchi Banda Gallaba; Treas: Anton D. Nallathamby. Past Pres: W.B. Dorakumbure. Exec.Council: 16
Staff   1 (paid), plus volunteers
Languages   Sinhala, Tamil, English
Established   1960, Colombo, as Ceylon Library Association, sponsored by the Department of Cultural Affairs with Unesco's encouragement; incorporated in 1974 under present name.
Major Fields of Interest   Libraries and librarianship
Major Goals and Objectives   To promote the establishment, extension, and improvement of library services in Sri Lanka and to set up professional standards; to represent the interests and welfare of librarians; to train librarians; to promote library cooperation nationally and internationally; to maintain a library of professional literature.
Structure   Governed by Executive Council. Affiliations: COMLA, IFLA.
Sources of Support   Membership dues, government subsidies.
Membership   Total members: 700. Sections: 4 (Special Libraries, Departmental Libraries, Academic Libraries, Public Libraries). Regional Groups: 3 (Western, Central and Northern Regions). Types of membership: Individual, institutional, honorary, student, affiliated, corresponding. Requirements: Members of the library profession or those interested in the aims of the Association. Dues (Sri Lanka Rupee): Individual, scaled according to income and working status; 30, institutional.
General Assembly   Entire membership meets annually in Colombo. 1989: Ceylon Institute of Scientific & Industrial Research, March 27.
Publications   *Official journal:* Sri Lanka Library Review (until 1974, Ceylon Library Review). 1962-. 2/yr. Free to members. Editor: Ms. S.N. Nawana. Address same as Association. Circ: 700+. Other publications: SLLA Newsletter, 4/yr.; annual reports, proceedings of conferences, etc.
Activities   Organizes conferences, seminars on specialized topics, such as "Current Trends in Information Technology" (1988, 1989), and other continuing education and training programs.
Bibliography   Goonetileke, H.A.I., "Sri Lanka," in ALA World Encyclopedia of Library and Information Services, 2nd. ed., pp. 784-785. Chicago: American Library Association, 1986; Khurshid, A., "Library Associations in Asia," Herald of Library Science 28 (1989):3-10; "Sri Lanka Library Association," COMLA Newsletter 65 (Sept. 1989):13.

Sudan

431   Sudan Library Association (SLA)

Address   PO Box 1361, Khartoum (permanent). Tel: 75100 ext.235.
Officers   Exec.Sec: Mohamed Omar.
Staff   None
Languages   Arabic, English
Established   1969, Khartoum, by members of the library staff at the University of Khartoum.
Major Fields of Interest   Library science and documentation; status of members; book publishing
Major Goals and Objectives   To promote library science and documentation; to advance the professional status of librarians; to encourage book publishing in Sudan.
Structure   Governed by Executive Council. Affiliations: The Association used to be a member of IFLA. Currently, only the Library of the University of Gezira (PO Box 20, Wad Medani) is an IFLA member.
Sources of Support   Membership dues.
Membership   Total members: Approx.180. Types of membership: Individual, institutional, student. Requirements: Open to all individuals and institutions interested in promoting the theory and practice of librarianship.
General Assembly   Entire membership meets once a year.
Publications   *Official journal:* Journal of the Sudan Library Association (supersedes Sudan Library Bulletin). 1975-. 1/yr. Free to members. Address same as Association. Circ: membership. Arabic, English.
Activities   No activities reported in the eighties. The British Council and the U.S. Information Center continue their support of Sudanese librarians by sponsoring meetings and colloquia (see M.M. Aman and S.A. Khalifa, p. 787 below).   This association appears to have been superseded by the newly formed Sudan Association for Library and Information Science (1988).
Bibliography   Aman, M.M., and Khalifa, Sha'Ban A., "Sudan," in ALA World Encyclopedia of Library and Information Services, 2nd. ed., pp. 786-787.   Chicago: American Library Association, 1986.

432   Sudan Association for Library and Information Science (SALIS)

Address   c/o Dr. Radia Adam, President, SALIS, School of Library and Information Studies, University of Khartoum, PO Box 321, Khartoum.
Officers   Pres: Dr. Radia Adam
Languages   Arabic, English
Established   Jan. 1988, at a conference addressed by the Prime Minister.
Major Fields of Interest   Library and information science, national information policy.
Major Goals and Objectives   To promote library and information science in the Sudan; to develop a national information policy; to promote the professional status and professional development of librarians and information scientists.
Structure   Governed by executive officers.
Sources of Support   Membership dues, government subsidies
Membership   Total members: Approx.300 (individual)
General Assembly   Entire membership meets once a year.
Publications   *Official journal:* Not yet established.

Activities   Association still in early stage of development; has been preparing papers on the need for a national information policy for a conference held by the National Council for Research in April 1989; is trying to establish links with professional associations in other countries.
Bibliography   "Sudan," FOCUS on International & Comparative Librarianship 20 (1989):9.

Swaziland

433   Swaziland Library Association (SWALA)

Address   PO Box 2309, Mbabane (permanent). Tel: 42633. Telex (c/o National Library) 2270.
Officers   Chair: Benjamin J.K. Kingsley; Sec: M.W.K. Gyimah; Treas: Esther Nxumalo. Exec.Comm: 7.
Staff   None
Languages   English
Established   1984, April 28, at Mbabane Library
Major Fields of Interest   Libraries and librarianship
Major Goals and Objectives   To promote the development of libraries and library services in Swaziland; to coordinate and improve national library services.
Structure   Governed by Executive Committee. Affiliations: COMLA, IFLA, LA (Community Services Group).
Sources of Support   Membership dues.
Membership   Total members: 72 (66 individual, 6 institutional). Requirements: Librarians, libraries, and other individuals and institutions interested in the aims of the Association. Dues (Lilangeni Rand): Approx. 3.2.
General Assembly   Entire membership meets once a year, usually the first week of June.
Publications   *Official journal:* SWALA Journal. 1984-. 1/yr. Free to members. Editor: Henry Oua-Agyemang. Address: The Library, University of Swaziland, Private Bag, Kwaluseni. Circ: Membership. English. Other publications: Proceedings of meetings, reports of seminars, workshops, a newsletter. All publications for sale.
Activities   Past achievements: (1) Forming the Association; (2) Organizing workshop on coordination and improvement of national information services, Mbabane, Feb. 1986; (3) organizing Eastern and Southern African Regional Branch of the International Council on Archives General Conference, at Mbabane, Nov. 1986. Current: (1) Establishing union catalogue; (2) organizing and hosting the Standing Conference of Eastern, Central and Southern African Librarians, SCECSAL VIII, July 1988 (Theme: Library and Information Services for the Disadvantaged). Future: (1) Adoption of legislation drafted in 1985; (2) formulation of National Information Policy. Association has been active in promoting library-related legislation, such as drafting the National Library Service Act of 1985.
Bibliography   Kuzwayo, A.W.Z., "Swaziland," in ALA World Encyclopedia of Library and Information Services, 2nd. ed., pp. 788-789. Chicago: American Library Association, 1986; "Swaziland Library Association Executive Committee 1986/87," COMLA Newsletter 55 (Mar. 1987):15.

Sweden

434   DIK Förbundet / The Swedish Federation of Employees in the Documentation and Cultural Fields (DIK Federation)

Address   Ryssviksvägen 2, S-13106 Nacka. Postal address: PO Box 760, S-13124 Nacka (permanent). Tel: 46 (8) 7162880.
Officers   Pres: Britt-Marie Häggström; VP: Thomas M. Larsson; Union Sec: Birgitta Rydell. Board of Management: 12
Staff   40 (paid)
Languages   Swedish
Established   1972, as the professional organization/union for those employed in the fields of documentation, information and culture (DIK = Dokumentation, Information, Kultur)
Major Fields of Interest   Documentation, information, culture; conditions of employment, salaries, education.
Major Goals and Objectives   All members should receive a salary which is commensurate with their education, their qualifications, and their responsibilities. Higher quality of education and training.
Structure   7 professional associations make up the DIK Federation, three of which are related to libraries and archives. These are: The Swedish Association of Employees in Archives and Record Offices (ARK), The Swedish Association of Public Librarians (Svenska Folkbibliotekarieförbundet/SFF), and The Association of Research Library Staff, Sweden (Vetenskapliga Bibliotekens Tjänstemannaförening/VBT). Federation is governed by a Congress of 60 delegates, meeting every third year, by a Representative Assembly of 20 delegates, meeting in intermediate years, and by a Board of Management of 12 members. Each member association has its own Board of Management. Affiliations: Swedish Confederation of Professional Associations, SACO-SR.
Sources of Support   Membership dues
Membership   Total members: 10,000 (individual). Sections: 8. Committees: 3 (Labor Market, Negotiating with Municipal, Governmental and Private Sectors, Educational). Types of membership: Individual. Requirements: University degree or qualified employment in documentation, information or cultural fields. Dues (Swedish Krona): 110 a month, fulltime employed individual; 60 a year, student. Dues include member's contribution to Unemployment Fund.
General Assembly   Member associations have their own annual general meetings. Delegates meet once a year in a representative assembly.
Publications   *Official journal:* DIK-forum. 1984-. 20/yr. (Swedish Krona) 125. Free to members. Address same as Federation. Circ: 11,000+. Swedish. Other occasional publications: A manual for new members, etc.
Activities   Past achievements: The organization has expanded and is now known among employers of all fields. Current: Through negotiation activities and promotion seeks to improve salaries and working conditions of members. Members include archivists, librarians, administrators, curators, etc. Works towards pay equality for employees in the municipal, governmental and private sectors, and for a six-hour working day for all employees. Quality education and training are considered most important areas, both basic and continuing education. Federation collaborates with other professional associations and trade unions. Carries out negotiations on behalf of members and gives general, professional and legal advice on interpretation of agreements and other matters of employ-

ment. Through the journal keeps members up-to-date on the labor market. Offers members a voluntary group insurance. Active in promoting legislation of concern to members.

435 Svenska Arkivsamfundet
(The Swedish Archival Association)

Address   c/o Riksarkivet, Box 12541, S-10229 Stockholm (permanent). Tel: 46 (8) 7376350
Officers   (elected for 1-yr.term) Pres: Sven Lundkvist; VP: Erik Norberg; Sec: Ulf Söderberg; Treas: Mára Eiche; Ed: Helmut Backhaus. Exec.Board: 15
Staff None
Languages   Swedish
Established   1952
Major Fields of Interest   Archives and archival studies
Major Goals and Objectives   To create and keep alive interest in public and private archives; to promote development of the care and maintenance of archives, and to spread information about archival matters.
Structure   Governed by executive officers. Affiliations: ICA
Sources of Support   Membership dues, sale of publications, research subsidies.
Membership   Total members: 520 (388 individual, 132 institutional). 5 countries represented. Requirements: Interest in goals and objectives of Association. Dues (Swedish Krona): 60.
General Assembly   Entire membership meets once a year.
Publications   *Official journal:* Arkiv, Samhälle och Forskning. 1/yr. (Swedish Krona) 60. Free to members. Editor: Helmut Backhaus. Address same as Association. Circ: Membership. Swedish.
Activities   Promoting the development of Swedish archives, records preservation and management, and making information on archival matters available to the public; publishing of journal. Association sponsors discussions and meetings.

436 Svenska Bibliotekariesamfundet (SBS)
(Swedish Association of University and Research Librarians)

Address   c/o Ume University Library, Box 1441, S-90124 Ume (not permanent). Tel: 46 (46) 107000 ext. 9212
Officers   Chair: T. Lidman; Past Chair: Birgit Antonsson; Sec: Ms. M. Nordström. Exec.Board: 14
Staff None
Languages   Swedish
Established   1921, at Uppsala University Library.
Major Fields of Interest   University and research libraries
Major Goals and Objectives   To create interest in the work and responsibilities of research libraries; to further education and training of members in the library and documentation field
Structure   Governed by Executive Council. Affiliations: IFLA, NVBF
Sources of Support   Membership dues, sale of publications. Budget (Swedish Krona): Approx. 150,000.
Membership   Total members: 1,000+ (individual). Sections: 5. Some Nordic countries represented. Requirements: Employment in research library or interest in documentation and library issues.
General Assembly   Entire membership meets once a year.

Publications *Official journal:* Bibliotekariesamfundet Meddelar (Communications). 1971-. 3-4/yr. Free to members. Editor: Kjell Nilsson. Address: Kungliga Biblioteket (The Royal Library), Box 5039, S-10241 Stockholm. Circ: Membership. Swedish. Other publications: Svenska bibliotekariesamfundets skriftserie (Series); Svenska bibliotekariesamfundet. Rapport (Reports). Publications for sale. No publications exchange program in effect.
Activities Past achievements: Expanded membership by including all staff members of research libraries regardless of professional status. Current and future: Sponsoring seminars, workshops and other continuing education programs.
Bibliography Tell, B., "Sweden," in ALA World Encyclopedia of Library and Information Services, 2nd ed., pp. 789-791. Chicago: American Library Association, 1986.

437 Svenska Folkbibliotekarieförbundet (SFF)
(Swedish Association of Public Librarians)

Address c/o DIK Förbundet, PO Box 760, S-13124 Nacka. Tel: 46 (8) 7162880.
Officers Pres. of DIK Förbundet: Britt-Marie Häggström (Uppsala Stadsbibliotek, PO Box 643, S-75127 Uppsala)
Languages Swedish
Established 1938, at annual meeting of the Swedish Library Association (Sveriges Allmänna Biblioteksförening)
Major Fields of Interest Economic status of public libraries and librarians
Major Goals and Objectives To gain better wages for librarians and to promote economic standards for public libraries
Structure Governed by Board of Managament, and Council of DIK Förbundet. Affiliations: One of the 7 member associations of DIK Förbundet.
Sources of Support Membership dues.
Membership Total members: 1,800+ (individual). Types of membership: Individual, student, emeritus. Requirements: Diploma from Library School.
General Assembly Entire membership meets once a year. In addition, delegates attend DIK Förbundet congresses.
Publications *Official journal:* Bibliofack. 1945-.
Activities Past achievements: Collective bargaining agreements for members. Current activities are mainly carried out through the DIK Förbundet.

438 Svenska Sektionen av AIBM
(Swedish Branch of the International Association of Music Libraries, Archives and Documentation Centres / IAML-Swedish Branch)

Address c/o Nybrokajen 11, S-11148 Stockholm (permanent). Tel: 46 (8) 117724
Languages Swedish, English, German
Established 1953, Stockholm
Major Fields of Interest Music librarianship
Major Goals and Objectives To encourage and promote the activities of music libraries, archives and documentation centers and to strengthen the cooperation among institutions and individuals in these fields of interest.
Structure Governed by Executive Committee. Affiliations: A national branch of IAML.
Sources of Support Membership dues, government subsidies.
Membership Total members: 80+ (50 individual, 30 institutional). Requirements: Any person or institution wishing to further the goals of the Association.

General Assembly   Entire membership meets once a year.
Activities   Carried out in coordination with those of IAML. Collaborated on Swedish cataloging rules and classification scheme for music and sound recording.

439   Sveriges Allmänna Biblioteksförening (SAB)
(Swedish Library Association)

Address   PO Box 3127, Drottninggatan 71b, S-10362 Stockholm (permanent). Tel: 46 (8) 7230082. Fax: 46-8-7230038.
Officers   Pres: B. Zachrisson; Sec: Ms. I. Domeij. Exec.Comm: 9
Staff   4 (paid)
Languages   Swedish
Established   1915, at Jönköping library meeting
Major Fields of Interest   Library development
Major Goals and Objectives   To support libraries and matters concerning the library system in Sweden
Structure   Governed by executive officers and membership. Affiliations: IFLA.
Sources of Support   Membership dues, sale of publications, conference fees. Budget (Swedish Krona): 1986: 2.483 million; 1987: 2.779 million.
Membership   Total members: 2,225 (1,500 individual, 725 institutional). Sections: 5. Requirements: Individual: Interest in library matters; Institutional: Institutions/organizations dealing with library matters, research, or school/educational matters. Dues (Swedish Krona): 120, individual; 400 to 7,860, institutional.
General Assembly   Entire membership meets once a year.
Publications   *Official journal:* Biblioteksbladet (BBL) (Library Journal). 1916-. 14/yr. (Swedish Krona) 210. Free to members. Editor: Barbro Blomberg. Address: PO Box 200, S-22100 Lund. Tel: (46) 140480. Circ: 5,500. Swedish, some English summaries. Other publications: Annual report, proceedings of seminars, workshops. Some publications for sale. No publications exchange program in effect.
Activities   Past achievements: Successful courses, conferences and annual meetings. Close contacts with Government and local authorities have also proven successful. Current and future: Continue and improve these activities. Implement new statutes by conducting campaigns to let people know more about the Association, the library system and the new library logotypes.
Use of High Technology   Computers (Macintosh etc.) for management.
Bibliography   "The Future of the Swedish Library Association," Biblioteksbladet 70 (1985):i-xvi (insert, in Swedish); Tell, B., "Sweden," in ALA World Encyclopedia of Library and Information Services, 2nd ed., pp. 789-791. Chicago: American Library Association, 1986; Andersson, L.G., "SAB - den oandliga historian," (SAB - a Story without an End), DF-Revy 9 (1986):38-41 (in Swedish).

440   Sveriges Vetenskapliga Specialbiblioteks Förening (SVSF)
(Swedish Association of Special Research Libraries)

Address   c/o Secretary, Utrikesdepartementets bibliotek, PO Box 15121, S-10323 Stockholm (not permanent)
Officers   Pres: Anders Ryberg; Sec: Birgitta Fridén
Staff   None
Languages   Swedish
Established   1945, Stockholm
Major Fields of Interest   Research libraries

Major Goals and Objectives To work for the development of special libraries and the education of librarians
Structure Governed by executive officers.
Sources of Support Membership dues.
Membership Total members: 270 (individual) from 20 libraries. Requirements: Open to all staff members of special libraries.
General Assembly Entire membership meets once a year in Stockholm.
Activities Sponsors meetings, seminars.

441 Swedish Association of Employees in Archives and Records Offices (ARK)

Address c/o DIK Förbundet, PO Box 760, S-13124 Nacka (permanent). Tel: 46 (8) 7162880
Languages Swedish
Major Fields of Interest Economic status of archives and records offices
Major Goals and Objectives To gain better wages and promote the economic status of archivists and records managers.
Structure Governed by Board of Management and the Council of DIK Förbundet. Affiliations: One of the 7 member associations of DIK Förbundet.
Sources of Support Membership dues.
Membership Requirements: Individuals working in archives and record offices
General Assembly Entire membership meets once a year. In addition, delegates attend DIK Förbundet congresses.
Activities Current activities are mainly carried out through DIK Förbundet.

442 Tekniska Litteratursällskapet (TLS)
(Swedish Society for Technical Documentation)

Address PO Box 5073, S-10242 Stockholm (permanent). Tel: 46 (8) 7912900. Telex: 17172. Fax: 46 (8) 215623.
Officers Pres: G. Lager; Sec: Birgitta Levin (appointed).
Staff 2 (paid)
Languages Swedish and other Scandinavian languages
Established 1936, Stockholm
Major Fields of Interest Documentation in industry
Major Goals and Objectives To promote documentation and to stimulate research and development in this field
Structure Governed by Executive Board. Affiliations: FID, IFLA
Sources of Support Membership dues, sale of publications, government subsidies.
Membership Total members: 1,000+ (individual and institutional). Requirements: Open to all those working in the field of technology and documentation.
General Assembly Entire membership meets twice a year.
Publications *Official journal:* Tidskrift för Dokumentation (TD) ("The Nordic Documentation Journal") (until 1948, Teknisk Dokumentation). 1945-. 4/yr. (Swedish Krona) 80. Free to members. Editor: Björn Tell. Address same as Association. Circ: 1,500+. Swedish, with English summaries. Indexed in Lib.Lit., LISA, Chem.Abst. Other publications: Newsletter, TLS Information (membership only); annual reports, proceedings of seminars, conferences; handbooks, bibliographies, scholarly works of documentation. Publications available for sale. Publications exchange program in effect.
Activities Sponsors seminars, meetings, and other continuing education programs, particularly for special librarians.

Bibliography   Bergsten, G., "Swedish Society for Technical Documentation. Fall Conference 1983," Tidskrift för Dokumentation 39 (1983):113-115 (in Swedish); Tell, B., "Sweden," in ALA World Encyclopedia of Library and Information Services, 2nd ed., pp. 789-791. Chicago: American Library Association, 1986.

**443   Vetenskapliga Bibliotekens Tjänstemannaförening (VBT)
(Association of Research Library Staff, Sweden)**

Address   c/o DIK Förbundet, PO Box 760, S-13124 Nacka, Sweden (permanent). Tel: 46 (8) 7152880
Officers   Pres: Anders Schmidt (Lund University Library, Box 3, S-22100 Lund. Tel: (46) 10700)
Languages   Swedish
Established   1958
Major Fields of Interest   University and research libraries and their staff
Major Goals and Objectives   To work for the economic and social status and interests of members, and for the general improvement of their working conditions.
Structure   Governed by Managing Board and Council of DIK Förbundet. Affiliations: One of the 7 member associations of DIK Förbundet.
Sources of Support   Membership dues.
Membership   Total members: 240+ (individual). Requirements: Individuals employed in research library.
General Assembly   Entire membership meets once a year. In addition, delegates attend DIK Förbundet congresses.
Publications   Members use publications of DIK Förbundet.
Activities   Current activities are mainly carried out through DIK Förbundet

Switzerland

444   Schweizerische Bibliophilen-Gesellschaft
(Swiss Society of Bibliophiles)

Address   c/o Dr. Conrad Ulrich, Voltastrasse 43, CH-8044 Zurich
Officers   (elected for indefinite term) Pres: Conrad Ulrich; Exec.Sec: Konrad Kahl
(Wolfbachstrasse 17, CH-8032 Zurich). Exec.Comm:10
Staff   None
Languages   German
Established   1921, Berne, uniting bibliophiles in Switzerland for the first time.
Major Fields of Interest   International and Swiss bibliophily; private and public book
collections; the work of illustrators and producers of books; problems of the book in the
modern world.
Major Goals and Objectives   To establish social contacts between Swiss bibliophiles;
to sponsor research in bibliophily; to publish reprints of rare books.
Structure   Governed by Executive Council. Affiliations: Association Internationale de
Bibliophilie.
Sources of Support   Membership dues, private gifts.
Membership   Total members: Approx. 750 (615 individual, 135 institutional). Types of
membership: Individual, institutional, student. Requirements: Written application to the
President of the Executive Council. Dues (Swiss Franc): 90, individual; 90, institutional;
30, students up to 27 years of age; 30, overseas.
General Assembly   Entire membership meets once a year.
Publications   *Official journal:* Librarium. 1958-. 3/yr. (Swiss Franc) 120. Free to mem-
bers. Editor: Werne G. Zimmermann. Address: Im Schilf 15, CH-8044 Zurich. Circ: 780.
German, French. Indexed in MLA. Other publications: Reprints of books. Publications
for members only, not available for sale or exchange.
Activities   Carried out according to the goals and objectives.

445   Schweizerische Musik-Archive / Archives Musicales Suisses
(Swiss Music Archives)

Address   c/o Bellariastrasse 82, CH-8038 Zurich (permanent). Tel: 41 (1) 457700.
Officers   Exec.Sec: Hans Steinbeck.
Staff   2 (paid)
Languages   German, French, English, Italian
Established   1942, Zurich, together with the Swiss Composers' Association.
Major Fields of Interest   Swiss music, especially contemporary.
Major Goals and Objectives   To promote Swiss music, especially contemporary music;
to document and disseminate information on Swiss music.
Structure   Association is a Department of the Swiss Performing Rights Society (SUISA).
Affiliations: IAML.
Sources of Support   Parent organization, SUISA.
Publications   Has no official journal. Publishes bibliographies and reference works on
Swiss music and composers. Publications for sale.
Activities   Publication program

446   Schweizerische Vereinigung für Dokumentation / Association Suisse de Documentation / Associazione Svizzera di Documentazione (SVD/ASD) (Swiss Association for Documentation)

Address   c/o BID GD PTT, CH-3030 Bern (permanent). Tel: 41 (31) 622749
Officers   (elected for indefinite term) Pres: Rolf Schmid; Sec/Treas: Walter Bruderer. Exec.Council: 73
Staff   7+ (volunteers)
Languages   French, German
Established   1939
Major Fields of Interest   Development of documental information.
Major Goals and Objectives   To support members; to further professional education and development; to promote information exchanges.
Structure   Governed by executive officers. Affiliations: EUSIDIC
Sources of Support   Membership dues. Budget (Swiss Franc): 1986/87: 30,000; 1987/88: 35,000; 1988/89: 39,000.
Membership   Total members: 550 (320 individual, 230 institutional). Regional Groups and Committees. Requirements: Open to all documentalists and to institutions engaged in documentation services. Dues (Swiss Franc): 50, individual; 100+, institutional.
General Assembly   Entire membership meets once a year.
Publications   *Official journal:* ARBIDO. 1986-. Issued in 2 parts: ARBIDO-R(Revue). 4/yr. (articles and book reviews); ARBIDO-B(Bulletin). 12/yr. (Association news). This is the official journal of 3 Swiss associations: VSA (Vereinigung Schweizerischer Archivare), VSB (Vereinigung Schweizerischer Bibliothekare), and SVD, (superseding the Nachrichten VSB/SVD and the Mitteilungen der Vereinigung Schweizerischer Archivare). (Swiss Franc) 40 (25 for ARBIDO-B alone). Editor: Edmond G. Wyss. Address: c/o Wander AG, Postfach 2747, CH-3001 Bern. Tel: 41 (31) 466710. German, French. Indexed in LISA. Other publications: Proceedings of meetings, conferences, etc. Annual reports appear in ARBIDO.
Activities   Sponsors meetings, seminars. Activities are carried out by various working groups in areas of media documentation, continuing education, patent documentation, economics documentation, etc. Some of the current issues are the impact of new technology on documentation access, user needs, etc.
Bibliography   Clavel, J.-P. and Médioni, J., "Switzerland," in ALA World Encyclopedia of Library and Information Services, 2nd ed., pp. 792-793. Chicago: American Library Association, 1986.

447   Vereinigung Schweizerischer Archivare / Association des Archivistes Suisses / Associazione degli Archivisti Svizzeri (VSA/AAS/AAS) (Association of Swiss Archivists)

Address   c/o Schweizerisches Bundesarchiv, Archivstrasse 24, CH-3003 Bern. Tel: 41 (31) 618989.
Officers   Pres: Anton Gössi; Treas: Otto Sigg.
Staff   None
Languages   German, French, Italian
Established   1922
Major Fields of Interest   Archives and records management
Major Goals and Objectives   To promote the development of archives in Switzerland; to facilitate contact among archivists; to promote their cooperation and to assist in their professional activities; to promote their professional development and status; to organize

colloquia on current problems in archives; to disseminate information on archival matters and archival studies in Switzerland and abroad through publications; to maintain contact and exchange information with other associations of similar interests, both Swiss and foreign.
Structure   Governed by executive officers. Affiliations: ICA.
Sources of Support   Membership dues
Membership   Total members: Approx. 200. Types of membership: Individual, institutional. Requirements: Open to archivists and archives. Dues (Swiss Franc): 25, individual; 50 +, institutional.
General Assembly   Entire membership meets annually. 1987: Schaffhausen, Sept.10-11; 1988: Glarus, Sept.1-2.
Publications   *Official journal:* ARBIDO. 1986-. (supersedes Mitteilungen der Vereinigung Schweizerischer Archivare); published jointly by 3 Swiss associations, VSA, VSB and SVD (see under Schweizerische Vereinigung für Dokumentation (SVD) for detailed information on journal). Annual reports published in ARBIDO; issues occasional monographs.
Activities   Carried out according to goals and objectives of Association; sponsors conferences, seminars, workshops, often jointly with the two other associations of librarians and documentalists (VSB and SVD).
Bibliography   Clavel, J.-P. and Médioni, J., "Switzerland," in ALA World Encyclopedia of Library and Information Services, 2nd ed., pp. 792-793. Chicago: American Library Association, 1986.

448   Vereinigung Schweizerischer Bibliothekare / Association des Bibliothécaires Suisses / Associazione dei Bibliotecari Svizzeri (VSB/ABS/ABS) (Swiss Librarians' Association)

Address   c/o Schweizerische Landesbibliothek, Hallwylstrasse 15, CH-3003 Bern (permanent). Tel: 41 (31) 618978. Telex: 912691. Fax: 41-31-618463.
Officers   (elected for 3-yr.term) Pres: J. Cordonier; Past Pres: Alois Schacher (Zentralbibliothek Luzern); VP: Philippe Monnier; Sec: Willy Treichler; Treas: Alfred Fasnacht. Exec.Board: 15
Staff   3 (paid)
Languages   German, French
Established   1895, Basel.
Major Fields of Interest   All areas affecting Swiss librarians and librarianship.
Major Goals and Objectives   Effective cooperation among all Swiss libraries; representation of common interests of librarians to authorities and the public; promotion of professional development and contact among librarians.
Structure   Governed by Executive Board. Affiliations: IFLA.
Sources of Support   Membership dues, sale of publications.
Membership   Total members: Approx.1,200 (1,000 individual, 200 institutional). Types of membership: Individual, institutional, life, emeritus, honorary. Requirements: Open to all persons working in libraries, and to all libraries and other institutions contributing to Swiss librarianship. Dues (Swiss Franc): 50, individual; 65, institutional.
General Assembly   Entire membership meets annually. 1988: Bern, Sept.15-17.
Publications   *Official journal:* ARBIDO. 1986- ; published jointly by 3 Swiss associations of archivists, librarians and documentalists, VSA, VSB and SVD (see under Schweizerische Vereinigung für Dokumentation (SVD) for detailed information on journal).
Activities   Carried out according to the goals and objectives of the Association. Current areas are: Education and training of library staff; a Union Catalog of Switzerland; interli-

brary cooperation through interlibrary loan; coordination of library automation; preservation of library material (theme of the 1988 annual conference). Sponsors conferences, workshops, continuing education programs, some jointly with the other associations.
Use of High Technology   Computers (IBM PC XT) for management.
Bibliography   Schneider, P., "Communications from the Swiss Association of Librarians (VSB)," VSB/ABS/ABS / Nachrichten/Nouvelles/Notizie 59 (1983):319-326 (in German); Clavel, J.-P. and Médioni, J. "Switzerland," in ALA World Encyclopedia of Library and Information Services, 2nd. ed., pp. 792-793. Chicago: American Library Association, 1986.
Additional Information   In 1980 the formation of an Association of Children's librarians was reported. See A. Libbrecht-Gourdet, "Swiss Children's Libraries Form an Association," VSB/SVD/ABS / Nachrichten/Nouvelles/Notizie 56 (Aug. 1980):175-180 (in French).

Syria

449   The Libraries and Documents Association of Syria

Address   This Association appears to be inactive. Leadership for professional organization and coordination in the country has been assumed by the Assad National Library, and some information is provided on professional activities in Syria. Postal address: Assad National Library, PO Box 3639, Damascus. Tel: 332883/338255/722409. Telex: 419134.
Officers   General Director: Ghassan Lahham; Sec: R. Kassab.   Exec.Board: 9
Staff   245 (paid)
Languages   Arabic
Established   1984
Major Fields of Interest   Syrian publications, Arabic manuscripts, selected Arabic and foreign works in all fields.
Major Goals and Objectives   Compilation and documentation of national works; promotion of librarianship in Syria; establishing the foundation for a national information network and its subsequent supervision.
Structure   Governed by Ministry of Culture and National Guidance. Affiliations: IFLA (since 1986).
Sources of Support   Government subsidies. Budget (Syrian Pound): Approx. 11.4 million.
Publications   No official journal. Publishes National Bibliography, 1/yr.; Analytical Index of Syrian Periodicals, 4/yr.; Internal Bulletin, 2/yr. Publications exchange program in effect.
Activities   (1) Legal Deposit Law for all Syrian publications; (2) organize courses for technical services in the Library;   (3) supervise the Library Association in Syria;   (4) hold general cultural lectures and symposia;   (5) supervise the establishment of the National Information Network;   (6) preservation and restoration of manuscripts.   Has been active in promoting library-related legislation.   Contributed to establishment of the Arab Federation for Libraries and Information   (AFLI).   Sponsors exhibits and continuing education programs.
Use of High Technology   Computers (international database services, such as DIALOG - Data Solve) for operations and management.
Bibliography   El Hadi, Mohamed M.,"Syria," in ALA World Encyclopedia of Library and Information Services, 2nd ed., pp. 794-795. Chicago: American Library Association, 1986; Khurshid, A., "Library Associations in Asia," Herald of Library Science 28 (1989):3-10.

Tanzania

450   Chama Cha Ukutubi, Tanzania / Tanzania Library Association (CUTA/TLA)

Address   PO Box 2645, Dar es Salaam (permanent). Tel: 255 (51) 26121. Telex: c/o tanlis

Officers   (elected for 2-yr.term) Chair: H.A. Mwenegoha; Past Chair: Theophilus E. Mlaki; Secs: Ms. M.K. Kasembe; H.I. Kiboya; Ms. M. Ngaiza. Exec.Comm: 6.

Staff   1 (volunteer)

Languages   English, Kiswahili

Established   1973, after the dissolving of the East African Library Association (EALA). Originally was a branch of EALA (1971-1972)

Major Fields of Interest   Librarianship

Major Goals and Objectives   To promote reading and literacy; to improve standards and level of library development; to increase competence of members; to conduct research and produce publications.

Structure   Governed by Executive Committee and Annual General Meeting of all members. Affiliations: COMLA, FID, IFLA, SCESCAL, Tanzania Professional Centre.

Sources of Support   Membership dues, sale of publications, course and seminar fees, private donations.

Membership   Total members: 255 (205 individual, 50 institutional). Requirements: Individuals working in libraries and documentation centers; institutions having libraries and documentation centers.

General Assembly   Entire membership meets once a year.

Publications   *Official journal:* Someni. 1973-. 2/yr. Free to members. Editor: K.J. Mchombu. Address same as Association. Circ: 1,000. English, Kiswahili. Indexed in LISA. Other publications: Series on Library Development; newsletter; annual reports, proceedings of meetings, reports of seminars, workshops. No publications exchange program in effect.

Activities   Past achievements: (1) Organizing courses; (2) improving and increasing membership; (3) starting publications program. Current: Offering courses; expanding publications; carrying out studies. Future: How to better manage and organize the Association. Sponsors continuing education seminars and workshops.

Bibliography   Kaungamno, E.E., "The Case of Tanzania Library Services," Canadian Library Journal 42 (1985):185-187; Kaungamno, E.E., "Tanzania," in ALA World Encyclopedia of Library and Information Services, 2nd ed., pp. 796-797. Chicago: American Library Association, 1986.

Thailand

451   Thai Library Association (TLA)

Address   273, 275 Vibhavadee Rangsit Road, Phyathai, Bangkok 10400. Tel: 66 (2) 2712084.
Officers   Pres: Ms. Kullasap Gesmankit; Past Pres: Ms. M. Chavalit; Sec: Ms. Karnmanee Suckcharoen
Staff   6 (paid)
Languages   Thai
Established   1954, Bangkok, with the aid of a grant from the Asia Foundation.
Major Fields of Interest   Library services.
Major Goals and Objectives   To encourage cooperation and assistance among members; to promote library education; to help with the growth and development of libraries throughout the country; to share professional knowledge and experiences with colleagues at home and abroad; to improve the status of librarians and safeguard their welfare; to help supervise the organization of any library upon request; to serve as a center to receive assistance from any source so as to obtain the objectives of the association.
Structure   Governed by Executive Council. Affiliations: CONSAL, IFLA.
Sources of Support   Membership dues, subsidy from the Asia Foundation.
Membership   Total members: Approx. 2,000 (individual, including about 550 librarians). Types of membership: Individual, associate, honorary, life. Requirements: For each category, specific requirements as to library education, job status, contributions to librarianship, etc.
General Assembly   Entire membership meets annually, in November or December, in Bangkok.
Publications   *Official journal:* The Thai Library Association Bulletin. 4/yr. Free to members. Address same as Association.   Other publications: Annual reports, proceedings of conferences, seminars, and other professional publications
Activities   Wide range of activities according to the goals and objectives of the Association. Sponsors conferences, seminars, and other continuing education programs.
Bibliography   Dhutiyabhodi, Uthai, "Thailand," in ALA World Encyclopedia of Library and Information Services, 2nd ed., pp. 799-801. Chicago: American Library Association, 1986; Khurshid, A., "Library Associations in Asia," Herald of Library Science 28 (1989):3-10.

Togo

452   Association Togolaise pour le Développement de la Documentation, des Bibliothèques, Archives et Musées
(Togo Association for the Development of Documentation, Libraries, Archives and Museums)

Address   c/o Bibliothèque de l'Université du Bénin, BP 1515, Lomé (permanent). Tel: (2) 14843.
Officers   Pres: H. Attignon; Exec.Sec: E.E. Amah.
Staff   None
Languages   French
Established   1959, as Togo Branch of the Association Internationale pour le Développement de la Documentation, des Bibliothèques et des Archives en Afrique (AIDBA, Section Togolaise).
Major Fields of Interest   Libraries, archives, documentation centres, and museums.
Major Goals and Objectives   To promote the development of libraries, archives, and documentation centres in Togo.
Structure   Governed by executive officers. Affiliations: IFLA.
Sources of Support   Membership dues.
Membership   Requirements: Open to all individuals and institutions interested in the aims of the Association.
General Assembly   Entire membership meets annually.
Activities   Carried out in accordance with the goals and objectives of the Association.
Bibliography   Jordan, A. and Comissiong, B., "Togo," in <u>ALA World Encyclopedia of Library and Information Services</u>, 2nd ed., pp. 502-803. Chicago: American Library Association, 1986.

Tonga

453   Tonga Library Association (TLA)

Address   c/o Library, Nuku'alofa
Languages   Tongan, English
Established   1987/88
Major Fields of Interest   Library services
Major Goals and Objectives   Promote library services in Tonga
Structure   Affiliations: COMLA
Sources of Support   Membership dues
General Assembly   Entire membership meets once year.
Publications   *Official journal:* Tonga Library Association Newsletter.
Activities   Sponsors meetings and various library-oriented projects, such as furnishing kindergartens in the Kingdom with writing and drawing materials.
Bibliography   "Tonga Library Association Appeal," COMLA Newsletter 55 (Mar. 1987):6.

Trinidad and Tobago

454   Library Association of Trinidad and Tobago (LATT)

Address   PO Box 1275, Port of Spain, Trinidad (not permanent).
Officers   (elected for 2-yr.term) Pres: Ms. L. Hannays; Sec: Ms. L. Elliott.
Staff   None
Languages   English
Established   1960
Major Fields of Interest   Librarianship
Major Goals and Objectives   To unite all qualified or practicing librarians and any persons or organizations connected with and interested in the promotion of librarianship and its related fields in Trinidad and Tobago.
Structure   Governed by executive officers. Affiliations: COMLA, IFLA.
Sources of Support   Membership dues.
Membership   Total members: Approx.170 (mostly individual). Types of membership: Individual, institutional, honorary, associate. Requirements: Open to librarians and all persons, groups, and organizations connected with and interested in the promotion of librarianship.
General Assembly   Entire membership meets annually in Trinidad between January and March 31.
Publications   *Official journal:* BLATT: Bulletin of the Library Association of Trinidad and Tobago. 1961-. 1/yr. Address same as Association.
Activities   Sponsors conferences, seminars, and other continuing education programs, sometimes jointly with the Department of Library Studies of the University of the West Indies.
Bibliography   Jordan, A., and Comissiong, B., "Trinidad and Tobago," in ALA World Encyclopedia of Library and Information Services, 2nd ed., pp. 803-804. Chicago: American Library Association, 1986; Williams, G. and DeFour-Sanatan, C., "Challenge to the Information Specialist in the Caribbean," COMLA Newsletter 57 (Sept. 1987):10, 12.

Tunisia

455   Association Tunisienne des Documentalistes, Bibliothécaires et Archivistes (ATD)
(Tunisian Association of Documentalists, Librarians and Archivists)

Address   BP 575, Tunis.
Officers   (elected for 1-yr.term) Pres: Mohamed Abdeljaoued; Exec.Sec: Rudha Tlili. Exec.Comm: 7
Staff   None
Languages   Arabic, French
Established   1965, at l'Institut Ali Bach Hamba.
Major Fields of Interest   Documentation, public and university libraries.
Major Goals and Objectives   To bring together all persons actively engaged in documentation; to promote knowledge of documentation throughout the nation; to establish cooperation and collaboration with international and other concerned organizations.
Structure   Governed by executive officers and committee. Affiliations: IFLA, Tunisian Committee of Unesco, UNISIST.
Sources of Support   Membership dues
Membership   Total members: Approx. 130 (individual). Types of membership: Individual, student. Requirements: Open to all professional librarians, documentalists, and archivists, and to third-year students in the field of documentation. Dues (Tunisian Dinar): 40.
General Assembly   Entire membership meets once a year.
Publications   *Official journal:* Bulletin de l'ATD. 1966-. 4/yr. Free to members. Editor: Mohamed Abdeljaoued. Address: 43 Rue de la Liberté, Le Bardo. Tel: (216) 261092. Circ: Membership. Arabic, French. All official reports of the Association appear in the official journal.
Activities   Works to improve the professional status of librarians, archivists, and documentalists in Tunisia; sponsors conferences, seminars, and other continuing education programs.
Bibliography   Habaili, H., "Development of Libraries and Information Services in Tunisia," The Arab Magazine for Information Sciences (Tunis: ALESCO, 1984); Habaili, H., "Tunisia," in ALA World Encyclopedia of Library and Information Services, 2nd ed., pp. 805-807. Chicago: American Library Association, 1986.

Turkey

456 Türk Kütüphaneciler Dernegi (TKD)
(Turkish Librarians' Association)

Address Elgün Sokagi 8/8, 06440 Yenisehir, Ankara (permanent). Tel: 90 (41) 301325.
Officers Pres: N. Sefercioglu; Exec.Sec: C. Tühkân; Gen.Sec: Aydin Kuran.
Staff 1 (volunteer)
Languages Turkish
Established 1949, Ankara.
Major Fields of Interest Library development, public libraries, library laws.
Major Goals and Objectives To develop library services and provide professional aid to libraries and librarians; to promote the development of the library profession in the country.
Structure Governed by Executive Committee. Affiliations: IFLA.
Sources of Support Membership dues, sale of publications.
Membership Total members: 1,200. Chapters: 51. Types of membership: Individual, institutional, student, honorary. Requirements: Professional librarians and others interested in the aims of the Association.
General Assembly Entire membership meets every 2 years.
Publications *Official journal:* Türk Kütüphaneciler Dernegi Bülteni (Bulletin of the Turkish Librarians' Association). 1952-. 4/yr. Free to members. Address same as Association. Circ: 2,000. Turkish. Other publications: Proceedings of conferences, seminars, and professional monographs. Publications for sale.
Activities Organizing conferences, seminars and workshops on library science, documentation and archives; sponsoring annual Turkish Library Week.
Bibliography Taner, S., "Turkey," in ALA World Encyclopedia of Library and Information Services, 2nd ed., pp. 807-809. Chicago: American Library Association, 1986; Khurshid, A., "Library Associations in Asia," Herald of Library Science 28 (1989):3-10.

457 Universite Kütüphanecilik Bölümü Mezunlari Dernei (KÜT-DER)
(Association of Library School Graduates)

Address c/o Bibliothèque Centrale de l'Université d'Istanbul, Takvimhane Caddesi 15, Beyazid-Istanbul (not permanent). Tel: (90) 222180.
Languages Turkish
Established 1970
Major Fields of Interest Library science; professional development
Major Goals and Objectives To promote professional status and professional development of librarians.
Structure Governed by Executive Council
Sources of Support Membership dues.
Membership Total members: Approx. 300 (individual). Requirements: Open to graduates of library schools.
General Assembly Entire membership meets once a year.
Publications Yeni Yayinlar - Aylik Bibliyografya Dergisi (New Publications - Monthly Bibliographical Journal). 12/yr.
Activities Sponsors meetings, seminars; publications.
Bibliography Siddique, Muhammad, comp., "Library Associations in the Muslim World," in Librarianship in the Muslim World 1984, vol.2, ed. by Anis Khurshid and Mal-

ahat Kaleem Sherwani, p.98. Karachi: University of Karachi, 1985; Taner, S., "Turkey," in <u>ALA World Encyclopedia of Library and Information Services</u>, 2nd ed., pp. 807-809. Chicago: American Library Association, 1986; Khurshid, A., "Library Associations in Asia," <u>Herald of Library Science</u> 28 (1989):3-10.

Uganda

458   Uganda Library Association

Address   PO Box 5894, Kampala (not permanent). Tel: (41) 65001 ext.4.
Officers   Chair: P.W. Songa; Exec.Sec: L.M. Sengero
Staff   9 (volunteers)
Languages   English
Established   1957, Nairobi, as a Regional Branch of the East African Library Association (EALA); when EALA was dissolved in order to enable strong national associations to develop, the present association was formed in 1972.
Major Fields of Interest   Establishment and development of libraries.
Major Goals and Objectives   To encourage the promotion, establishment, and improvement of libraries and library services, books and book production; to improve the standards of librarianship and the status of the profession; to bring together all those interested in libraries.
Structure   Governed by executive officers. Affiliations: COMLA, FID, IFLA, SCECSAL.
Sources of Support   Membership dues, government subsidies.
Membership   Total members: Approx.180. Types of membership: Individual, institutional. Requirements: Interest and involvement in libraries. Dues (Uganda Shilling): Individual, scaled to income; 40, institutional.
General Assembly   Entire membership meets every 2 years.
Publications   *Official journal:* Uganda Libraries (formerly Uganda Library Association Bulletin). 1971-. 2/yr. Address same as Association. English. Other publications: Annual reports, proceedings of conferences, seminars. Publications for sale.
Activities   Sponsors conferences, seminars and other continuing education programs; advises Government on establishing and developing more effective library and information services; establishes contacts with associations in other countries sharing similar goals and objectives.
Bibliography   Siddique, M., comp., "Library Associations in the Muslim World," in Librarianship in the Muslim World 1984, vol.2, ed. by Anis Khurshid and Malahat Kaleem Sherwani, p. 99. Karachi: University of Karachi, 1985; Kawesa, B.M., "Uganda," in ALA World Encyclopedia of Library and Information Services, 2nd ed., pp. 811-813. Chicago: American Library Association, 1986.

459   Uganda School Library Association (USLA)

Address   c/o Public Libraries Board, Bugunda Road, PO Box 4262, Kampala (not permanent)
Officers   Exec.Sec: J.W. Nabembezi
Staff   10 (volunteers)
Languages   English
Established   1968, Kampala, with assistance from British Council librarian.
Major Fields of Interest   School libraries
Major Goals and Objectives   (1) To promote libraries in schools and training colleges; (2) to provide an information service on running school and college libraries; (3) to arrange courses for teacher librarians; (4) to cooperate with other bodies providing library services to schools and colleges; (5) to provide a voice to speak for schools and colleges on library matters.

Structure   Governed by Executive Committee. Affiliations: Uganda Libraries Board
Sources of Support   Membership dues, private gifts.
Membership   Total members: Approx. 80 (20 individual, 60 institutional). Types of
membership: Individual, institutional. Requirements: Open to any school, college, or interested individual. Dues (Uganda Shilling): 10, individual; 20, primary school; 40, secondary school and college.
General Assembly   Entire membership meets once a year in April, in Kampala.
Publications   *Official journal:* Uganda School Library Association Newsletter. 1970-.
4/yr. Free to members. Address same as Association. Circ: Membership. English. Indexed
in LISA. Other publications: Annual reports, proceedings of conferences, seminars.
Activities   Running a Book Box Scheme for primary and secondary schools, and teacher
training colleges in remote areas (books supplied by British Council). Sponsors conferences, seminars, and other continuing education programs.
Bibliography   Siddique, M., comp., "Library Associations in the Muslim World," in Librarianship in the Muslim World 1984, vol.2, ed. by Anis Khurshid and Malahat Kaleem
Sherwani, p. 99. Karachi: University of Karachi, 1985.

460   Uganda Special Library Association

Address   PO Box 9, Entebbe (not permanent)
Officers   Pres: E.J. Orwiny; Sec: M. D'Mello.
Staff   5 (volunteers)
Languages   English
Established   1970, Entebbe
Major Fields of Interest   Special libraries
Major Goals and Objectives   To encourage and promote standards for special libraries
in Uganda; to facilitate the exchange of reference and bibliographical information; to
promote the service rendered by special libraries to researchers; to arrange for the orga-
nization of libraries not yet organized; to provide a voice to speak for special libraries; to
arrange with employers for the training of librarians and assistants.
Structure   Governed by Executive Council of 5 members.
Sources of Support   Membership dues, government subsidies.
Membership   Total members: Approx. 80. Types of membership: Individual, institutional, active, honorary, student, life. Requirements: Open to staff members of special li-
braries; all special libraries; other interested bodies.
General Assembly   Entire membership meets annually.
Publications   No official journal.
Activities   Sponsors library staff training program; sponsors workshops, seminars and
other continuing education offerings
Bibliography   Siddique, M., comp., "Library Associations in the Muslim World," in Li-
brarianship in the Muslim World 1984, vol.2, ed. by Anis Khurshid and Malahat Kaleem
Sherwani, p. 99. Karachi: University of Karachi, 1985.

Union of Soviet Socialist Republics

461   U.S.S.R. Library Council

Address   Ministry of Culture of the USSR, c/o The Lenin State Library of the USSR, 3 Prospect Kalinina, 101 000 Moscow (permanent). Tel: 7 (095) 2024056/2228551. Telex: 411167.
Officers   Pres: N.S. Kartashov; Sec: Ms. O. A. Diakonova.
Languages   Russian
Established   1959
Major Fields of Interest   Librarianship
Major Goals and Objectives   The current goal of the Council is to promote and improve the country's library services according to a plan for libraries, "The Fundamental Direction of Their Activities for 1986-1990 and for the Period through 2000."
Structure   The library profession in the USSR is centralized in the Council, which is under the jurisdiction of the Ministry of Culture. The Ministry approves and authorizes any decisions of the Council's plenary sessions before they become obligatory for implementation by all libraries in the Union Republics. The Council has various sections and committees, comprised of prominent librarians (Bibliography, Interlibrary Loan, Library Building and Equipment, Management, Library Service to Youth, International Relations, etc.). Interdepartmental Councils function similarly in the Republics and regions. Other Library Councils are set up with the Presidium of the Academy of Sciences of the USSR (including both librarians and scientists, and concerned with science information services), and the Ministry of Higher and Special Education (uniting university and high school libraries). An Interdepartmental Library Committee was set up by the Sate Committee for Science and Technology of the Council of Ministers of the USSR, to coordinate the activities of research and technical libraries of the different governmental departments. In addition, there are a number of standing conferences of directors of libraries for various subject areas (e.g. agriculture, medicine, etc.). Affiliations: IFLA.
Sources of Support   Government
General Assembly   Plenary sessions of the Council are held twice a year. The Council Bureau meets monthly. Plenary sessions are attended by representatives of all types of libraries. Attendance varies from 300 to 500.
Publications   Since 1964, a major part of publications is issued by Kniga, the government publisher. They cover all areas of library work. Some of the professional journals are: Bibliotekar (Librarian). 1923-. 12/yr. Circ: 150,000+, concerned with management of public libraries, articles arranged by subject; Sovetskoje bibliotekovedonie (Soviet Library Science; formerly Biblioteki SSSR, Libraries of the USSR). 1955-; Naucnye i tekhnicheskie biblioteki SSSR (Scientific and Technical Libraries of the USSR). 10-yr, concerned with science and technology librarianship; Naucnaja i tekhnicheskaja informatsija (Scientific and Technical Information), issued by VINITI (Union Institute for Scientific and Technical Information), concerned with information and documentation; Seriya 1: Organizatsiya i metodika informatsionnoi raboty (Organization and Methodology of Information Work); Seriya 2: Informatzionnye processy i systemy (Information Processes and Systems); Kniga. Issledovanija i materialy (Book Studies and Materials). 2/yr, concerned with problems of bibliography and librarianship; Sovetskaja bibliografija (Soviet Bibliography). 1933-. 6/yr., concerned with problems of theory, history, and methods of bibliography. Activities and developments in foreign libraries are reported in two journals published by the All-Union State Library of Foreign Literature (Ulyanovskaya 1, Moscow 109240): Bibliotekovedenie i bibliografija za rubezom (Librarianship and Bibli-

ography Abroad). 4/yr., and <u>Informacija o bibliotecnom dele i bibliografii za rubezom</u>. Aiding librarians in book selection are: <u>V mire knig</u> (In the World of Books), 12/yr., and <u>Kniznoe obozrenie</u> (Book Reviews), weekly. In addition, various specialized professional bulletins are published, with contributions from librarians working in these areas, and bulletins issued by the Republics and individual libraries.

Activities The library profession operates within an extensive library network that provides close cooperation and coordination of activities through exchange of information and experiences, and through directives for methods and performance. Librarians meet on an all-Union, Republican, regional, and municipal basis. They also participate in congresses of workers in the field of culture held by each Union Republic. There are also conferences for various types of libraries (academic, scientific, etc.). Most of these conferences are organized by central libraries (Republic, regional) jointly with government agencies. Monthly seminars for public, children's, and school libraries are organized in rural districts and cities as a form of continuing education and to improve library cooperation. There are frequent conferences and staff exchanges with other socialist countries, and growing activities at the international level.

Bibliography Nazmutdinov, I. (tr. T.L. Mann), "Union of Soviet Socialist Republics," in <u>ALA World Encyclopedia of Library and Information Services</u>, 2nd ed., pp. 818-822. Chicago: American Library Association, 1986.

United Kingdom

462   Agricultural Librarians in Colleges and Universities (ALCU)

Address   c/o Christopher Napper, Secretary, Silsoe College, Silsoe, Bedford, MK45 4DT (not permanent)
Officers   Sec: Christopher Napper
Languages   English
Established   1979
Major Fields of Interest   Agricultural librarianship at academic libraries
Major Goals and Objectives   To promote agricultural librarianship at college and university libraries; to provide a forum for exchange of information for agricultural librarians at such institutions; to improve the services of agricultural librarians at institutions of higher education.
Structure   Governed by executive officers.
General Assembly   Entire membership meets once a year. 1989: Lancashire College of Agriculture and Horticulture, July 12-14; 1990: Somerset College of Agriculture and Horticulture, July.
Bibliography   "ALCU Conference 1989," Aslib Information 17 (1989):245.

463   ARLIS UK & Eire: Art Libraries Society of the United Kingdom & the Republic of Ireland

Address   c/o Sue Price, ARLIS Secretary, Central School of Art and Design Library, Southampton Row, London WC1B 4AP (not permanent). Tel: 44 (1) 4051825 ext. 39
Officers   (elected for 1-yr. term) Chair: Beth Houghton; Sec: Sue Price; Treas: Carol Bagnall; Membership Sec: Linda Newington. ARLIS Council: 18.
Staff   None.
Languages   English.
Established   1969. Inaugural meeting held at Central School of Art, London.
Major Fields of Interest   Art and design librarianship.
Major Goals and Objectives   Corporate voice of art librarians in the promotion of all aspects of librarianship of the visual arts; make views known to appropriate professional and educational bodies.
Structure   Governed by ARLIS Council. Affiliations: IFLA.
Sources of Support   Membership dues, sale of publications.
Membership   Total members: 345 (180 individual, 165 institutional). Types of membership: Individual, institutional, student, honorary. Requirements: Open to all individuals and institutions interested in art librarianship, persons working in art libraries and institutions such as museums and galleries.
General Assembly   General membership meets once a year.
Publications   *Official journal:* Art Libraries Journal. 1976-. 4/yr. Free to members. Editor: Philip Pacey. Address: Lancashire Polytechnic Library, Preston PR1 2TQ. Circ: 480. English, some French and German. Other publications: ARLIS News-sheet. 1976-. 6/yr. Editor: Judith Preace. Address: School of Art & Design Library, NELP, 89 Greengate St., London E1B 0BG. Circ: Membership. English; ARLIS Union List of Periodicals on Art & Design and Related Subjects; User Education in Art & Design; ARLIS Directory, 1/yr.
Activities   Seminars, courses, conferences, visits, representation on committees (e.g., LA, British Library). The Association has been active in promoting library-related legislation.

Use of High Technology Computers (micros – BBC, Calterm) for management.
Bibliography Pacey, P., "ARLIS, the Art Libraries Society in the United Kingdom," Inspel 15 (1981):46-49.

464 Aslib, The Association for Information Management
(formerly The Association of Special Libraries and Information Bureaux)

Address Information House, 20-24 Old Street, London EC1V 9AP (permanent). Tel: 44 (1) 2534488. Telex: 23667 Aslib G. Fax: 44-1-4300514.
Officers Chief Executive: Roger Bowes (appointed, 1990-, replacing Dennis A. Lewis, 1981-89); Membership Sec: Sheila Williams; Marketing Manager: D.S. Wood. Chair of Council: Brian Dutton. Council: 40.
Staff 35 (paid).
Languages English.
Established 1924, Hoddesdon, Hertfordshire, at the first conference of representatives of UK special libraries and information bureaus, as Association of Special Libraries and Information Bureaux (Aslib); present name adopted in the 1980s.
Major Fields of Interest Provision and management of information, including librarianship and information science.
Major Goals and Objectives On July 20, 1989, the Aslib Council agreed upon the following Mission Statement and Corporate Goals: The mission of Aslib is to be the foremost organisation in the UK in promoting the concept that information is a corporate, organisational and social resource requiring the development and use of specialist skills. The Corporate Goals are: (1) to provide a forum whereby both library and information resource (LIR) professionals and others in the emerging information market may contribute to, and benefit from, a pool of knowledge on the practice and theory of information management; (2) to make effective representations to authorities and the media at appropriate local, regional, national and international level on issues of relevance to the information industry; (3) to bring the practice and profession of information management to public notice and to reinforce its identity and image; (4) to develop, promote and sell a range of high-quality products and services geared to the promotion, development and use of effective information management, thereby enabling organisations and individuals to achieve higher productivity and increased profits in the private sector, and improved services and greater sensitivity to need in the public and voluntary sectors; (5) to provide benefits for memberships through a mix of products and services, the cost of which is related to membership subscription income; (6) to achieve an overall net return on expenditure in order to provide finances for future development of the organisation (Adapted from Aslib Information 17 (1989):126).
Structure Governed by Council. Affiliations: IFLA, FID.
Sources of Support Membership dues, sale of publications, fees from courses, conferences, seminars. Budget (Pound Sterling): 1986/87: £1 million+; 1987/88: £1 million+.
Membership Total members: 2,200 (200 individual, 2,000 institutional). Special Interest Groups: 12 (Audiovisual; Biosciences (ABG); Chemical; Computer; Economic and Business Information (AEBIG); Electronics; Engineering Informatics - Advanced Information Systems; One Man Bands (OMB); Planning, Environment, Transport Information; Social Sciences Information; Technical Translation). 70 countries represented. Requirements: Interest in information management. Dues: Corporate: Depending on type of organization and number of employees; Associate: For students and employees of member organizations.
General Assembly General membership meets once a year. 1989: Windsor, June 23-25; 1990: London,

Publications   *Official journal:* Aslib Information. 1972-. 10/yr. (Pound Sterling) 30.
Free to members. Editor: Joyce Dundas. Address same as Association. English. Circ:
2,500. Indexed in Lib.Lit., etc. Proceedings of meetings and professional articles are
published in Aslib Proceedings. 1949-. 12/yr. (Pound Sterling) 75 (90 overseas). Free to
members. Editor: Joyce Dundas. Address same as Association. Circ: 3,500. English. Indexed in Lib.Lit., etc. Among some 11 specialist journals are Business Information
Times (12/yr.), Records Management Journal (4/yr.), CRITique (10/yr.), Online Notes
(12/yr.), IT Link incorporating Automation Notes (12/yr.), Program: Automated Library
and Information Systems (4/yr.), The Technical Translation Bulletin (3/yr.), Journal of
Documentation (4/yr.), Trend Monitor 2/yr., etc.; a wide range of directories, books and
practical guides, e.g. Webb, S.P., Creating an Information Service (2nd ed., 1989), Caw-
kell, A.E., ed., Evolution of an Information Society (1989), Online Management and
Marketing Databases 1989, Whitehead, J., ed., Information Management and Competi-
tive Success (1989), Online Bibliographic Databases (4th ed., comp. J.L. Hall), The
Translator's Handbook (2nd ed., ed. Catriona Picken, 1990), Directory of Information
Sources in the UK (2 v.), Who's Who in the UK Information World 1990 (2nd ed.), etc.
Publications for sale. Publications catalog with price lists available.
Activities   Specialized activities are further carried out by the various Groups and
Branches (Electronics, Engineering, Biosciences, Technical Translating, Social Sciences,
Economic and Business Information, Midlands Branch, etc.). Past achievements: Devel-
oped new range of publications, courses, seminars and advisory services. Current: Publishing, courses, conferences and seminars, and an advisory service for members on subjects such as online information retrieval, networking and library automation; planning
for "Information '90," the third major international conference and exhibition, 17-20
Sept. 1990, at Bournemouth International Centre. Future: Growth-related. Active in promoting copyright legislation. Sponsors exhibits. Extensive continuing education offerings
are coordinated by the Aslib Training Programme Manager.
Use of High Technology   Computers (IBM 34, Displaywriter & PCs) for management.
Fax for information dissemination.
Bibliography   Vickers, P.H., "Work of the Aslib Research Department," Aslib Proceed-
ings 33 (Sept. 1981):368-371; "Renaming Proposed for Aslib," Library Association Re-
cord 84 (1982):281; "Big Changes at Aslib," New Zealand Libraries 43 (1982):209;
"Changes at Aslib," Unesco Journal of Information Science, Librarianship and Archives
Administration 5 (1983):68-69; Lewis, D.A., "Role of the Professional Organisation," Aslib Proceedings 35 (1983):108-120; "Aslib, the Association for Information Mangement:
Some Recent Developments," Indexer 14 (1985):154; Lewis, D.A., "Aslib Development
Plan," Library Association Record 87 (1985):381; "Information '85: Aslib/IIS/LA/Society
of Archivists/SCONUL Conference," ibid.:382-383+; Harrison, K.C., "United Kingdom," in ALA World Encyclopedia of Library and Information Services, 2nd ed., pp.
823-830. Chicago: American Library Association, 1986; Sippings, G., "The Use of Information Technology by Information Services: The Aslib Information Technology Survey
1987," The Electronic Library 5 (1987):354-357; "60th Aslib Annual Conference; The
Information Business: Directions Forward," Aslib Proceedings 40 (1988):207-226.

465   Association of Assistant Librarians (AAL)

Address   c/o Avril E. Johnston, Secretary, The Scottish Council for Educational Technology, Dowanhill, 74 Victoria Crescent Road, Glasgow G12 9JN (not permanent). Tel:
44 (41) 9548287.

Officers   (elected for 1-yr. term, 1990) Pres: Roger Penny (Community Officer for Holmfirth, West Yorkshire); Past Pres: Martin Stone; Hon. Sec: Avril E. Johnston; Hon. Treas: Liz Buckle. Council: 13 officers plus divisional and student representatives.
Staff   None.
Languages   English.
Established   1895, London; reorganized in 1960. Until 1922 called Library Assistants' Association
Major Fields of Interest   Current awareness and professional involvement. Activities not limited to any particular field of librarianship, but concerned with the interests of students and younger members of the profession in all types of library and information services
Major Goals and Objectives   To provide a forum of expression for younger members of the profession, and to provide a platform for full and effective participation in professional affairs
Structure   Governed by Council consisting of elected officers, representatives from the divisions and student representatives from each library school. Affiliations: A Group of the Library Association.
Sources of Support   Membership dues, sale of publications. Budget (Pound Sterling): 1988: £97,941
Membership   Total members: 10,900. Divisions: 14. Requirements: Membership in Library Association.
General Assembly   General membership meets once a year, before July 15th. 1988: Llandudno, May 6; 1989: Nottingham, May 12.
Publications   *Official journal:* Assistant Librarian. 1898-. 12/yr. (Pound Sterling) 16 (17 overseas, US Dollar 32, North America). Editor: Nigel Ward. Address: Sherwood Library, Spondon Street, Mansfield Road, Nottingham NG5 4AB. Tel: 44 (602) 606680. Circ: 12,000 + . English. Other publications: Annual report; AAL Pointers, an introductory basic series for training and continuing education; Matthew, H., Community Information (1988); Rowley, J., Info-Tech? A Guide for Young Professional Librarians (1987); Drodge, S., Adult Education (1988); AAL Handbooks, a series: Johnson, I., Library School Leavers Handbook (1986), McKee, B., Public Libraries: Into the 1990's? (1987), Blanksby, M., Staff Training: A Librarian's Handbook (1988), Astbury, R., ed., Putting People First: Some New Perspectives on Community Librarianship (1988), etc.; AAL Bibliographic Series: Children's Books, Adult Books. Fiction Index, Picture Book Index, etc. Produces videos. Publications for sale. List available from AAL Publishing, Remploy Ltd., London Road, Newcastle-under-Lyme, Staffs ST5 1RX.
Activities   Past achievements: Worked on freedom of information policy of the profession and for society at large. Raised funds to stock a community library in Papua New Guinea. Current: Establishing an equal opportunity policy within the profession and within professional practice; recruiting new members. A review group was established to assess the Association's structure and activities, and to report to membership in early 1990. Sponsors Book Week activities, exhibits, and continuing education lectures, seminars, and workshops.
Bibliography   Montgomery, A., "Awareness, Action, Leadership: Report of AAL Council, London, Oct. 1986," Assistant Librarian 79 (1986):168-170; Macduff, Shiona, "Molding the Future: Report of AAL Council," Assistant Librarian 80 (1987):137-139; Frost, S., "Tries Hard, Could Do Better: Report of AAL Council," Assistant Librarian 81 (1988):29-32; Bennett, J., "Report from the Front: AAL Council, Jan. 1988," ibid.:60-61; Stone, M., "Presidential Address 1989," Assistant Librarian 82 (1989):159-161.

466   Association of British Library and Information Studies Schools (ABLISS)

Address   c/o School of Librarianship, Polytechnic of North London, 207-225 Essex Road, London N1 3PN (not permanent). Tel: 44 (1) 6072789 ext.2412. Telex: 25228.
Officers   (elected for 2-yr.term) Chair: K.J. McGarry
Languages   English
Established   1969, by heads of library schools in the United Kingdom and Eire, as Association of British Library Schools (ABLS). New name assumed in 1975
Major Fields of Interest   Education for librarianship and information studies
Major Goals and Objectives   To formulate and express the educational policy and attitudes of the library schools of the United Kingdom; to maintain contact with other bodies concerned with education for librarianship and information work
Structure   Governed by heads of library schools. Affiliation: Library Association
Sources of Support   Membership dues
Membership   Total members: 21 (institutional). Requirements: Open only to heads of library schools in the United Kingdom. Dues (Pound Sterling): 10
General Assembly   Entire membership meets four times a year, twice in London, twice in other areas
Publications   No official journal. Occasional publications
Activities   Works on professional qualifications in librarianship; sponsors workshops for teachers in library schools

467   Association of British Theological and Philosophical Libraries (ABTAPL)

Address   c/o Honorary Secretary, c/o Bible Society's Library, Cambridge University Library, West Road, Cambridge CB3 9DR (not permanent). Tel: 44 (223) 333000; Telex: 81395
Officers   (elected for 1-yr. term) Chair: Ms. M. Ecclestone (Partnership House Library, 157 Waterloo Road, London SE1 8XA); Past Chair: John Creasey; Hon. Sec: A.F. Jesson; Hon. Treas: M. Walsh. Exec.Comm: 11.
Staff   1 (volunteer).
Languages   English.
Established   1956, as the UK representative for the proposed International Association of Theological Libraries, which was not realized at that time.
Major Fields of Interest   Bibliography and librarianship of theology and philosophy.
Major Goals and Objectives   Promote the cause of librarianship in these special fields and disseminate information about techniques, collections and publications relevant to members.
Structure   Governed by membership in conference. Affiliations: Library Association, Conseil International des Associations de Bibliothèques de Théologie.
Sources of Support   Membership dues, sale of publications.
Membership   Total members: 100 (individual, mainly institutional). Requirements: Interest in the bibliography and librarianship of the subject fields. Dues (Pound Sterling): 8, libraries and personal members; 1, retired members.
General Assembly   General membership meets twice a year.
Publications   *Official journal:* Bulletin of the Association of British Theological & Philosophical Libraries. 1974-. (new series). 3/yr. (Pound Sterling) 8; (US Dollar 15). Free to members. Editor: Patrick J. Lamb. Address: c/o New College Library, Oxford OX1 3DN. Circ: 250. English. Other publications: Bibliographies and guides, e.g. Religious Bibliographies in Serial Literature: A Guide (1981); A Guide to the Theological Libraries of Great Britain and Ireland (1986). Publications for sale, listed in Journal. Has publications exchange program.

Activities   Past achievements: Compiled bibliographic literature which was published; continuing liaison through organizational affiliations between those working in the sub-ject fields in the UK and abroad. Current: Continuing conferences and publications. Sponsors continuing education lectures, seminars and workshops.
Bibliography   Collison, R.L., "SCOTAPL and ABTAPL: The Early Years," <u>Bulletin of the Association of British Theological and Philosophical Libraries</u> 34/35 (1986):13-15.

468   The Bibliographical Society

Address   c/o Mrs. Mirjam M. Foot, Hon. Sec., Preservation Service, The British Library, Great Russell Street, London WC1B 3DG (permanent). Tel: 44 (1) 6361544. Telex: 21462
Officers   (elected for various terms) Pres (2-yr.term): T. J. Brown; Hon.Sec (1-yr.term, renewable): Mirjam M. Foot; Hon.Treas (1-yr.term, renewable): R.A. Christophers; Hon. Editor (no fixed term): M.J. Jannetta; Hon. Librarian (no fixed term): R. Myers.
Staff   1 (part-time, paid); officers (volunteers)
Languages   English
Established   1892, London
Major Fields of Interest   Historical and textual bibliography
Major Goals and Objectives   (1) To promote and encourage study and research in the fields of historical, analytical, descriptive and textual bibliography, and the history of printing, publishing, bookselling, bookbinding and collecting; (2) to hold meetings at which papers are read and discussed; (3) to print and publish works concerned with bibliography; and (4) to form a bibliographical library.
Structure   Governed by Executive Council and executive officers
Sources of Support   Membership dues, sale of publications, grants from British Library, bequests, donations
Membership   Total members: 1,159 (859 individual, 300 institutional). 26 countries represented. Requirements: Membership is international and is open to all who, by reason of profession or private interest, are concerned with bibliography. It is conditional upon election by the Council. Candidates for membership should be proposed by a member and their names submitted through the Hon.Sec. Dues Pound Sterling): 18 (or $28.50 or DM63.00); 130, Life; 12, for over 65 (without publications).
General Assembly   A paper is read to members in London on the 3rd Tuesday of each month, October to April. The annual general meeting is held on the 3rd Tuesday in October.
Publications   *Official journal:* <u>The Library</u>. 1892-. 4/yr. (Pound Sterling) 27 (US Dollar 55). Free to members. Editor: M.J. Jannetta. Address: Humanities and Social Sciences, The British Library, Great Russell Street, London WC1B 3DG. Circ: 1,700. English. Indexed in <u>Abstracts of English Studies, Year's Work in English Studies, Index of Selected Bibliographical Journals</u> (1935-70). Extensive past and current publications program in accord with the aims of the Society includes monographs, small and large quartos, facsimiles, and folio monographs. Issues annual report, occasional papers, list of members. Price lists available. Publications listed in journal. Publications exchange program in effect.
Activities   Major accomplishments: Publication of revised edition of A.W. Pollard and G.R. Redgrave's <u>Short-Title Catalogue of English Books...1475-1640 (STC)</u> (first issued in 1926), vol.2, 1975, vol.1, 1988, to be followed by index vol.; publication of vol.1 of <u>Union Catalogue of Early Books in Cathedral Libraries</u>. Current and future: Monthly meetings; publication projects; setting-up endowment fund. Not active in promoting leg-

islation related to libraries, but has submitted a paper to the Department of Education
and Science on problems facing ecclesiastical libraries.
Use of High Technology   Computers (IBM-PC) for management
Bibliography   Retrospective sources: The Bibliographical Society: Studies in Retrospect.
London: The Society, 1945 (covers 1892-1942); Myers, R., "The First Fifty Years of the
Bibliographical Society, 1892-1942," Antiquarian Book Monthly Revue 5 (1979):148-153.

469   British and Irish Association of Law Librarians (BIALL)

Address   c/o Harding Law Library, University of Birmingham, PO Box 363, Birming-
ham B15 2TT (not permanent). Tel: 44 (21) 4721301 ext. 3122.
Officers   (elected for 1-yr. term) Chair: A.R.N. Noel-Tod; Hon. Sec: Ms. D.M. Blake;
Hon. Treas: D. Raper; Hon. Ed: B.M. Tearle. Exec.Board: 18.
Staff   None.
Languages   English.
Established   1969, Harrogate, Yorkshire, on the occasion of the Second Workshop on
Law Librarianship sponsoed by Leeds Polytechnic.
Major Fields of Interest   Law librarianship.
Major Goals and Objectives   To promote the better administration and utilization of
law libraries and legal information units, by further education and training, through the
organization of meetings and conferences, the publication of useful information, the en-
couragement of bibliographical study and research in law and librarianship, and cooperation with other organizations and societies.
Structure   Governed by the Council, which consists of 4 officers assisted by a committee
of five members, all annually elected.
Sources of Support   Membership dues, sale of publications.
Membership   Total members: 340 (196 individual, 144 institutional). 15 countries represented. Requirements: The individual/institution should be engaged in providing or
using legal or related materials and legal information. Associate membership available
for those not directly engaged as above. Dues (Pound Sterling): 15, individual (or associate member); 25, institutional (or associate).
General Assembly   General membership meets once a year. 1987: Wales, Aberystwyth; 1988: University of Leicester; 1989: University of Oxford.
Publications   *Official journal:* The Law Librarian. 1970-. 3/yr. (Pound Sterling) 13. Address same as Association. Editor: Ms. B.M. Tearle. Address: c/o The Library, University College of London, Gower Street, London WC1E 6BT. Circ: 800. English. Indexed in
Current Law Index, Legal Resource Index, Legal Information Management Index, LISA,
and Lib.Lit. Publications available to members only.
Activities   Past achievements: Increased membership, particularly from city law firms,
growth in active membership evidenced by attendance at courses and events. Recognized
by employers as advisory body on law library posts. Establishing regular short courses in
law librarianship; publishing annual salary survey of members. Active links with AALL
and CALL. Current: Work on publications, notably 2nd edition of Manual of Law Libraries and Bibliography of Commonwealth Law Reports. Offering course program
jointly with Polytechnic of Central London. Future: Strengthen education program and
links with overseas associations; consolidate membership base in growth areas and recruit
from minority areas such as public sector. BIALL has offered submissions to government
departments on relevant legislation, e.g., the reform of copyright law, and has generally
supported moves for the freedom of information and a national information policy.
Sponsors UK and American law publishers who offer significant support for conference
activities.

Bibliography   Moys, E.M., "BIALL Landmarks of the First Ten Years," The Law Librarian 11 (1980):3-5; Maiden, C., "BIALL - the 18th Annual Study Conference [Aberystwyth, 11-14 Aug. 1987]," Law Librarian 18 (1987):97-98; 19 (1988):33 (Addendum); Mineur, B.W., "Law and Librarianship," Law Librarian 19 (1988):1-4; Fletcher, V.A.A. and Francis, C., "BIALL Course: Teaching Law Students to Use Full Text Online Databases [Institute of Advanced Legal Studies, London, Mar.16, 1988]," Law Librarian 19 (1988):66-68.

470   British Business Schools Librarians Group (BBSLG)

Address   c/o The Librarian, Ashbridge Management College, Berkhamsted, Herts HP4 INS
Activities   No activities reported from the Association

471   British Records Association (BRA)

Address   The Charterhouse, London EC1M 6AU (permanent). Tel: 44 (1) 2530436
Officers   Chair of Council: G.H. Martin; Hon. Treas: A.J. Prescott; Hon. Sec: T.R. Padfield; Hon. Ed: J.D. Davies; Chair, Records Preservation Section Committee: C.R. Davey. Council: 47.
Staff   1 full-time, 2 part-time (paid).
Languages   English.
Established   1932, Nov., at conference of record and allied societies.
Major Fields of Interest   Preservation and use of records.
Major Goals and Objectives   To coordinate and encourage the work of all those individuals and bodies interested in the preservation and use of records, and to rescue records threatened with destruction or dispersal.
Structure   Governed by Council. Affiliations: International Council on Archives, Commonwealth Archivists Association.
Sources of Support   Membership dues, sale of publications, government subsidies, institutional donations.
Membership   Total members: 962. 29 countries represented. Dues (Pound Sterling): 10, individual; 6, retired or student; 15, institutional.
General Assembly   General membership meets once a year.
Publications   *Official journal:* Archives. 1949-. 2/yr. (Pound Sterling) 6. Address same as Association. Editor: J.D. Davies. Address: Reference Library, Public Libraries Dept., Birmingham B3 3HQ. Circ: 1,271. English. Other publications: Annual report; Sources for the History of Houses; Manorial Records; Sources for Irish History in the Public Records Office, etc. Publications available for sale.
Activities   Past achievements: Preservation and distribution to record offices of hundreds of historical documents; report on audiovisual records; worked on national archives policy. Current: National archives policy. Future: Records preservation. Sponsors exhibits and continuing education lectures.
Use of High Technology   Computers for management.
Bibliography   "Private Archives and Public Funding. British Records Association, Hatfield House Conference, 1981," Archives 15 (1982):131-147, 170-174; Davies, J., "Report of the Annual Conference 1985," Archives 19 (1986):41-42.

472   Circle of State Librarians (CSL)

Address   c/o M.J.D. Willsher, Honorary Secretary, Department of Library Services, British Museum (Natural History), Cromwell Road, London SW7 5BD (not permanent). Tel: 44 (1) 5896323 ext. 670

Officers (elected for 1-yr. term) Chair: Ms. S. Pantry; Sec: M.J.D. Willsher; Treas: Ms. M. Deighton. Exec.Comm: 15.
Staff None.
Languages English.
Established 1947.
Major Fields of Interest Government libraries and librarians
Major Goals and Objectives To cultivate a common interest in the cost-effective management of information among all staff working in UK government libraries, and to foster cooperation within the government service environment.
Structure Governed by Committee of 16 members.
Sources of Support Membership dues, sale of publications.
Membership Total members: 585 (individual). Requirements: Full member: Employment in UK government library; associate member: Interest in government librarianship. Dues (Pound Sterling): 1, full member; 6, associate.
General Assembly General membership meets once a year.
Publications *Official journal:* State Librarian. 1953-. 3/yr. (Pound Sterling) 5, (6 overseas). Editor: Ms. J. Driels. Address: Property Services Agency, Room 120, Lambeth Bridge House, Albert Embankment, London, SE1 7SP. Circ: 662. English. Indexed in LISA, Lib.Lit. Publications exchange program in effect.
Activities Meetings and publication of official journal.
Bibliography "Circle of State Librarians Conference on Government Libraries and the Challenge of Change," State Librarian 30 (1982):01-21; Driels, J., "Circle of State Librarians [1987] Conference on How to Manage More on Less: Cost Effective Management and Publicity for Today's Library and Information Services," State Librarian 36 (1988):2-13, 16-18; Willsher, M.J.D., "Comments on the 1987 Circle [of State Librarians] Conference," ibid.:25.

473   Institute of Information Scientists (IIS)

Address 44-45 Museum Street, London WC1A 1LY. Tel: 44 (1) 8318003/8633
Officers (elected for 3-yr. term) Chair of Council: Elspeth Scott; Exec.Sec (appointed): Sarah Carter; Hon.Sec: Diana Edmonds.
Staff 3 (paid)
Languages English
Established 1958, London
Major Fields of Interest Information science
Major Goals and Objectives To promote the value of information and of the information professional to employers; to make the views of the information community known through national and international committees and working groups; to help its members to carry out their work - the effective management and transfer of information - efficiently, and to develop their knowledge and skills
Structure Governed by Executive Council. Affiliations: CICI (Confederation of Information and Communications Industries), EUSIDIC, IFLA
Sources of Support Membership dues, sale of publications
Membership Total members: 2,400 (10% from outside the UK). Special Interest Groups and local Branches. Types of membership and requirements: Member (those with the necessary qualifications and experience); affiliate; student member; fellow (awarded to members who have made a significant contribution to information science, or to the work of the Institute). Dues: Vary according to status
General Assembly Entire membership meets annually.

Publications   *Official journal:* Journal of Information Science (JIS) (formerly The Information Scientist, 1967-78). 1979-. 4/yr. (Netherlands Guilder) 252. Free to members. Address: Elsevier Science Publishers B.V., PO Box 1991, 1000 BZ Amsterdam, The Netherlands. Editor: A. Guilchrist. Address same as Association. Circ: 2,500 (approx.). English. Indexed in Chem.Abs., ComputerRev., LISA, etc. Inform (newsletter). Other publications: Conference proceedings; Foundations of Information Science, a series of selected readings; Text Retrieval: A Directory of Software, etc. Publications for sale, price lists available.
Activities   Although, originally, members worked in scientific and technical fields, IIS members now further include members from commerce, finance, law, education and sociology. The Institute approves educational courses in information science, and influences structure and content of new courses. It carries out regular salary surveys, to keep a check on employment standards and provide a guide for use in negotiations with employers. It submitted and released policy statements on important issues such as copyright and data protection. Sponsors courses, seminars and meetings, to provide professional contacts for members and to enhance their professional skills. Continues to work for the recognition of the professional status of Institute members by employers.
Use of High Technology   Computers for management
Bibliography   Hayden, V., "Information Scientists and Librarians as a Market for Viewdata in the United Kingdom," Journal of Information Science 8 (1984):149-165; New Horizons for the Information Profession: Meeting the Challenge of Change. Proceedings of the Annual Conference of the Institute of Information Scientists, University of Warwick, 1987, ed. by H. Dyer and G. Tweng. Taylor Graham, 1988.

474   International Association of Music Libraries, Archives and Documentation Centres - United Kingdom Branch (IAML-UK)

Address   c/o Helen Mason, General Secretary, Lincolnshire County Library HQ, Music and Drama Library, Brayford House, Lucy Tower Street, Lincoln LN1 1XN (not permanent). Tel: 44 (522) 533541
Officers   (elected for 3-yr. term) Pres: Malcolm Jones (Birmingham City Libraries); Pres-Elect: Pam Thompson (Royal College of Music); Past Pres: Roger Crudge (Avon County Libraries); Gen.Sec: Helen Mason; Treas: Richard Priest (Allegro Music). Exec.Comm: 15.
Staff   None.
Languages   English.
Established   1953, London
Major Fields of Interest   Music libraries and librarianship.
Major Goals and Objectives   To represent the interests of music libraries and librarianship; to coordinate the work of music libraries and music librarians and to promote their status; to study and make effective music bibliography and music library science; to make available all the resources of British music libraries; to cooperate with other national and international organizations in related fields; to send delegates to conferences and to cooperate with the parent body in all possible ways.
Structure   Governed by Executive Committee. Affiliations: A national branch of IAML; Library Association.
Sources of Support   Membership dues, sale of publications.
Membership   Total members: 253 (121 individual, 132 institutional). Types of membership: Individual, institutional, life, student, honorary, retired, associate (for non–library organizations). Requirements: Interest in the work of the Association. Dues (Pound Sterling): 18, individual; 24.50, institutional; 5, retired, student, unemployed. (2 types of

membership, national and international, were introduced in 1987, and are under discussion with IAML).
General Assembly Entire membership meets once a year.
Publications *Official Journal:* BRIO. 1964-. 2/yr. (Pound Sterling) 15 (US Dollar 35).
Free to members. Address same as Association. Editor: Ian Ledsham. Address: 13
York Street, Harborne, Birmingham B17 OHG. Tel: 44 (21) 4720622. Circ: 600. English.
Indexed in Lib.Lit., LISA, RILM. Other publications: Newsletter. (Pound Sterling) 2.50
(US Dollar 5). Free to members. Address same as Association. Editor: Karen E. McAulay. Address: Royal Scottish Academy of Music and Drama; Annual Survey; annual report.
Activities Past achievements: Publication of British Union Catalogue of Orchestral
Sets, and British Union Catalogue of Music Periodicals. Established stronger links with
other organizations in the library and music world; established ERMUL Trust for music
librarians; statistical survey of music libraries. Current: Draft of international standard
music numbering; guide to obtaining voice sets on interlibrary loan; report on the availability of printed music; pack containing advice for those threatened with cuts in music
library services; commenting on new copyright proposals. Future: Publications series;
monitoring music library services through survey; bibliographical projects. Sponsors continuing education lectures, seminars and workshops.
Use of High Technology Computers for management.

475 Librarians' Christian Fellowship (LCF)

Address c/o Graham Hedges, Secretary, 34 Thurlestone Avenue, Seven Kings, Ilford,
Essex IG3 9DU. Tel: 44 (1) 5991310 (home), 44 (1) 8716351 (work).
Officers Sec: Graham Hedges
Staff None
Languages English
Major Fields of Interest Christian librarianship
Major Goals and Objectives To serve Christ in the library and the church
Structure Governed by membership Council. Affiliations: Library Association.
Sources of Support Membership dues, donations.
General Assembly Entire membership meets once a year. 1988: Bristol, April 22.
Membership Open to library, information and archive personnel of all kinds in Britain
and overseas
Publications *Official journal:* LCF Newsletter and Christian Librarian
Activities Meetings and special services, some together with the Fellowship of Christian
Librarians and Information Specialists (FOCLIS; c/o Paul Snezek, Secretary, Buswell Memorial Library, Wheaton College, 525 East Franklin, Wheaton, IL 60187, USA) during
the IFLA Congress in Brighton, 1987.
Bibliography Waller, Richard M., "Annual Report for 1986-87 by the Chairman and
Secretary of the Librarians' Christian Fellowship," Christian Librarian 11 (1987):4-6

476 The Library Association (LA)

Address 7 Ridgmont Street, London WC1E 7AE. Tel: 44 (1) 6367543; Telex: 21897
LALDN G; Fax: 44-1-4367218
Officers (elected for 1-yr. term, 1989-90) Pres: Alan White; Past Presidents: A. Wilson,
E.M. Broome, Jean Plaister; VPs: F.P. Richardson, T.M. Featherstone; Council Chair: N.
Higham; Exec. Comm. Chair: E.M. Broome; Hon. Treas: Stuart A. Brewer; Chief Exec:
George Cunningham (permanent appointment). Nominated for 1990-91 term: Pres: Maurice Line; VP (1990-92): R.G. Astbury. Exec.Comm: 10. Council: Approx.62.

Staff   100 (paid). The staff divides approximately equally between The Library Association proper and Library Association Publishing Ltd. (LAPL)
Languages   English.
Established   1877, London, at the First International Conference of Librarians; incorporated by Royal Charter 1898
Major Fields of Interest   All matters affecting the librarianship and information science profession and services.
Major Goals and Objectives   To unite all persons engaged in the profession and service of librarianship and information science; to promote the service of librarianship and information science in the UK and promote the librarianship and information science profession. In connection with those objectives, to campaign for improved legislation and government activity in these areas.
Structure   Governed by the Council. Affiliations: IFLA. Closely involved with the British Library as the UK affiliated member of FID. Operates in close consultation with all other relevant organizations in the UK and internationally
Sources of Support   Membership dues, sale of publications, investment revenue. Budget (Pound Sterling): 1986/87: Approx. 1.5 million; 1987/88: Approx. 3.5 million. Budget figures include LA Publishing Ltd.
Membership   Total members: 25,000 (24,248 individual, 752 institutional). Branches: 12 (geographical). Special Interest Groups: 23 (Association of Assistant Librarians, Audiovisual, Branch and Mobile Libraries, Cataloguing and Indexing, Colleges of Further and Higher Education, Community Services, Education Librarians, Government Libraries, Industrial, Information Services, Information Technology, International and Comparative Librarianship, Library History, Local Studies, Medical, Health and Welfare, Personnel Training and Education, Prison Libraries, Public Libraries, Publicity and Public Relations, Rare Books, School Libraries, University, College and Research Section, Youth Libraries). Committees: 9. 92 countries represented. Requirements: Work in librarianship and information science or interest in the aims and objectives of the Association. Chartered membership in The Library Association requires an academic qualification and an approved period of experience. Dues (Pound Sterling): 21-88, depending on salary, with reduced rates for students, unemployed, retired or overseas members. An overall increase of 7% was proposed in 1989, up to £115 for those with highest salaries, as well as the creation of a new class of Affiliated Members with dues of £15.
General Assembly   Entire membership meets once a year, but members meet in Branches and Groups more frequently. 1988: Blackpool, Nov.4-7; 1989: Brighton, Sept.4-7.
Publications   *Official journal:* Library Association Record. 1899-. 12/yr. (Pound Sterling) 53 (62 foreign) (US Dollar 123, North America). Free to members. Editor: Jane Jenkins. Address same as Association. Circ: 25,000. English. Indexed in LISA, Lib.Lit., Current Index to Journals in Education, etc. Other publications: Annual report, proceedings of meetings, reports of seminars, workshops. Extensive publication program of books and series: Library Association Yearbook; Library and Information Science Abstracts (12/yr.); Journal of Librarianship (4/yr.); Current Technology Index (12/yr.); British Humanities Index (12/yr.); Dyson, B., ed., The Modern Academic Library (1988); Usherwood, B., The Public Library as Public Knowledge (1988); Chapman, L., Buying Books for Libraries (1988); Gurnsey, J. and White, M., Information Consultancy (1988); Ryder, J., Library Services to Housebound People (1987); Thompson, J. and Carr, R., Introduction to University Library Administration (4th ed., 1987); Simpson, I.S., Basic Statistics for Librarians (3rd ed., 1987); Libraries in the U.K. and the Republic of Ireland (annual directory); British Librarianship and Information Work (series); Rowley, J.E.,

Abstracting and Indexing (2nd ed. 1988); Current Research for the Information Profession (international annual register), and others. Issues annual catalog of publications for sale. Publications exchange program in effect.

Activities   Past achievements: Working against cuts in library expenditures; successfully resisted the application of Value Added Tax (VAT) to books and other forms of literature in the UK; expanded continuing education program; hosted a successful IFLA Conference in 1987 at Brighton. Current: Supervises library and information science educational courses; continuing education program; active involvement in all professional issues nationally and internationally; find solution for the serious financial difficulties of the publishing company (LAPL). Future: Extend membership into the field of information managers in industrial and commercial units, and resist further reductions in library funding. Promoted legislation related to libraries and information services, such as copyright, obscenity legislation, and the Public Libraries and Museums Act 1964. Sponsors exhibits and an extensive program of continuing education lectures, seminars and workshops. The Association is preparing a major report on library and information activities within the European Community and the Council of Europe.

Use of High Technology   Computers for accounts, sales management, word processing and membership records.

Bibliography   "Cunningham: Wide Experience at High Levels," (succeeds Keith Lawrey as Chief Executive) Library Association Record 86 (1984):101, 145; "Group Proposes Changes in (British) Library Association," American Libraries 15 (1984):762-763; "Library Association Considers Sweeping Changes," Library Journal 110 (1985):96; Harrison, K.C., "Library Association," in ALA World Encyclopedia of Library and Information Services, 2nd ed., pp. 462-467. Chicago: American Library Association, 1986; Broome, E.M., "Presidential Address," Library Association Record 89 (1987):562-564; Cunningham, G., "Library Association," in ALA Yearbook 1988, pp. 192-193. Chicago: American Library Association, 1988; Marshall, A., "Green Paper and Poll Tax Main Issues for Library Campaign," Library Association Record 90 (1988):321; Plaister, J., "The New Morality [UK Legislation to Limit Freedom of Information]," New Zealand Libraries 45 (1988):245-246; Cunningham, G., "The Library Association (of the United Kingdom of Great Britain and Northern Ireland)," in ALA Yearbook 1989, p. 145. Chicago: American Library Association, 1989.

477   Map Curators Group of the British Cartographic Society

Address   c/o C.R. Perkins, Secretary, University Map Curator, University of Manchester, Manchester M13 9PL
Officers   Sec: C.R. Perkins
Languages   English
Major Fields of Interest   Map collections; map librarianship
Major Goals and Objectives   To promote the development of map collections; to provide a forum for map curators to exchange information.
Structure   Affiliations: A group of the British Cartographic Society
Sources of Support   Parent organization
Membership   Requirements: Open to members of the British Cartographic Society.
General Assembly   Entire membership meets during the conferences of the British Cartographic Society

478   Marine Librarians' Association (MLA)

Address   c/o Pauline N. Richards, Chairperson, c/o Marine Society, 202 Lambeth Road, London SEI 7JW

Officers   (elected annually) Chair: Pauline N. Richardson
Languages   English
Established   1971, as Nautical Librarians Association
Major Fields of Interest   Marine science and technology; shipping; shipbuilding; marine engineering and telecommunications; marine insurance; maritime law; ports and cargo handling; fisheries; offshore activities.
Major Goals and Objectives   (1) To promote contact and cooperation between librarians and information workers in the marine field; (2) to develop a body of professional expertise relevant to marine literature and information sources.
Sources of Support   Membership dues, sale of publications (to small extent)
Membership   Total number: 120 (individual). 10 countries represented. Requirements: Librarians and information workers interested in marine matters. Dues (reviewed annually) (Pound Sterling): 10
General Assembly   Entire membership meets once a year; regional meetings 3 times a year.
Publications   Publishes <u>Newsletter</u>. 3/yr. English. Circ: Membership. Other publications: Conference proceedings; membership directory; <u>Marine Transport: A Guide to Libraries and Sources of Information in Great Britain</u>. Publications available for sale are listed in <u>Seaways</u>, the journal of the Nautical Institute. Publications exchange program in effect.
Activities   Publications and meetings to provide a forum for discussion of problems and exchange of information.

479   Play Matters / The National Toy Libraries Association / ACTIVE   (Play Matters/NTLA)
(formerly the Toy Libraries Association)

Address   68 Churchway, London NW1 1LT (permanent). Tel: 44 (1) 3879592
Officers   (elected for 2-3-yr. terms) Chair: Ivan Horrocks; Vice-Chairs: Jenny Knight and Diane Underhill; Treas: Pat Clayton
Staff   8 (paid), 4 (part-time volunteers)
Languages   English
Established   1972, Enfield, Middlesex, as Toy Libraries Association; ACTIVE founded 1975; joined together in 1981, and became Play Matters in 1983.
Major Fields of Interest   Child development through play
Major Goals and Objectives   Toy libraries exist to promote the principle that play <u>does matter</u> for the developing child. They operate as a preventive service, filling gaps in the existing provision for all families with babies and young children, and for people with special needs. By offering a befriending, supportive service to parents, and by making available and lending appropriate toys, they extend the opportunity for shared play into the home. They function equally successfully in statutory and voluntary agencies and self-help groups. ACTIVE, within Play Matters, encourages the development of play, leisure and communication aids for disabled children and adults to enable them to lead more active and independent lives.
Structure   Governed by elected Council of management.
Sources of Support   Membership dues, sale of publications, government grants, donations from charitable trusts and other sources
Membership   Total members: 830 (individual and institutional). Requirements: Open to any interested individual, local authority, or toy library. Dues (Pound Sterling): 10, individual, toy library or ACTIVE group.
General Assembly   Entire membership meets once a year.

Publications *Official journal:* <u>ARK</u>, 1977-. 4/yr. Free to members. Editor: Lesley
Houlston, Information Officer. Address same as Association. Circ: Approx. 1,500. Eng-
lish. Price list of publications available. Journal exchanged with other voluntary organi-
zations in the UK.
Activities Activities as described in the goals and objectives of the Association.
Use of High Technology Computers (AMSTRAD PC 1512) for management
Bibliography Atkinson, P., "The Role of ACTIVE within PLAY MATTERS," <u>Ark:
Journal of Toy Libraries Association</u> (Summer 1988):4-5.

480   Private Libraries Association (PLA)

Address c/o Ravelston, South View Road, Pinner, Middlesex, HA5 3YD (permanent)
Officers (elected for 3-yr. term) Pres: Peter Eaton; Past Pres: John Russell Taylor;
Hon.Sec: Frank Broomhead; Hon.Treas: John Paton; Hon.Memb.Sec: John Allison (5
Criffel Ave., Streatham Hill, London SW2 4AY); Hon.Memb.Sec. for America: William
A. Klutts (145 East Jackson, Box 289, Ripley, Tennessee 38063, USA); Hon.Memb.Sec.
for Institut.Libraries: Frances Guthrie; Editor and Hon.Publ.Sec: David Chambers.
Exec.Comm: 13
Staff 8 (volunteers).
Languages English.
Established 1957, London, following a letter from Philip Ward to <u>The Observer</u>
Major Fields of Interest Book collecting.
Major Goals and Objectives To promote and encourage the awareness of the benefits
of book ownership; to publish works related to this field; and to serve as a forum for the
presentation of papers concerning book ownership.
Structure Governed by executive officers and council.
Sources of Support Membership dues, sale of publications.
Membership Total members: 1,200 (950 individual, 250 institutional). Worldwide
member representation. Requirements: Book collectors, i.e. collectors of rare books, fine
books, single authors, special subjects and, above all, collectors of books for the simple
pleasures of reading and ownership. Membership applications should be addressed to the
Hon. Membership Secretary. Dues (Pound Sterling): 20 (US Dollar 35).
General Assembly Entire membership meets once a year. 1987-1990 meetings
planned for London.
Publications *Official journal:* <u>The Private Library</u>. 1957-. 4/yr. (Pound Sterling) 20 (US
Dollar 35). Free to members. Editor: David Chambers. Address same as Association.
Circ: 1,200. English. Other publications: Series of illustrated pamphlets and books on
specialized aspects of bibliophilia; annual free book (sometimes every two years); <u>Private
Press Books</u> (annual checklist, 1960-); <u>The Exchange List</u>. 4/r. Editor: Peter Bond. Address: 23 Stanley Place, High Street, Chipping Ongar, Essex CM5 9SU, includes information on books members wish to donate, sell or obtain; <u>Members' Handbook</u>, listing addresses and collecting interests. Publications for sale, price lists available.
Activities Publication of journal, member books, and private press books. Correspondence within the Association is encouraged, and the Association attempts to provide useful information to members through its journal and other publications.
Use of High Technology Computers (PCs) for management.
Bibliography Chambers, D.J., "Twenty-five Years of the PLA, ...1968-1981," <u>Private
Libraries</u>, 3rd Ser., 4 (Summer 1981):73-86.

481   School Library Association (SLA)

Address   c/o Liden Library, Barrington Close, Liden, Swindon, Wiltshire SN3 6HF (not permanent). Tel: 44 (793) 617838.
Officers   (elected for 1-yr. term) Chair: Ms. J. Watts; Vice-Chair: Ms. K. Ryan; Hon. Sec: Keith Salkeld; Hon. Treas: Colin Pidgeon; Exec. Sec (appointed): Valerie Fea
Staff   3 (paid)
Languages   English.
Established   1937, incorporated 1955.
Major Fields of Interest   Development of school libraries (primary and secondary); training for school library work
Major Goals and Objectives   Recognition of the school library as the center of the curriculum; increase training opportunities for teachers and librarians in school library work; take action to prevent the decline in funds for school library resources; provide an information/advisory service from national headquarters and through publications.
Structure   Governed by executive officers and National Committee. Affiliations: IFLA, IASL, Joint Standing Committee with Library Association.
Sources of Support   Membership dues. Budget (Pound Sterling): Approx. 81,000.
Membership   Total members: 3,300 (approx.) (300 individual, 3,000 institutional). Branches: 31. 32 countries represented in membership. Requirements: Any individual, establishment, or organization with an interest in school libraries. Dues (Pound Sterling): 15, individual and institutional.
General Assembly   General membership meets once a year.
Publications   *Official journal:* School Librarian. 1937-. 4/yr. (Pound Sterling) 25. Free to members. Address same as the Association. Editor: Joan Murphy. Address: 5 Wilcote Lane, Ramsden, Oxon OX7 3BA. Circ: Membership plus approx. 500 subscribers. English. Indexed in Lib.Lit., LISA. Other publications: Annual reports. Publications for sale and listed in journal; price lists available.
Activities   Past achievements: Represented in Working Party set up by the Library and Information Services Council (LISC) to produce Report on School Library Services: LISC Report published in 1984. Meeting with Secretary of State for Education & Science, 1984. Support for school library services under threat of closure. Current: Development of information/advisory service; liaison with the Library Association in improving training opportunities for teachers and librarians in school library work; promoting the Association with the new publicity created by means of a Design Council grant in 1986 to produce a new image for the Association. Future: Develop a national center of information on school librarianship through grant aid; further development of information/advisory service; increase liaison with other professional organizations; extend range of publications with emphasis on practical guidelines. Sponsors exhibits and continuing education seminars on current school library issues.
Use of High Technology   Computers (Amstrad PCW 8512) for management
Bibliography   King, E.J., "The School Library Association of Great Britain: Its First Fifty Years," International Review of Children's Literature and Librarianship 2 (1987):82-94; Fea, V., "Change and Challenge - the School Library Association at Fifty," Education Libraries Bulletin 31 (Spring 1988):7-15.

482   Society of Archivists

Address   c/o Suffolk Record Office, County Hall, Ipswich, Suffolk 1P4 2JS (not permanent) Tel: 44 (473) 55801 ext. 4232

Officers   (elected for variable terms) Chair: K. Hall; Vice-Chair: V.W. Gray; Hon. Sec:
Ms. A.J.E. Arrowsmith; Hon. Asst. Sec: J.F. Wilson; Hon. Treas: P. Durrant; Hon. Ed: J.B.
Post. Exec. Council: 24
Staff   None
Languages   English
Established   1947, as Society of Local Archivists
Major Fields of Interest   Archival collections
Major Goals and Objectives   The preservation of archives and records; training and
professional standards of archivists, records managers and conservators.
Structure   Governed by Council. Affiliations: No formal affiliations, but has links
through representation with a number of organizations in the information field, including
FID
Sources of Support   Membership dues, sale of publications, conference/seminar fees.
Membership   Total members: 1,100 (individual only). Regions: 10. Groups: 4. Require-
ments: To be primarily occupied in the care or administration of archives and records.
Dues: Vary according to salary.
General Assembly   Entire membership meets twice a year, once in London and once
at another place.
Publications   *Official journal:* Journal of the Society of Archivists. 1947-. 2/yr. (Pound
Sterling) 12. Free to members. Editor: J.B. Post. Address: Public Record Office, Ruskin
Avenue, Richmond, Kew, Surrey TW9 4DU. English. Other publications: Annual report,
proceedings of meetings, reports of seminars, workshops, and others. Publications for
sale, price lists available.
Activities   Past achievements: Lobbying of government on local government bill; work
on national archives policy; recognition of university archival training courses. Current
and future: Completion of national archives policy work; establishment of professional
register; development of computer user group. Active in promoting legislation.
Use of High Technology   Microcomputers for management.
Bibliography   Hull, F., "The [British] Society of Archivists," Janus 2 (1985):7-9.

483   Society of County Librarians (SCL)

Address   Hampshire County Library, 81 North Walls, Winchester, Hants. SO23 8BY
(permanent). Tel: 44 (962) 60644. Telex: 47121
Officers   (elected for 3-yr. term) Pres: D. Harrison; English VP & Hon.Treas: G.E.
Smith; Welsh VP: W.G. Williams; Hon. Sec: J.C. Beard. Exec.Comm: 18
Staff   1 (volunteer)
Languages   English
Established   1954
Major Fields of Interest   Public librarianship in England and Wales
Major Goals and Objectives   To further the interests of county libraries in England
and Wales; to provide advice to the Association of County Councils on public library
matters.
Structure   Governed by Executive Committee. Affiliations: Federation of Local Au-
thority Chief Librarians
Sources of Support   Membership dues. Budget (Pound Sterling): 1987/88: 500 expen-
diture
Membership   Total members: 46 (individual). Types of membership: Individual. Requirements: County librarian in England or Wales. Dues (Pound Sterling): 5.
General Assembly   Entire membership meets once a year. 1987: Thorpe, Derbyshire;
1988: London; 1989: Thorpe, Derbyshire; 1990: London.

Publications   No official journal. Publishes   Newsletter. 1974-. 4/yr. Free to
members. Editor: P.D. Gee. Address: Director of Libraries and Museums, Cheshire
County Library, 91 Hoole Road, Chester. CH3 3NG. Circ: 50. English. Other publications: Annual report.
Activities   Past achievements: Argued the case for free public libraries; advised Association of County Councils on a number of matters, including service to children, technical
and information services. Current: Playing active role in setting up the Federation of Local Authority Chief Librarians; providing input to statistical data on funding for public
libraries. Future: Preparing case for the optimum size of public library authorities, if local government re-organization should become a live issue; arguing the case for better
public library services.

484   Standing Conference of Co-operative Library and Information Services (SCOCLIS)

Address   c/o The Editor, SCOCLIS News, Central Library, Surrey Street, Sheffield S1
1XZ
General Assembly   Entire membership meets once a year.
Publications   Official journal: Newsletter, SCOCLIS News. 1976-. 4/yr. Free to members. Editor: Angela M. Allott. Address same as Association. English.
Activities   The Standing Conference provides a forum for information exchange for
groups and institutions offering information services including networks.

485   Standing Conference of National and University Libraries (SCONUL)

Address   c/o SCONUL Secretariat, 102 Euston Street, London NW1 2HA (perma-
nent). Tel: 44 (1) 3870317
Officers   (elected for 1-yr. term) Chair: B. Naylor; Vice-Chair: Ms. A.M. McAulay; Hon.
Treas: A.G. Mackenzie; Sec. (appointed): Anthony J. Loveday. Exec.Comm: 10
Staff   2 (paid)
Languages   English
Established   1950, London, at a meeting of invited university and national library rep-
resentatives; incorporated 1979.
Major Fields of Interest   All aspects of university and national library administration
including SCONUL Advisory Committee on African Studies and SCONUL Advisory
Committee on American Studies (SACAS)
Major Goals and Objectives   To promote and advance the science and practice of li-
brarianship and to improve the overall standards of national and university libraries for
the benefit of the public.
Structure   Governed by Council (elected by full Conference of member institutions).
Affiliations: IFLA
Sources of Support   Membership dues. Budget (Pound Sterling): 1986/87: 61,000;
1987/88: 63,000.
Membership   Total members: 75 (institutional). Institutions from England, Scotland,
Wales, Northern Ireland, and Eire represented. Requirements: Membership by invitation.
Universities that hold University Charter, whose librarian is of professional status and
member of the Senate, and that have substantial provision for research needs. National
libraries with substantial collections, that function primarily as research libraries for the
general public. Dues: Graded subscription based upon a National Flat Rate (currently
£840).

General Assembly   Entire membership meets twice a year, in spring and fall. 1987:
University of Lancaster, April; and London, fall; 1988: University of Exeter, April 12-15;
and Univ. of York, Sept.19-22; 1989: Univ. of Southampton; London
Publications   No official journal. Publishes annual report, reports of seminars, workshops, SCONULOG, Statistics, etc.   Publications available for sale, price lists issued.
Activities   Representing academic libraries at various national committees. Sponsoring
conferences, and other continuing education programs. Active in promoting library-related legislation, e.g. Copyright Law, Public Lending Right, etc.   Bestows the Library Design Award for new major building or extension.
Use of High Technology   Computers (Exxon, Amstrad), databases for management;
setting up an Electronic Mail network on Telecom Gold.
Bibliography   Bowyer, T.H., "SCONUL: The Contribution of Geoffrey Woledge," Journal of Documentation 40 (1984):92-93; Munthe, G., "SCONUL/SCANDIA Meeting at
the University of Sussex," Synopsis 15 (1984):84; Loughridge, B., "The SCONUL Graduate Trainee Scheme as Preparation for Professional Education in Librarianship and Information Work: Results of a Survey," British Journal of Academic Librarianship 2
(1987):191-203; Loveday, A.J., "Statistics for Management and Trend Analysis: A SCO-
NUL Experiment," IFLA Journal 14 (1988):334-342.

486   Standing Conference of National and University Libraries. SCONUL Advisory Committee on American Studies (SACAS)

Address   c/o SCONUL Secretariat, 102 Euston Street, London NW1 2HA (perma-
nent). Tel: 44 (1) 3870317. Telex: 265871.
Officers   (elected for 1-yr. term) Chair: W.G. Simpson; Sec: J.R. Pinfold. Exec.Comm:
15
Staff   None
Languages   English
Established   1978, London, as American Studies Library Group (ASLG); later incorpo-
rated with SCONUL.
Major Fields of Interest   American studies
Major Goals and Objectives   To bring together librarians and libraries with American
studies interests; to advise on library provision for American studies; to initiate and
coordinate bibliographic projects to assist both scholars and librarians.
Structure   Governed by Committee composed of nominated members and SCONUL.
Affiliations: A committee of SCONUL; British Association of American Studies (BAAS);
European Association of American Studies.
Sources of Support   Membership dues, sale of publications, grants for specific pro-
jects. Supported by SCONUL.
Membership   Total members: 425 (325 individual, 100 institutional). Requirements: In-
terest in American studies. Dues: No dues for individuals; subscription to Newsletter for
institutions.
General Assembly   Entire membership meets once a year.
Publications   *Official journal:* American Studies Library Newsletter (formerly ASLG
Newsletter). 1978-. 3/yr. (Pound Sterling) 5. Address same as Association. Editor: Ms. A.
Cowden. Address: Institute of U.S. Studies, Tavistock Square, London WC1. Circ: 425.
English. Other publications: Proceedings of meetings; United States Guide to Library
Holdings in the U.K. (1982); Union List of American Studies Periodicals in U.K. Li-
braries (1983); Directory of American Studies Librarians in the U.K. (1984), etc. Publi-
cations available for sale. No publications exchange program in effect.

Activities   Past achievements: Publications, including a number of Bibliographic Guides and Union Lists; holding of annual conference on topics of American Studies interest. Current and future: Compilation of <u>Union List of Little Magazine Holdings in the U.K.</u> Sponsors Book Week, exhibits, lectures, seminars, workshops, and other continuing education programs.

United States of America

487   American Association of Law Libraries (AALL)

Address   53 W. Jackson Boulevard, Chicago, Illinois 60604 (permanent). Tel: 1 (312) 9394764. Fax: 1-312-4311097.
Officers   (elected for 1-yr.term, 1989-90) Pres: Richard Danner; VP/Pres.Elect: Penny Hazelton; Past Pres: Margaret A. Leary; Treas: Claire Engel; Sec: Paul Fu. Gitelle Seer; Exec.Dir: Judith Jenesen. Exec.Board: 11.
Staff   7 (paid)
Languages   English
Established   1906, Narragansett Pier, Rhode Island.
Major Fields of Interest   Law librarianship
Major Goals and Objectives   To promote law librarianship, to develop and increase the usefulness of law libraries, to cultivate the science of law librarianship, and to foster a spirit of cooperation among the members of the profession.
Structure   Governed by executive officers and council meetings. Affiliations: IFLA
Sources of Support   Membership dues, sale of publications.
Membership   Total members: 4,750. Chapters: 28. Special Interest Sections: 13 (Academic Law Libraries, Automation & Scientific Development, Contemporary Social Problems, Foreign, Comparative and International Law, Government Documents, Legal History and Rare Books, Legal Information Service to the Public, Micrographics & Audio/Visual, Online Bibliographic Services, Private Law Libraries, Readers' Services, Special-Interest Sections Council, State, Court and County Law Libraries, Technical Services). Committees: 32 (Copyright, Education, Preservation Needs of Law Libraries, Statistics, etc.). Type of membership: Individual, institutional, life, student, honorary, associate. Requirements: Persons officially connected with a law library, state library, or a general library maintaining a law section may become active individual members on payment of dues. Any library may become an institutional member. Dues: $115, active individual; $115, institutional; $115-220, associate; $25, student.
General Assembly   Entire membership meets annually. 1989: Reno, June 16-21; 1990: Minneapolis, June 17-20; 1991: New Orleans, July 14-17; 1992: San Francisco, July 19-22; 1993: Boston, July 20-23..
Publications   *Official journal:* Law Library Journal. 1908-. 4/yr. $50 ($55, foreign). Free to members. Editor: Richard A. Danner. Address: Duke University Law Library, Durham, NC 27706. Circ: 5,000+. English. Indexed in Lib.Lit., LISA. Other publications: AALL Newsletter (Editor: Mary Sworsky); AALL Directory; Directory of Law Libraries; Biographical Directory of Law Librarians; Index to Foreign Legal Periodicals; AALL Publication Series; Current Publications in Legal and Related Fields; Recruitment Checklist; annual reports, proceedings of conferences, seminars, etc. Price lists available.
Activities   Past achievements: Establishment of scholarship program; expansion of headquarters; appointment of first Executive Director in 1981; Professional Development Officer since 1988; Convention Manager for 1989 meeting. Current and future: To strengthen and coordinate educational activities with other professional organizations; two special committees are concerned with National Information Policy, and Preservation Needs of Law Libraries; Standing Committee on National Legal Resources works on outlining legal information needs for the rest of the century; awarding yearly some $53,000 in scholarships (including $3,500 for minorities); organizing special Conferences of Newer Law Librarians preceding the annual meetings, to orient new members. A job bank main-

tained by AALL Placement office. Sponsors conferences, seminars, workshops, and other
continuing education programs.
Use of High Technology   Computers for daily document production.
Bibliography   Rempel, S.P., "Quo Vadis?" Law Library Journal 77 (1985):151-156;
Howes, R., "American Association of Law Libraries," Law Librarian 16 (1985):121;
Marke, J.J.,"Law Libraries," in ALA World Encyclopedia of Library and Information Ser-
vices, 2nd ed., pp. 430-433. Chicago: American Library Association, 1986; "American Association of Law Libraries Special Committee on the Future of AALL 1983-1985: Final
Report Nov. 1985," Law Library Journal 78 (1986):351-361; Berring, R.C., "Dyspeptic
Ramblings of a Retiring Past President," Law Library Journal 79 (1987):345-350; "Reports from the 80th Annual Meeting of the American Association of Law Libraries, Held
in Chicago," Library of Congress Information Bulletin 46 (Nov.30, 1987): 512-518; Py-
rah, A., "'We the People' - 80th Annual Meeting of the AALL," Law Librarian 18
(1987):94-95; Wallace, M., "Statistics: Management and Political Tool [Future AALL-
sponsored survey of private law libraries]," Law Library Journal 80 (1988):329-338;
Leary, M.A., "American Association of Law Libraries," in ALA Yearbook 1989, pp.
21-22. Chicago: American Library Association, 1989; "American Association of Law Libraries," in The Bowker Annual: Library and Book Trade Almanac, 34th Edition
1989-90, pp. 631-633. New York: R.R. Bowker, 1989.

488   American Association of School Librarians (AASL)

Address   c/o ALA, 50 East Huron Street, Chicago, Illinois 60611 (permanent). Tel: 1
(312) 9446780. Fax: 1-312-4409374.
Officers   (elected for 1-yr.term) Pres: Retta B. Petrick (PO Box 22235, Little Rock, AR
72221; Tel: (501) 868-5740); Pres.-Elect: Winona Jones; Past Pres: Jacie Morris; Exec.Dir:
Ann Carlson Weeks. Exec.Board: 15.
Staff   5 (paid)
Languages   English
Established   1951, Chicago, during meeting of the American Library Association.
Major Fields of Interest   Library media services in schools, from kindergarten to 12th
grade.
Major Goals and Objectives   To establish a forum and voice for school librarians at
the national level; to plan a program of study and service for the improvement and extension of library media services in elementary and secondary schools as a means of
strengthening the educational program; evaluation, selection, interpretation, and utilization of media as used in the context of school programs; stimulation of continuous study
and research in the library field and to establish criteria of evaluation; synthesis of the activities of all units of the American Library Association in areas of mutual concern; representation and interpretation of the need for the function of school libraries to other educational and lay groups; stimulation of professional growth, improvement of the status of
school librarians, and encouragement of participation by members in appropriate type-of-
activity divisions.
Structure   Governed by Board of Directors and ALA Council. Affiliations: A Division
of ALA, NCATE (National Council for the Accreditation of Teacher Education), IASL,
and others.
Sources of Support   Membership dues, government subsidies (grants, project proposals). Budget: Approx.$312,500.
Membership   Total members: 6,973 (6,105 individual, 868 institutional). Sections: 3.
Types of membership: Individual, institutional, life, student. Requirements: Open to all

those interested in school library media programs and services. Dues: $35, plus ALA membership ($75).
General Assembly   Entire membership meets once a year during ALA Annual Conference. In addition, members meet at separate National Conferences every 3 years. 1989: Salt Lake City, Oct.18-22 (Fifth National Conference); 1990: Chicago; 1992: Baltimore (Sixth National Conference).
Publications   *Official journal:* School Library Media Quarterly. 1951-. 4/yr. $35. Free to members. Editors: Judy Pitts and Barbara Stripling. Address: Fayetteville High School Library, 1000 West Stone Street, Fayetteville, AR 72701). Circ: 9,000. English. Indexed in Lib.Lit. Other publications: AASL Presidential Hotline (2/yr. Circ: Membership); Information Power: Guidelines for School Library Media Programs (1988), a document prepared jointly with the Association for Educational Communications and Technology (AECT); Competencies for the Initial Preparation of School Library Media Specialists (guidelines); Focus on Issues and Trends, a monograph series; annual reports, proceedings of conferences, seminars, etc.
Activities   Expansion of membership; appointment of Donald Adcock to the new position of AASL Coordinator for Program Support, Sept. 1989, to provide staff support for AASL committees and sections, and advisory services to AASL members and the profession. Activities carried out by various interest groups, task forces and committees in areas such as: Media personnel development, media program development, public information, long-range planning, planning for the White House Conference on Libraries and Information Services, early childhood education, school library media programs in vocational/technical schools, student involvement in the Media Center, non-public schools, school library media educators and supervisors, liaison with other educational groups, issue of flexible scheduling, etc. A major AASL goal is to strengthen communication and cooperation with other professional associations and educational groups. Sponsors conferences, seminars, workshops, and other continuing education programs.
Use of High Technology   Computers for management.
Bibliography   Pond, P.B., American Association of School Libraries: The Origin and Development of a National Professional Association for School Libraries, 1896-1951. Unpubl. doctoral dissertation. University of Chicago, 1982; "AASL Studies Options for Future: Secession from ALA a Possibility," School Library Journal 30 (1984):9-10; "AASL's Report Listing ALA Constraints Offers These Options for Resolution," ibid.:8-9; Flagg, G., "AASL Answers the Challenge: Programs Take Precedence over Politics at the Division's Third National Conference in Atlanta," American Libraries 15 (1984):785 + ; Robb, F.C., "Future Connections: AASL and Main Trends," School Library Media Quarterly 12 (1984):120-126; Miller, M.L., "What Next, AASL?" School Library Journal 31 (1984):28-30; Lowrie, J.E.,"School Libraries/Media Centers," in ALA World Encyclopedia of Library and Information Services, 2nd ed., pp. 733-736. Chicago: American Library Association, 1986; Mancall, J.C. and Bertland, L.H., "Step One Reported: Analysis of AASL's First Needs Assessment for Continuing Education," School Library Media Quarterly 16 (1988):88-98; Hand, D., "Information Power Arrives in School Library/Media Centers [AASL/AECT Guidelines for School Library Media Programs]," Ohio Media Spectrum 40 (Spring 1988):4; "School Library Media Guidelines 1988 Define Elements of Effective Programs," School Library Journal 34 (1988):12; Weeks, A.C., "Information Power: Guidelines for School Library Media Programs," in ALA Yearbook 1988, pp. 27-28. Chicago: American Library Association, 1988; Kahler, J., "Information Power: Guidelines for School Library Media Programs: A Commentary," Texas Library Journal 64 (1988):69-70; Whitney, Karen A., "American Association of School Librarians," in ALA Yearbook 1989, pp. 22-25. Chicago: American Library Association, 1989; "Ameri-

can Library Association. American Association of School Librarians," in The Bowker Annual: Library and Book Trade Almanac, 34th Edition, 1989-90, pp. 637-639. New York: R.R. Bowker, 1989; Gaughan, T., "AALS Conference: Rugged Individuals Making Common Cause," American Libraries 20 (1989):1042-43.

489   American Federation of Information Processing Societies (AFIPS)

Address   1899 Preston White Drive, Reston, Virginia 22091. Tel: 1 (703) 6208900.
Officers   (elected for 1-yr.term) Pres: Howard L. Funk; VP: Seymour Wolfson; Sec: Arthur C. Lumb; Treas: Robert Hoadley; Manag.Dir: Dianne Edgar. Exec.Board: 23.
Staff   2 (paid), 100 (volunteers)
Languages   English
Established   1961; formerly National Joint Computer Committee.
Major Fields of Interest   Computer science
Major Goals and Objectives   To promote the profession of computer scientists; to serve as a national voice for the computing field; to advance knowledge of the information processing sciences.
Structure   Governed by Board of Directors. Affiliations: IFIP (International Federation for Information Processing); ASIS; American Statistical Association; Association for Computational Linguistics; Association for Computing Machinery, etc.
Sources of Support   Membership dues, sale of publications.
Membership   Total members: 11 (institutional, with about 1,500 individuals). Requirements: Interest in computer science.
General Assembly   Entire membership meets at the annual National Computer Conference (with exhibits).
Publications   *Official journal:* Washington Report. 6/yr. Free to members. Address same as Association. Other publications: Annual reports, proceedings of conferences, seminars, and occasional monographs. Publications for sale.
Activities   Activities carried out through various committees: Admissions, Awards, Education, Governmental Activities, History of Computing, and International Relations. Presents annual award for contribution to information processing. Sponsors conferences, seminars, workshops, and other continuing education programs.
Use of High Technology   Computers for management.

490   American Film and Video Association (AFVA)
(formerly Educational Film Library Association / EFLA)

Address   920 Barnsdale Road, Suite 152, La Grange Park, Illinois 60525. Tel: 1 (312) 4824000.
Officers   (elected for 1-yr.term) Pres: Sharon K. Chaplock; Pres-Elect: Mark Richie; Past Pres: Judy Gaston; Sec: Linda Artel; Treas: June McWatt; Exec.Dir: Ron MacIntyre. Exec.Board: 12.
Staff   8 (paid), 2 (volunteers)
Languages   English
Established   1943, Indiana, as Educational Film Library Association, Inc. (EFLA).
Major Fields of Interest   Non-theatrical educational films and videos
Major Goals and Objectives   To promote the production, distribution and utilization of educational films and videos, and other audiovisual materials.
Structure   Governed by executive officers.
Sources of Support   Membership dues, sale of publications, government subsidies.
Membership   Total members: 1,500. 20 countries represented. Types of membership: Individual, institutional. Requirements: Open to individuals and institutions interested in

the aims of the Association. Dues: $45, individual; $175, institutional; $265, commercial organization; $500, sustaining; $25, student and retiree.

General Assembly   Entire membership meets once a year.

Publications   *Official journal:* Sightlines. 1967-. 4/yr. $20. Free to members. Editor: Judith Trojan. Address same as Association. Circ: 4,000. English. Indexed in Film Literature Index, Lib.Lit., Media Review Digest. Other publications: American Film and Video Association Bulletin (4/yr.); American Film and Video Evaluations (2/yr.); American Film and Video Festival Program Guide (1/yr.); annual reports, proceedings of conferences, seminars, etc.

Activities   Ongoing American Film and Video Festival, the largest non-theatrical film/video festival. Extensive publications program; maintaining a reference library. Sponsors conferences, seminars, workshops, and other continuing education programs.

Use of High Technology   Computers for databases and electronic publishing.

Bibliography   Bickley, D., "American Film Festival's 25th Anniversary [and the 40th Anniversary of EFLA]," Sightlines 16 (Summer 1983):6-9; "American Film and Video Association," in The Bowker Annual: Library and Book Trade Almanac, 34th Edition 1989-90, p. 633. New York: R.R. Bowker, 1989.

491   American Friends of the Vatican Library (AFVL)

Address   157 Lakeshore Road, Grosse Pointe Farms, Michigan 48236 (permanent). Tel: 1 (313) 8858855.

Officers   (elected for 1-yr.term) Pres: Rev. Msgr. Francis X. Canfield; VP: Claudia Carlen, IHM; Sec: Elizabeth J. Flaherty, O.P.; Treas: Anne Lemhagen. Exec.Board: 18 (4 honorary).

Staff   1 (paid), 4 (volunteers)

Languages   English

Established   1981, to raise funds in support of the Vatican Library

Major Fields of Interest   Books, libraries, and research

Major Goals and Objectives   To operate exclusively for religious, charitable, scientific, literary, or educational purposes, especially for the benefit of the Biblioteca Apostolica Vaticana.

Structure   Governed by Board of Directors. Affiliations: Catholic Library Association.

Sources of Support   Membership dues, sale of publications; foundation grants, personal donations. Budget: 1986/87: $44,967; 1987/88: $43,682.

Membership   Total members: 800+. 4 countries represented. Requirements: Interest in things cultural and specifically the Vatican Apostolic Library and its work. Dues: $25, friend; $50, contributing; $100, sustaining; $500, patron; $1,000, founder.

General Assembly   No meetings of membership scheduled.

Publications   Official journal: AMICI (newsletter). 1982-. 4/yr. Free to members. Address same as Association. Editor: Yvonne Tata. Address: 420 N. Shore, St. Clair Shores, MI 48080. Circ: Membership. English. Other publications: Annual reports, pamphlets, brochures, etc., available to members only or as gifts. No publications exchange program.

Activities   Past achievements: Building up membership; sponsoring lectures; contributing funds for special accessions for the Vatican Library; contributing funds for new lighting in the Manuscript Reading Room of the Vatican Library. Current: Sponsoring fund raising activities; sponsoring lectures on the Vatican Library and the projects and publications sponsored by the Library. Future: Subsidizing special accessions for the Vatican Library; subsidizing research publications of the Vatican Library; setting up a Visiting Scholars Fund for young scholars working under the direction of a Vatican Library staff member. Sponsors lectures and exhibits.

Use of High Technology   Computers (IBM PC, PC Limited Turbo PC) for management.

492   American Indian Library Association (AILA)

Address   c/o ALA/OLOS, 50 East Huron Street, Chicago, Illinois 60611 (permanent). Tel: 1 (312) 9446780. Fax: 1-312-4409374
Officers   Pres: Rhonda Harris Taylor (Choctaw) (Henderson Library, Lon Morris College, Jacksonville, Texas 75766); VP: Janice M. Beaudin (College Library, 600 N. Park Street, Univ. of Wisconsin, Madison, WI 53706); Sec: Naomi Caldwell-Wood (Providence Public School, Ed.Tech.Dept., 480 Charles Street, Providence, Rhode Island 02904); Staff Liaison: Sibyl Moses (ALA Headquarters)
Staff   1 (paid)
Languages   English
Established   1979
Major Fields of Interest   Library services to American Indians
Major Goals and Objectives   To promote the development, maintenance, and improvement of libraries, library systems, and cultural and information services on reservations and in communities of Native Americans and Native Alaskans; to develop and encourage adoption of standards for Indian libraries; to provide technical assistance to Indian tribes on establishing and maintaining archives systems; to work for the enhancement of the capability of libraries to assist Indians who are writing tribal histories and to perpetuate knowledge of Indian language, history, legal rights, and culture; to seek support for the establishment of networks for the exchange of information among Indian tribes; to communicate the needs of Indian libraries to legislators and the library community; to coordinate the development of courses, workshops, institutes, and internships on Indian library services.
Structure   Governed by executive officers. Affiliations: ALA
Sources of Support   Membership dues, sale of publications.
Membership   Requirements: Interest in aims of Association.
General Assembly   Entire membership meets annually.
Publications   *Official journal:* American Indian Libraries Newsletter.
Activities   Carried out in accordance with goals and objectives.
Bibliography   Blumer, T.J., "Library Service for American Indian People and American Indian Library Association," Library of Congress Information Bulletin 42 (Sept. 10, 1984):296-298; Mathews, V.H., "American Indians," in ALA Yearbook 1989, pp. 25-26. Chicago: American Library Association, 1989.

493   American Library Association (ALA)

Address   50 East Huron Street, Chicago, Illinois 60611 (permanent). Tel: 1 (312) 9446780. Telex: 4909992000. Fax: 1-312-4409374.
Officers   (elected for 1-yr.term) Pres: Patricia Wilson Berger; Past Pres: F. William Summers; Pres.-Elect: Richard M. Dougherty; Treas: Carla J. Stoffle; Exec.Dir: Linda F. Crismon (appointed, 1989-); Dep.Exec.Dir: Roger H. Parent. Exec.Board: 13
Staff   250 (paid)
Languages   English
Established   1876, Philadelphia. ALA has influenced the course of American libraries since its inception in 1876, when such early library luminaries as Melvil Dewey and Justin Winsor issued a call to libraries to form a professional organization.
Major Fields of Interest   High quality library and information services

Major Goals and Objectives The mission of the American Library Association is to provide leadership for the development, promotion, and improvement of library and information services and the profession of librarianship in order to enhance learning and ensure access to information for all.

Structure Governed by Council, comprised of 174 members (100 elected at large, 52 by chapters, 11 by divisions, and 12 members of the Executive Board), meeting at the annual convention in summer and during midwinter. The Executive Board is the central management board of ALA. Affiliations: IFLA, American Association of Law Libraries, American Society for Information Science, Canadian Library Association, Medical Library Association, Laubach Literacy International, etc.

Sources of Support Membership dues, sale of publications, conference revenues. Budget: Approx. $22 million.

Membership Total members: 50,000+ (47,000 individual, 3,000 institutional). Divisions: 11 (see separate entries under names of Associations: American Association of School Librarians/AASL; American Library Trustee Association/ALTA; Association for Library Collections and Technical Services/ALCTS (formerly Resources and Technical Services Division/RTSD); Association for Library Service to Children/ALSC; Association of College and Research Libraries/ACRL; Association of Specialized and Cooperative Library Agencies/ASCLA; Library Administration and Management Association/ LAMA; Library and Information Technology Association/LITA; Public Library Association/PLA; Reference and Adult Services Division/RASD; Young Adult Services Division/YASD). Sections: 39. Round Tables: 15. Chapters: 52. 70 countries represented. Requirements: Open to any person, library or organization interested in library service and librarians. Dues: $38, first year, individual; $75, renewing individual; $26, non-salaried librarian; $34, trustee & associate member; $19, student; $45, foreign individual; $70-900, institutional, according to operating expenses of library. Special dues: $150, subscribing; $300, contributing; $500, sustaining; $1,000, patron.

General Assembly Entire membership meets annually in June/July. 1988: New Orleans, July 9-14; 1989: Dallas, June 24-29; 1990: Chicago, June 23-28; 1991: Atlanta, June 29-July 4.

Publications *Official journal:* American Libraries. 1907-. 11/yr. Subscription to institutions only: $50; $60 outside USA & Canada. Free to members. Editor: Tom Gaughan. Address same as Association. Circ: 47,000. English. Indexed in CIJE, Education Index, ISA, LISA, Lib.Lit., Magazine Index, DIALOG, etc. Other publications: ALA Handbook of Organization and Membership Directory (1/yr.); ALA Yearbook 1/yr.); Booklist (22/yr.); Choice (11/yr.); Library Video Magazine (4/yr.); Library Technology Reports (series); numerous professional monographs, e.g., some 1989-90 publications: Gorman, M., The Concise AACR2, 1988 Revision, Fink, D., Process and Politics in Library Research, Clack, D., Authority Control, Alshami, A., CD-ROM Technology for Information Managers, Karpisek, M., Policymaking for School Library Media Center Programs, Pay Equity: An Action Manual for Library Workers, Saffady, W., Introduction to Automation for Librarians (2nd ed., 1989), etc.; annual reports, proceedings of conferences, seminars, etc. Extensive publications program includes professional journals, monographs, and the ALANET Electronic Information Services. Complete information available from ALA Publishing Department. No publications exchange program.

Activities Besides a wide range of activities carried out by the Divisions, Sections, Committees and other ALA groups, many projects are initiated by ALA Headquarters Offices, e.g. the Office for Intellectual Freedom (OIF, Director: Judith F. Krug), Office for Research (OFR, Director: Mary Jo Lynch), Office for Library Personnel Resources (OLPR, Director: Margaret Myers), Office for Library Outreach Services (OLOS, Director: Sibyl E. Moses), and others. Conference programs are determined by the theme the incumbent President chooses for her/his term of office. Past achievements: $2,000 from National Endowment for the Humanities for "Let's Talk about It" Project; Strategic Long-Range Planning process completed; renovation of office space; ALANET, electronic mail information service implemented; expanding international activities through the "Library/Book Fellow Program" (Director: Robert P. Doyle), cosponsored with the US Information Agency, to place US librarians overseas to implement needed projects. Current: Major publisher of library and information science monographs; legislative information; conferences; focus on literacy, preservation, and access to information. ALA members are expected to play a leadership role in the planning of the second White House Conference on Library and Information Services (WHCLIS 2), scheduled for July 9-13, 1991. Future: Library Video Magazine - videocassette journal; library research project with OCLC; to develop family literacy projects and create a first association-wide literacy policy. Active in promoting library-related legislation, such as LSCA, HEA, WHCLIS 2. The ALA Washington Office (Director: Eileen D. Cooke, 110 Maryland Avenue NE, Box 54, Washington, DC 20002. Tel: 1 (202) 5474440. Fax: 1-202-5477363) publishes a newsletter to keep members informed on national legislation affecting libraries, including federal government actions and regulations. Presents a number of annual awards. Sponsors National Library Week, Banned Books Week, exhibits, conferences, seminars, workshops, and other continuing education programs.

Use of High Technology   Computers (Microdata 9000, Wang Word Processing, IBM & COMPAQ PCs) for management. ALANET: Electronic Information Service; Video Magazine.

Bibliography   Galvin, T.J., "ALA, Unesco and NWICO (New World Information and Communication Order)," Newsletter on Intellectual Freedom 33 (1984):63-64; Kraske, G.E., Missionaries of the Book: The American Library Profession and the Origins of United States Cultural Diplomacy. New York: Greenwood Press, 1985; Holley, E.G.,"American Library Association," in ALA World Encyclopedia of Library and Information Services, 2nd ed., pp. 43-49. Chicago: American Library Association, 1986; Wiegand, W.A., The Politics of an Emerging Profession: The American Library Association 1876-1917. New York: Greenwood Press, 1986; Sullivan, P., "ALA and Library Education: A Century of Changing Roles and Actors, Shifting Scenes and Plots," Journal of Education for Library and Information Science 26 (1986):143-153; "Strategic Plans for ALA and ACRL: A Comparison," College and Research Libraries News 47 (1986):709-712; Carroll, F.L., "International Relations of the American Library Association and R. Wedgeworth 1972-85," International Library Review 18 (1986):153-159; Kimmel, M.M., "The Committee on Accreditation: What It Can and Cannot Do," Top of the News 43 (1987):143-148; Cassell, K.A., "The Women's Rights Struggle in Librarianship: The Task Force on Women," in Activism in American Librarianship, 1962-1973, ed. by M.L. Bundy and F.J. Stielow, pp. 21-29. New York: Greenwood Press, 1987; "ALA and Its Divisions: Relationships Past, Present and Future," College & Research Libraries News 48 (1987):318-320; Melton, E.,"American Library Association," in ALA Yearbook 1989, pp. 27-28. Chicago: American Library Association, 1989; Chisholm, M.E., "American Library Asociation," in The Bowker Annual of Library and Book Trade Information, 1988, pp. 152-166. New York: R.R. Bowker, 1988; Wiegand, W.A. and Steffens, D.L, "Members of the Club: A Look at One Hundred ALA Presidents." University of Illinois at Urbana-Champaign. Grad. School of Libr. & Info. Science, 1988; Schuman, P.G., "ALA and Its Divisions," College & Research Libraries News 49 (1988):27-31; Sorensen, R.J., "Continuing Education in the American Library Association," School Library Media Quarterly 16 (1988):119-121; "ALA Urges Use of Permanent Paper," Wilson Library

<u>Bulletin</u> 62 (1988):12; "News from Annual Conference in New Orleans: Big But Not So Easy," <u>American Libraries</u> 19 (1988):658-660, 662-668, 701-708; "Information Literacy is Focus of ALA Report," <u>Library Journal</u> 114 (1989):20-21; Gerhardt, L.N., "That Motto of ALA ('The Best Reading, for the Largest Number, at the Least Cost')," <u>School Library Journal</u> 34 (1988):4; Summers, F. W., "American Library Association," in <u>The Bowker Annual: Library and Book Trade Almanac, 34th Edition 1989-90</u>, pp. 142-146; 634-637. New York: R.R. Bowker, 1989; Flagg, G. et al., "Issues of Reach and Grasp: ALA Faces up to Success," <u>American Libraries</u> 21 (1990):252-261 (Midwinter Meeting, Jan. 6-11, 1990, Chicago).

494   American Library Trustee Association (ALTA)

Address   c/o ALA, 50 East Huron Street, Chicago, Illinois 60611 (permanent). Tel: 1 (312) 9446780. Fax: 1-312-4409374.
Officers   (elected for 1-yr.term) Pres: Norma Buzan (3057 Betsy Ross Drive, Bloomfield Hills, Michigan 48013); 1st VP/Pres-Elect: Norman Kelinson (1228 Coffelt Ave., Bettendorf, Iowa 52722); 2nd VP: Wayne Moss; Past Pres: Gloria T. Glaser; Sec: Ira Harkavy; Exec.Dir: Sharon L. Jordan (appointed). Exec.Board: 18.
Staff   1 (paid).
Languages   English
Established   1961, as an ALA Division; based on earlier organization founded in 1890.
Major Fields of Interest   Library policies and services
Major Goals and Objectives   The development of effective library service for all people in all types of libraries; members are concerned, as policymakers, with organizational patterns of service, with the development of competent personnel, the provision of adequate financing, the passage of suitable legislation, and the encouragement of citizen support for libraries.
Structure   Governed by Board of Directors. Affiliations: A division of ALA.
Sources of Support   Membership dues, sale of publications.
Membership   Total members: 1,734+ (1,406 individual, 328 institutional). 12 countries represented. Various committees (Action Development, Awards, Education of Trustees, Intellectual Freedom, Legislation, Public Library Trusteeship, Specialized Outreach Services, etc.). Requirements: Open to all interested persons and organizations. Dues: $45 plus ALA membership.
General Assembly   Entire membership meets once a year at ALA Annual Conference.
Publications   *Official journal:* The ALTA Newsletter. 6/yr. Free to members. Editor: Nancy Stiegemeyer. Address: 215 Camelia Drive, Cape Girardeau, MO 63701). Circ: Membership only. English. Issues occasional publications; bibliographies, pamphlets, such as, "A Questionnaire to Evaluate Your Library and Library Board," "Major Duties, Functions, and Responsibilities of Public Library Trustees - An Outline," and "Library Boards - Who Are They and How Do They Get There? A Survey." No publications exchange program. Price lists available.
Activities   Specific responsibilities according to the aims of the Association are as follows: (1) A continuing and comprehensive educational program to enable library trustees to discharge their grave responsibilities in a manner best fitted to benefit the public and the libraries they represent; (2) continuous study and review of the activities of library trustees; (3) cooperation with other units within ALA concerning their activities relating to trustees; (4) encouraging participation of trustees in other appropriate divisions of ALA; (5) representation and interpretation of the activities of library trustees in contacts outside the library profession, particularly with national organizations and governmental agencies; (6) promotion of strong state and regional trustee organizations; (7) efforts to

secure and support adequate library funding; (8) promulgation and dissemination of recommended library policy; (9) assuring equal access to information for all segments of the
population; (10) encouraging participation of trustees in trustee/library activities, at local,
state, regional and national levels. Sponsors conferences, seminars, workshops, and other
continuing education programs. To commemorate the Association's 100 years of service,
an ALTA Centennial Endowment Fund was established in 1990, to continue and enhance
trustee education programs.
Bibliography   Miller, R.T., "ALTA's Workshop in Library Leadership," Show-Me Libraries (Missouri State Libraries) 35 (1984):9-11; Jordan, S.L., "American Library Trustee Association," in ALA Yearbook 1989, pp. 41-42. Chicago: American Library Association, 1989; "American Library Association. American Library Trustee Association," in
The Bowker Annual: Library and Book Trade Almanac, 34th Edition 1989-90, pp.
640-641. New York: R.R. Bowker, 1986.

495   American Merchant Marine Library Association (AMMLA)

Address   One World Trade Center, Suite 1365, New York, New York 10048 (perma-
nent). Tel: 1 (212) 7751038.
Officers   Pres: Hoyt S. Haddock; Chair, Exec.Comm: Talmage E. Simpkins; Sec: Ellen
Craft Dammond; Treas: Ulf K. Ghosh; Gen.Counsel: John I. Dugan. Exec.Comm: 40
Staff   3 (volunteers)
Languages   English
Established   1921; New York Board of Regents gave AMMLA its library charter. At
the end of World War II, the American Library Association asked Mrs. Henry Howard
(Alice Sturtevant Howard), chief of the social services library of the US Shipping Board,
to establish a continuing book service to serve American merchant ships.
Major Fields of Interest   Library services to seamen
Major Goals and Objectives   The only public library chartered to provide ship and
shore library service for American-flag merchant vessels, the Military Sealift Command,
the Coast Guard, and other waterborne operations of the U.S. government; to organize
books into "sea-going libraries" representing a variety of reading tastes and the educational and self-help needs of seamen; shipboard libraries to include hardcover and paper-
back books, current magazines, and some foreign language selections, in order to offer
crewmembers a diversion from daily routine and an opportunity to broaden educational
horizons.
Structure   Governed by Board of Directors. Affiliations: United Seamen's Service, Inc.
Sources of Support   Contributions. Budget: Approx. $100,000.
Activities   Carried out in accordance with the goals and objectives. Sponsors Annual
Book Drive for distribution on board of ships.
Bibliography   "American Merchant Marine Library Association," in The Bowker Annu-
al: Library and Book Trade Almanac, 34th Edition 1989-90, p. 662. New York: R.R. Bow-
ker, 1989.

496   American Society for Information Science (ASIS)

Address   1424 16th Street NW, Washington, DC 20036 (permanent). Postal address:
PO Box 554, Ben Franklin Station, Washington, DC 20044. Tel: 1 (202) 4621000. Fax:
1-202-4627494.
Officers   (elected for 3-yr.term) Pres: Toni Carbo Bearman; Past Pres: W. David Penni-
man; VP/Pres-Elect: Tefko Saracevic; Treas: N. Bernard (Buzzy) Basch; Exec.Dir: Richard
B. Hill (appointed). Exec.Comm: 5; Board of Directors: 13.

Staff   9 (paid)
Languages   English
Established   1937, Washington, D.C., as American Documentation Institute (ADI).
Major Fields of Interest   Information science and technology; information storage and retrieval; information policy.
Major Goals and Objectives   Organized for scientific, literary and educational purposes, and dedicated to the creation, organization, dissemination and application of knowledge concerning information and its transfer. Specifically, the Society aims to provide knowledge, education, training and awareness to, for and about information and its transfer; to provide a forum for the discussion, publication, and critical analysis of work dealing with the design, management, and use of information systems and technology.
Structure   Governed by Board of Directors, elected by membership. Affiliations: FID, NFAIS, and some 40 other organizations.
Sources of Support   Membership dues, sale of publications, revenues from meetings, continuing education seminars. Budget: Approx. $800,000.
Membership   Total members: 4,300 (4,180 individual, 120 institutional). Divisions: 22. Chapters: 27. Student Chapters: 29. Special Interest Groups (SIGs): 21 (Arts & Humanities/AH, Automated Language Processing/ALP, Biological & Chemical Information/BC, Behavioral & Social Sciences/BSS, Classification Research/CR, Computerized Retrieval Systems/CRS, Education for Information Science/ED, Foundations of Information Science/FIS, Information Analysis & Evaluation/IAE, International Information Issues/III, Library Automation Networks/LAN, Law & Information Technology/LAW, Medical Information Systems/MED, Management/MGT, Numeric Data Bases/NDB, Office Information Systems/OIS, Personal Computers/PC, Information Generation & Publishing/PUB, Storage & Retrieval Technology/SRT, Technology, Information and Society/TIS, User Online Interaction/UOI). Requirements: Any interested person who applies for membership and pays the prescribed dues. Institutional memberships are available to both profit and nonprofit organizations. Dues: $85, individual; $34, student; $350, institutional affiliate; $550, corporate patron.
General Assembly   Entire membership meets annually, in fall. 1988: Atlanta, GA, Oct. 23-27; 1989: Washington, DC, Oct. 29-Nov.2; 1990: Toronto, Canada, Nov. 4-8; 1991: Washington, DC, Oct.27-31; 1992: Pittsburgh, PA, Oct. 25-29.
Publications   *Official journal:* Journal of the American Society for Information Science (JASIS) (formerly American Documentation). 1950-. 6/yr. $140. $187 outside US. Free to members. Address: John Wiley & Sons, Inc., 605 Third Ave., New York, NY. 10158. Editor: Donald H. Kraft. Address: Department of Computer Science, Louisiana State University, Baton Rouge, LA 70803). Circ: 6,000 + . English. Indexed in Chem.Ab., ISA, Sci.Cit.Index, etc. Other publications: Bulletin of the American Society for Information Science (a news magazine concentrating on issues affecting the information field). 1974-. 6/yr. $55. Free to members. Editor: Richard B. Hill. Address same as Association. Circ: 6,000 + . English; ASIS Handbook and Directory (1/yr.); Annual Review of Information Science and Technology (ARIST). Editor: Martha Williams; Publisher: Elsevier Science Publishers, S. Burgerhartst 25, PO Box 1991, Amsterdam 100B2, Netherlands; Jobline (12/yr.); ASIS Monographs. Editor: Michael Koenig; annual reports, proceedings of conferences, seminars, etc. Publications available for sale.
Activities   As a multi-disciplinary society for the information profession, ASIS recruits members from virtually every industry, dedicated to improving access to information through the development and application of new policies, systems and techniques for information storage and retrieval. Members include lawyers, bankers, publishers, politicians, business people, social scientists, librarians, scientists and engineers, information

managers, computer scientists, etc., who wish to keep abreast of the latest research and developments in these fields. In 1987 and 1988, programs and publications reflected the 50th anniversary celebrations. Society provides a Placement Service, and bestows annual awards. Sponsors conferences, seminars, workshops, etc. as part of an extensive continuing education program.

Use of High Technology   Computers (IBM compatibles, Alpha Micro, Tandy) and databases for management.

Bibliography   Resnik, L., "American Society for Information Science Approaching 50 Years Young," Library Times International 3 (1986):17, 19; Elias, A.W., "Historical Note: Fifty Years of ASIS - Thirty-Eight Years of JASIS," Journal of the American Society of Information Science 38 (1987):385-386; Berry, J.N., "A New Social Concern at ASIS [technology is not ethically neutral]," Library Journal 112 (1987):79-81; Davis, M., "ASIS Mid-Year Meeting on Artificial Intelligence," LASIE 19 (1988):20-24; "ASIS Celebrates Its 50th Anniversary," Bulletin of the American Society of Information Science 14 (1988):10-13; Resnik, L., "ASIS Celebrates 50 Years of Services [anniversary conference]," ibid.:58-60; Resnik, L.,"American Society for Information Science," in ALA Yearbook 1989, pp. 42-44. Chicago: American Library Association, 1989; Resnik, L., "American Society for Information Science," in The Bowker Annual: Library and Book Trade Almanac, 34th Edition 1989-90, pp. 160-163. New York: R.R. Bowker, 1989; Sherwood, D., "Annual ASIS Meeting Looks to the 90's," Information Today (The Newspaper for Users and Producers of Electronic Information Services) 6 (Dec.1989):1, 14; "Inside ASIS: ASIS Members Share Insights and Knowledge on Management of Information and Technology [ASIS Annual Meeting, Washington, DC, Oct.1989]," Bulletin of the American Society for Information Science 16 (1990):4-8.

497   American Theological Library Association (ATLA)

Address   St. Meinrad School of Theology, Archabbey Library, St. Meinrad, Indiana 47577 (not permanent). Tel: 1 (812) 3576718.

Officers   (elected for 1-yr.term) Pres: Channing Jeschke; VP/Pres-Elect: H. Eugene McLeod; Past Pres: Rosalyn Lewis; Treas: Robert A. Olsen, Jr.; Exec.Sec: Simeon Daly, O.S.B. (appointed). Exec.Board: 10.

Staff   2 (paid)

Languages   English

Established   1947, Louisville, Kentucky, at a special joint meeting of the ALA Religious Books Round Table and the American Association of Theological Schools (now ATS).

Major Fields of Interest   Theological librarianship in general; theological bibliography; microreproduction of theological material; indexing of religious journals; theological library development; preservation of theological materials.

Major Goals and Objectives   To bring theological libraries into closer working relationships with each other; to improve theological libraries, and to interpret the role of such libraries in theological education; developing and implementing standards of library service; promoting research and experimental projects; encouraging cooperative programs that make resources more available; publishing and disseminating literature and research tools and aids; cooperating with organizations having similar aims; and otherwise supporting and aiding theological education.

Structure   Governed by Board of Directors. Affiliations: CNLA (Council of National Library Associations).

Sources of Support   Membership dues, sale of publications. Budget: Approx. $68,000.

Membership   Total members: 655 (490 individual, 165 institutional). Requirements: Open to persons actively engaged in professional library or bibliographic work in theological or related religious fields. Institutional membership for libraries or institutions with membership in the Association of Theological Schools in the U.S. and Canada. Dues: $30+, based on salary or income of institution, full and associate members.
General Assembly   Entire membership meets once a year. 1987: San Francisco, June 21-26; 1988: Wilmore, KY; 1989: Columbus, OH, June 18-23; 1990: Evanston, IL, June 25-30.
Publications   *Official journal:* ATLA Newsletter. 1947-. 4/yr. Free to members. Address same as Association. Circ: Membership. English. Other publications: Religion Index One: Periodicals Index to Book Reviews in Religion (1987); Religion Index Two: Multi-Author Works (1987); Research in Ministry: An Index to Doctor of Ministry Project Reports; annual reports, proceedings of conferences, seminars, etc. Price lists available.
Activities   Past achievements: Expansion of areas for bibliographies; Preservation Project; restructuring of the organization. Current and future: Preservation of theological materials 1850-1910; participation in the National Inventory Project, TUG (Theological Users Group on OCLC); Task Force on Strategic Planning. Sponsors conferences, seminars, workshops, and other continuing education programs.
Use of High Technology   Computers (IBM PC) for management.
Bibliography   Myers, S., "American Theological Library Association," in ALA Yearbook 1988, pp. 46-47. Chicago: American Library Association, 1988; Myers, S.,"American Theological Library Association," in ALA Yearbook 1989, p. 44. Chicago: American Library Association, 1989; "American Theological Library Association," in The Bowker Annual: Library and Book Trade Almanac, 34th Edition 1989-90, pp. 663-664. New York: R.R. Bowker, 1989.

498   Art Libraries Society of North America (ARLIS/NA)

Address   c/o Pamela J. Parry, Exececutive Director, 3900 East Timrod Street, Tucson, Arizona 85711 (permanent). Tel: 1 (602) 8818479. Fax: 1-602-3226778.
Officers   (elected for 2-3-yr.term) Chair: Clive Phillpot (Museum of Modern Art Library, 11 W. 53 Street, New York, NY 10019); VP/Pres-Elect: Lynette Korenic; Sec: Anita Gilden; Treas: Jack Robertson; Past Pres: Ann Abid; Exec.Dir: Pamela J. Parry (appointed). Exec.Board: 9.
Staff   1.5 (paid)
Languages   English, French, Spanish
Established   1972, Chicago, Illinois.
Major Fields of Interest   Art librarianship and visual resources curatorship.
Major Goals and Objectives   To provide leadership in the development and use of art libraries and visual resource collections, particularly by acting as a forum for the interchange of information and materials on the visual arts.
Structure   Governed by Executive Board. Affiliations: IFLA, College Art Association, Art Libraries Society/United Kingdom & Eire.
Sources of Support   Membership dues, sale of publications, conference fees. Budget: Approx. $165,000.
Membership   Total members: 1,312 (992 individual, 320 institutional). Chapters: 18. 15 countries represented. Requirements: An interest in and support for the fields of art librarianship and visual resources curatorship, e.g. professional librarians, students, library assistants, art book publishers, art book dealers, art historians, archivists, architects, slide and photograph curators, or retired associates in these fields.. Dues: $45, individual; $75,

institutional; $75, business affiliate; $20, student; $25, retired; $30, unemployed; $175, sustaining; $500, sponsor.

General Assembly   Entire membership meets once a year. 1987: Washington, DC; 1988: Dallas, TX; 1989: Phoenix, AZ.

Publications   *Official journal:* Art Documentation (formerly Art Libraries Journal). 1982-. 4/yr. $35 +. Free to members. Editor: Deirdre C. Stam. Address: School of Information Studies, Syracuse University, Syracuse, NY 13210. Circ: 1,400. English, French, Spanish. Indexed in Lib.Lit; LISA. Other publications: ARLIS/NA Update (newsletter, 4/yr.); Handbook and List of Members (1/yr.); Occasional Papers; annual reports, proceedings of conferences, seminars, etc. Publications available for sale. Publications exchange program in effect.

Activities   Past achievements: Established a solid financial base for the Society; superceded a five-time-per-year newsletter with a professional quarterly journal and a quarterly newsletter; greatly expanded continuing education opportunities at the annual conference; initiated series of regular regional conferences; inaugurated a new series of publications, the Occasional Papers; celebration of Society's fifteenth anniversary in 1987, including a membership recruitment drive and a fund drive to expand publications program. Current and future: Development of standards for physical facilities for art libraries and visual resources collections; supervising production of Occasional Paper, Historical Bibliography of Art Museum Serials; membership satisfaction survey; expanding continuing education programs. Sponsors exhibits, conferences, seminars and workshops. Active in promoting library-related legislation. Presents awards for publications in the visual arts, and to library students.

Use of High Technology   Computer (IBM AT) for management.

Bibliography   Haskins, K., "Decennalia: An Editorial Essay (ARLIS/NA)," Art Libraries Journal 7 (1982):6-10; "Art Librarians Meet at Los Angeles," Library Times International 1 (1985):74; Horrell, J.L.,"Art Libraries," in ALA Yearbook 1989, pp.47-48. Chicago: American Library Association, 1989; "Art Libraries Society of North America (ARLIS/NA)," in The Bowker Annual: Library and Book Trade Almanac, 34th Edition 1989-90, pp. 666-667. New York: R.R. Bowker, 1989.

499   Asian/Pacific American Librarians Association (APALA)

Address   c/o Conchita J. Pineda, President, APALA, Citicorp Information Center, One Citicorp Center, 153 East 53rd Street, New York, New York 10043 (not permanent). Tel: 1 (212) 5592826.

Officers   (elected) Pres: Conchita J. Pineda; VP: Ichiko T. Morita (1658 Neil Avenue, Ohio State University Libraries, Columbus, OH 43210); Treas: Abdul J. Miah; Sec: Dallas R. Shawkey (Brooklyn Public Library, 109 Montgomery Street, Brooklyn, NY 11225). Exec.Comm: 4

Staff   Volunteers

Languages   English

Established   1980

Major Fields of Interest   Asian/Pacific American librarians

Major Goals and Objectives   (1) To provide a forum for discussing problems and concerns of Asian/Pacific American librarians; (2) to provide a forum for the exchange of ideas by Asian/Pacific American librarians and other librarians; (3) to support and encourage library services to the Asian/Pacific American communities; (4) to recruit and support Asian/Pacific Americans in the library/information science professions; (5) to seek funding for scholarships in library/information science schools for Asian/Pacific

Americans; (6) to provide a vehicle whereby Asian/Pacific American librarians can cooperate with other associations and organizations having similar or allied interests.
Structure Governed by executive officers, committees, membership at-large. Affiliations: ALA.
Sources of Support Membership dues, advertisers' fees for conference publication. Budget: Approx. $4,000.
Membership Total members: 177+ (individual). 7 countries represented. Requirements: Open to all librarians/information specialists of Asian/Pacific descent working in US libraries/information centers and related organizations, and to others who support the goals and purposes of APALA. Asian/Pacific Americans are defined as those who consider themselves Asian/Pacific Americans. They may be Americans of Asian/Pacific descent, Asian/Pacific people with the status of permanent residency, or Asian/Pacific people living in the United States. Dues: $10, individual; $5, student; $25, institutional.
General Assembly Entire membership meets annually in conjunction with the ALA conference in summer, for the program meeting. Officers and members also meet during the ALA Midwinter meetings.
Publications *Official journal:* APALA Newsletter. 1980-. 4/yr. Free to members. Editor: Sharad Karkhanis. Address: Kingsborough Community College/CUNY, Manhatten Beach, Brooklyn, NY 11235. Circ: 200. English. Other publications: Annual reports, proceedings of conferences, seminars, bibliographies, e.g. "Books for Asian/Pacific Americans' Human Rights;" APALA Membership Directory (1/yr.); Collantes, Lourdes Y., ed., Asian/Pacific American Librarians Association: A Cross Cultural Perspective. Papers of the 1984 Program, June 25, 1984, Dallas, Texas (1985), etc. No publications exchange program.
Activities Past achievements: Preparation and publication of bibliographies of interest to the Asian/Pacific community; APALA's Distinguished Service Award, presented annually during the summer program (recipients include author Ved Mehta, Senator Samuel Hayakawa, Ambassador Haydon Williams, Dr. W. Tsuneishi, etc.). Current and future: Annual award program "to an individual for distinguished service and outstanding contributions to the better understanding of Asian/Pacific Americans and their contributions in America." Dissemination of information of value to the membership. Publication of 1986 conference-seminar, Human Rights: Minorities in New York City - a Microcosm of the World, and of 1987 conference, How to Avoid a Dead-End in Your Career: An Asian American Perspective and Library Services for the Asian American Community. Sponsors conferences, seminars, workshops, and other continuing education programs. Cooperates with like-minded organizations in promoting library-related legislation.
Use of High Technology Computers (Word processors, modem-computer systems) for management.
Bibliography Har Nicolescu, S. and Collantes, A., "Asian/Pacific American Librarians Association," Ethnic Forum: Journal of Ethnic Studies and Ethnic Bibliography 6 (1986):138-140; "Asians as 'Model Minority:' Myth, Reality, or Both," American Libraries 19 (1988):667; Pineda, C.J.,"Asian/Pacific American Librarians Association," in ALA Yearbook 1989, pp.48-49. Chicago: American Library Association, 1989; "Asian/Pacific American Librarians Association," in The Bowker Annual: Library and Book Trade Almanac, 34th Edition 1989-90, pp. 667-668.

500 Associated Information Managers (AIM)

Address 1776 E. Jefferson Street, 4th floor, Rockville, Maryland 20852 (permanent). Tel: 1 (301) 2317447.

Officers   (elected for 1-yr.term) Chair: Donald A. Marchand; Vice-Chair: Forest Woody Horton, Jr.; Sec-Treas: Molly A. Wolfe; Past Chair: Herbert R. Brinberg; Exec.Dir (appointed): Paul Oyer (3821-F S. George Mason Drive, Falls Church, Virginia 22041. Tel: 703-845-9150). Exec.Comm: 5. Board of Directors: 16.
Staff   1 (paid)
Languages   English
Established   1978, founded by Information Industry Association (IIA); incorporated in 1982.
Major Fields of Interest   Integration of information technologies and content; information management-related positions (including Chief Information Officer - CIO), and further development of these positions within private and public sector organizations.
Major Goals and Objectives   Goals: To realize an Information Manager/CIO position in all organizations; to realize an overall awareness of the importance of managing information in all organizations. Objectives: To provide educational forums enabling individuals interested in serving as Information Manager/CIO to further develop; to provide networking for information management-related individuals.
Structure   Governed by Board of Directors. Affiliations: Information Industry Association (IIA).
Sources of Support   Membership dues, sale of publications, conference registration proceeds. Budget: Approx. $100,000.
Membership   Total members: 623 (600 individual, 23 corporate). Chapters: 4. 7 countries represented. Requirements: Interest in information management. Members include corporate planners, vice presidents of communication and marketing, administration managers, online users; personnel involved in data processing, telecommunications, librarianship, records management, office automation, and management information systems (MIS), and any interested corporations and institutions. Dues: $85, individual; $35, student; $120, foreign individual; $500, contributing corporate; $1,000 supporting corporate; $3,000 sustaining corporate.
General Assembly   Entire membership meets annually.
Publications   No official journal. AIM Network, a biweekly newsletter. Free to members. Editor: Sheila Brayman. Address same as Association. Circ: Membership. English. Other publications: Who's Who in Information Management (1/yr., Membership Directory); Career Exchange Clearinghouse (biweekly announcements of job opportunities); Meltzer, M.F., Marketing Yourself in Your Organization; Solomon, R.J., ed., Partners in Fact: Information Managers and Markets Talk; AIM 1988 Membership Profile Survey; annual reports, proceedings of conferences, seminars, etc. Price lists available. No publications exchange program.
Activities   Past achievements: (1) Becoming an independent association, separate from founding association in 1981; (2) creating an awareness of the importance of information management; (3) the current recognition of the role and value of the Chief Information Officer (CIO). Current and future: Networking members; conducting a job clearinghouse; offering educational meetings; publishing. Sponsors exhibits, conferences, seminars, workshops, and other continuing education programs.
Use of High Technology   Computers for management are maintained by a computer service bureau.
Bibliography   "Association of Information Managers Now Independent Organization," Online 6 (1982):59-60; "A Lively Year is Ahead for Organizations," Government Computer News, Jan.17, 1986; "Associated Information Managers," in The Bowker Annual: Library and Book Trade Almanac, 34th Edition 1989-90, pp. 668-669. New York: R.R. Bowker, 1989.

501   Association for Federal Information Resources Management (AFFIRM)

Address   PO Box 28506, Washington, DC 20038 (permanent).
Officers   (elected for 1-yr.term) Chair: Margaret Skovira (US Department of the Treasury, Washington, DC 20239; Tel: 1-202-3764204); Exec.Vice-Chair/Chair-Elect: Leon Transeau (Department of the Interior); Vice-Chair, Finance: James Clancy; Vice-Chair, Admin: Phil Casto; Vice-Chair, Programs: Art Chantker. Exec.Board: 9
Staff   None
Languages   English
Established   1979
Major Fields of Interest   Information systems and resources in the Federal government
Major Goals and Objectives   To provide a forum for information resources management professionals in order to exchange ideas and to express opinions not subjected to official approval; to promote and advance the concept and practice of information resources management (IRM) in the government of the United States; to provide a forum for exploring new techniques to improve the quality and use of federal information systems and resources; to advocate effective application of IRM to all levels of the federal government, to enhance the professionalism of IRM personnel, and interact with state and local governments on IRM issues.
Structure   Governed by officers and Executive Board.
Sources of Support   Membership dues.
Membership   Total members: 250 (individual). Requirements: Professionals currently or formerly employed by the federal government in some capacity related to IRM. Other persons interested may join as associate members. Dues: $20, individual; $30, associate.
General Assembly   There are monthly program meetings with luncheon-speakers, at the George Washington University's Marvin Center, 21 Street, NW, Washington, DC; and annual one-day seminars in Information Resources Management, generally in fall.
Publications   *Official journal:* The AFFIRMation, newsletter. 1979-. 12/yr. Free to members. Address same as Association. Editor: Sarah Kadec. Address: PO Box 6786, Silver Spring, MD 20906. Circ: 300+. English. Publications exchange program in effect.
Activities   Current: To explore new concepts and techniques to improve the quality and use of federal information systems and resources. Sponsors conferences, seminars, workshops, and other continuing education programs.
Bibliography   "Association for Federal Information Resources Management (AFFIRM)," in The Bowker Annual: Library and Book Trade Almanac, 34th Edition 1989-90, p. 669. New York: R.R. Bowker, 1989.

**502   Association for Information and Image Management (AIIM)
(formerly National Micrographics Association)**

Address   1100 Wayne Avenue, Suite 1100, Silver Spring, Maryland 20910 (permanent). Tel: 1 (301) 5878202. Fax: 1-301-5872711.
Officers   (elected for 1-yr.term, 1989-90) Pres: David T. Bogue; VP: Roger Sullivan; Treas: Philip Trapp; Past Pres: John A. Lacy; Exec.Dir: Sue Wolk (appointed). Exec.Board: 18.
Staff   22 (paid)
Languages   English
Established   1943, as National Micrographics Association. Name changed to reflect the expansion into other imaging technologies.
Major Fields of Interest   Imaging technology, including information transfer, storage and retrieval on optical disk, computer imaging, document digitization, micrographics and data transmission

Major Goals and Objectives   To provide a forum which contributes to the effective development and application of information and image management systems through a Trade Association to benefit companies, and a Professional Society to benefit individuals; to provide opportunities, via the Annual Conference and Exposition and other meetings, for the interaction between trade and professional membership; to update membership on latest industry technology.

Structure   Governed by a Board of Directors, composed of prominent individuals in the imaging disciplines.

Sources of Support   Membership dues, sale of publications, annual conference and exposition revenues. Budget: $3 million+.

Membership   Total members: 8,000 (7,700 individual, 300 institutional). Divisions: 2. Chapters: 51. Worldwide representation in membership. Requirements: Member of the information and image processing community. Members are companies and individuals active in the design, creation, sale, and use of products and services for information and image management. Dues: $75, individual; $75, institutional AIIM trade member; $150, institutional, non AIIM trade member.

General Assembly   Entire membership meets annually. 1988: Chicago, April 11-14; 1989: Philadelphia, May 1-4; 1990: Chicago, April 9-12.

Publications   *Official journal:* INFORM: The Magazine of Information and Image Management. 1987-. 12/yr. (formerly JIIM: Journal of Information and Image Management and Journal of Micrographics, 1967-1986). $85 ($105, foreign). Free to members. Editor: Gregory E. Kaebnick. Address same as Association. Circ: Approx. 9,000. English.   Other publications: FYI/IM Newsletter. 12/yr. Free to members. Editor: Gregory E. Kaebnick. Address same as Association. Circ: 8,000. English.   Extensive publication program of professional monographs, e.g., Information and Image Management: The State of the Industry, 1989; Saffady, W., Optical Storage Technology 1989: A State of the Art Review; Hardy, J., Introduction to Micrographics; Micrographic Film Technology (3rd ed.);   Saffady, W., Micrographic Systems (3rd ed.); 1989 Information Management Sourcebook (annual Buying Guide and Membership Directory); Schantz, H.F., OCR/Imaging Systems in the Next Decade; Zakon, S., The Electronic Document; AIIM Standards Sets; Jordahl, G., Plugging into the Fax Track; Electronic Document Systems: User Evaluations;   annual reports, proceedings of conferences, seminars, etc. Publications catalog available upon request.

Activities   Past achievements: Broadening the scope of the Association to embrace technologies other than micrographics; creating a professional society and trade association which work together for the benefit of all.   Current: Meetings, shows, serial publications, standards, non-serial publications, market research, Resource Center services, government relations, seminars and public relations.   Future: New seminar programs, enhanced reference services, new publications.   Sponsors exhibits, conferences, seminars, workshops, and other continuing education programs, especially the AIIM Conference and Exposition ("The AIIM Show"). Presents annual awards.

Use of High Technology   Computers (Microdate, Altos, WANG) and databases for management.

Bibliography   Munro, K.G., "1985 Will be a Busy Year for Government Affairs," (AIIM legislative priorities) Journal of Information and Image Management 18 (1985):7; Steiger, B.A., "A Central Fact of Our Personal and Organizational Lives - Information Explosion Means Ever-Increasing Variety of Jobs," Washington Post, Sunday, Oct.5, 1986, High Technology Supplement; "Association for Information and Image Management," in The Bowker Annual: Library and Book Trade Almanac, 34th Edition 1989-90, p. 670. New York: R.R. Bowker, 1989.

503   Association for Library and Information Science Education (ALISE)
(formerly Association of American Library Schools)

Address   c/o Ilse Moon, Executive Secretary, 5623 Palm Aire Drive, Sarasota, Florida
34243 (permanent). Tel: 1 (813) 3551795.
Officers   (elected for 1-yr.term) Pres: Phyllis Van Orden (School of Library and Infor-
mation Studies, Florida State University, Tallahassee, FL 32306-2048. Tel: 1-904-6445775,
6448115, home. Fax: 1-904-6449763); Past Pres: Miles M. Jackson; VP/Pres-Elect: Eve-
lyn H. Daniel; Sec/Treas: Linda C. Smith; Exec.Sec: Ilse Moon (appointed). Exec.Board: 7
Staff   1 (paid)
Languages   English
Established   1915, Albany, New York, as Association of American Library Schools
(AALS).
Major Fields of Interest   Education for librarianship and information science
Major Goals and Objectives   Promote excellence in education for library and information science, as a means of increasing the effectiveness of library and information ser-
vices. To effect this goal, the objectives shall be: To provide a forum for the active inter-
change of ideas and information among LIS educators, and to promote research related
to teaching and to LIS; to formulate and promulgate positions on matters related to LIS
education; to cooperate with other organizations in matters of mutual interest.
Structure   Governed by Board of Directors. Affiliations: IFLA, ALA, ASIS, SLA, MLA.
Sources of Support   Membership dues, sale of publications. Budget: Approx. $85,000.
Membership   Total members: 686 (602 individual, 84 institutional). 20 countries represented. Requirements: Any library school with a program accredited by the ALA Committee on Accreditation, may become an institutional member. Any school that offers a
graduate degree in librarianship or a cognate field, but whose program is not accredited,
may become an associate institutional member. Any school outside the United States and
Canada offering a program comparable to that of institutional or associate institutional
membership, may become an international affiliate institutional member. Any faculty
member, administrator, librarian, researcher, or other individual employed full-time may
become a personal member. Any retired or part-time faculty member, student, or other
individual employed less than full-time, may become an associate personal member.
Dues: $40, individual; $20, associate individual; $250, institutional; $150, associate institutional; $75, international affiliate institutional.
General Assembly   Entire membership meets once a year.
Publications   *Official journal:* Journal of Education for Library and Information Science
(formerly Journal of Education for Librarianship). 1960-. 5/yr. $30 ($40, foreign). Free to
members. Address same as Association. Editor: Rosemary R. Du Mont. Address: School
of Library Science, Kent State University, Kent, OH 44242. Circ: 1,800. English. Indexed
in Current Contents, Education Index, ISA, LISA, Lib.Lit., etc. Other publications: The
Statistical Report (1/yr.); annual reports, proceedings of conferences, seminars, etc. Publications available for sale. No publications exchange program in effect.
Activities   Past achievements: Accreditation Conference; Centennial Symposium; annual
conferences; official journal. Current: Annual Conference; Awards and Honors Program;
Position Paper on Doctoral Programs; Participation in proposed White House Conference
on Library and Information Services. Future: Increased membership; more visibility on
an international level; computerized systems. Active in promoting library-related legislation, whenever feasible. Sponsors conferences, seminars, workshops, and other continuing education programs, particularly conferences that pertain to the interests of the Association. Supports National Library Week; cooperates with other library associations.
Use of High Technology   Computers (IBM PC) for management.

Bibliography   "AALS Changes Its Name," <u>Wilson Library Bulletin</u> 57 (1983):552; Berry, J. et al., "The Washington Week That Was: A Report on the Meetings of ALA, ALISE and the Urban Libraries Council, Jan. 5-12 [1984] in Washington, D.C.," <u>Library Journal</u> 109 (1984):537-543; Summers, F.W., "The Role of the Association for Library and Information Science Education," <u>Library Trends</u> 34 (1986):667-677; Berry, J., "Tension, Stress and Debate at the 1986 Annual Conference of ALISE," <u>Library Journal</u> 111 (1986):29-31; Berry, J., "Protecting Our Turf at the January 14-16 ALISE Conference," <u>Library Journal</u> 112 (1987):43-46; Estabrook, L.,"Association for Library and Information Science Education," in <u>ALA Yearbook 1989</u>, pp. 49-50. Chicago: American Library Association, 1989; "Association for Library and Information Science Education," in <u>The Bowker Annual: Library and Book Trade Almanac, 34th Edition 1989-90</u>, pp. 670-671. New York: R.R. Bowker, 1989; Berry, J.N., "ALISE in Washington (1989 Conference)," <u>Library Journal</u> 114 (1989):37-38; Berry, J. and De Candido, G.A., "Challenges and Concerns Confront ALISE," <u>Library Journal</u> 115 (1990):57-58.

504   Association for Library Collections & Technical Services (ALCTS) (formerly Resources and Technical Services Division - RTSD)

Address   c/o ALA, 50 East Huron Street, Chicago, Illinois 60611 (permanent). Tel: 1 (312) 9446780. Fax: 312-4409374.

Officers   Pres: Nancy R. John; Past Pres: Carolyn L. Harris; Exec.Dir: Karen Muller (appointed). Exec.Comm: 4.

Staff   2 (paid)

Languages   English

Established   1957, as Resources and Technical Services Division of ALA; new name adopted in 1989 to reflect the expansion of activities.

Major Fields of Interest   Library collections and technical services

Major Goals and Objectives   The mission of ALCTS is to provide leadership and to promote library service and librarianship in the areas of acquisitions, bibliographic description, subject analysis, preservation, and reproduction of library materials; and for those aspects of selection and evaluation of library materials relating to their acquisition and to the development of library collections. The goals are: (1) To implement the goals of ALA in the areas of ALCTS responsibility; (2) to ensure access to information by improving the development and management of collections and the bibliographic organization within libraries; (3) to promote research and publication in areas of divisional interest; (4) to provide forums for discussion and to advance the professional interests of librarians engaged in the development of library collections and in technical services; (5) to cooperate with other units of the American Library Association and with other national and international organizations in areas of mutual interest.

Structure   Governed by Board of Directors and Executive Committee. Affiliations: A division of ALA.

Sources of Support   Membership dues, sale of publications. Budget: Approx. $320,000.

Membership   Total members: 6,037 (4,979 individual, 1,058 institutional). Sections: 5 (Cataloging and Classification, Preservation of Library Materials, Reproduction of Library Materials, Resources, Serials). Committees: 28 (Audiovisual, Commercial Technical Services, Education, International Relations, Preservation Microfilming, Strategic Long-Range Planning, etc.). Discussion Groups: 26. Requirements: Open to members of the American Library Association who elect membership in this division according to the provisions of the bylaws. Dues: $35, individual, plus ALA dues.

General Assembly   Entire membership meets annually during ALA Conference.

Publications   *Official journal:* Library Resources and Technical Services. 4/yr. $30. Free to members. Address same as Association. Editor: Sheila S. Intner. Address: Box 53, Monterey, MA 01245. Circ: 8,000 +. English. Indexed in Lib.Lit., LISA.   Other publications: ALCTS Newsletter (formerly RTSD Newsletter) 1990-. 8/yr. $20. ($30, foreign). Free to members. Address same as Association. Interim Editor: Richard D. Johnson. Address: James M. Milne Library, State University College, Oneonta, NY 13820-4014. Circ: Approx.7,000. English. Indexed in Lib.Lit.; Walker, G., ed. Preservation Microfilming: Planning and Production: Papers from the RTSD Preservation Microfilming Institute, New Haven, Connecticut, April 21-23, 1988 (1989); Statistics for Managing Library Acquisitions; Merrill-Oldham, J., and Parisi, P., A Librarian's Guide to the Library Binding Institute Standard on Library Binding (1990); Guide for Written Collection Policy Statements (2nd ed.); annual reports, proceedings of conferences, seminars, etc.

Activities   Carried out by the various groups within the Association according to the goals and objectives through programs of continuing education, publication, standards development, research, legislation, equal opportunity, outreach and administration. ALCTS participates in the development of standards, guidelines, and codes, and promotes their use. Active in promoting library-related legislation, and provides expertise and support as appropriate for national, state, and local legislative efforts. Provides outreach by identifying and interfacing with appropriate groups within the private sector as well as professional associations. Sponsors conferences, seminars, workshops, and other continuing education programs.

Use of High Technology   Computers for management.

Bibliography   Reid, M.T.,"Resources and Technical Services Division," in ALA Yearbook 1989, pp.216-217. Chicago: American Library Association, 1989; "American Library Association. Resources and Technical Services Division," in The Bowker Annual: Library and Book Trade Almanac, 34th Edition 1989-90, pp. 658-659. New York: R.R. Bowker, 1989; Hirshon, A., "ALCTS Five-Year Financial Plan," RTSD Newsletter 14 (1989):60-63; "Mission and Priorities Statement [Revised Draft, Nov. 1989]: Introduction" by Marion T. Reid (Chair, ALCTS Strategic Long Range Planning Task Force) ALCTS Newsletter 1 (1990):5; Muller, K., "Division Financial Results," ibid.:6-7.

505   Association for Library Service to Children (ALSC)

Address   c/o ALA, 50 East Huron Street, Chicago, Illinois 60611 (permanent). Tel: 1 (312) 9446780. Fax: 1-312-4409374.

Officers   (elected for 1-yr.term) Pres: Barbara Immroth; Past Pres: Marilyn Berg Iarusso; Exec.Dir: Susan Roman (appointed). Exec.Comm: 13

Staff   2 (paid)

Languages   English, some publications in Spanish.

Established   1957, as Children's Services Division of ALA; present name adopted in 1977.

Major Fields of Interest   Services to children in all types of libraries.

Major Goals and Objectives   Improvement and extension of library services to children in all types of libraries. Responsible for the evaluation and selection of book and nonbook library materials for, and the improvement of techniques of, library service to children from preschool through eighth grade or junior high school age, when such materials or techniques are intended for use in more than one type of library.

Structure   Governed by Board of Directors. Affiliations: A division of ALA.

Sources of Support   Membership dues, sale of publications, private grants for projects. Budget:Approx. $250,000.

Membership   Total members: 3,578 (3,055 individual, 523 institutional). Priority Groups: 6 (Child Advocacy, Evaluation of Media, Professional Development, Social Responsibilities, Planning and Research, Awards). Committees: 50-60 (Library Service to Children with Special Needs, Competencies for Librarians Serving Youth, Computer Software Evaluation, Education, Film and Video Evaluation, Grants, Intellectual Freedom, International Relations, Legislation, Liaison with Mass Media, Preschool Services and Parents Education, Program Evaluation and Support, Research and Development, Selection of Children's Books and Materials from Various Cultures, National Planning of Special Collections, etc.). Discussion Groups: 6 (Managing Children's Services, Storytelling, Teachers of Children's Literature, etc.). Requirements: An interest in or a commitment to providing the best library service to children in all types of libraries. Dues: $58, first-year membership in ALSC and ALA, sliding scale thereafter.

General Assembly   Entire membership meets once a year during annual ALA conference.

Publications   *Official journal:* Journal of Youth Services in Libraries (JYSL) (formerly Top of the News / TON. 1946-88). 1988-. 4/yr. $30. Free to members. Issued jointly with YASD (Young Adult Services Division). Editor: Josette Anne Lyders. Address: 4222 Waycross Drive, Houston, TX 77035. Circ: 8,000. English. Indexed in Lib.Lit., LISA, Current Index to Journals in Education, etc. Other publications: ALSC Newsletter. 2/yr. Members only. Editor: Carla D. Hayden. Address: School of Library and Information Science, University of Pittsburgh, 135 N. Bellefield, Pittsburgh, PA 15260. Circ: Membership. English. Annual reports, proceedings of conferences, seminars, etc. Publications available for sale.

Activities   Carrying out projects within its area of responsibility. Cooperation with all units of ALA whose interests and activities have a relationship to library service to children. Interpretation of library materials for children and of methods of using such materials with children, to parents, teachers, and other adults, and representation of the librarians' concern for the production and effective use of good children's books to groups outside the profession. Stimulation of the professional growth of its members and encouragement of participation in appropriate type-of-library divisions. Planning and development of programs of study and research in the area of selection and use of library materials for children for the total profession. Development, evaluation, and promotion of professional materials in its area of responsibility. Presents a number of distinguished awards, such as the (Randolph) Caldecott Award (most distinguished American picture book for children), (John) Newbery Award (most distinguished contribution to American literature for children), Notable Children's Books (annual listing of notable children's books published), (Laura Ingalls) Wilder Award (author or illustrator who made a substantial and lasting contribution to literature for children), (Mildred L.) Batchelder Award (American publisher of the most outstanding children's book published in the US during preceding year, which was originally published abroad), etc. Sponsors conferences, seminars, workshops, and other continuing education programs.

Use of High Technology   Computers (attached to mainframe, and WANG word processing) for management.

Bibliography   Karrenbrock, M.H., "A History and Analysis of Top of the News, 1942-1987," Journal of Youth Services in Libraries 1 (1987):29-43; Jenkins, C. and Odean, K., "Recently Challenged Children's and Young Adult Books," Journal of Youth Services in Libraries 1 (1988):283-289; "Conference Highlights: Major Actions of the ALSC Board [and] YASD Board," Journal of Youth Services in Libraries 2 (1988):4-6; Somerville, M.R.,"Association for Library Service to Children," in ALA Yearbook 1989, pp. 50-51. Chicago: American Library Association, 1989; "American Library Association.

Association for Library Service to Children," in <u>The Bowker Annual: Library and Book Trade Almanac, 34th Edition 1989-90</u>, pp. 641-643. New York: R.R. Bowker, 1989.

506   Association for Recorded Sound Collections (ARSC)

Address   c/o Elwood A. McKee, President, 118 Monroe Street, # 610, Rockville, Maryland 20850 (not permanent).
Officers   (elected for 2-yr. term) Pres: Elwood A. McKee; Admin.Sec: Terry Montgomery (4560 Delafield Ave., New York, NY 10471). Exec.Board: 7.
Staff   4 (volunteers)
Languages   English
Established   1966, Syracuse, New York.
Major Fields of Interest   Management and preservation of audio collections
Major Goals and Objectives   To promote the organization, management and preservation of audio collections; to encourage and participate in research and development, exchange of information, and cooperative projects and programs having preservation of audio materials as their goal.
Structure   Governed by Executive Board. Affiliations: IASA, Music Library Association.
Sources of Support   Membership dues.
Publications   *Official journal:* ARSC Journal. Other publications: <u>ARSC Newsletter</u>; annual reports, proceedings of conferences, seminars, etc.
Activities   A major project has been carried out by its Associated Audio Archives (AAA) Committee, funded by the National Endowment for the Humanities, and which resulted in a final report on "Audio Preservation: A Planning Study" (Project Director: Elwood A. McKee). A reorganized and expanded AAA Committee participates in the development of a national preservation program for sound recordings and audio materials. Members also participate in a newly formed Subcommittee on Preservation and Restoration of Audio Materials of the Audio Engineering Society's Standards Committee (chaired by AAA representative William Storm of Syracuse University). Sponsors conferences, seminars, workshops, and other continuing education programs.

507   Association of Academic Health Sciences Library Directors (AAHSLD)

Address   c/o Houston Academy of Medicine - Texas Medical Center Library, 1133 M.D. Andersen Blvd., Houston Texas 77030 (permanent). Tel: 1 (713) 7971230.
Officers   (elected for 1-yr.term) Pres: Nina W. Matheson (Welch Medical Library, Johns Hopkins Univ. School of Medicine, 1900 E. Monument Street, Baltimore, MD 21205); Pres-Elect: Joan S. Zenan (Savitt Medical Library, University of Nevada, Reno, NV 89557); Sec-Treas: Karen L. Brewer; Past Pres: Shelley Bader; Admin.Assist: Ann Fenner. Exec.Board: 7
Staff   Volunteers, occasionally extra staff (paid).
Languages   English
Established   1978, Washington, D.C.
Major Fields of Interest   Biomedical information; medical education; medical librarianship
Major Goals and Objectives   To promote, in cooperation with educational institutions, other educational associations, government agencies, and other non-profit organizations, the common interests of academic health sciences libraries located in the United States and elsewhere, through publications, research, and discussion of problems of mutual interest and concern; to advance the efficient and effective operation of academic health sciences libraries for the benefit of faculty, students, staff, administrators, and practitioners.

Structure   Governed by Board of Directors.
Sources of Support   Membership dues. Budget: Approx.$34,000.
Membership   Total members: 119 (institutional). 2 countries represented. Types of membership: Institutional, associate. Requirements: Educational institutions which have an academic health sciences library. Dues: $300, institutional; $150, associate.
General Assembly   Entire membership meets once a year, usually in November. 1987: Washington, D.C., Nov.8-10; 1988: Chicago, Nov.12-17; 1989: Washington, D.C., Oct.28-Nov.2.
Publications   Association of Academic Health Sciences Library Directors NEWS. 1980-. 4/yr. $10. Free to members. Editor: Thomas D. Hydon. Address: Arizona Health Sciences Center Library, University of Arizona, 1501 N. Campbell Ave., Tucson, AZ 85724. Other publications: Directory; Annual Statistics of Medical School Libraries in the U.S. and Canada; Challenge to Action: Planning and Evaluation Guidelines for Academic Health Sciences Libraries; annual reports, proceedings of conferences, seminars, etc. Publications available for sale. No publications exchange program.
Activities   Past achievements: Development of guidelines for medical school libraries resulting in the publication Challenge to Action. Future: Commitee to work with medical school accrediting agency on establishment of appropriate criteria for evaluating libraries. Active in promoting library-related legislation; supports a Joint Legislative Task Force with MLA to support issues of importance to medical libraries, including the National Library of Medicine. Sponsors conferences, seminars, workshops, and other continuing education programs.
Use of High Technology   Computers and databases for analysis of statistical information.
Bibliography   "Association of Academic Health Sciences Library Directors," in The Bowker Annual: Library and Book Trade Almanac, 34th Edition 1989-90, pp. 671-672. New York: R.R.Bowker, 1989.

508   Association of Architectural Librarians (AAL)

Address   American Institute of Architects (AIA) Information Center, 1735 New York Avenue, NW, Washington, DC 20006. (permanent). Tel: 1 (202) 6267491.
Officers   (elected for unspecified term) Chair: Lamia Doumato; Sec: Sally Hanford; Newsletter Editor: Kathryn Wayne. Exec.Comm: 4
Staff   None
Languages   English
Established   1974, Washington, DC, by American Institute of Architects library staff.
Major Fields of Interest   Architectural librarianship in schools of architecture, architectural firms, architectural collections in special libraries.
Major Goals and Objectives   To provide a forum for architectural librarians to discuss their common problems; to promote information dissemination techniques in the fields of architecture, engineering, interior design, landscape architecture, and urban planning; to allow architectural librarians to meet once a year with members of the profession they serve at the annual AIA convention.
Structure   Governed by Executive Committee. Affiliations: American Institute of Architects.
Sources of Support   American Institute of Architects.
Membership   Total members: Approx.400 (individuals). Requirements: Open to any individual who works in an architectural library or is interested in the aims of the Association. Dues: None.
General Assembly   Entire membership meets once a year during AIA Convention.

Publications   *Official journal:* AAL Newsletter. 4/yr. Free to members. Address same as Association. Editor: Kathryn Wayne. Address: College of Architecture Library, University of Arizona, Tucson, AZ 85721. Circ: 400. English. No other publications.
Activities   Publishing newsletter and organizing annual conference.

509   Association of Christian Librarians (ACL)

Address   c/o Lynn A. Brock, Executive Secretary, PO Box 4, Cedarville College, Cedarville, Ohio 45314 (not permanent). Tel: 1 (513) 7662211.
Officers   (elected for 1-yr.term) Pres: William Abernathy (Ozark Christian College, Joplin, MO 64801); VP: Nancy Olson; Sec: Sharon Bull; Treas: Stephen Brown; Past Pres: David Wright. Exec.Sec: Lynn A. Brock (appointed). Exec.Board: 12
Staff   1 (paid)
Languages   English
Established   1957
Major Fields of Interest   Religion; Christian education; library work as related to Bible Colleges, Institutes, Christian Liberal Arts Colleges, and Christian Day Schools.
Major Goals and Objectives   To aid and assist librarians to do a more effective job in their work; to keep current with new trends in the library field; to meet the needs of evangelical Christian librarians serving in institutions of higher learning; to promote high standards of professionalism in library work as well as projects that encourage membership participation in serving the academic library community.
Structure   Governed by Board of Directors and Executive Committee. Affiliations: Council of National Library and Information Associations (CNLIA).
Sources of Support   Membership dues, sale of publications.
Membership   Total members: 300 (individual). 3 countries represented. Types of membership: Individual. Requirements: A full member shall be a Christian librarian subscribing to the aims of the Association, who is affiliated with an institution of higher learning. Associate members include those who are in agreement with the purposes of the Association, but who are not affiliated with institutions of higher learning, e.g. librarian at publishing houses or church libraries, or those who are nonlibrarians. Dues: $16-$37, based on salary scale.
General Assembly   Entire membership meets once a year, usually during second week of June.
Publications   *Official journal:* The Christian Librarian. 4/yr. $16. Free to members. Editor: Ron Jordahl. Address: Prairie Bible College, 3 Hills, Alberta, Canada TOM 2A0. Circ: Approx.500. English. Indexed in Christian Periodical Index, Social Sciences and Religion Index. Other publications: Christian Periodical Index (CPI); annual reports, proceedings of conferences, seminars, etc. Publications available for sale.
Activities   Past achievements: Publication of Christian Periodical Index (CPI) by automation; increased awareness of Association by Bible Colleges, Christian Liberal Arts Colleges, Church librarians, Christian Day Schools, and assistance to their librarians, many of whom are volunteers. Current: Continuing to set standards for librarians with AABC. Future: Continuing and enlarging publication of CPI. Sponsors conferences, seminars, workshops, and other continuing education programs.
Use of High Technology   Computers (Apple, IBM, and Inforonics,Inc.) for management.
Bibliography   "Association of Christian Librarians," in The Bowker Annual: Library and Book Trade Almanac, 34th Edition 1989-90, pp. 672-673. New York: R.R. Bowker, 1989.

510   Association of College and Research Libraries (ACRL)

Address   50 East Huron Street, Chicago, Illinois 60611 (permanent). Tel: 1 (312) 9446780. Fax: 1-312-4409374.
Officers   (elected for 1-yr.term, 1989-90) Pres: William A. Moffett; VP/Pres-Elect: Barbara J. Ford; Past Pres: Joseph A. Boissé; Exec.Dir: JoAn S. Segal (appointed). Exec.Comm: 12 (5 ex-officio, 7 elected)
Staff   11 (paid)
Languages   English
Established   1938, Kansas City, at the ALA Conference, replacing the College and Reference Section of ALA, founded in 1889.
Major Fields of Interest   Academic and research librarianship; higher education
Major Goals and Objectives   (1) To contribute to the total professional development of academic and research librarians; (2) to improve service capabilities of academic and research librarians; (3) to promote and speak for the interest of academic and research librarianship; (4) to promote study and research relevant to academic and research librarianship.
Structure   Governed by Board of Directors. Affiliations: A division of the American Library Association
Sources of Support   Membership dues, sale of publications. Budget: Approx. $2 million.
Membership   Total members: 10,170 (9,044 personal, 1,126 institutional). Sections: 14 (by subject-interest or types of library: Anthropology & Sociology, Art, Asian & African, Bibliographic Instruction, College Libraries, Community & Junior College Libraries, Education & Behavioral Sciences, Law & Political Science, Rare Books & Manuscripts, Slavic & East European, University Libraries, Western European Specialists, Women's Studies, etc.). Chapters: 39 (geographical). Requirements: Membership in ALA. Dues: $25 plus ALA dues.
General Assembly   Entire membership meets annually during ALA Conference and every 3 years at ACRL National Conference. 1989: 5th National Conference, Cincinnati, OH, April 5-8; 1992: 6th National Conference, Phoenix, AZ, April 1-4.
Publications   *Official journal:* College and Research Libraries 1939-. 6/yr. $45. ($55, foreign). Free to members. Address same as Association. Editor (until June 1990): Charles R. Martell. Address: California State University, Sacramento, CA 95819. Editor (June 1990-): Gloriana St. Clair (William Jasper Kerr Library, Oregon State University). Circ: Approx.12,000. English. Indexed in Lib.Lit., Current Index to Journals in Education, LISA, ISA, Social Sciences Citation Index, ERIC, etc. Official news magazine: College and Research Libraries News. 11/yr. $20. Free to members. Editor: George M. Eberhart. Address same as Association. Other publications: Choice (book review journal). 11/yr. $135 ($150, foreign). Editor: Patricia E. Sabosik. Address: 100 Riverview Ctr., Middletown, CT 06457; Rare Books and Manuscripts Librarianship. 2/yr. $25 ($35, foreign). Editor: Alice D. Schreyer. Address: University of Delaware Library, Newark, DE 19717-5267; ACRL Publications in Librarianship (occasional monograph series); ACRL University Library Statistics (biennial); College Library Information Packets (CLIP Notes), e.g. Collection Development Policies for College Libraries (1989; CLIP Note 11); Books for College Libraries III (1988); Ariel, J., ed., Building Women's Studies Collections: A Resource Guide (1987); Lehman, L.J. and Kiewitt, E.K., comps., Directory of Curriculum Materials Centers (1985); Mensching, T., Library Instruction Clearinghouses 1989: A Directory (1989); Academic Status: Statement and Resources (1988); 11 section newsletters; annual reports, proceedings of conferences, seminars, etc. Publications available for sale, listed in journal. No publications exchange program in effect

Activities   Past achievements: Held 5th National Conference in Cincinnati in 1989 with over 2,000 in attendance. Received grant from the National Endowment for the Humanities (NEH) to develop cooperative programs in the humanities in public and academic libraries. Completed revision of Standards for College Libraries. Current: Making links with other higher education associations; administering seven awards; working on NEH grant; developing output measures for academic libraries; offering professional education courses in local areas. Future: A membership survey and planning task force identified the 5 highest priorities of the Association: Publications, continuing education, standards and guidelines, alliances with other professional and scholarly organizations, chapters. Association has been active in promoting library-related legislation, such as, recommended need criteria to be used in allocation of HEA-Title II-A (College Resource Program) funds. Sponsors exhibits, conferences, seminars, workshops, and other continuing education programs.

Use of High Technology   Computers (IBM-compatible PC; CPT word processor) and databases for management. Electronic mail through ALANET (ALA).

Bibliography   Jones, W.G. and Ford, B.J., "Values and ACRL: What Do Our Leaders Report?" in <u>Academic Libraries: Myths and Realities</u>, pp. 141-145. Chicago: ACRL, 1984; Hogan, S.A. and Koyama, J.T., "ACRL Issues for the 80s," <u>College & Research Libraries News</u> 45 (1984):178, 181; Havens, S., "Academic Libraries: Myths and Realities: The ACRL's Third National Conference," <u>Library Journal</u> 109 (1984):1419-21; Segal, J.S.,"The Association of College and Research Libraries: What It Can Do for Academic Librarians in the 80's," <u>Show-Me Libraries</u> 36 (1984):8-12; Segal, J.S., "The Association of College and Research Libraries," <u>Library Times International</u> 2 (1986):74-75; Eswe, H.B., "ACRL Issues - An Action Agenda," (guest editorial) <u>ibid</u>.:76; "Strategic Plans for ALA and ACRL: A Comparison," <u>College & Research Libraries News</u> 47 (1986):709-712; "ACRL's Strategic Plan [Mission, Goals and objectives]," <u>College & Research Libraries News</u> 48 (1987):21-23, 25; "Strategic Planning for ACRL [first of a series of annual strategic planning reports]," <u>College & Research Libraries News</u> 49 (1988):292-294; Hilker, E., "Survey of Academic Science/Technology Libraries," <u>ibid</u>.:375-376; "Report from the ACRL Conference in Florence of Western Europeanists [April 4-8, 1988]," <u>Library of Congress Information Bulletin</u> 47 (July 11, 1988):293-294; Wand, P.A., "The Budget Process and ACRL Financial Issues," <u>College & Research Libraries News</u> 49 (1988):757-760; Euster, J.R., "Association of College and Research Libraries," in <u>ALA Yearbook 1989</u>, pp. 51-53. Chicago: American Library Association, 1989; "American Library Association. Association of College and Research Libraries," in <u>The Bowker Annual: Library and Book Trade Almanac, 34th Edition 1989-90</u>, pp. 644-647. New York: R.R. Bowker, 1989; Gordon, L., "'Futurists or Fossils?' is the Question for ACRL/NY," <u>Library Journal</u> 114 (1989):114; Segal, J.S., "The State of the Association," <u>College & Research Libraries News</u> 50 (1989): 693-696; "The Strategic Plan in Action: ACRL Looks to the Future," <u>ibid</u>.:711-712.

511   Association of Independent Information Professionals (AIIP)

Address   c/o Information Express, 324 E. Wisconsin Ave., Suite 1438, Milwaukee, Wisconsin 53202 (not permanent). Tel: 1 (414) 2725250

Officers   (elected for 1-yr.term) Pres: Helen Burwell; VP: Marilyn M. Levine; Rec.Sec: Rosemarie Falanga; Treas: Raymond Jassin. Exec.Board: 4

Staff   None

Languages   English

Established   June 4, 1987, Milwaukee, Wisconsin

Major Fields of Interest   Information services

Major Goals and Objectives   To enhance the professional interests of independent information professionals, etc. (Goals and Objectives are still in the process of being defined)
Structure   Governed by executive officers.
Sources of Support   Membership dues.
Membership   4 countries represented. Requirements: Independent information professionals.
General Assembly   Entire membership meets annually, usually in June in Milwaukee.
Publications   No publications program as yet.
Activities   Sponsors conferences. The association is still in the process of organizing into an international association.
Use of High Technology   Computers, databases and electronic mail for management.

512   Association of Information and Dissemination Centers (ASIDIC)

Address   PO Box 8105, Athens, Georgia 30603 (permanent). Tel: 1 (404) 5426820.
Officers   (elected for 1-yr.term) Pres: Marjorie Hlava; Past Pres: David Grooms; Sec-Treas: Taissa Kusma. Exec.Board: 6
Staff   0.25 (paid)
Languages   English
Established   1969, Columbus, Ohio, as Association of Scientific Information and Dissemination Centers. Present name adopted 1976
Major Fields of Interest   Computerized databases
Major Goals and Objectives   Better understanding of databases through discussing common problems in the operation of information dissemination centers
Structure   Governed by Executive Committee.
Sources of Support   Membership dues, fees from meetings. Budget: Approx. $25,000.
Membership   Total members: 130 (institutional). 5 countries represented. Requirements: Database vendor, database producer, or major online searcher. Dues: $50, full member; $30, associate member.
General Assembly   Entire membership meets twice a year.
Publications   *Official journal:* ASIDIC Bulletin. 1970-. 4/yr. Free to members. Address same as Association. Editor: Don Hawkins. Circ: Approx.150 (membership). English.
Activities   Sponsors conferences. Association is mainly involved in education and keeping track of developments in the industry affecting information centers and databases.
Use of High Technology   Computers used for management and by members.
Bibliography   Granick, L.W., "Emergence and Role of Common Interest Groups in Secondary Information," Journal of the American Society for Information Science 33 (1982):175-182.

513   Association of Information Systems Professionals (AISP)

Address   104 Wilmot Road, Suite 201, Deerfield, Illinois 60015-5195 (permanent). Tel: 1 (708) 9400361. Fax: 1-708-9407218.
Officers   Pres: Kitty McDuffy; Exec.Dir: Gayla McLean.
Staff   7 (paid)
Languages   English
Established   1972. Previous names: International Word Processing Association (1981); International Information/Word Processing Association (1983).
Major Fields of Interest   Information processing methods and systems
Major Goals and Objectives   To promote the development and dissemination of methods and techniques relating to the processing and flow of information in the automated

office environment; to encourage those who design, manage, and implement various types of information systems; to encourage exchange of ideas and experiences among members and the business community; to provide an innovative support system for information systems professionals through information on changes and advancements in the field, promotion of personal and professional growth, and lending active support to members.
Structure   Governed by executive officers.
Sources of Support   Membership dues, sale of publications. Budget: Approx. $1 million
Membership   Total members: Approx. 5,000. Chapters: 60 + . 2 countries represented. Requirements: Individuals involved in office information systems management, training, education, consulting, sales or support; companies/corporations interested in automated office equipment. Dues: $100 (120 Canadian Dollar), individual and corporate.
General Assembly   Entire membership meets at the Annual Syntopican Conference and exhibition. 1990: Syntopican XVIII, Phoenix, AZ, June 24-28.
Publications   *Official journal:* Dialogue (newsletter). 6/yr. Free to members. Address same as Association. English. Prompts. 12/yr. $19 for members; a monthly news digest of items of interest to PC users and word processing specialists. AISP Salary Survey (1/yr.), reporting on some 40 job titles in the information processing field throughout the country, $100 (members), $135 (non-members); free executive summary of this survey available to members. Other publications: Annual reports, proceedings of conferences, seminars, etc., mostly providing news and commentary on trends and technology, management and methods, people and productivity, including books, booklets, and tape programs designed to enhance professional development.
Activities   Association aims at providing a national and international network for members through chapter activities, and an opportunity to exchange ideas, concerns and solutions, while developing professional contacts and participating in educational programs. It cooperates with the Institute for Certification of Computer Professionals (ICCP) to help members acquire certification status. Many AISP programs are approved for re-certification credit. Sponsors exhibits, conferences, seminars, workshops, and other continuing education programs.
Use of High Technology   Computers for management

514   Association of Jewish Libraries (AJL)

Address   Postal address: c/o National Foundation for Jewish Culture, 330 Seventh Avenue, 21st floor, New York, New York 10001 (permanent).
Officers   (elected for 2-yr.term, 1988-90) Pres: Marcia Posner (Federation of Jewish Philanthropies Library, 130 E 59th St., New York, NY 10002. Tel: 1 (212) 8361506); Past Pres: Edith Lubetski; VP/Pres-Elect: Linda P. Lerman (Yale University, Sterling Memorial Library, PO Box 1603A, Yale Station, New Haven, CT 06520. Tel: 1 (203) 4324798); VP Membership: David J. Gilner; VP Publications: Ralph R. Simon; Treas: Toby G. Rossner; Corr.Sec: Tzivia Atik; Rec.Sec: Esther Nussbaum. Exec.Board: 8
Staff   20 (volunteers)
Languages   English, Hebrew, Yiddish
Established   1965, by merger of 2 groups, the Jewish Librarians Association (New York, 1946), and the Jewish Library Association (Cleveland, 1962). They now form the Association's 2 divisions: Research and Special Library Division (R&S) and Synagogue School & Center Division (SSC)
Major Fields of Interest   Judaica librarianship
Major Goals and Objectives   To inform, educate, and serve as a means of communicating the most advanced techniques in Judaica librarianship; to promote the improve-

ment of library services and professional standards in all Jewish libraries and collections of Judaica; to serve as a center of dissemination of Jewish library information and guidance; to encourage the establishment of Jewish libraries and collections of Judaica; to promote publication of literature which will be of assistance to Jewish librarianship; and to encourage people to enter the field of librarianship

Structure   Governed by the Executive Board. Affiliations: Council of National Library and Information Associations (CNLIA); Cataloging Committee of ALA

Sources of Support   Membership dues, sale of publications, private endowment (for book awards and manuscript competition).

Membership   Total members: 890. Divisions: 2 (1. Research and Special Library Division/R&S. Pres: Robert Singerman; 2. Synagogue, School & Center Division/SSC. Pres: Judith S. Greenblatt). Chapters: 7 (affiliated). Types of membership: Individual, institutional. Requirements: Anyone interested in Judaica librarianship and Judaica libraries. Dues: $25, individual and institutional; $18, students and retirees.

General Assembly   Entire membership meets once a year. 1989: Washington, DC, June 18-21; 1990: Israel.

Publications   *Official journal:* Judaica Librarianship. 1984-. 2/yr. $25. Free to members. Editors: Marcia Posner and Bella Hass Weinberg. Address: 19 Brookfield Rd., New Hyde Park, NY 11580. Circ: 890+. English, some Hebrew. Indexed in Genealogical Periodical Annual Index, Index of Articles on Jewish Studies, Index to Jewish Periodicals, ISA, LISA, Internationale Bibliographie der Zeitschriftenliteratur, etc. Other publications: AJL Newsletter. 4/yr. Free to members. Editor: Irene S. Levin. Address: 48 Georgia Street, Valley Stream, NY 11580; miscellaneous publications, such as, bibliographies, classification scheme, subject headings, basic library collections, reference material, library handbook, Index to Jewish Holiday Stories in Collections; Index to Jewish Values in Children's Literature, etc.; annual reports, proceedings of conferences, seminars, etc.

Activities   Past achievements: Establishment of reference award; funding of awards; establishment of the publications Judaica Librarianship; the Index to Jewish Values ("Juvenile Judaica"). Current: Compiling handbooks for officers and conventions; an organizational calendar; monthly newsletter for officers; increasing awareness of what is happening in the organization. Future: Increased collaboration/association with other library organizations; continuing education for professionals and para-professionals; rejuvenation of Chapters. Sponsors conferences, seminars, workshops, and other continuing education programs. Two book awards for children's literature, a book award for reference work, and a manuscript competition in children's literature.

Use of High Technology   Computers (IBM, Apple) for management (membership files and bibliographies).

Bibliography   Wiener, T., "Report from the Convention of the Association of Jewish Libraries," Library of Congress Information Bulletin 45 (Oct. 20, 1986):353-356; Wiener, T., "Report from the Association of Jewish Libraries," Library of Congress Information Bulletin 46 (Dec. 14, 1987):547-550; Kaganoff, N.M., "The American Jewish Historical Society as an Archival Agency," Judaica Librarianship 4 (1987/88):38-39; Posner, M., "Association of Jewish Libraries," in ALA Yearbook 1988, pp. 58-60. Chicago: American Library Association, 1988; Lerman, L.P., "Association of Jewish Libraries," in ALA Yearbook 1989, pp. 54-55. Chicago: American Library Association, 1989; "Association of Jewish Libraries," in The Bowker Annual: Library and Book Trade Almanac, 34th Edition 1989-90, p. 673. New York: R.R. Bowker, 1989; Wiener, T., "Association of Jewish Libraries Meets in Washington, DC," Library of Congress Information Bulletin 48 (Oct.9, 1989):351, 352-354.

515   Association of Librarians in the History of the Health Sciences (ALHHS)

Address   c/o Dorothy Whitcomb, President, Health Sciences Library, University of Wisconsin, Madison, Wisconsin 53706 (not permanent). Tel: 1 (608) 2622402
Officers   (elected for 1-yr.term) Pres: Dorothy Whitcomb; Pres-Elect: Glen Jenkins (Historical Div., Cleveland Health Sciences Library, 11000 Euclid Ave., Cleveland, OH 44106); Sec-Treas: Elizabeth Borst White (Houston Academy of Medicine Library, Texas Medical Center, Houston, TX 77030). Exec.Comm: 6
Staff   None
Languages   English
Established   1975, at annual meeting of the American Association for the History of Medicine (AAHM)
Major Fields of Interest   History of medicine; rare book librarianship; medical librarianship; preservation; computer application to the history of medicine
Major Goals and Objectives   To serve the professional interests of librarians, archivists, and other specialists actively engaged in the librarianship of the history of the health sciences by promoting an exchange of information and by improving standards of service, by identifying and making contact with persons similarly engaged, by providing opportunities to meet on appropriate occasions, by issuing a newsletter and such other materials as may seem appropriate to the association's interests, and by cooperating with other similar organizations in projects of mutual concern
Structure   Governed by officers and steering committees in annual meeting. Affiliations: AAHM.
Sources of Support   Membership dues. Budget: No fixed amount.
Membership   Total members: 65+ (60+ individual, 5 institutional). 5 countries represented. Requirements: Persons who have professional responsibilities for library and archives collections and services in the history of the health sciences (voting member); persons interested in the aims of the Association, e.g. booksellers, retired members, friends (non-voting member). Dues: $10, individual & institutional; $15, non-voting member.
General Assembly   Entire membership meets once a year. 1987: Philadelphia, PA, April 30; 1988: New Orleans, LA, May 3; 1989: Birmingham, AL.
Publications   *Official journal:* The Watermark. 1975-. 4/yr. Free to members. Editor: Judith Overmier. Address: Wangensteen Library, Diehl Hall, University of Minnesota, Minneapolis, MN 55455. Circ: Membership. English.
Activities   Past achievements: Annual program at AAHM; fellowship and nurture for new members. Current and future: Producing newsletter to keep in touch; continuing annual programs; preparing to raise program to acceptable level for continuing education credit. Sponsors conferences, and other continuing education programs.
Use of High Technology   Computers for mailing lists, desktop publishing and management.
Bibliography   "Association of Librarians in the History of the Health Sciences," in The Bowker Annual: Library and Book Trade Almanac, 34th Edition 1989-90, p. 674. New York: R.R. Bowker, 1989.

516   Association of Mental Health Librarians (AMHL)

Address   c/o Elizabeth Emily, President, Medical Library, Highland Hospital, PO Box 1101, Asheville, North Carolina 28802-1101 (not permanent). Tel: 1 (704) 2543201 ext. 266
Officers   (elected for 1-yr.term, 1990) Pres: Elizabeth Emily; VP/Pres.Elect: Mary L. Conlon (Medical Library, Cedarcrest Regional Hospital, 525 Russell Rd., Newington, CT

06111. Tel: 1-203-6667638); Past Pres: Ruth Stilman; Sec/Treas (2-yr.term): Mary E. Johnson (Library, Missouri Institute of Psychiatry, 5400 Arsenal St., St. Louis, MO 63139-1494. Fax: 1-314-6448839). Exec.Comm: 4
Staff None
Languages English
Established 1964, as Society of Mental Health Librarians, inactive between 1978-79, reorganized under present name, 1980, in Boston, during informal meeting with the Institute on Hospital & Community Psychiatry
Major Fields of Interest Mental health librarianship
Major Goals and Objectives To provide mental health librarians with an opportunity for exchange of information, continuing education, and collegiality
Structure Governed by executive officers. Affiliations: Institute on Hospital & Community Psychiatry of the American Psychiatric Association (APA)
Sources of Support Membership dues, sale of publications, meeting registrations.
Membership Total members: 139 (individual). 2 countries represented (US and Canada). Requirements: Employed in a mental health library or information center. Dues: $15.
General Assembly Entire membership meets once a year. 1987: Boston, MA, Oct.25-26; 1988: New Orleans, LA, Oct.22-24; 1989: Philadelphia, PA, Oct.14-16; 1990: Denver, CO, Oct. 6-8.
Publications No official journal. Other publications: <u>Directory of Mental Health Libraries and Information Centers</u>. Available for sale.
Activities Past achievements: Consolidating affiliation with Institute on Hospital & Community Psychiatry of the APA; broadening the core of serious and active membership. Current and future: Yearly meetings; small grants program to assist research projects; updating of <u>Directory</u>; expanding membership by enlisting more Canadian interest. Sponsors conferences, seminars, workshops, and other continuing education programs.
Use of High Technology Computers for management (membership lists, etc.)

517   Association of Research Libraries (ARL)

Address 1527 New Hampshire Avenue, NW, Washington, DC 20036 (permanent). Tel: 1 (202) 2322466. Fax: 1-202-9627849.
Officers (elected for 1-yr.term) Pres: Martin D. Runkle; Past Pres: Charles E. Miller; VP/Pres.Elect: Marilyn J. Sharrow; Exec.Dir: Duane E. Webster (appointed). Exec.Board: 3
Staff 20 (paid)
Languages English
Established 1932, Chicago, by chief librarians of 43 research libraries
Major Fields of Interest Issues confronting large research libraries (university and non-university libraries), such as development, organization, management, and access to information sources.
Major Goals and Objectives To initiate and develop plans for strengthening research library resources and services in support of higher education and research.
Structure Governed by officers and Board of Directors. Affiliations: ALA, IFLA
Sources of Support Membership dues, sale of publications, research grants. Budget: Approx. $900,000
Membership Total members: 119 (institutional). Types of membership: Institutional. Requirements: Membership eligibility is determined by membership criteria adopted by the ARL membership. Dues: $8,440, institutional.
General Assembly Entire membership meets twice a year.

Publications   *Official journal:* ARL Newsletter. 1965-. 5/yr.+ $15. Free to members. Address same as Association. Circ: Approx. 150. English. Other publications: ARL Annual Salary Survey; ARL Statistics (1/yr.); Rising Serials Prices and Research Libraries (1988); Guidelines for Retrospective Conversion of Bibliographic Records for Monographs; Preserving Knowledge: The Case for Alkaline Paper; Meeting the Preservation Challenge (1988); Technology & U.S. Government Information Policies: Catalysts for New Partnerships (1987); Linked Systems; Toward Telecommunications Strategies in Academic and Research Libraries; Selection of the University Librarian; The Automation Inventory of Research Libraries (1988); Preservation Planning Resources Notebook (1987); annual reports, proceedings of conferences, seminars, etc. The ARL Office of Management Services (OMS; until 1988, Office of Management Studies) continues publishing the series SPEC Kits (System and Procedures Exchange Center) on current topics of interest, e.g., performance appraisals, approval plans, preservation, remote access to online catalogs, search procedures for administrators, fundraising, use surveys, electronic mail, etc. Publications for sale. Price lists available.

Activities   The Association's activities were centered on implementing its Five-Year Plan, 1984-89, and on preparing a new plan to meet the needs of large research libraries. A serials pricing study was carried out in 1988 due to rising costs affecting member libraries. The North American Collections Inventory Project (NCIP) ended in 1988, and developed an online inventory of North American research library collections through a database managed by the Association. Preservation, with related activities, continues to be a major objective. The Association is actively involved in promoting library-related legislation, e.g. funding for library programs, increased funding for library preservation efforts, access to information, copyright, including electronic formats. Assisted members in self-studies through its Academic Library Program. Sponsors conferences, seminars, workshops, and other continuing education programs, such as OMS Management Skills Institutes, Analytical Skills Institutes, Managing the Learning Process Institutes, Special Focus Workshops, and the Creativity to Innovation Workshop, introduced in 1988.

Use of High Technology   Computers and databases for management.

Bibliography   Welsh, W.J., "ARL Holds 50th Anniversary Meeting," Library of Congress Information Bulletin 40 (June 18, 1982):183-184; Molyneux, R., "Growth at ARL Member Libraries 1962/63 to 1983/84," Journal of Academic Librarianship 12 (1986):211-216; Hewitt, J.A. and Shipman, J.S., "Cooperative Collection Development among Research Libraries in the Age of Networking: Report of a Survey of ARL Libraries," in Advances in Library Automation and Networking v. 1. pp. 189-232. Jai Press, 1987; "Joint ARL-Library of Congress Project to Produce Machine-Readable National Register of Microform Masters," Library of Congress Information Bulletin 47 (Jan. 4, 1988):2; Dougherty, R.M. and Barr, N.E., "Paying the Piper: ARL Libraries Respond to Skyrocketing Journal Subscription Prices," The Journal of Academic Librarianship 14 (1988):4-9; Stubbs, K., "Apples and Oranges and ARL Statistics [library statistics invite the unwary to draw illicit conclusions from mismated numbers]," Journal of Academic Librarianship 14 (1988):231-235; Gyeszly, S., "Reserve Departments and Automation: A Survey of ARL Libraries," Information Technology and Libraries 7 (1988):401-410; "ARL Receives Preservation Grant," Wilson Library Bulletin 63 (1989):13; Daval, N.,"Association of Research Libraries," in ALA Yearbook 1989, pp. 55-61. Chicago: American Library Association, 1989; Daval, N., "Association of Research Libraries," in The Bowker Annual: Library and Book Trade Almanac, 34th Edition 1989-90, pp. 155-159. New York: R.R. Bowker, 1989; "ACRL," ibid.:674-676.

518   Association of Specialized and Cooperative Library Agencies (ASCLA)

Address   50 East Huron Street, Chicago, Illinois 60611 (permanent). Tel: 1 (312) 9446780. Fax: 1-312-4409374.

Officers   Pres: William G. Asp; Past Pres: Joseph F. Shubert; Acting Exec.Dir: Evelyn Shaevel. Exec.Board: 12

Staff   2 (paid)

Languages   English

Established   1977, through a merger of 2 ALA Divisions: Association of State Library Agencies, and Health and Rehabilitative Library Services Division

Major Fields of Interest   State library agencies, specialized library agencies, and multitype library cooperatives

Major Goals and Objectives   To represent state library agencies, specialized library agencies, and multitype library cooperatives and assist in the development and evaluation of their plans, and to coordinate activities with other appropriate ALA units. The specific objectives are: (1) Development and evaluation of goals and plans for member groups to facilitate the implementation, improvement and extension of library activities designed to foster improved user services, coordinating such activities with other appropriate ALA units; (2) representation and interpretation of the role, functions, and services of these agencies and cooperatives within and outside the profession, including contact with national organizations and government agencies; (3) development of policies, studies, and activities in matters affecting these agencies and cooperatives; (4) establishment, evaluation, and promotion of standards and service guidelines relating to the concerns of the association; (5) identifying the interests and needs of all persons, encouraging the creation of services to meet these needs within the areas of concern of the association, and promoting the use of these services provided by the agencies and cooperatives; (6) stimulating the professional growth and promoting the specialized training and continuing education of library personnel at all levels in the areas of concern of the association; (7) assisting in the coordination of activities of other units within ALA with related concerns; (8) granting recognition for outstanding library service; (9) acting as a clearinghouse for the exchange of information and encouraging the development of relevant materials, publications and research.

Structure   Governed by Executive Board. Affiliations: A division of ALA.

Sources of Support   Membership dues. Budget: Approx. $55,000.

Membership   Total members: 1,363 (1,012 individual, 351 institutional). Sections: 3 (Libraries Serving Special Populations/LSSPS; Multitype Library Networks and Cooperatives/Multi-LINCS; State Library Agency/SLAS). Committees: 18 (Legislation, Library Personnel and Education, Research, Standards Review, etc.). Requirements: Membership in ALA. Dues: $25 plus ALA dues.

General Assembly   Entire membership meets annually during ALA conference.

Publications   *Official journal:* Interface. 4/yr. $10. Free to members. Editor: Mary Redmond. Address: Principal Librarian, State Library, Legislative & Government Service, Cultural Education Center, Albany, NY 12230. Circ: 1,400+. English. Other publications: Bibliotherapy Forum Newsletter. 4/yr. $5, members; $7, nonmembers. Editor: Lethene Parks. Address: 8520 State Road, State Highway 302 NW, Gig Harbor, WA 98335; The State Library Agencies: A Survey Project Report (7th ed., 1988, biennial); The Report on Library Cooperation (6th ed., 1988, biennial); Publications for sale.

Activities   Carried out through the sections and committees, covering a wide range of issues in accordance with the goals and objectives of the Association. Some activities deal with matters involving state and local library legislation, state grants-in-aid and appropriations, and relationships among state, federal, regional, and local governments. Much

attention is given to the development of standards, such as preparing revisions of <u>Standards for Juvenile Correctional Institutions</u>, the <u>Library Standards for Jails and Detention Centers</u>, and <u>Standards for Adult Correctional Institutions</u>. Sponsors conferences, seminars, workshops, and other continuing education programs, on topics such as consulting skills, automation activities, youth services, services to the impaired elderly, AIDS information, bibliotherapy, health care, managing effective programs for disabled persons, etc..
Use of High Technology   Computers used for management
Bibliography   "ALA Unit [ASCLA] Awarded $.9 Million for Literature Project," <u>American Libraries</u> 14 (1983):696+; Daniels, B.E., "Association of Specialized and Cooperative Library Agencies," in <u>ALA Yearbook 1989</u>, pp. 61-62. Chicago: American Library Association, 1989; "American Library Association. Association of Specialized and Cooperative Library Agencies," in <u>The Bowker Annual: Library and Book Trade Almanac, 34th Edition 1989-90</u>, pp. 647-648. New York: R.R. Bowker, 1989.

519   Association of Visual Science Librarians (AVSL)

Address   c/o Bette Anton, Librarian, Optometry Library, University of California, Berkeley, California 94720 (not permanent). Tel: 1 (415) 6421020.
Officers   (elected for 2-yr.term) Chair: Bette Anton; Past Chair: Laurel Gregory; Treas: Alison Howard; Archivist: Maria Dablemont. Exec.Board: 5
Staff   None
Languages   English
Established   1968, Beverly Hills, California.
Major Fields of Interest   Vision science
Major Goals and Objectives   To foster development of individual libraries, improve access to vision information, develop reference and bibliographic tools, and promote standards for visual science libraries.
Structure   Governed by executive officers and members. Affiliations: American Academy of Optometry
Sources of Support   Sale of publications. No specific budget.
Membership   Total members: 65 (6 individual, 59 institutional). 8 countries represented. Requirements: An interest in some aspect of the literature of vision. Dues: None.
General Assembly   Entire membership meets once a year, in December, in conjunction with the annual meeting of the American Academy of Optometry. 1989: New Orleans, LA; 1990: Boston, MA. Members also meet with the Medical Library Association.
Publications   No official journal. Other publications: <u>Union List of Vision-Related Serials</u> (5th ed.,1985); "Standards for Academic Visual Science Libraries," <u>American Journal of Optometry and Physiological Optics</u> 63(1986):559-566; <u>Opening Day Book Collection - Visual Science</u>; <u>PhD Theses in Physiological Optics</u> (irreg.).
Activities   Publications program, including revision of Union list; sponsors conferences.
Use of High Technology   Computers (IBM PC, Apple IIe, Macintosh) for management.
Bibliography   "Association of Visual Science Librarians," in <u>The Bowker Annual: Library and Book Trade Almanac, 34th Edition 1989-90</u>, pp. 676-677. New York: R.R. Bowker, 1989.

520   Bibliographical Society of America (BSA)

Address   Postal address: PO Box 397, Grand Central Station, New York, New York 10163 (permanent). Tel: 1 (212) 6387957. Headquarters: 794 Carroll Street, Brooklyn, NY 11215 (permanent).

Officers   (elected for 2-yr.term) Pres: Ruth Mortimer (Smith College); VP: William Matheson; Sec: John Bidwell; Treas: R. Dyke Benjamin; Exec.Sec./Asst.Treas: Irene Tichenor (appointed). Exec.Council: 12
Staff   1 (paid)
Languages   English
Established   1904, New York City.
Major Fields of Interest   Descriptive and analytical bibliography; printing, publishing, bookselling and other book trade history; textual editing; codicology and related manuscript studies
Major Goals and Objectives   To support bibliographical inquiry in all areas listed above.
Structure   Governed by Council. Affiliations: American Council of Learned Societies.
Sources of Support   Membership dues, sale of publications, endowed funds. Budget: Approx. $220,000.
Membership   Total members: 1,400 (730 individual, 670 institutional). 34 countries represented. Requirements: Open to all individuals and institutions interested in bibliographical problems and project. Dues: $30, individual & institutional; $50, contributing; $150, sustaining; $750, life.
General Assembly   Entire membership meets once a year, in late January.
Publications   *Official journal:* Papers of the Bibliographical Society of America. 1904-. 4/yr. Subscription through membership only. Free to members. Address same as Association. Editors: William S. Peterson and John Lancaster. Address: William S. Peterson, Department of English, University of Maryland, College Park, MD 20742. Circ: 1,400 (membership). English. Publishes monographs and contributed many major bibliographical works. Some recent publications: Adams, T.R., The American Controversy: A Bibliographical Study of the British Pamphlets about the American Disputes, 1764-1783; Wolfe, R.J., Early American Music Engraving and Printing: A History of Music Publishing in America from 1787 to 1825...; Christianson, C. P., A Directory of London Stationers and Book Artisans 1300-1500 (1988), etc.
Activities   In accordance with the aims of the Society, activities promote bibliographical research and relevant publications. Initiated fellowship program. Continuing publication of quarterly journal and preparing manuscripts for publication as monographs. Some projects are being carried out jointly with related associations, e.g. a comprehensive survey of repositories of printing and publishing archives to result in the publication of a guide to the resources for bibliographical research in the US. Active in promoting library-related legislation, e.g., participated with other constituents of the American Council of Learned Societies in supporting re-authorization of the National Endowment for the Humanities. Awards short-term fellowships to encourage scholarship in bibliography. Sponsors regional meetings (lectures and exhibitions) with other bibliographical institutions.
Use of High Technology   Computers and databases for management.
Bibliography   Wiegand, A.A., "Library Politics and the Organization of the Bibliographical Society of America," The Journal of Library History, Philosophy and Comparative Librarianship 21 (1986):131-157; "Bibliographical Society Meets," Antiquarian Bookman (AB) 81 (1988):1496-98; "Bibliographical Society of America," in The Bowker Annual: Library and Book Trade Almanac, 34th Edition 1989-90, p. 679. New York: R.R. Bowker, 1989.

521   Catholic Library Association (CLA)

Address   461 West Lancaster Ave., Haverford, Pennsylvania 19041 (permanent). Tel: 1 (215) 6495250
Officers   (elected for 1-yr.term) Pres: Brother Emmett Corry, OSF; Past Pres: Irma C. Godfrey; VP/Pres.Elect: Rev. Paul J. DeAntoniis; Exec.Dir: Natalie A. Logan (appointed, 1989-). Exec.Board: 7
Staff   8 (paid)
Languages   English
Established   1921, Cincinnati, Ohio. Originally founded as a section of the National Catholic Educational Association, becoming independent in 1931 and legally incorporated in 1955.
Major Fields of Interest   Catholic library and information science fields
Major Goals and Objectives   The promotion and encouragement of Catholic literature and library work through cooperation, publications, education, and information.
Structure   Governed by Executive Board, assisted by Advisory Council.
Sources of Support   Membership dues, sale of publications. Budget: Approx. $700,000.
Membership   Total members: 3,250 (2,750 individual, 500 institutional). Sections: 6 (Archives, Children's Libraries, Academic Libraries, High School Libraries, Library Education, Parish and Community Libraries). Chapters: 27 (geographical). Round Tables: 2 (Cataloging and Classification, Public Libraries). 18 countries represented. Requirements: Open to anyone interested in the aims of the Association. Dues: $45, individual, regular; $10-$500, various categories for individual, from student to life; $45-$105, institutional, scaled according to expenditures.
General Assembly   Entire membership meets once a year. 1988: New York City, Apr. 4-7; 1989: Chicago, IL, March 27-30; 1990: Toronto, Canada, Apr. 16-19; 1991: Boston, MA, Apr. 1-4.
Publications   *Official journal:* Catholic Library World. 1929-. 10/yr. $60. Free to members. Editor: Michael W. Rechel. Address same as Association. Circ: 3,500. English. Indexed in Lib.Lit., LISA,etc. Other publications: CLA Handbook and Membership Directory; The Catholic Periodical and Literature Index (subscription); Corrigan, J.T. Guide for the Organization and Operation of a Religious Resource Center (rev.ed., 1986); Gallagher, M.E., Young Adult Literature: Issues and Perspectives (1988), and other religious reference tools and specialized publications (e.g. bibliographies of books for elementary and secondary Catholic schools). Publications available for sale.
Activities   The Association strives to initiate and foster any activity or library program that will promote literature and libraries not only of a Catholic nature, but also of an ecumenical spirit. Maintains representation to other professional associations having library/ information service interests. Active in promoting library-related legislation, such as, obtaining Federal aid for Catholic school libraries, etc. Provides 2 scholarships annually to encourage promising students to enter the library profession, and presents other awards. Current and future: Increase of publications program to meet membership needs; computerization of membership services and publications; sponsorship of the American Catholic Heritage project; cooperative activities with other similar associations; increase of continuing education programs for members. Sponsors conferences, seminars, workshops, and exhibits.
Bibliography   Lynch, Sister M.F., "Structuring CLS's Mission for the Future," Catholic Library World 56 (1985):270-271; Corrigan, J.T.,"Catholic Library Association," in ALA Yearbook 1989, pp. 87-88. Chicago: American Library Association, 1989; "Catholic Library Association," in The Bowker Annual: Library and Book Trade Almanac, 34th Edition 1989-90, pp. 682-683. New York: R.R. Bowker, 1989.

522   Center for Research Libraries (CRL)

Address   6050 S. Kenwood Ave., Chicago, Illinois 60640 (permanent). Tel: 1 (312) 9554545
Officers   Chair: Richard J. Talbot; Vice-Chair: Kenneth R.R. Gros Louis; Sec: Roger Hansen; Treas: James Govan. Exec.Comm: 15.
Staff   75 (paid)
Languages   English
Established   1949, as Midwest Inter-Library Center, with grants from the Carnegie Corporation and Rockefeller Foundation. Organized under new name in 1966.
Major Fields of Interest   Library cooperation in research materials
Major Goals and Objectives   To supplement and complement major American research collections by maintaining a collection of important research materials.
Structure   The Center is a nonprofit organization operated and maintained by its member institutions. Members are represented on the Council by two persons, the head librarian (ex officio) and a nonlibrarian appointed by the president of the member institution. Associate members are not represented.
Sources of Support   Membership dues.
Membership   Total members: 150 (institutional). Requirements: Any institution supporting research or having a research library. Dues: Depend on size of library acquisitions expenditures over 5 years and number of volumes held.
General Assembly   Entire membership meets once a year.
Publications   *Official journal:* Focus on The Center for Research Libraries (newsletter); 1980-. 6/yr. Free to members. Editor: Sally Brickman. Address same as Association. Circ: 150. English. Other publications: Handbook of collections, bibliographies, annual reports, proceedings of conferences, seminars, etc.
Activities   Past achievements: Systematic review of CRL's Collection and Services Program; preservation studies and microfilming of newspaper collections; review of the Center's internal operations, and reorganization. Current and future: To strengthen communication and promotion of the Center's services to members and potential members as a central resource-sharing facility for less frequently needed materials.
Use of High Technology   Computers used for management and electronic publishing.
Bibliography   "Center for Research Libraries: Meeting the Opportunity to Fulfill the Promise: A Symposium," Journal of Academic Librarianship 9 (1983):258-269; "Center for Research Libraries is Newest Member of CONSER Program," Library of Congress Information Bulletin 46 (June 22, 1987):286.

523   Chief Officers of State Library Agencies (COSLA)

Address   c/o Thomas F. Jaques, Chairperson, State Librarian, State Library of Louisiana, Box 131, Baton Rouge, Louisiana 70821 (not permanent). Tel: 1 (504) 3424923.
Officers   (elected for 2-yr.term, 1988-90) Chair: Thomas F. Jaques; Vice Chair/Chair-Elect: Richard Cheski (State Librarian, State Library of Ohio, 65 S. Front St., Columbus, OH 43266-0334); Sec: Gary J. Nichols (Maine State Library, State House, Sta. #64, Augusta, ME 04333); Treas: James Nelson. Exec.Board: 10
Staff   None
Languages   English
Major Fields of Interest   Cooperation among state library agencies
Major Goals and Objectives   To provide a means for cooperative action among its state and territorial members to strengthen the work of the respective state and territorial agencies; to provide a continuing mechanism for dealing with the problems faced by the

heads of these agencies, which are responsible for state and territorial library development.
Structure Governed by Executive Board. Affiliations: ALA, ASCLA
Sources of Support Membership dues.
Membership Membership consists solely of the chief library officers of the 50 states and one territory, who are variously named state librarians, directors, commissioners, or executive secretaries.
General Assembly Entire membership meets annually at the ALA conference.
Publications No publications program.
Activities Various committees carry out liaison activities with government agencies and other organizations.
Use of High Technology Computers for management.
Bibliography Miller, R.T., "Cherry Blossoms, Chief Officers of State Library Agencies and Congress," Show-Me Libraries 37 (1986):3-4; "Chief Officers of State Library Agencies," in The Bowker Annual: Library and Book Trade Almanac, 34th Edition 1989-90, pp. 683-684. New York: R.R. Bowker, 1989.

524 Chinese-American Librarians Association (CALA)

Address c/o Eveline L. Yang, Executive Director, CALA, c/o Auraria Library, University of Colorado, 1100 Lawrence Street, Denver, Colorado 80204. Tel: 1 (303) 5562911. Headquarters: 1712 Barrington, Ann Arbor, Michigan 48103 (permanent).
Officers (elected for 1-yr.term, 1989-90) Pres: Peter R. Young (Faxon Institute, 15 Southwest Park, Westwood, MA 02090. Tel: 1 (617) 3292250); VP/Pres-Elect: Amy D. Seetoo (University Microfilms International, 300 North Zeeb Road, Ann Arbor, MI 48106-1346); Treas: Susan Ma; Exec.Dir (appointed): Eveline L. Yang. Exec.Board: 21
Staff 1 (partially paid)
Languages English
Established 1973, at Rosary College, River Forest, Illinois.
Major Fields of Interest Sino-American librarianship; international exchanges of information and library personnel
Major Goals and Objectives To provide a medium through which Chinese-American librarians may cooperate with other associations and organizations: (1) To promote better communication among Chinese-American librarians; (2) to serve as a forum for the discussion of mutual problems and professional concerns among Chinese-American librarians; (3) to promote the development of Chinese and American librarianship.
Structure Governed by Executive Board members elected by the general membership. Affiliations: ALA
Sources of Support Membership dues, sale of publications. Budget: Approx. $25,000.
Membership Total members: 450 (individual). Chapters: 5 (regional). 4 countries represented (USA, China, Taiwan, Hongkong). Requirements: Any individual or corporate body interested in the goals of the Association. Dues: $15, individual; $45, institutional; $200, life; $7.50, student.
General Assembly Entire membership meets once a year during the annual ALA conference.
Publications *Official journal:* Journal of Library and Information Science. 1975-. 2/yr. $15. Free to members. (Published jointly with the Department of Social Education, National Taiwan Normal University, Taiwan). Address: Chinese Culture Service, Inc., PO Box 444, Oak Park, IL 60303. Editor: Nelson Chou. Address: Librarian, East Asian Library, Rutgers University, New Brunswick, NJ 08890. Tel: (217) 8933955. Circ: 1,000. English, Chinese. Indexed in Lib.Lit., Index to Chinese Periodicals, ISA, LISA, PAIS. etc.

Other publications: <u>Chinese-American Librarians Association Newsletter</u>. 1973-. 3/yr.
Editors: Ingrid Hsieh-Yee (910 Primrose Road, #203, Annapolis, MD 21403) and May
Chan Rathbone (University of Washington Libraries, FM-25, Seattle, WA 98195); <u>Areas
of Cooperation in Library Development in Asian and Pacific Regions</u>; annual reports,
proceedings of conferences, seminars, etc. Publications available for sale.
Activities   Past achievements: Sponsoring annual programs as an effective means to
raise funds for research grants and scholarships, and library acquisitions matching grants
for ethnic reading materials. Current: Co-sponsoring ALA's presidential programs. Preparing a series of "Chinese American Resources Directories (CARD)." Future: To promote intellectual freedom, equal access to information and library services to ethnic minorities and new Americans, and bridge the information gap between the USA and
China. Active in promoting library-related legislation, e.g. support of library services to
non-English speaking persons, support of English literacy programs among new Americans. Sponsors Book Week, exhibits, conferences, seminars, workshops, and other continuing education programs, and promotes writers, publishers and book sellers so that
they can reach a larger audience.
Use of High Technology   Computers (IBM PC) and databases for management (e.g.,
mailing labels).
Bibliography   Wan, W.W., "Chinese American Librarians Association: An Overview,"
<u>Ethnic Forum: Journal of Ethnic Studies and Ethnic Bibliography</u> 6 (1986):141-143; Seet-
oo Wilson, A., "Chinese-American Librarians Association (CALA)," in <u>ALA Yearbook
1989</u>, p. 98. Chicago: American Library Association, 1989.

525   Church and Synagogue Library Association (CSLA)

Address   c/o Lorraine E. Burson, Executive Director, PO Box 19357, Portland, Oregon
97219 (permanent). Tel: 1 (503) 2446919
Officers   (elected for 1-yr.term) Pres: Lin Wright (27 Magna Drive, Gillette, NJ 07933);
Past Pres: Anne Greenwood; VP: Eleanor S. Courtney; Treas: Vera G. Hunter. Exec.Dir:
Lorraine E. Burson (appointed). Exec.Board: 15
Staff   3 (paid)
Languages   English
Established   1967, Philadelphia, during ALA conference, by Protestant, Catholic and
Jewish librarians
Major Fields of Interest   Church and synagogue librarianship
Major Goals and Objectives   To provide educational guidance in the establishment
and maintenance of library service in churches and synagogues; to act as a unifying core
for the many existing church and synagogue libraries; to provide the opportunity for a
mutual sharing of practices and problems; to inspire and encourage a sense of purpose
and mission among church and synagogue librarians; to study and guide the development
of church and synagogue librarianship toward recognition as a formal branch of the library profession.
Structure   Governed by Executive Board. Affiliations: None
Sources of Support   Membership dues, sale of publications. Budget: Approx. $65,000.
Membership   Total members: 1,820 (1,234 individual, 586 institutional). Chapters: 23.
Committees: 8. 8 countries represented. Requirements: Interest in aims of Association
and payment of dues. Dues: $12, individual; $23, church or synagogue; $50, affiliated;
$75, institutional; $100, contributing.
General Assembly   Entire membership meets once a year. 1987: Philadelphia, PA,
June 28-30; 1988: Oberlin, OH, June 19-21; 1990: Portland, OR, July 1-3.

Publications   *Official journal:* Church & Synagogue Libraries. 1967-. 6/yr. $15. Free to
members. Editor: Lorraine E. Burson. Address same as Association. Circ: 3,500. English.
Indexed in Christian Periodical Index. Other publications: A numbered series of Guides
to aid in the establishment and operation of congregational libraries, e.g., Pritchett, J.
Providing Reference Service in Church and Synagogue Libraries (1988; No.15);   Archives
in the Church or Synagogue Library (No.10);   Standards for Church and Synagogue Libraries (No.6), etc.;   A Basic Book List for Church Libraries (3rd ed., B.E. Deitrick);
Church and Synagogue Library Resources (4th ed., R. Kohl & D. Rodda);   Church and
Synagogue Library Resources: Annotated Bibliography;   annual reports, proceedings of
conferences, seminars, etc. Publications available for sale.
Activities   Past achievements: Growth in membership, chapters, and publications; computerization of procedures.   Current and future: Publication of bi-monthly journal and
monographs on church and synagogue librarianship; annual conference for all church and
synagogue librarians; awards to outstanding religious libraries; provision of scholarships
for courses in church and synagogue librarianship; establishment of a permanent office
and enlarged staff; establishment of self-evaluation certification program; establishment
of self-study programs in church and synagogue librarianship. Sponsors exhibits, conferences, seminars, workshops, and other continuing education programs.
Use of High Technology   Computers (IBM PC) for management.
Bibliography   Harvey, J.F., ed., Church and Synagogue Libraries. Metuchen, NJ: Scarecrow Press, 1980; Hannaford, C.,"The Church and Synagogue Library Association: Fif-
teen Years of Ecumenical Concern for Quality Service in Religious Libraries," Special Libraries 74 (1983); "Church and Synagogue Librarians Meet," Library Times International
2 (1985):3; Vanderhoof, A., "Church and Synagogue Library Association in Texas," Texas
Library Journal 62 (1986):32-33; Karabinus, K., "Ohio Welcomes CSLA's Annual Conference," Church and Synagogue Libraries 21 (1988):1, 5l; "Church and Synagogue Library Association," in The Bowker Annual: Library and Book Trade Almanac, 34th Edition 1989-90, pp. 684-685. New York: R.R. Bowker, 1989.

526   Committee on East Asian Libraries of the Association for Asian Studies, Inc. (CEAL)

Address   c/o Karl K. Lo, Chair, Committee on East Asian Libraries, Head, East Asia
Library, University of Washington, Gowen Hall D0-27, Seattle, Washington 98195 (not
permanent). Tel: 1 (206) 5434490
Officers   (elected for 3-yr.term) Chair: Karl K. Lo; Exec.Group: 9 members (John
Yung-hsiang, Chae-Jin Lee, Masato Matsui, Vivienne B. Shue, Kevin Lin, Richard Ho-
ward, Min-chih Chou, Maureen H. Donovan, Richard T. Wang), elected
Staff   None
Languages   English
Established   As a Committee of the Association for Asian Studies, Inc.
Major Fields of Interest   East Asian librarianship
Major Goals and Objectives   (1) To further the profession of East Asian librarianship;
(2) to serve as a faculty librarians' forum for the discussion of problems of common con-
cern and to recommend programs for the improvement of library facilities; (3) to pro-
mote the development of library resources and bibliographic controls; (4) to improve in-
terlibrary and international cooperation and services.
Structure   Governed by Executive Group consisting of 3 faculty members and 6 librarians, serving staggered terms of not more than 3 years. Affiliations: Association for Asian
Studies.
Sources of Support   Membership dues (through the Association for Asian Studies)

Membership   Total members: Approx. 270 (210 individual, 60 institutional). Subcommittees: 5 (Resources and Development, Technical Processes, Union Catalog, Liaison with Chinese Libraries, Japanese Material). Requirements: Open to institutions in America with library collections on East Asia and to members of the Association for Asian Studies. Membership approved by Executive Group upon written application. Dues: $15, individual; $25, institutional.

General Assembly   Entire membership meets once a year during the annual meeting of the Association for Asian Studies.

Publications   *Official journal:* CEAL Bulletin. 1964-. 3/yr. Free to members. Address same as Association. Editor: Diane Perushek. Address: Curator, Gest Oriental Library, Princeton University, Princeton, NJ 08540. Circ: Membership. English.   Other publications: CEAL Directory.

Activities   Initiated Chinese Cooperative Catalog, issued monthly by the Library of Congress. Activities carried out through subcommittees. Projects involving institutional cooperation are voted on by institutional members only.

527   Committee on South Asian Libraries and Documentation of the Association for Asian Studies, Inc. (CONSALD)

Address   c/o Kenneth R. Logan, Chair, South Asia Librarian, South/Southeast Asia Library, 438 Main Library, University of California, Berkeley, CA 94720 (not permanent). Tel: 1 (415) 6423095

Officers   (elected for 2-yr.term) Chair: Kenneth R. Logan. Exec.Board: 7

Staff None

Languages   English

Established   1970, as Committee of the Association for Asian Studies, Inc.

Major Fields of Interest   South Asian studies

Major Goals and Objectives   Identification, location, acquisition and availability of resources for the scholarly research on South Asia (India, Pakistan, Nepal, Sri Lanka, Bangladesh and Afghanistan) in North America.

Structure   Governed by Executive Board, appointed by the South Asia Council of the Association for Asian Studies (Ann Arbor, MI). Affiliations: Association for Asian Studies.

Sources of Support   Membership dues (through the Association for Asian Studies).

Membership   Total members: Approx. 65 (individual). Requirements: Interest in South Asia research materials in North American libraries. Dues: Membership in Association for Asian Studies.

General Assembly   Entire membership meets once a year at the annual meeting of the Association for Asian Studies. 1988: San Francisco, March 25-27.

Publications   *Official journal:* South Asia Library Notes and Queries. 1978-. 2/yr. $8. Editor: James H. Nye. Address: South Asia Collection, Room 560, University of Chicago Library, 1100 East 57th Street, Chicago, IL 60637. Circ: Membership. English.

Activities   Coordination and cooperation between South Asia research collections in the USA.

528   Continuing Library Education Network and Exchange Round Table of the American Library Association (CLENERT)

Address   50 East Huron Street, Chicago, Illinois 60611 (permanent). Tel: 1 (312) 9446780 ext.425. Fax: 1-312-4409374.

Officers   (elected for 1-yr.term) Pres: Mary Y. Moore; VP/Pres-Elect: Gail J. McGovern; Sec: Gary R. Purcell; Staff Liaison: Elaine K. Wingate. Exec.Board: 9

Staff   1 (paid by ALA)
Languages   English
Established   1984, as Round Table of ALA. Originally, Continuing Library Education Network and Exchange, Inc. (CLENE), founded in 1975 in San Francisco.
Major Fields of Interest   Continuing education
Major Goals and Objectives   (1) To provide a forum for the exchange of ideas and concerns among library and information personnel responsible for continuing library education, training, and staff development; (2) to provide learning activities and material to maintain the competencies of those who provide continuing library education; (3) to provide a force for initiating and supporting programs to increase the availability of quality continuing library education; (4) to create an awareness of, and sense of need for, continuing library education on the part of employees and employers.
Structure   Governed by Executive Board. Affiliations: A Round Table of ALA.
Sources of Support   Membership dues (through ALA).
Membership   Total members: 378 (304 individual, 74 institutional). Requirements: Open to all ALA members. Dues: $15, individual; $50, institutional; plus ALA dues.
General Assembly   Entire membership meets once a year during annual ALA conference.
Publications   *Official journal:* CLENExchange (newsletter). 1965-. 4/yr. $20 ($25, foreign). Free to members. Address same as Association. Editor: Gail J. McGovern. Address: State Library, Suite 300, Sacramento, CA 95714-3324. Circ: Approx.500. English.
Activities   Sponsors conferences, seminars, workshops, and other continuing education programs.
Use of High Technology   Computers for management
Bibliography   Snyder, S.E., "Continuing Library Education Network and Exchange Round Table," in ALA Yearbook 1989, pp. 100-101. Chicago: American Library Association, 1989.

529   Council of National Library and Information Associations, Inc. (CNLIA)

Address   c/o Sister Marie Melton, Secretary/Treasurer, Library Director, St. John's University, Grand Central and Utopia Parkways, Jamaica, NY 11439 (not permanent). Tel: 1 (718) 9906161.
Officers   (elected for 1-yr.term, 1989-90) Chair: Thomas Kemp (Library Director, Historical Society of Pennsylvania, 1300 Locust Street, Philadelphia, PA 19107. Tel: 1 (215) 7326200. Fax: 1-215-7322680); Vice-Chair: Sherman Clarke (Rhode Island School of Design Library, 2 College Street, Providence, RI 02903. Tel: 1 (401) 3313511, ext. 294. Fax: 1-401-8317106); Past Chair: Theodore Wiener (Hebraic Division, Library of Congress, Washington, DC 20546); Sec/Treas: Sister Marie Melton. Board of Directors: 7
Staff   1 (volunteer)
Languages   English
Established   1942, New York City, as Council of National Library Associations, Inc. (CNLA), with 14 library associations as charter members.
Major Fields of Interest   National library and information science associations in North America
Major Goals and Objectives   To provide a forum for discussion and cooperation among library/information associations and other professional organizations of the United States and Canada in promoting matters of common interest.
Structure   Governed by Board of Directors.
Sources of Support   Membership dues. Budget: Approx.$5,000.

Membership   Total members: 20 (institutional). Requirements: National library/information associations and organizations with related interests, of the US and Canada. Dues: Graded structure according to size of organization.
General Assembly   Entire membership meets twice a year, in fall and spring
Publications   *Official journal:* CNLIA Update. 1942-. Irreg. Free to members. Address same as Association. Circ: 100. English.
Activities   Past achievements: Ad Hoc Committee on Copyright Practice and Implementation; Joint Committee on Specialized Cataloging; establishment of the National Information Standards Organization Z39 (NISO) (formerly ANSI Committee Z39). Current and future: Continuing committee work; Joint Committee on Library Legislation; Ad Hoc Committee on White House Conference on Library Services; searching for new directions to assist member associations in such areas as preservation policies and practices, association conference planning, developing association newsletters and other publications, the question of public lending rights, etc. Active in promoting library-related legislation. Sponsors conferences, publication of The Bowker Annual (originally started by CNLIA), and the work of the National Information Standards Organization Z39 (NISO).
Use of High Technology   Computers used for management.
Bibliography   Corrigan, J.T., "Council of National Library and Information Associations, Inc.," in The Bowker Annual of Library and Book Trade Information, 1984, 29th ed., pp. 167-169. New York: R.R. Bowker, 1984; "Report from A Meeting of the CNLIA," Library of Congress Information Bulletin 45 (Jan. 20, 1986):39; Lerner, A.A., "The Council of National Library and Information Associations," in The Bowker Annual of Library and Book Trade Information, 1987, 32nd ed., pp. 208-214. New York: R.R. Bowker, 1987; Wiener, T., "Report from the Council of National Library and Information Associations," Library of Congress Information Bulletin 46 (July 6, 1987):303 + ; Wiener, T.,"Report from a Meeting of CNLIA," Library of Congress Information Bulletin 47 (June 20, 1988):244-245; (Sept. 19, 1988):381; "Council of National Library and Information Associations," in The Bowker Annual: Library and Book Trade Almanac, 34th Edition 1989-90, p. 686. New York: R.R. Bowker, 1989.

530   Council of Planning Librarians (CPL)

Address   1313 East 60th Street, Chicago, Illinois 60637-2897 (permanent). Tel: 1 (312) 9479007.
Officers   (elected for 1-yr.term) Pres: Catherine K. Harris; VP/Pres-Elect: June Crowe; Past Pres: Katherine G. Eaton; Sec: Deborah Thompson-Wise; Treas: Jane McMaster. Exec.Comm: 6
Staff   1 (paid)
Languages   English
Established   1957, Chicago, at meeting of the American Institute of Planners
Major Fields of Interest   Urban and regional planning
Major Goals and Objectives   To bring together librarians, professional planners, and institutions interested in the organization and dissemination of literature in the field of community and regional planning; to provide mutual support among planning librarians, planning professionals, and academic planning programs; to provide an opportunity for exchange among those interested in problems of library organization and research and in the dissemination of information about city and regional planning; to sponsor programs of service to the planning profession and librarianship; to advise on library organization for new planning programs; to aid and support administrators, faculty, and librarians in their efforts to educate the public and their appointed or elected representatives on the need for strong library programs in support of planning.

Structure   Governed by Executive Committee. Affiliations: American Planning Association, CNLIA.
Sources of Support   Membership dues, sale of publications. Budget: Approx.$100,000.
Membership   Total members: 200 (120 individual, 80 institutional). 5 countries represented. Requirements: Open to any individual or institution supporting the aims of the Council, upon written application and payment of dues. Dues: $25, individual; $45, institutional; $5, student.
General Assembly   Entire membership meets once a year.
Publications   *Official journal:* CPL Newsletter. 1960-. 4/yr. Free to members. Editor: Lynne DeMerritt. Address: 1313 East 60th Street, Chicago, IL 60637. Circ: Membership. English. Other publications: CPL Bibliographies Series. 24 issues/yr. $255, or individual issues. Editor: Patricia Coatsworth (Merriam Center Library, 1313 E. 60 St., Chicago, IL 60637); some of the current topics covered are agricultural policy, land value taxation and urban land use planning, groundwater quality, automobile trip characteristics, environmental consciousness, innovators in urban planning, port planning, etc.
Activities   Publication of the Bibliographies Series.
Bibliography   "Council of Planning Librarians, Publications Office," in The Bowker Annual: Library and Book Trade Almanac, 34th Edition 1989-90, p. 687. New York: R.R. Bowker, 1989.

531   Council on Botanical and Horticultural Libraries, Inc. (CBHL)

Address   c/o Jayne MacLean, Secretary, National Agricultural Library, Beltsville, Maryland 20705 (permanent). Tel: 1 (301) 3443705.
Officers   (elected for 1-yr.term) Pres: Geraldine C. Kaye; VP: Meryl Miasek; Co-VPs: Judith Diment and Virginia A. Henrichs; Permanent Officers: Sec: Jayne T. MacLean; Treas: John Reed. Exec.Comm: 6
Staff   None
Languages   English
Established   1970, at Hunt Institute, Pittsburgh, PA, after a feasibility meeting in 1969 at the Massachusetts Horticultural Society, Boston, MA.
Major Fields of Interest   Botanical and horticultural libraries, literature, publications, information
Major Goals and Objectives   To encourage and facilitate communication among individuals and institutions in our fields of interest.
Structure   Governed by Executive Committee.
Sources of Support   Membership dues, sale of publications.
Membership   Total members: 250+. 11 countries represented. Types of membership: Individual, institutional. Requirements: Individuals interest in the field and botanical and horticultural libraries of any size, worldwide. Dues: $20, individual; $50, institutional.
General Assembly   Entire membership meets once a year. 1987: Chapel Hill, NC, Apr.22-25; 1988: Pittsburgh, PA, June; 1989: St. Louis, MO.
Publications   *Official journal:* CBHL Newsletter. 1972-. 3-4/yr. Free to members. Editor: Bernadette G. Callery. Address: Hunt Institute, Carnegie-Mellon University, Pittsburgh, PA 15213. Circ: 250+. English. Other publications: Membership list, Plant Bibliography (series). Publications exchange program in effect of duplicate books and journals. Publications available for sale.
Activities   Past achievements: Completion of a national survey of locations and holdings of old nursery and seed catalogs, reported in Nursery and Seed Catalogs: A Directory of Collections (available in Plant Bibliography series). Current and future: Preparation of a CBHL history and a manual for meeting organizers; organization of a European chapter

at the 14th International Botanical Congress, Berlin, July 1987. Sponsors biennial Oberly
Award for botanical/agricultural bibliography.
Bibliography   Callery, B.G. et al., Directory of Member Libraries. Bronx, NY: The As-
sociation, 1983.
Additional Information   "This is an informal group operated entirely by volunteer ef-
fort; little formal structure or services are involved." (Geraldine C. Kaye, President)

532   Council on Library Resources, Inc. (CLR)

Address   1785 Massachusetts Ave., NW, Washington, DC 20036 (permanent). Tel: 1
(202) 4837474.
Officers   Pres: Warren J. Haas; Sec-Treas: Mary Agnes Thompson; Board of Directors:
25
Staff   9.5 (paid)
Languages   English
Established   1956, by the Ford Foundation "for the purpose of aiding in the solution of
the problems of libraries generally, and of research libraries in particular."
Major Fields of Interest   Research on the effect of the information revolution on schol-
arship, research and teaching; preservation of library resources; bibliographic systems; eq-
uitable access to information; the profession of librarianship
Major Goals and Objectives   CLR is a private foundation that supports work on matters pertinent to library service and information systems, with the special objective of im-
proving the quality and performance of academic and research libraries.
Structure   Governed by Board of Directors.
Sources of Support   Grants from private foundations and the National Endowment for
the Humanities.
Membership   Council consists of a 25-member Board of Directors.
Publications   *Official journal:* CLR Reports (newsletter, formerly CLR Recent Develop-
ments). 1972-. irregular. Free to members. Editor: Jane A. Rosenberg. Address same as
Association. Circ: 4,000. English. Other publications: Annual Report. Publications avail-
able for sale.
Activities   Past achievements: Establishment of several major programs: The Biblio-
graphic Service Development Program and the Linked Systems Project; the Professional
Educational and Training for Research Librarianship Program; the establishment of the
National Commission for Preservation and Access. Current and future: The Research
Program; continued work on preservation and access projects; attention to library educa-
tion, and library management. Sponsors conferences, seminars, workshops, and other
continuing education programs.
Use of High Technology   Computers and databases for management.
Bibliography   Gwinn, N.E., "CLR and Preservation," College & Research Libraries 42
(1981):104-126; Rosenberg, J.A.,"The Council on Library Resources, Inc.," in The Bow-
ker Annual of Library and Book Trade Information, 31st ed., pp.235-241. New York:
Bowker, 1986; "Council on Library Resources, Inc.," in The Bowker Annual: Library and
Book Trade Almanac, 34th Edition 1989-90, p. 688. New York: R.R. Bowker, 1989.

533   Council on Library/Media Technicians (COLT)

Address   423 E. 112th Street, Cleveland, Ohio 44108 (permanent). Tel: 1 (216)
2496480. Headquarters: Cuyahoga Community College, Attn: SC 126, 2900 Community
College Ave., Cleveland, Ohio 44115

Officers   (elected for 2-yr.term) Pres: Audrey V. Jones (11257 Colombia Pike, Silver Spring, MD 20901); Exec.Sec: Margaret R. Barron; Past Pres: Joanne Wolford. Exec.Board: 14

Staff   None

Languages   English

Established   1965, as Council on Library Technical Assistants. 1976 became the Council on Library/Media Technical-Assistants, with new Constitution and Bylaws.

Major Fields of Interest   Support staff in all types of libraries and information centers

Major Goals and Objectives   To serve as a voice and a home for support staff in all types of libraries: Public, school, university, and all special; to improve the education and general welfare of support staff.

Structure   Governed by Board of Officers plus Regional Directors and Standing Committee Chairpersons. Affiliations: ALA.

Sources of Support   Membership dues, sale of publications. Budget: $10,000+

Membership   Total members: 450 (300 individual, 150 institutional). Regional Chapters: 5. 5 countries represented. Requirements: Open to anyone interested in the aims of the Association. Dues: $20, individual; $10, student; $35, US institution; $40, institution outside US.

General Assembly   Entire membership meets once a year. 1988: New Orleans; 1989: Dallas; 1990: Chicago.

Publications   *Official journal:* COLT Newsletter. 1970-. 6/yr. Free to members. Address: 5049 8th Street, NE, Washington, DC 20017. Editor: Myron Allman. Address: 10505 Cedarville Road, 11-4, Brandywine, MD 20613. Circ: 450. English. Other publications: COLT Membership Directory; Job Descriptions for Library Support Personnel; Paraprofessional Library Employees Booklet; reports of seminars, workshops, etc. No publications exchange program. Publications available for sale.

Activities   Past achievements: Building new local chapters; 1985, joint conference in Chicago with 2 other library associations; study of certification for technicians. Current and future: Exploration of workshops with CTE (continuing education) credit; exploration of certification of technicians; 20-year celebration at annual conference in San Francisco, 1987; completion of study and implementation of certification of library technicians. Sponsors exhibits, conferences, seminars, workshops, and other continuing education programs.

Bibliography   Halsted, D.D. and Neeley, D.M., "The Importance of the Library Technician," Library Journal 115 (1990):62-63

534   Evangelical Church Library Association (ECLA)

Address   PO Box 353, Glen Ellys, Illinois 60138 (permanent). Tel: 1 (312) 6680519

Officers   (elected for 3-yr.term) Pres: Mary K. Bechtel; VP: Ruth Fischer; Sec-Treas: Nancy Dick. Exec.Board: 10.

Staff   1 (volunteer)

Languages   English

Established   1970

Major Fields of Interest   Church libraries

Major Goals and Objectives   The establishment and growth of church libraries in evangelical churches through encouragement given in the quarterly Librarian's World, annual conference, personal assistance and resource materials.

Structure   Governed by Board of Directors.

Sources of Support   Membership dues, sale of publications.

Membership   Total members: 650 (individual and institutional). Chapters: 5. 2 countries represented. Requirements: Open to interested individuals and institutions or organizations. Dues: $12, individual, church school or organization; $15, foreign; $15, bookstore, $30, publisher.
General Assembly   Entire membership meets once a year. 1988: Wheaton, IL, Nov. 5.
Publications   *Official journal:* Librarian's World. 1970-. 4/yr. $12. Free to members. Editor: Nancy Dick. Address same as Association. Circ: 700. English.
Activities   Encouraging church librarians by means of the quarterly journal, an annual conference in fall, and assistance with problems through letters and phone calls. Some resource material is also made available. Future: Organization of a local chapter; possible affiliation with another evangelical organization.

535   Federal Librarians Round Table (FLRT)

Address   50 East Huron Street, Chicago, Illinois 60611 (permanent). Tel: (312) 9446780. Fax: 312-4409374.
Officers   (elected for 1-yr.term) Pres: Nancy Cummings Liston; Sec-Treas: Shirley Loo; Past Pres: Doria Beachell Grimes; Staff Liaison: Anne A. Heanue. Exec.Board: 6
Staff   1 (paid by ALA)
Languages   English
Established   1972, Chicago, during the ALA Conference; previous acronym FLIRT.
Major Fields of Interest   Federal libraries and information activities
Major Goals and Objectives   To promote library and information service and the library and information profession in the federal community; to promote appropriate utilization of federal library and information resources and facilities; to provide an environment for the stimulation of research and development relating to the planning, development, and operation of federal libraries and information activities.
Structure   Governed by Executive Board. Affiliations: A round table of ALA
Sources of Support   Membership dues (through ALA), sale of publications.
Membership   Total members: 472 (386 individual, 86 institutional). Requirements: Any member of ALA may become a member upon payment of dues. Dues: $8, individual; $10, institutional.
General Assembly   Entire membership meets once a year during the annual ALA conference
Publications   *Official journal:* The Federal Librarian. 1979-. 3/yr. Free to members. Editor: Grace T. Waibel. Address: 2500 Wisconsin Ave., NW, Apt.852, Washington, DC 20007. Circ: Membership. English.
Activities   Current issues are the urgent need to modernize the dissemination of federal information, alternative salary scales for librarians, and privatization. Sponsors conferences, seminars, workshops, and other continuing education programs.
Use of High Technology   Computers for management.
Bibliography   Grimes, D.B.,"Federal Librarians Round Table," in ALA Yearbook 1989, pp.109-110. Chicago: American Library Association, 1989.

536   Federal Library and Information Center Committee (FLICC)

Address   c/o Mary Berghaus Levering, Acting Executive Director, Library of Congress, Washington, DC 20540 (permanent). Headquarters: Room 1026C, John Adams Building, 2d and Independence Avenue SE, Washington, DC 20540. Tel: 1 (202) 7076055. Fax: 1-202-7072171

Officers   Chair: James H. Billington (The Librarian of Congress); Chair Designate: Ruth Ann Stewart; Acting Exec.Dir: Mary Berghaus Levering; Admin.Off: Christina Zirps. Exec.Advisory Comm: 8
Staff   19 (paid; 4 by FLICC, 15 by FEDLINK / Federal Library & Information Network)
Languages   English
Established   1965, by the Library of Congress and the Bureau of the Budget to provide leadership in policy issues affecting the provision of information to government employees and the general public. Established as Federal Library Committee. Reorganization in 1984 brought changes in name (FLICC), mission, and membership.
Major Fields of Interest   Library information
Major Goals and Objectives   To achieve better utilization of library and information center resources and facilities; to provide more effective planning, development, and operation of federal libraries and information centers; to promote an optimum exchange of experience, skill, and resources; to promote more effective service to the nation at large; to foster relevant educational opportunities.
Structure   Governed by Executive Advisory Committee and FLICC membership. Affiliations: FLICC is administratively under the Library of Congress.
Sources of Support   Government appropriations and FEDLINK membership users fees. Budget: Govt. approp: Approx.$190,000; FEDLINK users fees: Approx.$850,000.
Membership   Total members: 40 Federal departments and agencies, and 1,000+ FEDLINK participants and members. Requirements: FLICC membership: 40 predesignated federal departments and agencies as listed in the Federal Register notice. FEDLINK: Any library or organization in the US Federal Government that uses one of FEDLINK services. Dues: Users fees for FEDLINK
General Assembly   Entire membership meets four times a year for FLICC, and twice a year for FEDLINK.
Publications   *Official journal:* FLICC Newsletter. 1965-. 4/yr. Free upon request. Editor: Christina Zirps. Address same as FLICC. Circ: 2,500. English. Other publications: Annual FLICC Forum on Federal Information Policies; FEDLINK Technical Notes (newsletter, 12/yr.). Circ: 1,000+; Managing Information Resources (Washington: Library of Congress, 1984); Federal Information Policies: The International Flow of Scientific and Technical Information (1985); Price, D. Federal Information Policies: The Congressional Initiative (1989); annual reports. No publications exchange program.
Activities   FLICC's operating network is FEDLINK (the Federal Library and Information Network), the nation's largest library network. FLICC makes recommendations on federal library and information policies, programs, and procedures to federal agencies and to others concerned with libraries and information centers. Past achievements: Increased educational programs; increased cooperative programs among various federal libraries and information centers, and increased use of automation in the federal information community with savings to the government in dollars in the area of retrieval services and contracts; large increase in use of OCLC, the national bibliographic utility, by federal libraries and information centers. Current and future: Educational programs for the federal information sector and the nation at large; cooperative collection development pilot project; expert system pilot project; IDEA/LIST project (Investigation, Development, Early Application of Library and Information Systems Technology); increased information databases and services under contract for use by federal members; 7th annual Forum on Federal Information Policies, March 21, 1990; additional automated and other services to the federal sector, and establishing long-term goals for FLICC.
Use of High Technology   Computers (microcomputers), databases, electronic publishing, and electronic bulletin board for management

Bibliography   "FLICC to Hold Forum on Federal Information Access Policy," Library of Congress Information Bulletin 45 (Jan. 27, 1986):43-44; "FLICC to Hold Technology Seminars around the Country," ibid. (Mar. 31, 1986):94; "FLICC Sponsors Session on Laser Disk Technology," ibid. (Apr. 28, 1986):125; Zirps, C., "1986 FLICC Forum Considers Federal Information Policies," ibid. (May 19, 1986):177-178; "FLICC Cosponsors Seminars with USDA to Brief Federal Librarians on New Trends," ibid. (Aug. 11, 1986):281-282; "FLICC Issues New Publication," Library of Congress Information Bulletin 46 (Feb. 9, 1987):59-60; "Federal Library and Information Center Committee (FLICC)," in The Bowker Annual: Library and Book Trade Almanac, 34th Edition 1989-90, pp. 688-689. New York: R.R. Bowker, 1989; "Librarian Backs Interagency Cooperation: FLICC Elevated in Reorganization Plans," FLICC Newsletter 150 (1989):1-2; "Access is the Key: Forum Explores Future of Federal Information Policies," FLICC Newsletter 151 (1990):7.

537   Friends of Libraries U.S.A. (FOLUSA)

Address   50 East Huron Street, Chicago, Illinois 60611 (permanent). Tel: (312) 9446780. Fax: 1-312-44609374.
Officers   Pres: Frank W. Miller; VP: Fred A. Philipp; Sec: Robert S. Runyan; Treas: Paul W. Karr; Past Pres: Richard C. Torbert; Exec.Dir: Sandy F. Dolnick (1420 Locust Street, Apt.131, Philadelphia, PA 19102; appointed); Staff Liaison: Peggy Barber. Exec.Board: 20
Staff   1 (paid)
Languages   English
Established   1979, Dallas, during annual ALA conference.
Major Fields of Interest   Development and support of Friends of Library groups, to encourage better library services; to increase public awareness of libraries
Major Goals and Objectives   To encourage and assist the formation and development of local, state, national and international Friends of Library groups; to provide avenues of communication between Friends, and to the library world; to provide recognition and awareness of those who have rendered outstanding service.
Structure   Governed by Board of Directors. Affiliations: ALA; Center for the Book (Library of Congress).
Sources of Support   Membership dues, corporate support. Budget: Approx. $50,000.
Membership   Total members: 1,200 (majority institutional). 6 countries represented. Requirements: Payment of annual membership dues. Dues: $10, individual; $15, Friends group: 1-100 members; $25, 101-499 members; $35, 500+ members; $25, library or association; $50, sustaining; $100, patron, $250-999, sponsor, $1,000+, benefactor.
General Assembly   Entire membership meets once a year at annual ALA conference
Publications   *Official journal:* Friends of Libraries U.S.A. National Notebook. 1978-. 4/yr. Free to members. Address same as Association. Editor: James Houck. Address: Department of English, Youngstown State University, Youngstown, OH 44555. Circ: 1,200 (membership). English. Other publications: Idea Bank. 4/yr.; Making Friends (videotape); Dolnick, S., ed., Friends of Libraries Sourcebook (ALA, 1980, under revision); Fact Sheets on how Friends can help with literacy issues in their communities, how to organize a book and author event, etc.
Activities   Past achievements: Expansion of publications program; growth of Friends of Libraries groups; development of state Friends groups; moving into videotaping with a how-to series; fulltime staffer; speaker's bureau. Current: Program planning, publications development, speakers' bureau; videotaping of programs; merchandise for Friends; inform members about current legislation. Future: Regional activity; expanding state Friends; broadening base of support; inclusion of all types of libraries. Active in promot-

ing library-related legislation. Legislative alerts are sent out regularly, and there is a publication explaining how to lobby. Sponsors exhibits; author's luncheon at ALA conference, with presentation of annual awards to outstanding Friends groups.
Use of High Technology   Databases used for management.
Bibliography   Torbert, R., "Friends of Libraries," in <u>ALA Yearbook 1988</u>, pp. 142-144. Chicago: American Library Association, 1988; Miller, F.W., "Friends of Libraries," in <u>ALA Yearbook 1989</u>, p.118. Chicago: American Library Association, 1989.

538   Independent Research Libraries Association (IRLA)

Address   c/o Edmund C. Carter II, Chair, Librarian, American Philosophical Society, 105 South 5th Street, Philadelphia, Pennsylvania 19106-3386 (not permanent). Tel: 1 (215) 6270706.
Officers   Chair: Edmund C. Carter II; Past Chair: Louis L. Tucker (Director, Massachusetts Historical Society, Boston, MA 02115. Tel: 1 (617) 5361608)
Staff   None
Languages   English
Established   1972, at the Newberry Library, Chicago
Major Fields of Interest   Research libraries; humanities
Major Goals and Objectives   To strengthen the programs of member institutions
Structure   Governed by members and Chair; an informal body. Affiliations: Informal affiliations with ACLS (American Council of Learned Societies), ARL, and other relevant groups.
Sources of Support   Membership dues.
Membership   Total members: 15 (institutional). Requirements: Library must be an independent institution, not subordinate to another organization; must have a collection of international importance with emphasis on specialized research materials; must be used by a national, or preferably, international group of readers. Dues: $500.
General Assembly   Entire membership meets once or twice a year at various locations.
Publications   No official journal. Issues <u>IRLA Handbook,</u> a membership directory.
Activities   Meetings at least once a year to exchange ideas and discuss issues of common interest; joint fund raising; no formal program.

539   International Association of Music Libraries, Archives, and Documentation Centres - United States Branch (IAML-US)

Address   c/o Sibley Music Library, Eastman School of Music, Rochester, New York 14604 (not permanent). Tel: 1 (716) 2753046.
Officers   (elected for 3-yr.term) Pres: Don L. Roberts; Sec-Treas: Charles Lindahl. Exec.Board: 7
Staff   None
Languages   English
Established   1951
Major Fields of Interest   Music librarianship; music bibliography
Major Goals and Objectives   Development of music libraries, music librarianship, and music bibliography
Structure   Governed by executive officers and Executive Board. Affiliations: IAML, IFLA
Sources of Support   Membership dues. Budget: Approx.$14,000.
Membership   Total members: 400 (200 individual, 200 institutional). Requirements: Interest in aims of Association. Dues: $26, individual; $41, institutional.

General Assembly Entire membership meets once a year. 1988: Minneapolis, MI; 1989: Cleveland, OH
Publications *Official journal:* Fontes Artis Musicae (official journal of IAML). 1954-. 4/yr. Free to members. Editor: Brian Redfern. Address: 27 Plantation Rd., Leighton Buzzard, Bedfordshire, LU7 7HJ, United Kingdom. Circ: Approx.1,900. English, French, German. Indexed in Music Index, RILM Abstracts.
Activities Similar to those of parent association.
Use of High Technology Computers for management
Bibliography Brook, B.S. and Ratliff, N., "International Association of Music Libraries, Archives and Documentation Centres (IAML)," in ALA World Encyclopedia of Library and Information Services, 2nd ed., pp. 369-370. Chicago: American Library Association, 1986.

540 Librarians for Nuclear Arms Control (LNAC)

Address PO Box 60552, Pasadena, California 91106 (permanent). Tel: 1 (818) 7957331.
Officers Pres: Victoria Kline; Exec.Officers: Janet C. Jenks, Alice Fisher, Ami Kirby. Exec.Board: 4
Staff 2 (volunteers)
Languages English
Established 1983
Major Fields of Interest Nuclear arms race; defense; nuclear weapons
Major Goals and Objectives To inform the public about the effects and dangers of nuclear war.
Structure Governed by Board and Chapters.
Sources of Support Membership dues.
Membership Chapters: 3. Requirements: Interest in aims of Association. Dues: $15, individual; $30, contributing; $100, sponsor; $5, student.
General Assembly Entire membership usually meets during state and national conventions
Publications *Official journal:* LNAC Almanac. 1984-. 3/yr. $10. Free to members. Address same as Association. English.
Activities Publishing newsletter; providing free information to the public and other librarians; publishing subject bibliographies on various topics.
Use of High Technology Computers for newsletter production and bibliographic searching.

541 Library Administration and Management Association (LAMA)

Address 50 East Huron Street, Chicago, Illinois 60611 (permanent). Tel: 1 (312) 9446780. Fax: 1-312-4669374.
Officers (elected for 1-yr.term) Pres: Dallas Y. Shaffer; Exec.Dir: John W. Berry (appointed). Past Pres: Maureen Sullivan. Exec.Comm: 4; Board of Directors: 25
Staff 3.25 (paid)
Languages English
Established 1957, Chicago
Major Fields of Interest Administration and management in all types of libraries
Major Goals and Objectives To provide an organizational framework for encouraging the study of administrative theory, for improving the practice of administration in libraries, and for identifying and fostering administrative skills in all types of libraries, including organizational structure, financial administration, personnel management and training, buildings and equipment, and public relations.

Structure   Governed by Board of Directors. Affiliations: A division of ALA
Sources of Support   Membership dues, sale of publications. Budget: Approx.$240,000.
Membership   Total members: 5,074 (4,225 individual, 849 institutional). Sections: 7
(Buildings & Equipment, Fund Raising & Financial Development; Library Organization
& Management; Personnel Administration; Public Relations; Statistics; Systems & Services). Committees, Task Forces, and Discussion Groups. 6 countries represented. Requirements: Open to ALA members upon payment of divisional dues. Dues: $25, individual and institutional, plus ALA dues.
General Assembly   Entire membership meets twice a year during ALA Midwinter and
annual conferences.
Publications   *Official journal:* Library Administration & Management (LA&M; formerly
LAMA Newsletter). 1975-. 4/yr. $35 ($45 foreign). Free to members. Address same as
Association. Editor: Charles Lowry. Address: Director of Libraries, University of Texas at
Arlington, Arlington, TX. Circ: 6,000+. English. Indexed in Lib.Lit. Other publications:
Statistical Applications in Library Technical Services: An Annotated Bibliography (1987);
Automation Projects: The Evaluation Stage (1988); Checklist of Library Building Design
Considerations (1988); Library Buildings Consultants List (1989); Staff Development: A
Practical Guide (1988); Miller, D., Working with Government Authority (1989); Lowry,
M., Preservation and the Small Library (1989); annual reports, proceedings of conferences, seminars, etc. Publications for sale, listed in journal. Price lists available. No publications exchange program.
Activities   Past achievements: (1) Initiation of new journal, LA&M in Jan. 1987 (founding editor: Donald E. Riggs) to replace the LAMA Newsletter; (2) development of a catalog of Regional Institutes (10+ currently approved), dealing with leadership survival,
financial management, library building planning process, managing youth services, etc.
Current: Expanding publications program; marketing Regional Institutes; preparing for
LAMA National Conference in 1991; planning for Leadership Issues Forum in 1990, focusing on the importance of effective communication in leadership. Future: National
Conferences; further development of journal; expansion of publications and Regional Institutes program. Active in sponsoring library-related legislation through its Governmental Affairs Committee. Sponsors conferences, seminars, workshops, and other continuing
education programs.
Use of High Technology   Computers (Wang, Macintosh) and electronic mail for management.
Bibliography   Kendrick, B.L., "Library Administration and Management Association,"
Library of Congress Information Bulletin 43 (Sept. 1984):315-317; Burdash, D.H., "Making the Corporate Connection: LAMA PRS Friends, Volunteers, Advocates Committee
Annual Conference Program," in ALA Yearbook 1988, pp. 188-190. Chicago: American
Library Association, 1988; Eastman, A.H., "Library Administration and Management Association," in ALA Yearbook 1989, pp. 140-144. Chicago: American Library Association,
1989; "American Library Association. Library Administration and Management Association," in The Bowker Annual: Library and Book Trade Almanac, 34th Edition 1989-90,
pp. 649-651. New York: R.R. Bowker, 1989.

542   Library and Information Technology Association (LITA)

Address   50 East Huron Street, Chicago, Illinois 60611 (permanent). Tel: 1 (312)
9446780. Fax: 1-312-4409374.
Officers   (elected for 1-yr.term) Pres: Carol A. Parkhurst; Past Pres: Sherrie Schmidt;
Exec.Dir: Linda J. Knutson (appointed). Exec.Board: 12
Staff   2.25 (paid)

Languages English
Established 1966, at ALA Midwinter Conference in Chicago.
Major Fields of Interest Information dissemination in the areas of library automation, video and cable communications, telecommunications, and audiovisuals.
Major Goals and Objectives Concerned with the planning, development, design, application, and integration of technologies within the library and information environment. Major focus is on interdisciplinary issues and emerging technologies. Within these areas, LITA encourages and fosters research, promotes the development of appropriate technical standards, monitors new technologies with potential applications in information science, develops models of library systems and networks, examines the effects of automation on people, disseminates information, and provides a forum for the discussion of common concerns. The Association views itself as a source of leadership linking librarians and information specialists to technology for access to information.
Structure Governed by Board of Directors, with authority specified by the ALA Council. Affiliations: A division of ALA, National Information Standards Organization (NISO), ASIS.
Sources of Support Membership dues, sale of publications, fees from conferences,institutes. Budget: Approx.$280,000.
Membership Total members: 4,829 (3,904 individual, 925 institutional). Committees, Interest Groups. Requirements: Open to members of ALA. Dues: $25, for all categories, plus ALA dues.
General Assembly Entire membership meets twice a year during the ALA Midwinter and annual conference. In addition, there are LITA National Conferences, the 2nd held in Boston, Oct. 2-6, 1988.
Publications *Official journal:* Information Technology and Libraries (ITAL) (formerly Journal of Library Automation, 1968-81). 1982-. 4/yr. $35. Free to members. Editor: William G. Potter. Address: Hayden Library, Arizona State University, Tempe, AZ 85287. Circ: 5,000 +. English. Indexed in ISA, Lib.Lit., CompuMath Citation Index, etc. Other publications: LITA Newsletter. 4/yr. $15. Free to members. Editor: Walt Crawford (Research Libraries Group, Jordan Quadrangle, Stanford, CA 94305); various monographs and packets; annual reports, proceedings of conferences, seminars, etc. Publications available for sale. Limited publications exchange program in effect.
Activities LITA's activities were reorganized several years ago around an interest group structure, involving more members in programming and other activities. Interest groups successfully promote discussion and present programs on topics of current interest, such as on-line catalogs, expert systems, authority control, retrospective conversion, telecommunications, distributed systems, library consortia sharing automated systems, use of technology to fight illiteracy, etc. Presents awards. Sponsors exhibits, conferences, seminars, workshops, and other continuing education programs.
Use of High Technology Computers (Compaq) and electronic mail used for management
Bibliography Berry, J.N., "Constant Change: The LITA Message [first national conference]," Library Journal 108 (Oct. 15, 1983):1898; Brandenhoff, S.E., "First National LITA Conference: Library Technology on Stage," American Libraries 14 (Nov. 1983):672 +; Fenly, C., "Report on the Institute on Technology at the Library of Congress in the 1980's," Library of Congress Information Bulletin 45 (Aug. 4, 1986):276-278; "Interest Groups Two Years Later: How They are Working," LITA Newsletter 9 (Winter 1988):11-13; Boydston, J.M.K., "On the Conference Circuit: Whose Computer Revolution is It? - A Review [of LITA program]," Technicalities 8 (Nov. 1988):10-11; "Library Service, New Products Focus of LITA's Conference," Library Journal 113 (Dec. 1988):24;

Welsch, E.K., "The LITA Conference: Digitized Images," <u>Computers in Libraries</u> 9 (Jan. 1989):32-33; Potter, W.G.,"Library and Information Technology Association," in <u>ALA Yearbook 1989</u>, p.144. Chicago: American Library Association, 1989; "American Library Association. Library and Information Technology Association," in <u>The Bowker Annual: Library and Book Trade Almanac, 34th Edition 1989-90</u>, pp. 651-653. New York: R.R. Bowker, 1989.

543 Library Public Relations Council (LPRC)

Address c/o New York Library Association, 15 Park Row, Suite 434, New York, New York 10038 (permanent).
Officers (elected for 1-yr.term) Pres: Sheldon Tarakan; Sec: Leanna Povilaitus; Treas: Sharon Karmazan; Past Pres: Sue Fontaine. Exec.Board: 7
Staff None
Languages English
Established Constitution adopted May 26, 1944
Major Fields of Interest Public relations; marketing; communications
Major Goals and Objectives Professional development for library staff members in the fields of public relations and communications
Structure Governed by elected Board.
Sources of Support Membership dues.
Membership Total members: 284 (individual and institutional). 3 countries represented (USA, Australia, Canada). Requirements: Interested in aims of Association.
General Assembly Entire membership meets once a year during annual ALA conference, and 3 times a year in Metropolitan New York.
Publications No official journal. Publishes proceedings of meetings, reports of seminars, workshops.
Activities Past achievements: (1) Juried packets of public relations (PR) materials from selected libraries are mailed to all members annually ("LPRC Packets Competition"); (2) L'Percy Award for the best PR material in selected categories. Current: (1) Continuing the above two competitions; (2) four dinner meetings with professional speakers (one the general meeting at ALA conference which includes the L'Percy Award presentation). Future: A continuing education project, such as internship or scholarship. Active in promoting library-related legislation, with members participating in library lobbying efforts nationally and locally. Sponsors conferences, seminars, workshops, and other continuing education programs; maintains a booth at ALA conference with "Swap & Shop" program.
Bibliography Eldredge, J., "Public Relations and Marketing," in <u>ALA Yearbook 1989</u>, pp. 191-194. Chicago: American Library Association, 1989.

544 Lutheran Church Library Association (LCLA)

Address 122 Franklin Avenue, Minneapolis, Minnesota 55404 (permanent). Tel: 1 (612) 8703623.
Officers (elected for 1-yr.term, 1989-90) Pres: L. Edwin Wang; VP: Elaine Hanson; Sec: Gloria Landborg; Treas: Robert Kruger; Exec.Dir: Wilma Jensen (3620 Fairlawn Drive, Minnetonka, MN 55345. Tel: 1-612-4735965). Exec.Board: 11
Staff 4 (paid), many volunteers
Languages English
Established 1958, Minneapolis, at a special meeting of all interested church librarians.
Major Fields of Interest Church libraries
Major Goals and Objectives To promote the growth of church libraries by publishing a quarterly journal, <u>Lutheran Libraries</u>, furnishing lists of books recommended for Lu-

theran church libraries, assisting member libraries with the technical problems of setting up and operating a library, and providing meetings for mutual encouragement, assistance, and exchange of ideas among members.

Structure   Governed by executive officers and Executive Council meeting at least twice a year. Affiliations: CNLIA.

Sources of Support   Membership dues, private donations, grants from Lutheran churches. Budget: Approx.$40,000.

Membership   Total members: 1,800 (70 individual, 1,730 institutional). Chapters: 32.   8 countries represented. Requirements: Open to church libraries, individuals, libraries, church organizations, and to any congregation that is planning to start a church library. Dues: $20, individual, institutional (churches); $30, contributor; $100, donor; $500, patron; $1,000, guarantor.

General Assembly   Entire membership meets once a year.

Publications   *Official journal:* Lutheran Libraries. 1958-. 4/yr. $12. Free to members. Editor: Ron Klug. Address: 115 South Division Street, Northfield, MN 55057. Circ: 2,000+. English. Other publications: Annual reports, proceedings of conferences, seminars, basic booklists, service bulletins, etc. Publications exchanged with other library associations.

Activities   Activities carried out by 6 committees (Advisory, CNLIA, Finance, Library Services Board, Membership, Publications). Sponsors conferences, seminars, workshops, and other continuing education programs.

Bibliography   "Lutheran Church Library Association," in The Bowker Annual: Library and Book Trade Almanac, 34th Edition 1989-90, pp. 691-692. New York: R.R. Bowker, 1989.

545   The Manuscript Society

Address   350 North Niagara Street, Burbank, California 91505 (permanent). Tel: 1 (818) 8405424

Officers   Exec.Dir: David R. Smith. Exec.Board: 20

Staff   None

Languages   English

Established   1948

Major Fields of Interest   Autographs and manuscripts

Major Goals and Objectives   To foster an interest in manuscripts

Structure   Governed by Executive Board.

Sources of Support   Membership dues, sale of publications.

Membership   Total members: 1,350 (1,125 individual, 225 institutional). 17 countries represented. Requirements: Interest in manuscripts. Dues: $25, individual; $30, institutional.

General Assembly   Entire membership meets once a year.

Publications   *Official journal:* Manuscripts. 1948-. 4/yr. $25. Free to members. Editor: David R. Chesnutt. Address: Department of History, University of South Carolina, Columbia, SC 29208. Circ: 1,350+. English. Other publications: News (3/yr.); Directory; George Washington's Expence Account (facsimile); Manuscripts: The First 20 Years; annual reports, proceedings of conferences, seminars, etc.

Activities   Chief activity: Three-day annual meeting, held in a community offering good manuscript resources for viewing. Programs feature panel discussions, speakers of note, exhibitions, etc.

Use of High Technology   Computers (Macintosh) for management.

Bibliography   Fields, J.E., "Founding the Manuscript Society," AB Bookman's Weekly 73 (1984):785-786; Sifton, P.G., "Manuscript Society Meeting," Library of Congress Information Bulletin 43 (July 9, 1984):238-239; Filby, P.W., "Manuscript Society Views Rhode Island Treasures," AB Bookman's Weekly 76 (1985):240-242.

546   Medical Library Association (MLA)

Address   Six North Michigan Avenue, Suite 300, Chicago, Illinois 60602 (permanent). Tel: 1 (312) 4199094. Fax: 1-312-4198950.
Officers   (elected for 1-yr.term, 1989-90) Pres: Frances Goen; VP/Pres.Elect: Lucretia W. McClure; Finance Comm.Chair: Frieda O. Weise; Exec.Dir: Raymond A. Palmer (appointed); Past Pres: Eloise C. Foster. Exec.Board: 12
Staff   18 (paid)
Languages   English
Established   1898, Philadelphia; incorporated 1934.
Major Fields of Interest   Medical librarianship
Major Goals and Objectives   To influence the quality of available health information resources and provide timely, accurate, and relevant information; to improve the knowledge and skill of members; to develop and maintain information systems and resources; to broaden health information research; and to promote a legislative agenda that supports access to the world's health sciences information.
Structure   Governed by Board of Directors and Executive Committee. Affiliations: ALA, IFLA.
Sources of Support   Membership dues, sale of publications. Budget: Approx.$1.5 million.
Membership   Total members: 5,053 (3,758 individual, 1,295 institutional). Sections: 23. Chapters: 14. 31 countries represented. Requirements: Persons actively engaged in professional library or bibliographic work in medical or allied scientific fields or who hold the Association's Certificate of Medical Librarianship; other persons interested in medical or allied scientific libraries may become associate members. Institutional members are medical and allied scientific libraries. Dues: $95, individual; $22, student; $32, emeritus; $95, associate; $1,900, life; $160-375, institutional, based on number of subscriptions.
General Assembly   Entire membership meets once a year. 1987: Portland, OR, May 15-21; 1988: New Orleans, LA, May 20-26; 1989: Boston, MA, May 26-June 1; 1990: Detroit, MI, May 18-24; 1991: San Francisco, CA, May.
Publications   *Official journal:* Bulletin of the Medical Library Association. 1911-. 4/yr. $102. Free to members. Editor: Irwin H. Pizer. Address same as Association (Tel: 1-312-7511343). Circ: 6,000+. English. Indexed in Hospital Literature Index, Index Medicus, Lib.Lit., etc. Other publications: MLA News. 1961-. 10/yr. $39.50. Free to members. Editor: Julie Kesti (University of Mexico), International News Editor: Janet Fisher (East Tennessee State University); MLA Directory (1/yr.); Handbook of Medical Library Practice (vols.1-3); McCarthy, S., Personal Filing Systems: Creating Information Retrieval Systems on Microcomputers (1988); Snow, B., Drug Information: A Guide to Current Resources (1988); Hospital Library Management; Introduction to Reference Sources in the Health Sciences; MEDLINE: A Basic Guide to Searching; annual reports, proceedings of conferences, seminars, etc. List of publications available from Association headquarters. Publications exchange program in effect. All major MLA publications are printed on acid-free paper that conforms to paper permanence standards of the American National Standards Institute.
Activities   Past achievements: Initiated strategic planning; strengthened and integrated all association programs: professional development, including continuing education, cre-

dentialling, honors & awards, information services and annual meeting; publications; information issues & policy; standards & practices. Developed and installed a computer system to handle membership, annual meeting, continuing education, and accounting functions. Current: Providing programs and services in the following areas: Professional development, publications, standards and practices, and information issues and policy. Future: Developing new and revised programs and services to support the design, development, and management of information systems; creation and provision of information services and education for health information users; research in health information science. Active in promoting library-related legislation. Sponsors exhibits, conferences, seminars, workshops, and other continuing education programs. The Continuing Education Committee is responsible for high quality courses, covering topics such as preserving endangered collections, designing expert systems, managing microcomputers, writing procedures manuals, offering workshops, etc. Presents a number of annual awards and scholarships; contributes to ALA National Library Week.

Use of High Technology   Computers (Microdata, IBM PC), databases, electronic publishing used for management

Bibliography   Echelman, S., "Role of the Medical Library Association in Education, Standards and Other Support Services for Members," Inspel 16 (1982):49-57; Poland, U.H., "Reflections on the Medical Library Association's International Activities," Medical Library Association Bulletin 70 (1982):359-368; Shafer, R., "Equal Opportunities for Health Sciences Librarians: A Report on the 1986 Medical Library Association Annual Meeting," Library Journal 111 (1986):42-45; "Medical Libraries," in ALA World Encyclopedia of Library and Information Services, 2nd ed., pp. 522-541. Chicago: American Library Association, 1986; Love, E., "The Science of Medical Librarianship: Investing in the Future," Bulletin of the Medical Library Association 75 (1987):302-309; Mayfield, M.K. and Palmer, R.A., "Organizational Change in the Medical Library Association: Evolution of the Continuing Education Program," ibid.:326-332; "Medical Library Association Launches Credentialing Academy [of Health Information Professionals]," American Libraries 19 (1988):433; Walter, P.L., "MLA: Strategic Planning and All That Jazz," Library Journal 113 (1988):51-55; Palmer, R.A.,"Medical Library Association," in ALA Yearbook 1989, pp. 159-161. Chicago: American Library Association, 1989; "Medical Library Association," in The Bowker Annual: Library and Book Trade Almanac, 34th Edition 1989-90. New York: R.R. Bowker, 1989.

Additional Information   The formation of a new association, the American Medical Informatics Association (AMIA), during the annual meeting of the Symposium on Computer Applications in Medical Care (SCAMC), was announced, with Donald A.B. Lindberg, Director of the National Library of Medicine, as first president. This new professional group will be concerned with medical informatics, will hold annual meetings, and will establish a College of recognized leaders in this field. Address: 1101 Connecticut Avenue, NW, Suite 700, Washington, DC 20036. Tel: 1 (202) 8571190 ("New Informatics Association," Information Retrieval & Library Automation (IRLA) 25 (1990):9-10).

547   Music Library Association, Inc. (MLA)

Address   PO Box 487, Canton, Massachusetts 02021 (permanent). Tel: 1 (617) 8288450.
Officers   (elected for 2-yr.term) Pres: Susan T. Sommer (New York Public Library, 111 Amsterdam Ave., New York, NY 10023); Treas: Sherry L. Vellucci; Rec.Sec: Jean Geil; Exec.Sec: A. Ralph Papakhian (Music Library, Indiana University, Bloomington, IN 47405); Past Pres: Lenore Coral. Exec.Board: 11
Staff   3 (part-time, paid)
Languages   English

Established   1931, at Yale University School of Music Library. Initial meeting to found association was held to discuss the common problems facing librarians and musicologists.
Major Fields of Interest   Music librarianship, bibliography
Major Goals and Objectives   To promote the establishment, growth, and use of music libraries; to encourage the collection of music and musical literature in libraries; to increase the effectiveness of music library services; to further studies in music bibliography.
Structure   Governed by Board of Directors. Affiliations: ALA, CNLIA, American Musicological Society, Music Publishers Association, IAML.
Sources of Support   Membership dues, sale of publications. Budget: Approx. $250,000
Membership   Total members: 2,125 (1,355 individual, 770 institutional). Committees: 14 (Bibliographic Control, Development, Education, Legislation, Preservation, Public Libraries, Reference and Public Service, Resource Sharing & Collection Development, etc.). Roundtables: 12. Regional Chapters: 12. 28 countries represented. Requirements: All persons or institutions actively engaged in library work or interested in the purposes of the Association. Dues: $50, individual; $25, student and retired; $65, institutional; $35, associate; $100, sustaining.
General Assembly   Entire membership meets once a year in winter or early spring. 1988: Minneapolis, MN, Feb.8-13; 1989: Cleveland, OH, Mar.11-19; 1990: Tucson, AZ, Feb.21-24.
Publications   *Official journal:* Notes. 1945-. 4/yr. $45. Free to members. Editor: Michael Ochs. Address: Music Library, Harvard University, Cambridge, MA 02138. Circ: 3,000. English. Indexed in LISA, Lib.Lit., Music Index, RILM Abstracts, etc. Other publications: MLA Newsletter. 4/yr. Free to members. Editor: James Farrington; Membership Directory; Technical Reports Series; Index and Bibliography Series; Music Cataloging Bulletin; annual reports, proceedings of conferences, seminars, etc. Publications for sale; listed in Notes; price lists available. Publications exchange program in effect.
Activities   Past achievements: Reviewed and revised many internal organizational procedures, resulting in improved management. Current and future: Publications program. Many activities are centered around committee structure: Committees on Bibliographic Control, Preservation, Legislation, Resource Sharing and Collection Development, Reference and Public Service, and Administration have produced papers and reports benefitting music librarians and libraries. Much work carried out in conjunction with other related organizations in music and library science. MLA strives to recruit and educate qualified persons for music librarianship, and sends out brochures upon request. Sponsors exhibits, conferences, seminars, workshops, and other continuing education programs. Presents 4 awards at annual meeting.
Use of High Technology   Computers for management
Bibliography   Bradley, C.J., "Music Library Association: The Founding Generation," Music Library Association Notes 37 (1981):763-822; 39 (1982):490-491; Coral, L., "Music Library Association," in ALA Yearbook 1988, pp. 214-215. Chicago: American Library Association, 1988; Sommer, S.T., "Music Library Association," in ALA Yearbook 1989, pp. 162-163. Chicago: American Library Association, 1989; "Music Library Association," in The Bowker Annual: Library and Book Trade Almanac, 34th Edition 1989-90, pp. 695-696. New York: R.R. Bowker, 1989.

548   National Association of Government Archives and Records Administrators (NAGARA)

Address   c/o Bruce W. Dearstyne, Executive Director, New York State Archives, Room 10A75 Cultural Education Center, Albany, New York 12230 (not permanent). Tel: 1 (518) 4746926/4738037

Officers   Pres: John Burns; VP: Roy Tryon; Sec: William Ptacek; Treas: Deborah Skaggs. Exec.Dir: Bruce W. Dearstyne. Exec.Comm: 5
Staff   None
Languages   English
Established   1984, as successor to the National Association of State Archives and Records Administrators, established in 1974.
Major Fields of Interest   Government archival and records management
Major Goals and Objectives   To unite local, state, and federal archivists and records administrators, and others interested in improved care and management of government records; to promote public awareness of government records and archives management programs; to encourage interchange of information among government archives and records management agencies; to develop and implement professional standards of government records and archival administration; to encourage study and research into records management problems and issues.
Structure   Governed by executive officers. Affiliations: Adjunct member of the Council of State Governments, Lexington, Kentucky.
Sources of Support   Membership dues, grants, revenues from annual meetings.
Membership   Total members: 265 (230 individual, 35 institutional). 3 countries represented. Requirements: Open to local governments, federal agencies, and to any individual or organization interested in improved government records programs. State archival and records management agencies are sustaining members. Dues: $20, individual; $600, state archives and records management agencies.
General Assembly   Entire membership meets once a year. 1990: Boston, MA, July 25-28.
Publications   Official journal: The Clearinghouse. 1982-. 4/yr. Free to members. Address same as Association. Editor: David Olson. Address: Department of Cultural Resources, Division of Archives and History, 109 East Jones Street, Raleigh, NC 27611. Circ: Membership. English. Other publications: Government Records Issues; Program Reporting Guidelines for Government Records Programs; Reports, e.g., Information Clearinghouse Needs of the Archival Profession; Preservation Needs in State Archives. Publications for members only. No publications exchange program.
Activities   Publications program. Active in promoting library-related legislation, e.g., the appointment of the Archivist of the USA. Sponsors conferences.
Use of High Technology   Computers (word processing) for management
Bibliography   "National Association of Government Archives and Records Administrators (NAGARA)," in The Bowker Annual: Library and Book Trade Almanac, 34th Edition 1989-90, p. 696. New York: R.R. Bowker, 1989.

549   National Federation of Abstracting and Information Services (NFAIS) (formerly National Federation of Abstracting and Indexing Services)

Address   1429 Walnut Street, Philadelphia, Pennsylvania 19102 (permanent). Tel: 1 (215) 5632406
Officers   (elected for 1-yr.term, 1990-91) Pres: Kent Smith (National Library of Medicine); VP/Pres.Elect: David Weisgerber (Chemical Abstracts Service); Past Pres: Sec: Kurt Mulholm; Treas: Kent A. Smith; Past Pres: Bonnie Lawlor (Institute for Scientific Information); Exec.Dir: Betty Unruh (appointed). Exec.Board: 11
Staff   4 (paid)
Languages   English
Established   1958, Washington, DC

Major Fields of Interest Indexing; abstracting; databases; electronic publishing; information industry

Major Goals and Objectives To unite organizations that produce abstracting and indexing services in all areas, in print or database formats, or that are otherwise involved in the instruction or use of secondary information services; to promote secondary (abstracting and indexing) services and their use; to encourage information dissemination and exchange, nationally and internationally.

Structure Governed by Board of Directors and Member Assembly. Affiliations: ASIS, SLA, etc.

Sources of Support Membership dues, sale of publications, meeting registration fees. Budget: $300,000.

Membership Total members: 60+ (institutional). 4 countries represented. Requirements: Open to information organizations that publish or manage the publication of bibliographic information. Dues: Full members (secondary services), dues scale dependent on revenue; associate members: $3,000.

General Assembly Entire membership meets once a year. 1988: Philadelphia, PA, Feb.28-Mar.3 (30th Anniversary Conference); 1990: Washington, DC, Mar.14-16.

Publications *Official journal:* NFAIS Bulletin (formerly NFAIS Newsletter. 1958-89). 1990-. 12/yr. $98 ($113, foreign). Free to members. Editor: Wendy Schipper; Exec.Editor: Betty Unruh. Address same as Association. Circ: 600. English. Indexed in Lib.Lit., LISA. Other publications: NFAIS Membership Directory (1/yr.); Brenner, E.H. and Saracevic, T., Indexing and Searching in Perspective (2nd ed., 1985); Unruh, B. and Cornog, M., eds., Forms and Responses: Library/Acquisitions, Editorial, and Production (1986); Neufeld, M. L. and Cornog, M., Abstracting and Indexing Career Guide (2nd ed., 1986); Bremner, J. and Miller, P., The Guide to Database Distribution: Legal Aspects and Model Contracts (1987); Unruh, Betty and Cornog, Martha, eds., Human Resources Survey (1987); Unruh, B. and Cornog, M., eds., NFAIS Directory of Consultants and Contractors (1987); The Information Marketing Handbook (1988); Unruh, B., Effective Exhibiting: A Practical Guide (1988); Information Industry Terms & Conditions (1989); annual reports, proceedings of conferences, seminars, etc. Price lists available. Publications exchange program in effect.

Activities Past achievements: Expansion of publications and seminars; focus of Federation on needs of database producers, while expanding membership eligibility to for-profit and non-US organizations. Current and future: Annual conference, seminars, publications, committee/task force work on relevant issues, e.g., clarifying copyright registration for automated databases, work for hire and copyright. Sponsors conferences, seminars, workshops, and other continuing education programs.

Use of High Technology Computers (Vectorgraphic PC) and databases used for management

Bibliography "New Name: NFAIS is Now the National Federation of Abstracting and Information Services," Indexer 13 (1982):82; Keenan, S.V., "NFAIS Silver Anniversary," Indexer 14 (1983):251-252; Neufeld, N.F. et al., eds. Abstracting and Indexing Services in Perspective: Miles Conrad Memorial Lectures, 1969-1983; Commemorating the 25th Anniversary of the National Federation of Abstracting and Information Services. Washington, DC: Information Resources Press, 1983 (contains bibliography); Neufeld, M. L. and Cornog, M., "Abstracting and Indexing," in ALA World Encyclopedia of Library and Information Services, 2nd ed., pp. 1-4. Chicago: American Library Association, 1986; Unruh, B.L., "Abstracting and Indexing," in ALA Yearbook 1989, pp. 13-14. Chicago: American Library Association, 1989.

550   National Librarians Association (NLA)

Address   PO Box 586, Alma, Michigan 48801 (permanent). Tel: 1 (517) 4637227.
Officers   (elected for 1-yr. term, 1989-90) Pres: Margareth Gibbs (-6/91); VP/Pres-Elect: Lawrence W.S. Auld (-6/92); Sec/Treas: Peter Dollard (-6/92); Past Pres: Peter B. Kaatrude (-6/90). Exec.Board: 9.
Staff   1 (volunteer)
Languages   English
Established   1975, Greensboro, North Carolina, to provide an organization where all professional librarians may voice their concerns.
Major Fields of Interest   Professional concerns of librarians
Major Goals and Objectives   To provide a forum for the identification and articulation of issues of professional concern to librarians; to promote and advance the professional interests of librarians.
Structure   Governed by Executive Board. Affiliations: ALA, CNLIA.
Sources of Support   Membership dues, sale of publications. Budget: Approx.$6,000.
Membership   Total members: 200 (individual). Chapters: 2. Requirements: Any person insterested in librarianship and libraries who holds a graduate degree in library science (MLS) (or presents evidence of outstanding professional contributions) may become a member upon election by the Executive Board. Dues: $20, individual; $35 for 2 years; $10, student, retired, and unemployed.
General Assembly   Entire membership meets once a year during the annual ALA conference
Publications   Official journal: The National Librarian. 1976-. 4/yr. $15. Free to members. Editor: Peter Dollard. Address same as Association. Circ: 600. English. Indexed in LISA. No publications exchange program.
Activities   Program at annual ALA conferences; developing position papers on certification, ethics, professional welfare, and pay equity.
Use of High Technology   Computers (DEC POP II) for management.
Bibliography   "National Librarians Association: A Forum for Librarians," in Bowker Annual of Library and Book Trade Information 1980, pp. 156-162. New York: Bowker, 1980; "National Librarians Association: Constitution and By-Laws," National Librarian 14 (1989):4-5; "National Librarians Association," in The Bowker Annual: Library and Book Trade Almanac, 34th Edition 1989-90, pp. 697-698. New York: R.R. Bowker, 1989.

551   Public Library Association (PLA)

Address   50 East Huron Street, Chicago, Illinois 60611 (permanent). Tel: 1 (312) 9446780. Fax: 312-4409374.
Officers   (elected for 1-yr.term, 1989-90) Pres: Sarah A. Long; Exec.Dir: Eleanor Jo Rodger; Past Pres: Melissa Buckingham. Exec.Comm: 4
Staff   8 (paid)
Languages   English
Established   1946
Major Fields of Interest   All concerns shared by public librarians and others about public libraries
Major Goals and Objectives   To advance the development and effectiveness of public library service and public librarians: (1) To raise the awareness of public librarians about the issues related to free and equal access to information; (2) to develop a coordinated program for continuing education which includes conference programming, preconferences, regional workshops, and publications; (3) to provide a Public Library Information

Service for inquiries on public library issues; (4) to initiate, support, and disseminate information on new research projects on public library service or management; (5) to develop and implement a public relations program at the national level to increase awareness of the diverse nature and value of public library services; (6) to provide public libraries with planning and evaluation tools, and to advocate and encourage the utilization of these tools; (7) to ensure that ALA and other units within ALA keep literacy as a high priority; (8) to develop a strategic plan to address public library funding issues; (9) to develop a plan to assist PLA in addressing member interests regarding distinct constituencies of the public library.

Structure Governed by Board of Directors. Affiliations: A division of ALA, IFLA (through ALA)

Sources of Support Membership dues, sale of publications, conference fees. Budget: Approx. $480,000.

Membership Total members: 6,298 (5,577 individual, 721 institutional). Sections: 6 (Alternative Education Programs/AEPS, Armed Forces Library/AFLS, Community Information/CIS, Metropolitan Libraries, Public Library Systems, Small and Medium-Sized Libraries). Many Committees, Discussion Groups, and an Affiliate Network of state library associations. Requirements: Open to ALA members with an interest in public libraries. Dues: $35, plus ALA dues.

General Assembly Entire membership meets once a year during annual ALA conference. In addition, the PLA National Conference meets every 3 years. 1988: Pittsburgh, PA; 1991: San Diego, CA, March 20-23..

Publications Official journal: Public Libraries (formerly PLA Newsletter). 1961-. 6/yr. (4/yr. until 1988). $40 ($50 foreign). Free to members. Editor: Kathleen H. Heim. Address: Louisiana State University, School of Library and Information Science, Coates Hall, Room 267, Baton Rouge, LA 70803. Circ: 7,000. English. Indexed in Lib.Lit., Current Index to Journals in Education, LISA. Other publications: Materials Availability Study, 1987 (1988); Referral Promotional Samples, Public Library Data Service Statistical Report, 1988 (1988); EIC Linkletter (newsletter produced by the PLA Education Information Project with support from the W.K. Kellogg Foundation); Latchkey Children in the Public Library (a position paper of the Service to Children Committee, completed in collaboration with ALSC); annual reports, proceedings of conferences, seminars, etc. List of publications for sale available. No publications exchange program.

Activities Past achievements: Public Library Development Program (development and implementation); National Conferences; Public Library Trusteeship: An investment program for public libraries (development and implementation). Current and future: Establishment of Public Library Data Service; strategies to recruit public librarians; work with Internal Revenue Service to enhance the Income Tax Form Distribution Program. Presents a number of annual awards. Works with ALA's Washington Office to promote library-related legislation. Sponsors conferences, seminars, workshops, and other continuing education programs.

Use of High Technology Computers (ALANET) used for management

Bibliography Berry, J.N., "Council on Public Library Resources?" (First National Conference of ALA's Public Library Association) Library Journal 108 (1983):770; Mills-Fischer, S., "The Public Library Association," Library Times International 2 (1986):82-83; Godwin, M.J., "Building Bridges in Pittsburgh," Wilson Library Bulletin 62 (1988):91-92; Plotnik, A., "PLA Conference Report: A Marathon of Problem-Sharing," American Libraries 19 (1988):27; McCarty, A., "The Public Library Association's Small and Medium-sized Libraries Section," Public Libraries 27 (1988):67-68; Stoltz, D., "The Public Library Association's Third National Conference - An Album," Public Libraries 27

(1988):113-117; "PLA Votes Down Public Library Accreditation," Library Journal 113
(1988):18; Balcom, K.M., "Public Library Association," in ALA Yearbook 1989, pp.
190-191. Chicago: American Library Association, 1989; "American Library Association.
Public Library Association," in The Bowker Annual: Library and Book Trrade Almanac,
34th Edition 1989-90, pp. 653-655. New York: R.R. Bowker, 1989.

**552   REFORMA (National Association to Promote Library Services to the Spanish
Speaking)**

Address   c/o ALA/OLOS, 50 East Huron Street, Chicago, Illinois 60611 (permanent).
Tel: 1 (312) 9446780. Fax: 1-312-4469374. Postal address: c/o Liz Rodriguez Miller, Li-
brary Administration, Tucson Public Library, PO Box 27470, Tucson, Arizona 85726.
Officers   (elected for 1-yr.term) Pres: Ingrid Betancourt (Newark Public Library, 5
Washington St., PO Box 630, Newark, NJ 07101-0630); Sec: Rhonda Ries Kravitz; Treas:
Rene Amaya. Exec.Board: 16
Staff   4 (volunteers)
Languages   English
Established   1971, Dallas, Texas, during ALA conference.
Major Fields of Interest   Library service and programs for the Spanish speaking
Major Goals and Objectives   Improve the full spectrum of library and information ser-
vices for the approximately 19 million Spanish-speaking and Hispanic people in the
United States, promote the development of library collections to include Spanish-lan-
guage and Hispanic-oriented materials, recruit more bilingual and bicultural library professionals and support staff, develop library services and programs which meet the needs
of the Hispanic community, establish a national information and support network among
individuals who share our goals, educate the US Hispanic population regarding the availability and types of library services, and lobby to preserve existing library resource centers
serving the interests of Hispanics.
Structure   Governed by Executive Board. Affiliations: ALA
Sources of Support   Membership dues.
Membership   Total members: 658 (individual and institutional). Chapters: 8. Affiliate: 1
(Bibliotecas Para la Gente Adella Lines, San Francisco Public Library). Requirements:
Open to all interested persons and institutions. Dues: $20, individual; $40, institutional;
$10, student.
General Assembly   Entire membership meets twice a year during ALA Midwinter and
annual conference.
Publications   *Official journal:* Newsletter. 4/yr. Free to members. Other publications:
Membership Directory; annual reports, proceedings of conferences, seminars, etc.
Activities   A REFORMA Long Range Planning Task Force presented its final report in
1988 after surveying membership on issues of concern, priorities and future direction, and
targeted five areas for strategic planning. A plan of action is being prepared to set long-
and short-term goals. Works closely with other units of ALA to sponsor relevant programs. Developed a Mentor Program with the University of California at Los Angeles, so
that more bilingual/bicultural librarians could be trained. The chapters function autono-
mously, working through their local library systems and state library associations to
achieve local objectives. Carries out annual scholarship drive to award a $1,000 scholar-
ship to a library school student interested in pursuing a career in library service to the
Spanish speaking. Publication of the newsletter, which keeps members abreast of the latest developments in the organization and in library services to Hispanics; the annual
membership directory has in fact established a national network of librarians, library
trustees, community and library school students with mutual concerns. Sponsors confer-

ences, seminars, workshops, and other continuing education programs which focus on service to Hispanics.
Bibliography   Gloriod, B., "Latin American Books and Hispanic Immigrants are Subjects of REFORMA Meeting," Library of Congress Information Bulletin 46 (Feb. 2,
1987):52; Betancourt, I., "REFORMA," in ALA Yearbook 1989, pp. 206-208. Chicago:
American Library Association, 1989.

553   Society of American Archivists (SAA)

Address   600 South Federal Street, Suite 504, Chicago, Illinois 60605 (permanent). Tel:
1 (312) 9220140
Officers   (elected for 1-3-yr.term) Pres: John A. Fleckner; Treas: Linda Henry;
Exec.Dir: Donn C. Neal (appointed); Past Pres: Frank B. Evans. Exec.Council: 12 (3
elected each year for 3-year terms)
Staff   9 (paid)
Languages   English
Established   1936, at a meeting in Providence, Rhode Island
Major Fields of Interest   Archives
Major Goals and Objectives   To promote sound principles of archival economy and to
facilitate cooperation among archivists and archival agencies. Through its publications,
annual meetings, workshops, and Sections, the Society provides a means for contacts,
communication, and cooperation among archivists and archival institutions.
Structure   Governed by Officers and Council.
Sources of Support   Membership dues, sale of publications, grants. Budget: Approx.
$500,000.
Membership   Total members: 4.400 (2,800 individual, 800 institutional, 800 subscribers). Sections (based on functions): 6 (Acquisitions & Appraisal; Conservation; Description; Oral History; Reference, Access and Outreach; Visual Materials). Sections (based
on institutional affiliation): 5 (Business Archives; College & University Archives; Government Records; Manuscript Repositories; Religious Archives). Many Committees, Roundtables and Task Forces. Requirements: Persons and institutions interested in the preservation and use of archives, manuscripts, current records and machine-readable records,
films, maps, etc. Dues: $45-75, individual, scaled according to salary; $30, student; $65,
institution; $150, sustaining; $40 (domestic) and $50 (foreign), subscriber.
General Assembly   Entire membership meets once a year. 1987: New York, Sept.2-6;
1988: Atlanta, GA, Sept.28-Oct.2; 1989: St.Louis, MO, Oct.23-29.
Publications   *Official journal:* The American Archivist. 1938-. 4/yr. $40 ($50 foreign).
Free to members. Editor: David Klaassen. Managing Editor: Teresa Brinati. Address
same as Association. Circ: 4,600. English. Indexed in Lib.Lit. Other publications: SAA
Newsletter. 6/yr. Membership. Editor: Teresa Brinati; annual reports, proceedings of conferences, seminars, and numerous monographs. Publications for sale. Issues publications
catalog, "SAA Bookcase." No publications exchange program.
Activities   Past achievements: Expansion of publications program; major initiatives in
professional education; thorough review of goals and priorities for the profession. Current and future: Membership services; publications; education; advocacy; information-
sharing; commercial expansion. Presented the archival profession with a certification plan
based upon an objective standard of archival competence. The plan involves 2 phases of
certification of individual archivists: By petition (possible until 1989), and by an examination process. It will entitle a certified archivist to 8 years of certification, and to periodic
renewal after that. Certification fee has been set to $275. SAA bestows several annual
awards. Active in promoting relevant legislation, such as independent status of the Na-

tional Archives. Sponsors conferences, seminars, workshops, and other continuing education programs.

Use of High Technology   Computers (Adds Mentor) for management.

Bibliography   Quinn, P.M., "Regional Archival Organizations and the Society of American Archivists," American Archivist 46 (1983):433-440; Brown, T.E., "Society of American Archivists Confronts the Computer," in American Archivist 47 (1984):366-382; Neal, D.C., "The Society of American Archivists," Illinois Libraries 69 (1987):538-542; Davis, S.E., "Development of Managerial Training for Archivists," American Archivist 51 (1988):278-285; Ericson, T.L., "Professional Associations and Archival Education: A Different Role, or a Different Theater?" ibid.:298-311; "Guidelines for Graduate Archival Education Programs," ibid.:380-389; "Archival Research Agendas [special issue]," American Archivist 51 (1988):16-105; Neal, D.C., "Archives," in ALA Yearbook 1989, pp. 44-46. Chicago: American Library Association, 1989; Neal, D.C., "Society of American Archivists," in The Bowker Annual: Library and Book Trade Almanac, 34th Edition 1989-90, pp. 152-154. New York: R.R. Bowker, 1989; "Society of American Archivists," ibid. p.699.

554   Society of Bibliophiles

Address   c/o Bruce Northrup, President, 2132 Niskayuna Drive, Schenectady, New York 12309 (not permanent). Tel: 1 (518) 3771478.

Officers   (elected for 1-yr.term) Pres: Bruce Northrup; Treas: Marion Munzer (34 Colonial Ave., Albany, NY 12203); Corr.Sec: John Stevenson; Rec.Sec./Archivist: Harriet Dyer Adams. Exec.Board: 5.

Staff   None

Languages   English

Established   1966

Major Fields of Interest   Book collecting and the arts of the book

Major Goals and Objectives   To promote book collecting and the arts of the book, and provide a forum for members to discuss matters of common interest and concern

Structure   Governed by executive officers.

Sources of Support   Membership dues.

Membership   Total members: 100 (95 individual, 5 institutional). Requirements: Open to any interested persons, such as hobbyists, librarians, antiquarian booksellers, and others interested in books.

General Assembly   Entire membership meets monthly.

Publications   *Official journal:* Society of Bibliophiles Newsletter. 1985-. 12/yr. Free to members. Editor: Bruce Northrup. Address same as Association. Circ: 100. English. Brochures and sample newsletter available upon request.

Activities   Past achievements: Association has regional sponsor of lectures which foster awareness and appreciation of books - as reading matter, collectibles, archival and art objects, etc. Through tours of historically and technically-related facilities, and participation in the annual Albany Book Fair, the Association hopes to encourage public interest and support in this field. Current and future: Continue the ongoing lecture program on topics such as William Morris, the art of papermaking. Sponsors conferences, seminars, workshops, and other continuing education programs.

Use of High Technology   Computers (Macintosh Plus and Image-Writer) for management and newsletter. A laser-writer will be acquired for improved printing quality.

555   Special Libraries Association (SLA)

Address   1700 18th Street, NW, Washington, DC 20009 (permanent). Tel: 1 (202) 2344700. Fax: 1-202-2659317
Officers   (elected for 1-yr.term, 1989-90) Pres: Muriel B. Regan; VP/Pres-Elect: Ruth K. Seidman; Sec: James B. Tchobanoff; Treas: Catherine A. Jones; Past Pres: Joe Ann Clifton; Exec.Dir: David R. Bender (appointed). Exec.Board: 14
Staff   28 (paid)
Languages   English
Established   1909, Brettenwoods, New Hampshire, during July meeting of ALA, with 56 charter members.
Major Fields of Interest   All aspects of special librarianship and information science
Major Goals and Objectives   The mission of SLA is to advance the leadership role of special librarians in putting knowledge to work in our information society. "To provide an association of individuals and organizations having a professional, scientific, or technical interest in library and information science, especially as these are applied in the recording, retrieval, and dissemination of knowledge and information in areas such as the physical, biological, technical and social sciences, the humanities, and business, and to promote and improve the communication, dissemination, and use of such information and knowledge for the benefit of libraries or other educational organizations" (Rev. Bylaws, 1974).
Structure   Governed by Board of Directors. Affiliations: IFLA, CNLIA, etc.
Sources of Support   Membership dues, sale of publications, annual conference, exhibits, and advertising revenue from publications. Budget: Approx. $1.6 million
Membership   Total members: 12,500 (individual). Divisions: 29. Chapters: 55. Requirements: Individual: MLS or equivalent degree or 3 years of professional experience in special libraries; faculty members with 7 years experience in educating students in topics relating to special librarianship; Institutional (sustaining): Institutions and organizations wishing to support the objectives and programs of the Association. Dues: $75, individual; $15, student & retired; $75, associate; $300, sustaining.
General Assembly   Entire membership meets once a year. 1988: Denver, CO, June 11-15; 1989: New York, NY, June 10-15; 1990: Pittsburgh, PA, June 9-14; 1991: San Antonio, TX.
Publications   *Official journal:* Special Libraries. 1910-. 4/yr. $48. Free to members. Editor: Elaine Hill. Address same as Association. Circ: 12,000 +. English. Indexed in Lib.Lit., LISA, ISA, etc. Other publications: SpeciaList (newsletter). 12/yr. $8. Free to members. Editor: Maria C. Barry. Address same as Association; Who's Who in Special Libraries (1/yr.); SLA Guide Series; SLA Research Series: From the Top: Profiles of U.S. and Canadian Corporate Libraries and Information Centers (1989), Survey of SLA Software Users (1988), SLA Triennial Salary Survey 1989, Valuing Corporate Libraries: A Senior Management Survey (1990), Powering Up: A Technological Assessment of the SLA Membership (1990), etc.; SLA Information Kits: Disaster Planning and Recovery (1989), Managing Small Special Libraries (1988), Perspectives on Special Library Automation (1989), Ladner, S., comp., Networking and Special Libraries (1990), etc.; numerous monographs, e.g., Tools of the Profession (1988), Winning Marketing Techniques: An Introduction to Marketing for Information Professionals (1990), Mount, E., Special Libraries and Information Centers: An Introductory Text (2nd ed., 1990), Masyr, C., Space Planning for Special Libraries (1990), Jorensen, M.A., comp., Directory of Selected Research and Policy Centers Working on Women's Issues (5th ed., 1989), Rix, S.E., The American Woman 1990-91: A Status Report (1990), etc.; annual reports, pro-

ceedings of conferences, seminars, etc. Annual publications catalog with price list available upon request. Publications exchange program in effect.

Activities   Past achievements: Continued growth of the Association; move to permanent headquarters in Washington, DC; expanded services, including government relations, public relations, and professional development; computerization of the Information Resources Center; implementation of the Association's Long-Range Plan. Current: Investigation of new member services; implementation of the State-of-the-Art Institute; membership development; research continued growth of all program areas, including publications and professional development. Future: Continued implementation of the Association's Long-Range Plan; participation in the graduate library/information management education process; increased professional development opportunities, government relations, public relations, and research in information-related areas. Expansion of SLA Student Groups, including a Student Group Newsletter produced since 1988. Preparation of two new membership brochures to assist in recruitment. Presents annual awards and scholarships. Active in promoting library-related legislation, e.g., supported changes in the US copyright law, and monitors copyright law in Canada, opposed tariffs on information products and privatization of NTIS. Sponsors conferences, seminars, workshops, and other continuing education programs, particularly the Annual Conference and Exhibit, and the annual Winter Education Conference. Sponsored a meeting on "National Information Policies: Strategies for the Future," in Washington, Dec. 14-15, 1989. Supports federal funding of a National Research and Education Network (NREN) and the inclusion of the library community in its development.

Use of High Technology   Computers (IBM System 36) used for management. The Information Resources Center uses 2 IBM PCs, and is in the process of automating the card catalog and serials control.

Bibliography   Molholt, P., "75 Years of [SLA] Service: Reconsider, Redefine, Reconfirm," Special Libraries 74 (1983):298-301; Williams, R.N. and Zachert, M.J.K., "Knowledge Put to Work: SLA at 75," ibid.:370-382; Arterbury, V.J., "SLA's Long Ranging Objectives: A Vision for the Future," Special Libraries 75 (1984):61-68; Christianson, E.B., "Special Libraries," in ALA World Encyclopedia of Library and Information Services, 2nd ed., pp. 772-782. Chicago: American Library Association, 1986; Avallone, S., "The SLA Success Story: Annual Conference in Boston, June 7-12, 1986," Library Journal 111 (1986):55-60; "Transcending Its Specialism," American Libraries 17 (1986):586-588; Arterbery, V.J., "Accreditation: A Blueprint for Action," Special Libraries 77 (1986):230-234; Malinak, D., "SLA: A History Rich in Tradition: A Future Bright with Promise," Library Times International 3 (1987):81-82; Bender, D.R., "SLA: Prepared to Meet the Future," (Guest Editorial) ibid.:82; Shaw, R.V., "Report from the 78th Annual Conference of SLA in Anaheim, Calif.," Library of Congress Information Bulletin 46 (Nov. 23, 1987):501-503; Mobley, E.R., "Special Libraries Association," in ALA Yearbook 1988, pp. 313-315. Chicago: American Library Association, 1988; DeCandido, G.A., "SLA: High Energy & Social Concerns," Library Journal 113 (1988):43-47; Scheeder, D., "The SLA Government Relations Program," Special Libraries 79 (1988):184-188; Shaw, R.V., "Report from the Special Libraries Association Annual Conference, Denver, June 11-15," Library of Congress Information Bulletin 47 (Sept. 12, 1988):370-371; Clifton, J.A., "Special Libraries Association," in ALA Yearbook 1989, pp. 232-234. Chicago: American Library Association, 1989; Malinak, D., "Special Libraries Association," in The Bowker Annual: Library and Book Trade Almanac, 34th Edition 1989-90, pp. 147-151. New York: R.R. Bowker, 1989; "Special Libraries Association," ibid. pp. 699-700; "A Visionary Framework for the Future: SLA's Strategic Plan 1990-2005," SpeciaList 13 (1990), insert;

Scheeder, D., "Special Libraries - The International Scene," Special Libraries 81 (1990):1-2; Spaulding, F.H., "Internationalism of SLA and IFLA 1989," ibid.:3-9.

556   Theatre Library Association (TLA)

Address   111 Amsterdam Avenue, New York, New York 10023, Attention: Richard M. Buck, Secretary/Treasurer (permanent). Tel: 1 (212) 8701644
Officers   (elected for 2-yr.term) Pres: Mary Ann Jenson; VP: James B. Poteat; Sec/ Treas: Richard M. Buck; Rec.Sec: Lois Erickson McDonald. Exec .Board: 15
Staff   None
Languages   English
Established   1937, New York City
Major Fields of Interest   Theater, film, television, radio, and all other performing arts except classical music
Major Goals and Objectives   To advance the interests of all those involved in collecting and preserving theatrical materials and in utilizing those materials for purposes of scholarship.
Structure   Governed by Board of Directors and officers. Affiliations: ALA, American Society for Theatre Research, International Federation for Theatre Research, SIBMAS (International Association of Libraries and Museums of the Performing Arts)
Sources of Support   Membership dues, sale of publications, donations from members. Budget: Approx.$15,000.
Membership   Total members: 526 (274 individual, 252 institutional). 10 countries represented. Requirements: Interest in collections about the performing arts. Dues: $20, individual; $25, institutional.
General Assembly   Entire membership meets once a year. 1988: New York, Oct. 21
Publications   *Official journal:* Broadside (The Quarterly Newsletter of the Theatre Library Association). 1940-. 4/yr. Free to members. Editor: Alan J. Pally. Address same as Association. Circ: Membership. English. Other publications: Performing Arts Resources (PAR) (1/yr. Editor: Barbara Naomi Cohen-Stratyner); annual reports, proceedings of conferences, seminars, etc. Publications available for sale.
Activities   Past achievements: Publication of papers of 1982 Conservation conference; continuing annual publication of PAR; continuing selection and presentation of the Freedley and TLA Awards. Current: Planning of occasional publications to be given or sold to members and sold to the interested public, e.g., a Style Manual. Future: More and better publications; enlargement of membership by publications and other efforts. Sponsors conferences, seminars, workshops, and other continuing education programs.
Bibliography   Buck, R.M., "Theatre Library Association," in ALA Yearbook 1989, pp. 239-241. Chicago: American Library Association, 1989; "Theatre Library Association," in The Bowker Annual: Library and Book Trade Almanac, 34th Edition 1989-90, p. 701. New York: R.R. Bowker, 1989.

557   Ukrainian Library Association of America, Inc./Ukrains'ke Bibliotechne Tovarystvo Ameryky (ULAA/UBTA)

Address   c/o 49 Windmill Lane, New York, New York 10956 (permanent Headquarters).
Officers   (elected for 3-yr.term, 1987-90,June) Pres: Vasyl H. Luchkiw (headquarters); Pres-Elect: Bohdan Yasinsky (Preservation Microfilming Office, LMG05 Library of Congress, Washington, DC 20540); Exec.Sec: Valentina Limonchenko (Voice of America Library, 301 4th Street, SW, Room 324, Washington, DC 20547); Past Pres: Dmytro M. Shtohryn, PO Box 3295, Champaign, IL 61821). Exec.Board: 12

Staff   None
Languages   English, Ukrainian
Established   1961, Cleveland, Ohio, at the annual ALA conference.
Major Fields of Interest   Ukrainian libraries and archives
Major Goals and Objectives   To promote and coordinate research in Ukrainian librarianship; to foster and encourage scholarly and cultural activities among members.
Structure   Governed by Executive Board. Affiliations: ALA, ACRL.
Sources of Support   Membership dues.
Membership   Requirements: Interest in aims of the Association.
General Assembly   Entire membership meets once a year.
Publications   *Official journal:* Ukrains'ka Knyha (Ukrainian Book). 4/yr.; Bulletin. 2/yr.
Activities   Planning of annual conferences, yearly book week, and exhibitions of Ukrainian books and periodicals. Plans to index all Ukrainian periodicals published in the United States.

558   Urban Libraries Council (ULC)

Address   c/o Keith Doms, Executive Director, 3101 West Coulter Street, Philadelphia, Pennsylvania 19129 (permanent). Tel: 1 (215) 8483550.
Officers   (elected for 2-yr.term) Pres: Phil E. Dessauer (3720 South Birmingham, Tulsa, OK 74105); Past Pres: Paulette H. Holahan (6417 Fleur de Lis Drive, New Orleans, LA 70124); Sec: Donald J. Sager; Treas: Roslyn S. Kurland; Exec.Dir: Keith Doms. Exec.Board: 15
Staff   1 (part-time, paid)
Languages   English
Established   1971, Chicago, during annual ALA conference
Major Fields of Interest   Legislative and financial support for urban public libraries
Major Goals and Objectives   To improve legislative and financial support at the state and federal levels for urban library programs; to collect relevant data; to facilitate the exchange of ideas; to develop programs to supply the informational needs of new urban populations.
Structure   Governed by Executive Board. Affiliations: ALA
Sources of Support   Membership dues, sale of publications. Budget: Approx.$28,000.
Membership   Total members: 185 (institutional). Requirements: Urban libraries serving cities of 50,000 or more individuals located in a standard metropolitan statistical area in the US. Dues: $100, cities with population of 50,000 to 249,000; $250, for 250,000 to 499,999; $500, for 500,000 and above.
General Assembly   Entire membership meets once a year in conjunction with annual ALA conference.
Publications   *Official journal:* Urban Libraries Exchange (formerly The Lamp, 1975-1983). 1984-. 12/yr. Free to members. Address same as Association. Editor: Roy H. Millenson. Address: 1156 15th Street, NW, Washington, DC 20005. Circ: 225. English. Other publications are issued at irregular intervals. No publications exchange program.
Activities   Past achievements: Improved newsletter; increased legislative activity; organized two seminars; collection and publication of State Aid and Public Library Statistics. Current and future: In-depth review of funding concerns. Active in library-related legislation, e.g., addition of MURLS program to LSCA. Sponsors conferences, seminars, workshops, and other continuing education programs.
Bibliography   Berry, J. et al., "The Washington Week That Was: A Report on the Meetings of ALA, ALISE and the Urban Libraries Council, Jan. 5-12 [1984] in Washington,

DC," Library Journal 109 (1984):537-543; Doms, K., "Urban Libraries Council," in ALA Yearbook 1989, p. 245. Chicago: American Library Association, 1989.

559   White House Conference on Library and Information Services Taskforce (WHCLIST)

Address   901 Brookside Drive, Greensboro, North Carolina 27408 (not permanent). Tel: 1 (919) 2727102/2724635.
Officers   (elected for 2-yr.term) Chair: Mary Kitt Dunn; Vice Chair: Joe B. Forsee; Sec: Joan Ress Reeves; Treas: Dorothy Mahoney. Exec.Board: 14
Staff   1 (volunteer)
Languages   English
Established   Sept. 15-17, 1980. Called for by 2 of the 54 resolutions passed at the White House Conference on Library and Information Services (WHCLIS) in Washington, DC, Nov.15-19, 1979, this committee of 1 lay and 1 professional representative from each state and territory of the US was formed to plan and monitor implementation of the WHCLIS results.
Major Fields of Interest   Implementation of the results of the 1979 WHCLIS, including the resolution which called for another conference every decade.
Major Goals and Objectives   To educate and instruct the public concerning library and information services, including the status of resolutions adopted by the 1979 conference.
Structure   Governed by a Steering Committee composed of 4 officers and 1 lay and 1 library professional representative from each of 5 regions representing states, territories, the American Indians and the federal library community. Affiliations: Cooperates with NCLIS (the National Commission on Libraries and Information Science), ALA, ALTA, Friends of Libraries USA, and Urban Libraries Council.
Sources of Support   Membership dues, grants and contributions from individuals and corporations interested in WHCLIST aims. Budget: Approx.$5,000.
Membership   Total members: 200 (195 individual, 5 institutional). Requirements: 118 delegates (1 library/information professional and 1 lay member elected from each state and territory) and associate members who are composed of individuals, organizations and businesses supporting WHCLIST goals. Dues: $10, delegate and associate; $100, corporate, business and organization; $500, benefactor.
General Assembly   Entire membership meets once a year.
Publications   *Official journal:* LISTEN ("Library & Information Services Taskforce Educational Newsletter"). 1980-. irregular. Free to members. Editor: Mary Kitt Dunn. Address same as Association. Circ: 500. English. Other publications: Annual Report from the States, proceedings of meetings (available on ERIC); "WHCLIST Five Year Review of Progress Made Toward Implementation of the Resolutions Adopted at the 1979 White House Conference on Library and Information Services" (available from WHCLIST and NCLIS).
Activities   Past achievements: Providing leadership in promoting implementation of the 1979 White House Conference resolutions including support of legislation for the next conference and testifying before Congress on this and other needs; producing two conferences (1985, Princeton, NJ and 1986, Phoenix, AZ) designed to serve as prototypes for conferences within the states to address issues related to a second White House Conference. Current and future: Working for the second White House Conference on Library and Information Services to be held at the Washington, DC Convention Center, July 9-13, 1991, and creating a network of associations interested in having a voice in it; securing (1) authorizing legislation, and (2) appropriations for the White House Conference. WHCLIST has been active in promoting relevant legislation: Since its organization

in 1980, nearly one third of the WHCLIST delegates have testified before Congress concerning LSCA reauthorization, rural library service, etc.

Bibliography Cooper, B., "WHCLIST: A View from the States," Library Journal 110 (1985):98-99.

Additional Information WHCLIST is a unique, independent association of citizens and library/information professionals organized following the first White House Conference and supported entirely through volunteer efforts. Its membership includes leaders in the state and national library community and citizens who have organized and led statewide citizens' councils or Library Friends groups. Trustee members often serve on state library commissions or LSCA advisory councils. The chair is a lay person, while the vice chair is traditionally head of a state library agency. The National Commission on Libraries and Information Science (NCLIS) sponsored the organization of WHCLIST, and both a Commissioner and a staff member act as liaisons to WHCLIST.

560   Women's National Book Association (WNBA)

Address   160 Fifth Avenue, New York, New York 10010 (permanent). Tel: 1 (212) 6757805

Officers   (elected for 2-yr.term) Pres: Marie Cantlon; VP: Patti Breitman; Sec: Lou Carter Keay; Treas: Susan B. Trowbridge; Past Pres: Cathy Rentschler. Exec.Board: 5

Staff   2 (volunteer)

Languages   English

Established   1917

Major Fields of Interest   Books, publishing and retailing, women's affairs, libraries, education

Major Goals and Objectives   Advancement of women in the world of books; education of women and men about the book world, especially publishing; education of members of allied organizations about the way publishing works; study of the role of the publisher in society.

Structure   Governed by Board of Directors. Affiliations: National Library Week Partner of ALA

Sources of Support   Membership dues.

Membership   Total members: 927 (900 individual, 27 institutional). Local Chapters: 8. Requirements: Individuals interested in aims of Association; institutions willing to support the Association. Dues: Each chapter has its own dues schedule, e.g., $15-35, individual, depending on income; $250, sustaining institutions.

General Assembly   Entire membership meets for a breakfast program meeting during annual ALA conference; Chapters design their own programs and meetings.

Publications   *Official journal:* The Bookwoman. 3/yr. Free to members. Editor: Nancy Musorafite-Lutz. Address: 5222 St. Genevieve Place, Alexandria, VA 22310. Circ: 1,000. English. In addition, chapters produce their own newsletters.

Activities   Past achievements: The WNBA Bookwoman Award to 70 women who made contributions to the world of books on the occasion of the 70th Anniversary of the Association in 1987, at the New York Public Library. Current: Presentation of awards: The biennial WNBA Award, honoring an American bookwoman "for an outstanding contribution to the world of books and, through books, to the society in which we live;" the annual Lucile Michels Pannell Award to a creative children's bookstore. Chapters carry out extensive programs of interest to the diverse membership of writers, editors, designers, book and magazine producers, booksellers, librarians, educators, and readers. Chapters sponsor conferences, seminars, workshops, lectures, and other continuing education events, often jointly with other groups sharing common interests, e.g., Women in Scholar-

ly Publishing, Modern Language Association, American Booksellers Association, etc.
Some current topics of programs: Censorship and Book Banning in America, High Tech
in the Book World, Independent Bookstores, University Presses, Publishing Mergers,
Magazine Editing, etc.
Use of High Technology   Computers (Radio Shack) for management.
Bibliography   Rentschler, C., "Women's National Book Association," in ALA Yearbook
1989, p. 254. Chicago: American Library Association, 1989.
Additional Information   "WNBA is the only organization in the book world open to
women and men in all occupations allied to the publishing industry. Since it represents
no special interest group, WNBA offers educational and literary programs for all. Publishers, wholesalers, and other organizations support the work of WNBA as sustaining
members." (C. Rentschler, see Bibliography, above)

Uruguay

561 Agrupación Bibliotecológica del Uruguay (ABU)
(Library Science Association of Uruguay)

Address Calle Cerro Largo 1666, Montevideo (permanent). Tel: 598 (2) 405740.
Officers (elected for 4-yr.term) Pres: Luis Alberto Musso. Exec.Comm: 5
Staff None
Languages Spanish
Established 1945
Major Fields of Interest Library science, bibliography, archival studies, numismatics.
Major Goals and Objectives To publish in the fields of interest; to promote the profession and professional development; to support research; to compile bibliographies, etc.
Structure Governed by Executive Committee.
Sources of Support Membership dues; grants for contract work and research.
Membership Total members: 230 (individual). Requirements: To have a degree in librarianship or related field; or student in the same fields..
General Assembly Entire membership meets every 2 years.
Publications No official journal. Extensive publication program of bibliographies and surveys: Bibliografía uruguaya sobre Brasil; Aportes para la historia de la bibliotecología en el Uruguay; Bibliografía y documentación en el Uruguay (Bibliography and Documentation in Uruguay); Bibliografía bibliográfica y bibliotecologica del Uruguay (Bibliography of Bibliography and Library Science in Uruguay); Archivos des Uruguay (Archives of Uruguay); Bibliografía Uruguaya de Numismática (Bibliography of Numismatics in Uruguay), and others. Price lists and some free copies available upon request.
Activities Compiling extensive bibliographies and surveys in library science and archival studies. Active in promoting library-related legislation: Participated in the passage of a law for the creation of a library school, and a law for the protection of the national inheritance. Sponsors exhibits, symposia, workshops, seminars, and other continuing education programs.

562 Asociación de Bibliotecarios del Uruguay (ABU)
(Association of Librarians of Uruguay)

Address c/o Biblioteca Nacional del Uruguay, 18 de Julio 1790, Casilla de Correo 452, Montevideo
Established 1945
Major Fields of Interest Library profession
Major Goals and Objectives To further the professional status of librarians and to promote librarianship in Uruguay.
Activities The Association was active between 1945 and 1973, and contributed to raising the status of librarians in Uruguay. The Association was also a member of IFLA and participated in international activities. In 1978, the Asociación de Bibliotecólogos y Afines del Uruguay was founded, became a member of IFLA in 1980, and is the active library association in Uruguay now.
Bibliography Acerenza, E., "Uruguay," in ALA World Encyclopedia of Library and Information Services, 2nd ed., pp. 838-839. Chicago: American Library Association, 1986.

563 Asociación de Bibliotecólogos y Afines del Uruguay
(Uruguayan Library Association)

Address Dante 2255, Casilla de Correo 1315, Montevideo.

Officers   Pres: Ms. S. Gil;   Sec: Ms. S. Tavarez.
Staff   None
Languages   Spanish
Established   1978
Major Fields of Interest   Libraries and library profession
Major Goals and Objectives   To promote the development of libraries and library science in Uruguay; to promote the professional status and professional development of members; to participate in national and international professional activities.
Structure   Governed by executive officers. Affiliations: IFLA.
Sources of Support   Membership dues.
Membership   Total members: 390 (individual). Requirements: Librarians with a professional diploma/degree.
General Assembly   Entire membership meets annually.
Publications   *Official journal:* Actualidades Bibliotecológicas. 2/yr.; Boletín. 12/yr.
Activities   Sponsors conferences, continuing education programs, and other activities according to the goals and objectives of the Association.
Bibliography   Acerenza, E., "Uruguay," in ALA World Encyclopedia of Library and Information Services, 2nd ed., pp. 838-839. Chicago: American Library Association, 1986.

Venezuela

564   Asociación Interamericana de Bibliotecarios y Documentalistas Agrícolas, Filial Venezuela (AIBDA, Filial Venezuela)
(Inter-American Association of Agricultural Librarians and Documentalists, Venezuela Branch)

Address   c/o Universidad de Los Andes, Facultad de Ciencias Forestales, Biblioteca, Merida (not permanent)
Officers   Pres: Mayra de Burgos; Sec-Treas: Celmira Tirade
Staff   None
Languages   Spanish
Established   1971, Maracay
Major Fields of Interest   Agricultural documentation
Major Goals and Objectives   To maintain and increase relations between agricultural libraries at the national, regional, and international levels; to encourage government authorities, universities, and private organizations to assist in agricultural library development; to involve members in efforts to improve the professional status of librarians and documentalists.
Structure   Governed by executive officers. Affiliations: National member of AIBDA.
Sources of Support   Membership dues, subsidies.
Membership   Types of membership: Individual, institutional, honorary. Requirements: Open to all personnel of agricultural libraries and documentation centers, persons and institutions interested in the aims of the Association. Dues (Bolivar): 8.
General Assembly   Entire membership meets twice a year, in July at Barquisimeto, in November at Maracay.
Publications   No official journal; Boletín of AIBDA used as official journal.
Activities   Sponsors meetings, seminars, and other activities aimed at raising the professional status of librarians and documentalists.

565   Asociación Venezolana de Archiveros
(Venezuelan Association of Archivists)

Address   c/o Archivo General de la Nación, 15 Avenida Urdaneta, Apartado 5935, Caracas 101
Officers   Pres: José Daniel Vera Custodio
Languages   Spanish
Major Fields of Interest   Archival profession
Major Goals and Objectives   To promote the development of archives and the professional status of archivists in Venezuela.
Sources of Support   Membership dues

566   Colegio de Bibliotecólogos y Archivólogos de Venezuela (COLBAV)
(Association of Libraries and Archives of Venezuela)

Address   Apartado 6283, Caracas. Tel: 58 (2) 7813245.
Officers   Pres: Ms. O. Ruíz la Scalea; Exec.Sec: Zunilde Nuñez de Rojas
Staff   None
Languages   Spanish
Established   1962, from the Asociación Venezolana de Bibliotecarios (founded 1954) and the Asociación Bibliotecaria Venezolana (founded 1956).

Major Fields of Interest   Libraries and archives
Major Goals and Objectives   To promote and improve library and archival services, and represent the professional interests of members.
Structure   Governed by Executive Board. Affiliations: ACURIL, FID, IFLA.
Sources of Support   Membership dues, sale of publications, donations.
Membership   Total members: Approx. 700. Types of membership: Individual, charter, active, associate, honorary. Requirements: Professional librarians and those interested in the aims of the Association, on written application.
General Assembly   Entire membership meets once a year.
Publications   *Official journal:* COLVAR.
Activities   Sponsors conferences, seminars, workshops, and other continuing education programs. As the main professional association for librarians and archivists in Venezuela, it represents the professions and participates in international organizations and meetings.
Bibliography   Matza, M., "Venezuela," in ALA World Encyclopedia of Library and Information Services, 2nd ed., pp. 841-843. Chicago: American Library Association, 1986.

Wales

567   Cymdeithas Llyfrgelloedd Cymru / Welsh Library Association (WLA)

Address   c/o B. Jones, Honorary Secretary, National Library of Wales, Aberystwyth, Dyfed, Wales SY23 3BU United Kingdom (not permanent). Tel: 44 (970) 3816. Telex: 35165.
Officers   (elected for 3-yr.term) Pres: B.F. Roberts (National Library of Wales); Chair: Ms. E. A. Mitcheson (Gwynedd); Past Chair: Ms. A. Croft; Hon.Sec: B. Jones (National Library of Wales); Hon.Treas: G.W.F. Ewins (Polytechnic of Wales). Exec.Comm: 17
Staff   None
Languages   Welsh, English
Established   A Branch of The Library Association (LA) (founded 1877); became Wales and Monmouthshire Branch of the Library Association in 1933, and assumed present name in 1971.
Major Fields of Interest   Librarianship and information science
Major Goals and Objectives   Same aims as the parent body, the Library Association (LA) of the United Kingdom.
Structure   Governed by executive officers within the LA structure. Affiliations: A national branch of LA; member of IFLA through LA.
Sources of Support   Membership dues, sale of publications. Budget (Pound Sterling): Approx. 3,000.
Membership   Total members: 903 (individual). Types of membership: Individual. Requirements: Basic membership of The Library Association (UK); working in Welsh libraries or information services, or, if retired, residing in Wales. Dues: Personal subscription regulated by amount of annual salary.
General Assembly   Entire membership meets 3 times a year.
Publications   *Official journal:* Y Ddolen: Cylchgrawn Cymdeithas Llyfrgelloedd Cymru/ Journal of The Welsh Library Association. 1970-. 3/yr. Free to members. Address same as Association. Editor: R.E. Huws. Circ: Approx.950. Welsh, English. Other publications: Jones, B., A Bibliography of Anglo-Welsh Literature 1900-65 (1970); Huws, G., Ffynonellau gwybodaeth am Gymru a'r iaith Gymraeg: Rhestr ddethol/Information Sources Relating to Wales and the Welsh Language: Select List (1984); WLA Index Series, WLA Bibliographies Series, annual reports, proceedings of meetings, conferences, etc. Publications available for sale from Honorary Secretary. No publications exchange program in effect.
Activities   Past achievements: (1) Publications program; (2) funding research projects from Kathleen Cooks bequest. Current: (1) Supporting activities of Groups of WLA; (2) arranging general meetings; (3) sponsoring research of library and information science projects. Sponsors Book Week activities, exhibits.

568   Cymdeithas Llyfrgellwyr Iechyd Cymru / Association of Welsh Health Librarians (AWHL)

Address   c/o The Secretary, AWHL, The Friars, Friars Road, Newport, Gwent, Wales NP9 4EZ United Kingdom (not permanent). Tel: 44 (633) 52244 ext.4661/2
Officers   (elected for 3-yr.term) Chair: Ms. L. Shewring; Vice-Chair: D.A. Matthews; Sec: G.D.C. Titley; Treas: Ms. V. Baker. Exec.Comm: 12
Staff   None
Languages   Welsh, English

Established   1981, Cardiff, inaugural meeting.
Major Fields of Interest   Health sciences
Major Goals and Objectives   To raise the standard of library and information services offered to health personnel in Wales; to improve the conditions and career structure of those working in the field; to offer a forum for the exchange of ideas and experiences through discussion.
Structure   Governed by Executive Committee, elected by members. Affiliations: Library Association; Library Association Medical Health and Welfare Libraries Group (LAMHWLG).
Sources of Support   Membership dues. Budget (Pound Sterling): Approx.200.
Membership   Total members: 40 (individual). Requirements: To be working in health sciences libraries in Wales. Dues (Pound Sterling): 6, individual; 4, associate.
General Assembly   Entire membership meets 3-4 times a year.
Publications   *Official journal:* AWHL Newsletter. 1983-. Irreg. Free to members. Address: c/o Secretary of Association. Circ: Membership. English.
Activities   Continuing the promotion of Welsh health sciences libraries and librarianship; continuing work in the education and training of health sciences library staff.
Bibliography   "Welsh Health," Library Association Record 83 (1981):566.

Western Samoa

569   Library Association of Western Samoa

Address   c/o Nelson Memorial Public Library and Mobile Service, PO Box 598, Apia
Languages   Samoan, English
Established   1987
Major Fields of Interest   Libraries and library services
Major Goals and Objectives   To promote library services in Western Samoa
Structure   Governed by executive officers. Affiliations: COMLA
Sources of Support   Membership dues
Membership   Total members: Approx. 30 (29 individual, 1 institutional).
General Assembly   Entire membership meets once a year.
Activities   Organizing conferences, workshops, training courses (with assistance from Unesco); compiling a directory of libraries in the country.
Bibliography   "Library Association of W. Samoa," <u>COMLA Newsletter</u> 55 (Mar. 1987):7.

Yugoslavia

570 Arhiv Hrvatske (Association des Archivistes de la R.S. de Croatie) (Association of Archivists of Croatia)

Address Marulicev trg. 21, YU-41000 Zagreb
Languages Serbo-Croatian
Major Fields of Interest Archives
Major Goals and Objectives To further the development of archives in Croatia; to represent the interests of Croatian archivists

571 Arhiv SR Slovenije (Association of Archivists of Slovenia)

Address Zvezdarska 1, YU-61000 Ljubljana
Languages Slovenian
Major Fields of Interest Archives
Major Goals and Objectives To further the development of archives in Slovenia; to represent the interests of Slovenian archivists.

572 Arhiv Srbje (Association of Archivists of Serbia)

Address c/o Archives d'État de la R.P. de Serbie, Karnedzcjeva 2, YU-11000 Belgrade
Languages Serbo-Croatian
Major Fields of Interest Archives
Major Goals and Objectives To further the development of archives in Serbia; to represent the interests of Serbian archivists.

573 Drustvo Arhivskih Radnika Bosne i Hercegovine (DAR BiH) (Association of Archivists of Bosnia and Hercegovina)

Address Arhiv ViH, S. Kovacevica br.6, YU-71000 Sarajevo. Tel: (38) 213657/214555.
Officers Sec: Mirhana Djokic. Exec.Board: 9
Staff None
Languages Serbo-Croatian
Established 1951, Sarajevo
Major Fields of Interest Archives; history of Bosnia and Hercegovina
Major Goals and Objectives To promote the development of archives and archival research in the history of Bosnia and Herzegovina; to organize conferences to provide opportunity for exchange of experiences; to promote and develop archival services in Bosnia and Herzegovina; to facilitate contact and cooperation among archivists and give assistance in their professional activities; to support and publish a journal; to establish relations with similar associations in the Province and outside.
Structure Governed by Executive Board. Affiliations: ICA, Unesco.
Sources of Support Membership dues, sale of publications, government subsidies.
Membership Total members: Approx. 150. Types of membership: Individual, institutional. Requirements: Individual, all staff members employed in archives; institutional, all archives in Bosnia and Hercegovina. Dues (New Yugoslavian Dinar): 15 a month, individual; institutional varies.

General Assembly Entire membership meets once a year.
Publications *Official journal:* Glasnik Arhiva i Drustva Arhivskih Radnika BiH (Information about Archives and the Association of Archivists of Bosnia and Hercegovina). 1961-. 1/yr. Free to members. Address same as Association. Circ: 200. Serbo-Croatian, with German summaries. Journal exchanged with other associations, museums, and institutions.
Activities Sponsors meetings, lectures, seminars, and specialized projects, according to the goals and objectives of the association.

574 Drustvo Biblioteckih Radnika Srbije (Society of the Library Workers of Serbia)

Address Skerliceva 1, YU-11000 Belgrade (permanent). Tel: 38 (11) 451242/43
Officers (elected for 2-yr.term) Pres: B. Popovic; Exec.Sec: Ljiljana Popovic. Past Pres: Dragan Cirovic. Exec.Comm: 11.
Staff 1 (paid)
Languages Serbo-Croatian
Established 1948
Major Fields of Interest Librarianship, information science, library research.
Major Goals and Objectives To promote librarianship, information science, and library research in Serbia; to represent the interests of members and promote their professional development.
Structure Governed by Executive Committee. Affiliations: FID, IFLA.
Sources of Support Membership dues.
Membership Total members: 2,470 (including over 1,000 professional librarians). 8 countries represented.
General Assembly Entire membership meets once a year, in Belgrade.
Publications *Official journal:* Bibliotekar (The Librarian). 1949-. 6/yr. (New Yugoslavian Dinar) 300. Free to members. Address same as Association. Circ: Approx. 2,600. Serbo-Croatian, with summaries in English, Russian, French. Indexed in LISA.
Activities Organizing library network and cooperation between members. Sponsors conferences, seminars, workshops, and other continuing education programs.
Bibliography Kort, R.L., "Yugoslavia," in ALA World Encclopedia of Library and Information Services, 2nd ed., pp. 853-865. Chicago: American Library Association, 1986.

575 Drustvo Bibliotekara Bosne i Hercegovine (DB BiH) (Association of Librarians of Bosnia and Hercegovina)

Address Narodna i univerzitetske biblioteka Bosne i Hercegovine, Obala 42, YU-71000 Sarajevo (permanent). Tel: (38) 36047.
Officers Exec.Sec: Amra Residbegovic
Staff 1 (paid)
Languages Serbo-Croatian
Established 1949, Sarajevo
Major Fields of Interest Library service, professional education of library workers
Major Goals and Objectives To improve library and information services in Bosnia and Hercegovina; to establish a network of libraries and information services; to promote the professional education and development of members; to contribute to the cultural development of Bosnia and Hercegovina.
Structure Governed by executive officers. Affiliations: Union of Librarians' Associations of Yugoslavia.

Sources of Support   Membership dues, sale of publications, government subsidies.
Membership   Total members: 468 (individual). 180 members are librarians with professional degrees. Types of membership: Individual, honorary. Requirements: Open to any person working in a library or retired from the library profession. Dues (New Yugoslavian Dinar): 60.
General Assembly   Entire membership meets irregularly, as necessary.
Publications   *Official journal:* Bilten Drustva Bibliotekara Bosne i Hercegovine (Bulletin of the Association of Librarians of Bosnia and Hercegovina); Bibliotekarstvo Godisnjak Drustva Bibliotekara Bosne i Hercegovine (Library Science Annual of the Association of Librarians of Bosnia and Hercegovina). Both publications free to members. Address same as Association. Circ: 550. Serbo-Croatian.
Activities   Sponsors conferences, seminars, and other continuing education programs, to raise professional standards and improve library services in accordance with the goals and objectives of the Association.
Bibliography   Kort, R.L., "Yugoslavia," in ALA World Encyclopedia of Library and Information Services, 2nd ed., pp. 864-865. Chicago: American Library Association, 1986.

576   Drustvo Bibliotekara Crne Gore
(Association of Librarians of Montenegro)

Address   Njegoseva 100, YU-81250 Cetinje. Tel: 38 (86) 21137.
Languages   Serbo-Croatian
Established   1952
Major Fields of Interest   Librarianship
Major Goals and Objectives   To promote the development of libraries and library services in Montenegro
Structure   Governed by executive officers. Affiliations: Union of Librarians' Associations of Yugoslavia.
Sources of Support   Membership dues, government subsidies.
Membership   Total members: 120.
General Assembly   Entire membership meets annually.
Publications   *Official journal:* Le Courrier Bibliographique: Revue de l'Association des Bibliothécaires du Monténégro et de la Bibliothèque nationale de la R.S. de Monténégro à Cetinje
Activities   Sponsors conferences, seminars, workshops, and other continuing education programs.
Bibliography   Kort, R.L., "Yugoslavia," in ALA World Encyclopedia of Library and Information Services, 2nd ed., pp. 864-865. Chicago: American Library Association, 1986.

577   Drustvo Bibliotekara SAP Vojvodine (Association des Bibliothécaires de Vojvodina)
(Association of Librarians of Vojvodina)

Address   c/o Bibliothèque Centrale de la Faculté des Lettres et des Sciences de l'Université de Novi Sad, Rue Njegoseva 1, YU-21000 Novi Sad. Tel: 38 (21) 24333.
Officers   Pres: R. Vukoslavovic; Sec: D. Stojanovic.
Staff   None
Languages   Serbo-Croatian
Established   1972
Major Fields of Interest   Libraries

Major Goals and Objectives To promote librarianship and library development in Vojvodina; to represent the interests of librarians.
Structure Governed by executive officers. Affiliations: IFLA, Union of Librarians' Associations of Yugoslavia.
Sources of Support Membership dues, sale of publications, government subsidies.
General Assembly Entire membership meets annually.
Publications No official journal.
Activities Sponsors conferences, seminars, workshops, and other continuing education programs.
Bibliography Kort, R.L., "Yugoslavia," in <u>ALA World Encyclopedia of Library and Information Services</u>, 2nd ed., pp. 864-865. Chicago: American Library Association, 1986.

**578 Drustvo Dokumentalistov in Informatojev Slovenije
(Association of Documentalists and Information Scientists of Slovenia)**

Address Yegova 4, YU-61000, Ljubljana. Tel: 38 (61) 214326.
Languages Slovenian
Established 1964
Major Fields of Interest Documentation and information science.
Major Goals and Objectives To promote the development of documentation and information services in Slovenia; to establish, in cooperation with other similar associations and organizations, a network of documentation and information services in Slovenia; to promote professional education and development of members.
Structure Governed by executive officers.
Sources of Support Membership dues, government subsidies.
Membership Total members: 170 (individual).
General Assembly Entire membership meets annually.
Publications No official journal.
Activities Sponsors conferences, seminars, workshops, and other continuing education programs.
Bibliography Kort, R.L., "Yugoslavia," in <u>ALA World Encyclopedia of Library and Information Services</u>, 2nd ed., pp. 864-865. Chicago: American Library Association, 1986.

**579 Hrvatsko Bibliotekarsko Drustvo (HBD)
(Croatian Library Association)**

Address Marulicev trg. 21, YU-41000 Zagreb. Tel: 38 (41) 446322. Telex: 22206 YU BICH.
Officers (elected for 2-yr.term) Pres: Anisja Cecuk; Sec: Daniela Zivkovic; Treas: Mate Sikic; Past Pres: Dora Secic. Exec.Board: 17
Staff 3 (volunteers)
Languages Croatian
Established 1948, at the Constitutional Congress in Zagreb
Major Fields of Interest Librarianship
Major Goals and Objectives To promote librarianship and library services in the country; to encourage the establishment and development of libraries in Croatia; to protect the interests, education and training of Croatian librarians.
Structure Governed by Executive Council. Affiliations: IFLA, Union of Librarians' Associations of Yugoslavia.
Sources of Support Membership dues, sale of publications, government subsidies.

Membership   Total members: 1,000 (individual). Divisions: 12. Types of membership: Individual. Requirements: Librarians or persons interested in the promotion of librarianship.
General Assembly   Entire membership meets annually.
Publications   *Official journal:* Vjesnik Bibliotekara Hrvatske (Croatian Librarians' Bulletin). 1951-. 2/yr. Free to members. Address same as Association. Editor: Aleksandra Malnar. Address: Lenjinov trg.2, YU-41000 Zagreb. Circ: 1,500. Croatian. Other publications: Knjiga i Citaoci (Books and Readers); professional monographs. Publications for sale. No publications exchange program in effect.
Activities   Past achievements: Education and training of new librarians; publication of cataloging rules by Eva Verona; standards for school libraries; supporting drive for building national library and establishing a national information system. Current and Future: Continuing education of librarians; UAP (Universal Availability of Publications) program; preparing standards for academic libraries. Association has been active in promoting library-related legislation. Sponsors conferences, seminars, workshops, exhibits, and other continuing education programs.
Bibliography   Kort, R.L., "Yugoslavia," in ALA World Encyclopedia of Library and Information Services, 2nd ed., pp. 864-865. Chicago: American Library Association, 1986.

580   Savez Arhivskih Radnika Jugoslavije (SARJ)
(Association of Archivists of Yugoslavia)

Address   Karnedzijeva 2, YU-11000 Belgrade (permanent). Tel: 38 (11) 324489.
Officers   (elected for 1-yr.term) Pres: Miodrag Cankovic; Exec.Sec: Radomir Jemuovic. Exec.Comm: 18
Staff   2 (volunteers)
Languages   Serbo-Croatian
Established   1954
Major Fields of Interest   Archival management
Major Goals and Objectives   To promote the professional work in archives and the organization of archival services; to assist in solving professional problems in archives; to coordinate the activities of member archives.
Structure   Governed by Executive Committee. Affiliations: ICA, etc.
Sources of Support   Membership dues, sale of publications, government subsidies; support from local archives and archives of the Republic. Budget (New Yugoslavian Dinar): 1986/87: 7 million; 1987/88: 9 million.
Membership   Total members: 9 (institutional). Sections: 10. Members are archives of the Republics, representing the Federal Archives, 6 Republic Archives, and 2 Provincial Archives.
General Assembly   Entire membership meets once a year, and every 4 years for a National Congress.
Publications   *Official journal:* Arhivist. 1951-. 2/yr. (Yugoslavian Dinar) 5,000. Free to members. Editor: Bogdan Lekic. Address same as Association. Circ: 1,500. Serbo-Croatian and other languages of nationalities in Yugoslavia. Other publications: Reports of seminars, workshops; monograph series on archives, etc. Publications listed in journal; price lists available. Publications exchange program in effect.
Activities   Past achievements: Publication of archives series (over 10 volumes so far); organizing professional meetings and the National Congress on Archives. Current and Future: Publication of further volumes in series; attending International Congress on Archives in Paris; working for a national information system. Association has been active in

promoting library-related legislation. Sponsors book week activities, exhibits, conferences, seminars, workshops, and other continuing education programs.
Bibliography   Kort, R.L., "Yugoslavia," in ALA World Encyclopedia of Library and Information Services, 2nd ed., pp. 864-865. Chicago: American Library Association, 1986.

581   Sojuz na Drustvata na Arhivskite Rabotnici na Makedonija (SDARM) (Union of the Associations of Macedonian Archivists)

Address   c/o Arhiv na Makedonija, Kej Dimiter Vlahov bb, PO Box 496, YU-91000 Skopje (permanent). Tel: 38 (91) 237211/234461.
Officers   (elected for 2-yr.term) Pres: Kiro Dejeinovski; Sec: Alenka Lape. Exec.Comm: 15.
Staff   All volunteers
Languages   Macedonian
Established   1955, as Association of Archivists of Macedonia; in 1980 reconstituted under present name.
Major Fields of Interest   Archives
Major Goals and Objectives   The unification of archival work in Macedonia; modern archival techniques in Macedonian archives; development of archival studies and their application to archives; professional development of archivists; contacts among Macedonian associations of archivists and with other similar associations in Yugoslavia.
Structure   Governed by Executive Committee. Affiliations: ICA; Intermediate Yugoslav Archival Union.
Sources of Support   Membership dues, sale of publications, government subsidies. Budget (US Dollar): Approx. 2,400.
Membership   Total members: 190 (180 individual, 10 associations). Requirements: Active archival worker or interested in archives.
General Assembly   Entire membership meets every 2 years.
Publications   *Official journal:* Makedonski Arhivist (Macedonian Archivist). 1972-. 1/yr. (US Dollar) 3, foreign. Free to members. Address same as Association. Circ: Membership. Macedonian. No other publications program. Journal available for subscription.
Activities   Past achievements and current: Standardizing archival processes; preparing guidelines for archival work in industry and state institutions; organizing conferences: An inter-republic conference of Macedonian and Serbian archivists (biennial), a federal conference of Yugoslav archivists, and a conference of Macedonian archivists (biennial). Sponsors conferences, seminars, workshops, and other continuing education programs, and an "Archives Week."

582   Sojuz na Drustvata na Bibliotékarite na SR Makedonija (Union of Librarians' Associations of the SR of Macedonia)

Address   c/o Narodna i Univerzitetska Biblioteka "Kliment Ohridski," Bul. "Goce Delcev," br. 6, PO Box 566, YU-91000 Skopje (permanent). Tel: 38 (91) 232122.
Officers   Pres: Slobodanka Dueva; Sec: Zivka Spasovska
Staff   None
Languages   Macedonian
Major Fields of Interest   Librarianship
Major Goals and Objectives   To coordinate the activities of the associations of librarians of Macedonia; to promote the development of libraries in Macedonia
Structure   Governed by executive officers. Affiliations: IFLA.
Sources of Support   Membership dues, government subsidies.

Membership   Comprised of library associations in Macedonia.
General Assembly   Entire membership meets every 2 years.
Publications   *Official journal:* Bibliotekarska Iskra.
Activities   Sponsors conferences, seminars, workshops, and other continuing education programs.
Bibliography   Kort, R.L., "Yugoslavia," in ALA World Encyclopedia of Library and Information Services, 2nd ed., pp. 864-865. Chicago: American Library Association, 1986.

583   Zveza Bibliotekarskih Drustev Slovenije
(Library Association of Slovenia)

Address   Turjaska 1, YU-61000 Ljubljana. Tel: 38 (61) 332853/332825.
Officers   Pres: Tomaz Kobe; Exec.Sec: Stanislav Bahor.
Languages   Slovenian
Established   1947
Major Fields of Interest   Librarianship
Major Goals and Objectives   To promote the development of library science; to improve the status of librarians; to improve library facilities; to establish a network of library and information services; to coordinate the activities of librarians; to represent the members on the national and international level; to offer continuing education programs; to promote library-related legislation.
Structure   Governed by executive officers. Affiliations: IFLA.
Sources of Support   Membership dues, sale of publications, government subsidies.
Membership   Total members: Approx. 920.
General Assembly   Entire membership meets annually.
Publications   *Official journal:* Knjiznica (The Library). 4/yr.
Activities   Carried out according to the goals and objectives of the Association. Sponsors conferences, seminars, workshops, and other continuing education programs.
Bibliography   Kort, R.L., "Yugoslavia," in ALA World Encyclopedia of Library and Information Services, 2nd ed., pp. 864-865. Chicago: American Library Association, 1986.

584   Zveza Drustev Bibliotekarjev Jugoslavije [Slovenian] /
Savez Drustava Bibliotekara Jugoslavije [Serbo-Croatian] /
Sojuz na Drustvata na Bibliotékarite na Jugoslavija [Macedonian] /
(Union of Librarians' Associations of Yugoslavia)

Address   c/o Narodna i univerzitetna knjiznica, Turjaska 1, pp 259, YU-61001 Ljubljana (not permanent). Tel: 38 (61) 332853, 213052. Headquarters rotate every 2 years together with official title.
Officers   (elected for 2-yr. term) Pres: T. Martelanc; Sec: D. Balazic. Exec.Comm: 19
Staff   Volunteers
Languages   Slovenian, Serbo-Croatian, Macedonian
Established   1949, Ljubljana
Major Fields of Interest   Library organizations in Yugoslavia
Major Goals and Objectives   To coordinate the activities of library organizations of Yugoslavia, and to represent them abroad.
Structure   Governed by Executive Council. Affiliations: IFLA.
Sources of Support   Membership dues.
Membership   Composed of eight library associations of the six Socialist Republics: Serbia, Croatia, Bosnia and Hercegovina, Macedonia, Slovenia, Montenegro, and two Socialist Autonomous Provinces of Yugoslavia: Kossovo and Vojvodina (totaling over 3,000 members).

General Assembly   Entire membership meets every 2 years.
Publications   *Official journal:* Informativen Bilten, a newsletter. The associations of the Republics have their own publications: Serbia, Bibliotekar; Bosnia and Hercegovina, Bibliotekarstvo; Croatia, Vjesnik Bibliotekarstva Hrvatske; Slovenia, Knjiznica; Macedonia, Bibliotekarska Iskra; Montenegro, Bibliografski Vjesnik; Vojvodina, Bilten and Bibliotekarski godisnjak. Other publications: Proceedings of meetings. No publications exchange program.
Activities   Coordinates activities of its member associations; operates within the framework of these groups. Activities are centered in various standing commissions (standards and library development, automation, education, cataloging, bibliography, children's and school libraries, library buildings and equipment); works to coordinate library legislation in the Republics and provinces; to coordinate education for library documentation and information science. Works for the development of a uniform library system with adopted standards for a network of public libraries and improved library services. Sponsors conferences, seminars, workshops, and other continuing education programs.
Bibliography   Kort, R.L., "Yugoslavia," in ALA World Encyclopedia of Library and Information Services, 2nd ed., pp. 864-865. Chicago: American Library Association, 1986.

Zaire

585   Association Zaïroise des Archivistes, Bibliothécaires, Documentalistes et Muséologues (AZABDOM)
(Zairian Association of Archivists, Librarians, Documentalists and Museum Curators)

Address   BP 125, Kinshasa 1 (permanent). Tel: 30123 / 30124. Telex: 142
Officers   Exec: Sec: E. Kabeba-Bangasa. Exec.Comm: 6
Staff   6 (volunteers)
Languages   French
Established   1968, Kinshasa, as Association Zaïroise des Archivistes, Bibliothécaires et Documentalistes (AZABDO).
Major Fields of Interest   Archives, libraries, documentation centers, museums.
Major Goals and Objectives   To promote the development of archives, libraries, documentation centers, and museums in Zaire and to improve their services; to represent the professional interests of members.
Structure   Governed by Executive Committee. Affiliations: AIDBA, FID, IFLA, ICA.
Sources of Support   Membership dues, private donations.
Membership   Total members: Approx.300 (285 individual, 15 institutional). Divisions: 3. Types of membership: Individual, institutional, student, honorary. Requirements: Open to those interested in the field of librarianship and services in libraries, archives, and documentation centers, and those interested in museum work.
General Assembly   Entire membership meets twice a year. Congress held every 3 years.
Publications   *Official journal:* Mukanda. 1975-. Free to members. Address same as Association. French. Indexed in LISA. Other publications: Annual reports, proceedings of seminars, conferences and workshops.
Activities   Sponsors conferences, seminars, workshops, and other continuing education programs.
Bibliography   "Zaire," in ALA World Encyclopedia of Library and Information Services, 2nd ed., pp. 865-866. Chicago: American Library Association, 1986; Komba, M., "Formation des Documentaliste-Bibliothécaires au Zaïre," Documentaliste: Sciences de l'Information 23 (1986):189-191.

Zambia

586 Zambia Library Association (ZLA)

Address c/o Maurice C. Lundu, Executive Secretary, Librarian, University Library, University of Zambia, PO Box 32379, Lusaka (not permanent). Tel.: (1) 213221. Telex: 44370.
Officers (elected for 1-yr.term) Chair: Max Banda; Exec.Sec: Maurice C. Lundu.
Staff Volunteers
Languages English
Established 1967, at the headquarters of the Zambia Library Services in Lusaka. The history of the Association is linked with the political history of the area. 1962-63, there was a Library Association of Rhodesia and Nyasaland, which became the Library Association of Central Africa in 1964, when the Federation of Rhodesia and Nyasaland was dissolved. With the creation of an independent Zambia, the Association became the Zambia Branch of the Library Association of Central Africa in 1965. This Association was replaced by the independent Zambia Library Association in 1967.
Major Fields of Interest Development of librarianship in Third World nations, especially Africa. Appropriate library technology for developing countries.
Major Goals and Objectives (1) To unite all persons engaged in library work or interested in libraries in Zambia; (2) to encourage the establishment and development of libraries and library cooperation in Zambia; (3) to improve standards in all aspects of librarianship, bibliography, and documentation in Zambia; (4) to act as an advisory and public relations body in all matters pertaining to libraries, bibliography, and documentation in Zambia; (5) to stimulate an awareness among central and local government bodies and other institutions of their responsibilities in providing adequate library services and facilities; (6) to promote whatever may tend to the improvement of the position and qualifications of librarians; (7) to undertake activities (e.g., meetings, conferences, publications) that will further the above objectives.
Structure Governed by Executive Council. Affiliations: Adult Education Association of Zambia, COMLA, IFLA.
Sources of Support Membership dues.
Membership Total members: Approx. 250 (individual, institutional). Requirements: Open to all individuals interested in librarianship, upon payment of dues. No formal application required. Open to all institutions upon payment of prescribed fee. Dues (Kwacha): 20, individual; 40, institutional (less for students and persons with lower income).
General Assembly Entire membership meets once a year for the Annual General Meeting, and also at the monthly lecture series.
Publications *Official journal:* Zambia Library Association Journal (ZLAJ). 1968-. Free to members. Address same as Association. Circ: Membership. English. Indexed in LISA. Zambia Library Association Newsletter (ZLAN). 1979-. 6/yr. Other publications: Annual reports, proceedings of conferences, and Occasional Publications Series. Publications for sale. Publications exchange program in effect.
Activities Past achievements: Presented a national information policy document to the government on May 5, 1987, after 5 years' work on this issue. Project was carried out with support from Unesco and prepared by a Working Party on the National Information Policy for Zambia, chaired by Maurice C. Lundu. Sponsors conferences, seminars, workshops, and other continuing education programs.

Bibliography   Phiri-Zilole, M.K., "Performance of the Library Profession in Zambia," International Library Review 18 (1986):259-266; Mohamedali, O.N.,"Zambia," in ALA World Encyclopedia of Library and Information Services, 2nd ed. pp. 867-869. Chicago: American Library Association, 1986; Lundu, M. C., "National Information Policy for Zambia Proposals," COMLA Newsletter 57 (Sept. 1987):5.

Zimbabwe

587 Zimbabwe Library Association (ZLA)

Address PO Box 3133, Harare (permanent). Tel: 263 (4) 692741. Headquarters: University of Zimbabwe Library, Mount Pleasant, Harare. Tel: 263 (4) 303211.
Officers (elected for 1-yr.term) Chair: G.C. Motsi; Past Chair: S.M. Made; Vice Chair: R.W. Doust; Treas: L. Mavudzi; Sec: Ms. D. E. Barron. Exec.Comm: 8
Staff None
Languages English
Established 1947, as the Central African Branch of the South African Library Association (CABSALA); 1959, established as the Library Association of Rhodesia and Nyasaland (now Zimbabwe, Zambia and Malawi); 1964, became the Library Association of Central Africa; 1967, Rhodesia Library Association, and 1980, Zimbabwe Library Association, when the country's name changed from Rhodesia to Zimbabwe.
Major Fields of Interest Libraries and librarianship
Major Goals and Objectives To unite all persons engaged in library services; to encourage the establishment and development of libraries; to improve standards in librarianship; to make governing bodies aware of their responsibility to provide adequate library and documentation services.
Structure Governed by Executive Council. Affiliations: FID, IFLA.
Sources of Support Membership dues, sale of publications.
Membership Total members: 270 (130 individual, 140 institutional). Divisions: 2. 3 countries represented. Types of membership: Individual, institutional, life, student. Requirements: Open to all persons or institutions engaged in library or documentation work and interested in the aims of the Association. Dues (Zimbabwe Dollar): Scale based on salary, individual; 10, institutional; 6, unemployed librarians.
General Assembly Entire membership meets once a year. Branches of Mashonaland (Chair: Ms. S. Mabaso-Kwalo) and Matabeleland (Chair: A. Ngwenya) meet monthly.
Publications *Official journal:* Zimbabwe Librarian (formerly Rhodesia Librarian, 1969-79). 1980-. 2/yr. (Zimbabwe Dollar) 20 (US Dollar 20, foreign). Free to members. Address same as Association. Editor: Devi Pakkiri. Address: Acquisitions Librarian, University of Zimbabwe Library, Harare. Circ: 350. English. Indexed in LISA. Other publications: Annual reports, proceedings of conferences, seminars, workshops; Chiware, E.R.T. and Matsika, K., A Handbook for Teacher-Librarians in Zimbabwe (1989). Publications for sale.
Activities Past achievements: Association worked for the concept of a National Library and Documentation Service (NLDS), with an emphasis on providing library services to rural areas not well served. Increased international participation, e.g., hosted SCECSAL VI meeting at the University of Zimbabwe, 17-21 Sept. 1984. Involved in the establishment of a Department of Library and Information Science at the Harare Polytechnic in 1985, and the planning of its educational program. Current and future: Continue improvement of library services to all through the establishment of Culture Houses (district libraries) throughout the country; promote education and training of more qualified personnel. Acted as pressure group for governmental recognition of librarianship as a profession. Continues working for improved library services and literacy programs. Sponsors conferences, seminars, workshops, and other continuing education programs.
Bibliography Mazikana, P.C., "Towards an Association for Librarians, Archivists and Other Information Scientists," Zimbabwe Librarian 14 (1982):51-53; Barnshaw, A., "Establishing and Maintaining Professional Standards in Zimbabwe Libraries," Zimbabwe

Librarian 16 (1984):8-9; Johnson, N., "Zimbabwe," in ALA World Encyclopedia of Library and Information Services, 2nd ed., pp. 869-870. Chicago: American Library Association, 1986; Pakkiri, D., "The Zimbabwe Library Association: From CABSALA to ZLA," COMLA Newsletter 65 (Sept. 1989):8-9,11.

General Bibliography: 1981-1990

I. Monographs and Series

ALA World Encyclopedia of Library and Information Services, ed. by Robert Wedgeworth. 2nd ed. Chicago: American Library Association, 1986. 895 pp. A comprehensive source on current library and information services developments throughout the world, including professional associations.

ALA Yearbook for Library and Information Services. 1976-. Vol. 1-. Chicago: American Library Association, 1976-. Includes current information on associations.

Author's Guide to Journals in Library and Information Science, ed. by Norman D. Stevens and Nora B. Stevens. New York: Haworth Press, 1982. 283 pp.

Bibliographic Services throughout the World: Supplement 1983-1984 / Les services bibliographiques dans le monde: Supplément 1983-1984, by Marcelle Beaudiquez. Paris: Unesco, 1987. 319 pp.

The Bowker Annual: Library and Book Trade Almanac, 34th Edition 1989-90. New York: R. R. Bowker, 1989. 783 pp.

The Community of the Book: A Directory of Selected Organizations and Programs, 2nd ed. comp. by Maurvene D. Williams, ed. and with an Introduction by John Y. Cole. Washington, DC: Library of Congress, 1989. 140 pp.

Comparative and International Librarianship, ed. by P. S. Kawatra. New York: Envoy Press, 1987. 216 pp.

Directory of Associations in Canada (DAC) 1989, 10th ed. Toronto: Micromedia Limited, 1989.

Directory of British Associations and Associations in Ireland, ed. by G. P. Henderson and S. P. A. Henderson, 9th ed. Beckenham, Kent: CBD Research Ltd., 1988. 548 pp.

Directory of European Associations, ed. by I. G. Anderson, 3rd ed. Part I: *National Industrial, Trade, and Professional Associations*. Part II: *National Learned, Scientific, and Technical Societies*. Detroit: Gale Research Inc., 1981, 1984.

Encyclopedia of Associations 1989, 23rd ed. Vol. 1: *National Organizations of the U.S.* In 3 Parts. Detroit: Gale Research Inc., 1988.

Encyclopedia of Associations: International Organizations 1989, 23rd ed. Companion to Vol. 1 in 2 Parts and a Supplement. Detroit: Gale Research Inc., 1989.

Encyclopedia of Information Systems and Services, ed. by Amy F. Lucas and Nan Soper, 9th ed. 3 vols. Vol. 1: U.S. Listings, Vol. 2: International Listings, Vol. 3: Indexes. Detroit: Gale Research Inc., 1989.

Encyclopedia of Library and Information Science, ed. by Allen Kent, et al. New York: Marcel Dekker, 1968-. Extensive articles on countries and various national and international associations.

The Europa World Year Book 1989. 2 vols. London; Europa Publications, 1989. "International Organizations," Vol. 1, part 1.

Fang, Josephine R., and Songe, Alice H. *International Guide to Library, Archival and Information Science Associations*, 2nd ed. New York: R. R. Bowker, 1980. 448 pp. Useful for retrospective information and bibliographies up to 1980.

A Guide to Information Resources Management (IRM) Associations, 2nd ed. comp. by Sarah T. Kadec and Rhoda R. Mancher. Silver Spring, MD: Kadec Information Management Products, 1987.

Guides to International Organizations, ed. by the Union of International Associations. 4 vols. Munich/New York: K. G. Saur, 1984-85.

A Handbook of Comparative Librarianship, ed. by Monique MacKee. 3rd rev. and enl. ed. London: Bingley, 1983. 567 pp.

Harrison, K. C. *International Librarianship*. Metuchen, NJ: The Scarecrow Press, 1989.

IFLA Annual. 1969-. The Hague: International Federation of Library Associations and Institutions. Published by K. G. Saur, Munich/New York.

IFLA Directory 1990/91. The Hague: IFLA Secretariat, 1990. 226 pp. Published annually.

International Directory of Archives, ed. by André Vanrie. New York: K. G. Saur, 1988. 397 pp.

International Directory of Library, Archives and Information Science Associations, 2nd rev. ed. Paris: General Information Programme and UNISIST, 1986 (PGI-86/WS/20). 160 pp. [in French, English and Spanish]

International Encyclopedia of Abbreviations of Organizations, comp. by Paul Spillner and Peter Wennrich. 3rd ed. 6 vols. Munich/New York: K. G. Saur, 1989-.

International Literary Market Place 1988-1989. New York: R. R. Bowker, 1988. 598 pp. Includes information on professional associations.

Library and Information Science Journals and Serials, comp. by Mary Ann Bowman. Westport, CT: Greenwood Press, 1985.

The Library Association Yearbook 1989, comp. by R. E. Palmer and L. M. Davies. London: The Library Association, 1989 (*Yearbook* published since 1965).

Montgomery, A. C., comp. *Acronyms & Abbreviations in Library & Information Work: A Reference Handbook of British Usage*, 3rd ed. London: The Library Association, 1986.

New International Dictionary of Acronyms in Library and Information Science and Related Fields, ed. by Henryk Sawoniak and Maria Witt. Munich/New York: K. G. Saur, 1988. 459 pp.

Sauppe, Eberhard. *Dictionary of Librarianship. Including a Selection from the Terminology of Information Science, Bibliology, Reprography, and Data Processing. German-English. English-German...*. Munich/New York: K. G. Saur, 1988. 428 pp.

World Guide to Libraries, ed. by Helga Lengenfelder et al. 9th ed. Munich/New York: K. G. Saur, 1989. 1275 pp.

World Guide to Scientific Associations and Learned Societies / Internationales Verzeichnis Wissenschaftlicher Verbände und Gesellschaften, ed. by Helmut Opitz. 4th ed. Munich/New York: K. G. Saur, 1984. 947 pp. (*Handbook of International Documentation and Information*, Vol. 13)

The World of Learning, 1989, 39th ed. London: Europa Publications, 1989. 1988 pp.

Yearbook of International Organizations 1989/90, ed. by the Union of International Associations. 26th ed. 3 vols. Munich/New York: K. G. Saur, 1989.

II. Serials

Aslib Information. 1972-. 10/yr. London: Aslib.

*BLIBAD, Bulletin de Liaison à l'Intention des Bibliothécaires, Archivistes et Documental-
istes Africains.* 1976-. 3/yr. École des Bibliothécaires, Archivistes et Documentalistes de
l'Université de Dakar, B.P. 3252, Dakar, Senegal.

Education for Information. 1981-. 4/yr. Amsterdam: Elsevier Publishers.

FID News Bulletin. 1951-. 12/yr. The Hague: International Federation for Information
and Documentation.

Focus on International and Comparative Librarianship. 1967-. 3/yr. London: The Library
Association, International and Comparative Librarianship Group.

IFLA Journal. 1974-. 4/yr. Munich/New York: K.G. Saur.

Information: Reports and Bibliographies. 1972-. 6/yr. New York: Science Associates International, Inc. Selected contents from leading journals in the library and information
sciences.

Information Hotline. 1976-. 10/yr. New York: Science Associates International, Inc.

Information Science Abstracts (ISA). 1969-. 6/yr. American Society for Information Science.

Inspel: International Journal of Special Libraries. 1966-. 4/yr. IFLA Special Libraries Section, Technische Universität Berlin, Universitätsbibliothek, D-1000 Berlin, Federal Republic of Germany.

International Forum on Information and Documentation. 1975-. 4/yr. The Hague: International Federation for Information and Documentation.

International Library Review. 1969-. 4/yr. New York: Academic Press.

Journal of Library and Information Science. 1976-. Delhi: University of Delhi, Department
of Library Science.

Journal of Library and Information Science. 1975-. 2/yr. Chinese Culture Service, P.O. Box
444, Oak Park, Illinois 60303.

Libraries & Culture: A Journal of Library History. 1988-. 4/yr. University of Texas Press,
P.O. Box 7819, Austin, Texas 78713 (formerly *Journal of Library History, Philosophy and
Comparative Librarianship.* 1966-1987).

Library and Information Science Abstracts (LISA). 1969-. 6/yr. London: The Library Association.

Library Literature. 1933-. 6/yr. New York: H. W. Wilson Co.

Library and Information Science Research: An International Journal. 1983-. 4/yr. Ablex
Publishing Corp., 355 Chestnut Street, Norwood, New Jersey 07648 (formerly *Library
Research: An International Journal.* 1979-1982).

Library of Congress Information Bulletin. 1941-. Biweekly. Public Affairs Office, Library of
Congress, Washington, DC 20540. Includes reports on many association conferences.

Libri: International Library Review. 1950-. 4/yr. Copenhagen: Munksgaard.

Research Review in Information and Documentation. 1989-. 4/yr. The Hague: International
Federation for Information and Documentation (replaces *R & D Projects in Documentation and Librarianship.* 1971-1988).

III. Articles in Serials and Monographs

Auster, E. "Organizational Behavior and Information Seeking: Lessons for Librarians." *Special Libraries* 73 (1982):173-182.

Baker, Sharon L., and Powell, Ronald R. "The Research Efforts of Major Library Organizations." In *Library and Information Science Annual*, Vol. 4, 1988, pp. 45-50.

"Les Bibliothèques et les Communautés européennes." *Documentaliste* 24 (1987):37.

Bowden, R. "Library Associations on the Move." *IFLA Journal* 8 (1982):141-146. (Report on two programs considering the management, organizational and administrative problems of library associations).

Carosella, Maria-Pia. "Le secteur documentaire en Europe," *Documentaliste* 25 (1988):33-35.

Chavan, U. A. "Professional Associations: Their Role and Utility in the Development Programme of Library Education." *Herald of Library Science* 20 (1981):65-68.

Dollard, P. "National Librarians Associations and Association Credibility." *Colorado Libraries* (1981):27-32.

"Entwurf eines Modells zur Kooperation bibliothekarischer Verbände der Bundesrepublik Deutschland." [Outline of a Model Plan for the Cooperation of Library Associations in the Federal Republic of Germany] *Bibliotheksdienst* 21 (1987):281-286.

Ernestus, Horst. "Annahme, Anspruch und Wirklichkeit: Die Bibliotheksverbände der USA und Grossbritanniens - ein Beitrag zur Diskussion in der Bundesrepublik." [Assumption, Demand and Reality: The Library Associations of the USA and the UK - a Contribution for Discussion in the Federal Republic of Germany] *Buch und Bibliothek* 38 (1986):928-931, 934-936, 938.

"FID/ICA/IFLA Consultative Meeting for UNESCO/PGI on the Establishment of Interprofessional Organizations of Documentalists, Librarians and Archivists at the Regional Level." *IFLA Journal* 13 (1987):303-305.

Gassol de Horowitz, Rosario. "Report of the Caracas Seminar, 1-5 June 1987 (on Latin American Regional Library Cooperation that Will Help Strengthen the Role of Library Associations)." *IFLA Journal* 14 (1988):89-92.

Granick, L. W. "Emergence and Role of Common Interest Groups in Secondary Information." *Journal of the American Society for Information Science* 33 (1982):175-182.

Holley, Edward G., and Havener, W. Michael. "American Library Associations." *Journal of Educational Media & Library Science* 25 (1988):132-153.

Kurshid, Anis. "Library Associations in Asia." *Herald of Library Science* 28 (1989):3-10.

"Major Professional Organizations and Professional Literature." In *The Library in Society*, ed. by A. R. Rogers and K. McChesney, pp. 219-228. Littleton, CO: Libraries Unlimited, 1984.

Nafees, N. "Role of Library Associations in the Development of School Libraries." *Pakistan Library Bulletin: Urdu Section* 12 (1981):1-16 [in Urdu].

Nagakura, Mieko. "The Roles of International Organizations in School Librarianship." *Toshokan-Kai* 38 (1987):260-265 [in Japanese]. Contribution to an issue commemorating the 52nd General Conference of IFLA [1986].

"Organizations and Associations in North America." In *Educational Media and Technology Yearbook*, Vol. 14, 1988. Littleton, CO: Libraries Unlimited, 1988.

Pacey, P. K. D. "Art Libraries Associations Worldwide: Their History and Future." *Inspel* 16 (1982):10-20.

Parent, R. H. "Strategic Planning for Library Associations [experiences of the American Library Association]." *IFLA Journal* 14 (1988):343-353.

Rayward, W. Boyd. "International Library and Bibliographical Organizations." In *ALA World Encyclopedia of Library and Information Services*, 2nd ed., pp. 381-385. Chicago: American Library Association, 1986.

Shank, R. "IFLA, ALA and Issues in International Librarianship." *Library Journal* 107 (1982):1299-1301.

Siddique, Muhammad, comp. "Library Associations in the Muslim World." In *Librarianship in the Muslim World 1984*, Vol. 2, ed. by Anis Khurshid and Malahat Kaleem Sherwani, pp. 94-99. Karachi: Islamic Library Information Centre, Library and Information Science Department, University of Karachi, 1985.

Singleton, A. K. J. "Learned Societies and Journal Publishing." *Journal of Information Science* 3 (1981):211-224.

Sontag, Helmut. "Vorschlag zur Konzentration bibliothekarischer Verbandsarbeit." [Proposal for Strengthening the Work of Library Associations] *Bibliotheksdienst* 19 (1985):791-799.

Tees, M. H. "Needs of the Special Librarian and the Library Association." *Inspel* 15 (1981):189-196.

Van Zoen, Leo. "Wat doen instanties voor het o. b.-werk." [The Work of National Associations for Public Library Services] *Bibliotheek en Samenleving* 15 (1987):171-172 [in Dutch]

Xu, Z. "Working for the Chinese Library of the Future: A Report on Latest Developments in China." *Library Association Record* 89 (1987):590.

Yungmeyer, Elinor. "The Role of Professional Associations in Achieving Excellence." *Journal of Education for Librarianship* 23 (1983):264-272.

Selected Information Sources on Librarianship in the Third World

Aboyade, O. "Towards a Rural Development Information System." *Quarterly Bulletin of IAALD* 28 (1983):63-70.

Adimorah, E. N. D. "Information and Documentation for Integrated Rural Development in Africa." *Quarterly Bulletin of IAALD* 29 (1984):21-28.

Aithnard, K. M. "La bibliothèque, source d'information dans les pays en voie de développement?" (The Library, Source of Information in Developing Countries?) *Bulletin d'Information de l'A.B.F.* [Association des Bibliothécaires Français] 137 (1987):39-42.

Alexander, P. N., and Pessek, E. "Archives in Emerging Nations: The Anglophone Experience." *American Archivist* 51 (1988):120-131.

Allen, L. L. "Considerations on the Training of Information Specialists from Developing Countries." In *Education and Training in Developed and Developing Countries*, pp. 23-27. The Hague: International Federation for Documentation, 1983.

Altbach, P. G., and Rathgeber, E. M. *Publishing in the Third World: Trend Report and Bibliography.* New York: New Praeger Publications, 1983. 186 pp.

Anderson, D. P. "Waiting for Technology: An Overview of Bibliographic Services in the Third World." *IFLA Journal* 9 (1983):285-295.

Baldwin, C. M., and Varady, R. G. "Information Access in Niger: Development of a West African Special Library." *Special Libraries* 80 (1989):31-38.

"Canadian Librarians and the Third World." *Canadian Library Journal* 42 (1985):181-220 [special issue].

Dosa, M. L. "Information Transfer as Technical Assistance for Development." *Journal of the American Society for Information Science* 36 (1985):146-152.

Dulong, A. "For Systematic Studies of Policies for Development of the Means for Information and Documentation." *Documentaliste* 19 (1982):50-53 (in French).

Education and Training in Developed and Developing Countries, with Particular Attention to the Asia Region. The Hague: FID, 1983. 218 pp. (Papers presented at the FID/ET Workshop in Hong Kong, 6-9 September 1982)

Eres, B. K. "Socioeconomic Conditions Related to Information Activity in Less Developed Countries." *Journal of the American Society for Information Science* 36 (1985):213-219.

_____ and Noerr, K. B. "Access to Primary and Secondary Literature from Peripheral or Less Developed Countries." *Journal of the American Society for Information Science* 36 (1985):184-191.

Harris, Gordon. "The Attempt of Library Associations to Assist Third World Librarianship." *IFLA Journal* 12 (1986):291-295.

Harrison, K. C. "Satisfying Third World Book Needs." *Library Association Record* 86 (1984):33-65.

Havard-Williams, P. "Libraries and Information in Developing Countries." In *International Association of Technological University Libraries Conference, Lausanne, Switzerland, 1981. Libraries and the Communication Process*, pp. 73-90. The Association, 1981.

Hogling, G., and Limberg, L. "Role of School Libraries in Providing Information about Developing Countries." *Biblioteksbladet* 66 (1981):251-252 [in Swedish].

Jackson, M. M. "Usefulness of Comparative Librarianship in Relation to Non-industrialized Countries." *IFLA Journal* 7 (1981):339-343; revised version in *International Library Review* 14 (1982):101-106.

Kaungamno, E. E. "Books and Libraries in the Third World: Problems and Prospects." In *The Library in Society*, ed. by A. R. Rogers and K. McChesney, pp. 255-276. Littleton, CO: Libraries Unlimited, 1984.

Lemos, A. A. B. de. *Portrait of Librarianship in Developing Societies*. Urbana, IL: University of Illinois Graduate School of Library and Information Science, 1981. 46 pp.

Lindley, J. A. "Third World Parliaments and Their Libraries." *Inspel* 22 (1988):169-172.

Lundu, M. C. "Library Education and Training: At Home or Abroad? A Personal Assessment." *International Library Review* 14 (1982):363-378.

Lungu, C. B. M. "Serial Acquisition Problems in Developing Countries: The Zambian Experience." *International Library Review* 17 (1985):189-202.

Martin, W. J. "The Potential for Community Information Services in a Developing Country." *IFLA Journal* 10 (1984):385-392 [Paper delivered at the 1984 IFLA Conference]

Mchombu, K. J. "On the Librarianship of Poverty." *Libri* 32 (1982):241-250.

Moll, P. "International Professional Organisations and the Third World." *Focus on International and Comparative Librarianship* 17 (1986):6-10.

_____. "Should the Third World have Information Technology?" *IFLA Journal* 9 (1983):296-308.

Nahari, A. M. *Role of National Libraries in Developing Countries with Special Reference to Saudi Arabia*. London: Mansell, 1984. 166 pp.

Namponya, C. R. "Agricultural Development and Library Services." *International Library Review* 18 (1986):267-274.

Ndiaye, A. R. "Oral Culture and Libraries." *IFLA Journal* 14 (1988):40-46.

Pachevsky, T. "Problems of Scientific and Technological Information in Small Developed and Developing Countries." *Journal of Library and Information Science* 9 (1983):201-231.

Paker, Y. "Report of a Workshop on Information Science and Technology for Developing Countries: London, 26-28 June 1984." *Program* 19 (1985):89-92.

Saracevic, T. et al. "Issues in Information Science Education in Developing Countries." *Journal of the American Society for Information Science* 36 (1985):192-199.

Sardar, Z. "Between GIN (Global Information Network) and TWIN (Third World Information Network): Meeting the Information Needs of the Third World." *Aslib Proceedings* 33 (1981):53-61; 263 (discussion).

Slamecka, V. "Information Technology and the Third World." *Journal of the American Society for Information Science* 36 (1985):178-183.

Official Journals of Associations

The official journals and selected newsletters published by the associations. Each entry is followed by the name and identification number of the association in parenthesis, and the page number to which the user is directed for full bibliographical information.

AAL Newsletter, (Association of Architectural Librarians 508), 393

ABDOSD-Mitteilungen, (Arbeitsgemeinschaft der Bibliotheken und Dokumentationsstellen der Osteuropa-, Südosteuropa- und DDR-Forschung 234), 173

ACCESS, (Australian School Library Association 097), 75

Actualidades Bibliotecológicas, (Asociación de Bibliotecólogos y Afines del Uruguay 563), 443

ACURIL Newsletter/Carta Informativa, (Association of Caribbean University, Research and Institutional Libraries 021), 14

The AFFIRMation, (Association for Federal Information Resources Management 501), 385

Afghan Library Association Bulletin, (Afghanistan Library Association 077), 63

Afribiblios, (African Standing Conference on Bibliographic Control 001), 3

African Archivist: Journal of WARBICA, (West African Regional Branch of the International Council on Archives 076), 60

African Journal of Academic Librarianship
(Standing Conference of African University Libraries 069), 56
(Standing Conference of African University Libraries, Eastern Area 070), 57
(Standing Conference of African University Libraries, Western Area 071), 57

African Research & Documentation, (Standing Conference on Library Materials on Africa 074), 59

AGORA, (Canadian Association of Special Libraries and Information Services 154), 118

AGRIASIA, (Agricultural Information Bank for Asia 002), 4

Agrícolas, (Federaçao Brasileira de Associaçoes de Bibliotecários – Comissao Brasileira de Documentaçao Agrícola 131), 101

AIDA Informazioni, (Associazione Italiana per la Documentazione Avanzata 299), 221

AIM Network, (Associated Information Managers 500), 384

AINTD - Story, (Association de l'Institut National des Techniques de la Documentation 220), 161

Alam al-Maktabát, (Egyptian Library and Archives Association 204), 149

ALAP News, (Agricultural Libraries Association of the Philippines 398), 297

ALASA Newsletter, (African Library Association of South Africa 422), 315

ALEBCI Informa, (Asociación Latinoamericana de Escuelas de Bibliotecología y Ciencias de la Información 012), 9

Allgemeine Mitteilungen, (Arbeitsgemeinschaft der Archive und Bibliotheken in der Evangelischen Kirche 233), 172

The ALTA Newsletter, (American Library Trustee Association 494), 377

The American Archivist, (Society of American Archivists 553), 433

American Indian Libraries Newsletter, (American Indian Library Association 492), 374

American Libraries, (American Library Association 493), 375

American Studies Library Newsletter, (Standing Conference of National and University Libraries. SCONUL Advisory Committee on American Studies 486), 367

Australian Journal of Toy Libraries for the Handicapped, (Australian Association of Toy Libraries for the Handicapped 091), 70

Australian Law Librarians' Group Newsletter, (Australian Law Librarians' Group 093), 71

Australian Library Journal, (Australian Library and Information Association 094), 72

Australian Library News, (Australian Library Promotion Council 095), 74

AWHL Newsletter, (Association of Welsh Health Librarians 568), 447

B

B.L.A. Newsletter, (Bophuthatswana Library Association 423), 316

Belize Library Association Bulletin, (Belize Library Association 118), 92

Beta Phi Mu Newsletter, (Beta Phi Mu [International Library Science Honor Society] 024), 16

Bibliofack, (Svenska Folkbibliotekarieförbundet 437), 328

The Bibliographical Society of Australia and New Zealand Bulletin, (Bibliographical Society of Australia and New Zealand 025), 17

Bibliophile, (Library Writers' Bureau, Pakistan 387), 287

Bibliotek 70, (Bibliotekarforbundet 190), 141

Biblioteka Bulteno, (Tutmonda Esperantista Biblioteka Asocio 075), 59

Bibliotekar, (Drustvo Biblioteckih Radnika Srbije 574), 450

Bibliotekariesamfundet Meddelar, (Svenska Bibliotekariesamfundet 436), 328

Bibliotekarska Iskra, (Sojuz na Drustvata na Bibliotékarite na SR Makedonija 582), 455

Biblioteksbladet (BBL), (Sveriges Allmänna Biblioteksförening 439), 329

Bibliotheca Medica Canadiana, (Canadian Health Libraries Association 157), 120

Le Bibliothécaire: Revue d'Information Culturelle et Bibliographique, (Association des Bibliothécaires Belges d'Expression Française 112), 88

Bibliotheek en Samenleving [Library and Society], (Nederlands Bibliotheek en Lektuur Centrum 357), 266

Bibliotheek- en Archiefgids, (Vlaamse Vereniging voor het Bibliotheek-, Archief- en Documentatiewezen 117), 91

Bibliotheksdienst, (Deutscher Bibliotheksverband e.V. 250), 182

Bibliotheksverband Aktuell, (Bibliotheksverband der Deutschen Demokratischen Republik 231), 170

Bilten Drustva Bibliotekara Bosne i Hercegovine, (Drustvo Bibliotekara Bosne i Hercegovine 575), 451

BLATT: Bulletin of the Library Association of Trinidad and Tobago, (Library Association of Trinidad and Tobago 454), 341

BLOC-Notes, (Association Professionnelle des Bibliothécaires et Documentalistes 114), 89

Bogens Verden, (Danmarks Biblioteksforening 191), 142

Boletín
(Asociación Panameña de Bibliotecarios 392), 290
(Colegio de Bibliotecarios de Chile A.G. 170), 128

Boletín de ACB, (Asociación Costarricense de Bibliotecarios 182), 135

Boletín de la ABUEN, (Asociación de Bibliotecas Universitarias y Especializadas de Nicaragua 373), 278

Boletín de la ANABAD, (Asociación Española de Archiveros, Bibliotecarios, Museólogos y Documentalistas 427), 319

Cadernos de Biblioteconomia, Arquivística e Documentaçâo, (Associaçâo Portuguesa de Bibliotecários, Arquivistas e Documentalistas 410), 305

Cahiers de la Documentation/Bladen voor de Documentatie, (Association Belge de Documentation 111), 87

Canadian Association of Law Libraries Newsletter/Bulletin de l'Association Canadienne des Bibliothèques de Droit, (Canadian Association of Law Libraries 150), 115

Canadian Journal of Information Science/Revue Canadienne des Sciences de l'Information, (Canadian Association for Information Science 147), 113

Canadian Library Journal, (Canadian Library Association 159), 122

Caribbean Archives, (Caribbean Archives Association - Regional Branch of the International Council on Archives 026), 17

Carta al Bibliotecario, (Asociación Colombiana de Bibliotecarios 177), 132

Carta Informativa, (Asociación Peruviana de Bibliotecarios 399), 296

Cátálogo de Préstamo, (Asociación de Bibliotecarios y Archiveros de Honduras 267), 196

Catholic Library World, (Catholic Library Association 521), 405

CBHL Newsletter, (Council on Botanical and Horticultural Libraries, Inc. 531), 413

CEAL Bulletin, (Committee on East Asian Libraries of the Association for Asian Studies, Inc. 526), 410

Christian Librarian, (Librarians' Christian Fellowship 475), 359

The Christian Librarian, (Association of Christian Librarians 509), 393

Church & Synagogue Libraries, (Church and Synagogue Library Association 525), 409

The Clearinghouse, (National Association of Government Archives and Records Administrators 548), 428

CLENExchange, (Continuing Library Education Network and Exchange Round Table of the American Library Association 528), 411

CLR Reports, (Council on Library Resources, Inc. 532), 414

CLTA Newsletter, (Canadian Library Trustees Association 161), 123

CNLIA Update, (Council of National Library and Information Associations, Inc. 529), 412

College and Research Libraries, (Association of College and Research Libraries 510), 394

COLT Newsletter, (Council on Library/Media Technicians 533), 415

COLVAR, (Colegio de Bibliotecólogos y Archivólogos de Venezuela 566), 445

COMLA Newsletter, (Commonwealth Library Association 030), 20

Commonwealth Archivists Association Newsletter, (Commonwealth Archivists Association 029), 19

Communiqué, (Canadian Association of Research Libraries 153), 118

Continuo, (International Association of Music Libraries, Archives and Documentation Centres, Australian Branch 100), 77

Le Courrier Bibliographique: Revue de l'Association des Bibliothécaires du Monténégro et de la Bibliothèque nationale de la R.S. de Monténégro à Cetinje, (Drustvo Bibliotekara Crne Gore 576), 451

CPL Newsletter, (Council of Planning Librarians 530), 413

Crescendo, (International Association of Music Libraries, Archives and Documentation Centres, New Zealand Branch, Incorporated 371), 276

D

Daigaku Toshokan Kenkyu (Journal of College and University Libraries), (Kokuritsu Daigaku Toshokan Kyogikai 313), 229

Knijiznica, (Zveza Bibliotekarskih Drustev Slovenije 583), 455

Kodomo no Toshyokan (Children's Library), (Jidou Toshokan Kenkyukai 311), 227

Kontakten, (Kommunale Bibliotekarbeideres Forening 381), 283

Kouritsu Daigaku Kyokai Toshokan Kyogikai Kaihou [KODAIKYO Bulletin], (Kouritsu Daigaku Kyokai Toshokan Kyogikai 314), 229

L

The Law Librarian, (British and Irish Association of Law Librarians 469), 355

Law Library Journal, (American Association of Law Libraries 487), 369

LCF Newsletter, (Librarians' Christian Fellowship 475), 359

Lektuurgids, (Nationaal Bibliotheekfonds 115), 89

Lesotho Books and Libraries, (Lesotho Library Association 340), 249

Liaison, (Council of Federal Libraries 165), 126

Liaison – AMBAD, (Association Mauritanienne des Bibliothécaires, des Archivistes et des Documentalistes 349), 259

LIBER Bulletin, (Ligue des Bibliothèques Européennes de Recherche 059), 48

LIBER News Sheet, (Ligue des Bibliothèques Européennes de Recherche 059), 48

Librarian's World, (Evangelical Church Library Association 534), 416

Librarium, (Schweizerische Bibliophilen-Gesellschaft 444), 332

Library Administration & Management (LA&M), (Library Administration and Management Association 541), 421

Library and Information Science, (Mita Toshokan Joho Gakkai 316), 231

Library Association Record, (The Library Association 476), 360

Library Lines, (Church Library Association 163), 125

Library Resources and Technical Services, (Association for Library Collections & Technical Services 504), 389

The Library, (The Bibliographical Society 468), 354

LISTEN, (White House Conference on Library and Information Services Taskforce 559), 439

LNAC Almanac, (Librarians for Nuclear Arms Control 540), 420

LOGIN, (Nederlandse Vereniging van Gebruikers van Online Informatiesystemen 361), 269

Lutheran Libraries, (Lutheran Church Library Association 544), 424

M

Ma'ase Cho-shev, (Information Processing Association of Israel 293), 216

Majalah Ikatan Pustakawan Indonesia, (Ikatan Pustakawan Indonesia 285), 210

Majallah Perpustakaan Malaysia, (Persatuan Perpustakaan Malaysia 345), 254

Makedonski Arhivist, (Sojuz na Drustvata na Arhivskite Rabotnici na Makedonija 581), 454

Maktaba (Libraries), (Kenya Library Association 331), 242

MALA Bulletin, (Malawi Library Association 344), 253

Maltechnik-Restauro: Mitteilungen der IADA, (Internationale Arbeitsgemeinschaft der Archiv-, Bibliotheks-, und Graphikrestauratoren 058), 47

Manuscripts, (The Manuscript Society 545), 424

Yad–La–Koré, (Israel Archives Association 295), 217

Yakugaku Toshokan (Pharmaceutical Library Bulletin), (Nihon Yakugaku Toshokan Kyogi-kai 322), 235

Yeni Yayinlar – Aylik Bibliyografya Dergisi, (Universite Kütüphanecilik Bölümü Mezunlari Dernei 457), 343

Z

Zambia Library Association Journal (ZLAJ), (Zambia Library Association 586), 458

Zeitschrift für Bibliothekswesen und Bibliographie
(Verein der Diplom-Bibliothekare an Wissenschaftlichen Bibliotheken e.V. 257), 187
(Verein Deutscher Bibliothekare e.V. 259), 189

Zimbabwe Librarian, (Zimbabwe Library Association 587), 460

Zväzovy Bulletin, (Zväz Slovenskych Knihovníkov a Informatikov 188), 140

Official Names of Associations

An index of all associations described in the book, both national and international, usually by the official name, but occasionaly by the English version, if the official name was not available. The country of origin (or "International") and the entry number of the association are listed in parenthesis, followed by the page number.

Asociación de Bibliotecarios de El Salvador, (El Salvador 206), 151

Asociación de Bibliotecarios del Paraguay, (Paraguay 394), 292

Asociación de Bibliotecarios del Uruguay, (Uruguay 562), 442

Asociación de Bibliotecarios en Instituciónes de Enseñanza Superior e Investigación, (Mexico 351), 261

Asociación de Bibliotecarios Graduados de la República Argentina, (Argentina 084), 67

Asociación de Bibliotecarios Graduados del Istmo de Panamá, (Panama 391), 290

Asociación de Bibliotecarios Profesionales, (Argentina 085), 68

Asociación de Bibliotecarios Universitarios del Paraguay, (Paraguay 395), 292

Asociación de Bibliotecarios y Archiveros de Honduras, (Honduras 267), 196

Asociación de Bibliotecarios y Documentalistas Agrícolas del Perú, (Peru 397), 294

Asociación de Bibliotecas Públicas de América Latina y el Caribe, (International 009), 7

Asociación de Bibliotecas Universitarias y Especializadas de Nicaragua, (Nicaragua 373), 278

Asociación de Bibliotecólogos y Afines del Uruguay, (Uruguay 563), 442

Asociación Dominicana de Bibliotecarios, Inc., (Dominican Republic 199), 147

Asociación Ecuatoriana de Administradores de Documentos y Archivos, (Ecuador 201), 148

Asociación Ecuatoriana de Bibliotecarios, (Ecuador 202), 148

Asociación Española de Archiveros, Bibliotecarios, Museólogos y Documentalistas, (Spain 427), 319

Asociación General de Archivistas de El Salvador, (El Salvador 207), 151

Asociación Interamericana de Bibliotecarios y Documentalistas Agrícolas, (International 010), 7

Asociación Interamericana de Bibliotecarios y Documentalistas Agrícolas, Filial Venezuela, (Venezuela 564), 444

Asociación Internacional de Bibliotecas de las Universidades Tecnológicas, (International 051), 39

Asociación Latinoamericana de Archivos, (International 011), 9

Asociación Latinoamericana de Escuelas de Bibliotecología y Ciencias de la Información, (International 012), 9

Asociación Mexicana de Bibliotecarios, A.C. (Asociación Civil), (Mexico 352), 261

Asociación Nacional de Bibliotecas Públicas, (Colombia 178), 133

Asociación Nicaragüense de Bibliotecarios y Profesionales Afines, (Nicaragua 374), 278

Asociación Panameña de Bibliotecarios, (Panama 392), 290

Asociación Peruana de Archiveros, (Peru 398), 295

Asociación Peruviana de Bibliotecarios, (Peru 399), 295

Asociación Venezolana de Archiveros, (Venezuela 565), 444

Asociatia bibliotecarilor din Republica Socialistâ România, (Romania 412), 307

Associaçao Brasileira de Escolas de Biblioteconomía e Documentaçao, (Brazil 123), 97

Associaçao dos Arquivistas Brasileiros, (Brazil 124), 97

Associaçâo Portuguesa de Bibliotecários, Arquivistas e Documentalistas, (Portugal 410), 305

Associaçao Profissional de Bibliotecários do Estado do Rio de Janeiro, (Brazil 126), 99

Associaçio Paulista de Bibliotecários, (Brazil 125), 98

Associated Information Managers, (USA 500), 383

Association Belge de Documentation, (Belgium 111), 87

Association Canadienne des Bibliothèques de Collège et d'Université, (Canada 149), 114

Association Canadienne des Bibliothèques de Droit, (Canada 150), 115

Association Canadienne des Bibliothèques Musicales, (Canada 151), 115

Association Canadienne des Études Supérieures en Bibliothéconomie, Archivistique, et Sciences de l'Information, (Canada 146), 111

Association Canadienne des Sciences de l'Information, (Canada 147), 112

Association Congolaise pour le Développement de la Documentation, des Bibliothèques et des Archives, (Congo 181), 134

Association de l'École Nationale Supérieure des Bibliothécaires, (France 219), 160

Association de l'Institut National des Techniques de la Documentation, (France 220), 161

Association des Archivistes Français, (France 221), 162

Association des Archivistes Suisses, (Switzerland 447), 333

Association des Archivistes, Bibliothécaires, et Documentalistes Francophone de la Caraïbe, (International 013), 9

Association des Bibliothécaires Belges d'Expression Française, (Belgium 112), 87

Association des Bibliothécaires de la République Socialiste de Roumanie, (Romania 410), 307

Association des Bibliothécaires Français, (France 222), 162

Association des Bibliothécaires Laotiens, (Laos 338), 247

l'Association des Bibliothécaires Parlementaires au Canada, (Canada 143), 109

Association des Bibliothécaires Suisses, (Switzerland 448), 334

Association des Bibliothècaires, Archivistes, Documentalistes et Muséographes du Cameroun, (Cameroon 107), 107

Association des Bibliothécaires–Documentalistes de l'Institut Supérieur d'Études Sociales de l'État, (Belgium 113), 88

Association des Bibliothèques de Judaica et Hebraica en Europe, (International 023), 15

Association des Bibliothèques de l'Enseignement Supérieur de l'Afrique de l'Ouest, (International 014), 10

Association des Bibliothèques de la Santé du Canada, (Canada 157), 120

Association des Bibliothèques de Recherche du Canada, (Canada 153), 117

Association des Bibliothèques Ecclésiastiques de France, (France 223), 163

Association des Bibliothèques Internationales, (International 022), 15

Association des Bibliothèques Libanaises, (Lebanon 339), 248

Association des Cartothèques et des Archives Canadiennes, (Canada 142), 108

Association des Diplômés de l'École de Bibliothécaires–Documentalistes, (France 224), 164

Association for Federal Information Resources Management, (USA 501), 385

Association for Health Information and Libraries in Africa, (International 015), 10

Association for Information and Image Management, (USA 502), 385

Association for Library and Information Science Education, (USA 503), 387

Association for Library Collections & Technical Services, (USA 504), 388

Conseil International des Archives, (International 033), 22

Conseil International des Associations de Bibliothèques de Théologie, (International 034), 24

Consejo Interamericano de Archivos, (International 035), 25

Conselho Federal de Biblioteconomia, (Brazil 127), 99

Continuing Library Education Network and Exchange Round Table of the American Library Association, (USA 528), 410

Council of Administrators of Large Urban Public Libraries, (Canada 164), 125

Council of Federal Libraries, (Canada 165), 125

Council of Libraries, (Albania 078), 64

Council of National Library and Information Associations, Inc., (USA 529), 411

Council of Planning Librarians, (USA 530), 412

Council on Botanical and Horticultural Libraries, Inc., (USA 531), 413

Council on Library Resources, Inc., (USA 532), 414

Council on Library/Media Technicians, (USA 533), 414

Cumann Leabharlann na h-Éireann, (Ireland 289), 213

Cumann Leabharlannaithe Scoile, (Ireland 290), 214

Cymdeithas Llyfrgelloedd Cymru, (Wales 567), 446

Cymdeithas Llyfrgellwyr Iechyd Cymru, (Wales 568), 446

Cyprus Association of Professional Librarians, (Cyprus 185), 137

D

Danmarks Biblioteksforening, (Denmark 191), 142

Danmarks Forskningsbiblioteksforening, (Denmark 192), 143

Danmarks Skolebibliotekarforening, (Denmark 193), 144

Danmarks Skolebiblioteksforening, (Denmark 194), 144

Dansk Arkivselskab, (Denmark 195), 144

Dansk Musikbiblioteksforening, (Denmark 196), 145

Deutsche Bibliothekskonferenz, (Germany, Federal Republic of 248), 180

Deutsche Gesellschaft für Dokumentation e.V., (Germany, Federal Republic of 249), 181

Deutscher Bibliotheksverband e.V., (Germany, Federal Republic of 250), 182

Deutscher Verband Evangelischer Büchereien e.V., (Germany, Federal Republic of 251), 183

DIK Förbundet, (Sweden 434), 326

Drustvo Arhivskih Radnika Bosne i Hercegovine, (Yugoslavia 573), 449

Drustvo Biblioteckih Radnika Srbije, (Yugoslavia 574), 450

Drustvo Bibliotekara Bosne i Hercegovine, (Yugoslavia 575), 450

Drustvo Bibliotekara Crne Gore, (Yugoslavia 576), 451

Drustvo Bibliotekara SAP Vojvodine, (Yugoslavia 577), 451

Drustvo Dokumentalistov in Informatojev Slovenije, (Yugoslavia 578), 452

E

East Asian Librarians Association of Australia, (Australia 099), 77

Eastern and Southern Africa Regional Branch of the International Council on Archives, (International 036), 25

Egyptian Association for Scientific and Technical Libraries and Information Centres, (Egypt 203), 149

Egyptian Library and Archives Association, (Egypt 204), 149

Egyptian School Library Association, (Egypt 205), 150

Enosis Ellenon Bibliothekarion, (Greece 263), 192

Ente Nazionale per le Biblioteche Popolari e Scolastiche, (Italy 301), 221

Ethiopian Library Association, (Ethiopia 208), 152

European Association for Health Information and Libraries, (International 037), 25

European Association of Information Services, (International 038), 26

Evangelical Church Library Association, (USA 534), 415

Ex Libris Association, (Canada 166), 126

F

Federaçao Brasileira de Associaçoes de Bibliotecários, (Brazil 128), 100

Federaçao Brasileira de Associaçoes de Bibliotecários – Comissao Brasileira de Bibliotecas Centrais Universitárias, (Brazil 129), 100

Federaçao Brasileira de Associaçoes de Bibliotecários – Comissao Brasileira de Bibliotecas Públicas e Escolares, (Brazil 130), 101

Federaçao Brasileira de Associaçoes de Bibliotecários – Comissao Brasileira de Documentaçao Agrícola, (Brazil 131), 101

Federaçao Brasileira de Associaçoes de Bibliotecários – Comissao Brasileira de Documentaçao Biomédica, (Brazil 132), 102

Federaçao Brasileira de Associaçoes de Bibliotecários – Comissao Brasileira de Documentaçao em Ciências Sociais e Humanidades, (Brazil 133), 102

Federaçao Brasileira de Associaçoes de Bibliotecários – Comissao Brasileira de Documentaçao Jurídica, (Brazil 134), 102

Federaçao Brasileira de Associaçoes de Bibliotecários – Comissao Brasileira de Documentaçao Tecnológica, (Brazil 135), 103

Federaçao Brasileira de Associaçoes de Bibliotecários – Comissao Brasileira de Processos Técnicos, (Brazil 136), 103

Federación Española de Sociedades de Archivística, Biblioteconomía, Documentación y Museística, (Spain 428), 319

Federación Internacional de Información e Documentación. Comisión Latino–americana, (International 039), 27

Federal Librarians Round Table, (USA 535), 416

Federal Library and Information Center Committee, (USA 536), 416

Federatie van Organisaties op het Gebied van het Bibliotheek–, Informatie– en Documentatiewezen, (Netherlands 356), 265

Fédération des Associations de Documentalistes–Bibliothécaires de l'Education Nationale, (France 228), 166

Fédération Internationale d'Information et de Documentation, (International 040), 27

Fédération Internationale des Archives du Film, (International 041), 30

Fédération Internationale des Associations de Bibliothécaires et des Bibliothèques, (International 055), 42

Federation of Indian Library Associations, (India 278), 205

Federazione Italiana delle Biblioteche Popolari, (Italy 302), 222

Library Association of Antigua and Barbuda, (Antigua and Barbuda 079), 65
Library Association of Bangladesh, (Bangladesh 108), 84
Library Association of Barbados, (Barbados 109), 85
Library Association of Bermuda, (Bermuda 120), 94
Library Association of China, (China 174), 131
Library Association of Cuba, (Cuba 184), 136
The Library Association of Ireland, (Ireland 289), 213
Library Association of Malaysia, (Malaysia 345), 254
Library Association of Singapore, (Singapore 421), 313
Library Association of the Democratic People's Republic of Korea, (Korea, Democratic People's Republic of 332), 243
Library Association of Transkei, (South Africa 424), 316
Library Association of Trinidad and Tobago, (Trinidad and Tobago 454), 341
Library Association of Western Samoa, (Western Samoa 569), 448
The Library Association, (United Kingdom 476), 359
The Library Association, Northern Ireland Branch, (Northern Ireland 378), 281
Library Promotion Bureau, (Pakistan 386), 286
Library Public Relations Council, (USA 543), 423
Library Science Society, (China 175), 131
Library Writers' Bureau, Pakistan, (Pakistan 387), 286
Ligue des Bibliothèques Européennes de Recherche, (International 059), 48
Lutheran Church Library Association, (USA 544), 423

M

Magyar Könyvtárosok Egyesülete, (Hungary 270), 199
Malawi Library Association, (Malawi 344), 253
Maldives Library Association, (Maldives 346), 255
Map Curators Group of the British Cartographic Society, (United Kingdom 477), 361
Marine Librarians' Association, (United Kingdom 478), 361
The Manuscript Society, (USA 545), 424
Mauritius Library Association, (Mauritius 350), 260
Medical Library Association, (USA 546), 425
Middle East Librarians Association, (International 060), 49
Mita Toshokan Joho Gakkai, (Japan 316), 230
MTESZ Tájékoztatási Tudományos Tanács, (Hungary 271), 200
Music Library Association, Inc., (USA 547), 426

N

Nationaal Bibliotheekfonds, (Belgium 115), 89
National Association of Archivists, Librarians, Documentalists, Booksellers, Museologists and Museographers of Benin, (Benin 119), 93
National Association of Government Archives and Records Administrators, (USA 548), 427
National Federation of Abstracting and Information Services, (USA 549), 428

Society of County Librarians, (United Kingdom 483), 365

Sojuz na Drustvata na Arhivskite Rabotnici na Makedonija, (Yugoslavia 581), 454

Sojuz na Drustvata na Bibliotékarite na Jugoslavija, (Yugoslavia 584), 455

Sojuz na Drustvata na Bibliotékarite na SR Makedonija, (Yugoslavia 582), 454

South African Institute of Librarianship and Information Science, (South Africa 425), 316

South African Institute of Librarianship and Information Science. South West Africa/Namibia Branch, (Namibia 355), 264

South and West Asian Regional Branch of the International Council on Archives, (International 066), 54

Southeast Asian Regional Branch of the International Council on Archives, (International 067), 54

Special Libraries Association, (USA 555), 435

Sri Lanka Library Association, (Sri Lanka 430), 322

Standing Conference of African Library Schools, (International 068), 55

Standing Conference of African University Libraries, (International 069), 56

Standing Conference of African University Libraries, Eastern Area, (International 070), 56

Standing Conference of African University Libraries, Western Area, (International 071), 57

Standing Conference of Co-operative Library and Information Services, (United Kingdom 484), 366

Standing Conference of Eastern, Central and Southern African Librarians, (International 072), 58

Standing Conference of National and University Libraries, (United Kingdom 485), 366

Standing Conference of National and University Libraries. SCONUL Advisory Committee on American Studies, (United Kingdom 486), 367

Standing Conference of Pacific Librarians, (International 073), 58

Standing Conference on Library Materials on Africa, (International 074), 58

State Librarians' Council of Australia, (Australia 101), 78

Stowarzyszenie Archivistów Polskich, (Poland 408), 303

Stowarzyszenie Bibliotekarzy Polskich, (Poland 409), 303

Sudan Association for Library and Information Science, (Sudan 432), 323

Sudan Library Association, (Sudan 431), 323

Suid-Afrikaanse Instituut vir Biblioteek en Inligtingwese, (South Africa 425), 316

Suomen Kirjastoseura – Finlands Biblioteksförening, (Finland 215), 156

Suomen Tieteellinen Kirjastoseura r.y. – Finlands Vetenskapliga Biblioteksamfund r.f., (Finland 216), 157

Svenska Arkivsamfundet, (Sweden 435), 327

Svenska Bibliotekariesamfundet, (Sweden 436), 327

Svenska Folkbibliotekarieförbundet, (Sweden 437), 328

Svenska Sektionen av AIBM, (Sweden 438), 328

Sveriges Allmänna Biblioteksförening, (Sweden 439), 329

Sveriges Vetenskapliga Specialbiblioteks Förening, (Sweden 440), 329

Swaziland Library Association, (Swaziland 433), 325

Swedish Association of Employees in Archives and Records Offices, (Sweden 441), 330
The Swedish Federation of Employees in the Documentation and Cultural Fields, (Sweden 434), 326

T

Tanzania Library Association, (Tanzania 450), 337
Tekniska Litteratursällskapet, (Sweden 442), 330
Thai Library Association, (Thailand 451), 338
Theatre Library Association, (USA 556), 437
Tietopalveluseura, (Finland 217), 158
Tiraisan'ny Mpikajy ny Harentsain'ny Tirenena, (Madagascar 343), 251
Tonga Library Association, (Tonga 453), 340
Toshokan Mondai Kenkyukai, (Japan 327), 238
Transvaal School Media Association, (South Africa 426), 317
Transvaalse Skoolmediavereniging, (South Africa 426), 317
Türk Kütüphaneciler Dernegi, (Turkey 456), 343
Tutmonda Esperantista Biblioteka Asocio, (International 075), 59

U

U.S.S.R. Library Council, (USSR 461), 347
Uganda Library Association, (Uganda 458), 345
Uganda School Library Association, (Uganda 459), 345
Uganda Special Library Association, (Uganda 460), 346
UKB (Samenwerkingsverband van de Universiteitsbibliotheken, de Koninklijke Bibliotheek en de Bibliotheek van de Koninklijke Nederlandse Akademie van Wetenschappen, (Netherlands 362), 270
Ukrainian Librarians Association of Canada, (Canada 169), 127
Ukrainian Library Association of America, Inc., (USA 557), 437
Ukrains'ke Bibliotechne Tovarystvo Ameryky, (USA 557), 437
Universite Kütüphanecilik Bölümü Mezunlari Dernei, (Turkey 457), 343
Urban Libraries Council, (USA 558), 438
Ustrední Knihovnická Rada CSR, (Czechoslovakia 187), 139

V

Verband Deutscher Werkbibliotheken e.V., (Germany, Federal Republic of 254), 184
Verband Österreichischer Archivare, (Austria 106), 82
Verein Angehörige des Mittleren und Nichtdiplomierten Bibliotheksdienstes e.V., (Germany, Federal Republic of 255), 185
Verein der Bibliothekare an Öffentlichen Bibliotheken e.V., (Germany, Federal Republic of 256), 186
Verein der Diplom–Bibliothekare an Wissenschaftlichen Bibliotheken e.V., (Germany, Federal Republic of 257), 187
Verein Deutscher Archivare, (Germany, Federal Republic of 258), 188
Verein Deutscher Bibliothekare e.V., (Germany, Federal Republic of 259), 188
Verein Deutscher Dokumentare e.V., (Germany, Federal Republic of 260), 189

Chief Officers

An index of the presidents or chairpersons of the associations, with the country (or "International") and entry number of the corresponding association in parenthesis, followed by the page number.

Rodríguez de M., Lupita, (International 010), 7

Rodwell, John, (Australia 093), 71

Römer, Gerhard, (Germany, Federal Republic of 244), 178

Ronsin, Albert, (France 227), 166

Rosenqvist, Kerstin, (Finland 212), 155

Rouamba, Louis Aristide, (Burkina Faso 139), 106

Rumschöttel, Hermann, (Germany, Federal Republic of 258), 188

Runkle, Martin D., (USA 517), 400

Ryberg, Anders, (Sweden 440), 329

S

Said, Hakim Mohammed, (Pakistan 390), 288

Sakai, Y., (Japan 328), 239

Sakálová, Elena, (Czechoslovakia 188), 140

Samanez Alzamora, D., (Peru 397), 295

Sämann, Jörg, (Germany, Federal Republic of 261), 190

Sánchez, Efraín Virreira, (Bolivia 121), 95

Santos Pita Leite, Maria Stela, (Brazil 123), 97

Sarjeant, Barbara, (International 038), 26

Savva, Andreas, (Cyprus 185), 137

Sawamoto, Takahisa, (Japan 316), 230; (Japan 318), 232

Scalea, O. Ruíz la, (Venezuela 566), 444

Schmid, Rolf, (Switzerland 446), 333

Schmidt, Anders, (Sweden 441), 331

Schmitz-Esser, Winfried, (Germany, Federal Republic of 260), 189

Schoots, P. J. Th., (Netherlands 356), 265

Schuursma, Rolf L., (Netherlands 362), 270

Schwenger, Frances, (Canada 152), 116

Scott, E., (Scotland 414), 308

Scott, Elspeth, (United Kingdom 473), 357

Scott, Marianne, (Canada 165), 125; (International 031), 21

Sefercioglu, N., (Turkey 456), 343

Sen, Sankar, (India 280), 205

Seria, L. M., (Philippines 406), 301

Shaffer, Dallas Y., (USA 541), 420

Shapira, I., (Israel 294), 216

Shaw, Dennis F., (International 051), 39

Shewring, L., (Wales 568), 446

Simmons, D., (Fiji 209), 153

Simpson, W. G., (United Kingdom 486), 367

Simunovic, Marcia Marinovic, (Chile 170), 128

Sison, Josephine C., (International 002), 3

Skandali, N., (Greece 263), 192

Skovira, Margaret, (USA 501), 385

Smethurst, J.M., (International 059), 48

Smith, David R., (USA 545), 424

Smith, Kent, (USA 549), 428

Smits, Jan, (Netherlands 367), 272

Soemartini, Dra, (International 067), 54

Solimine, G., (Italy 298), 219

Sommer, Susan T., (USA 547), 426

Songa, P. W., (Uganda 458), 345

Sorensen, Bent, (Denmark 191), 142

Sprudzs, Adolf, (International 044), 32

Stefanache, C., (Romania 412), 307

Steinbeck, Hans, (Switzerland 445), 332

Stephanou, Costas D., (Cyprus 186), 137

Stephenson, Wenda R., (Guyana 266), 195

Stockmarr, Mette, (Denmark 192), 143

Strachar, Stuart, (New Zealand 369), 275

Strebl, Magda, (Austria 107), 82

Sugita, K., (Japan 325), 237

Sunny, Nellie Haji, (Brunei Darussalam 137), 104

T

Talbot, Richard J., (USA 522), 406

Tarakan, Sheldon, (USA 543), 423

Taylor, Rhonda Harris, (USA 492), 374

Terry, Marta, (Cuba 184), 136

Thomas, Abator, (Sierra Leone 419), 312

Thomas, Lucille C., (International 049), 36

Thomson, Sharon, (International 045), 33

Subject Index

Subjects listed are followed first by the total number (in parentheses) of associations concerned with that subject, then by the identification number for each cited association.

Countries with International Associations

List of countries in which international association are currently located. The entry number for each association, followed by the page number, are provided.

Countries with National Associations

Statistical Data

	1976 Number	1976 %	1980 Number	1980 %	1990 Number	1990 %
Total number of associations listed	361	100%	509	100%	587	100%
International	44	12	59	12	76	13
National	317	88	450	88	511	87
Associations with paid staff	89	25	111	22	154	26
Associations affiliated with: IFLA	132	37	172	34	199	33
Other organizations	*	*	204	40	276	47
Associations receiving government aid	68	19	93	18	78	13
Associations with publications exchange programs	81	23	121	24	43	7
Associations with continuing education programs	*	*	*	*	308	52
Associations involved in library legislation	56	16	157	31	121	21
Associations using High Technology in management	*	*	*	*	129	22
Total membership	310,000 up	100	374,840 up	100	536,030 up	100**
Individual	173,000 up	56	287,509 up	76	411,317 up	77
Institutional	42,000 up	14	56,328 up	15	95,772 up	18
Not established	95,000 up	31	32,003 up	9	28,941 up	5
Membership of international associations	25,000 up	8	24,612 up	7	43,679 up	8
Membership of national associations	285,000 up	92	351,228 up	93	492,351 up	92
Official journals	256	100	301	100	406	100
International associations	25	10	37	12	47	12
National associations	231	90	264	88	359	88
Journals indexed and/or abstracted	94	37	103	34	208	51
in *LISA*	71	28	73	24	76	19
in *Library Literature*	52	21	58	19	49	12
in *ISA*	29	12	20	6	19	5
in other sources	24	9	52	17	64	16

*Statistics not available
**Membership figures were available for 438 associations (out of a total of 587)

Series IFLA Publications
Edited by Willem R.H. Koops

K·G·Saur München·London·New York·Paris
K·G·Saur Verlag · Postfach 71 10 09 · 8000 München 71 · Tel. (0 89) 7 91 04-0

Series IFLA Publications
Edited by Willem R.H. Koops

37 Paula A. Baxter
**International Bibliography of Art
Librarianship**
An annotated compilation

1987. V, 94 pages. Bound
DM 40.00 (IFLA members DM 32.00)
ISBN 3-598-21767-6

**38 Automated Systems for Access to
Multilingual and Multiscript Library
Materials**
Pre-Conference Seminar held at Nihon
Daigaku Kaikan Tokyo, Japan, August
1986
Ed. Willem R.H. Koops
1987. 225 pages. Bound
DM 68.00 (IFLA members DM 51.00)
ISBN 3-598-21768-4

39 Adaption of Buildings for Library Use
Proceedings of the Seminar held in
Budapest June 3-7, 1985
Ed. Michael Dewe
1988. 263 pages. Bound
DM 58.00 (IFLA members DM 43.50)
ISBN 3-598-21769-2

40/41 Preservation of Library Materials
Conference held at the National Library of
Austria, Vienna, Austria, April 7-10, 1986
Ed. Merrily A. Smith
1987. 2 vols. Bound. Cplt. DM 132.00
(IFLA members DM 102.00)
ISBN 3-598-21770-0 (Vol.1)
ISBN 3-598-21771-4 (Vol.2)

**42 World Directory of Biological and
Medical Sciences Libraries**
Ed.Ursula H. Poland
1988. XII, 203 pages. Bound
DM 48.00 (IFLA members DM 36.00)
ISBN 3-598-21772-2

**43 Education and Research in Library and
Information Science in the Information
Age: Means of Modern Technology and
Management**
IFLA Post-Conference Seminar, Beijing,
China, 1986
Ed. Miriam H. Tees
1988. 202 pages. Bound
DM 68.00 (IFLA members DM 51.00)
ISBN 3-598-21773-0

K·G·Saur München·London·New York·Paris
K·G·Saur Verlag · Postfach 71 10 09 · 8000 München 71 · Tel. (0 89) 7 91 04-0

Series IFLA Publications
Edited by Willem R.H. Koops

44 Open Systems Interconnection
The Communications Technology of the
1990's

Ed. Willem R. Koops
1988. 254 pages. Bound
DM 68.00 (IFLA members DM 51.00)
ISBN 3-598-21774-9

45/46 Newspaper Preservation and Access
Symposium, London, 1987

Ed. Ian Gibb
1988. 2 vols. Cplt. VI,449 pages. Bound
DM 68.00/vol.(IFLA members DM 51.00)
ISBN 3-598-21775-7 (Vol.1)
ISBN 3-598-21776-5 (Vol.2)

47 A l'écoute de l'oeil
Les collections iconographiques et les
bibliothèques
Actes du colloque organisé par la Section
des Bibliothèques d'Art de l'IFLA,
Genève, 1985

Ed. Huguette Rouit and J.-P. Dubouloz.
1989. 348 pages. Bound
DM 88.00 (IFLA members DM 66.00)
ISBN 3-598-21777-3

**48 Library Buildings: Preparations for
Planning**
Proccedings of the Seminar held in
Aberystwith, August 1978
Ed. Michael Dewe
1989. 278 pages. Bound
DM 68.00 (IFLA members DM 51.00)
ISBN 3-598-21778-1

**49 Harmonisation of Education and
Training Programmes for Library,
Information and Archival Personnel**
Proceedings of an International
Colloquium, London, August 9-15, 1987

Ed. Ian M. Johnson, Fall A. Correra,
Richard J. Neill, Matha B. Terry
Vol. 1: 1989. 164 pages. Bound
DM 68.00 (IFLA members DM 51.00)
ISBN 3-598-21779-X
Vol. 2: 1989. Pages 165-374. Bound
DM 68.00(IFLA members DM 51.00)
ISBN 3-598-21780-3

In Preparation:
Manual for Map Librarians

Ed. Hans van de Waal
1990. Ca. 300 pages. Bound
ISBN 3-598-20390-X

K·G·Saur München·London·New York·Paris
K·G·Saur Verlag · Postfach 71 10 09 · 8000 München 71 · Tel. (0 89) 7 91 04-0